March 3–4, 2012
London, England, UK

Association for
Computing Machinery

Advancing Computing as a Science & Profession

VEE'12

Proceedings of the ACM SIGPLAN/SIGOPS International Conference on Virtual Execution Environments

Sponsored by:

ACM SIGPLAN & ACM SIGOPS

Supported by:

CITRIX, Morgan Stanley, VMWare, Microsoft Research, and Technicolor

Advancing Computing as a Science & Profession

The Association for Computing Machinery
2 Penn Plaza, Suite 701
New York, New York 10121-0701

ISBN: 978-1-4503-1175-5 (Digital)

ISBN: 978-1-4503-1373-5 (Print)

Additional copies may be ordered prepaid from:

ACM Order Department
PO Box 30777
New York, NY 10087-0777, USA

Phone: 1-800-342-6626 (USA and Canada)
+1-212-626-0500 (Global)
Fax: +1-212-944-1318
E-mail: acmhelp@acm.org
Hours of Operation: 8:30 am – 4:30 pm ET

Printed in the USA

Chairs' Welcome

It is our great pleasure to welcome you to the *8th ACM SIGPLAN/SIGOPS Conference on Virtual Execution Environments (VEE'12).* We are delighted to present the community with a strong program covering a wide range of virtualization topics.

This year we received 53 complete submissions. The program committee comprised 18 leading researchers active in virtualization-related aspects of programming languages and operating systems. All papers received at least 3 reviews, and the PC held an (appropriately) virtual meeting to make the final selection. In the end, 20 papers were selected for presentation at the conference. In addition, the program includes a keynote presentation by Jason Nieh, and an invited talk by Evangelos Kotsovinos. We hope that these proceedings will serve as a valuable reference for researchers and practitioners in the area of virtualization.

VEE'12 is once again co-located with the International Conference on Architectural Support for Programming Languages and Operating Systems (ASPLOS'12). Both conferences are being held at the buildings of The Royal Society, London – a learned society which includes Isaac Newton as a past president.

On behalf of the organizers, we are delighted to welcome you to London, and wish you all an enjoyable, educational and generally edifying stay!

Steven Hand	**Dilma da Silva**
VEE'12 General Chair	*VEE'12 Program Chair*
University of Cambridge, UK	*IBM Research, USA*

Table of Contents

VEE 2012 Conference Organization

General Chair: Steven Hand *(University of Cambridge, UK)*

Program Chair: Dilma da Silva *(IBM T. J. Watson Research Center, USA)*

Steering Committee:
Vikram Adve *(University of Illinois, Urbana-Champaign, USA)*
David F. Bacon *(IBM T. J. Watson Research Center, USA)*
Brian Bershad *(University of Washington, USA)*
Marc Fiuczynzki *(Princeton University, USA)*
David Gregg *(Trinity College Dublin, Ireland)*
Steven Hand *(University of Cambridge, UK)*
Anthony Hosking *(Purdue University, USA)* (**chair**)
Orran Krieger *(Boston University, USA)*
Doug Lea *(State University of New York at Oswego, USA)*
Brian Noble *(University of Michigan, USA)*
Erez Petrank *(Technion, Israel Institute of Technology, Israel)*
Andrew Warfield *(University of British Columbia, Canada)*

Program Committee:
Muli Ben-Yehuda *(Technion, Israel Institute of Technology, Israel)*
Angela Demke Brown *(University of Toronto, Canada)*
Dave Dice *(Sun Labs at Oracle, USA)*
Alexandra Fedorova *(Simon Fraser University, Canada)*
Michael Franz *(University of California Irvine, USA)*
Ada Gavrilovska *(Georgia Institute of Technology, USA)*
Ajay Gulati *(VMware, USA)*
David Gregg *(Trinity College Dublin, Ireland)*
Robert Grimm *(New York University, USA)*
Tim Harris *(Microsoft Research Cambridge, UK)*
Galen Hunt *(Microsoft Research Redmond, USA)*
Herman Härtig *(TU Dresden, Germany)*
Chandra Krintz *(University of California Santa Barbara, USA)*
Doug Lea *(State University of New York at Oswego, USA)*
Jason Nieh *(Columbia University, USA)*
Ian Rogers *(Google, USA)*
Dilma da Silva *(IBM T. J. Watson Research Center, USA)*
Dan Tsafir *(Technion, Israel Institute of Technology, Israel)*

VEE 2012 Sponsors & Supporters

Supporters:

Morgan Stanley

Microsoft Research

Challenges in Building a Real, Large Private Cloud

Evangelos Kotsovinos
Morgan Stanley
London, UK
evangelos.kotsovinos@ms.com

Abstract

Virtualization and internal cloud are often touted as the solution to many challenging problems, from resource underutilization to data-center optimization and carbon emission reduction. However, the hidden costs of cloud-scale virtualization, largely stemming from the complex and difficult system administration challenges it poses, are often overlooked. Reaping the fruits of internal Infrastructure as a Service cloud requires the enterprise to navigate scalability limitations, revamp traditional operational practices, manage performance, and achieve unprecedented cross-silo collaboration..

Categories & Subject Descriptors: C.2.4 [**Computer-Communication Networks**]: Distributed Systems

General Terms: Management, Performance, Design, Reliability, Standardization

Bio

Evangelos is a vice president at Morgan Stanley, where he leads virtualization and cloud computing engineering. His areas of interest include massive-scale provisioning, predictive monitoring, scalable storage for virtualization, and operational tooling for efficiently managing a global cloud. He also serves as the chief strategy officer at Virtual Trip, an ecosystem of dynamic start-up companies, and is on the Board of Directors of NewCred Ltd. Previously, Evangelos was a senior research scientist at T-Labs, where he helped develop a cloud-computing R&D project into a VC-funded Internet start-up. A pioneer in the field of cloud computing, he led the XenoServers project, which produced one of the first cloud-computing blueprints. He holds a PhD from the University of Cambridge and is the author of several patents and peer-reviewed publications.

VEE'12, March 3–4, 2012, London, England, UK.
ACM 978-1-4503-1175-5/12/03.

Modeling Virtualized Applications using Machine Learning Techniques

Sajib Kundu
Florida International University
skund001@cs.fiu.edu

Raju Rangaswami
Florida International University
raju@cs.fiu.edu

Ajay Gulati
VMware
agulati@vmware.com

Ming Zhao
Florida International University
zhaom@cs.fiu.edu

Kaushik Dutta
National University of Singapore
duttak@nus.edu.sg

Abstract

With the growing adoption of virtualized datacenters and cloud hosting services, the allocation and sizing of resources such as CPU, memory, and I/O bandwidth for virtual machines (VMs) is becoming increasingly important. Accurate performance modeling of an application would help users in better VM sizing, thus reducing costs. It can also benefit cloud service providers who can offer a new charging model based on the VMs' performance instead of their configured sizes.

In this paper, we present techniques to model the performance of a VM-hosted application as a function of the resources allocated to the VM and the resource contention it experiences. To address this multi-dimensional modeling problem, we propose and refine the use of two machine learning techniques: artificial neural network (ANN) and support vector machine (SVM). We evaluate these modeling techniques using five virtualized applications from the RUBiS and Filebench suite of benchmarks and demonstrate that their median and 90th percentile prediction errors are within 4.36% and 29.17% respectively. These results are substantially better than regression based approaches as well as direct applications of machine learning techniques without our refinements. We also present a simple and effective approach to VM sizing and empirically demonstrate that it can deliver optimal results for 65% of the sizing problems that we studied and produces close-to-optimal sizes for the remaining 35%.

Categories and Subject Descriptors D.4.8 [*Operating Systems*]: Performance; C.4 [*Performance of Systems*]: Modeling techniques

General Terms Management, Performance

Keywords Virtualization, Cloud Data Centers, VM Sizing, Machine Learning, Performance Modeling

VEE'12. March 3–4, 2012, London, England, UK.

1. Introduction

With the proliferation of private and public cloud data centers, it is quite common today, to create or buy virtual machines to host applications instead of physical machines. Cloud users typically pay for a statically configured VM size irrespective of the actual resources consumed by the application (e.g., Amazon EC2). It would be highly desirable for users to size their VMs based on actual performance needs, to reduce costs. At the same time, cloud service providers can benefit from a performance-based charging model built around an application service-level agreement (SLA), thereby eliminating the need for guess work or over-provisioning by the customers [25]. Doing so could increase customer willingness to pay a higher price for better service compared to paying a flat fee based on the size of their VMs. Moreover, cloud service providers would now have the flexibility to dynamically optimize the resources allocated to VMs based on actual demand.

The complexity of meeting application-level SLAs and doing performance troubleshooting in virtual environments has been mentioned in many recent studies [15, 21, 32]. The primary source of this complexity lies in finding accurate relationships between resource allocation and desired application performance targets. First, the performance of many real-world applications depend upon the simultaneous availability levels of several resource types, including CPU, memory, and storage and network I/O performance. Performance model are therefore *multi-dimensional* and *complex*. Second, while some types of resources (e.g., CPU time, memory capacity) are easy to partition, other types (e.g., storage and network I/O bandwidths) are not. Virtualization magnifies this impact due to the inherent, underlying sharing and contention [21]. Our proposed modeling approach explicitly addresses storage I/O contention, local or networked. We do not address (non-storage) network I/O contention in this work. While host-level NIC bandwidth is typically not a bottleneck, there is little control over in-flight packets once they leave the host. Datacenter level solutions are necessary to manage network I/O contention.

In this paper, we create per-application performance models that can then be used for VM resource provisioning. Our models use parameters that are based on widely available control knobs for allocating resources to a VM within commodity virtualization solutions. We make the following contributions in this paper.

1. We identify and study the impact of key VM resource allocation and contention parameters that affect the performance of virtualized applications. In doing so, we find that the I/O latency observed by the virtual machine is a good indicator of I/O con-

Modeling Technique	*Strengths*	*Weaknesses*	*Applications*
		Queuing & Control Theory based Techniques	
Queueing Theory	Usability, Speed	Restrictive assumptions	Predicting response times of internet services [14]
Control Theory	Simplicity	Computational complexity	Linear MIMO models to manage resource for multi-tier applications [26]
		Machine Learning (ML) Techniques	
Regression Analysis	Usability, Transparency	Limited scope	Memory resource modeling [35], Translating physical models to virtual ones [36], Fingerprinting problems [10]
Bayesian Networks	Extensibility, Transparency	Binary decisions, Domain-based	Fingerpointing for SLA violations [12], Signature construction of systems history [13]
Fuzzy Logic	Extensibility	Usability, Stability	Predicting resource demand of virtualized web applications [37]
Reinforcement Learning (RL)	Exploratory	Value predictions not supported	CPU/memory resource allocation for VMs [27]
Kernel Canonical Correlation Analysis (KCCA)	Multivariate analysis	Sensitivity to outliers	Predict Hadoop job execution time [16]
Artificial Neural Networks	Powerful	Opacity, Configuration, Computational complexity, Overfitting	Performance prediction for virtualized applications [22]
Support Vector Machines	Powerful	Opacity, Configuration	Workload modeling in shared storage systems [29], Estimating power consumption [24]

Table 1. A compendium of related work on application performance modeling

tention in a shared storage environment. We empirically demonstrate that it is possible to model the performance of virtualized applications accurately using just three simple parameters.

2. We apply and extensively evaluate two machine learning techniques, Artificial Neural Network (ANNs) and Support Vector Machine (SVM), to predict application performance based on these parameters. We develop *sub-modeling*, a clustering-based approach that overcomes key limitations when directly applying these machine learning techniques.

3. We implement and evaluate our modeling techniques for five complex benchmark workloads from the RUBiS [7] and Filebench [2] suites for the VMware ESX hypervisor [33]. The median and 90th percentile prediction errors are 4.36% and 29.17% respectively (averaged across these applications). The higher prediction errors appear mainly within areas of low resource allocation and consequently low performance.

4. We present a simple and effective approach to sizing the resource requirements for VMs in the presence of storage I/O contention based on the performance models that we develop. Our VM sizing experiments deliver optimal results for 65% of the sizing problems that we studied and produces sizes that are close to optimal for the remaining 35%.

2. Background

Creating performance models for applications as a function of underlying system parameters is a well researched area. Many previous studies have focused on predicting an application's performance based on low level performance counters related to cache usage, allocation, and miss rates [14, 28]. Utilizing such models is difficult in virtualized environments because the support of hardware performance counters is not widely available in production hypervisors. However, virtualized environments provide an unique opportunity to model an application's performance as a function of the size of the VM or underlying hardware resource allocation. The resources allocated to a VM are fungible and can be changed in an online manner. For example, VMware's vSphere utility allows changing the minimum reservation and maximum allocation or relative priority of CPU, memory, and I/O resources available to a VM at runtime. We now examine the work related to application performance modeling as a function of one or more resources.

2.1 Related Work

We classify the related work into two categories: (1) Queuing & control theory based techniques and (2) Machine learning techniques. Table 1 provides a summary of the related work which we elaborate on below.

Queuing and Control Theoretic Models. Doyle *et al.* [14] used queueing theory based analytical models to predict response times of Internet services under different load and resource allocation. Bennani *et al.* [9] proposed multi-class queuing networks to predict the response time and throughput for online and batch virtualized workloads. The effectiveness of these solutions is restricted by their simplified assumptions about a virtualized system's internal operation based on closed-form mathematical models.

Another related class of solutions have applied control theory to adjust VM resource allocation and achieve the desired application performance. Such solutions often assume a linear performance model for the virtualized application. For example, first-order autoregressive models are used to manage CPU allocation for Web servers [23, 34]. A linear multi-input-multi-output (MIMO) model is used to manage the multi-type resources for multi-tier applications [26]. A similar MIMO model is also used to allocate CPU resource for compensating the interference between concurrent VMs [25]. Such linear models are not sufficient to accurately capture the nonlinear behaviors of virtualized applications, which are demonstrated and addressed in this paper.

Machine Learning Approaches. Machine learning techniques have been extensively studied for performance analysis and troubleshooting. The CARVE project employs simple regression analysis to predict the performance impact of memory allocation [35]. Wood *et al.* use regression to map a resource usage profile obtained from a physical system to one that can be used on a virtualized system [36]. However, the accuracy of regression analysis has been shown to be poor when used for modeling the performance of virtualized applications [22].

Cohen *et al.* [12] introduced Tree-Augmented Bayesian Networks to identify system metrics attributable to SLA violations. The models enable an administrator to forecast whether certain values for specific system parameters are indictors of application failures or performance violations. In subsequent work, the authors used bayesian networks to construct signatures of the performance problems based on performance statistics and clustering similar signatures to support searching for previously recorded instances of observed performance problems [13].

Bodik *et al.* [10] challenged the usefulness of Bayesian classifiers and proposed logistic regression with L1 regularization to derive indicators. This was shown to be effective for automatic performance crisis diagnosis and in turn facilitating remedial actions. The above techniques address bottleneck identification and forecasting whether certain resource usage and/or application metrics would lead to SLA violations. However, they do not address how much SLA violation would be incurred or how resources should be allocated to prevent future violation. In contrast, we specifically address performance prediction: given a set of controllable/observable parameters, what would be the application's performance? Such prediction can then be used within an optimized resource allocation or VM sizing framework.

Xu *et al.* use fuzzy logic to model and predict the resource demand of virtualized web applications [37]. The VCONF project has studied using reinforcement learning combined with ANN to automatically tune the CPU and memory configurations of a VM in order to achieve good performance for its hosted application [27]. These solutions are specifically targeted for the CPU resource. In addition to CPU, we address memory and I/O contention explicitly.

To address such "what-if" questions, ANN models were proposed in our own previous work [22]. However, subsequent investigations revealed several drawbacks. First, we observed that the parameter to capture I/O contention in shared storage platform can lead to arbitrary inaccuracy in the model (as demonstrated in section 3.3). Second, we observed that the proposed approach of constructing a single model encompassing the entire parameter space in a multi-dimensional model was also severely deficient. In this paper, we propose new modeling techniques that overcome these limitations and evaluate them on a wide set of realistic virtualized server workloads. Further, we demonstrate that our models can also be applied easily for accurate VM sizing.

We explore the use of both ANN and SVM approaches to machine learning for performance modeling. Although SVMs are generally applied as a powerful classification technique, SVM-based regression (SVR) is gaining popularity in systems data modeling. In [29], SVR was used to build models to predict response time given a specified load for individual workloads co-hosted on shared storage system. SVR has also been used to model power consumption as a function of hardware and software performance counters [24]. To the best of our knowledge, SVR has not been used before for performance prediction of virtualized applications.

2.2 Building Models

We propose to use advanced machine learning methods to model the relationship between the resource allocation to a virtualized application and its performance using a limited amount of training data. Such a model can then be used to predict the resource need of an application to meet its performance target. One of the questions in this approach is when and how the model is built. Since our approach requires collecting application performance data for a wide range of resource allocation choices, it is difficult to build the model quickly based only on observations from production runs. One option is to have a staging area where a customer can deploy the application and run a sample workload against various resource allocation configurations to facilitate modeling. We can also leverage recent work like *justrunit* [38] where authors provided a framework for collecting training data by running cloned VMs and applications in an identical physical environment. The modeling techniques that we propose can complement and enhance a such a system which used simple linear interpolation to predict performance results for unavailable allocations.

3. Model Parameters Selection

Choosing appropriate control knobs to manage a VM's resource allocation is critical to create a robust performance model. The purpose of this section is two fold. First we identify the knobs in the form of VM resource allocation parameters that can be used to directly control application performance. Second, we demonstrate that the relationship between these controls and the application performance is quite complex and hard to model.

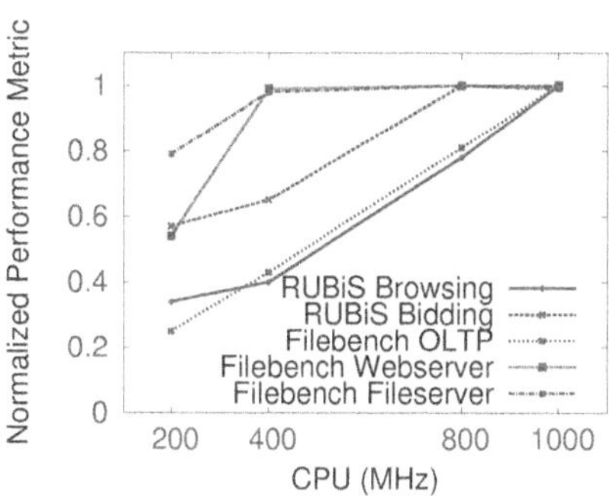

Figure 1. Impact of *CPU limit.*

We focus our discussion on control knobs available on the VMware ESX hypervisor [30]. Similar knobs are available in other hypervisor solutions as well. Throughout this paper, we use five virtualized benchmark applications to both motivate and evaluate our modeling approach. These applications are representative of various enterprise workloads that consume different physical resources (CPU, memory, and I/O) in a complex fashion, and are described in more detail in Section 6. The performance metrics associated with the RUBiS workloads are *requests/sec* and those for the Filebench workloads are *operations/sec.*

3.1 CPU Limit

ESX provides three control knobs for CPU allocation to VMs: *reservation, limit,* and *shares* [31]. Reservation guarantees a minimum CPU allocation expressed in MHz. Limit (in MHz) provides an upper bound on the CPU allocation. Share provides a mechanism for proportional allocation during time periods when the sum of the CPU demands of the currently running VMs exceeds the capacity of the physical host. We chose *reservation* and *limit*, both set to the same value as our control knob, to enforce the physical segregation of CPU resources across multiple VMs running on a single physical machine and to ensure that the VM will never get any allocation more than the set value as well.

Even with such physical segregation for the CPU, the relationship between application performance and the CPU limit is complex. We measured the performance of the five virtualized applications while varying the VM's CPU limit from 200 MHz to 1 GHz keeping the memory allocations high enough to ensure that memory is not the bottleneck. We used a VMFS [11] data store on a local disk of the ESX host to store the virtual disks of the VMs. Figure 1 shows the normalized performance of these applications. Both the RUBiS workloads behave non-linearly; the performance slope varies based on CPU allocation ranges. The three personalities of Filebench: OLTP, webserver, and fileserver behave quite differently. While the webserver and fileserver performances saturate quickly at 400MHz, OLTP performance, on the other hand, varies almost linearly with CPU allocation. Overall, this data reveals that virtualized workloads can have quite different performance curves with respect to CPU allocation.

3.2 Memory Limit

Similar to the knobs for CPU, the ESX hypervisor provides three controls for memory allocation: *reservation, limit,* and *shares.* The semantics of these knobs are similar to the ones for CPU. We set the reservation equal to limit and used this as the control parameter to guarantee a specific memory allocation and no more.

Figure 2 shows the normalized performance of these applications as we vary the memory limit from 256 MB to 1 GB. The CPU allocation was kept at a sufficient level to avoid saturation, and there was no I/O contention at the storage. In the case of the

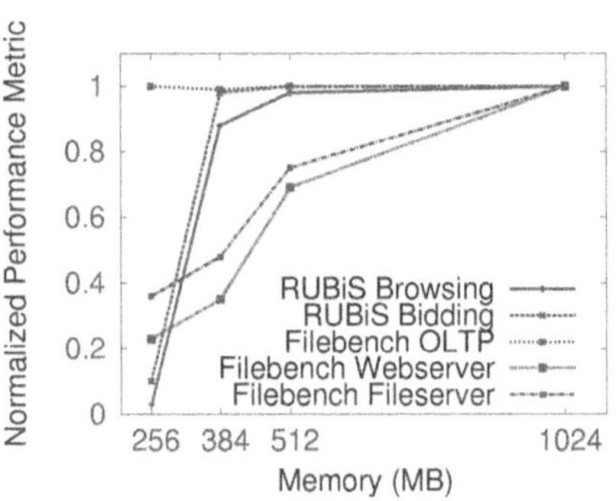

Figure 2. Impact of *memory limit*.

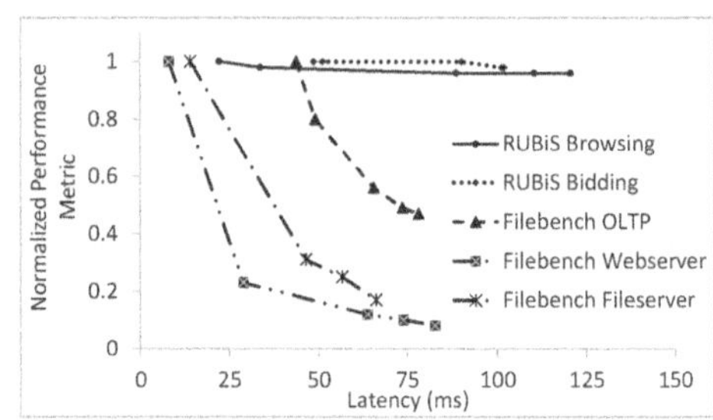

Figure 3. Performance impact of *VM I/O latency*.

I/O Type	Postmark TPS	CDIOPS	I/O latency [ms]
Seq	49	6016	48.08
Seq	52	8483	48.43
Seq	46	8303	46.14
Rand	13	154	77.14
Rand	13	155	70.06
Rand	11	165	81.9

Table 2. Comparison between CDIOPS vs. I/O latency for modeling I/O contention.

RUBiS browsing mix workload, performance improves sharply between 256 MB and 512 MB, and remains almost flat afterwards. This behavior can be attributed to the fact that working set size of the workload fits into the memory after a certain allocation. A similar observation can also be made in the case of the RUBiS bidding mix workload, where the working set fits within 384 MB of memory. The Filebench-OLTP workload shows almost no memory dependency and the performance remains flat when the VM's memory allocation ranges from 256 MB to 1 GB. The performance of the Filebench webserver and fileserver rises gradually as more of the working set fits in memory.

Overall, these workloads show varied behavior. Some are insensitive to VM memory allocation, while others show either a sudden or gradual increase in performance as the entire or an increasing fraction of the working set fits in memory.

3.3 Virtual Disk I/O Latency

Strict performance isolation and guaranteed I/O allocation in virtualized environments are challenging because storage arrays are accessed in a distributed manner and the allocation is not under direct control of the hypervisor [17, 18]. I/O allocation can be controlled or modeled in several ways: measuring or controlling the number of I/O operations/sec (IOPS), MB/sec, or I/O latency. In our previous work [22], we used the competing disk IOPS (CDIOPS) issued by other VMs to the shared storage as a measure of I/O contention for a VM. However, there are two main drawbacks to this. First, obtaining the true CDIOPS value when using shared networked storage requires explicit communication either with other hosts or the storage device; this may not be feasible or if so, would incur substantial overhead to keep the information up-to-date. Second, when there is high variance in I/O sizes from competing workloads, the CDIOPS metric can be substantially inaccurate in capturing the actual I/O contention. Large I/O requests would keep the CDIOPS low while causing high device latencies for all VMs. Finally, even the sequentiality characteristics of competing I/O can lead to inaccuracies when using a single CDIOPS value for modeling sequential versus random I/Os which have different costs.

To illustrate the limitations of CDIOPS for modeling I/O contention, we ran Postmark [20] in a VM running on a ESX host and generated I/O contention using *fio* [3] on a different VM. We fixed the I/O size at 4KB and and issued 4 outstanding I/Os at a time. Keeping the CPU and memory allocation levels constant, we configured the fio VM to issue either random or sequential I/O. We recorded the data for three different instances in each case. Table 2 reports the VM I/O latency, CDIOPS, and the resulting transactions-per-second (TPS) for Postmark. When the competing I/O is sequential, in spite of the higher CDIOPS values, the application performance is better than it is when the competing I/O is random and the CDIOPS values are lower. This simple experiment clearly indicates the inadequacy of CDIOPS as a measure of I/O contention. A similar example can be constructed for bandwidth (in MB/sec) based modeling by using small and large sized I/Os.

I/O latency-based measure of I/O contention. We explored the use of the VM *I/O latency* itself, a direct measure of modeling the I/O performance of a VM in the presence of contention. This metric directly reflects the impact of I/O contention irrespective of its complexity as well as the performance of the underlying device. Table 2 demonstrates that using the VM I/O latency more accurately reflects the performance impact of I/O contention on the Postmark workload.

To understand how VMs behave as I/O contention (as captured by I/O latency) varies, we ran each of the five applications in one of the VMs (*appVM*) and ran the competing fio workload in another VM (called *fioVM*) both sharing the same storage. The load is varied from the fioVM to create different levels of I/O contention and cause different I/O latencies perceived by the appVM. Figure 3 shows normalized performance as the I/O latency is varied from 20 ms to 120 ms. Most of the applications suffer significant performance degradation when the average I/O latency seen by the appVM increases. The RUBiS Bidding and Browsing workloads generate very few number of I/Os (because their working set is small and fits well in the memory) which made them largely insensitive to the I/O contention.

Controlling I/O latency. IO latency observed by a VM can be controlled in many ways. Techniques like PARDA [17] and mClock [18] have been proposed for I/O performance isolation among VMs. With PARDA [17], each virtual disk can be assigned an I/O share value which determines the relative weight of the I/Os from its virtual disk as compared to others. VMs with higher I/O shares get higher IOPS and lower latency. mClock provides additional controls of reservation and limit to control VM latency. Due to a lack of access to these technologies, we used the intensity of contending workloads to control I/O latency for our experiments.

Our analysis in this section reveals that the performance of various applications varies in a non-linear and complex manner as the allocation of resources for the VM is changed. We also noticed that the relationship with respect to one resource is dependent on the availability of other resource as well. For example, performance of the RUBiS bidding workload seems almost independent of I/O latency in Figure 3. However, under low memory allocations (256 MB) the performance is impacted by the changes in VM I/O latency. When operating at 256 MB, the performance changed from 1.5 requests/sec under high latency (80-100 ms) to

Benchmark	% Avg.	% Med.	Stdev.	90p.
RUBiS Browsing	68.57	5.23	119.73	340.00
RUBiS Bidding	19.30	2.29	45.86	60.18
Filebench OLTP	11.59	8.82	12.63	21.08
Filebench Webserver	19.85	12.88	30.36	38.60
Filebench Fileserver	12.89	6.80	18.64	28.78

Table 3. Prediction errors when using a single ANN Model.

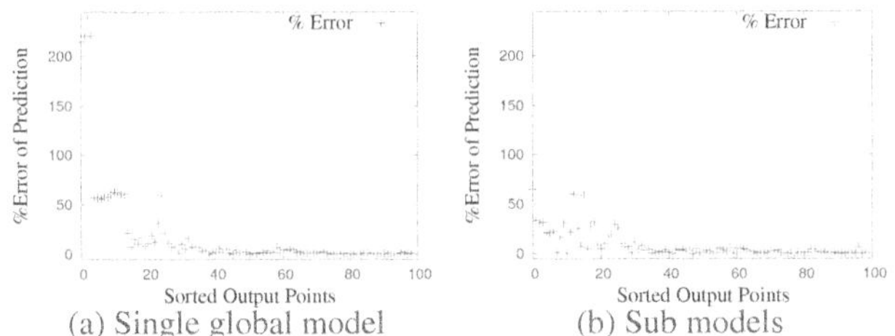

(a) Single global model (b) Sub models

Figure 4. % Error in prediction for points sorted in increasing order of obtained performance for RUBiS bidding mix.

6 requests/sec under low latency (25-35 ms); an increase of 300%. On the other hand, the performance remains saturates at 59-60 requests/sec when operating under 1024 MB, regardless of the the VM I/O latency level. Such behaviors clearly emphasize the complexity of modeling performance when taking I/O contention into account.

4. Model Design

In our previous work [22], we showed the limitations of standard regression analysis techniques for modeling virtualized applications due to their inability to capture the complex behavior; we confirmed these behaviors in the previous section. Specifically, our study demonstrated that the non-linear dependence of performance on resource levels and the complex influence of contention cannot be represented using simple functions. The study also motivated and justified the choice of Artificial Neural Networks (ANN) based modeling for virtualized applications. In this paper, we demonstrate that a simple application of ANN-based technique for modeling can produce large modeling errors when used for complex applications and when possible resource allocations span a wider range (as typical in cloud data centers) than those explored in that study. We introduce the use of another popular machine learning model, Support Vector Machine (SVM) which has gained more popularity recently and find that it has similar limitations as ANN when used directly for modeling. We analyze the root cause of why ANN and SVM techniques are still not sufficient and propose improved use of these tools to substantially increase modeling accuracy.

4.1 Limitations of a Single Global Model

Table 3 summarizes error statistics when using ANNs for modeling a set of workloads. We note that prediction errors can be high in some cases, for instance, the RUBiS workloads. We registered identical observations by applying SVM modeling as well. Further analyzing the data revealed that large errors were mostly concentrated in a few sub-regions of the output value space, indicating a single model's inability to accurately characterize changes in application behavior as it moves across critical resource allocation boundaries. We demonstrate this behavior in Figure 4(a) where we plot the % error in performance prediction across different testing points of RUBiS bidding mix benchmark (specified by resource allocation and I/O latency levels) when sorted by actual obtained performance in *requests/sec*. Note that the % errors are quite different across the range of output values and higher errors are concentrated in the region with smaller output values.

4.2 Creating Multiple Models with Sub-modeling

To overcome the limitations posed by a single model, we explored the use of multiple models that target specific regions of the input parameter space. Our proposed *sub-modeling* technique divides the input parameter space into non-overlapping sub-regions and builds individual models for each sub-region. For performance prediction, the sub-model corresponding to the sub-region containing the input parameters can be used. One approach to sub-modeling is subdividing the space into several equal-sized regions. However, this seemingly simple approach is inadequate. First, it is difficult to determine how many sub-models to use. A small number of submodels may not improve prediction accuracy. Whereas a large number of sub-models would be impractical in terms of collecting sufficient training data points for each to ensure high accuracy. Second, since applications behave non-linearly and non-smoothly with respect to resource allocations, merely building sub-models for equally divided regions may not always be effective in isolating and capturing unique behaviors.

To create robust sub-models, we employ classical clustering techniques whereby the data points are separated into clusters based on a chosen indicator parameter. We used an improved version of K-means clustering technique (*pamk* function in the fpc [4] package of R [6]) that automatically identifies the optimal number of clusters based on the observed values. We used *application output values* and *prediction error values* (from using the global model) as two choices for the clustering indicator parameter. To verify that the clustering results were useful, we checked whether the cluster boundaries can be clearly identified based on the input parameter values. In other words, a well-defined cluster should be defined by continuous ranges in the input parameter space. In Section 6, we demonstrate that output-value based clustering indeed produces well-defined regions at the input space with negligible overlapping. After the clustering stage, we segregate the training data points into buckets based on cluster boundaries and build separate sub-models corresponding to each cluster.

Predicting for a given resource assignment entails checking the input parameter values and determine which sub-model to use. When clusters do not overlap, for points in the boundary regions, we use ensemble averaging of the two consecutive clusters that these points straddle. If clusters overlap in the input parameters space; we use one of two methods to identify the model to use. The first method uses ensemble averaging of predictions using all the overlapping sub-models. The second method coalesces the overlapping clusters and builds a single sub-model for the merged cluster. In general, for applications with high prediction errors either distributed across the entire parameter space or simply concentrated in a single sub-region, the sub-modeling technique can help reduce prediction errors substantially in comparison to a single global model over both ANN and SVM techniques. We demonstrate the effectiveness of the output value based sub-modeling optimization in Section 6.

Apart from evaluating clustering based on *output values*, we also performed clustering based on *prediction error values* from the single global model. This choice was motivated by the skewing of high prediction error values towards low allocation values for several of the applications (e.g., in the case of RUBiS bidding mix). At low resource allocation, the sensitivity of the error computation with respect to predicted values is higher when using a single model for the entire range because the application performance drops significantly in this range for most workloads. For instance, requests/sec for RUBiS workloads drops to very low values when the memory assignment of the VM nears 256 MB. Figure 4(a) confirms that the large errors are concentrated in the lower output region of RUBiS bidding mix which corresponds to the application output with less than or equal to 256 MB. We made a similar observation for the RUBiS browsing workload. We created multiple models based on the clustering results on the % prediction error values obtained from the global model. Figure 4(b) demonstrates that error based clustering can substantially reduce the % errors in the lower output regions. In fact, the 90th percentile errors for RUBiS browsing mix dropped from 340% to 27.28%. For the bidding mix, the reduction is from 60.18% to 25.80%.

In general, if large errors are concentrated within a specific region of input parameters space, sub-models based on prediction error values from a single global model become valuable. However, this trend does not hold across all the workloads. Except the RUBiS workload mixes, error-based clustering did not lead to well-defined sub-regions and resulted in high overlap in the corresponding input parameter spaces, rendering the clusters practically unusable. On the other hand, sub-modeling based on output values produced robust models across all the workloads we examined. We evaluate output value based sub-modeling in more detail in Section 6.

5. Model Configuration

In this section, we scrutinize both the ANN-based modeling and SVM-based modeling and identify the key internal parameters that need to be tuned for robust modeling. In addition, we provide details of how the model trainings are performed.

5.1 Model Training

During the training process, a machine learning model gradually tunes its internal network by utilizing the *training data set*. The accuracy of any model is contingent upon selection of a proper training data set and is evaluated using a different *testing data set*. Briefly, the training starts with a boot-strapping phase which requires system administrators to identify the best-case and worst-case resource allocation considered feasible across each resource dimension (CPU limit, memory limit, and virtual disk I/O latency) for the workload on the target hardware. The input parameter set is then chosen by first including these boundary allocation values and selecting additional values obtained by equally dividing the range between the lowest and highest values across each resource dimension. This input parameter set and the corresponding output values (obtained by running the workload on the target system) are chosen as the initial training data set.

After this initial training, the modeling accuracy with the initial training data set is measured by predicting for the testing data set. If satisfactory accuracy (defined as an administrator chosen bound on prediction error) is achieved, the training process concludes. Otherwise, additional allocation values are computed by preferentially varying highly correlated input parameters (based on the correlation coefficient calculated using any statistical tool) by further subdividing the allocation range with the goal of populating the training set with allocation values that represent the output parameter range more uniformly.

5.2 Model Configuring

We highlight some of the intricacies of model configuration when using ANN and SVM for modeling VM-hosted applications.

5.2.1 Configuring ANNs

Hidden Layer and Hidden Neurons An ANN has multiple layers of neurons which include at least one input layer and one output layer and a tunable number of hidden layers, each with a tunable number of hidden neurons associated with it. The number of hidden layers and hidden neurons at each layer play an integral role in determining the accuracy of an ANN model. However, choosing the number of hidden neurons at each hidden layer is not straightforward. If the number of hidden neurons is too small, the model may not assign enough importance to the input parameters and hence suffer from under-fitting. Conversely, if this number is too large, the model may amplify the importance of input parameters and suffer from over-fitting. We evaluated an automated incremental approach of determining the hidden layers and hidden neurons in the training process. We start with one hidden layer and three hidden neurons (because of three input parameters in our environment) at each hidden layer to accommodate the three modeling parameters. We grow the network by adding more neurons on the single hidden layer. We grow the network by adding more layers if we find that increasing number of hidden neurons does not improve modeling accuracy. If adding more neurons or layers does not lead to improved accuracy, we pick the least number of layers/neurons which provided the best accuracy.

For an example, the above process led to an ANN configured with 2 hidden layers and 15 hidden neurons at each hidden layer for the RUBiS bidding mix workload. Table 4 summarizes the average and standard deviation of errors for 59 testing data set points using a single global ANN model for RUBiS bidding mix workload under various combinations of hidden layers and hidden neurons at each layer. We applied the same incremental procedure for other workloads to derive the best possible layer/neuron combination for each.

(hlayer,hneurons)	% Avg. Error	Std. dev.
(1,4)	13.59	13.30
(1,8)	3.25	5.43
(1,12)	6.07	10.61
(2,4)	6.10	9.04
(2,8)	5.17	6.12
(2,12)	9.46	18.83
(2,15)	2.52	3.52
(2,20)	10.34	17.48

Table 4. ANN model errors when varying hidden layers (hlayers) and hidden neurons at each layer (hneurons) for the RUBiS bidding mix workload.

Model	% Avg. error	% Median error	Std. dev.
ANN1	64.67	6.50	105.23
ANN2	84.62	9.31	140.82
ANN3	85.80	9.68	140.87
ANN4	58.95	7.72	107.35
ANN5	63.09	8.70	104.93
Ensemble	68.57	5.23	119.73

Table 5. Errors across individual and ensemble ANN models on RUBiS browsing workload.

Activation Function It defines the mapping function from the input to the output for each node. Our previous study [22] already confirmed that *ELLIOT* activation function (a faster version of sigmoidal function) is the best choice for this environment. We observed the same trend and hence used ELLIOT activation function for all the benchmarks.

Ensemble Averaging Since the initial weight distributions are randomly selected, non-identical models are created across multiple training runs even if the tunable ANN parameters and the training set are the same. We found that the prediction from the testing data can vary significantly across such similarly trained models. One approach to tackle such variability is to generate multiple models and average their predicted output. Such *ensemble averaging* using multiple ANN models is a well-known technique which turns out to be quite effective [19]. Table 5 demonstrates how ensemble averaging reduces prediction variability across a set of ANN models generated using the same training data set, training procedure, and identical internal configuration of the ANN. Errors are shown for same testing data points of the RUBiS browsing mix workload. It is important to clarify that ensemble averaging reduces the variations in prediction accuracy across different training runs and does not always deliver to the most accurate predictions.

5.2.2 Configuring SVMs

At high-level, SVM-based regression technique works by first mapping the inputs to a multi-dimensional vector space using some form of non-linear function and finally a linear regression is performed in this mapped space. We specifically used ϵ-regression implementation of e1071 package which provides an interface to the libsvm [5] in R. There are several parameters that need to be tuned for getting accurate modeling with SVM - kernel, gamma, cost. We experimented with a set of kernel functions (linear, polynomial, radial, sigmoid), out of which *radial basis function* turned out to be effective for our data set. Gamma and cost values were calculated by a *tune()* function which does a grid search over the training data to figure out the best possible values of those two parameters. It is important to understand the influence of these two parameters, because the accuracy of a SVM model is largely dependent on their selection. For example, if the cost is too large, we have a high penalty for nonseparable points and we may store many support vectors and overfit. Conversely, a very small value may lead to underfitting [8].

6. Evaluation

Our evaluation focuses on addressing the accuracy of our sub-modeling techniques using both the ANN and SVM approaches and contrasting these with regression techniques. We compare each of these modeling techniques when used to create a single global model and as well as clustering based sub-models. We also evaluate the prediction confidence by examining how prediction errors are distributed in the parameter space. Finally, we evaluate the sensitivity of modeling accuracy to training data set size, its robustness to noise in measurements, and the overhead incurred in modeling.

For our experiments, we used an AMD-based Dell PowerEdge 2970 server with dual socket and six 2.4 GHz cores per socket. The server has 32 GB of physical memory and ran VMware ESX-4.1 hypervisor. All the VMs ran Ubuntu-Linux-10.04. VMs were restricted to use only four of the cores (0-3). All the virtual disks for VMs, and the ESX install were on a VMFS [11] (VMware's clustered file system) data-store on local 7200 RPM SAS drives from Seagate. We used a VMware vSphere client running on a separate physical machine for managing the resource allocations of individual VMs. The statistics were collected using `esxtop` utility and transferred to a separate Dell PowerEdge T105 machine with a quad-core AMD Opteron processor (1.15GHz$\times$4), 8 GB of physical memory, 7.2k rpm disk, running Ubuntu-Linux-10.10, for analysis. All modeling tasks were also done using this machine.

To simulate I/O contention, we used a separate Ubuntu-Linux VM with 1000 MHz of VCPU and 512 MB of memory to run *fio* [3] - a Linux-based I/O workload generation tool co-located with the virtualized application being modeled. The number of outstanding I/Os and other workload parameters (e.g., sequentiality) were varied to create different levels of I/O contention on the shared VMFS data-store. A different VM on the same host was used to run Perl-based scripts for changing the allocation parameters for the VMs running the benchmarks. Our choice of following workloads used for evaluation were guided by their representation of data center server workloads and their diversity in resource usage:

Benchmark	Training points	Testing points
RUBiS Browsing	160	79
RUBiS Bidding	198	99
Filebench OLTP	135	75
Filebench Webserver	160	80
Filebench Fileserver	68	68

Table 6. Training and Testing data set sizes.

RUBiS Browsing. A Java servlet based RUBiS [7] Browsing workload was used for the experiments. Client requests were handled by a Tomcat web server and the underlying database was MySQL. The webserver, database, and clients were run on the same VM to minimize network effects that we do not address in this work. 1000 clients were run simultaneously. The Browsing mix consists of 100% read-only interactions. After each run, RUBiS reported average throughput as requests/sec, chosen as the application performance metric.

RUBiS Bidding. A similar set up was used for RUBiS Bidding Mix workload with 15% writes. The performance metric was average requests/sec with 400 clients running simultaneously were used and Both the RUBiS profiles are CPU and memory intensive. They generate a small number of I/Os and are largely insensitive to the I/O contention.

Filebench OLTP. Filebench [2] is a widely used benchmark for creating realistic I/O intensive workloads such as OLTP, webserver, mail server, etc. We used the Linux based Filebench tool and ran the OLTP application profile which emulates a transaction processing workload. This profile tests for the performance of small random reads and writes, and is sensitive to the latency of moderate (128k+) synchronous writes to the log file. We configured the benchmark to create 32 reader threads and 4 writer threads; I/O size was set to 2KB with a 10GB dataset. We took the Operations per Second (Ops/Sec) reported by Filebench as the application performance metric for this workload.

Filebench Webserver. We also used the Webserver profile that performs a mix of open, read, close on multiple files in a directory tree, accompanied by a file append to simulate the web log. We created a fileset of total size 10GB and used 32 user threads. The application performance metric used was the operations per second (Ops/sec) performed.

Filebench Fileserver The Filebench Fileserver workload performs a sequence of creates, deletes, appends, reads, writes and attribute operations on the file system. A configurable hierarchical directory structure is used for the file set. Again, we used a dataset of 10GB and 32 simultaneous threads, and used Ops/sec as the application performance metric.

6.1 Modeling Accuracy

We evaluated the modeling techniques for overall accuracy across the workloads. Table 6 shows the training and testing data set size used for each benchmark; the training data set was obtained by following the training procedure described in Section 5. A peculiarity of the ANN Elliot function that we use within the core of our ANN models is that it requires the output values to be mapped in the range of 0 to 1. In order to map application performance metric values to this range, we normalized all observed values relative to the observed application performance obtained with the highest resource allocation and no I/O contention and including an additional headroom of 10% to account for outliers. No such translation was necessary for any of the other modeling techniques. We compared the ANN and SVM approaches with the following regression based approaches.

Regression linear(L) is the simplest of the regression family which attempts to establish a relationship between the output and the input parameters by considering only first degree terms of the input

Benchmark	# clusters	% Overlap of consecutive clusters
RUBiS Browsing	2	1.25
RUBiS Bidding	4	0.37
Filebench OLTP	8	1.09
Filebench Webserver	2	0.63
Filebench Fileserver	2	1.47

Table 8. Number of clusters and the average % overlap betwee consecutive cluster pairs, measured using the Jaccard coefficient.

variables.

Regression quadratic(Q) allows both first order and second order terms for the input variables.

Regression linear interactive(LI) captures the combined combined influence of pairs of parameters on the application output (e.g. Memory and I/O Latency) using the first degree of input variables with pairwise interactive terms.

6.1.1 Single Global Model

Table 7 summarizes the error statistics for all benchmarks and modeling techniques; we focus on average, median, and 90th percentile values of the error distribution. The classical regression techniques largely fail to deliver usable accuracy while using a single global model. This result confirms that the non-linear and non-smooth application behavior cannot be characterized well using simpler mathematical models. Similarly, the ANN global model and the SVM global model also suffer from high average and variance in prediction errors, especially for the RUBiS benchmarks and Filebench webserver, confirming that that global models have limitations when modeling complexity.

6.1.2 Sub-Modeling

Recall that sub-modeling requires clustering of the training data points and then defining cluster boundaries using the corresponding input parameters before creating sub-models for each cluster. Our evaluation focuses on output value based clustering; we found it to be more broadly applicable than error based clustering. We first report the number of clusters and the degree of overlap in consecutive clusters for each benchmark in Table 8. If the total number of clusters is *n*, the number of consecutive pairs of clusters is *n-1*. Sub-modeling is only viable when there is less overlap in the input dimensions of the clusters formed. We consider two consecutive clusters overlap only if one or more points in both the clusters overlap in all three input dimensions (CPU, Memory and I/O latency). The output-value based clustering is able to produce well-defined clusters as the average overlaps for all the benchmarks is about 1% as calculated using the Jaccard coefficient.

Table 7 presents the error statistics for sub-modeling based on output value clustering for each benchmark. For all workloads and modeling techniques, sub-modeling successfully reduces the mean, median, and 90th percentile of the error distribution when compared to using a single global model. Interestingly, even simple regression models provided greater accuracy using sub-modeling relative to a global model in most cases. This uniform trend clearly indicates that the complexity of these applications cannot be reduced to a single consistent representation as a global model would be forced to adhere to. As the sub models are confined to smaller ranges of the applications performance metric space, they can offer constrained, but more accurate, representations of behavior. Although sub-modeling with clustering increases the attractiveness of simpler regression based models, the power and utility of using the machine learning based models are evident when we consider error variance. We found, in particular, that the effectiveness of regression based modeling is tied to the effectiveness of clustering. When the clusters are bigger, regression models typically perform poorly (average error of 42.78% for R-Browsing using regression-Q) . On the other hand, ANN and SVM are able to provide reasonable accuracy in all the scenarios with average errors ranging from 5.90% to 15.95% and 5.65% to 21.51% respectively. To provide a more detailed view of accuracy when using sub-modeling with ANN and SVM, Fig 5 shows the actual and predicted output values for each of the testing points for benchmark. For clarity, we present the actual and predicted values sorted in increasing order of actual performance obtained. Predicted values closely follow the actual values in the majority of the cases.

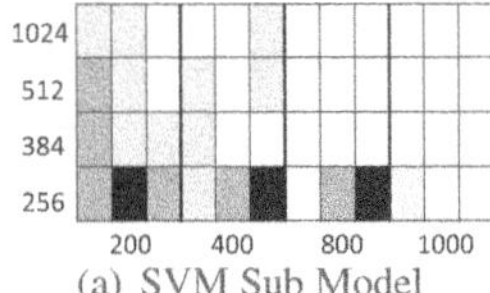

(a) SVM Sub Model

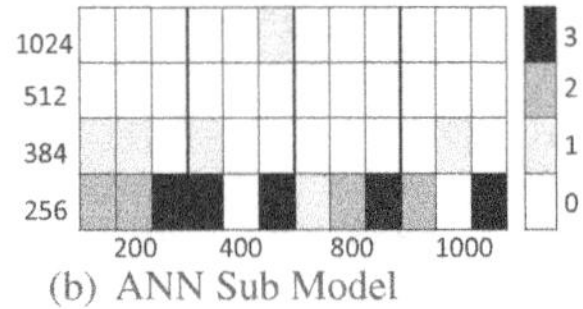

(b) ANN Sub Model

Figure 6. Error Distribution of RUBiS Bidding Mix when using sub models for prediction. The X axis represents CPU Limit (MHz); the Y axis represents Memory Limit (MB). Each box is divided into three columns - representing low, medium, and high (from left to right) VM I/O latency. Error value 0-3% = white, 3-9% = light grey, 9-27% = dark grey, 27% and more = black.

6.1.3 Summary

Based on our analysis with the five virtualized server benchmarks, we conclude that accurately designing and configuring ANN and SVM based models are critical to effectively address the VM performance modeling problem. We find that creating multiple sub models is a necessary step in achieving high accuracy predictions. For instance, even with as few as 68 training data points, both the ANN and SVM based sub-models improve the prediction accuracy for the filebench-fileserver benchmark substantially.

In summary, these new techniques substantially improve the prediction accuracy and reduce the average and 90th percentile prediction errors from 26.48% and 101.68% respectively (averaged over all applications) for a correctly configured single ANN global model to 11.04% and 29.17% by using sub-modeling with ANN. Similarly for SVM, the average and 90th percentile prediction errors drop from 34.19% and 66.91% respectively for a single global model to 12.96% and 33.46% using sub models. We also emphasize that between ANN and SVM, there is no clear winner. Although Table 7 shows that ANN is slightly better in prediction statistics than SVM for most of the workloads, these differences are not statistically significant.

6.2 Measures of Confidence

While summary error metrics are valuable indicators, the distribution of error values across various combinations of input parameters can be a useful guide to the system administrator while choosing a specific set of allocation values. Particularly, if it is known that in certain regions of the resource allocation space, the modeling error tends to be higher, system administrators can choose to compensate with a greater degree of over-provisioning. Figure 6 shows a heatmap of error distributions for qRUBiS bidding mix workload using SVM and ANN based sub-modeling as an example to illustrate this point. The higher errors are concentrated towards the region of low memory allocations (256 MB) with both techniques, informing administrators of caution while choosing allocations around that range of memory allocations. While we do not address this in our work, it is possible to modify predictions to be conservative for regions prone to higher prediction errors within

Bench mark	Modeling	Regression-L			Regression-Q			Regression-LI			SVM			ANN		
		% prediction error			*% prediction error*			*% prediction error*			*% prediction error*			*% prediction error*		
		avg.	**med.**	**90p.**	**avg.**	**med.**	**90p.**	**avg.**	**med.**	**90p.**	**avg.**	**med.**	**90p.**	**avg.**	**med.**	**90p.**
RUBiS	Global	397.08	36.05	1366.83	323.81	23.94	867.77	327.27	35.47	1090.05	55.78	12.78	142.67	68.57	5.23	340.00
Browsing	Sub-Model	106.11	17.74	340.60	42.78	4.16	145.01	103.39	18.78	332.80	21.51	5.19	68.44	**15.95**	**2.94**	45.87
RUBiS	Global	314.05	30.87	1096.58	110.53	21.81	341.54	317.52	29.37	1126.94	68.86	14.21	100.67	19.52	1.97	80.00
Bidding	Sub-Model	9.19	2.43	34.72	8.37	1.94	34.64	9.10	2.39	35.08	7.38	**1.79**	**22.50**	**7.18**	**1.79**	30.01
Filebench	Global	18.33	15.75	33.41	17.82	12.63	35.58	14.02	10.41	28.74	7.40	4.70	13.14	11.59	8.82	21.08
OLTP	Sub-Model	6.31	2.74	13.42	9.47	3.44	29.48	7.55	3.57	10.95	**5.65**	**2.90**	15.19	5.90	3.02	**13.66**
Filebench	Global	76.03	62.99	138.31	50.54	44.91	96.71	51.44	33.41	113.78	25.02	15.57	53.50	19.85	12.88	38.60
Webserver	Sub-Model	32.13	21.85	53.01	27.83	20.31	55.09	29.85	20.72	55.79	19.38	12.25	36.02	**15.57**	**8.49**	**33.07**
Filebench	Global	49.02	30.70	98.18	54.94	21.20	123.36	27.59	21.10	55.75	13.87	9.38	24.56	12.89	6.80	28.78
Fileserver	Sub-Model	21.34	13.63	46.48	16.22	8.91	42.64	18.35	11.26	38.91	10.89	6.72	25.14	**10.60**	**5.57**	**23.22**

Table 7. % Error statistics (average, median, and 90th percentile) for different modeling techniques by using global models and sub models.

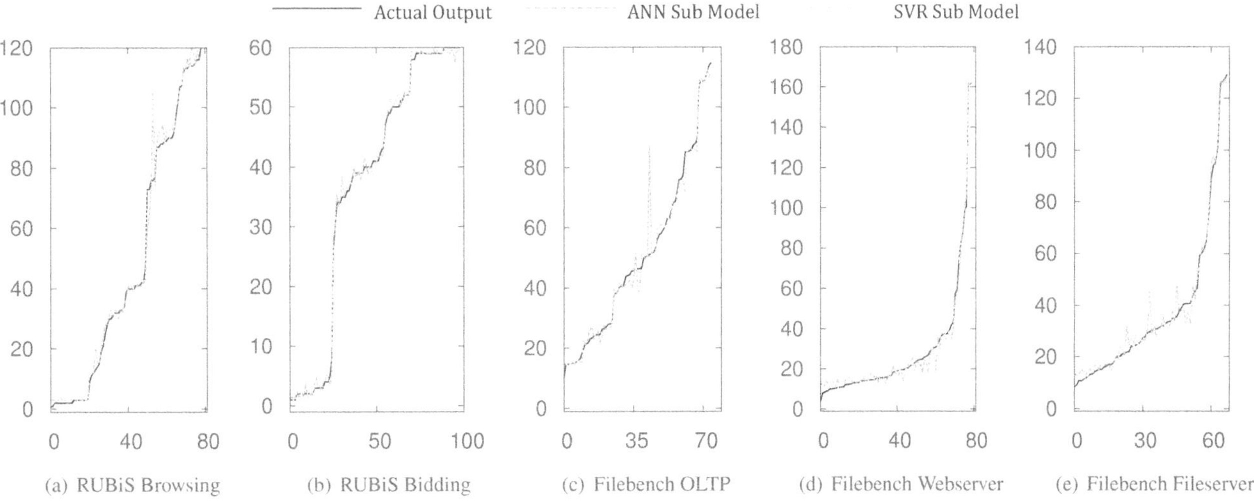

Figure 5. Actual performance and predictions using ANN and SVM based sub-models. The x-axis enumerates data points sorted by increasing performance values. The y-axes represent performance (requests/sec for RUBiS and operations/sec for Filebench respectively).

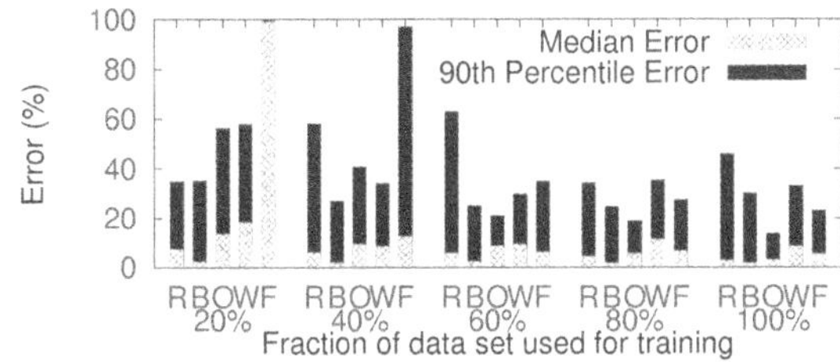

Figure 7. Sensitivity of accuracy to training data set size using ANN based sub-modeling. The x-axis represents the percentage size of final training set and the y-axis represents the median and 90th percentile errors for each benchmark. R-RUBiS Browsing, B-RUBiS Bidding, O-Filebench OLTP, W-Filebench Webserver, F-Filebench Fileserver.

the modeling framework itself once the error distribution is known using a sample set of testing points.

6.3 Sensitivity to the Training Data Set Size

To understand the implications of the training data set size on modeling accuracy, we performed a sensitivity study. We collected a fraction of the final training data set and created sub-models which we then evaluated for prediction accuracy. We repeated the same procedure several times but by changing the fraction of the training set data while retaining the same testing data set each time. The fractional training data sets were chosen so as to span the output parameter space as much as possible. Figure 7 shows the resulting modeling accuracy for ANN sub-models. We conclude that a careful selection of the fraction of the training data set results in low median errors even when the fraction is as small as 20% for most workloads. The only exception is Filebench Fileserver wherein the total number of points in the training data set was small resulting in only 13 data points in the 20% fractional training set. A similar trend was observed with SVM with sub-modeling. These results indicate that our techniques provide reasonable accuracy even with relatively fewer training data points.

6.4 Robustness to Noise

Our experiments thus far were performed in a controlled environment. However, production environments can pose additional challenges, especially with respect to performance variability due to noise. To evaluate the effectiveness of our models in the presence of noise, we simulated noise in 10% of our training data set points. To do so, we perturbed observed performance values by randomly varying these within a fixed percentage specified by the *degree of noise*. For example, if the degree of noise is 20%, the original value was changed by either +20% or -20%. The testing data set was unmodified across these experiments. In Figure 8, we report the median % modeling errors for each benchmark as we vary the degree of noise when using the ANN-based sub-modeling technique. Trend lines indicate a largely linear dependency between noise and

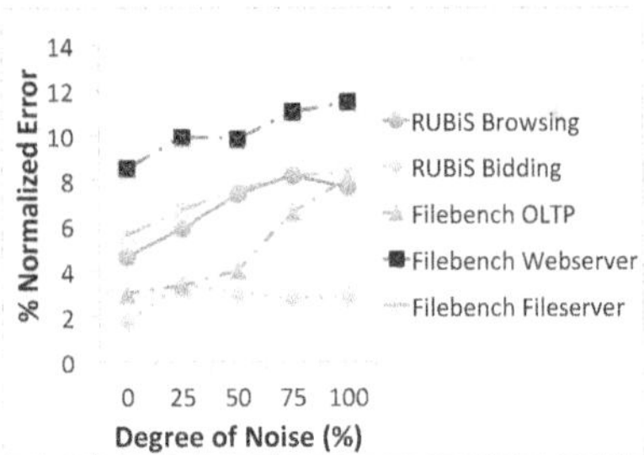

Figure 8. Change in median error when noise is introduced in the training data set.

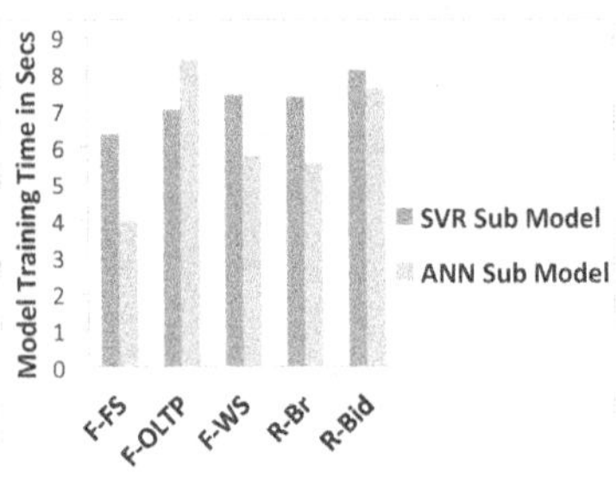

Figure 9. Training time. Benchmarks appear in increasing training data set size from left to right

error. Additionally, a key take away from this analysis is that even after 100% modifications of as much as 10% of the training data points, the modeling accuracy does not suffer substantially. In the case of RUBiS bidding workload, the % median error just increased from 1.79% (in case of perfect data) to 2.91% (in case of ±100% change of 10% of the points in the original training data set). In the case of Filebench Webserver, the degradation is from 8.49% to 11.48%. This validates one aspect of robustness under noise as is possible in a production environment.

6.5 Modeling Overhead

The time for training a model is proportional to the number of points in the training data set. We show the modeling time for each technique in Figure 9 with benchmarks sorted by their training data set size, appearing from left to right. We see that the modeling overhead for the largest training data set (198 points) is limited to 8 seconds using SVM sub-modeling. The training time for ANN is calculated as an aggregate of five different model runs, as required by ensemble averaging. We believe that the presented overhead is sufficiently low to make these models usable in an online fashion within a production environment where a model is possibly (re)trained at regular intervals.

7. VM Sizing

Cloud service providers (e.g. Amazon EC2) charge customers based on the rented computing capacity . For the sake of simplicity, capacity is usually represented using coarse-grained choices (e.g. small, large, and extra-large for standard on-demand instances in Amazon's EC2 cloud service [1]) that map to a certain amount of CPU, memory and other resources. These choices have proportional as well as skewed allocation of resources, where one can even get an instance with more CPU and less memory. In private virtualized environments, administrators have more flexibility in assigning the resource allocations for a VM. In either case, it is the customers' responsibility to determine the VM sizes (CPU and memory capacity) that they need to meet application-level performance targets. Given the lack of application-based model customers choose more conservative sizes and over-provision to avoid any performance problems. This leads to sub-optimal sizing and higher costs throughout the life of the VM. A fine-grained, tailored sizing of VMs, on the other hand, can allow meeting target performance while minimizing over-provisioning.

In this section, we show that given a target application performance metric and a VM I/O latency level available to the application, our performance models can be used to find the optimal CPU and memory sizes. We used a specific I/O latency as an input because it is not configurable in many cloud environments. However, our modeling can even determine a desired I/O latency value so as to minimize the overall cost of the VM. We experimentally demonstrate that, for a range of performance targets across RUBiS Browsing and Filebench webserver workload, the suggested CPU and memory sizes indeed deliver the required performance in all the cases.

7.1 VM Sizing Problem Definition

We define the optimal VM sizing problem as follows:
Problem definition: Given a performance target P_{target} and a VM I/O latency $iolat$ and a performance model PM, the VM sizing algorithm generates suggested CPU c and a memory m which are able to meet P_{target} and satisfy the following constraints:

$$\frac{P_{c,m,iolat}}{P_{target}} \geq 1 \tag{1}$$

subject to:

$$c_{min} \leq c \leq c_{max} \tag{2}$$

$$m_{min} \leq m \leq m_{max} \tag{3}$$

$$\frac{P_{c-\delta_c,m,iolat}}{P_{target}} < 1 \tag{4}$$

$$\frac{P_{c,m-\delta_m,iolat}}{P_{target}} < 1 \tag{5}$$

under the following assumptions:

$$P_{c+\delta_c,m,iolat} \geq P_{c,m,iolat}; P_{c,m+\delta_m,iolat} \geq P_{c,m,iolat} \tag{6}$$

$$P_{c-\delta_c,m,iolat} \leq P_{c,m,iolat}; P_{c,m-\delta_m,iolat} \leq P_{c,m,iolat} \tag{7}$$

Intuitively, these constraints force us to find a VM size such that less of any resource would make us miss the performance target. Equation 1 ensures that application performance for the suggested c, m, and $iolat$ values should be at least equal to or greater than P_{target}. Equations 2 and 3 bound allocations to the feasible range; additionally, allocation choices for CPU and memory in these range can only be made in units of δ_c and δ_m respectively. Equation 4 guarantees that the performance achieved for a smaller CPU allocation fails to meet P_{target}. Similarly, equation 5 checks for memory optimality. Finally, we assume that allocating additional resources to a VM will not degrade its performance (Equation 6) and taking away resources cannot improve performance (Equation 7).

7.2 Model-based VM Sizing

We follow a simple approach to VM sizing, i.e., determining the values of c and m. First, assuming a memory allocation of m_{max}, the maximum possible memory allocation, we use binary search on c to determine its optimal value that would allow meeting the application's performance target by querying the performance model PM using the given **iolat (input)**, m_{max}, and c. After the optimal value of c is obtained, we perform a second binary search as above fixing c for various values of m.

To handle modeling inaccuracy, we use a query performance target 10% higher than the actual performance target P_{target}. To accommodate our hardware platform, we used c_{min}=200MHz,

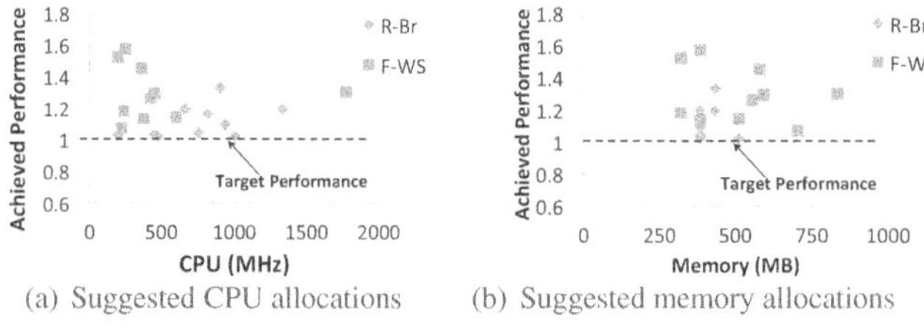

(a) Suggested CPU allocations (b) Suggested memory allocations

Figure 10. Observed application performance relative to performance target for model-based VM sizing. Each point represents a specific sizing query.

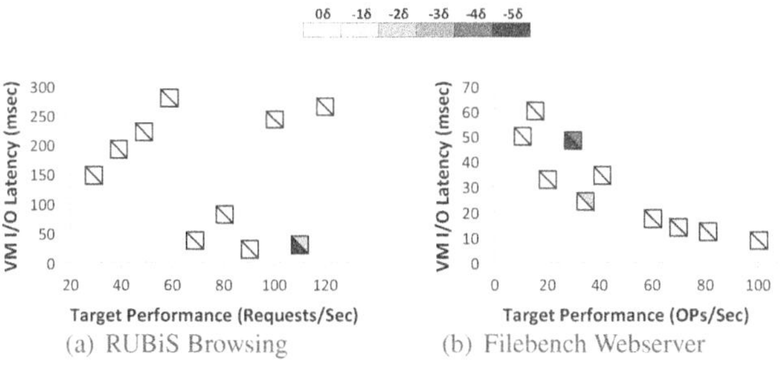

(a) RUBiS Browsing (b) Filebench Webserver

Figure 11. Optimality of VM sizing given a target performance and a target VM I/O latency. Each point is a box divided into two triangles - the lower triangle represents optimality of CPU while the upper one represents optimality of memory. The degree of optimality is based on the grayscale code (top).

c_{max}=2GHz, m_{min}=256MB, and m_{max}=2GB. We use δ_c=100 MHz and δ_m=64 MB in our experiments.

We experimented with two workloads for VM sizing: RUBiS Browsing and Filebench Webserver workloads. We randomly selected 20 performance targets and VM I/O latency levels as inputs to evaluate the accuracy of our models and sizing algorithm. We validate the results by running individual workloads with the CPU and memory allocation suggested by our sizing technique. VM I/O latency is controlled by issuing I/Os from a contending VM to the same storage LUN.

Figure 10 demonstrates that P_{target} is met or exceeded for all the 20 configurations using our sizing technique; P_{target} is normalized to 1 in all the cases. In other words, the charts plot the $\frac{P_{achieved}}{P_{target}}$ for each performance target; essentially showing how far are the experimentally observed performances obtained under suggested CPU, memory allocations from the respective target queries. The X-axis in the two plots marks the suggested CPU and memory sizes for each query. The wide range of suggested sizes indicates that the required memory and CPU may vary quite significantly based on the target performance over most of the available allocation range, underscoring the need for fine grained VM sizing.

To demonstrate the optimality of the suggested allocations, we run each workload with smaller CPU (c-δ) and memory (m-δ) allocations. We deem sizing results as *optimal* with respect to a specific resource dimension (CPU or memory) if a δ reduction in allocation results in the performance target P_{target} being violated. If P_{target} is met under a reduced allocation, we investigate the degree of sub-optimality by running the workload under varying number of δ reductions. In Figure 11, we depict sizing optimality along CPU and memory dimensions separately. Out of 20 randomly selected performance targets for a wide range of chosen VM I/O latency values, the performance models deliver optimal results on both dimensions in 65% cases; rest of the points are within 2δ of the optimal, except for two cases where allocations are sub-optimal by 4δ or 5δ.

This analysis indicates that our model-based VM sizing approach can suggest optimal sizes in the majority of cases while meeting performance targets. In some cases, we suggested a higher size but that is still better than picking a size without any information. The higher can also be attributed to the fact that we set a higher performance target and we want to be conservative in picking our sizes so that performance is not impacted. This is very critical to increase the confidence of administrators in such a tool and over time one can make the estimate more aggressive.

8. Discussion

In this section, we expand on some of the assumptions that are built into our work and clarify the scope of usage for the performance models.

One implicit assumption in our work is that the platform used when training the model is the same as where the VM is executed, because differences in the underlying software (hypervisor) and hardware (CPU frequency, memory bandwidth, and cache size) can influence the model. We believe that this is a reasonable assumption as most cloud systems today are mainly based on homogeneous clusters. However, over time, heterogeneity is bound to occur, which means a virtualized application's performance model has to be retrained every time it is deployed (or migrated) to a different platform. While one approach is to retrain performance models in the new execution platform, cross-platform models can possibly help eliminate this need. We plan to investigate cross-platform performance prediction models in the future.

In this paper, we focus on the average performance of an application's execution, assuming its behavior to be stable, and the offline modeling of such performance. Such a performance model is valuable for a variety of applications that are mainly concerned with average performance and have static workloads. However, for applications that service very dynamic workloads, online training of the performance model is necessary. A key challenge in such environments is to distinguish between the long-term change and the short-term change. We believe that our proposed approach can be extended to work in a dynamic setting primarily because of the relatively low training time, as shown in Section 6. Retraining the model at regular intervals and using aging of observed performance and I/O latency and optionally aging of the model itself can help to overcome these challenges.

A final point worth mentioning is that our performance models can be used to find optimal VM I/O latency as well, i.e., perform sizing for VM I/O latency. Since current storage systems and hypervisors do not provide fine-grained control of latency, we did not explore this direction in this paper. In the future, we anticipate that storage I/O latency will be virtualized and allocated similar to CPU and memory resources. This is attractive for both the cloud service providers who can then charge for various levels of I/O performance as well as the customer who can expect a specific I/O performance for their VMs. If I/O latency control is available, the critical question that might arise is trading-off between memory size and I/O latency since these two are inter-dependent. We did not face this problem in current set up since CPU and memory can be treated independently. Nevertheless, our robust modeling techniques will be able to handle the mutual inter-dependence between the control variables because we train the models under various combinations of memory and observed VM latency values.

9. Conclusions

Accurate modeling of an application's performance is very useful both for users and cloud service providers. However, the non-linear relationship of resource allocations to application performance, the interplay of resource usage across different types of resources, and resource contention in a virtualized environment makes it very difficult to create such models. We identified three VM resource control parameters as sufficient inputs for creating performance models. We also evaluated the effectiveness of artificial neural network (ANN) and Support Vector Machine (SVM) techniques for modeling and demonstrated that these are superior to conventional regression-based approaches. In order to further increase the accuracy of these techniques, we presented a sub-modeling technique that substantially reduced prediction errors across five virtualized benchmark workloads from the RUBiS and Filebench suites. Median and 90th percentile prediction errors using ANNs were reduced from 7.14% and 101.68% respectively (averaged across the workloads) for a correctly configured single global model to 4.36% and 29.17% with sub-modeling. Finally, when our models were used in VM sizing experiments, they delivered optimal results for 65% of the sizing problems we studied and produced sizes that were close to optimal for the remaining 35%. We expect that cloud users and service providers can benefit from the ability to create accurate performance models for their virtualized workloads and utilize such models for accurate VM sizing and placement.

References

[1] Amazon elastic compute cloud (amazon EC2). http://aws.amazon.com/ec2/.

[2] *Filebench: a framework for simulating applications on file systems.* http://www.solarisinternals.com/wiki/index.php/FileBench.

[3] *fio: Flexible I/O tester.* http://freshmeat.net/projects/fio/.

[4] *fpc: Flexible procedures for clustering.* http://cran.r-project.org/web/packages/fpc/index.html.

[5] *LIBSVM: A Library for Support Vector Machines.* http://www.csie.ntu.edu.tw/ cjlin/libsvm/.

[6] *The R Project for Statistical Computing.* http://www.r-project.org/.

[7] *RUBiS: Rice University Bidding System.* http://rubis.ow2.org/.

[8] E. Alpaydin. *Introduction to machine learning.* MIT Press, 2004.

[9] M. N. Bennani and D. A. Menascé. Resource allocation for autonomic data centers using analytic performance models. In *ICAC*, pages 229–240. IEEE Computer Society, 2005.

[10] P. Bodik, M. Goldszmidt, A. Fox, D. B. Woodard, and H. Andersen. Fingerprinting the datacenter: Automated classification of performance crises. In *EuroSys '10 Proceedings of the 5th European conference on Computer systems*, pages 111–124, 2010.

[11] A. T. Clements, I. Ahmad, M. Vilayannur, and J. Li. Decentralized Deduplication in SAN Cluster File Systems. In *Proc. of USENIX ATC*, June 2009.

[12] I. Cohen, M. Goldszmidt, T. Kelly, J. Symons, and J. S. Chase. Correlating instrumentation data to system states: A building block for automated diagnoses and control. In *Proc. of the 6th USENIX OSDI)*, 2004.

[13] I. Cohen, S. Zhang, M. Goldszmidt, J. Symons, T. Kelly, and A. Fox. Capturing, indexing, clustering, and retrieving system history. In *Proc. of ACM SOSP*, 2005.

[14] R. P. Doyle, J. S. Chase, O. M. Asad, W. Jin, and A. Vahdat. Model-based resource provisioning in a web service utility. In *USENIX Symposium on Internet Technologies and Systems*, 2003.

[15] U. Drepper. The Cost of Virtualization. *ACM Queue*, Feb. 2008.

[16] A. Ganapathi, Y. Chen, A. Fox, R. Katz, and D. Patterson. Statistics-driven workload modeling for the cloud. In *SMDB*, 2010.

[17] A. Gulati, I. Ahmad, and C. Waldspurger. PARDA: Proportionate Allocation of Resources for Distributed Storage Access. In *Proc. of USENIX FAST*, Feb. 2009.

[18] A. Gulati, A. Merchant, and P. Varman. mClock: Handling Throughput Variability for Hypervisor IO Scheduling. In *9th USENIX OSDI*, October 2010.

[19] S. Haykin. *Neural Networks: A Comprehensive Foundation.* Prentice Hall, 2nd edition, 1998.

[20] J. Katcher. Postmark: A new file system benchmark. Technical report, Network Appliance, 1997.

[21] E. Kotsovinos. Virtualization: Blessing or Curse? *ACM Queue*, Jan. 2011.

[22] S. Kundu, R. Rangaswami, K. Dutta, and M. Zhao. Application Performance Modeling in a Virtualized Environment. In *Proc. of IEEE HPCA*, January 2010.

[23] X. Liu, X. Zhu, S. Singhal, and M. F. Arlitt. Adaptive entitlement control of resource containers on shared servers. In *IM*, pages 163–176. IEEE, 2005.

[24] J. C. McCullough, Y. Agarwal, J. Chandrashekar, S. Kuppuswamy, A. C. Snoeren, and R. K. Gupta. Evaluating the effectiveness of model-based power characterization. In *Proc. of USENIX Annual Technical Conference*, 2011.

[25] R. Nathuji, A. Kansal, and A. Ghaffarkhah. Q-clouds: managing performance interference effects for qos-aware clouds. In *EuroSys '10*, pages 237–250, 2010.

[26] P. Padala, K.-Y. Hou, X. Zhu, M. Uysal, Z. Wang, S. Singhal, A. Merchant, and K. G. Shin. Automated control of multiple virtualized resources. In *Proceedings of the 4th ACM European conference on Computer systems/EuroSys*, pages 13–16, 2009.

[27] J. Rao, X. Bu, C.-Z. Xu, L. Y. Wang, and G. G. Yin. VCONF: a reinforcement learning approach to virtual machines auto-configuration. In *ICAC*, pages 137–146. ACM, 2009.

[28] C. Stewart, T. Kelly, A. Zhang, and K. Shen. A dollar from 15 cents: Cross-platform management for internet services. In *Proceedings of the USENIX Annual Techinal Conference*, pages 199–212, 2008.

[29] S. Uttamchandani, L. Yin, G. A. Alvarez, J. Palmer, and G. Agha. Chameleon: a self-evolving, fully-adaptive resource arbitrator for storage systems. In *Proc. of USENIX Annual Technical Conference*, 2005.

[30] VMware, Inc. *Introduction to VMware Infrastructure.* 2010. http://www.vmware.com/support/pubs/.

[31] VMware, Inc. *vSphere Resource Management Guide: ESX 4.1, ESXi 4.1, vCenter Server 4.1.* 2010.

[32] W. Vogels. Beyond Server Consolidation. *ACM Queue*, Feb. 2008.

[33] C. A. Waldspurger. Memory resource management in vmware esx server. In *Proc. of USENIX OSDI*, 2002.

[34] Z. Wang, X. Zhu, and S. Singhal. Utilization and slo-based control for dynamic sizing of resource partitions. In *Proc. of 16th IFIP/IEEE Distributed Systems: Operations and Management (DSOM)*, October 2005.

[35] J. Wildstrom, P. Stone, and E. Witchel. CARVE: A cognitive agent for resource value estimation. In *ICAC*, pages 182–191. IEEE Computer Society, 2008.

[36] T. Wood, L. Cherkasova, K. Ozonat, and P. Shenoy. Profiling and modeling resource usage of virtualized applications. In *Proc. of ACM/IFIP/USENIX Middleware*, 2008.

[37] J. Xu, M. Zhao, J. A. B. Fortes, R. Carpenter, and M. S. Yousif. Autonomic resource management in virtualized data centers using fuzzy logic-based approaches. *Cluster Computing*, 11(3):213–227, 2008.

[38] W. Zheng, R. Bianchini, G. J. Janakiraman, J. R. Santos, and Y. Turner. JustRunIt: Experiment-Based Management of Virtualized Data Centers. In *Proceeding of the USENIX Annual Technical Conference*, 2009.

Virtualization Challenges: A View from Server Consolidation Perspective

Hui Lv, Yaozu Dong, Jiangang Duan, Kevin Tian

Intel Asia-Pacific Research & Development Ltd.
{hui.lv eddie.dong jianggang.duan kevin.tian}@intel.com

Abstract

Server consolidation, by running multiple virtual machines on top of a single platform with virtualization, provides an efficient solution to parallelism and utilization of modern multi-core processors system. However, the performance and scalability of server consolidation solution on modern massive advanced server is not well addressed.

In this paper, we conduct a comprehensive study of Xen performance and scalability characterization running SPECvirt_sc2010, and identify that large memory and cache footprint, due to the unnecessary high frequent context switch, introduce additional challenges to the system performance and scalability. We propose two optimizations (dynamically-allocable tasklets and context-switch rate controller) to improve the performance. The results show the improved memory and cache efficiency with a reduction of the overall CPI, resulting in an improvement of server consolidation capability by 15% in SPECvirt_sc2010. In the meantime, our optimization achieves an up to 50% acceleration of service response, which greatly improves the QoS of Xen virtualization solution.

Categories and Subject Descriptors

D.4.8 [**Operating Systems**]: Performance—Measurement
D.2.8 [**Software Engineering**]: Metric—Performance measures

General Terms

Measurement, Performance, Design

Keywords

Virtualization; server consolidation; SPECvirt_sc2010, scheduler, performance optimization

1. Introduction

As the computing industry enters the multi-core era and more and more CPU cores are integrated into one single die [1] [2], how to efficiently use the core resources becomes a big challenge to software. The CPU cycles, used for synchronization among CPU cores (for example, OS kernel spin-lock), may increase dramatically as the core number increases. On the other hand, finding concurrency in a program for efficient parallel computing to take the advantage of core resources, requires excessive engineering effort and may be not applicable for many software [38][39].

Virtualization offers a solution to improve efficiency of parallelism and core usage by consolidating multiple independently running virtual machines (VMs) into a single physical machine. In virtualization, a new layer of software, named as hypervisor or virtual machine monitor (such as VMWare [3], Hyper-V [4] KVM [5] and Xen [6], etc.), runs on top of bare metal hardware to provide multiple illusions of virtual machine (VM) to run guest OSs. Virtualization enables a new usage model to commodity the elastic computing resources (that is VMs), for example pay-as-you-use cloud service. A virtualization system, such as Xen, often over commits the CPU resources (that is the total number of virtual CPUs is larger than physical CPUs), which depends on a hypervisor scheduler to map the physical CPUs to different virtual CPUs in a timeshared manner. However, the performance and scalability of virtualization solution for server consolidation and the impact of its scheduling policy, on modern massive advanced server, remains to be challenging.

SPECvirt_sc2010 is a standard benchmark to measure the capability of virtualization solution for server consolidation [7]. It runs as many as possible tiles (a set of VMs) of typical server workloads, consisting of a Web server, a mail server, and a JAVA server to complete certain amount of transactions, and use the number of tiles it can run to indicate the throughput of the virtualized system. The response time, or QoS, is another indicator in Specvirt_sc2010, reflecting the fact that most transactions in server workload are latency sensitive. The performance of SPECvirt_sc2010 is critical for a hypervisor targeting server consolidation usage model, such as data center and cloud computing environment, however, the characterization of SPECvirt_sc2010 and the impact of hypervisor scheduling on SPECvirt_sc2010, on massive advanced server, are not well studied yet.

In this paper, we conduct a comprehensive study of Xen server consolidation capability running SPECvirt_sc2010, and share our findings of the performance overhead on massive advanced server, and optimizations to improve the performance and scalability of Xen from server consolidation perspective. The major contributions of our work are as follows.

1) We conduct a comprehensive study of Xen performance and scalability characterization running SPECvirt_sc2010 on top of a state of the art 2-socket Xeon 5680 system (which is one of, if not the most, the advanced servers in massive production). The result shows that Xen scales badly (the CPU cycle per instruction, or CPI, increases sharply, and the response time increases exponentially), when the number of VMs increases (that is the tile number goes up in Specvirt_sc2010).
2) We present a thorough analysis on the virtualization overhead, and identify the scalability issue as a result of large memory

VEE'12, March 3–4, 2012, London, England, UK.

and cache footprint, due to the unnecessary high frequent context switch. The further analysis reveals that the high frequency is a result of a) inefficient processing of interrupts, and b) over aggressive hypervisor scheduling.

3) Optimizations to improve the efficiency of interrupt processing and to limit the over aggressive hypervisor scheduling, are proposed. Dynamically-allocable tasklets is used to eliminate the unnecessary involvement of hypervisor scheduling to idle VM context, and adaptive hypervisor scheduling rate control is adopted to limit the context switch if the scheduling frequency exceeds certain threshold.

The results show the improved memory and cache efficiency with reduction of the overall CPI, resulting in the improvement of server consolidation capability by 15% in SPECvirt_sc2010. In the meantime, our optimization achieves an up to 50% acceleration of service response, which greatly improves the QoS of Xen virtualization solution.

The rest of this paper is organized as follows. Section 2 presents the background of server consolidation including a brief introduction of Xen VMM and the consolidation workload we use. Section 3 introduces the experimental configuration. In Section 4, we present the detailed overhead breakdown, followed by the illustration of two optimizations to address the high frequency context switch issue in Section 5. The performance benefits of our optimization are shown in Section 6. Section 7 describes related work, and Section 8 concludes this paper.

2. Background

2.1 Server Consolidation

Multiple virtual machines are allowed to run on the same physical hardware in system virtualization, so as to increase system utilization and thus reduce cost. Server consolidation reduces the number and variety of components in the environment. This may not be limited to servers but also to other physical elements such as tapes, disks, network devices and connections, operating systems, and peripherals involved in the server consolidation. It becomes easy to move and change systems, applications, and peripherals with fewer hardware and software standards to manage. Although the physical hardware is shared across the virtual machines, the virtual machines are completely isolated from each other and each virtual machine runs a separate operating system instance with its own applications.

Performance characterization and analysis for server consolidation [8] [9] [11] [32] is important for deployment with fair sharing of resources, providing feedback to IT administrators and platform architects, projecting and optimizing future platform performance and so on. In this paper, SPECvirt_sc2010[1] is adopted for performance analysis of server consolidation.

2.2 Xen Virtual Machine Monitor

A virtual machine monitor [12] [13] [14] [15] allows multiple operating systems to share a single machine safely. It isolates operating systems and controls accesses to hardware resources. We use open source VMM, Xen, which is widely adopted as a representative VMM in both academia and industry, for our study. The organization of Xen [6] is depicted in Figure 1. Xen consists of two elements: hypervisor and the driver domain. The hypervisor provides an abstraction layer between the guest operating systems and the actual hardware. The driver domain, a privileged VM, called domain0, manages other guest VMs, called domainU. One of the major functions of the driver domain is to conduct real I/O operations to a bare device on behalf of domainU to implement a reliable I/O architecture [16] [17] [18] [19]. With hardware assistance, Single Root I/O Virtualization and Sharing (SR-IOV) [23][24], which enables efficient sharing of a single I/O device among multiple VMs, provides a foundation for efficiently utilization of I/O resources as reaching near-native I/O performance. Although this paper is based on Xen, the problem addressed here is not limited to this specific hypervisor. We have observed the same issue in KVM.

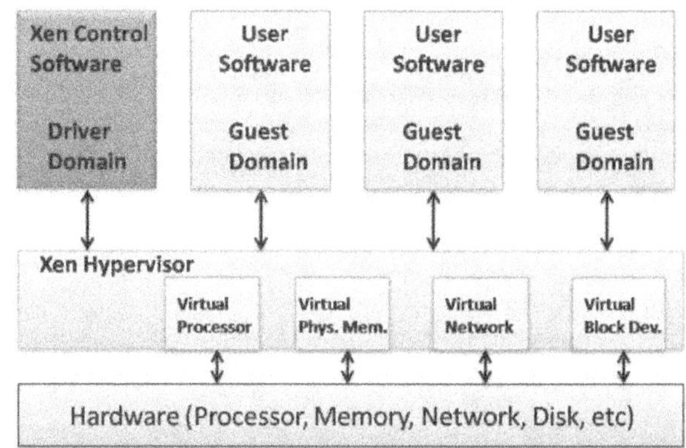

Figure 1. The Xen virtual machine environment

2.3 SPECvirt_sc2010 Benchmark

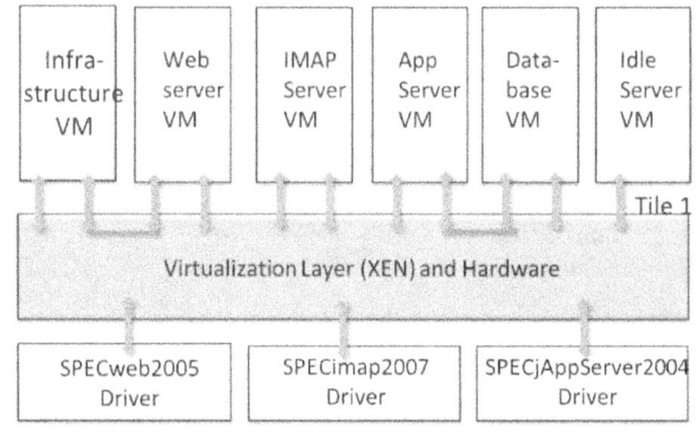

Figure 2. SPECvirt_sc2010 block diagram

SPECvirt_sc2010 [7] is SPEC's first benchmark addressing performance evaluation of datacenter servers used in virtualized server consolidation. The benchmark utilizes several SPEC workloads, to complete certain amount of transactions, representing applications that are common targets of virtualization and server consolidation as shown in Figure 2. Each of these standard workloads is modified to match a typical server consolidation scenario of CPU resource requirements, memory, disk I/O, and network

[1] The benchmark runs discussed here are for our research and non-compliant with the SPEC run-rules. The data presented here are only to illustrate the points discussed in this paper and cannot be compared with any other SPECvirt_sc2010 results

utilization. These workloads are modified versions of SPECweb2005, SPECjAppServer2004, and SPECmail2008. Scaling is achieved by running additional sets of virtual machines, called "tiles", until overall throughput reaches a peak. One tile consists of 6 different hardware-assistant VMs (HVM). All workloads must continue to meet required quality of service (QoS) criteria. The compliant results are necessary to meet all the Qos requirements. Performance metrics (throughputs) are obtained by calculating the arithmetic mean of the 3 normalized values per tile and summing up the scores for all tiles.

3. Experiment Configuration

The server under test is the latest Intel Xeon 5680 server with two 3.33GHz processors. Each processor has 6 cores, 12 threads with Hyper-Threading technology [20] on and 12MB shared L3 cache. Xen 4.1.0 is selected as the virtual machine monitor. We allocate enough storage and network devices to make sure that there are no hardware bottlenecks. One LSI HBA is used to connect to an external disk enclosure. Each tile is assigned 4x64GB Intel solid status disk as storage. Due to the public availability of SR-IOV network card & iSCSI [33] in data centers and the performance advantage of hardware-assisted virtualization solution, we use SR-IOV & iSCSI [33] in our experiment environment. As depicted in Figure 3, all the disk storages are placed at the remote iSCSI target machine, directly linked through 10 GB network card to the server under test. All VMs, running under server side, select host's SR-IOV virtual functions as their networks. Each guest accesses its VFs directly. In this way, IO requests from disks are exchanged for network bandwidth, walking through the software layer with the assistance of SR-IOV and iSCSI.

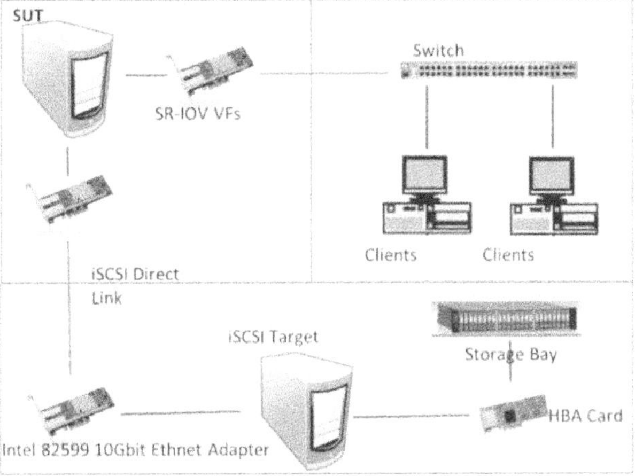

Figure 3. SR-IOV & iSCSI solution

4. Characterization and Analysis

In this Section, we adopt well-designed profiling methodologies to thoroughly investigate hypervisor's overhead and show the challenges met under server consolidation. Accordingly, several possible solutions are presented as the initial steps in section 5 to conquer such challenges. Although this work is based on the Xen hypervisor, we believe the analysis methods and challenges raised are equally applicable to other hypervisors.

4.1 Scalability Challenges

To provide insights into behaviors of server consolidation, we present the load scalability of SPECvirt_sc2010 on the latest 2-way commercial server. As shown in Figure 4, when the system load is low, the overall system CPU utilization scales up linearly with the system throughput. 2-tile load provides 99% increase in CPU utilization over 1-tile and 4-tile achieves 111% CPU utilization increase over 2-tile. These numbers indicate relatively good CPU utilization scalability. However, 8-tile consumes 219% more CPU resources than 4-tile, indicating a sharp increase of CPU utilization. The increase ratio becomes even greater at peak performance implying underlying high overhead of scalability as the system load is overwhelming. As mentioned in Subsection 2.3, SPECvirt_sc2010 workload cares not only about the throughputs, but also about QoS. As illustrated in Figure 4, the total response time (geometric mean result of three sub-workload's response time) keeps relatively low until close to the peak throughput from 0.13ms to 0.32ms (146% increase), an exponential-like increase from 8-tile to 9-tile configuration. The dramatic increase of the total response time near the peak performance implies potential bottlenecks existing with high system load, as the hypervisor is unable to function efficiently under such condition.

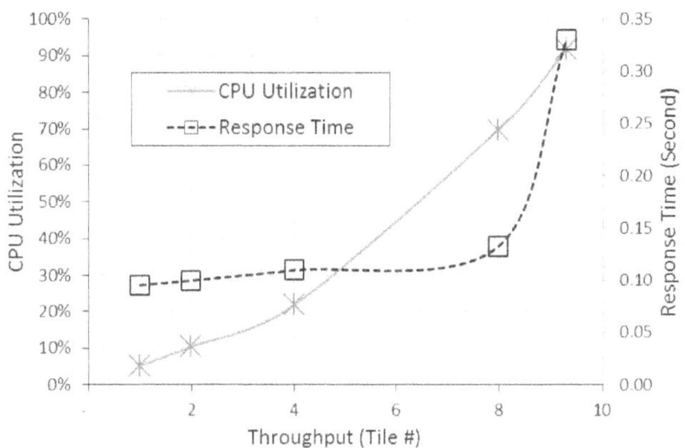

Figure 4. CPU utilization & response time trend with throughput

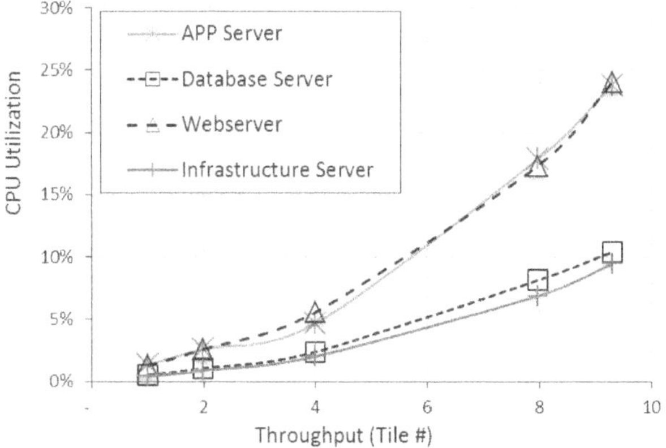

Figure 5. CPU utilization for each VM with throughput

The breakdown of CPU utilization scalability for each VM is shown in Figure 5 (Idle server is not illustrated here due to low

CPU utilization number). VMs of webserver and JAVA application server scale worse than those of database server and infrastructure server when system load becomes heavy. Interestingly, both webserver and java application server are assigned two virtual CPUs for a single VM to satisfy CPU requirements, while the rest VMs are assigned only one virtual CPU due to less consumption. One possible reason is that more number of virtual CPUs brings the extra overhead such as the inter-communication between different virtual CPUs, which causes the worse scalability of related VMs. It also implies the efficiency of current hypervisor that manages multiple virtual CPUs drops, as the number of VM increases.

Turning our attention to the cause of the high CPU utilization consumption with heavy system stress shown in Figure 4, the overall system CPU utilization is divided into four different parts – guest user, guest kernel, hypervisor and domain0. Because these four parts are running in different privilege levels – the guest part (HVM guest) runs in non-root mode and hypervisor and domain0 (PV guest) run in root mode – we can easily breakdown them by programing the hardware performance counter separately. Guest parts are the valuable work while hypervisor and domain0 are so called virtualization overhead. As illustrated in Figure 6, all components, except domain0, increase sharply as tile number increases. At the peak throughput, hypervisor part occupies more than 25% of the total CPU cycles – much higher than expected. It is equally to say that the hypervisor needs to occupy 6 cores of the total 24 logical cores at the peak performance, which is identified to be a big overhead.

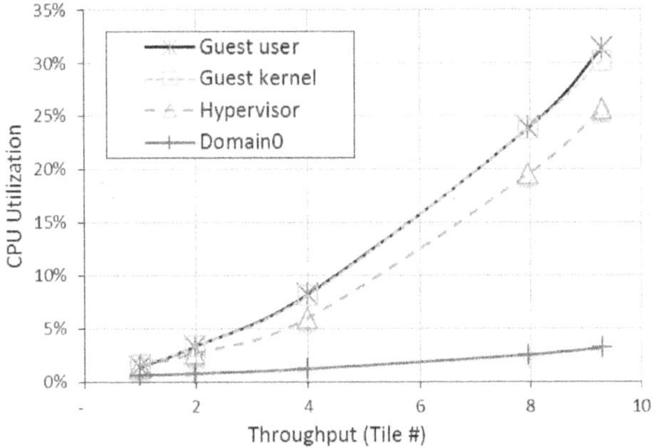

Figure 6. System CPU utilization breakdown

Equation 1 shows cycles per throughput are decided by the multiplicative of Cycles per instruction (CPI) and Path Length (PL). CPI refers to the number of clock cycles that happens when an instruction is being executed, used to describe a processor's performance from one aspect. PL refers to instructions required per transaction, deemed as a measurement of the software's performance on particular computer hardware. As displayed in Figure 7, the trend of PL keeps relatively flat when system load is low, but increases slightly (5.9% increase from 4-tile to 8-tile), when reaching the peak throughput, implying less efficient software execution when system stress is heavy. Whereas CPI increases sharply as throughput grows (88% increase from 1-tile to 9-tile). Obviously, the dramatic increase of CPI is the major contributor for non-linear CPU utilization increase of both guest and hypervisor parts.

$$Cycles/Throughput = CPI \times PL \qquad (1)$$

Among various aspects which may impact the value of CPI, data from hardware performance counter points out that the increase of cache miss rate such as LLC and TLB, depicted in Figure 8, plays the vital role to the increase of overall CPI. Cache miss rate of LLC increases by 2.67x and that of TLB increases by 0.38x from 1-tile to 9-tile. High cache miss rate was caused by larger memory and cache footprint under server consolidation as VM number goes up. In other words, as the number of consolidated VMs grows, the memory footprint consumed by both VMs and hypervisor becomes greatly increased so that current hardware resource like hierarchical cache and TLB cannot process efficiently, resulting in slow instruction execution. Besides the hardware approach of enlarging the cache size, there are software ways to reduce the footprint, such as to merge the same page together as KSM [35]. Also a well-tuned scheduler to achieve better context switch frequency – satisfy latency/throughput at the same time – is another software approach.

Without effective cache usage on multicore platform, such caches can cause thrashing that severely degrades system performance. Some cache-aware schedulers have been discussed and developed recently in the native system [34]. However, in virtualization environment, it becomes more complex as the intrusion of isolation of various VMs running to share the same hardware resource. A well-designed scheduler in virtualization should not only efficiently isolate various VMs to make them access the underlying hardware resource fairly, but also treat the hardware as a whole to maximize the throughput. For example, as one of the practical implementations, KSM allows to share equal anonymous memory across different processes and in turn also across different KVM virtual machines. The object of KSM is to increase memory density, or conversely, to reduce the memory size with the same number of running VMs

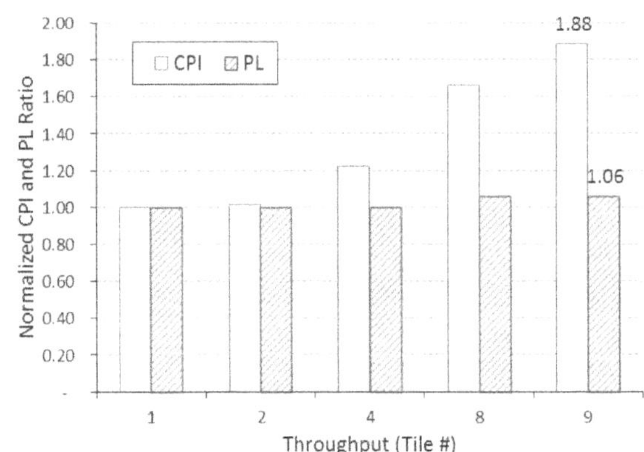

Figure 7. CPI and Path Length trend with throughput

To resolve the feckless usage of cache in virtualization, controlling context switches frequency by eliminate unnecessary ones is another important approach to be worthy considered. Unnecessary context switches result in unnecessary cache flush, thus causing extra overhead. Low frequency of context switch among VMs will produce small overhead of hypervisor and assure cache hot thus reduce cache footprint. But it may result in the QoS issue, especially for latency sensitive workloads. High frequency of context switch will otherwise satisfy the QoS requirement to some extent, but impair the cache performance thus consume high CPU utilization. So how to select the right frequency is the key issue scheduler should solve. In section 5, we will show in detail that current scheduler in virtualization lacks considerations to eliminate unnecessary context switch and impairs the overall performance. Meanwhile, as the first step to conquer these challenges, a scheduler with fine control of context switch frequency is implemented to showcase the benefits from both the CPI and PL sides.

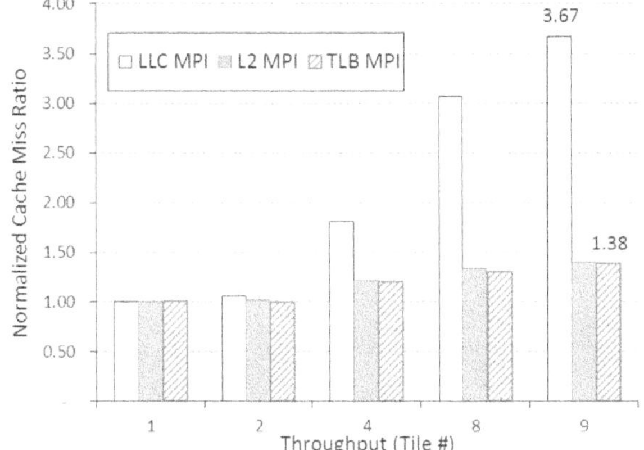

Figure 8. Cache miss rate trend with throughput

4.2 Hypervisor Overhead Breakdown

Scalability issue, as observed in Figure 4, is primarily caused by the sharp increase of CPI, which can be mitigated by either hardware or software ways. We mainly focus on software solutions, so that it's worthwhile to dig into the behaviors of hypervisor to find out the clues.

To further investigate the hypervisor's overhead, we need to firstly clarify the terminology – VMExit. When the running VMs are HVM guests, a VMExit marks the point at which a transition is made between the VM currently running and the hypervisor that executes the sensitive instructions on behalf of guest system. In other words, when a VMExit event happens, related physical CPU migrates from non-root mode to root mode, henceforth, hypervisor performs its system management functions according to the VMExit reasons. With the assistance of tracing tools – XenTrace – we breakdown the hypervisor's overhead (25% of the overall system CPU cycles as shown in Figure 6) according to such categories (56 VMExit reasons in total). Thus it helps to detect which VMExit event causes the big overhead in hypervisor.

Figure 9 depicts hypervisor's detailed CPU cycles breakdown according to the VMExit number at peak performance. The VMExit event of 'External Interrupt' consumes the largest portion, more than 12% CPU cycles. The following major parts are 'APIC Access', 'HLT' and 'IO instruction' which consume 4.78%, 3.73% and 2.94% respectively. The rest 52 VMExit only contribute less than 2% CPU utilization. Regarding such distribution, the major overheads of hypervisor are centralized in a small amount of VMExit events. In the following paragraphs, we will take a look into the reasons of top three VMExit events and propose possible ways to reduce the overhead.

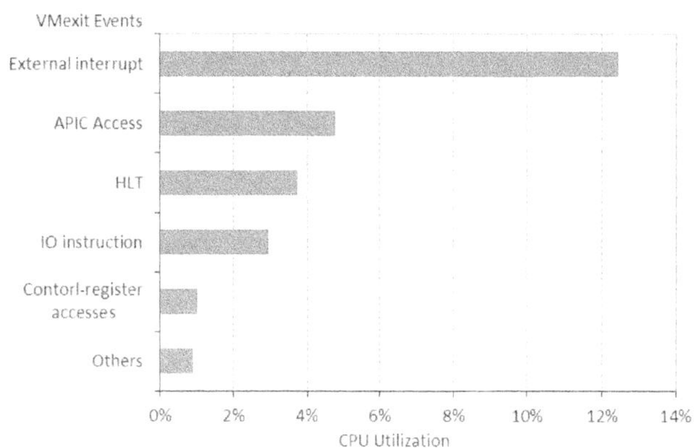

Figure 9. Hypervisor CPU utilization breakdown according to VMExit number

a) 'External Interrupt' VMExit Event

'External Interrupt' VMExit event responds to the handling process of system interrupt requests (IRQs) including handler's top and bottom halves. In our experiment, the software emulated network and disk are passed through by SR-IOV NIC and iSCSI disk solutions, which produce lots of network IRQs. It is readily to understand that the 'External Interrupt' VMExit event composes a large portion of the hypervisor's overhead.

IRQs could happen at any time in the following cases: a) system 'Halt' period; b) virtual CPU running state or c) 'Hypervisor' running state. Only in case b) will system generate the 'External Interrupt' VMExit event and transition from guest to hypervisor context to handle it. In other cases, system enters hypervisor directly without such event happening. Therefore, as system load is heavy, interrupts are more probably to interrupt current virtual CPU's running state. One issue emerges here for external interrupt handling process. If the current running virtual CPU, disrupted by the external interrupt, is the target virtual CPU to which external interrupt delivers, a virtual IRQ will be injected directly when this virtual CPU enters from hypervisor to its running state. However, if the target VM is running on a different physical CPU, an inter-processor interrupt (IPI) will be imperatively sent to the target physical CPU to interrupt it and inject virtual IRQ. In addition, if the target virtual CPU is not running, a scheduling request should be raised to wake it up. Such extra procedures, caused by IPIs and scheduling requests, will possibly aggrandize and thus impair the running streamline of VMs and cause performance turbulence, especially under the condition with large scales of VMs. From the tracing data at peak performance, lots of IPIs and scheduling events, happening during the handling process of 'External Interrupt' VMExit, demonstrate such problem. Sending interrupts to the wrong core or waking up target virtual CPU frequently are the major causes of the high overhead in processing 'External Interrupt' VMExit.

In [30], it proposed an interrupt migration method to avoid most of IPIs by marking target core status at virtual CPU migration. Interrupts are deliver to the right core with this information except for the condition that the target VM migrates to another core, in which an IPI is needed to be sent to the original core to clear the old vector. Consequently, if the frequency of virtual CPU migration is high with lots of VMs consolidating on one system, the mitigation degree will be relatively small. In such situation, the scheduler should comply with the handling process of external interrupts to balance both efficiency and fairness. As a practical example, we enhance current Xen schedule's capability in section 5 to overcome the scalability issue caused by excessive scheduling during external interrupt handling process.

b) 'APIC Access' VMExit Event

Accesses to the APIC-access page inside the guest VMs are considered as virtualized APIC accesses, causing VMExit event during which register access operations, such as EOI and ICR, are emulated by hypervisor. The procedure of software emulation consumes lots of CPU cycles as shown in Figure 9. In [30], it is observed that, EOI access accounts for most percentage of all kinds of 'APIC Access' emulations under SR-IOV condition. By passing instruction fetch/emulation stage, it shortens the code path of vEOI emulation greatly, resulting in decrease of total CPU usage. However, the overhead of 'APIC Access' VMExit is still high when the number of IRQs is large for consolidation workloads.

c) 'HLT' VMExit Event

'HLT' VMExit event occurs when the current VM is idle and executes HALT instruction. Hypervisor marks the current VM's state as 'blocked' and enters scheduling procedure. If there are no available VMs to run at this time, system will enter idle state. The CPU cycles consumed in 'HLT' VMExit as shown in Figure 9 were calculated by eliminating the idle state. It is the real overhead consumed by hypervisor to process scheduling. For CPU intensive workloads, rare number of 'HLT' VMExit events is triggered due to long running time slice. Whereas for IO intensive and client-server type workloads, such as SPECvirt_sc2010, large number of 'HLT' VMExit events is produced due to intermittent running-state exchanges of virtual CPUs. Apparently, scheduling work is considered as the vital factor to reduce the overhead in this process. For example, if the pattern of tasks running inside VMs can be detected, then a deliberate scheduling scheme can be carried out to maximize the efficiency of cache usage.

The above analysis of hypervisor's behaviors demonstrates that scheduler is one of the vital factor in the constitution of virtualization overhead. Current scheduling scheme in Xen shows bottlenecks on the massive advanced system with heavier load (more VMs and heavier stress) as shown in Figure 4. In the following section 5, a close analysis related to scheduling challenges will be presented with specified identification. Then two optimizations are presented to showcase the performance benefits.

5. Optimization Methods

In this section, we analyze the performance of Xen's credit scheduler and propose two solutions, dynamically-allocable tasklets and context-switch rate controller, to optimize the scalability performance. The result shows the improvement of server consolidation capability by 15% in SPECvirt_sc2010. In the meantime, our optimization achieves an up to 50% acceleration of service response.

5.1 Challenges in Scheduler

In order to exactly identify the software scalability bottlenecks, code level profiling tools are necessary. OProfile is a system-wide profiler for Linux systems, capable of profiling all running code at low overhead. It is based on statistical profiling – continually sampling currently executing code at every fixed hardware events. Large set of sample approximating to the real hardware event distribution are employed. Xenoprofile [14] extends to Xen and Oprofile to fully profile across multiple domains and cover code in user processes, kernel and hypervisor. We strengthen Xenoprofile's functionalities by enabling call-graph to obtain the full picture of callees constitution for specified functions. As shown in Figure 11, for each function entry in the left column, the right side functions are called by this entry. We also see a special entry with a '[self]' marker. This records the normal samples for the function itself, but the percentage becomes relative to all callees. This allows comparing time spent on the function itself with that on functions it calls. In order to reduce the profiling overhead, we choose 4 as the call-graph depth.

As shown in Figure 10, cycles of top four functions increase as system load and throughput grow. It makes sense for 'vmx_asm_do_vmentry' to consume the biggest part of CPU resource due to the primary path walked when the system transits from VM to hypervisor. The 'Schedule' function consumes the second largest part. Moreover, the following functions, such as 'do_softirq' and 'context_switch, are all related to the scheduling process. For example, the majority amount of 'softirq' is raised to trigger the scheduling process as listed in Figure 11.

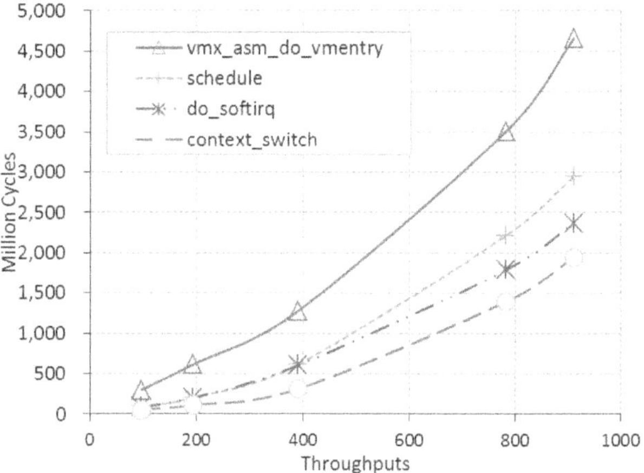

Figure 10. Top functions call-graph trend with throughput

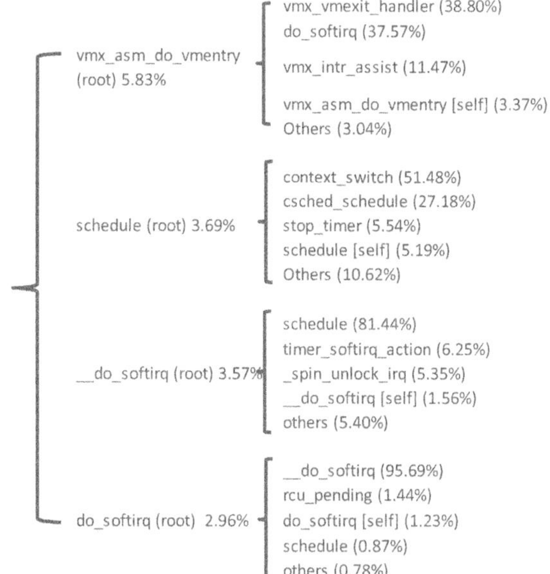

Figure 11. Top hot functions call-graph distribution

By tracing each scheduling process from the beginning to the end, cycles utilized by the context switch procedure are obtained. Table 1, cycles consumed by the context switch process occupy more than 27% of total hypervisor cycles at peak performance. From the frequency side, data in Table 1, collected by counting based tools, shows the procedure of scheduling (Sched: scheduler) is triggered 29 thousand times per second per physical core, and 26 thousand of which cause context switches (Sched: context switches). Context switch here refers to the process of de-schedule the current running virtual CPU and schedule in the next virtual CPU. One question is that is it reasonable to trigger so many context switches – approximately 26 thousand per second for one physical thread at peak performance? Stated differently, the average running tile slice for a virtual CPU once scheduled in is far less than tenth of a microsecond.

Table 1. Scheduler events number & CPU utilization at peak

Scheduler events	Number/second/thread
Sched: scheduler	29,819
Sched: context switches	26,551
Hypervisor	CPU Utilization
Total	26.23%
Context switches	7.28%

From the cause number distribution of context switch shown in Figure 12, most of the context switches take place in the 'External Interrupt' VMExit events, constituting 65% of the total number. Subsequently, 21% context switches occur in the 'HLT' VMExit events. Since 'HLT' VMExit occurs when the current VM is idle and executes HALT instruction, hypervisor primarily activates the scheduling process. However, the high frequency of context switches in the 'External Interrupt' VMExit events is unreasonable. From the code path of handling pass-through 'IRQ' (produced by SR-IOV devices) in Table 2, hypervisor raises the 'SCHEDULE_SOFTIRQ' to trigger a scheduling operation during 'External Interrupt' handler. Thus, system switches to the idle virtual CPU's context to process such tasklets. Basically, the idle virtual CPU shares the same context as the original one so that the overhead should be small. However, if the number of external interrupts is large enough, such kind of transition overhead cannot be ignored anymore.

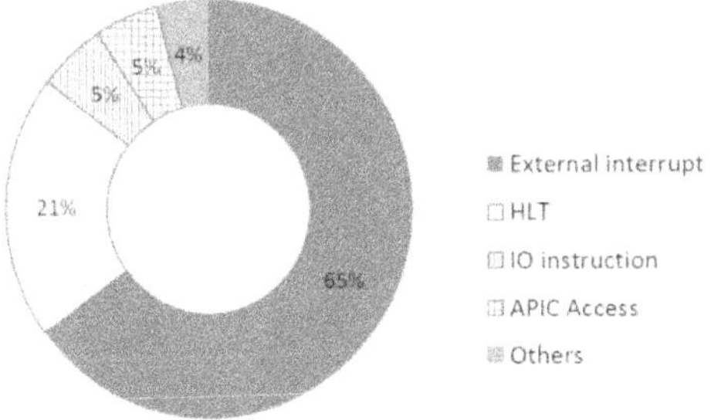

Figure 12. The Cause of Context switch

On the other hand, in virtualization environment, all external interrupts are handled by hypervisor that physical IRQs designated to some VMs are injected as virtual IRQs. Correspondingly, hypervisor kicks related VCPUs by raising scheduling requests combined with IPIs in some conditions, as discussed in section 4.2. Therefore, if the number of IRQ is very huge, the scheduling happens more frequently which explains the scheduling distribution in Figure 12. For current scheduler in Xen, there is no scheme to control the scheduling rate to eliminate the unnecessary scheduling requests so as to cause high frequency of context switch.

Table 2. IRQ pass-through delivery code path

```
Hvm_do_IRQ_dpci
-->|tasklet_schedule(&dpci->dirq_tasklet)
-->|-->|tasklet_schedule_on_cpu(t, smp_processor_id());
-->|-->|-->|tasklet_enqueue(t)
-->|-->|-->|-->cpu_raise_softirq(cpu, SCHEDULE_SOFTIRQ);
```

Therefore, scheduler in Xen meets bottlenecks, which originate from the following two aspects: a) inefficient interrupt handling process mechanism and b) lack of context switch frequency control. In next paragraphs, as the first step to conquer the scheduling challenges for virtualization under server consolidation, two optimizations are proposed, aiming to reduce the context switch frequency thus improve the overall throughput.

5.2 Dynamically-allocable tasklets

Considering the first bottleneck, since not all tasklet users need to run in virtual CPU context (more specifically, the idle virtual CPU context), the best fix is to make it per-tasklet configurable. Based on what we observed, the method of dynamically-allocable tasklets is devised. In this new mechanism, tasklets are dynamically-allocable tasks, running in either virtual CPU context or in softirq context on at most one CPU at a time. Softirq versus virtual CPU context execution is specified during per-tasklet initialization. This method avoids all tasklets running in virtual CPU context at the same time. Consequently, a number of unnecessary context switches is expected to be reduced.

By adopting the dynamically-allocable tasklets method, the number of context switches at peak performance is reduced by 54%, which is a significant improvement to the efficiency of interrupt processing, as shown in Table 3. However, the scheduling number is still high, more than 13k per second per thread, which means the average running time slice for one virtual CPU is still below 0.1 million second. A context switch rate controller is further proposed to solve this issue in the next paragraph.

Table 3. Context switch number comparison at peak performance

Scheduler events (#/send/thread)	Original	Configurable tasklet	Reduction(%)
Sched: scheduler	29819	13668	54.16%
Sched: context switches	26551	12006	54.78%

5.3 Context-Switch Rate Controller (CSRC)

Three different CPU schedulers were introduced in recent years – Borrowed Virtual Time (BVT) [28], Simple Earliest Deadline First (SEDF) [10] and Credit Scheduler [26] [29] – all of which allow the user to specify CPU allocation via CPU share (weights). The credit scheduler, Xen's latest scheduler, is a proportional share scheduler with a load balancing feature for SMP systems. The virtue of the credit scheduler is the simplicity of the operation with reasonable fairness guarantee and performance.

Figure 13 displays the flow of Xen's credit scheduler. There are two major parts in this flow: 1) pick up the next running virtual CPU and 2) do context switch when selecting a new different running virtual CPU. Since credit scheduler sorts run queue according to priority instead of credit, the current running virtual CPU is added to the tail of the run-queue with the same priority. Therefore, if the run-queue with the same priority as current virtual CPU is not empty, the current virtual CPU will be scheduled out and the head virtual CPU in the run queue will be scheduled in. It explains the data in Table 3 why the number of context switch (12006) is very close to the number of scheduler triggered (13668). At peak throughput, the numbers of virtual CPU and physical CPU are in the high ratio 60:24, so it is possible that there are runnable candidate virtual CPUs in the run-queue as the scheduling process is triggered. In this condition, the current virtual CPU is more probably to be scheduled out, following the context switch process.

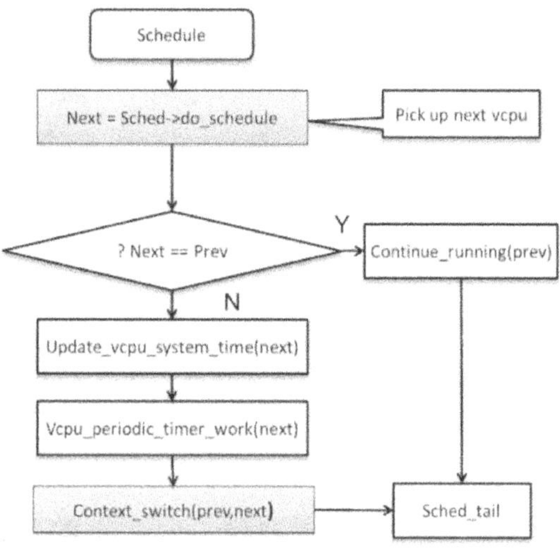

Figure 13. Flow of credit scheduler

Considering excessive number of hypervisor scheduling in Xen's current scheduler, we carry out one proposal to reduce the scheduling's overhead by controlling the frequency of context switch, called Context-Switch Rate Controller (CSRC). The basic philosophy is to reduce the context switch number, if possible, when the rate of VCPU scheduling exceeds the threshold. Two criterions are presented here: 1) to skip the current scheduling process, if the frequency of context switch is bigger than the threshold during last period (10 million second) under the condition that the last running virtual CPU is still runnable (not blocked). The frequency number, counted during the last 10 million second period is applied to judge whether the scheduling frequency is too high. 2) if the last running virtual CPU runs less than some time slice (1million second for example) and is still runnable, to skip this scheduling process, aiming to elongate the running slice for specified virtual CPUs whose running time slice is too short.

Taking the flow in Figure 14 for example, the current running virtual CPU is vcpu1 and the system is under hypervisor's environment. When the scheduler is triggered at some point, it will first judge whether the frequency of scheduling is too high. If yes, it will check whether vcpu1 is still runnable. If it is still yes, vcpu1 will return directly to skip the following scheduling process. If the scheduling frequency is below the threshold, it will check whether vpu1's last running slice is less than 1 million second, if so and vcpu1 is still runnable, it will return to continue its running stage directly.

After applying the CSRC method, the number of context switch at peak performance (with CSRC method, system obtains higher performance than previous result) reduces slightly as shown in Table 4, but the number of context switch reduces almost by 20%, demonstrating CSRC method effectively reduces the frequency of context switch. Detailed performance benefits, brought by the proposed methods, are to be exhibited in section 6.

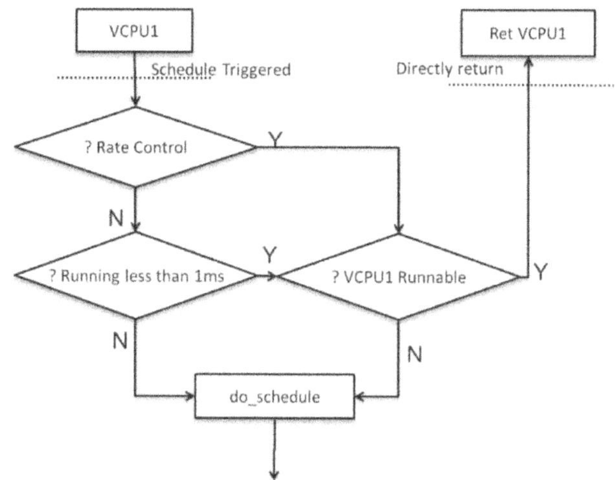

Figure 14. Proposals of SRC scheme

Table 4. Context switch number comparison at peak performance

Scheduler events (#/s/thread)	Configurable tasklet	CSRC & Configurable tasklet	Reduction(%)
Sched: scheduler	13668	13616	0.38%
Sched: context switches	12006	9685	19.33%

6. Evaluation

As depicted in Figure 16, by adopting the method of dynamically-allocable tasklet, the CPU utilization decreases from 92% to 89% comparing to the original result at peak performance (9-tile). After supplying CSRC method, the system CPU utilization decreases even more, about 81% at the same throughput comparing to the original peak results. Furthermore, due to lower CPU utilization, more loads can be added to achieve higher throughput with CSRC. When considering the compliant results – achieving QoS requirements – the peak performance (throughput per CPU utilization) with CSRC is improved by 15% comparing to the original result, as shown in Figure 15. There is no obvious performance change when system load is light. SPECvirt_sc2010 workload takes both throughput and QoS into consideration. In Figure 17, it reveals that proposed methods of dynamically-allocable tasklets and CSRC shorten the response time significantly when close to peak performance, explaining that such methods achieve higher throughput with qualified QoS. It is also observed that, when system load is light, the response time of proposed methods is slightly higher than original results due to relative less frequent scheduling when applying CSRC method. However it has little influence on the overall performance.

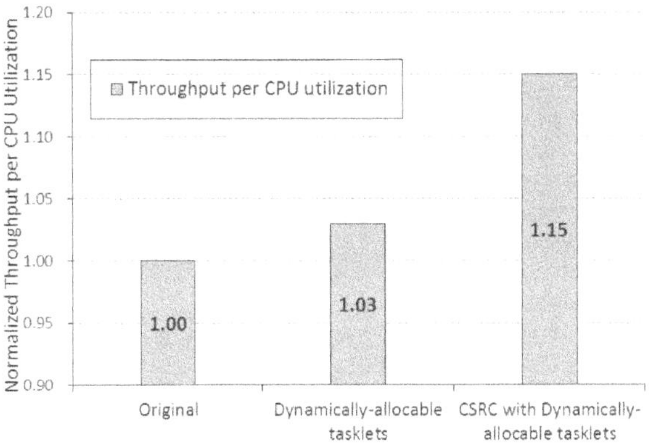

Figure 15. Peak throughput per CPU utilization comparison

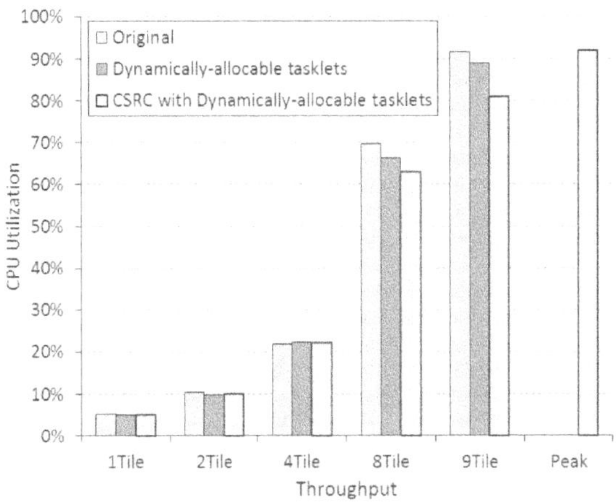

Figure 16. Proposals of dynamically-allocable tasklets and CSRC improve reduce CPU utilization and improve overall throughputs

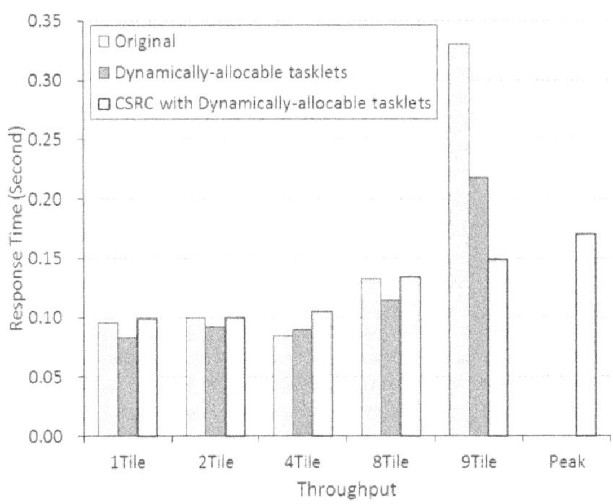

Figure 17. Proposals of dynamically-allocable tasklets and CSRC shorten the response time significantly when close to peak performance

As displayed in Figure 18, PL of the optimized CSRC method at peak performance (9-tile) reduces by 4%, implying more efficient software execution – less number of context switches reduces the instructions required for each function. From the CPI side shown in Figure 19, CPI of optimized CSRC method obtains 6% reduction than original result at 9-tile. Less number of context switches reduces the cache miss ratio – 6% reduction for LLC and 15% for TLB, resulting in lower CPI. All above prove that CSRC benefits from both hardware and software aspects.

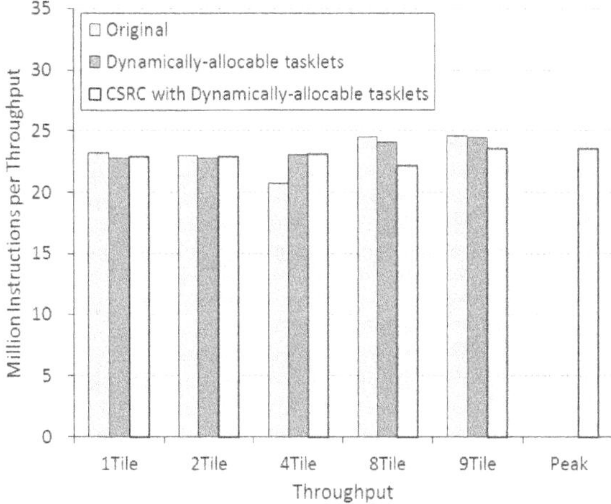

Figure 18. Path length trend comparisons

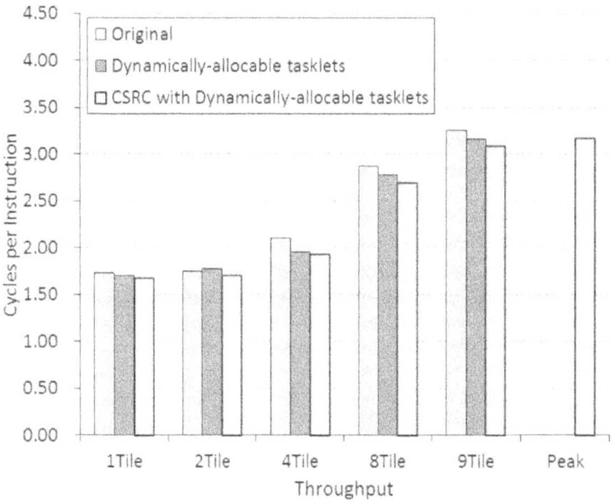

Figure 19. CPI trend comparisons

Finally, from the CPU utilization breakdown of different privilege levels as shown in Figure 20, both guest and hypervisor parts obtain lower CPU utilization when applying CSRC methods. CPU utilization at the same throughput (9-tile) reduces significantly from 92% to 81% by controlling the context switch rate. The hypervisor part contributes 6% and the guest part contributes the other 5%. As discussed above, CPU utilization reduction of guest part is primarily caused by the lower CPI and hypervisor part is caused by both PL and CPI.

To sum up, integrated with the two methods proposed in this section, the overall system throughput of SPECvirt_sc2010 is improved by 15%. The optimized methods obtains lower CPU utilization by reducing both CPI and PL, benefited from less number of context switches. The results show that, current frequency of context switch is so high that impair the server consolidation's performance, which can be partially solved by fine-grained scheduling rate controller. There are still more considerations for scheduler in virtualization, such as to reduce memory and cache footprint, to be aware of running tasks in running VMs, to fairly and efficiently allocate and utilize the underlying hardware resources and so on.

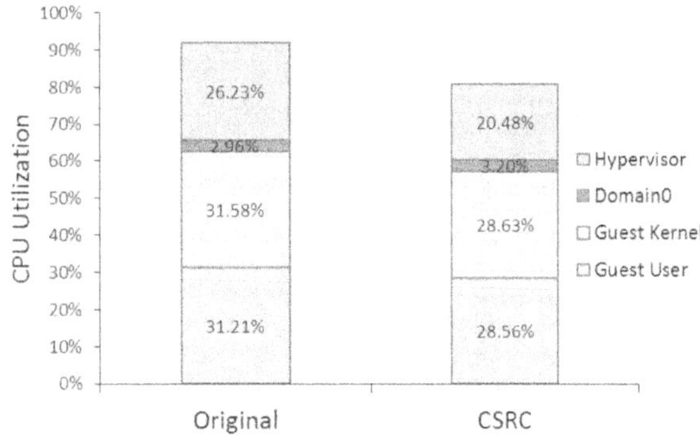

Figure 20. CPU utilization breakdown comparisons at same throughput (9-tile)

7. Related Work

Analyzing and improving virtual consolidation performance is a popular topic in the research community. There are many studies performed to improve virtualization's performance [29] [36] [31] [27]. In software, Liao et al. [29] [36] proposed some scheduling optimizations to improve I/O performance. Besides software optimizations, hardware-assisted solutions, such as VMDq [31], self-virtualized devices [27] and SR-IOV [24] are proposed in virtualization to achieve high-performance.

Studies for better hypervisor resource scheduler [19] [25] [28] are covered in several previous works. Using Xen as hypervisor, Cherkasova et al. [25] studied the impact that three different schedulers have on the throughput of three I/O-intensive benchmarks. In addition to the Credit and SEDF schedulers, their study also addressed Xen's BVT [28] scheduler. They evaluated how a single instance of these applications was affected by the choice of scheduling policy. In effect, they evaluated how the scheduler divided the processing resources between the guest domain and the driver domain. Ongaro et al. [19] explored the relationship between domain scheduling in a hypervisor and I/O performance using multiple guest domains concurrently running different types of applications. In addition, their work examined a number of new and existing extensions to Xen's credit schedule targeted at improving I/O performance. Finally, their study showed that latency-sensitive applications perform best if they are not combined in the same domain with a computing intensive application, but instead are placed within their own domain.

Compared to previous research work leveraging simple workload and hardware, we conducted our measurements and analysis with the state of art hardware. The workload we used is also modified through complex industry benchmark, thus representative enough of real virtual consolidation environments. We believe our performance data and conclusion are more realistic and can be used as a reference for real IT product system design.

8. Conclusion and Future Work

In this paper, through analyzing performance scalability of a representative consolidation workload on the latest 2-way X86 multiple core architecture, we identify both challenges and opportunities for virtualization performance under server consolidation condition: i) large memory and cache footprint caused by high frequency context switch brings in notable bottlenecks, and ii) the current scheduler can be improved with a finer control algorithm. Regarding these, we propose two potential optimization opportunities: applying a dynamically-allocable tasklets method brings in great context switch number reduction and a context switch rate control prototype results in total 15% performance improvement and up to 50% acceleration of service response. However, there is still great headroom for improvement. In future work, a guest-level sensitive scheduler considering its internal workloads and with finer control on priorities is arguably better in allocating the hardware resources between virtual machines to achieve a better overall system level performance. Long term fairness between virtual machines should also be considered in the scheduler design.

Acknowledgements

We would like to thank Keir Fraser for his contributions to compose the dynamically-allocable tasklets algorithm for this study.

References

[1] Intel Corporation. Terascale computing. http://www.intel.com/research/platform/terascale/index.htm.

[2] Intel Corporation. Intel Develops Tera-Scale Research Chips. http://www.intel.com/pressroom/archive/releases/20060926corpb.htm.

[3] VMware. http://www.vmware.com/.

[4] Microsoft Virtual Server, http://www.microsoft.com/hyper-v-server/

[5] Kernel Based Virtual Machine http://www.linux-kvm.org/

[6] P. Barham, B. Dragovic, K. Fraser, S. Hand, T. Harris, A. Ho, R. Neugebauer, I. Pratt, and A. Warfield. Xen and the art of virtualization. In Proceedings of the Symposium on Operating Systems Principles (SOSP), Oct. 2003

[7] SPECvirt_sc2010 http://www.spec.org/virt_sc2010/

[8] P. ApparaoNewell, Towards Modeling & Analysis of Consolidated CMP Servers, Workshop on the Design, Analysis, and Simulation of Chip Multi-Processors (dasCMP), 2007

[9] Jeffrey P. Casazza, Redefining server performance characterization for virtualization benchmarking, Intel Technology journal August 2006

[10] I. M. Leslie, D. Mcauley, R. Black, T. Roscoe, P. T. Barham, D. Evers, R. Fairbairns, and E. Hyden. The Design and Implementation of an Operating System to Support Distributed Multimedia Applications. IEEE Journal of Selected Areas in Communications, 1996

[11] VMmark http://www.vmware.com/products/vmmark/

[12] M. Rosenblum. VMware's Virtual Platform: A virtual machine monitor for commodity PCs. In Hot Chips 11: Stanford University, Stanford, CA, August 15–17, 1999

[13] K. Fraser, S. Hand, R. Neugebauer, I. Pratt, A. War_eld, and M. Williamson. Safe hardware access with the Xen virtual machine monitor. In 1st Workshop on Operating System and Architectural Support for the on demand IT InfraStructure (OASIS), Oct 2004

[14] A. Menon, J. R. Santos, Y. Turner, G. J. Janakiraman, and W. Zwaenepoel. Diagnosing performance overheads in the Xen virtual machine environment. In Proceedings of the First ACM/USENIX International Conference on Virtual Execution Environments (VEE), pages 13–23, June 2005

[15] Selvamuthukumar Senthilvelan and Murugappan Senthilvelan. Study of content-based sharing on the xen virtual machine monitor http://www.cs.wisc.edu/~remzi/Classes/736/Spring2005/Projects/Muru-Selva/cs736-report.pdf.

[16] Wiegert, J., et al.: Challenges for Scalable Networking in a Virtualized Server. In: 16th International Conference on Computer Communications and Networks

[17] A. Menon, A.L. Cox, and W. Zwaenepoel. Optimizing network virtualization in Xen. In Proceedings of the 2006 USENIX Annual Technical Conference, pages 15–28, June 2006

[18] L. Cherkasova and R. Gardner. Measuring CPU overhead for I/O processing in the Xen virtual machine monitor. In USENIX Annual Technical Conference, Apr. 2005

[19] Diego Ongaro , Alan L. Cox , Scott Rixner, Scheduling I/O in virtual machine monitors, Proceedings of the fourth ACM SIGPLAN/SIGOPS international conference on Virtual execution environments, March 05-07, 2008, Seattle, WA, USA

[20] Susan J. Eggers , Joel S. Emer , Henry M. Levy , Jack L. Lo , Rebecca L. Stamm , Dean M. Tullsen, Simultaneous Multithreading: A Platform for Next-Generation Processors, IEEE Micro, v.17 n.5, p.12-19, September 1997

[21] Xudong Zheng, Jiangang Duan, Shameem F Akhter, Zhidong Yu, Hui Lv, A Consolidation Workload Characterization Study on Modern Platform, CMG'09

[22] UHLIG, R., NEIGER, G., RODGERS, D., SANTONI, A. L., MARTINS, F. C. M., ANDERSON, A. V., BENNETT, S. M., KAGI, A., LEUNG, F. H., AND SIMTH, L. 2005. Intel Virtualization Technology. IEEE Computer. 38, 5, 48–56

[23] Yaozu Dong, Zhao Yu, Greg Rose: SR-IOV Networking in Xen: Architecture, Design and Implementation. Workshop on I/O Virtualization 2008

[24] DONG, Y., YANG, X., LI, X., LI, J., TIAN, K., AND GUAN, H. 2010. High Performance Network Virtualization with SR-IOV. In Proceeding of the 16th IEEE International Symposium on High-Performance Computer Architecture (HPCA'10). IEEE, Bangalore, India, 271-280

[25] L. Cherkasova, D. Gupta, and A. Vahdat. Comparison of the Three CPU Schedulers in Xen. ACM SIGMETRICS Performance Evaluation Review, 35(2):42–51, 2007

[26] Credit Scheduler.

http://wiki.xensource.com/xenwiki/CreditScheduler

[27] RAJ, H., AND SCHWAN, K. 2007. High performance and scalable I/O virtualization via self-virtualized devices. In Proceeding of the 16th international symposium on high performance distributed computing (HPDC'07). ACM, Monterrey, CA, 179-188

[28] K. J. Duda and D. R. Cheriton. Borrowed-virtual-time (BVT) scheduling: supporting latency-sensitive threads in a general-purpose scheduler. In Proceedings of the 17th ACM SOSP, 1999.

[29] GUO, D., LIAO, G., AND BHUYAN, L. N. 2009. Performance characterization and cache-aware core scheduling in a virtualized multi-core server under 10GbE. In Proceeding of 2009 IEEE International Symposium on Workload Characterization (IISWC'09). IEEE, Austin, TX, 168-177

[30] Yaozu Dong, Xiaowei Yang, Xiaoyong Li, Jianhui Li, Kun Tian, Haibing Guan. High performance network virtualization with SR-IOV. HPCA'2010. pp.1~10

[31] SANTOS, J. R., TURNER, Y. JANAKIRAMAN, G., AND PRATT, I. 2008. Bridging the gap between software and hardware techniques for I/O virtualization, In Proceeding of the USENIX Annual Technical Conference (USENIX'08). USENIX, Boston, MA, 29-42.

[32] Hui Lv, Xudong Zheng, Zhiteng Huang, Jiangang Duan, Tackling the Challenges of Server Consolidation on Multi-Core Systems. IISWC'2010

[33] Open-iscsi project http://www.open-iscsi.org/

[34] J. Calandrino and J. Anderson. On the design and implementation of a cache-aware multicore real-time scheduler. In Proceedings of the 21st Euromicro Conference on Real-Time Systems, July 2009.

[35] Arcangeli, Andrea ; Eidus, Izik ; Wright, Chris: Increasing memory density by using KSM. http://www.kernel.org/doc/ols/2009/#19-28. Version: 2009

[36] LIAO, G., BHUYAN, L. N., WU, W., YU, H., AND KING, S. R. 2010. A new TCB cache to efficiently manage TCP sessions for Web servers. In Proceeding of the 6th ACM/IEEE Symposium on Architecture for Networking and Communication Systems (ANCS'10). ACM, San Diego, CA, 1-10.

[37] Jun Nakajima, Qian Lin, Sheng Yang, Min Zhu, Shang Gao, Mingyuan Xia, Peijie Yu, Yaozu Dong, Zhengwei Qi, Kai Chen, Haibing Guan: Optimizing virtual machines using hybrid virtualization. SAC 2011: 573-578

[38] A. J. Bernstein, Program Analysis for Parallel Processing, IEEE Trans. on Electronic Computers". EC-15, pp. 757–62, 1966

[39] X. Zhang, A. E. Eichenberger, Y. Luo, K. O'Brien , K. O'Brien, Exploiting Parallelism with Dependence-Aware Scheduling, In Proceedings of the 18th International Conference on Parallel Architecture and Compilation Techniques (PACT'09) (Raleigh, NC, USA, Sept. 2009), ACM, pp. 193–202

REEact: A Customizable Virtual Execution Manager for Multicore Platforms

Wei Wang
University of Virginia
wwang@virginia.edu

Tanima Dey
University of Virginia
td8h@virginia.edu

Ryan W. Moore
University of Pittsburgh
rmoore@cs.pitt.edu

Mahmut Aktasoglu
Pennsylvania State University
msa203@cse.psu.edu

Bruce R. Childers
University of Pittsburgh
childers@cs.pitt.edu

Jack W. Davidson
University of Virginia
jwd@virginia.edu

Mary Jane Irwin
Pennsylvania State University
mji@cse.psu.edu

Mahmut Kandemir
Pennsylvania State University
kandemir@cse.psu.edu

Mary Lou Soffa
University of Virginia
soffa@virginia.edu

Abstract

With the shift to many-core chip multiprocessors (CMPs), a critical issue is how to effectively coordinate and manage the execution of applications and hardware resources to overcome performance, power consumption, and reliability challenges stemming from hardware and application variations inherent in this new computing environment. Effective resource and application management on CMPs requires consideration of user/application/hardware-specific requirements and dynamic adaption of management decisions based on the actual run-time environment. However, designing an algorithm to manage resources and applications that can dynamically adapt based on the run-time environment is difficult because most resource and application management and monitoring facilities are only available at the operating system level. This paper presents REEact, an infrastructure that provides the capability to specify user-level management policies with dynamic adaptation. REEact is a virtual execution environment that provides a framework and core services to quickly enable the design of custom management policies for dynamically managing resources and applications. To demonstrate the capabilities and usefulness of REEact, this paper describes three case studies—each illustrating the use of REEact to apply a specific dynamic management policy on a real CMP. Through these case studies, we demonstrate that REEact can effectively and efficiently implement policies to dynamically manage resources and adapt application execution.

Categories and Subject Descriptors D.4.1 [*Process Management*]: Multiprocessing/multiprogramming/multitasking

General Terms Performance, Management, Design

Keywords Chip multiprocessor, Resource management, Runtime adaptation, Virtual Execution Environment

1. Introduction

As the core counts and sophistication of modern chip multiprocessors (CMPs) increases, adaptive resource management techniques are needed to realize the full potential of these microarchitectural advances. There have been a flurry of such techniques proposed by the research community, such as cache contention management [8, 17, 34], processor temperature management [31, 32], and process variation management [29, 30]. While these and other adaptive policies have shown significant promise, *Users*, such as system administrators, application developers, and other technical experts, are in need of a platform to create, customize, and deploy adaptive resource management policies that address a myriad of design goals and requirements. These policies must also be *plug and play* as user-specific, application-specific and hardware-specific goals change.

For example, consider two users. The users are executing the same application on two identical machines (i.e., the same CMP architecture). However, the users have two distinct requirements. $UserA$ has a tight power budget and prefers a management policy that focuses on minimizing power consumption. $UserB$ desires a management policy that prioritizes performance over power consumption. These goals are contradictory and require distinct management policies. Given the wide range of distinct requirements, it is desirable that management frameworks support flexibility as user requirements, or application requirements, or even hardware characteristics, change.

Currently, most resource management policies are implemented in the operating system (OS) kernel. However, the OS is not well-suited for implementing and incorporating custom policies for two reasons:

1. The OS is not designed to take into account application-specific information when making management decisions. However, with application-specific information, user-level management policies can adjust the execution of applications in a way that is not possible with current OSes. For example, consider an application that uses work-stealing. Work-stealing allows the number of worker threads spawned by the application to be dynamically adjusted. If details of the work-stealing design are known, the management policy can dynamically increase the number of the application's worker threads when the system

is underutilized, and reduce the number of threads for better fairness when the system is over-utilized (see Section 4.2).

2. The complexity of modifying OS policies or adding new ones to the OS is high, which can prevent users from designing their own policies. Even after a custom policy is implemented and carefully tested, much effort has to be made when the same policy is ported to another OS or the user-goal is changed. Furthermore, custom policies may introduce security issues if they are not carefully designed and tested.

Implementing resource management policies at the user-level is easier, and it allows utilization of application-specific information. Previous work has proposed different techniques for user-level resource management [3, 9, 13, 35]. However, these techniques do not necessarily provide easy customization by the user, and some techniques only target a subset of resource management problems of CMPs. Moreover, some techniques do not provide the means to utilize online performance monitoring technology available in modern CMPs. This monitoring capability is widely used by many policies to monitor the system and dynamically adjust management decisions [8, 17, 29–32, 34].

In this paper, we advocate using a user-level virtual execution environment (VEE) to provide a framework for easy integration and development of custom CMP resource management policies. To design a user-level VEE framework, there are several challenges to overcome. The first challenge is to provide the necessary resource management facilities to allow easy development of customized resource management policies. These facilities include allocating hardware resources, adjusting application execution, and collecting run-time information about the resource landscape and application status. Furthermore, the VEE-implemented policies should dynamically adapt based on the actual run-time environment. Additionally, the VEE should be carefully designed so that management overhead does not outweigh the benefit of a custom management policy.

This paper presents a *Customizable Virtual Execution Manager* (REEact) which provides the flexibility to implement dynamic custom resource management policies. Situated between applications and the OS and hardware, REEact is active at run time, and can use both application and hardware run-time information to manage and coordinate the applications running in the system.

REEact provides the capability to specify custom management policies that need dynamic adaptation. It offers basic services for resource and application management to permit the incorporation of different management and coordination policies and mechanisms, including those that are customized to a workload, computing environment and/or system goals. These services are exposed through easy-to-use application programming interfaces (API), allowing quick development and testing without the burden or difficulty of modifying global OS policies.

With REEact, custom policies can be easily ported across platforms, so long as a few basic facilities are available on the target platform, such as thread pinning and access to hardware performance counters. Currently, REEact supports two operating systems, Linux and Solaris, and two ISAs, x86 and SPARC. Moreover, although we introduce a new layer into the system, REEact is very lightweight. Its overhead is typically less than 3% (see Section 3).

To demonstrate REEact's capabilities and usefulness for runtime management, we present three case studies. The first case study examines how REEact can implement a custom thermal management policy for a malfunctioning machine. The second case study illustrates REEact in the context of an application-specific policy that aims to maximize utilization while avoiding unfairly starving other programs from execution. The last case study describes using REEact to dynamically control hardware prefetchers to reduce power consumption without sacrificing performance.

The contributions of this paper include:

1. The REEact framework that provides the capability to easily write user-specific, application-specific and hardware-specific management policies with dynamic adaptation. We describe REEact's software architecture, which is designed to be easy-to-use, extensible, configurable and portable. REEact also permits the implementation of policies that consider application semantics.
2. A thorough evaluation of the overhead and scalability of REEact on a 32-core CMP platform. We demonstrate that, by careful design and implementation, a user-level virtual execution environment, like REEact, can perform aggressive and fine-grained on-line monitoring, dynamic adaptation and multi-application/thread coordination with very low overhead (<3%) and high scalability (64 thread contexts).
3. Presentation of three case studies that demonstrate REEact's flexibility for providing custom dynamic resource management. Evaluation of the three custom policies show the flexibility, effectiveness and low overhead of REEact. The results also highlight the benefits of customization. Over conventional systems, case study 1 improves performance by up to 16%; case study 2 improves the fairness of processor time allocation significantly without sacrificing overall processor utilization; and case study 3 improves performance by up to 69%, energy consumption by up to 43%, and energy-delay-product by up to 142%.

This paper is organized as follows. Section 2 presents the high-level structure and operation of REEact. Section 3 evaluates the overhead of REEact. Section 4 illustrates the operation and utility of REEact by presenting three case studies where REEact manages the use of CMP resources as by specified policies. Section 5 discusses related work and Section 6 concludes the paper.

2. REEact Framework

This section provides an overview of the REEact software architecture, and it describes the design of the framework and implementation choices.

2.1 REEact Software Architecture Overview

Figure 1 sketches the flow of using REEact to implement the specified policies. In REEact, a specified policy requires the implementation of two procedures using the API provided by REEact: a global procedure that manages the execution of multiple applications, and a local procedure that manages the execution of an application (and its threads).

The modification to an existing application to use REEact is straightforward—the main program of the application is modified to include a call to the REEact execution manager. This call essentially places the control of the main thread of execution (as well as subsequent threads the application may create) under the control of REEact. No further modification to the application is required.

During execution, REEact is initialized and it invokes the two procedures of the custom policy, and carries out the specified operations. By coordinating with the OS and the hardware, these operations manage applications and hardware resources.

To illustrate REEact's structure and operation, we first present a simple example. In this example, REEact manages the execution of three multi-threaded applications on a 16-core CMP. For ease of explanation, each core has a single execution context (i.e., simultaneous multi-threading or hyper-threading is not supported). For this example, REEact manages the use of the computation resources (i.e., the cores) and dynamically allocates or deallocates

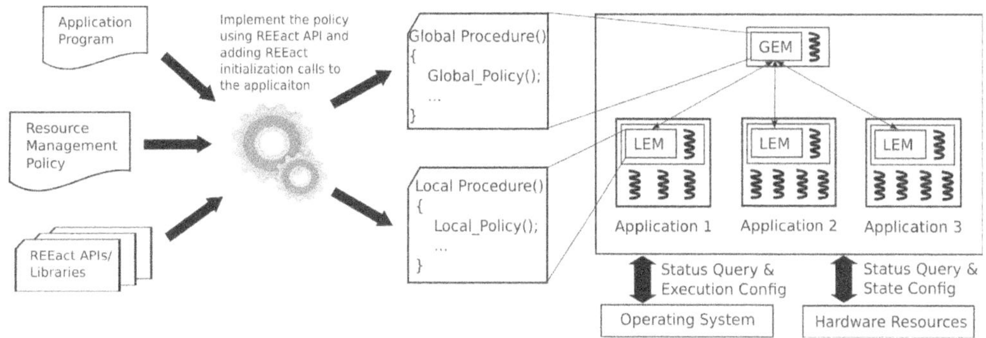

Figure 1. A custom policy requires implementing two procedures using the REEact API, and adding REEact's initialization calls to the application.

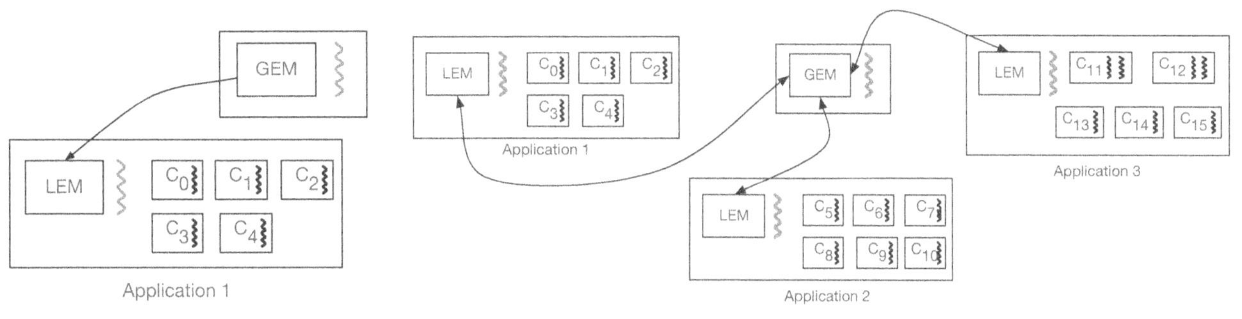

(a) REEact management of a single, multi-threaded application.

(b) REEact management of three, multi-threaded applications.

Figure 2. REEact dynamically allocated/deallocated resources (i.e., cores) using a custom FCFS policy.

them during thread creation and termination following a specified first-come, first-served (FCFS) policy.

In this example, the three applications, App_1, App_2, App_3, create five, six, and seven threads, respectively. We assume that App_1 acquires all its resources before App_2 begins execution, and App_2 acquires all its resources before App_3 begins execution.

Initially, REEact initiates a global execution manager (GEM), which invokes the global procedure to manage multiple applications. In this example, all 16 cores are managed by the GEM. Since GEM's execution has very low overhead, it is allowed to execute on any core (even a core that is allocated to an application thread). When App_1 begins execution, it calls the REEact initialization API routine. This call creates a local execution manager (LEM), which invokes the local procedure to manage the application. The first action of the LEM is to communicate with the GEM and request a core. From this point on, the LEM executes on any core that has been allocated to it (at this point it has one core).

As App_1 executes, it creates other threads. REEact intercepts thread creation calls, and notifies the LEM. The LEM communicates to the GEM requesting another core (recall the policy is FCFS). At this point, the GEM has available cores and one is allocated to this LEM. As application execution continues, additional threads are created and cores are allocated in a similar manner.

Figure 2(a) illustrates the structure of REEact at this point. In the figure, five cores (C_0–C_4) have been allocated to App_1—one for each thread of the application. The LEM thread, like the GEM thread, has low overhead and it is permitted to run on any of the cores allocated to the application (i.e., C_0–C_4).

When App_2 starts, the same process occurs. Here, App_2 creates six threads and is therefore allocated six cores (C_5–C_{10}). Then App_3 begins execution and requests cores (there are now five unallocated cores remaining). The first five thread creations result in a core being allocated for each thread. However, the sixth thread creation results in the GEM informing App_3's LEM that no core is available. The LEM then must map this thread to a core already allocated to it. The process is similar for the seventh and final thread. The final state of execution is illustrated in Figure 2(b). The last two threads of App_3 are mapped to cores C_{11} and C_{12}, respectively.

Note that during the execution of an application, a thread may terminate. REEact intercepts thread termination and notifies the applications' LEMs. If the termination of a thread frees a core, the core may be dynamically reallocated to other threads. The LEM may map an existing thread to the core, or return the core to the GEM for global reallocation. In this example, if a thread in App_1 terminates, the core is returned to the GEM which makes a global decision to offer it to App_3. App_3 can then map one of the threads that is sharing a core to its own core.

REEact supports managing applications with multiple policies. Currently, individual policies are combined manually. REEact also permits the co-existence of multiple GEMs, where each GEM controls some applications and resources using different policies.

2.2 REEact Design

2.2.1 REEact Components

REEact provides the framework and services to enable the implementation of management policies (essentially the global and local procedure). These services, such as GEM/LEM communication and thread mapping, are provided through various REEact components.

API Component	API Methods	Notes
	sendMessage	
Communicator	getMessage	blocking
	timeoutGetMessage	non-blocking with timeout
	readPMUperThread	
	readPMUperCore	
	getCoreTemperature	
Monitor (HW Status)	getTemperatureThreshold1	threshold temperature of DVFS
	getTemperatureThreshold2	threshold temperature of core shutdown
	getCoreFrequency	
	getHWComponentState	e.g. whether prefetcher or L2 cache is disabled?
Monitor (Sys. Util.)	getCoreUtilization	
	getSystemLoad	
SW Actuator	pinAppsToCores	
	pinThreadsToCores	
HW Actuator	enableHWComponent	e.g. enable or disable hardware prefetchers
	adjustFrequency	adjust processor/core frequency or duty cycle
	getUnallocCores	
	getAllocCores	
App. State Tbl. (GEM)	allocOrDeallocCore	
	getTotalCoreCount	get the total number of cores
	getCoresofCache	get the cores that share a cache
	getAllL2Caches	get a list of available L2 caches
App. State Tbl. (LEM)	getCurrentlyUsingCores	get the cores allocated to this LEM
	getAppThreads	

Table 1. API component and their associated methods currently provided by REEact

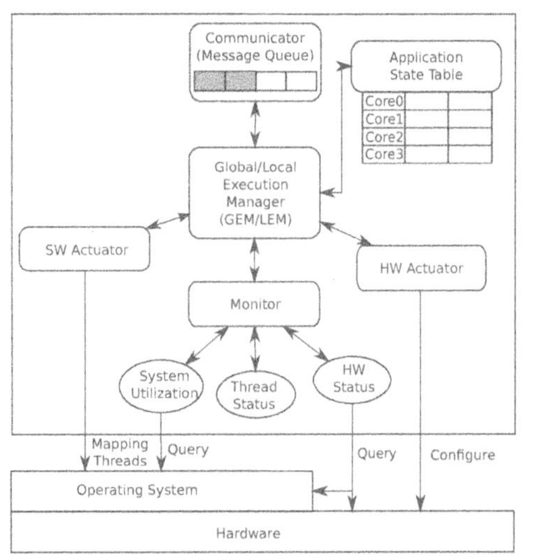

Figure 3. Essential components of REEact.

Figure 3 shows the essential components of REEact. Because proper resource management decisions have to be made based on the actual states of applications and hardware resources, REEact has monitors to collect their run-time status. Hardware and software actuators are provided to adjust resource allocation and application execution. A GEM makes global management decisions based on the run-time information collected by the LEMs, and the communication component provides facilities for communication between GEMs and LEMs. REEact also provides application status tables so that GEM/LEM can keep track of resource allocation. The following paragraphs briefly describe each component.

The **Global/Local Execution Managers (GEM/LEMs)** have three major duties. First, they initialize and release REEact component objects during application start-up and termination. Second, they maintain the tree structure introduced in Section 2.1 (Figure 2(b)). Third, they execute customized policy procedures.

The GEM and LEMs are instantiated during application start-up. When several applications execute simultaneously, the application that starts first becomes the "master" which creates the GEM and the first LEM. Applications that start later only create LEMs. The GEM and LEM perform all necessary operations to create other REEact components. A LEM also identifies the GEM and creates a two-way communication link between them. And lastly, the GEM/LEM invokes the specified policy procedures (see Figure 1).

The **Communicator** transfers data among the GEM and LEMs asynchronously. It is designed as a message queue attached to a GEM/LEM. Each message is composed of three parts: a sender ID, a message type and the message body. The actual meaning of the message is policy dependent.

The **Monitor** provides capabilities to monitor the status of both the hardware and the applications. It collects information about the hardware, system utilization, and the status of threads.

Hardware information that can be collected includes the output of performance monitoring units (PMU), core frequency, core temperature, and whether a particular hardware component (e.g., prefetchers, L2 caches, etc.) is enabled.

The system utilization information includes the load (utilization) of each core, and the overall load. REEact also monitors the status of application threads, such as thread creation, termination and suspension.

The **SW Actuator** configures the execution of applications. The SW actuators map both applications and threads to cores. How cores are allocated depends on the policy used.

The **HW Actuator** configures a hardware (HW) component. A HW actuator can enable or disable a hardware component of a core (e.g., prefetchers), or adjust processor frequency by setting special bits of model specific registers (MSR).

The **Application Status Table (AST)** contains the current states of hardware resources and applications. Each GEM and LEM has its own AST, which contains the information about the resources and threads that it controls. ASTs can be extended to include policy-required information.

2.2.2 REEact API

REEact components are represented as objects and their services are exposed through methods that operate on these objects. The core of REEact is the GEM and LEM classes and associated methods.

Table 1 lists the methods currently provided. For communication among the multiple applications, we provide methods to send and receive messages as part of the communicator component. There are two methods for receiving messages—a blocking method and method with timeout. Currently, the methods for monitors and actuators are designed to provide access to typical resource controls [18–20, 28, 32–34]. We provide the methods for the monitor component to collect the profiling information either per-core or per-application-thread basis. There are additional methods to obtain current temperature, temperature threshold, frequency and other hardware status of the individual physical cores. We also provide methods to gather information about core utilization. The methods for the software actuator component enable the control of the application using software, including on which core an application's threads run. The methods for a hardware actuator enable the control of the state of a particular hardware device, for example, to enable or disable the hardware prefetchers. The methods for the application state table enable the gathering of information about all the applications running in the system for the GEM and one application for LEMs. Additional services and features will be added as REEact expands to support more operating systems and architectures.

2.3 REEact Implementation

The next paragraphs describe the actual implementation of REEact components on Linux-x86 and Solaris-SPARC.

Global/Local Execution Manager (GEM/LEM): A GEM/LEM is implemented as a helper thread, which is created during REEact initialization at the beginning of application execution (recall that to use REEact, a REEact initialization call is added to the application's main program).

Communicator: The communicator is implemented using shared memory and semaphores. The message queue of a GEM or LEM is essentially a portion of memory that is shared by all GEM/LEMs. Therefore, posting a message or reading a message is an access to this shared memory. Each queue is associated with a semaphore, which notifies the GEM/LEM on arrival of a message.

Monitor: On Linux-x86, the monitor uses Perfmon2 to read PMU data [14]. On Solaris-SPARC, the monitor uses "Libcpc" to read PMU data.

On x86 architectures, the core frequency, temperature and other hardware component states are acquired by reading MSRs. REEact reads the MSRs through a special driver that we designed and implemented. On SPARC, these hardware states are acquired from the OS.

System utilization information (e.g., processor utilization) is acquired from the OS. For example on Linux, this information can be read through the "stat" file (per-core) or "loadavg" file (all-cores) under "/proc". On Solaris-SPARC, this information can be acquired from library "Libkstat".

To intercept thread status changes (e.g., thread creation, termination, suspension), we link application thread functions (e.g., pthread_create, pthread_join) to REEact's thread functions. Once a thread status change is detected, the monitor notifies the GEM and LEM by sending messages to them.

SW Actuator: For thread mapping, the SW actuator uses the core-affinity system call. Core/processor affinity is readily available in today's commodity operating systems, including Linux, Solaris and Windows. Once a thread is mapped to a set of cores, the OS does not move the thread to use any other cores. Less rigid mechanisms could also be used; for example, a mechanism could be provided to convey scheduling and allocation hints about thread co-location to the operating system. These mechanisms could be targeted by a user policy in REEact to guide OS management decisions.

HW Actuator: The HW actuators enable/disable hardware components, and adjust core frequency by setting special bits of MSRs. We implement a driver that allows reading and writing MSRs at the user-level.

Application Status Table (AST): In the default implementation, the ASTs are lists that store resource allocation information. Policies can define their own lists (or other data structures) to store any data they need.

3. REEact Overhead Evaluation

This section evaluates the overhead of the REEact framework implementation. REEact incurs overhead when reading hardware performance counters, by monitoring and managing thread creation, and through communication between the LEMs and GEM.

To determine the run-time overhead of REEact, we chose several multithreaded applications from PARSEC [6], and we measured REEact's overhead as we scaled the total number of threads and applications. The experiments were run on a CMP machine that has four Intel Xeon X7550 processors each of which has eight cores. As the processors are hyper-threaded, each core has two thread contexts and consequently the machine supports 64 thread contexts. Each physical core has a private 32KB L1-cache, a 256KB L2-cache and one 16MB L3-cache shared by eight physical cores. This machine is running Linux 2.6.32.

We conducted a series of experiments with workloads consisting of different numbers of randomly chosen PARSEC benchmarks. The benchmarks used in the experiments are: *blackscholes (BS)*, *bodytrack (BT)*, *canneal (CN)*, *dedup (DD)*, *facesim (FA)*, *ferret (FE)*, *fluidanimate (FL)*, *streamcluster (SC)* and *swaptions (SW)*. To measure the overhead of reading performance counters, we varied the period of reading counters from 10 milliseconds to 32 seconds for a fixed number of applications and threads per application. As we increased the period, REEact's overhead decreased because of less frequent access to the performance counters.

To measure REEact's overhead, we varied the number of applications from 1 to 16 and threads per application from 1 to 8, for a fixed counter-reading period. We set the counter-reading period to 10 milliseconds. We experimentally checked PARSEC and SPEC, and discovered that no benchmark has a phase shorter than 10ms (similar results are also reported by previous research [10]). Therefore, 10ms is small enough in practice to capture phase changes in the application threads. If an application does have phases less than 10ms, then phase changes may go undetected, and there could be some penalty. However, as the phases are short ($<$ 10ms), any penalty should not be high/significant. We ran experiments with four one-application, four two-application, three four-application, one eight-application and one sixteen-application workload with different number of threads under REEact control. The benchmarks used in the workloads are described in Table 2. For each workload, the overhead was measured by calculating the average percentage difference in each application's execution time normalized with respect to the native execution (i.e., no REEact).

Table 3 shows the overhead results. We did not measure the overhead for 16 applications with 8 threads per application as the total number of threads exceeds the number of thread contexts for

Workload size	Benchmark Initials used in each workload
$\|WL\|$=1	{BS}, {BT}, {CN}, {FA}
$\|WL\|$=2	{BS, BT}, {BS, CN}, {BS, FA}, {BS, SW}
$\|WL\|$=4	{BS, BT, CN, FA}, {BS, CN, FA, SW}, {BS, BT, CN, FA}
$\|WL\|$=8	{BS, BT, CN, FA, FE, FL, SC, SW}
$\|WL\|$=16	{BS, BT, CN, FA, FE, FL, SC, SW, BS, BT, CN, FA, FE, FL, SC, SW}

Table 2. The benchmarks used in each workload for measuring REEact overhead. $|WL|$ denotes the number of applications in a workload, e.g., $|WL| = 2$ means two applications in a workload. For each workload size, each set in the next column represents one workload composed by $|WL|$ number of PARSEC benchmarks (indicated by the acronym).

	Number of threads			
	1	2	4	8
$\|WL\|$=1	0.77	1.36	1.46	2.74
$\|WL\|$=2	0.79	1.82	1.45	0.63
$\|WL\|$=4	0.6	0.84	0.94	2.49
$\|WL\|$=8	1.43	1.07	1.18	1.37
$\|WL\|$=16	1.27	1.47	1.32	—

Table 3. Total overhead (in percentage) as the number of applications and threads per application is varied, for counter-reading period=10 milliseconds. $|WL|$ denotes the number of applications in a workload, e.g., $|WL| = 2$ means two applications in a workload.

the experimental machine. From the table, we observe that for a particular workload size, as the number of threads increases (reading across a column), the overhead slightly increases. The increase is due to the increased number of messages. For a fixed number of threads, as we increase the number of applications, the overhead varies slightly. This slight variation is caused by the differences in the workloads. For all 19 experiments, the average overhead of the REEact framework is at most 3%, which is acceptably small. Note that, the overall overhead of REEact given in Table 3 includes the overhead of sending messages across processors. The low overall overhead (less than 3%) implies that the use of cross-processor messaging has low overhead and is not a bottleneck for the machines we examined.

4. Case Studies

This section describes three case study policies that are implemented in REEact to demonstrate its flexibility and usefulness. These policies tackle diverse problems: thermal management, fairness among parallel applications, and performance/energy-consumption management.

4.1 Case Study 1: Fighting the Broken Screw

In the first case study, we demonstrate how to use REEact to implement a policy that reacts to thermal emergencies. We have a CMP computer that frequently experiences overheating. This computer has an Intel Q6600 quad-core processor. The processor has four cores. Each core has 32KB L1 I-cache and 32 KB L1 D-cache. Every two cores of this processor shares one 4MB L2 cache. The machine is running Linux 2.6.25.

In this machine, one of the four screws that fasten the heat sink and fan to the chip is broken, causing some cores (especially *core0*) to easily reach a very high temperature. Most CMP processors have hardware mechanisms to prevent overheating. For this processor, it uses dynamic voltage/frequency scaling (DVFS) and voluntary core shutdown. By reading the on-die digital thermal sensors (DTS), this processor monitors its cores' temperatures. If any core's temperature exceeds a factory predefined threshold T_1, the core's frequency and/or voltage are reduced. If a core's temperature keeps climbing and reaches the critical temperature T_2, the core is shutdown temporarily. Although these mechanisms prevent

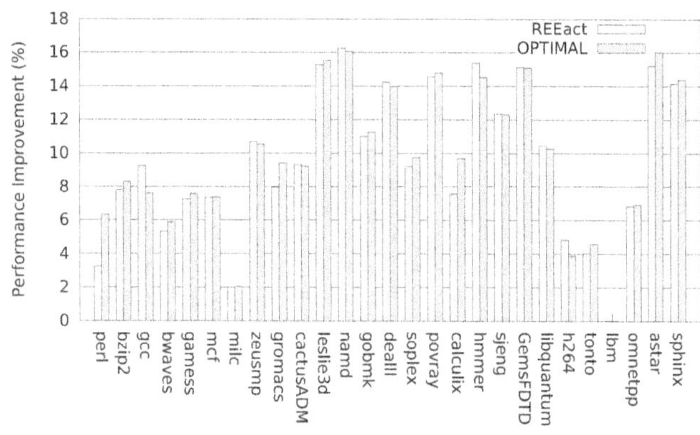

Figure 4. Performance (execution time) improvement of SPEC with REEact broken-screw policy and manually tuned optimal execution, compared to the Linux default scheduler.

catastrophic overheating, they have negative impact on system performance. If we can detect cores that are vulnerable to overheating, and schedule the threads to use these cores less frequently, then we can achieve better performance as well as prevent unnecessary overheating of the cores.

REEact's monitoring methods support reading core temperatures (using MSR "IA32_THERM_STATUS"), as well as dynamically detecting threshold temperatures T_1 and T_2. To solve the broken-screw thermal problem, we developed a custom policy using REEact. In this policy, the GEM and LEMs work together to detect overheating and migrate application threads appropriately. Policy 1.a and 1.b give the pseudocode for the global (GEM) and local (LEM) procedures respectively. When an application first requests a core for its newly created thread (through its LEM), the GEM randomly allocates a free core to it. During execution, the LEM periodically (every 10 seconds) checks if any of its cores are overheating. Depending on the level of overheating, the LEM requests different cores:

1. If the overheating core's temperature is between T_1 and T_2, the LEM asks the GEM for a core with temperature below T_1 (Policy 1.b line 16). If the GEM finds such a core (Policy 1.a lines 11-19), it responds with the new core (Policy 1.a lines 35-37), to which LEM maps its threads (Policy 1.b line 21).

2. If the overheating core's temperature is equal to or higher than T_2, the LEM marks this core as a hot core, and asks the GEM for the coolest non-marked core (Policy 1.b line 13-14). Once the GEM responses with a new core (Policy 1.a lines 21-31), the LEM re-maps its threads to it (Policy 1.b line 21). If the GEM fails to find a core, the LEM and its threads stay on the hot core.

We evaluated this policy using the SPEC2006 benchmarks. Figure 4 shows the performance (execution time) improvement of SPEC benchmarks controlled by REEact with the overheating prevention policy, as well as manually tuned optimal execution, compared to the Linux default scheduler, which does not consider core temperature and can freely use any core. The optimal execution time is determined by trying all possible thread-to-core mappings, and choosing the one with the minimum execution time.

The maximum speedup of REEact over the Linux default scheduler is 16%, and the average speedup is 9.5%. The results show the benefit of using REEact framework by implementing this adaptive policy customized for this specific machine. The results also show that REEact and this policy has very low overhead, with at most 3% slowdown compared to optimal results. This slowdown is partially caused by the reactive nature of the policy: it only migrates threads when overheating actually occurs. The policy can be further refined to be proactive instead of being reactive [32].

Policy 1.a Fighting the broken screw: GEM policy procedure (bold-faced functions are REEact methods)

```
/* input parameters: ref to all LEM objs, ref to GEM obj, ref to monitor and ref to
   GEM's app state table */
INPUT: List lemList, Gem gem, Monitor m, AppStatTbl ast
List freeCores ← ast.getUnallocCores();
Int T1 ← m.getTempThreshold1();
Int T2 ← m.getTempThreshold2();
LOOP
   Message msg ← gem.getMessage();
   Lem lem ← msg.sender;
   Core oldCore ← msg.value;
   Core newCore ← oldCore;
   IF msg.type = TemperatureAboveT1 THEN
      /* search for a core that has a temperature below T1 */
      FOR ALL c IN freeCores DO
         Int t ← m.getCoreTemperature(c);
         IF t < T1 THEN
            newCore← c;
            BREAK;
         END IF
      END FOR
   ELSE IF msg.type = TemperatureAboveT2 THEN
      Int lowestT ← T2;
      /* List of cores that "lem" has used and had thermal issue (core temperature
         above T2) */
      List hotCores ← lem.ast.getCoresAboveT2();
      /* search for an unallocated core that has lowest temperature and no thermal
         issue for "lem" yet */
      FOR ALL c IN freeCores DO
         t ← m.getCoreTemperature(c);
         IF hotCores.doNotHave(c) AND (t < lowestT) THEN
            newCore ← c;
            lowestT ← t;
         END IF
      END FOR
   END IF
   /* ask LEM "lem" to run on newCore */
   IF newCore ≠ oldCore THEN
      lem.sendMessage(runOnCore, newCore);
      freeCores.add(oldCore);
      freeCores.remove(newCore);
   END IF
END LOOP
```

4.2 Case Study 2: Maximizing Utilization without Penalty

We next demonstrate a REEact policy that maximizes the utilization of a multicore system without unnecessarily starving other applications from execution.

Consider a shared, heavily utilized multicore server, where diverse CPU-intensive workloads arrive without notice. The run times may be unknown and multi-threaded workloads likely can run with a user-specified number of threads.

Recognizing that new workloads are likely to arrive, a user may restrict the number of threads a multi-threaded program uses, leaving CPU resources for future workloads. However, it may be difficult or impossible to know when future workloads will arrive or what their properties will be. Consequently, at times the system may be underutilized.

Policy 1.b Fighting the broken screw: LEM policy procedure (bold-faced functions are REEact methods)

```
/* input parameters: ref to this LEM obj, ref to GEM obj, ref to monitor and ref to
   this LEM's app state table */
INPUT: Lem lem, Gem gem, Monitor m, AppStatTbl ast
Int T1 ← m.getTempThreshold1();
Int T2 ← m.getTempThreshold2();
/* extend ast with a new list for the cores on which this LEM has thermal issue
   (core temperature above T2) */
List ast.CoresAboveT2 ← new List();
LOOP
   /* single-threaded app has only one thread and one core*/
   Core curCore ← ast.getCurrentlyUsingCores();
   Thread appThread ← ast.getAppThreads();
   Int coreT ← m.getCoreTemperature(curCore);
   IF coreT ≥ T2 THEN
      ast.CoresAboveT2.add(curCore);
      gem.sendMessage(TemperatureAboveT2, curCore);
   ELSE IF coreT ≥ T1 THEN
      gem.sendMessage(TemperatureAboveT1, curCore);
   END IF
   /* Get message with timeout "timeout" (non-blocking)*/
   Message msg ← LEM.timeoutGetMessage(timeout);
   IF (msg ≠ NULL) AND (msg.type = runOnCore) THEN
      lem.pinThreadstoCores(appThread, msg.value);
      sleep(timeout);
   END IF
END LOOP
```

Alternatively, the user may assume that no new workloads will arrive. The initial workload can then use as many threads as there are CPUs (assuming CPU bound threads). Future workloads, if any, may be starved for CPU time if they generate fewer number of threads than the first application. A better policy is to dynamically adapt each program in response to system utilization.

A multi-threaded program on an otherwise idle system should use all available cores. If workloads arrive, current workloads should reduce their CPU usage (e.g., by shutting down worker threads). If workloads exit, existing workloads should expand to use the newly freed CPU resources. In this way, the system is consistently at 100% utilization, yet no program is unnecessarily starved of CPU time.

We developed a policy, called AutoMax, to dynamically expand and shrink running programs in REEact. Policy 2.a shows the global policy procedure as implemented in the GEM. Policy 2.b shows the local policy procedure as implemented in the LEM.

The GEM determines a minimum and maximum amount of utilization that the system should try to achieve (lines 4-5). It then monitors overall load, as given by the OS (line 7). The load is a measure of how many cores the system would need to properly run the current workload.

Each application is launched under the GEM's control with a LEM as described in Section 2. AutoMax obtains and permutes the list of current LEMs for the current workload (line 8). The LEM list is permuted to avoid favoring one application over another. A permuted list on average will balance the number of shrink and expand requests sent across applications and is also simple and fast to implement.

If the utilization is below a minimum threshold (line 10), a LEM is randomly selected to expand (line 11). Similarly, if the utilization is above the maximum threshold (line 12), a LEM is chosen randomly to shrink. The LEM may elect not to expand or shrink, in which case the next LEM in the list, if any, is given a chance to expand or shrink (lines 19-26).

The GEM then pauses for a few seconds (line 27). This pause (5 seconds) allows applications to shrink or expand before rebalancing is again considered. How a LEM responds to a request to expand or shrink is application specific (Policy 2.b). Applications may require a minimum number of threads or have a maximum number of threads to run (i.e., due to a limited amount of parallelism). It is up to the LEM to reject expand or shrink messages as appropriate.

We conducted experiments to compare the performance of applications using static thread allocation versus the AutoMax policy. We modified *blackscholes* from PARSEC to support AutoMax. The modification required having worker threads perform work-stealing from a global queue of uncompleted work units. An expand request creates a new worker thread. Once a thread has received a work unit, it must complete the work unit before obtaining more work, or shutting down due to a shrink request. The modification of *blackscholes* was easy since it has a global thread number counter that explicitly tells the benchmark how to distribute their work. As developers embrace libraries that abstract away explicit thread creation and work allocation (e.g., OpenMP, Intel Thread Building Blocks), AutoMax will become more easily applicable.

Policy 2.a AutoMax: GEM Policy Procedure (boldfaced functions are REEact methods)

```
/* input parameters: ref to LEM objs, ref to GEM obj, ref to monitor, ref to app state table */
INPUT: List lemList, Gem gem, Monitor m, AppStatTbl ast

Double minUtilization ← ast.getTotalCoreCount() - ε_1
Double maxUtilization ← ast.getTotalCoreCount() + ε_2
LOOP
  Double curUtilization ← m.getSystemLoad()
  List permutedLL ← permute(lemList)
  /* Depending on system load, ask apps to expand or shrink their threads */
  IF curUtilization < minUtilization THEN
    MSGTYPE msgType = expand
  ELSE IF curUtilization > maxUtilization THEN
    MSGTYPE msgType = shrink
  ELSE
    permutedLL.removeAll() /* No app must change */
  END IF
  /* loop until an app has expanded or shrunk, or until no app can be changed */
  Bool didExpandOrShrink ← FALSE
  REPEAT
    Lem lem ← permutedLL.getFirst&Remove()
    lem.sendMessage(msgType, NULL)
    Message msg ← gem.getMessage()
    IF msg.type = changeResponse AND
    msg.sender = lem THEN
      didExpandOrShrink ← msg.value
    END IF
  UNTIL didExpandOrShrink OR permutedLL.isEmpty()
  sleep(time);
END LOOP
```

Policy 2.b AutoMax: LEM Policy Procedure (boldfaced functions are REEact methods)

```
/* input parameters: ref to this LEM obj, ref to GEM obj, ref to monitor and ref to this LEM's app state table */
INPUT: Lem lem, Gem gem, Monitor m, AppStatTbl ast

LOOP
  Message msg ← lem.getMessage();
  IF msg.type = expand OR msg.type = shrink THEN
    /* the application decides its response */
    Bool canChange ← canExpandOrShrink(msg.type);
    IF canChange THEN
      /* the application decides how to expand or shrink */
      expandOrShrink(msg.type);
    END IF
    gem.sendMessage(changeResponse, canChange)
  END IF
END LOOP
```

The experiments were conducted on a 4-core CMP machine. This machine has one Intel Xeon E5335 processor. The processor has four cores. Each core has 64KB L1 I-cache and 64KB L1 D-cache, and every two cores share one 4MB L2 cache. The machine uses Linux 2.6.29.

To evaluate our policy, we ran *blackscholes* on this machine and injected synthetic single-threaded programs. Each synthetic program instance performs a fixed amount of CPU-intensive work, taking 50s on an idle system. After the synthetic programs finish, we waited 30s before starting the next period. In total, 3 waves of injections occured. The waves represent users periodically running one or more short running tasks. Figures 5(a), 5(b), and 5(c) show these results. We give the arithmetic average execution time of the synthetic programs.

As *blackscholes* is statically assigned more threads, its execution time decreases, eventually starving the synthetic programs for CPU time. In contrast, AutoMax avoids harming the performance of the synthetic programs.

With one single-threaded synthetic program active in a wave (Figure 5(a)), AutoMax *blackscholes* has an execution time closest to that of *blackscholes* when statically allocated 4 threads. When no synthetic programs are running, *blackscholes* can create new threads and use all cores on the system. The synthetic programs have an execution time closest to that of when *blackscholes* is statically allocated 3 threads (leaving a core for their use). Thus, AutoMax is able to maximize the performance of the synthetic programs without penalizing the execution time of *blackscholes*.

With two synthetic program active in a wave (Figure 5(b)), AutoMax *blackscholes* has a run time closest to that of *blackscholes* when statically allocated 3 threads. The synthetic programs have an execution time closest to that of when *blackscholes* is statically allocated 3 threads. An ideal policy would have the synthetic programs' execution time be as if *blackscholes* was statically allocated 2 threads, leaving 2 cores available for each synthetic program.

With three synthetic program instances active in a wave (Figure 5(c)), AutoMax *blackscholes* has a run time closest to that of *blackscholes* when statically allocated 3 threads. The synthetic programs have an execution time closest to that of when *blackscholes* is statically allocated 2 threads. A policy which does not impact the performance of the synthetic benchmarks would cause the synthetic programs to have the same execution time as if run alongside an instance of *blackscholes* that is statically allocated 1 core.

Based on the results shown in Figures 5(a), 5(b), and 5(c), the AutoMax version of *blackscholes* is adapting itself to other workloads on the system (i.e., the synthetic programs).

4.3 Case Study 3: Reducing Energy Usage without Performance Penalty

In the third case study, we present a REEact policy for reducing system energy consumption. This policy is based on the following observations: hardware prefetchers may have no or negative performance impact if many cache lines prefetched are not used by the application [26]. However, fetching these useless cache lines requires extra energy. Therefore, we can disable the prefetchers when they do not improve performance to save energy. With REEact, we can dynamically examine how the applications use prefetchers, and control the prefetchers accordingly.

Policy 3.a and 3.b give the pseudo-code for the global (GEM) and local (LEM) procedures. When a new thread is created or unblocked (from synchronization wait), REEact's thread status monitor sends a new message to the GEM (Policy 3.a line 6). Upon receiving this message, the GEM starts to test two configurations: one with prefetchers enabled and one with prefetchers disabled. The GEM also notifies the LEMs to collect the number of instructions retired for these two configurations (Policy 3.a lines 7-27). Each configuration is executed for 0.5 seconds and each LEM reports the number of instructions retired to GEM (Policy 3.b lines

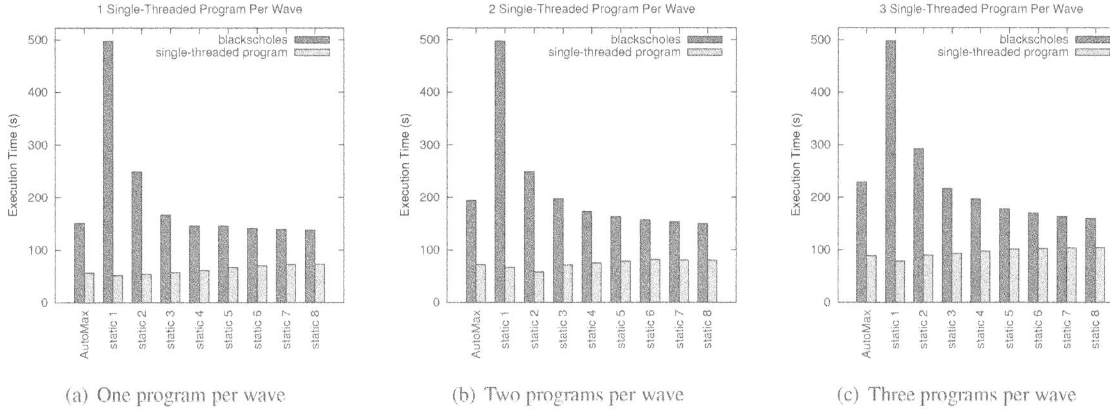

(a) One program per wave (b) Two programs per wave (c) Three programs per wave

Figure 5. AutoMax compared to static policies. The number after "static" means the number of statically created blackscholes threads (not controlled by REEact).

Policy 3.a REEact Power management: GEM policy procedure (boldfaced functions are REEact methods)

```
1: /* input parameters: ref to all LEM objs, ref to GEM obj, ref to monitor, ref to
   GEM's app state table, ref to HW actuators */
2: INPUT: List lemList, Gem gem, Monitor m, AppStatTbl ast, HWActuator hwAct
3: Int coreCnt ← m.getTotalCoreCount();
4: LOOP
5:   Message msg ← gem.getMessage();
6:   IF msg.type = ThreadActivated THEN
7:     /* start sampling configuration with prefetchers on*/
8:     /* enable prefetchers on all cores */
9:     hwAct.enableHWComponent(c, prefetcher, on);
10:    FOR ALL lem IN lemList DO
11:      lem.sendMessage(readInsnRetired, NULL);
12:    END FOR
13:    Int insnPfOn ← 0;
14:    FOR ALL lem IN lemList DO
15:      Message msg ← gem.getMessage();
16:      insnPfOn ← insnPfOn + msg.value;
17:    END FOR
18:    /* start sampling configuration with prefetchers off*/
19:    hwAct.enableHWComponent(c, prefetcher, off);
20:    FOR ALL lem IN lemList DO
21:      lem.sendMessage(readInsnRetired, NULL);
22:    END FOR
23:    Int insnPfOff ← 0;
24:    FOR ALL lem IN lemList DO
25:      Message msg ← gem.getMessage();
26:      insnPfOff ← insnPfOff + msg.value;
27:    END FOR
28:    /* Comparing two configuration */
29:    BOOL switch ← off;
30:    IF insnPfOn > insnPfOff × 1.02 THEN
31:      switch ← on;
32:    END IF
33:    hwAct.enableHWComponent(c, prefetcher, switch);
34:  END IF
35: END LOOP
```

8-13). The GEM compares the results, and disables the prefetchers if the configuration with enabled prefetchers does not retire more instructions (Policy 3.a lines 28-33). To avoid measurement errors from PMUs, the configuration with enabled prefetchers is considered superior only if it has at least 2% more instructions retired.

We evaluated this policy on a computer with an Intel quad-core processor Q9550. Each core has 32KB L1 I-cache and 32KB L1 D-cache. There are two 6MB L2 caches each shared by two cores. For each L1 cache, there are two prefetchers (DCU and IP) that prefetch data into it. For each L2 cache, there are also two prefetchers (hardware prefetcher and adjacent cache line prefetcher) that prefetch data into it. The DCU prefetcher and the adjacent cache line prefetcher prefetch the next cache line of the missed cache line into the cache. The IP prefetcher and the hardware prefetcher look for a stride in the memory access pattern and prefetch the next expected data [2]. We tested eleven PARSEC benchmarks individually. Each benchmark was configured to run with four threads using native input sets. We ran each benchmark for three iterations and computed the average energy consumption and execution time of PARSEC's "region of interest" (parallel region). We collected the energy consumption of the processor using the methodology from Esmaeilzadeh et al. [15].

Figure 6 shows the results of seven benchmarks running under REEact, as well as two other static configurations where prefetchers are always enabled or disabled. Four benchmarks, *bodytrack*, *raytrace*, *vips* and *blackscholes*, are omitted because configuring prefetchers does not impact their performance or energy consumption. The results show that REEact always provides the best performance and lowest energy consumption. Compared to always enabling prefetchers, REEact improves execution time by up to 8%. It improves energy consumption by 12% and the energy-delay-product (EDP) by up to 19%. Compared to always disabling prefetchers, REEact improves execution time by up to 69%, energy consumption by 43% and EDP by up to 142%. The results show that REEact has little (at most 1%) overhead over the best static prefetcher configuration.

Policy 3.b REEact power management: LEM policy procedure (boldfaced functions are REEact methods)

```
/* input parameters: ref to this LEM obj, ref to GEM obj, ref to monitor and ref to
   this LEM's app state table */
INPUT: Lem lem, Gem gem, Monitor m, AppStatTbl ast
List appThreads ← ast.getAppThreads();
LOOP
  Message msg ← lem.getMessage();
  Double time = 0.5; /* sample for 0.5 seconds */
  IF msg.type = readInsnRetired THEN
    /* read InsnRetired for all the threads of this LEM */
    List insnCnts ← insnCnt +
      m.readPMUperThread(appThreads, InsnRetired, time);
    gem.sendMessage(InsnRetiredValue, insnCnts.sum());
  END IF
END LOOP
```

5. Related Work

There has been much work in designing and implementing virtual execution environments (VEEs) for various purposes. Nesbit

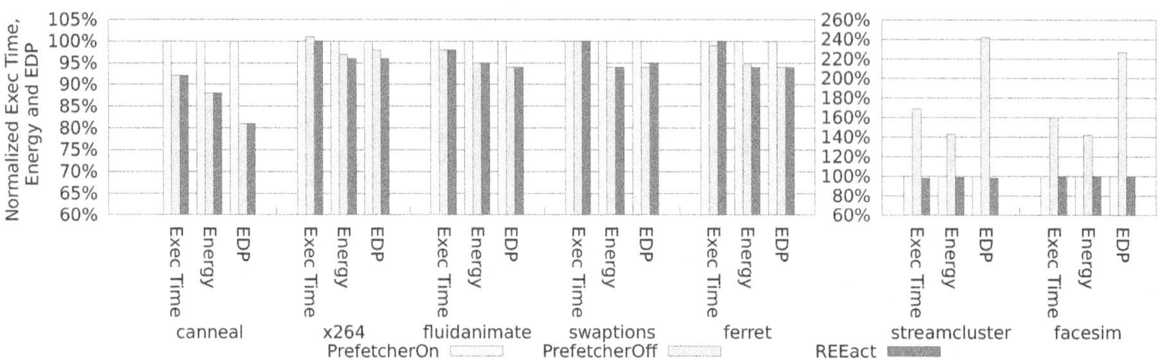

Figure 6. Execution time, energy consumption and EDP for PARSEC benchmarks running under REEact and two static configurations where prefetchers are always enabled or disabled (normalized to the configuration where prefetchers are always enabled; the lower bar is better).

et al. proposes virtual private machine (VPM) as an abstraction for managing spatial and temporal resources in multicore systems [22]. These VPMs consist of several software policies for managing resources which translate system-level requirements into different hardware mechanisms. In other work, the Xen hypervisor is extended to create a framework for supporting application-specific resource management in many core systems [23]. Cuvillo describes a Thread Virtual Machine (TVM) in the form of a thread library to allow applications to achieve full resource utilization [9]. AKULA is a tool-set for experimenting and testing scheduling algorithms that mitigate shared cache contention among single-threaded applications [35]. Noll et al. describes a virtual machine to allow programmers to use higher level programming constructs and mimic the behavior of a homogeneous shared memory multiprocessor, hiding the heterogeneity in the underlying Cell processors [24]. Similar to these researchers, we advocate the use of VEEs to dynamically manage applications and hardware resources on CMPs. However, these VEEs are usually specialized for a particular purpose (mostly for shared resource management) or an architecture, while our REEact is designed to provide a generic framework and a wide variety of services that can be used for a range of diverse purposes. Multikernel shares the same application and architecture-specific management spirit with us, but it focuses on improving the OS kernel design [5]. Log-based architecture (LBA) is similar to REEact in that LBA also constantly monitors on-line applications [7]. The difference is that LBA focuses more on application security and correctness. REEact shares the spirit of user-level application management with scheduler activation [3] and shares the spirit of application-specific resources management with exokernel [13]. However, for CMP resource/application management, extensive user-level/kernel-level thread interactions and application-specific resource abstractions are not always necessary.

There has been prior work on virtualization and hypervisors. Xen is a hypervisor that allows the existance of large number of guest OSes on the same machine with low overhead and safe resource isolation [4]. This work describes a virtualization architecture consisting of a microhypervisor and environment that provides operating system functionality including virtual-machine monitors (VMM) in user-level [27]. This user-level VMM allows execution of unmodified guest OSes in the virtual machine. On the other hand, REEact provides a VEE that supports the design and implementation of customizable user-level resource management policies for the execution of applications.

There also has been prior work addressing the problems described in the three case studies. Kadin et al. describes centralized and distributed dynamic thermal management for CMPs [18]. A low overhead thermal manager using core swapping has been proposed to address thermal emergencies [20]. A proactive dynamic temperature management technique is described by Yeo et al. [32]. Most of these software techniques can be easily implemented with REEact. Prior work has also been done in having multi-threaded programs automatically adapt their behavior. Libraries like Intel's Threading Building Blocks [25] abstract away the work of threads, and use techniques such as work stealing and/or a task scheduler to ensure that all threads (and cores) in a system are active. Our AutoMax policy differs from [25] in that applications have their own policy (in the LEM) and are able to choose how to respond, instead of being limited to the Intel task scheduler's available policy/policies. Works such as [21] are orthogonal to our approach, and might allow for the automatic creation of LEM policies. Java's thread pool preallocates a pool of worker threads [1]. An application can then use these pre-created threads to process its tasks. It can also return the threads to the pool if there are no more tasks to do. Thread pool helps minimizes the overhead due to thread creations and terminations. Thread pool can be included in REEact to help design management policies like case study 2. Several recent studies address the over-aggressiveness of current prefetchers. Zhang et al. proposed throttling processor's duty cycle and prefetchers to improve resource sharing fairness, which can be implemented with REEact [33]. A similar hardware solution was proposed by Ebrahimi et al. [12]. New hardware prefetcher designs are also proposed to reduce the negative performance impact [11, 16, 26].

6. Summary

Various user requirements, application behaviors, and hardware configurations, have greatly complicated the management of CMP hardware resources and applications. Management policies addressing such variations depends on user/application/hardware-specific requirements and require dynamic adaptation. This paper tackles these management problems by enabling the design and implementation of custom resource management policies with REEact, a user-level VEE framework. This framework provides several services for dynamic management and coordination of hardware resources and applications. REEact allows easy development of custom policies to meet different user requirements. It also facilitates the development of policies that consider application-specific information and hardware characteristics. We describe the design and implementation of REEact, and use it with three case studies, each focusing on distinct issues on CMPs—thermal management, resource efficiency and fairness, and power management. These case studies highlight the benefits brought by REEact, such as flexibility, effectiveness, ease-of-use, and separation of concerns. Through these case studies, we also demonstrate that a carefully designed user-level VEE, like REEact, can effectively manage resources and applications with little run-time overhead.

Acknowledgments

This research is supported by National Science Foundation grants CCF-0811689, CNS-1012070, CCF-0811295, CCF-0811352, CCF-1147388, CNS-1017882, CCF-0963839 and CCF-0811687. We appreciate the insightful comments and constructive suggestions from the anonymous reviewers. We would also like to thank Jason Mars and Lingjia Tang for their valuable input.

References

[1] Java(TM) 2 Platform Standard Edition 5.0 API Specification. `http://java.sun.com/j2se/1.5.0/docs/api/`.

[2] Intel 64 and IA-32 architecture software developer's manual, 2011.

[3] T. E. Anderson, B. N. Bershad, E. D. Lazowska, and H. M. Levy. Scheduler activations: effective kernel support for the user-level management of parallelism. In *Proc. of the Thirteenth ACM Symposium on Operating Systems Principles*, pages 95–109, 1991.

[4] P. Barham, B. Dragovic, K. Fraser, S. Hand, T. Harris, A. Ho, R. Neugebauer, I. Pratt, and A. Warfield. Xen and the art of virtualization. In *Proc. of the Nineteenth ACM Symposium on Operating Systems Principles*, pages 164–177, 2003.

[5] A. Baumann, P. Barham, P.-E. Dagand, T. Harris, R. Isaacs, S. Peter, T. Roscoe, A. Schüpbach, and A. Singhania. The multikernel: a new OS architecture for scalable multicore systems. In *Proc. of the 22nd ACM Symposium on Operating Systems Principles*, pages 29–44, 2009.

[6] C. Bienia, S. Kumar, J. P. Singh, and K. Li. The PARSEC benchmark suite: characterization and architectural implications. In *Proc. of the 17th Int'l Conf. on Parallel Architectures and Compilation Techniques*, pages 72–81, 2008.

[7] S. Chen, B. Falsafi, P. B. Gibbons, M. Kozuch, T. C. Mowry, R. Teodorescu, A. Ailamaki, L. Fix, G. R. Ganger, B. Lin, and S. W. Schlosser. Log-based architectures for general-purpose monitoring of deployed code. In *1st Workshop on Architectural and System Support for Improving Software Dependability*, pages 63–65, 2006.

[8] S. Chen, P. B. Gibbons, M. Kozuch, V. Liaskovitis, A. Ailamaki, G. E. Blelloch, B. Falsafi, L. Fix, N. Hardavellas, T. C. Mowry, and C. Wilkerson. Scheduling threads for constructive cache sharing on CMPs. In *Proc. of the Nineteenth Annual ACM Symposium on Parallel Algorithms and Architectures*, pages 105–115, 2007.

[9] J. del Cuvillo. *Breaking away from the OS Shadow: A Program Execution Model Aware Thread Virtual Machine for Multicore Architectures*. PhD thesis, University of Delaware, Newark, DE, USA, 2008.

[10] E. Duesterwald, C. Cascaval, and S. Dwarkadas. Characterizing and Predicting Program Behavior and its Variability. In *Proc. of the 12th Int'l Conf. on Parallel Architectures and Compilation Techniques*, pages 220–231, 2003.

[11] E. Ebrahimi, O. Mutlu, C. J. Lee, and Y. N. Patt. Coordinated control of multiple prefetchers in multi-core systems. In *Proc. of the 42nd Annual IEEE/ACM Int'l Symposium on Microarchitecture*, pages 316–326, 2009.

[12] E. Ebrahimi, C. J. Lee, O. Mutlu, and Y. N. Patt. Fairness via source throttling: a configurable and high-performance fairness substrate for multi-core memory systems. In *Proc. of the Fifteenth Edition of ASPLOS on Architectural Support for Programming Languages and Operating Systems*, pages 335–346, 2010.

[13] D. R. Engler, M. F. Kaashoek, and J. O'Toole, Jr. Exokernel: an operating system architecture for application-level resource management. In *Proc. of the Fifteenth ACM Symposium on Operating Systems Principles*, pages 251–266, 1995.

[14] S. Eranian. Perfmon2: A flexible performance monitoring interface for Linux. In *Ottawa Linux Symposium*, pages 269–288, 2006.

[15] H. Esmaeilzadeh, T. Cao, Y. Xi, S. M. Blackburn, and K. S. McKinley. Looking back on the language and hardware revolutions: measured power, performance, and scaling. In *Proc. of the Sixteenth Int'l Conf. on Architectural Support for Programming Languages and Operating Systems*, pages 319–332, 2011.

[16] I. Hur and C. Lin. Memory Prefetching Using Adaptive Stream Detection. In *Proc. of the 39th Annual IEEE/ACM Int'l Symposium on Microarchitecture*, pages 397–408, 2006.

[17] L. Jin and S. Cho. SOS: A Software-Oriented Distributed Shared Cache Management Approach for Chip Multiprocessors. In *Proc. of the 2009 18th Int'l Conf. on Parallel Architectures and Compilation Techniques*, pages 361–371, 2009.

[18] M. Kadin, S. Reda, and A. Uht. Central vs. distributed dynamic thermal management for multi-core processors: which one is better? In *Proc. of the 19th ACM Great Lakes Symposium on VLSI*, pages 137–140, 2009.

[19] S. Kim, D. Chandra, and Y. Solihin. Fair Cache Sharing and Partitioning in a Chip Multiprocessor Architecture. In *Proc. of the 13th Int'l Conf. on Parallel Architectures and Compilation Techniques*, pages 111–122, 2004.

[20] E. Kursun, G. Reinman, S. Sair, A. Shayesteh, and T. Sherwood. Low-Overhead Core Swapping for Thermal Management. In *Workshop on Power-Aware Computer Systems*, 2004.

[21] J. Lee, H. Wu, M. Ravichandran, and N. Clark. Thread tailor: dynamically weaving threads together for efficient, adaptive parallel applications. In *Proc. of the 37th Annual Int'l Symposium on Computer Architecture*, pages 270–279, 2010.

[22] K. J. Nesbit, J. Laudon, and J. E. Smith. Virtual private machines: A resource abstraction. Technical report, In University of Wisconsin - Madison, ECE TR, 2007.

[23] D. Nikolopoulos, G. Back, J. Tripathi, and M. Curtis-Maury. VT-ASOS: Holistic system software customization for many cores. In *IEEE Int'l Symposium on Parallel and Distributed Processing*, pages 1–5, 2008.

[24] A. Noll, A. Gal, and M. Franz. CellVM: A Homogeneous Virtual Machine Runtime System for a Heterogeneous Single-Chip Multiprocessor. In *Workshop on Cell Systems and Applications*, 2008.

[25] C. Pheatt. Intel®threading building blocks. *J. Comput. Small Coll.*, 23(4):298–298, 2008. ISSN 1937-4771.

[26] S. Srinath, O. Mutlu, H. Kim, and Y. N. Patt. Feedback Directed Prefetching: Improving the Performance and Bandwidth-Efficiency of Hardware Prefetchers. In *Proc. of the IEEE 13th Int'l Symposium on High Performance Computer Architecture*, pages 63–74, 2007.

[27] U. Steinberg and B. Kauer. Towards a scalable multiprocessor user-level environment. In *Workshop on Isolation and Integration for Dependable Systems*, 2010.

[28] D. K. Tam, R. Azimi, L. B. Soares, and M. Stumm. RapidMRC: Approximating L2 miss rate curves on commodity systems for online optimizations. In *Proc. of the 14th Int'l Conf. on Architectural Support for Programming Languages and Operating Systems*, pages 121–132, 2009.

[29] R. Teodorescu and J. Torrellas. Variation-aware application scheduling and power management for chip multiprocessors. In *Proc. of the 35th Annual Int'l Symposium on Computer Architecture*, pages 363–374, 2008.

[30] J. Winter and D. Albonesi. Scheduling algorithms for unpredictably heterogeneous CMP architectures. In *IEEE Int'l Conf. on Dependable Systems and Networks With FTCS and DCC*, pages 42 –51, 2008.

[31] J. Yang, X. Zhou, M. Chrobak, Y. Zhang, and L. Jin. Dynamic Thermal Management through Task Scheduling. In *IEEE Int'l Symposium on Performance Analysis of Systems and Software*, pages 191–201, 2008.

[32] I. Yeo, C. C. Liu, and E. J. Kim. Predictive dynamic thermal management for multicore systems. In *Proc. of the 45th Annual Design Automation Conference*, pages 734–739, 2008.

[33] X. Zhang, S. Dwarkadas, and K. Shen. Hardware execution throttling for multi-core resource management. In *Proc. of the 2009 Conf. on USENIX Annual Technical Conference*, pages 23–23, 2009.

[34] S. Zhuravlev, S. Blagodurov, and A. Fedorova. Addressing shared resource contention in multicore processors via scheduling. In *Proc. of the Fifteenth Edition of ASPLOS on Architectural Support for Programming Languages and Operating Systems*, pages 129–142, 2010.

[35] S. Zhuravlev, S. Blagodurov, and A. Fedorova. AKULA: a toolset for experimenting and developing thread placement algorithms on multicore systems. In *Proc. of the 19th Int'l Conf. on Parallel Architectures and Compilation Techniques*, pages 249–260, 2010.

DVM: Towards a Datacenter-Scale Virtual Machine

Zhiqiang Ma Zhonghua Sheng Lin Gu
Department of Computer Science and Engineering
The Hong Kong University of Science and Technology
Hong Kong
{zma,szh,lingu}@cse.ust.hk

Liufei Wen Gong Zhang
Huawei Technologies
Shenzhen, China
{wenliufei,nicholas}@huawei.com

Abstract

As cloud-based computation becomes increasingly important, providing a general computational interface to support datacenter-scale programming has become an imperative research agenda. Many cloud systems use existing virtual machine monitor (VMM) technologies, such as Xen, VMware, and Windows Hypervisor, to multiplex a physical host into multiple virtual hosts and isolate computation on the shared cluster platform. However, traditional multiplexing VMMs do not scale beyond one single physical host, and it alone cannot provide the programming interface and cluster-wide computation that a datacenter system requires. We design a new instruction set architecture, DISA, to unify myriads of compute nodes to form a big virtual machine called DVM, and present programmers the view of a single computer where thousands of tasks run concurrently in a large, unified, and snapshotted memory space. The DVM provides a simple yet scalable programming model and mitigates the scalability bottleneck of traditional distributed shared memory systems. Along with an efficient execution engine, the capacity of a DVM can scale up to support large clusters. We have implemented and tested DVM on three platforms, and our evaluation shows that DVM has excellent performance in terms of execution time and speedup. On one physical host, the system overhead of DVM is comparable to that of traditional VMMs. On 16 physical hosts, the DVM runs 10 times faster than MapReduce/Hadoop and X10. On 256 EC2 instances, DVM shows linear speedup on a parallelizable workload.

Categories and Subject Descriptors D.1.3 [*PROGRAMMING TECHNIQUES*]: Concurrent Programming—Parallel programming; C.2.4 [*COMPUTER-COMMUNICATION NETWORKS*]: Distributed Systems

General Terms Design, Performance, Experimentation

Keywords Datacenter, Virtualization, Cloud Computing

1. Introduction

Emerging as a paradigm shifting technology, cloud-based computation has demonstrated tremendous capability in web applications and a wide range of computational tasks, such as business intelligence, bioinformatics, computational finance, chemical analysis, and environmental sciences [17, 18, 21, 42, 43], especially for processing large data sets [10, 20, 27]. Cloud-based systems rely on abundantly provisioned datacenters strategically distributed in geographic regions [7, 24]. A datacenter usually contains tens of thousands of compute servers made of commodity hardware, employs high-bandwidth switching networks, and often utilizes virtualization and distributed services to manage resources and provide a scalable computing platform [1, 2, 10].

It is believed that virtualization is a fundamental component in cloud technology. Particularly, ISA-level virtual machine monitors (VMM) are used by major cloud providers for packaging resources and enforcing isolation [1, 3], sometimes providing underlying support for higher-level language constructs [2]. However, the traditional VMMs are typically designed to work on a single physical host and multiplex it to be several virtual machine instances [8, 30, 46]. Though it is possible to build management or single system image (SSI) services to coordinate multiple physical or virtual hosts [12, 38, 46], they fall short of providing the functionality and abstraction that allow users to develop and execute programs as if the underlying platform were a single big "computer" [9]. Extending traditional ISA abstractions beyond a single machine has only met limited success. For example, vNUMA extends the IA-64 (Itanium) instruction set to a cluster of machines [14], but finds it necessary to simplify the memory operation semantics and shows difficulty in scaling to very large clusters.

On the other hand, exposing the distributed detail of the platform to the application layer leads to increased complexity in programming, decreased performance, and, sometimes, loss of generality. In recent years, application frameworks [20, 27] and productivity-oriented parallel programming languages [4, 15, 40, 48] have been widely used in cluster-wide computation. For example, MapReduce and its open-source variant, Hadoop, are perhaps the most widely-used application framework in the datacenter environment [34]. Without completely hiding the distributed hardware, MapReduce requires programmers to partition the program state so that each map and reduce task can be executed on one individual host, and enforces a specific control flow and dependence relation to ensure correctness and reliability. This leads to a restricted programming model which is efficient for "embarrassingly parallel" programs, where data can be partitioned with minimum dependence and thus the processing is easily parallelizable, but makes it difficult to design sophisticated and general applications [21, 34, 41, 47]. The language-level solutions, such as X10 [15], Chapel [13] and Fortress [4], are more general and give programmers better control over the program logic flows, parallelization and synchronization, but the static locality, programmer-specified synchronization, and the linguistic artifacts influence such solutions to perform well with one set of programs but fail to deliver performance, functionality, or ease-of-programming with another. It remains an open problem to design an effective system architec-

VEE'12, March 3–4, 2012, London, England, UK.

ture and programming abstraction to support general, flexible, and concurrent application workloads with sophisticated processing.

Considering that ISAs indeed provide a clearly defined interface between hardware and software and allow both layers to evolve and diversify, we believe it is effective to unify the computers in a datacenter at the instruction level, and present the programmers the view of a big virtual machine that can potentially scale to the entire datacenter. The key is to overcome the scalability bottleneck in traditional instruction sets and memory systems. Hence, instead of porting an existing ISA, we design a new ISA, Datacenter Instruction Set Architecture (DISA), for datacenter-scale computation. Through its instruction set, memory model and parallelization mechanism, the DISA architecture presents the programmers an abstraction of a large-scale virtual machine, called the DISA Virtual Machine (DVM), which runs on a plurality of physical hosts inside a datacenter. It defines an interface between the DVM and the software running above it, and ensures that a program can execute on any collection of computers that implement DISA.

Different from existing VMMs (e.g. VMware [46], Xen [8], vNUMA [14]) on traditional architectures (e.g., x86), DVM and DISA make design choices on the instruction set, execution engine, memory semantics and dependence resolution to facilitate scalable computation in a dynamic environment with many loosely coupled physical or virtual hosts. There are certainly many technical challenges in creating an ISA scalable to a union of thousands of computers, and backward compatibility used to constrain the application of new ISAs. Fortunately, the cloud computing paradigm presents opportunities for innovations at this basic system level—first, the datacenter is often a controlled environment where the owner can autonomously decide internal technical specifications; second, major cloud-based programming interfaces (e.g., RESTful APIs, RPC, streaming) require minimum instruction-level compatibility; finally, there is only a manageable set of "legacy code". The goals of our design of DVM are:

- **General**. DVM should support the design and execution of general programs in datacenters.
- **Efficient**. DVM should be efficient and deliver high performance.
- **Scalable**. DVM should be scalable to run on a plurality of hosts, execute a large number of tasks, and handle large datasets.
- **Portable**. DVM should be portable across different clusters with different hardware configurations, networks, etc.
- **Simple**. It should be easy to program the DVM; DISA should be simple to implement.

With the design goals stated, we revisit the approach and rationale of unifying the computers in a datacenter at the ISA layer. The programming framework, language, and system call/API are also possible abstraction levels for large-scale computation. However, as aforementioned, the frameworks and languages have their limitations and constraints. Hence, they fall short of providing the required *generality* and *efficiency*. Using system calls/APIs to invoke distributed system services can be *efficient* and reasonably *portable*. However, an abstraction on this level creates dichotomized programming domains and requires the programmers to explicitly handle the complexity of organizing the program logic around the system calls/APIs and filling any semantic gap, which fails to provide the illusion of a "single big machine" to the programmers and leads to a far less *general* and *easy-to-program* approach than what we aim to. The existing ISAs, designed for a single computer with up to a moderate number of cores, can hardly provide the *scalability* required by the "machine" that scales to the datacenter size. On the other hand, the design of the DVM is motivated by the necessity of developing a next-generation datacenter computing technology that overcomes several important limitations in current solutions. The DVM should provide the basic

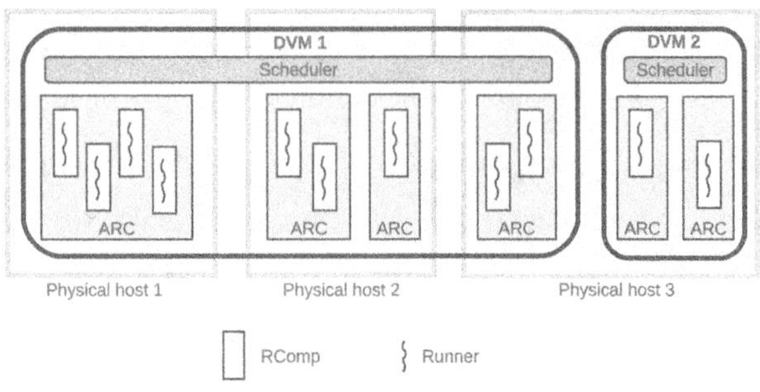

Figure 1. DVM architecture. Two DVMs run on top of three physical hosts in this example.

program execution and parallelization substrate in this technology, and should meet all the goals on *generality*, *efficiency*, *scalability*, *portability*, and *ease-of-programming* (with compilers' help). This leads us to choose the ISA layer to construct a unified computational abstraction of the datacenter platform. To break the *scalability* bottleneck in traditional ISAs and retain the advantages of *generality* and *efficiency*, we design the new ISA, DISA, and build the DVM on this architecture. The design of DISA, the DVM system, and the evaluation of these designs (refer to Section 5) show that the performance of the programs benefits much from the ISA-level abstraction.

We implement the DVM on top of commodity computers and virtual machines, and evaluate it on several platforms with a set of workloads. The results show that DVM can be more than 10 times faster than Hadoop and X10 on certain workloads with moderately iterative logic, and that DVM scales well with near-linear speedup up to at least 256 compute nodes with parallelizable workloads.

The structure of this paper is as follows. We give an overview of DVM in Section 2. Section 3 presents the designs of DISA, memory space, runners, scheduling, etc. Section 4 describes the implementation. We show the evaluation results in Section 5, and discuss related work in Section 6. Section 7 concludes the paper and discusses future work.

2. System overview

The architecture of DVM is shown in Figure 1. A DVM runs on top of one, multiple, or many physical hosts. We abstract a group of computational resources including processor cores and memory to be an *available resource container* (ARC). In its simplest form, an ARC is a physical host. However, it can also materialize as a traditional virtual machine or other container structure, given the container provides an appropriate programming interface and adequate isolation level. Although one ARC is exclusively assigned to one DVM during one period of time, the ARCs in one physical host may belong to one or more DVMs and one DVM's capacity can be dynamically changed by adding or removing ARCs to or from the DVM as needed. Hence, the capacity of a DVM is flexible and scalable—a DVM can share a single physical host with other DVMs, or exclusively include many physical hosts as its ARCs.

2.1 System organization

A DVM accommodates a set of tasks running in a unified address space. Depending on the required resources, multiple DVMs can co-exist on a single physical host, or a single DVM may scale to run on a large number of physical hosts. Although DVMs may have different capacity and the size of a DVM can grow to very large, the DVMs provide the same architectural abstraction of a "single computer" to programs through the Datacenter Instruction Set Architecture (DISA). The programs in DVMs are in DISA

Table 1. DISA instructions

Instruction	Operands	Effect
mov	*D1, M1*	Move [*D1*] to *M1*
add	*D1, D2, M1*	Add [*D1*] and [*D2*]; store the result in *M1*
sub	*D1, D2, M1*	Subtract [*D2*] from [*D1*]; store the result in *M1*
mul	*D1, D2, M1*	Multiply [*D1*] and [*D2*]; store the result in *M1*
div	*D1, D2, M1*	Divide [*D1*] by [*D2*]; store the result in *M1*
and	*D1, D2, M1*	Store the bitwise AND of [*D1*] and [*D2*] in *M1*
or	*D1, D2, M1*	Store the bitwise inclusive OR of [*D1*] and [*D2*] in *M1*
xor	*D1, D2, M1*	Store the bitwise exclusive OR of [*D1*] and [*D2*] in *M1*
br	*D1, D2, M1*	Compare [*D1*] and [*D2*]; jump to *M1* depending on the comparing result
bl	*M1, M2*	Branch and link (procedure call)
newr	*M1, M2, M3, M4*	Create a new runner
exit		Exit and commit or abort

M means this operand is a memory address; *D* means this operand is a memory address or immediate value; [*D*] means the immediate value (when *D* is an immediate value) or the value stored in the memory address (when *D* is a memory address)

instructions and a program running inside a DVM instantiates to be a number of tasks called *runners* executing on many processor cores and computers.

Inside an ARC, many runners, each residing in one *runner compartment* (RComp), can execute in parallel. The RComp is a semi-persistent facility that provides various system functions to runners and the meta-scheduler (discussed later) to facilitate and manage runners' execution. Specifically, the RComp accepts the meta-scheduler's commands to prepare and extend runners' program state and start runners, helps the memory subsystem handle runners' memory accesses, facilitates the execution of instructions such as `newr` (see Table 1), sends scheduling-related requests to the meta-scheduler, and provides I/O services. As these functions are tightly correlated with other subsystems of DVM, we introduce pertinent details of the RComp design along with the treatise of the other system components in Section 3. Suffices it at present to understand that one RComp contains at most one runner at a specific time, and it becomes available for assigning a new runner to after the current incumbent runner exits.

The DVM contains an internal meta-scheduler (or, simply, scheduler) to schedule tasks (runners) executing in RComps. The scheduler is a distributed service running on all constituent hosts of a DVM, with one scheduler master providing coordination and serialization functions. The scheduler dispatches runners to execute in RComps, prepares runners' memory, and handles runners' requests to create new runners.

2.2 Programming in DISA

In this section, we use one example to illustrate how to write a simple program on a DVM using DISA. Details of the DISA architecture will be introduced in Section 3, and a more complex example will be introduced in Section 4.2.

The following DISA code performs a sum operation of two 64-bit integers by a *sum_runner* runner. The starting address of the memory range storing the two integers is in `0x100001000`, and the result's address is in `0x100001008`. The lines starting with "#" are comments and the runners' names are in italic.

```
sum_runner:
add (0x100001000):q, 8(0x100001000), (0x100001008)
                                      # :q indicates 64-b data
mov:z $1:q, 8(0x100001008):q          # set exit code
exit:c                                # exit and commit
```

With an emphasis on instruction orthogonality, DISA allows the instruction to freely choose memory addressing modes to reference the first and second operands. The second instruction sets the exit code to indicate the result is ready (`:z` means "zero extend"). The last instruction makes the runner exit and commit (`:c`) the changes.

3. Design

We design DISA as a new ISA targeting a large-scale virtual machine running on a plurality of hosts connected through the network inside a datacenter and build the DVM above this architectural abstraction. In this section, we first introduce the design of DISA's instructions then present DISA's memory model in Section 3.2 and the parallelization mechanism in Section 3.3.

3.1 DISA

Given the system goals of the DVM design as listed in Section 1, the goals of the DISA are as follows.

1. DISA should support a memory model and parallelization mechanism scalable to a large number of hosts.
2. DISA programs should efficiently execute on common computing hardware used in datacenters, which are usually made of commodity products. Certain hardware may provide native support to DISA in the future, although we emulate DISA instructions using x86-64 instructions in our current implementation.
3. DISA instructions should be able to express general application logic efficiently.
4. DISA should be a simple instruction set with a small number of instructions so that it is easy to implement and port.
5. DISA should be Turing-complete.

In summary, DISA should be scalable, efficient, general, simple, and Turing-complete. To ensure programmability, simplicity and efficiency, DISA, as shown in Table 1, includes a selected group of frequently used instructions. The `newr` and `exit` instructions in DISA facilitate construction of concurrent programs with a plurality of execution flows.

We show the Turing completeness of DISA by using DISA to emulate a Turing-complete `subleq` machine [39]. The emulator accepts an arbitrary `subleq` program and generates the corresponding output. The DISA implementation is as follows (each `subleq` instruction is encoded as a triple of 64-bit integers representing its three parameters).

```
loop: mov:z (pc):q, addr1:q
      mov:z 8(pc):q, addr2:q
      sub (addr2):q, (addr1), (addr2)
      br:l $0:q, (addr2), next
      mov:z 16(pc):q, addr3:q
      mov (addr3):q, pc
      br:j loop
next: add pc:q, $24, pc
      br:j loop
```

Here `pc`, `addr1`, `addr2` and `addr3` are mnemonic names of the addresses of special variables used by the emulator. `pc` initially points to the start address of the input `subleq` program. The third instruction means "jump to *next* if `0` is less than the value in

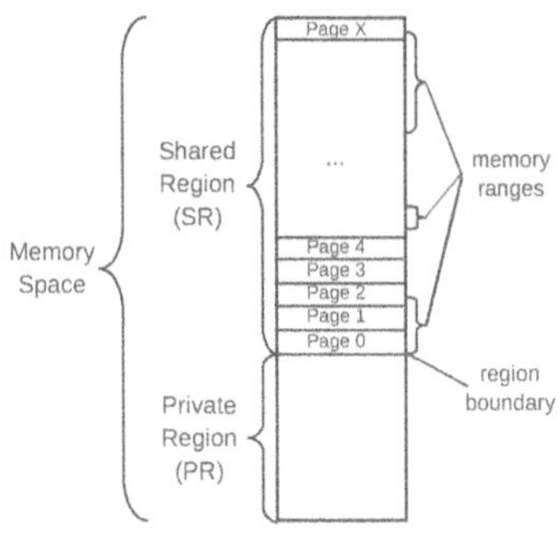

Figure 2. Organization of the memory space

the 64-bit memory range whose address is stored in addr2". Being Turing-complete, DISA is capable of implementing any computable application logic.

DISA's architecture does not explicitly contain registers. This design provides a unified operand representation yet does not prevent register-based optimization because the memory model allows some addresses to be affiliated with registers. A DISA instruction may use options to indicate specific operation semantics, such as the :z and :c in the *sum_runner* example, and the operands can refer to immediate values or memory content using direct, indirect or displacement addressing mode.

3.2 Unified memory space

To facilitate the illusion of programming on a single computer, DISA provides a large, flat, and unified memory space where all runners in a DVM reside. The memory space of a DVM is divided into two regions–the private region (PR) and the shared region (SR). The starting address of the SR is the region boundary (RB) which is just after the address of PR's last byte. The memory layout is shown in Figure 2.

A write in an individual runner's PR does not affect the content stored at the same address in the other runners' PRs. In contrast, the SR is shared among all the runners in the sense that a value written by one runner can be visible to another runner in the same DVM with DISA's memory consistency model controlling when values become visible. A runner can use the PR to store temporary or buffered data because of its very small overhead, and use the SR to store the main application data which may be shared among runners. In our implementation on the x86-64 platform, we set RB to 0x400000000 and an application can use a 46-bit memory address space. Therefore, programs can potentially store around 64TB data in SR and each runner can store several gigabytes of data in its PR, which is sufficient for most of the applications in datacenters.

The consistency model of DISA plays a critical role on the programmability and the scalability. DISA provides a snapshot-based consistency model that relaxes the read/write order on different snapshots. In DISA, a snapshot is a set of memory ranges instantiated with the memory state at a particular point in time. A memory range is a sequence of consecutive bytes starting from a memory address. After a snapshot is created for a runner, later updates to the associated memory ranges by other runners do not affect the state of the snapshot. Hence, when reading data from a snapshot, a runner always receives the value the runner itself has written most recently or the value stored at the time the snapshot is taken. The consistency model of DISA permits concurrent accesses optimistically, and detects write conflicts automatically. With this consistency model, it is possible to implement atomic writes of a group of data, which are commonly used in transactional processing and other reliable systems requiring ACID properties.

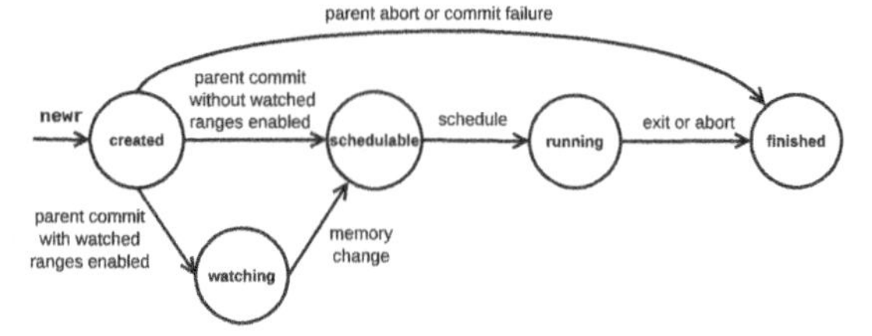

Figure 3. State transition of the runner and watcher

To assist the runners in using the shared and snapshotted SR in the unified memory space, components of the DVM cooperate to manage the snapshots and facilitate the memory accesses by runners. The snapshots are managed by the scheduler for runners and serialized by the memory subsystem. The scheduler creates a snapshot for a runner on its interested memory ranges before scheduling it for execution. The snapshot is associated with the runner throughout its lifetime and the snapshot can be extended only by the scheduler when it is needed. At the end of the runner's execution, the scheduler commits the changes made by the runner to the DVM memory. The commit operation is atomic and the updates are made visible to all the snapshots created thereafter.

The RComps facilitate the memory subsystem to handle the runners' memory accesses. An individual runner's PR is implemented as the local memory ranges on the RComp where the runner resides. The SR is shared among all the runners and distributed across the RComps. The memory subsystem reuses the virtual memory hardware to detect memory accesses in the SR and service remote data following established practices [29, 32].

As locality is crucial for performance in large clusters [49], we design a simple yet general mechanism to coordinate runners to execute on RComps based on the memory range usage history to improve locality for various workloads. The scheduler proactively assigns a runner to the RComp that recently used the SR ranges needed by the runner if such an RComp exists. In the mean time, the users or programmers need not to know or make specific arrangements for the physical memory allocation and distribution.

As updates by one runner only affect the content of the associated snapshot, most of the memory accesses are handled locally at native speed. The order of read/write by different runners is relaxed and concurrent accesses and updates are permitted in this memory model. This makes the system easily scalable with both the number of runners and the data size. In the mean time, the memory subsystem only serializes the committing of memory ranges when runners exit. Hence, the DVM can efficiently manage a large number of snapshots for the runners in the system.

3.3 Tasking and scheduling

We design DVM's parallelization mechanism so that it is easier to develop not only "embarrassingly parallel" programs, but also more sophisticated applications, and the programs can efficiently execute in a datacenter environment. Our goal is to provide a scalable, concurrent, and easy-to-program task execution mechanism with automatic dependence resolution. To achieve the goal, we design a many-runner parallelization mechanism for scalable and efficient concurrent execution, a scheduler to manage the runners and the many-runner execution, and watchers to express and resolve task dependences.

3.3.1 Runner

Runners are the abstraction of the program flows in a DVM. A runner is created by its parent runner and terminates after it exits or aborts. Figure 3 summarizes the state transitions in a runner's life cycle. The parent runner creates a new runner by executing

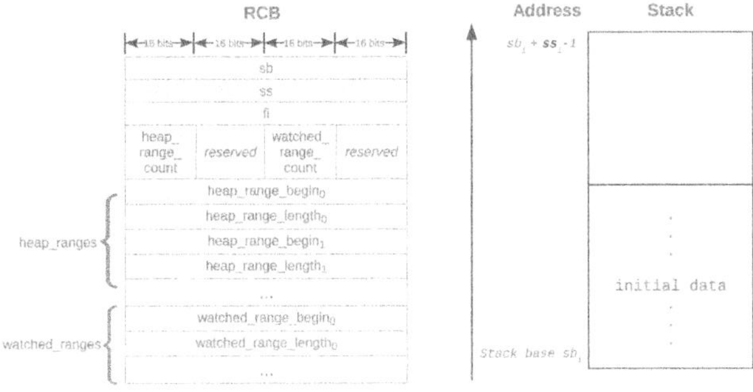

Figure 4. Runner i's initial stack and RCB

the `newr` instruction. A "created" runner moves to "schedulable" state after the parent runner exits and commits successfully. The runner moves to the "running" state after being scheduled and to the "finished" state after it exits or aborts. The "watching" state applies only to a class of special runners called "watchers", which are to be introduced in Section 3.3.4.

Each runner uses a range of memory as its stack range (stack for short), changes to which are discarded after the runner exits, and multiple ranges of memory as its heap ranges. Runners in a DVM are started by the scheduler. Therefore, the scheduler needs to know certain control information about the runner, such as the location of code and the runner's stack and heap ranges. DVM uses a Runner Control Block (RCB) to store the control information needed by the scheduler to start a runner. Figure 4 shows the content of a runner's RCB as well as the runner's initial stack. The RCB contains the stack base address sb and stack size ss. A 64-bit pointer, fi, specifies the address of the first instruction from which the runner starts to execute. The $heap\_ranges$ and $heap\_range\_count$ fields stores the locations and the number of the heap ranges, respectively. The $watched\_ranges$ and $watched\_range\_count$ fields are used by the watcher mechanism which will be discussed later.

Every runner resides in one RComp. Providing system functions related to the management and operations of runners, the RComp reduces the overhead of dispatching and starting a runner. RComps interact with other parts of the DVM system, and hide the complexity of the system so that the runners can focus on expressing the application logic on the abstraction provided by DISA. Because RComps are reused, a large portion of the runner startup overhead, such as loading modules and setting up memory mapping, is incurred only once in the lifetime of a DVM. To start a runner, the RComp only needs to notify the memory subsystem to set up the runner's snapshot, and the supporting mechanisms, such as the network connections, can be reused. Hence, RComps make it efficient to start runners in a DVM. Section 5 quantitatively studies the overhead of creating and starting runners.

3.3.2 Scheduling

In a complex program, myriads of runners may be created dynamically and exit the system after completing their computation. RComps, on the other hand, represent a semi-persistent facility to support runners' execution. Hence, there can be more runners than RComps in a DVM, and the scheduler assigns runners to RComps, as well as manages and coordinates the runners throughout their life cycles. Specifically, the scheduler is responsible for deciding when runners should start execution, assigning runners to RComps, preparing runners' memory snapshots, handling runners' requests to create new runners, and managing the runners that the DVM does not have resources (RComps) to execute currently. As the child runners created by a parent runner are not schedulable until the parent runner exits and commits successfully, the scheduler also maintains the "premature" runners (the runners in the "created" state) in the DVM. The scheduler also implements the DVM's watcher mechanism (to be discussed in Section 3.3.4).

The scheduler is a distributed service running on all constituent hosts of DVM. Specifically, the scheduler of a DVM consists of two parts: the scheduler master (the master) and the scheduler agent. There is a single scheduler master in a DVM, and there are many scheduler agents residing in RComps. The master and the agents communicate with each other through the datacenter network. The master makes high-level scheduling decisions, such as dispatching runners for execution and assigning them to RComps, and commands the agents to handle the remaining runner management work, such as preparing and updating runners' snapshots. In the other direction, an RComp can send scheduling-related requests to its associated agent and the agent may ask the master for coordination if it is needed.

The scheduler dispatches multiple runners from its pool of schedulable runners according to the scheduling policy, which takes locality along with other factors into consideration, to an RComp when it is free (no runner is running in it), creating a memory snapshot for the runner and notifying the RComp to execute the runner. A runner may create as many child runners as the entire DVM (or datacenter) can handle. When a runner requests to create new runners, the scheduler constructs RCBs for the child runners, and extends the parent runner's memory snapshot so that the parent can access and construct the child runners' stacks. After the parent exits and commits successfully, the scheduler adds the child runners to the runner and watcher pools, and the newly created runners in the runner pool become schedulable.

Although there is only one scheduler master in a DVM, it has not been found that the single master constrains the DVM's scalability. As aforementioned, the master is only responsible for high-level decisions and occasional coordination and arbitration, and is, consequently, very lightweight. Most of the work is handled in parallel by the scheduler agents in the RComps. Hence, the scheduler does not constitute bottleneck in the DVM in practice. Several large-scale systems, such as MapReduce [20], GFS [23], and Dryad [27], follow a similar single-master design pattern.

3.3.3 Many-runner parallel execution

The DVM should be able to accommodate a large number of runners and execute them in parallel to exploit the aggregate computing capacity of many physical hosts. This requires the parallelization mechanism to provide scalable, concurrent and efficient task execution and a flexible programming model to support many-runner creation and execution.

DVM uses the shared-memory model to simplify the program development and hides the underlying distributed system details from programmers. All runners inside one DVM share a common memory region (SR) as discussed in Section 3.2. While a runner may write multiple memory ranges in the SR during its execution, the runner may not want to apply all the changes made by it to the global memory space—for example, some ranges may only provide input or temporary data which are not used by other runners. DISA's memory subsystem enables programmers to control the behaviors of memory ranges so that it can support common cases of memory usage. A runner mainly obtains its input from its initial state comprising its stack and heap ranges, and can also read data from I/O channels during its execution. The runner's initial stack state is constructed by its parent runner, and its output is written into its heap ranges and I/O channels if it is needed. We call this memory usage scheme the SIHO (Stack-In-Heap-Out) model.

Upon completion, a runner specifies whether it wants to commit or abort its changes to the heap ranges. If it commits, the changes to the heap ranges by the runner are applied to the global memory space, given no conflicts with other runners' memory updates exist. If it aborts, the changes are discarded. The changes to a runner's stack are always discarded upon completion of the runner. As a runner operates on its own snapshot independently of other runners', a large number of runners in a DVM can execute in parallel optimistically assuming there are no conflicts. In the case that conflicts occur, the DVM system automatically detects conflicts, delays execution, and aborts runners, if necessary, to ensure correct memory semantics.

To support many-runner parallel execution on the ISA level, the runner creation and dispatching mechanism must be lightweight and highly efficient. We design an instruction-level runner creation mechanism. To create a new runner and prepare it for execution, the program only needs to specify the fi and the heap ranges for the new runner, issue a "`newr`" instruction, and instantiate the stack.

We use an example to show how a runner creates a new runner and how the DVM handles the runner creation. When a runner, R_i, creates a new runner, R_j, R_i executes the instruction "`newr`" with addresses of R_j's stack range, heap ranges and fi, as operands. $RComp(R_i)$, the RComp in which R_i runs, sends R_j's control information specified by these operands to the scheduler. As R_i may write the input data into R_j's stack and a memory range can be used by R_i only after $RComp(R_i)$ has the range's snapshot, the scheduler creates a snapshot of R_j's stack and merges the snapshot into R_i's current one. After the memory range for R_j's stack is ready, R_i writes the initial application data into R_j's stack. The scheduler constructs and records R_j's RCB along with the RCBs of the other runners created by R_i.

When R_i exits and commits, the scheduler starts the newly created runners by R_i, including R_j, according to the recorded RCBs. Using R_j as an example, we specify the runner start-up procedure in Algorithm 1.

Algorithm 1 Start a new runner R_j

$RComp(R_j)$ = the RComp chosen by the scheduler for R_j
A = snapshot of R_j's stack range and heap ranges, created by the scheduler according to RCB_j
The scheduler sends A and RCB_j to $RComp(R_j)$
The scheduler commands $RComp(R_j)$ to start R_j
$RComp(R_j)$ sets R_j's local context according to RCB_j
R_j starts from fi to execute in $RComp(R_j)$

3.3.4 Task dependency

Task dependency control is a key issue in concurrent program execution. Related to this, synchronization is often used to ensure the correct order of the operations, avoid race conditions, and, with execution order constrained, guarantee that the concurrent execution does not violate dependence relations. For example, X10 provides barriers through the `finish` statement and `clock` operations to conduct synchronization and, consequently, control the execution order [15]. A MapReduce application's map workers' output is the reduce workers' input, which, in turn, implicitly requires dependence be handled in this way. Dryad requires the programmer or compiler to explicitly specify the dependency graph of the programs using a DAG (directed acyclic graph) [27].

As an important goal in the DVM design, the DISA architecture should provide a task dependency representation and resolution mechanism with which task-level dependence can be naturally expressed, concurrent tasks can proceed without using synchronization mechanisms such as locks [11], and sophisticated computation logic can be processed effectively with dynamically scheduled parallelism. The aforementioned approaches have their limitations and constraints: the synchronization mechanisms are not natural or efficient to represent dependence [16, 45]; MapReduce employs a restricted programming model and makes it difficult to express sophisticated application logic [21, 41, 47]; DAG-based frameworks incur non-trivial burden in programming, and automatic DAG generation has only been implemented for certain high-level languages [48]. Departing from existing solutions, we design a watcher mechanism in the DISA architecture to provide a flexible way of declaring dependence and enable the construction of sophisticated application logic. A watcher is a runner that depends on other runners and watchers: a watcher W is not schedulable until other runners or watchers change specific memory ranges that are "watched" by W. We call these ranges W's "watched ranges", and we use the $watched\_range\_count$ field in the RCB (refer to Figure 4), which stores the number of watched ranges (0 for a regular runner), to distinguish a watcher from a regular runner. The watcher-specific data structures impose almost no space overhead for regular runners as the $watched\_ranges$ list, which stores the watched ranges, is variable-size.

Suppose a runner, R, has created the watcher W. When R exits and commits, W is enabled by the scheduler (transition to the "watching" state in Figure 3). Different from a regular runner, W is in the "watching" state, is not schedulable, and stays in the watcher pool. When some other runners or watchers write W's watched ranges and commit the changes to the global memory space, the memory subsystem notifies the scheduler, and the scheduler moves W to the runner pool, making it schedulable.

With the watcher mechanism, the programs focus on and naturally express the true dependence among tasks (runners) and data. Therefore, programmers can easily construct programs for not only embarrassingly parallel but also complex, iterative, or even interactive computation. The DVM system automatically resolves the dependence and efficiently executes the program with parallelization.

3.4 I/O, signals and system services

We design the I/O mechanism to enable runners to read and write data on I/O channels. For simplicity and flexibility, DISA adopts the memory mapped I/O for DVM to operate on I/O channels. This design does not require additional instructions—all DISA's memory access instructions can also be used for I/O. We can use this mechanism to support many kinds and a large number of I/O channels which may be distributed in many RComps. In the evaluation discussed in Section 5, we use I/O channels to input the dataset to the k-means program.

Signals are notifications of the state changes in a DVM. We design the signal mechanism to enable runners to catch the information of its interested events in the system. We design the signal mechanism above the watcher mechanism and the system services (to be discussed below). The signals are represented as changes to specific memory ranges, and runners (watchers) can "watch" these memory ranges to get notified.

Several distributed system services collaborate with the scheduler and RComps to support system functions. For example, the I/O services on RComps manage I/O channels, and the "system state" service broadcasts "system state changing" signals. On top of the compact and efficient core parts of the DVM as described, it is easy to implement various system services to provide a rich set of functions.

4. Implementation and programming notes

We have implemented DVM and DISA on x86-64 hosts. The implementation of the DISA and DVM comprises around 11,510 lines of C and assembly code. On each host, the DVM runs in conjunction with a local Linux OS as the base system, which manages local resources including CPUs and local file systems. The distribution of the code in each part of DVM is shown in Table 2.

Table 2. Implementation of DVM

Sub-system	LOC	Size of binary code (KiB)
Scheduler	2861	59
Memory	3220	72
RComp	715	40
Translator	4714	73

Figure 5. The CCMR research testbed

4.1 Implementation and portability

We have implemented and run DVM on three platforms—a research testbed, an industrial testbed, and the Amazon Elastic Compute Cloud (EC2). Although the three platforms have quite different underlying hardware configurations and slightly different Linux kernels, it proves to be straightforward to port DISA to all these platforms by adding logic to match specific kernel data structures. Application programs do not need to be changed at all on three platforms. Our experience shows that DISA and DVM are highly portable.

We emulate DISA instructions on x86-64 machines in our current implementation using two mechanisms. One is to translate the DISA assembly to x86-64 assembly and compile it to object code. The other is to conduct binary translation to convert x86-64 code on the fly during the execution of a DISA program. Which emulation mode to use in a DVM can be configured at compilation time. In our evaluation discussed in Section 5, we manually encode the microbenchmark programs to run on a DVM. As one direction of future work, we will build compilers for the DISA architecture.

Our main development and evaluation platform is the CCMR research testbed which we can fully control. Shown in Figure 5, the CCMR testbed is constructed for cloud computing research, and is composed of 50 servers with Intel Quad-Core Xeon processors. The testbed has two additional servers providing GPU acceleration, but they are not used in our evaluation.

To verify the performance results in industrial environments, we repeat some experiments on the industrial cluster. The industrial testbed comprises 32 servers, each of which has one Intel Core 2 Duo processor.

To test DVM's scalability in a larger scale, we conduct part of the experiments on Amazon EC2 virtual machines. The results on EC2 also show the portability of DISA in a virtualized and heterogeneous environment.

4.2 How to program

We extend the *sum_runner* example (introduced in Section 2.2) to illustrate how to write a parallel program with data dependence in DISA. The example uses 10,240 runners to compute sums of 20,480 integers in parallel. The execution graph is shown in Figure 6. Each vertex in the graph represents one runner that sums two integers and stores the result in the global memory space.

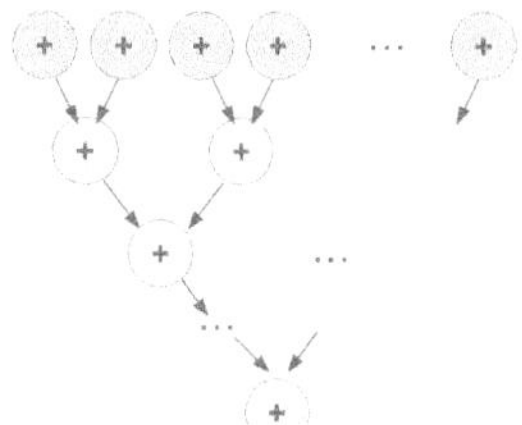

Figure 6. The execution graph of the parallel sum

4.2.1 Parallelism

The following code starts 10,240 *sum_runner* runners to compute 10,240 partial sums. The calculation of the final sum requires additional rounds of sum operations following data dependence, which will be introduced later.

```
main_runner:
# create 10,240 sum_runner runners:
# store the addresses of ranges for stacks and heaps
#    in 0x100001008 and 0x100001010 (omitted)
mov:z $0:q, 0x100001000:q                  # i = 0
j_do:
# suppose the addresses of the runner's control information
#   are in 0x1f0000100, 0x1f0000108, 0x1f0000110 and 0x1f0000118
mov:z 0x100001008:q, (0x1f0000100):q       # set stack base
mov:z $0x1000:q, 8(0x1f0000100):q          # set stack size
mov:z $1:q, (0x1f0000108):q                # set heap range count
mov:z 0x100001010:q, 8(0x1f0000108):q      # heap range
mov:z $0x1000:q, 16(0x1f0000108):q         # heap range's length
mov:z $0:q, (0x1f0000110):q                # watched range count
mov:z $sum_runner:q, (0x1f0000118):q       # set code
# create the new runner:
newr 0x1f0000100, 0x1f0000108, 0x1f0000110, 0x1f0000118
# initialize the stack (omitted here)
add $0x1000:uq, 0x100001008, 0x100001008 # update stack base
add $0x1000:uq, 0x100001010, 0x100001010 # update heap range
add $1:uq, 0x100001000, 0x100001000        # i++
br:l 0x100001000:uq, $10240, j_do          # while i < 10240
exit:c                                     # exit and commit
```

In this example, *main_runner* creates 10,240 *sum_runner* runners by executing the `newr` instruction with the new runners' control information as operands. The new runners will be schedulable after *main_runner* exits and commits (the `exit:c` instruction).

From this example, we can see that programs can create new execution flows efficiently at the DISA instruction level, and programmers can easily design and effectively express distributed and parallel programs with the DISA instruction set.

4.2.2 Data dependence

Each of the runners represented as white vertices in Figure 6 depends on the output of two other runners as indicated by the edges in the graph. We show in the following code how to express this data dependence using the "watcher" mechanism.

```
sum_watcher:
# read the heap addresses of the depended runners or watchers and
#   the address to store the result from the stack, and stores
#   them in 0x100001000, 0x100001008, and 0x100001010 (omitted)
# check whether the depended data is ready
br:e $0:uq, 8(0x100001000), create_self
br:e $0:uq, 8(0x100001008), create_self
# sum the two integers as the sum_runner
add (0x100001000):uq, (0x100001008), (0x100001010)
mov:z $1:q, 8(0x100001010):q               # exit code
exit:c
create_self:
```

```
# create sum_watcher with the same control information
#   as itself (omitted)
exit:c

main_runner:
# creates 10,240 sum_runner as in the previous part (omitted)
# creates 10,239 sum_watcher watchers:
mov:z $0:q, 0x100001000:q               # i = 0
j_do2:
# suppose the addresses of the watcher's control information are
#  in 0x1e0000100, 0x1e0000108, 0x1e0000110 and 0x1e0000118,
#  and the watched ranges are calculated according to i and
#  stored in the memory range starting from 0x100001018
# set the stack range, the heap ranges, and the code (omitted)
mov:z 0x100001018:q, 8(0x1e0000110):q    # set watched range 1
mov:z 0x100001020:q, 16(0x1e0000110):q   # set range 1's length
mov:z 0x100001028:q, 24(0x1e0000110):q   # set watched range 2
mov:z 0x100001030:q, 32(0x1e0000110):q   # set range 2's length
# create the new watcher:
newr 0x1e0000100, 0x1e0000108, 0x1e0000110, 0x1e0000118
# initialize the stack (omitted)
# update stack base and heap ranges (omitted)
add $1:uq, 0x100001000, 0x100001000      # i++
br:l 0x100001000:uq, $10239, j_do2       # while i < 10239
exit:c                                   # exit and commit
```

The *main_runner* creates 10,239 *sum_watcher* watchers together with the 10,240 *sum_runner* runners. The *sum_watcher* is activated after the data it depends on are changed by other runners or watchers. As the *sum_runner* (or the *sum_watcher*) writes "1" as the exit code which is also used as the "marker" to indicate that it has committed its heap ranges, the *sum_watcher* can check the exit codes to determine whether both operands for the sum operation are ready. The watcher creates itself again to continue "watching" the data it depends if either of the two depended runners or watchers has not exited and committed.

This example shows that programs can express task dependence easily by watchers on the ISA level without using synchronization mechanisms. The dependences are automatically resolved by the scheduler and watcher-related mechanisms in the DVM.

5. Evaluation

We measure the virtualization and tasking overhead of DVM, compare the performance of DVM with Hadoop and X10, and inspect the scalability of the DVM. We choose Hadoop and X10 for comparison because they are representatives of two mainstream approaches to datacenter computing and their implementations are relatively mature and optimized. Hadoop represents a class of MapReduce-style programming frameworks such as Phoenix [41], Mars [25], CGL-MapReduce [21], and MapReduce online [19], and has been used extensively by many organizations [5]. X10 represents a class of language-level solutions, including Chapel [13] and Fortress [4], targeting "non-uniform cluster computing" environments [15].

For each technical solution in comparison, we apply the highest performance setting among the standard configurations. For example, X10 programs are pre-compiled to native executable programs to give the best performance, and we write the x86-64-based microbenchmark programs in comparison in the assembly language to optimize the baseline to our best. We use measurement programs and two computational workloads to evaluate the DVM on the three platforms presented in Section 4.1, examine the execution time and speedup, and compare DVM's results with other technologies'. Note that the platforms have different performance characteristics. To make the comparison fair, we indicate the platform on which the evaluation is conducted, use the same set of compute nodes and the same network topology and configuration to run comparative experiments on each platform, and repeat the experiments to make sure results are consistent.

Table 3. Microbenchmark results

Benchmark	Solution	Time (second)
Arithmetic and logic operation	Native	7.13
	DVM	7.14
	Xen	7.14
	VMware	7.35
Memory operation	Native	110.60
	DVM	126.41
	Xen	112.43
	VMware	128.37

Table 4. Time for creating and executing a runner

Operation	Operation step	Time (ms)
Create a runner	Create snapshot	0.4
	Create the runner	0.4
	Update RComp	0.5
	Overall	1.3
Execute a runner (empty runner)	Create snapshot	0.4
	Update RComp (NULL)	0.4
	Update RComp	0.5
	Invoke the runner	0.2
	Commit snapshot	0.9
	Overall	2.4

The evaluation results show that DVM is one order of magnitude faster than the other technologies on workloads with moderate sophistication, runs reliable across different environments, and scales easily to hundreds of computer nodes.

5.1 Microbenchmarks

We run microbenchmarks to measure the virtualization overhead of DVM and compare the results with traditional virtual machine monitors. We also measure the overhead of creating and executing runners in a DVM.

5.1.1 Virtualization overhead

We measure the arithmetic and logic operation performance to assess the overhead of CPU virtualization. A microbenchmark program is created to execute totally 2^{34} *add* operations, and implemented in x86-64 assembly and DISA. We execute the microbenchmark programs in Xen, VMware Player, native Linux, and a DVM on the same physical host. To achieve the best performance, the x86-64 assembly implementation heavily uses registers. The DISA implementation is assembled into DISA binary code, and the binary translator of DVM translates DISA instructions into x86-64 instructions during the execution.

Memory is another important subsystem in the DVM, and we shall verify that the large-scale, distributed and shared memory system does not incur dramatic overhead on one machine. We measure the memory operation performance with another microbenchmark program that writes 2^{29} 64-bit integers (4 GB in total) to the memory for 256 times and then read them for 256 times. We implement the microbenchmark in x86-64 assembly and DISA and execute the microbenchmark on the same physical host.

Table 3 shows the results of the microbenchmarks. From the result, we can see that the virtualization overhead for arithmetic, logic and memory operation of DVM is 0.1–15% over native execution on the physical host, which is comparable to traditional VMMs. In particular, DVM exhibits even higher performance than VMware on one physical host. For the memory microbenchmark, the time on DVM includes 7.47 seconds for creating and committing the memory snapshot for the runner.

5.1.2 Runner overhead

Task creation, scheduling, and termination are important and frequent operations in a task execution engine. To examine DVM's performance in this aspect, we measure the overhead of creating and executing a runner. We use one runner to create 1000 new empty runners and execute these runners. To measure the overhead accurately, we force the tasking operation to be serial by conducting the experiment using one RComp on one working node so that we can obtain the average execution time of each operation.

Table 4 shows the overhead of creating and executing a runner and the time used in each step—create snapshot for the runner, initialize the RComp's memory (update RComp with a NULL snapshot), prepare the memory (update RComp), invoke the runner and commit the snapshot after the runner exits. From the results, we can see that the overhead of creating and executing a runner in a DVM is only several milliseconds. The small overhead enables DVM to handle thousands of runners efficiently, and gives programmers the flexibility to use a large number of runners as they want.

5.2 Workloads

To evaluate DVM's performance of parallel execution, we design and run the prime-checker which uses 1000 runners to check the primality of 1,000,000 numbers. To show DVM's performance on widely used algorithms that are less easy to parallel, we implement the k-means clustering algorithm [35] which iteratively clusters a large number of 4-dimensional data points into 1000 groups and reflects known problem configurations in related work [28, 31, 50].

Prime-checker We use the prime-checker to evaluate DVM's scalability and portability. A runner (the main runner) creates 1000 runners and each runner checks 1000 large numbers. To show the ease of programming with shared memory, we design the program in the way that all the runners use the same global parameters by sharing a memory range so that each runner can calculate its set of numbers to be checked. As the prime-checker is highly parallelizable, we use this arithmetic application to evaluate the scalability of the DVM—whether DVM can achieve near-linear speedup as we add more working nodes.

K-means clustering K-means clustering is an algorithm used for partitioning a data set into k clusters iteratively [35], which is commonly used for data mining. Various software and libraries implement the k-means algorithm [6, 36, 44]. Researchers also use k-means algorithm to evaluate MapReduce for machine learning and data intensive analytics [18, 21]. The k-means process starts with k initial clusters and iteratively refines the clusters by reassigning points to the closest cluster and updating the clusters' means. We implement the k-means algorithm mainly following the widely used ones from Mahout [6] and X10's distribution. To achieve reasonably optimized performance results, we optimize the implementations for all three technologies, Hadoop, X10, and DVM, with the methods used in related work [18, 51]. Our implementations are downloadable from `http://baijia.info/dvm/kmeans.tar`. In addition to the same implementation and optimization method, we use the same data set and identical configurations for the three technologies, including the number of iterations, the initial cluster centroids and the value of k.

5.3 Performance comparison

We run the performance evaluation programs with the same dataset on different numbers of working nodes on the research testbed to compare the performance and scalability of the three technologies. To verify the results, we run all the tests on the industrial testbed and compare the results with those on the research testbed. We also increase the size of the input data and test with a fixed number of

Table 5. Execution time for prime-checker

Number of nodes	Hadoop (second)	DVM (second)
1	16661	15795
2	8352	7885
4	4169	3950
8	2090	1975
16	1112	986

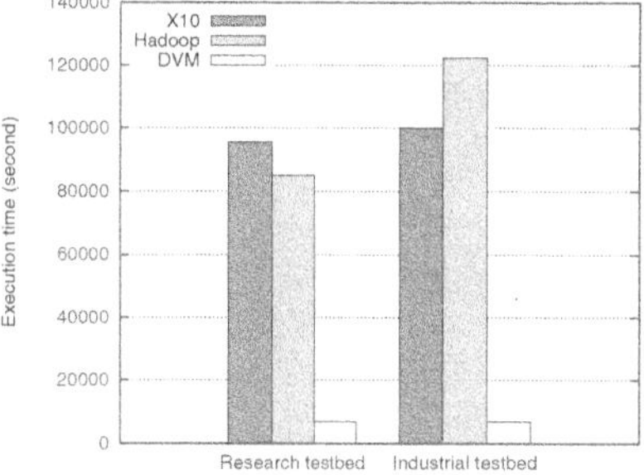

Figure 7. Execution time for k-means on 1 node

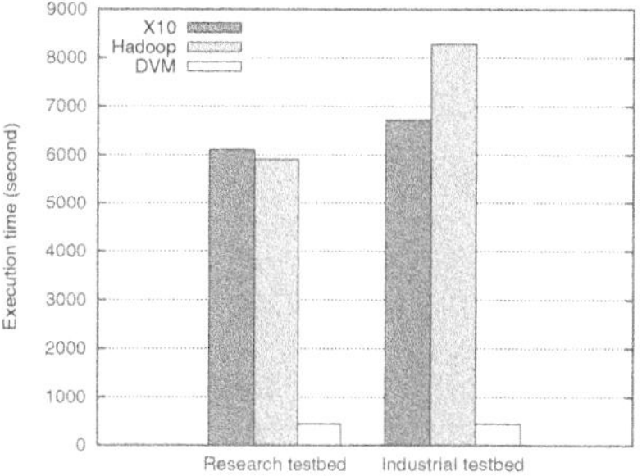

Figure 8. Execution time for k-means on 16 node

working nodes on the research testbed to evaluate DVM's scalability with data size.

Table 5 shows the time of prime-checker on Hadoop and DVM. We conduct the test on the research testbed and scale the number of working nodes to 16 physical hosts. The results show that both Hadoop and DVM scale linearly as prime-check is easy to parallelize. For simple ALU-intensive workloads, both DVM and Hadoop are efficient, but DVM provides slightly higher performance in spite of DVM's advanced instruction set features and memory model.

Figure 7 presents the execution time of k-means on Hadoop, X10 and DVM with one working node on the research testbed and industrial testbed. The execution time on Hadoop and X10 is 11 times more than that on DVM in both research and industrial environments. As shown in this evaluation, DVM quickly exhibits superiority in efficiency as the complexity of application grows. Figure 8 shows the results on 16 working nodes and we can see that DVM is at least 13 times faster than Hadoop, an indication of good scalability for DVM.

Figure 7 and Figure 8 present that DVM exhibits tremendous speed gains over Hadoop and X10, although Table 5 shows that DVM only provides slightly better performance than Hadoop with simple ALU-intensive workloads. This observation, in fact, illustrates the advantages of the DVM technology. When the computation is composed of one or two stages of easily parallelizable processing, the MapReduce/Hadoop frameworks can already accomplish algorithmically optimal performance. The DVM can still

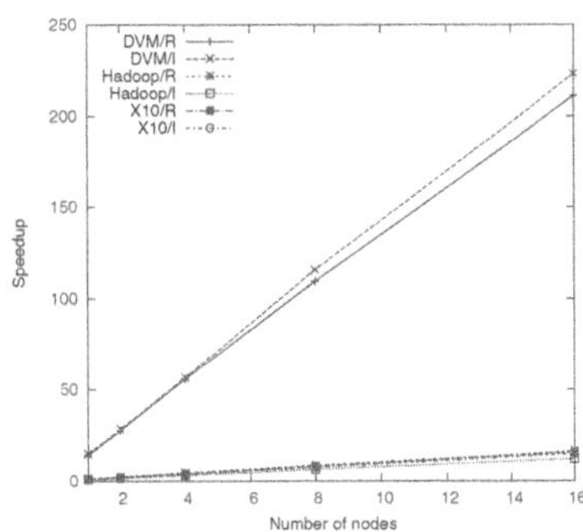

Figure 9. Speedups of k-means as the number of working nodes grows

provide slightly higher performance due to its efficient instruction-level abstraction. Moreover, the DVM quickly outperforms existing technologies when the computation becomes more complex—i.e., containing iterations, more dependence, or non-trivial logic flows, which are common cases in programs. The system design of DVM aims to provide strong support for general programs, and the speed gains of DVM shown in Figure 7 and Figure 8 reflect DISA's generality, efficiency and scalability.

Figure 7 and Figure 8 also show that the Hadoop program on the industrial testbed is slower than on the research testbed. Hadoop transfers data through HDFS [20], the underlying data persistence layer which stores data in working nodes' hard drives, and the working nodes in the research testbed are equipped with higher-end hard drives than the industrial testbed. We believe that the disk I/O contributes to the difference of the program execution time between the research testbed and the industrial testbed. In a cluster with high-speed network (such as 10Gbps Ethernet), which we believe will become more popular in datacenters in the future, the disk I/O speed has certainly an impact on the system performance. On the other hand, DVM uses shared memory for data communication which does not rely on hard drives. From the results, we can see that the performance data of DVM in both environments are close to each other.

It may appear that the DVM's memory-based data processing is the main reason for its superiority in performance. This is, in fact, an over-simplified view of the technical design space. X10 also handles program data through memory with PGAS (Partitioned Global Address Space) [15]. As shown in Figure 7 and Figure 8, however, the DVM is one order of magnitude faster than both Hadoop and X10. In fact, disk I/O does not necessarily outweight other factors, such as network bandwidth and CPU capacity, in a datacenter computing environment. In our evaluation, we have implemented the same algorithm in all the three technologies and applied salient optimizations for each of them—e.g., compiling X10 programs to native x86-64 instructions—to ensure the workloads are comparable with the three implementations. It is the holistic design and the simple yet effective mechanisms in the DVM that lead to the significant speedup over existing technologies, and it is the ISA-level abstraction that enables such a design and the mechanisms. As the result, DVM performs at least as well as other technologies on all workloads, and delivers much better performance than others for complex programs.

Figure 9 shows the speedups for three technologies on the research testbed ("/R" in the figure) and industrial testbed ("/I" in the figure) as we scale the number of working nodes. All speedups are calculated with respect to the X10 performance on one working node for each workload.

The speedup of the k-means computation on DVM is near-linear in the number of compute nodes used, which highlights the good scalability of the design and implementation of DVM. We can also observe that the overhead of DVM is small, taking into consideration the near-linear speedup and the fact that the execution time on DVM in the 16-node experiment is very short compared to the time on Hadoop or X10. The DISA program sequentially reads the input from I/O in our current implementation, and the I/O time is also included in the overall execution time. The k-means computation on DVM should achieve a larger speedup if DVM implemented the parallel I/O which is one direction of future work.

Figure 7, Figure 8, and Figure 9 also show that the execution time and speedups are consistent on the industrial testbed and the research testbed, which verifies the applicability of the DVM technology in industrial environments and reflects DVM's portability.

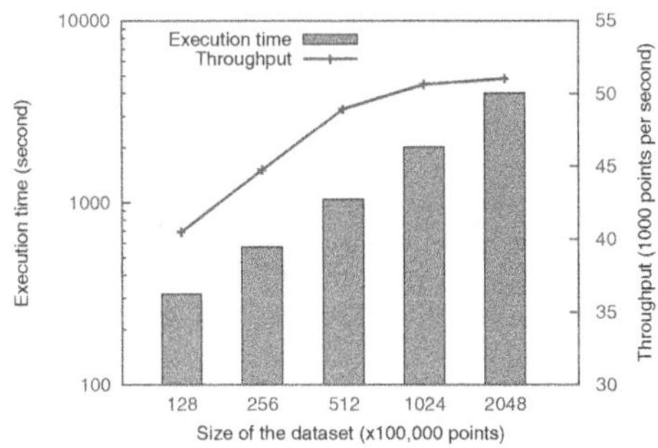

Figure 10. Execution time and throughput of k-means as the size of dataset grows

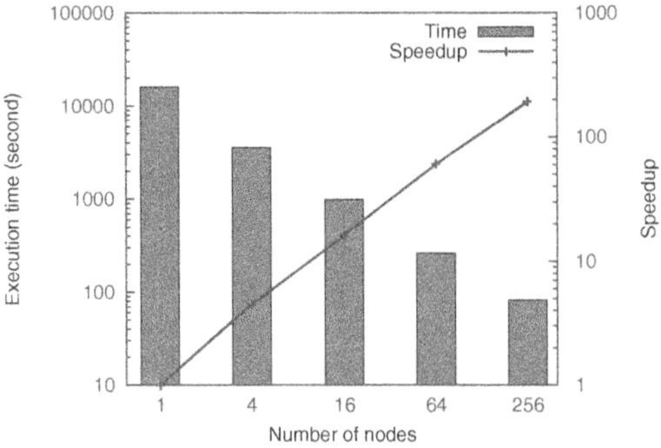

Figure 11. Speedup and execution time of prime-checker as the number of working nodes grows

5.4 Scalability

We run k-means on DVM with 50 working nodes on the research testbed to evaluate DVM's scalability with the data size. Figure 10 presents the execution time and throughput. We scale the dataset from 12,800,000 points to 204,800,000 points (16 times). The throughput is calculated by dividing the number of points by the execution time. From the result, we can see that, on the same number of working nodes, the execution time grows slower than linear growth with the data size while the throughput increases. Hence, DVM scales well with the data size.

To evaluate DVM's scalability and also test DVM's performance in a public cloud, we test the prime-checker on a DVM running on Amazon EC2 with up to 256 virtual machine instances. Figure 11 shows the execution time and speedup with respect to the performance on one instance. The results show that the DVM scales very well to 256 working nodes—the speedup is near-linear as we increase the number of instances. Our ability to perform tests with larger-scale and more sophisticated workloads is limited by the concurrent instance cap stipulated by EC2. In our future work, we will communicate with Amazon to explore opportunities of larger-scale tests. In the mean time, the current result on 256 instances already shows that, although prime-checker is a relatively easy-to-parallelize program, the DISA architecture and the DVM design easily scale to hundreds of compute nodes without showing signs of slowdown or obvious system bottlenecks. The experiment on EC2 also proves the good portability of DVM in a virtualized environment, and that the DVM can be used independently of or in combination with traditional virtual machine monitors.

6. Related work

Many systems, programming frameworks, and languages are proposed and designed to exploit the computing power of constellations of compute servers inside today's gigantic datacenters and help the programmers design parallel programs easily and efficiently. Dean et al. have created the MapReduce programming model to process and generate large data sets inside Google's datacenter environment [20]. MapReduce exploits a restricted programming model so that the execution engine can automatically run the programs in parallel and provide fault-tolerance. Dryad takes a more general approach by allowing an application to specify an arbitrary "communication DAG (directed acyclic graph)" [27]. While these frameworks are successful in large data processing, the restricted programming model is not general enough to cover many important application domains and makes it difficult to design sophisticated and time-sensitive applications [21, 34, 41, 47]. Different from the previous solutions, DVM allows programmers to easily design general-purpose applications running on a large number of compute nodes by providing a more flexible yet highly scalable programming model.

Although programming frameworks provide simple programming models and interfaces for designing and developing large distributed applications, a new language may help programmers write clearer, more compact and more expressive programs. High-level languages, such as Sawzall and DryadLINQ, which are implemented on top of programming frameworks (MapReduce and Dryad), make the data-processing programs more easier to design [40, 48]. However, these languages also suffer from the limitation of the underlying application frameworks although they allow programmers to design parallel programs using a higher-level abstraction. Charles et al. design X10 to write parallel programs in non-uniform cluster computing system, taking both performance and productivity as its goals [15]. The language-level approach gives the programmers more precise control of the semantics of parallelization and synchronization. DVM provides a lower level abstraction by introducing a new ISA—DISA. On top of DISA, we may implement various programming languages easily using DVM's the parallelization and concurrency control mechanism along with the memory model.

Different from the frameworks and languages that make the data communication transparent to programmers, message passing-based technologies [22] require that the programmer handle the communication explicitly [33]. This can simplify the system design and improve scalability, but often imposes extra burden on programmers. In contrast, the distributed shared memory (DSM) keeps the data transportation among computers transparent to programmers [37]. The DSM systems, such as Ivy [32] and Treadmark [29], combine the advantages of "shared-memory systems" and "distributed-memory systems" to provide a simple programming model by hiding the communication mechanisms [37], but incur a cost in maintaining memory coherence across multiple computers. In order to reduce overhead and enhance scalability, DVM provides snapshotted memory, and the memory consistency model of DISA permits concurrent accesses optimistically. In contrast to the traditional ways of providing DSM in middleware which provide a limited illusion of shared memory, vNUMA uses virtualization technology to build shared-memory multiprocess (SMM) system and provides a single system image (SSI) on top of workstations connected through an Ethernet network that provides "sender-oblivious total-order broadcast" [14]. This also differs from widely used virtualization systems, such as Xen and VMware on the x86 ISA, which divide the resources of a single physical host into multiple virtual machines [8, 46]. Both vNUMA and the emerging "inverse virtualization" [26] aim to merge a number of compute nodes to be one larger machine. Different from vNUMA, which is designed to be used on a small cluster [14], DVM virtualizes the servers at the ISA level and allows programs to scale up to thousands of logic flows across a large number of nodes.

7. Conclusions and future work

Cloud computing is an emerging and important computing paradigm backed by datacenters. However, developing applications running in datacenters is challenging. We design and implemented DVM as an approach to building datacenter-size virtual machines. Giving programmers an illusion of a "big machine", we design the DISA as the programming interface and abstraction of DVM. We implement and evaluate DVM on research, industrial and public clusters, and show that DVM is one order of magnitude faster than Hadoop and X10 for moderately complex applications, and can scale to hundreds of computers.

Beyond the current implementation of DVM, we see a number of interesting future research directions and several of them are as follows. First, we believe that the DISA architecture can scale to larger-scale clusters, and will actively explore opportunities for evaluations of DVM on 1000 or more compute nodes. Second, we shall certainly not require all the programmers write application in DISA. A compiler that "understands" DISA well to generate efficient code is needed on DVM. Third, we may scale a DVM to run across datacenters, so that DVM can use more computing resources and recover from disasters that may possibly render a datacenter inoperable.

8. Acknowledgments

This work was supported in part by the Huawei Technologies research grant HUAW17-15G00510/11PN and HKUST research grants REC09/10.EG06 and DAG11EG04G. We thank Yanling Zheng, Mengmeng Cheng, Chengqi Song and Yanqun Zhang for their help in various aspects of this project, and the Amazon AWS research grant for the support in the EC2 based evaluation. Finally, we are thankful to our shepherd, Ada Gavrilovska, and the reviewers for their reviewing effort and valuable feedback.

References

[1] Amazon Elastic Compute Cloud – EC2. `http://aws.amazon.com/ec2/`. [last access: 11/2, 2011].

[2] Windows Azure. `http://www.microsoft.com/windowsazure/`. [last access: 11/2, 2011].

[3] Rackspace. `http://www.rackspace.com/`. [last access: 11/2, 2011].

[4] E. Allen, D. Chase, J. Hallett, V. Luchangco, J. Maessen, S. Ryu, G. Steele Jr, S. Tobin-Hochstadt, J. Dias, C. Eastlund, et al. The Fortress language specification. `https://labs.oracle.com/projects/plrg/fortress.pdf`, 2008. [last access: 11/2, 2011].

[5] Apache Hadoop. Hadoop Users List. `http://wiki.apache.org/hadoop/PoweredBy`. [last access: 11/2, 2011].

[6] Apache Mahout. Mahout machine learning libraries. `http://mahout.apache.org/`. [last access: 11/2, 2011].

[7] M. Armbrust, A. Fox, R. Griffith, A. D. Joseph, R. Katz, A. Konwinski, G. Lee, D. Patterson, A. Rabkin, I. Stoica, and M. Zaharia. Above

the clouds: A Berkeley view of cloud computing. *UC Berkeley Technical Report UCB/EECS-2009-28*, February 2009.

[8] P. Barham, B. Dragovic, K. Fraser, S. Hand, T. Harris, A. Ho, R. Neugebauer, I. Pratt, and A. Warfield. Xen and the art of virtualization. In *Proceedings of the 19th ACM symposium on Operating Systems Principles*, pages 164–177, 2003.

[9] L. Barroso and U. Hölzle. The datacenter as a computer: An introduction to the design of warehouse-scale machines. *Synthesis Lectures on Computer Architecture*, 4(1):1–108, 2009.

[10] L. Barroso, J. Dean, and U. Hoelzle. Web search for a planet: The Google cluster architecture. *IEEE Micro*, 23(2):22–28, 2003.

[11] K. Birman, G. Chockler, and R. van Renesse. Toward a cloud computing research agenda. *SIGACT News*, 40(2):68–80, 2009.

[12] R. Buyya, T. Cortes, and H. Jin. Single system image. *Intl. Journal of High Performance Computing Applications*, 15(2):124, 2001.

[13] B. Chamberlain, D. Callahan, and H. Zima. Parallel programmability and the Chapel language. *International Journal of High Performance Computing Applications*, 21(3):291, 2007.

[14] M. Chapman and G. Heiser. vNUMA: A virtual shared-memory multiprocessor. In *Proceedings of the 2009 conference on USENIX Annual technical conference*, 2009.

[15] P. Charles, C. Grothoff, V. Saraswat, C. Donawa, A. Kielstra, K. Ebcioglu, C. Von Praun, and V. Sarkar. X10: an object-oriented approach to non-uniform cluster computing. In *ACM SIGPLAN Notices*, volume 40, pages 519–538, 2005.

[16] D.-K. Chen, H.-M. Su, and P.-C. Yew. The impact of synchronization and granularity on parallel systems. In *Proceedings of the 17th annual intl. symposium on Computer Architecture*, pages 239–248, 1990.

[17] Y. Chen, D. Pavlov, and J. F. Canny. Large-scale behavioral targeting. In *Proc. of the 15th ACM SIGKDD intl conf. on Knowledge discovery and data mining*, pages 209–218, 2009.

[18] C.-T. Chu, S. K. Kim, Y.-A. Lin, Y. Yu, G. Bradski, A. Y. Ng, and K. Olukotun. Map-Reduce for machine learning on multicore. In *Proc. of NIPS'07*, pages 281–288, 2007.

[19] T. Condie, N. Conway, P. Alvaro, J. Hellerstein, K. Elmeleegy, and R. Sears. MapReduce online. In *Proceedings of the 7th USENIX conf. on networked systems design and implementation*, pages 21–21, 2010.

[20] J. Dean and S. Ghemawat. MapReduce: simplified data processing on large clusters. In *the 6th Conference on Symposium on Operating Systems Design & Implementation*, volume 6, pages 137–150, 2004.

[21] J. Ekanayake, S. Pallickara, and G. Fox. MapReduce for data intensive scientific analysis. In *Fourth IEEE International Conference on eScience*, pages 277–284, 2008.

[22] M. P. I. Forum. MPI: A message-passing interface standard. `http://www.mpi-forum.org/docs/mpi-2.2/mpi22-report.pdf`, 2009. [last access: 11/2, 2011].

[23] S. Ghemawat, H. Gobioff, and S.-T. Leung. The Google file system. In *Proc. of the 9th ACM Symposium on Operating Systems Principles (SOSP'03)*, pages 29–43, 2003.

[24] B. Hayes. Cloud computing. *Communications of the ACM*, 51(7): 9–11, 2008.

[25] B. He, W. Fang, Q. Luo, N. Govindaraju, and T. Wang. Mars: a MapReduce framework on graphics processors. In *Proceedings of the 17th international conference on parallel architectures and compilation techniques*, pages 260–269, 2008.

[26] B. Hedlund. Inverse virtualization for internet scale applications. `http://bradhedlund.com/2011/03/16/inverse-virtualization-for-internet-scale-applications/`. [last access: 11/2, 2011].

[27] M. Isard, M. Budiu, Y. Yu, A. Birrell, and D. Fetterly. Dryad: distributed data-parallel programs from sequential building blocks. In *EuroSys '07: Proceedings of the 2nd ACM SIGOPS/EuroSys European Conference on Computer Systems 2007*, pages 59–72, 2007.

[28] H. Jégou, M. Douze, and C. Schmid. Improving bag-of-features for large scale image search. *International Journal of Computer Vision*, 87(3):316–336, 2010.

[29] P. Keleher, A. Cox, S. Dwarkadas, and W. Treadmarks. Distributed shared memory on standard workstations and operating systems. In *Proc. 1994 Winter Usenix Conference*, pages 115–131, 1994.

[30] A. Kivity, Y. Kamay, D. Laor, U. Lublin, and A. Liguori. KVM: the linux virtual machine monitor. In *Proceedings of the Linux Symposium*, volume 1, pages 225–230, 2007.

[31] D. Lee, S. Baek, and K. Sung. Modified k-means algorithm for vector quantizer design. *Signal Processing Letters, IEEE*, 4(1):2–4, 1997.

[32] K. Li and P. Hudak. Memory coherence in shared virtual memory systems. *ACM Trans. Comput. Syst.*, 7(4):321–359, 1989.

[33] H. Lu, S. Dwarkadas, A. Cox, and W. Zwaenepoel. Message passing versus distributed shared memory on networks of workstations. In *Proc. of the IEEE/ACM Supercomputing 95 Conf.*, page 37, 1995.

[34] Z. Ma and L. Gu. The limitation of MapReduce: A probing case and a lightweight solution. In *Proc. of the 1st Intl. Conf. on Cloud Computing, GRIDs, and Virtualization*, pages 68–73, 2010.

[35] J. MacQueen. Some methods for classification and analysis of multivariate observations. In *Proceedings of the fifth Berkeley symposium on mathematical statistics and probability*, volume 1, page 14, 1967.

[36] MathWorks. Inc. Matlab. `http://www.mathworks.com/products/matlab/`. [last access: 11/2, 2011].

[37] B. Nitzberg and V. Lo. Distributed shared memory: A survey of issues and algorithms. *Computer*, 24(8):52–60, 1991.

[38] D. Nurmi, R. Wolski, C. Grzegorczyk, G. Obertelli, S. Soman, L. Youseff, and D. Zagorodnov. The Eucalyptus open-source cloud-computing system. In *Proc. of the 9th IEEE/ACM Intl. Symposium on Cluster Computing and the Grid*, pages 124–131, 2009.

[39] P. J. Nurnberg, U. K. Wiil, and D. L. Hicks. A grand unified theory for structural computing. *Metainformatics*, 3002:1–16, 2004.

[40] R. Pike, S. Dorward, R. Griesemer, and S. Quinlan. Interpreting the data: Parallel analysis with Sawzall. *Sci. Program.*, 13(4):277–298, 2005.

[41] C. Ranger, R. Raghuraman, A. Penmetsa, G. Bradski, and C. Kozyrakis. Evaluating MapReduce for multi-core and multiprocessor systems. In *Proc. of the 2007 IEEE 13th Intl Symposium on High Performance Computer Architecture*, pages 13–24, 2007.

[42] Salesforce.com. `http://www.salesforce.com`. [last access: 11/2, 2011].

[43] M. C. Schatz. CloudBurst: highly sensitive read mapping with MapReduce. *Bioinformatics*, 25:1363–1369, 2009.

[44] The R Project. The R Language. `http://www.r-project.org/`. [last access: 11/2, 2011].

[45] C. Tseng. Compiler optimizations for eliminating barrier synchronization. In *ACM SIGPLAN Notices*, volume 30, pages 144–155, 1995.

[46] C. A. Waldspurger. Memory resource management in VMware ESX server. *SIGOPS Oper. Syst. Rev.*, 36(SI):181–194, 2002.

[47] H.-C. Yang, A. Dasdan, R.-L. Hsiao, and D. S. Parker. Map-Reduce-Merge: simplified relational data processing on large clusters. In *SIGMOD '07: Proceedings of the 2007 ACM SIGMOD international conference on Management of data*, pages 1029–1040, 2007.

[48] Y. Yu, M. Isard, D. Fetterly, M. Budiu, Ú. Erlingsson, P. K. Gunda, and J. Currey. DryadLINQ: A system for general-purpose distributed data-parallel computing using a high-level language. In *the 8th Conference on Symposium on Operating Systems Design & Implementation*, pages 1–14, 2008.

[49] M. Zaharia, D. Borthakur, J. Sen Sarma, K. Elmeleegy, S. Shenker, and I. Stoica. Delay scheduling: a simple technique for achieving locality and fairness in cluster scheduling. In *EuroSys '10: Proceedings of the 5th European conference on computer systems*, pages 265–278, 2010.

[50] R. Zhang and A. Rudnicky. A large scale clustering scheme for kernel k-means. *Pattern Recognition*, 4:40289, 2002.

[51] W. Zhao, H. Ma, and Q. He. Parallel k-means clustering based on mapreduce. In *roceedings of the First International Conference on Cloud Computiong (CloudCom)*, pages 674–679, 2009.

SimTester: A Controllable and Observable Testing Framework for Embedded Systems

Tingting Yu, Witawas Srisa-an, and Gregg Rothermel

Department of Computer Science and Engineering
University of Nebraska-Lincoln
256 Avery Hall
Lincoln, NE 68588-0115
{tyu,witty,grother}@cse.unl.edu

Abstract

In software for embedded systems, the frequent use of interrupts for timing, sensing, and I/O processing can cause concurrency faults to occur due to interactions between applications, device drivers, and interrupt handlers. This type of fault is considered by many practitioners to be among the most difficult to detect, isolate, and correct, in part because it can be sensitive to execution interleavings and often occurs without leaving any observable incorrect output. As such, commonly used testing techniques that inspect program outputs to detect failures are often ineffective at detecting them. To test for these concurrency faults, test engineers need to be able to *control interleavings* so that they are deterministic. Furthermore, they also need to be able to *observe faults as they occur* instead of relying on observable incorrect outputs. In this paper, we introduce *SimTester*, a framework that allows engineers to effectively test for subtle and non-deterministic concurrency faults by providing them with greater *controllability* and *observability*. We implemented our framework on a commercial virtual platform that is widely used to support hardware/software co-designs to promote ease of adoption. We then evaluated its effectiveness by using it to test for data races and deadlocks. The result shows that our framework can be effective and efficient at detecting these faults.

Categories and Subject Descriptors D.2.5 [*Software Engineering*]: Testing and Debugging—Testing tools, Tracing; D.3.4 [Programming Languages]: Processor—Run-time environments

General Terms Reliability, Experimentation, Languages

Keywords Testing, Concurrency, Kernels, Device Drivers

1. Introduction

Concurrency faults such as data races, atomicity violations, and deadlocks are difficult to detect, isolate, and correct. This is because these faults are sensitive to execution interleavings; therefore, they often occur intermittently and unpredictably. Furthermore, certain classes of concurrency faults such as data races and atomicity violations do not always produce visible failures; therefore, techniques that inspect program outputs to detect failures are often ineffective at detecting them. As such, we have seen many instances of concurrency faults that remain dormant during testing and debugging periods and then appear during deployment [3, 10, 34].

In software for embedded systems, the frequent use of interrupts for timing, sensing, and I/O processing can cause concurrency faults to occur due to interactions between applications and interrupt handlers. As an example, occurrences of data races between interrupt handlers and applications have been reported in a previous release of *uCLinux*, a Linux OS designed for real-time embedded systems. In this particular case the serial communication line can be shared by an application through a device driver and an interrupt handler. In common instances, the execution of both the driver and the handler would be correct. However, in an exceptional operating scenario, the driver would execute a rarely executed path. If an interrupt occurs at that particular time, simultaneous transmissions of data is possible. (Section 3 provides further details).

Traditional techniques for testing for such concurrency faults require that engineers repeatedly execute a program. It is hoped that during such testing, a particular execution interleaving can reveal faults. There are two major problems with this approach. First, to reveal faults, tests must produce *observable* incorrect outputs. The absence of observable incorrect outputs, however, does not mean that there are no concurrency faults in the program. In the example described above, when data races occur, there is no guarantee that incorrect outputs are generated (e.g., in one scenario the interrupt handler wins the race and completely overwrites data written by the application). Therefore, for engineers to effectively test for data races in this case, they must be able to *observe the simultaneous transmissions and not just rely on the presence of incorrect outputs*.

As a second requirement for revealing faults, engineers must be able to exercise specific execution interleavings. However, engineers often do not have *control* over execution sufficient to exercise interleavings that are likely to expose faults. In the examples we describe in Section 3, engineers need to be able to *force an interrupt to occur at a particular location of a program*. Unfortunately, existing approaches for randomly forcing interrupts [38] are not powerful enough to support such a precise requirement. In the ideal case in which randomly invoking interrupts does expose faults, it may miss faults that can occur due to other interleavings.

There are existing techniques that can *precisely* detect concurrency faults such as data races as they occur instead of waiting to analyze the output [7, 20]. However, many of these techniques require significant source code modifications to record access sequences, monitor lock usage and track data reads and writes. Major code modifications make such approaches expensive; i.e., execution slowdown can be as high as a factor of 12. Moreover, extensive

VEE'12, March 3–4, 2012, London, England, UK.

code modifications make adopting these approaches in real-world software development environments challenging.

To achieve greater execution control, several existing approaches have tried to abstract away scheduling non-determinism. For example, there are techniques that perform dynamic analysis to permute execution interleavings [13]. There are also approaches based on model checking that can exhaustively explore execution interleavings [35]. Last, there are approaches that tightly control scheduling orders to make execution more deterministic [11]. One characteristic that these approaches have in common is that they require additional tools and runtime support that are not commonly used by real-world practitioners. As such, they have not been widely adopted by the software development community.

A further drawback with the foregoing techniques is that they have rarely been adapted to work in scenarios in which concurrency faults occur due to asynchronous interrupts. It is unclear whether these approaches can work in such a scenario for two reasons. First, controlling interrupts requires *fine-grained* execution control; that is, it must be possible to control execution at the machine code level and not at the program statement level, which is the granularity at which many existing techniques operate [13, 41]. Second, occurrences of interrupts are highly dependent on hardware states; that is, interrupts can occur only when hardware components are in certain states. Existing techniques are often not cognizant of hardware states [24, 38].

In this paper, we introduce a testing framework, *SimTester*, that provides *observability* and *fine-grained controllability* features sufficient to allow test engineers to detect concurrency faults that occur due to interactions between software and hardware. SimTester takes advantage of many features readily available in many virtual platforms to tackle the challenges of testing for concurrency errors in embedded software. Particularly, we can achieve the level of observability and controllability needed to test such systems by utilizing the virtual platform's abilities to interrupt execution without affecting the states of the virtualized system, to monitor function calls, variable values and system states, and to manipulate memory and buses directly to force events such as interrupts and traps. As such, SimTester is able to stop execution at a point of interest and force a traditionally non-deterministic event to occur. Our system then monitors the effects of the event on the system and determines whether there are any anomalies.

As stated earlier, many existing approaches for detecting concurrency faults are not widely used because they require significant deployment efforts. We have designed SimTester to overcome deployment obstacles by implementing it on a commercial virtual platform called Simics [18, 23, 45]. We chose *Simics* for several reasons. First, similar to other full-system simulators, *Simics* provides functional and behavioral characteristics similar to those of the *target hardware system*, enabling software components to be developed, verified, and tested as if they are executing on the actual systems. Second, through a rich set of *Simics* APIs, software engineers have the ability to non-intrusively observe and control various system behaviors without ever needing the source code. Third, due to its powerful device modeling infrastructure, *Simics* already plays a critical role in hardware/software (HW/SW) co-designs; therefore, adding the proposed capabilities to it will enable adoption without requiring much effort [43]. Thus, we envision that SimTester will allow several aspects of product integration testing to be moved up to the co-design phase of system development. Fourth, licensing of *Simics* is free for academic institutions, making it a good platform for research.

SimTester is implemented for applications running on x86/Linux environments. There are four major components that interact with Simics:

- A **configuration repository** stores initialization scripts containing information that includes execution break-points and variable locations that must be observed.
- An **execution controller** is an external module that can be attached to Simics. It invokes callback functions when events of interest occur (e.g., interrupts, memory read/write operations).
- An **execution observer** is another external module that can be attached to Simics. It monitors information generated by the execution controller and then records it in a file.
- An **oracle repository** stores test oracle files in the form of property requirements.[1] For example, the oracle can specify in which condition data races or deadlocks occur. Each log file is compared against an oracle file to detect a particular type of anomalous execution behavior.

By using SimTester, engineers can directly observe races and causes of deadlocks as they occur. They can also precisely control the occurrences of interrupts so that they can test every variable that can be accessed by both the application and interrupt handler for vulnerabilities to concurrency faults. SimTester yields precise detection of data races; that is, it produces no false positives. It is also effective; that is, if races or deadlocks are possible on a shared variable under test, they can be found more easily than with testing approaches that do not incorporate our framework. To evaluate the potential usefulness of SimTester we apply it to test for two classes of errors. These include data races (using an approach similar to that introduced by Higashi et al. [24] but with additional optimization) and deadlocks between device drivers and interrupt handlers. Our results show that SimTester can be effective and efficient.

The remainder of this paper is organized as follows. Section 2 provides an overview of SimTester, and Section 3 provides further details and a description of the approach by which engineers use it. Section 4 describes our evaluation of SimTester, and Section 5 provides details on related work. Finally, Section 6 concludes.

2. Introducing *SimTester*

Figure 1 depicts the overall architecture of the SimTester framework. There are four major components in the framework in addition to Simics itself. As stated earlier, Simics provides APIs that can be accessed via Python scripts; thus, all components except the test oracles are Python scripts.

The first component is the *configuration* script, the content of which includes information such as locations at which to set execution breakpoints, addresses of variables that need to be monitored, and machine instructions that need to be monitored.

The second component is the *execution controller* program. This program specifies certain events to be invoked at particular points in executions. It can generate data that can cause the system to take different execution paths. As an example, the framework can artificially create I/O interrupts simply by writing data to I/O bus or memory locations that have been mapped to hardware devices. It can also force the system to execute a particular exception handling routine by artificially creating that exception. Finally, it can force the system to execute a particular path by specifically setting a conditional value.

The third component is the *execution observer* program, which monitors and generates information that can either be recorded into a file for offline analyses (used to detect data races) or fed directly into the test oracles for online analyses (used to detect deadlocks). Any anomalies are reported in the *result file*.

[1] In the testing literature, a *test oracle* is the device by which engineers determine whether a test has elicited a failure in a system.

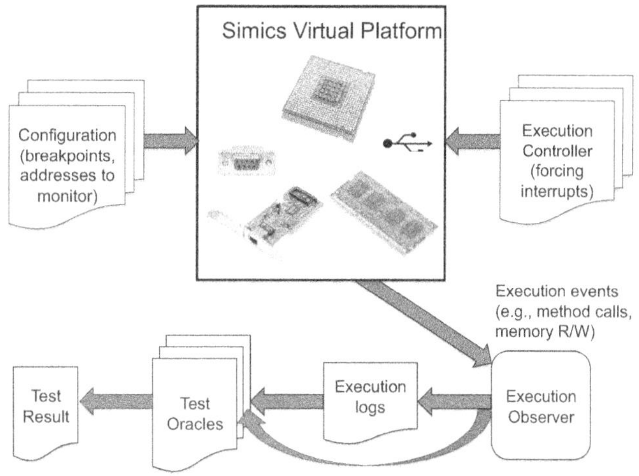

Figure 1. Overview of the SimTester architecture.

To use the framework, a test engineer first configures Simics to model the system to be tested. The engineer then writes a configuration script to set up breakpoints and a variable watch list, and specific instructions to be monitored (e.g., procedure calls and return instructions). In addition, the engineer also writes a script to specify actions to be taken when monitored events occur (Simics refers to these actions as *handlers*.) As an example, a handler for reaching an execution breakpoint could be firing a timer interrupt. Another possible handler for writing to a monitored address could make the written data available for logging or on-line analysis. Any generated information is processed by the execution observer.

In addition to the components illustrated in Figure 1, a test driver is also needed to automate the testing process. Typically, engineers conduct testing by running test programs on a system. A test driver is a program that automates the process of running test programs in a suite and managing the generated log files.

After a test driver executes a test case an event log file is generated. Log files can then be analyzed to detect anomalies, or saved for further off-line analysis. Typically, in a testing process that detect faults by analyzing a program's output, the test oracle is the correct output of the program. On the other hand, if a testing process detects faults by analyzing execution behaviors, then the test oracle can consist of properties that specify correct execution behaviors [47]. In this paper, we compare both types of oracles.

3. Utilizing *SimTester*

In this section, we describe and illustrate how *SimTester* can be used to test for two significant classes of concurrency faults: data races and deadlocks. These two classes of faults have been identified as the most "nasty" faults to test for in embedded software [17]. When we conduct testing for data races, the components under test include the main application, the UART device driver, and the ISRs that are associated with specified serial ports. The focus of our illustration is testing for races that occur when the application coupled with the device driver interact with an ISR.

Note that in the illustration that we present, interrupts are not nested, but our algorithms do also support nested interrupts. Also note that our illustration considers only a single ISR but our algorithm can be generically applied to handle multiple ISRs; however, in that case it is more difficult to isolate events related to any one particular ISR. In addition, because our framework forces interrupts to occur, we would like to distinguish between interrupts that occur naturally as part of program execution and forced interrupts issued by the execution control module of *SimTester*. We refer to the former type of interrupts as *self-generated*, and to the latter as *controlled*.

3.1 Data Race Detection

In prior releases of *uCLinux* version 2.4, there is a particular data race that occurs between the UART driver program `uart_start` and the UART ISR `serial8250_interrupt`. As it turns out, a similar error also existed in the early version of the 2.6 Linux kernel [26]. We provide the code snippets that illustrate the error in Figure 2.

The error can be summarized as follows. Under a normal operating condition, the ISR is always responsible for transmitting data. Routine `serial8250_startup` is responsible for initializing the UART port and assigning the ISR. To ensure that an ISR is assigned correctly, it issues an interrupt and monitors the response from the ISR. Several sources have shown that problems such as races with other processors on the system or intermittent port problems can cause the response from the ISR to get lost or cause a failure to correctly install the ISR, respectively [26, 27]. When that happens, the port is registered as "buggy" (line 5 in Figure 2) and workaround code based on polling instead of using interrupts is used (lines 8-11). Unfortunately, interrupts are not disabled in the workaround code region so by the time the workaround code is executed, it is possible for both the ISR and the workaround code to be transmitting or receiving data through the same serial port at the same time. As such, a race in this illustration occurs when:

1. the program is preempted by the ISR *immediately* after a shared memory access before it can proceed to next instruction;
2. the ISR manipulates the content of this shared memory.

Higashi et al. [24] introduce an approach to test for this fault by controlling invocations of interrupts. In that work, they used an ARM-based processor simulator and modified version of *uCLinux* with the same fault so that it could run on that simulator. Their

```
static int serial8250_startup(...)
  { ...
  if (lsr & UART_LSR_TEMT &&
         iir & UART_IIR_NO_INT) {
    if (!(up->bugs & UART_BUG_TXEN)) {
       up->bugs |= UART_BUG_TXEN;
}

static void serial8250_start_tx(...)
  { ...
  if (up->bugs & UART_BUG_TXEN) {
     ...
     transmit_chars(up);
  } ...
}
```

Figure 2. Faulty code that can cause data races in the UART driver in Linux.

modifications included porting the code over from PPC to ARM and removal of irrelevant code to reduce the simulation time. Their methodology was to invoke an interrupt at every memory read and write operation.

For this illustration, we replicated the fault found in Fedora Core 2.6.15. We also recreated a similar testing system based on *SimTester* with two additional optimization techniques. In the first optimization technique, we apply static program analysis to detect the resources that can be affected by the UART driver and the ISR. With this optimization, we invoke interrupts only when these shared resources are accessed. Second, we also check the system states to ensure that it is possible to invoke interrupts when those resources are accessed. These two optimizations should significantly reduce the time required to conduct testing. Next, we discuss the configuration of *SimTester* that allows engineers to test for this fault.

Configuration of the Test System

To test for data races we need to provide two components to the system under test: the test input and conditions governing when to invoke interrupts from within the system. In this case, a *test case* is used as the test input for the program under test (PuT) (which in this case includes the application and any device driver running under non-interrupt service routine context that is called by the application.) In the case we are considering, the PuT includes an application that interacts with a serial port and the UART driver. We refer to the interrupt service routine for the tested UART port as the ISR. Note that test cases for the PuT can be generated based on various criteria. We discuss the criteria we use in the next section.

Next, we need to describe each *interrupt condition* (*IC*). We express IC as a tuple: $< loc, pin >$. The first element loc specifies a code location at which to invoke an interrupt. The second element pin specifies an *Interrupt Request* (*IRQ*) line number at which to invoke the interrupt. This is needed because typically, an interrupt service routine can be associated with multiple IRQ lines. ICs are used only when the controllability module is enabled.

Observer Module. We configure the observer module so that it records runtime information that can be used by test engineers to perform off-line analysis for races. In this example, the generated information includes:

- when functions of the PuT and ISR execute and when they return, and
- when SVs are accessed by the PuT and written by the ISR.

As such, one of our configuration tasks is to set execution breakpoints in Simics to detect when functions in the PuT and ISR execute and when SVs are accessed. The algorithms to accomplish this task are provided next.

```
procedure BasicConfig()
1: begin
2: for each function f in the PuT and ISR
3:     set execution breakpoint at entry point function_addr of f
4: endfor
5: set execution breakpoint on function return instruction ret
6: set execution breakpoint on interrupt return instruction iretd
7: end
```

```
procedure RaceObserver()
require: procedure BasicConfig()
begin
for each SV in list l_SV
    set memory read/write breakpoint at SV
endfor

switch (breakpoint)
  case function_addr:
     func_list.push({func_addr, ebp, esp})
     if func_addr == ISR_entry
        log "ISR_entry"
        is_ISR = true
     endif
  case ret:
     if esp == func_list.top[index_esp]
        if func_list.top[index_func] == ISR_entry
           is_ISR = false
           log "ISR_exit"
        endif
        func_list.pop()
     endif
  case iretd:
     if ebp == ebp_switch
        log "iretd"
        /*log program counter in next instruction*/
        next_pc()
     endif
  case SV:
     /*check if SV is accessed by the PuT*/
     if ebp == func_list.top[index_ebp]
        if is_ISR == false
           log "PuT", SV, SV_access, pc
           /*save Reg[ebp] content*/
           ebp_switch = ebp
        else /*interrupt handler context*/
           if SV_access == write
              log "ISR", SV, SV_access
           endif
        endif
     endif
end
```

Execution memory breakpoints are set in *BasicConfig*, including function entry addresses $function\_addr$ (line 3), function return instructions ret in the PuT and ISR (line 5), and interrupt return instructions $iretd$ (line 6). Races occur when both the PuT and ISR access the same memory location, so a memory breakpoint for

```
...
PuT, $xmit->tail$, read, pc1
ISR entry
ISR, $xmit->tail$, write
ISR exit
IRETD
pc1+1
...
```

Figure 3. Sample trace information for race detection.

each SV address is set in callback function *RaceObserver*, which is invoked whenever the execution reaches a breakpoint.

One challenge in setting up a breakpoint for each SV is that we need to be able to obtain the dynamic address of that SV. One option for doing this is to parse the symbol table. However, the symbol table provides only global variable addresses so our system may miss other shared variables such as local pointers. To obtain the address of each SV that has been identified by our static analysis (Section 4), we first create an instrumented version of the ISR so that it dynamically prints each SV address. We then iteratively inject data into the device port or adjust the device's register so that we can obtain the addresses of all SVs in the ISR stored in l_{SV}. Our function *RaceObserver* sets breakpoints at these shared variable addresses in line 3 of *RaceObserver*.

To isolate the PuT and ISR from other applications in the system or other ISR invocations, we statically identify all function names in the PuT and their entry addresses. We also identify the entry address to the ISR. These addresses can be obtained by parsing the symbol tables. Furthermore, we monitor the function return instruction (*ret* in X86) to determine whether a function or the ISR has returned, and the interrupt return instruction (*iretd* in X86) to determine whether the PuT has been recovered from the interrupt context.

At runtime, we keep a *calling stack* named $func\_list$. When a function or an ISR is invoked its <address, frame pointer, stack pointer> is added to *calling stack* (line 7). When a shared variable is accessed, we compare the current frame pointer *ebp* with the frame pointer on top of *calling stack* (line 28). This mechanism allows us to ignore those shared variables that might be accessed by a different ISR or a different program on the same ISR. If a ret instruction is encountered, by comparing the current stack pointer esp with the stack pointer on top of *calling stack* (line 13), we can determine whether the current function or the ISR has returned.

A function is popped from *calling stack* if its ret instruction is reached. Program counter pc is recorded twice to determine whether the PuT is actually preempted between a shared variable access and its following instruction. The first time is when a shared variable is accessed (line 30) under a non-interrupt service routine context, and the second time is after an interrupt returns (line 24). An interrupt return instruction $iretd$ is recorded to indicate termination of an interrupt context. Note that the mere presence of an $iretd$ does not imply that an interrupt will jump back to the PuT, because more than one device can issue interrupts and call $iretd$ instructions. To overcome this problem, an $iretd$ is logged only when its frame pointer is equal to the frame pointer when a shared variable is accessed in the PuT (line 22).

In summary, events logged for testing race conditions include: (1) read/write accesses to shared variables (SV_{access} by the PuT); (2) entry to the ISR; (3) a write to an SV by the ISR; (4) return from the ISR; (5) context switches from the ISR to the PuT. Figure 3 illustrates a sample of trace information recording these events for this example.

Note that there is a race in the trace given in Figure 3. By observing the program counter when SV is accessed by the PuT and the interrupt recovery point, we can determine that an interrupt occurs right after $xmit->tail$ is read by the PuT.

Controller Module. When engineers enable the controller module *RaceController*, a *controlled* interrupt is invoked right after a shared variable access by the PuT. Simics provides a $simple\_interface$ API to issue an interrupt on a specific IRQ line. This interface guarantees that the interrupt happens before the subsequent instruction. As such, when our test system reaches a memory breakpoint, the observer module is called. If the controller module is enabled, the observer module tries to invoke an interrupt right after the access to SV.

It is not always realistic, however, to invoke an interrupt whenever we want. For example, the interrupt enable register and possibly other control registers have to be set to enable interrupts. Even if interrupts are enabled, they can be temporarily disabled. The following routine is the routine in *RaceController* used to determine whether it is possible to issue an interrupt.

---

procedure *ISR_enabled(int p)*
/*p is the pin number for a certain interrupt*/
1: **begin**
2: **if** eflags[9] != 0 and ioapic.redirection[p] == 0
    and ioapic.pin_raised[p] == LOW:
3: *return* $true$
4: **else**
5: *return* $false$
6: **endif**
7: **end**

There are two general steps that our system takes prior to invoking a *controlled interrupt*. First, the controller module checks the status of the local interrupt and global interrupt bits to see if interrupts are enabled. In an X86 architecture the global interrupt bit is the ninth bit of the eflags register (line 2 of *ISR_enabled*). When this bit is set to 1, the global interrupt is disabled, otherwise it is enabled. For local interrupts, Simics uses the Advanced Programmable Interrupt Controller (APIC) as its interrupt controller. As such, our system checks whether the bit controlling the UART device is masked or not. Our system also checks whether a *self-generated* interrupt is about to be issued by examining the current pin status. If this is true, the *controlled* interrupt will not be invoked.

Second, our system invokes only one *controlled* interrupt per test run. This is done to avoid *fault masking* effects, which may occur in cases where multiple interrupts fire and cause a failure that would be evident in the presence of a single interrupt to be "masked" by the presence of the second. Thus, our system needs to first check a flag to determine whether a controlled interrupt has already been invoked in the current run. If it has, the test system does not monitor any further events in this run. Once it has been determined that there has not been any invocation of a controlled interrupt in this run, the system then checks to see whether the last accessed SV has already been tested in prior runs. If it has not, the system enables the control register for UART and then calls the $simple\_interrupt$ API.

Note that, given the foregoing approach, there can be multiple runs of each test case, and the number of runs depends on the number of SVs that must be tested. With the controller module disabled, the PuT runs $|tc|$ times during a testing process, where $|tc|$ is the number of test cases. With the controller module enabled, the number of runs is $|tc| * (|int| + 1)$, where $|tc|$ is the number of test cases and $|int|$ is the number of controlled interrupts issued. We also need to run the PuT one additional time for each test case to determine whether all SVs have been accessed.

```
void xhci_watchdog(...)
{
        xhci = ep->xhci;
         ...
        spin_lock(&xhci->lock);
        ...
        spin_unlock(&xhci->lock);
}
irqreturn_t interrupt(int irq, void *dev_id)
{
        xhci = get_dev(dev_id);
        ...
        spin_lock(&xhci->lock);
        ...
}
```

Figure 4. Faulty code that can cause deadlocks.

3.2 Deadlock Detection

It is common for interrupt handlers to use non-preemptive mechanisms such as spin-locks instead of preemptive mechanisms such as semaphores to protect critical code regions. This is because typically, ISR code is not allowed to sleep. As such, interrupt code is short and deterministic so the amount of time that a task must wait to enter the critical region should be predictably short [15]. That said, there are many real world examples including the one used in this illustration that show how incorrect usage of spinlocking mechanisms can cause priority inversions and ultimately deadlocks between the PuT and ISR. In the example of Figure 4, deadlocks occur because:

- the PuT is preempted by the ISR while the PuT is holding a spin lock,
- the ISR tries to acquire the same spinlock and becomes stuck in the spinlock loop.

Because the ISR has higher priority, it can become stuck in this loop. To test for such deadlocks, we configure our test system in a manner similar to that used to test for races. However, test cases for the system are generated to adequately cover *spin_lock* and *spin_unlock* pairs in the PuT instead of shared variables. In this illustration, we assume that *spin_lock* and *spin_unlock* are properly paired. Next, we describe the configurations of the execution observer and execution controller.

Configuration of the Test System

In a uniprocessor environment, an observer does not increase fault detection effectiveness because deadlocks can be easily observed (e.g., systems hang or show no responses). However, the proposed test system can still be useful in informing testers of the sources of deadlocks. Furthermore, it can support deadlock detection in multiprocessor systems where deadlock might cause one or more processors to stop making execution progress but other processors continue to do useful work.

Observer Module. We configure the observer module so that it records runtime information that can be used to both issue a runtime warning and log for offline analysis. In this deadlock example, the generated information includes:

- when functions of the PuT and ISR execute and return;
- when a spinlock is acquired by the PuT and by ISR, and
- when a spinlock is released by the PuT.

As in the above example, when the spinlock is acquired by the the PuT, the observer sets the lock condition to true. If the ISR tries to obtain the same lock, the observer first checks whether the lock condition is true, and then compares the requested lock with that held by the PuT. If they are the same, we have a deadlock. In this case, the observer issues a warning once the deadlock is detected. In both environments, it also records the event so that engineers can perform analysis offline. Function *DeadlockObserver* describes our algorithm to detect deadlocks.

```
procedure DeadlockObserver()
require: procedure BasicConfig()
1: begin
2: set execution breakpoint on entry point of spin_lock and spin_unlock
3: switch (breakpoint)
4:    case func_addr:
5:        func_list.push({func_addr, ebp, esp, lock_obj})
6:        if func_addr == ISR_entry
7:            is_ISR = true
8:        endif
9:    case spin_lock:
10:       if ebp == func_list.top[index_ebp]
11:           if is_ISR and is_lock and eax == lock_obj
12:               print"deadlock occurs"
13:           else
14:               func_list.push({func_address, ebp, esp, eax})
15:           endif
16:       endif
17:   case spin_unlock:
18:       if ebp == func_list.top[index_ebp]
19:           func_list.push({func_address, ebp, esp, eax})
20:       endif
21:   case ret:
22:       if esp == func_list.top[index_esp]
23:           if func_list.top[index_func] == ISR_entry
24:               is_ISR = false
25:           endif
26:           if fun_list.top[index_func] == spin_lock
27:               /*spinlock returns*/
28:               if !is_ISR
29:                   is_lock = true
30:                   lock_obj = func_list.top[index_eax]
31:               endif
32:           endif
33:           if fun_list.top[index_func] == spin_unlock
34:               if !is_ISR
35:                   is_lock = false
36:                   lock_obj = null
37:               endif
38:           endif
39:           func_list.pop()
40:       endif
41: end
```

Functions *spin_lock* and *spin_unlock* are commonly used by various applications. As such, we need to isolate calls to these two functions that come from the PuT and ISR. Again, we use the *calling stack* to dynamically store information on called functions during virtualization (lines 5, 14, 19).

Initially, lock_obj is set to *null*. The lock is acquired after *spin_lock* returns (line 29), and released after *spin_unlock* returns (line 35). Besides the frame pointer and stack pointer, each function in *calling stack* carries a lock object, indicating whether the current running function is holding a lock or which lock it is holding. As such, a locked object can always be obtained by examining the top of stack (line 30).

A deadlock occurs under three conditions (line 10): (1) the ISR is executing; (2) a lock is held by the PuT; (3) the ISR is stuck in the same spinlock loop as the object of the held lock.

Deadlock detection is different from race detection in that a deadlock warning is issued instead of simply recording deadlock information. Once a deadlock is detected, the test script terminates execution and reinitializes the test system for the next test run. Because a lock object is passed as a parameter to *spin_lock* or *spin_unlock*, the object can be obtained by reading the CPU eax register in the X86 architecture. Note that this is architecture and compiler dependent. However, the approach should be generalizable to other architectures and compilers as long as we know how the lock object is passed.

Controller Module. The controller module *DeadlockController* is implemented following the same steps as the controllability module for race conditions, except that an interrupt is issued after a spinlock is acquired by the PuT instead of invoking interrupts on each shared variable access.

4. Evaluation

To evaluate SimTester, we applied our approach to the UART device driver on a preemptive kernel version of Fedora Core 2.6.15. The driver includes two files, serial_core.c and 8250.c, containing 1896 and 1445 lines of non-comment code, respectively. The main application transmits character strings to and receives character strings from console via the UART port. Note that in this paper we apply our testing process only to the UART driver. However, the same process is also applicable to other types of device drivers.

Our approach requires the use of existing test cases, so we generated test cases for the system based on a code-coverage-based test adequacy criterion. To generate test cases relevant to race conditions, we first statically identified shared variables (SVs) between the PuT and ISR. We use the precise shared variable detection algorithm proposed in [29], but we are interested only in shared variables that are read by the PuT and written by the ISR, or written by both the PuT and the ISR. We label each shared variable as a "definition" or "use" through our analysis. After SVs are identified, we generate a set of test cases that cover the feasible SVs (SVs for which there exists a possible execution of the program which executes them) in the PuT. This process produced 12 test cases.

To generate test cases relevant to deadlocks, we sought to find test cases that adequately cover *spin_lock* and *spin_unlock* pairs in the PuT instead of shared variables. (In the case of our target program, we know that all occurrences of *spin_lock* and *spin_unlock* are properly paired; in practice a static analysis could initially determine this and flag unpaired occurrences for attention by the test engineer.) In the case of our target program, which contains only three spin-lock pairs, this process resulted in two test cases (one of which covered two of the pairs).

To better assess the cost and effectiveness of our approach, we considered both the approach and two alternative baseline approaches. In the discussion that follows, we refer to our approach as the *conditional controllability* approach, because it involves issuing controlled interrupts under certain conditions. The second approach that we considered, *no controllability*, involves testing the program without any controlled interrupts; this is the approach that test engineers would normally use. The third approach that we consider, *random controllability*, involves issuing controlled interrupts at random program locations after shared variable accesses and without checking interrupt conditions.

We measured execution times for the foregoing approaches by embedding a timer in the Simics module. As such, the reported times are the actual times spent by Simics to execute the program.

4.1 Testing for Race Conditions

We begin by considering the target program as given, and evaluate the effectiveness and efficiency of our race condition testing approach on that program.

We first applied conditional controllability together with observability. Under this approach, across the 12 test cases utilized, 84 controlled interrupts were applied, and for each test case, one extra run was needed to determine whether all shared variables had been accessed. Thus, 96 test runs were required to finish testing the target program with an average execution time of 77.91s per test run. Including self-generated interrupts, the number of interrupts generated for the target program was 352. In the course of applying the approach, we detected a race in function *uart_write_room* of serial_core.c, which we later determined had been corrected in subsequent versions of the system. By running the system with observability turned off, we determined that this fault can be detected only with observability enabled; in other words, it is a fault that did not propagate to output on our particular test inputs.

We next tested our target program with no controllability. In this case, the only interrupts that occur are self-generated interrupts. Because runs of each given test can conceivably differ, we ran each test on the program 500 times. The total number of interrupts observed was 16,500. Over the 6000 total test runs, average execution time was 74.08s per test, only 3.83 seconds less than with controllability added. None of these test runs detected the race condition detected by our first approach, however, either with observability enabled or disabled.

Finally, we tested our target program using the random controllability approach. For each test case, we ran the target program three times more than the number of runs performed under the conditional controllability approach, on each run generating an interrupt at a randomly selected program location. The total number of test runs was 288 and the number of interrupts generated was 1044. In this case the average execution time per test case was 75.17s, only 2.74 seconds less than with controllability added. Again, the race was not detected, either with observability enabled or disabled.

One important characteristic of our technique is that checking is performed before issuing a controlled interrupt. When a shared variable is accessed in the main program, the controllability module first checks to see whether it is possible to issue an interrupt, and if not, it proceeds to the next possible location. This approach can save test runs, but at the cost of checking. To quantify the tradeoffs involved, we also applied our conditional controllability approach without the checking step enabled. Recall that with checking enabled, 96 test runs were needed to issue controlled interrupts, with an average execution time of 77.91s per test. With checking disabled, on the other hand, 1428 test runs were needed to issue controlled interrupts, with an average execution time of 75.66s per test. Clearly, the checking approach saves time overall.

A second characteristic of our technique is that interrupts are issued only after shared memory accesses, and this can be much less expensive than issuing interrupts after each memory access, which is the approach used by Higashi et al. [24]. For our target program, there are 94,941 data accesses made in the course of running the 12 test cases. If an interrupt were issued after each data access, we would need 82.6 days to finish testing the target program.

4.2 Testing for Deadlock

We next consider the target program as given, and evaluate the effectiveness and efficiency of our deadlock testing approach on that program. (In this case, because our experiment is running on a uniprocessor and observability does not increase fault detection power, we consider only the effects of controllability, not the effects of observability.)

We began by running our two deadlock test cases on the target program under conditional controllability. Under this approach, only two controlled interrupts were generated, and they detected one deadlock in function $serial8250\_handle\_port$ of 8250.c, which had been reported [30] and corrected in later versions. The average execution time was 69.88s per test run.

We next ran the target program with no controllability. For each test case, we ran the program 500 times; the 1000 tests had an average execution time of 75.24s, and 4000 self-generated interrupts were observed. However, no deadlocks were detected.

Finally, we ran the program using the random controllability approach. Here we ran the program three times as many as the number of runs performed for conditional controllability, issuing an interrupt at a random program location. The total number of controlled interrupts was six and the total number of interrupts generated was 15. The average run time was 75.24s per test. Here also, no deadlocks were detected.

Notice that the average execution times of the latter two approaches are higher than that of the conditional controllability approach. This result, at first, appears counter-intuitive. However, in our experiment with conditional controllability, we terminated the execution once a deadlock has been detected. On the other hand, the latter two approaches did not detect deadlocks, so the program ran to completion.

4.3 Fault Detection Effectiveness

While the results of the foregoing studies are encouraging, the numbers of naturally occurring faults found in the target program was low, rendering comparisons of the fault detection effectiveness of the approaches less meaningful. To further investigate fault detection effectiveness we followed a process often utilized in the software testing research community [2]; namely, the use of seeded faults.

In this case, we injected 12 potential race condition faults and 11 potential deadlock faults into 8250.c by making syntactic changes to the code. For race conditions, we removed statements corresponding to critical section protection (e.g., $spin\_lock$, $spin\_lock\_irq$). For deadlock, we changed statements corresponding to interrupt disable and enable pairs (e.g., $spin\_lock\_irq$ and $spin\_unlock\_irq$) into pure spin lock pairs (e.g., $spin\_lock$, $spin\_unlock$). Of the 23 potential faults thus created, further examination revealed that seven of the potential race condition faults, and seven of the potential deadlock faults, could not possibly be triggered on the system on its given hardware platform, so we removed those. This left us with five potentially revealable race condition faults and four potentially revealable deadlock faults.

Given the faults thus seeded, we ran our test cases on the faulty systems using conditional and random controllability, and in the case of race detection, with observability enabled and disabled. For the race condition detection approach, conditional controllability detected two of the five faults. One of these faults was detected both with and without observability. The same fault was also detected with random controllability, but only with observability enabled because in this case the fault does not propagate to output. This occurred because interrupts issued by conditional controllability visited more unprotected shared variables that can cause incorrect output, and these shared variables are not visited by random controllability.

The second fault revealed in our race detection trial was revealed not through observability, but rather, through output, for both conditional controllability and random controllability. The reason this occurred is because the fault was not actually caused by our defined race condition, but rather, by another type of atomicity violation. In particular, a read-write SV pair in the main program is supposed to be atomic, but the ISR read this SV before it was updated in the main program. This outcome shows that, while our approach does not specifically target other types of faults, it may catch them as byproducts.

We also inspected the three potential race condition faults that were not detected by any techniques. We determined that the reason for their omission was that the interrupt handler in each of the versions does not share variables or read variables with the main program. This does not mean that the code regions involved do not need to be protected, because other ISRs may share memory locations, or programmers may intentionally cause the regions to execute without interruption.

Where deadlock faults were concerned, we discovered that conditional controllability detected all four, while random controllability detected two.

5. Further Discussion

Our observer module considers one type of definition of a race condition. In practice, testers can adopt different definitions because there is not a single general definition for the class of race conditions that occur between an ISR and a PuT. As noted above, for the four faulty versions on which the ISR and the PuT do not share read-write and write-write variables, we still found one fault with controllability enabled. This fault is related to an atomicity violation, as a code region in the main program is supposed to execute atomically, e.g., before a shared variable is updated in the main program, and an interrupt occurs and the wrong data is read.

Our approach injects data into device ports and forces an interrupt handler to execute one path. The data we inject is the same as the test input given to the program. For example, if an application sends the string "hello" to the UART console passed by UART *transmitter buffer*, a controllability module would inject "world" into the UART *transmitter buffer* to force an interrupt to occur after a certain access. It is also possible to have multiple paths by which shared variables can exist in interrupt handlers. Testers can extend our method by forcing interrupt handlers to execute different paths, which may increase the probability of revealing faults.

However, no faults are left undetected due to missing shared variables or spin locks in the other paths of the ISR in our target program. It is also possible to force an interrupt handler to execute only the paths that have definition-use relationships with the main program. This may further reduce the number of controlled interrupts and test runs. To do this, the value schedule approach proposed by Chen et al. [13] could be adapted.

To force an interrupt to occur, our controllability module issues a new interrupt. However, races and deadlocks can occur relative to the interrupt generated by the target program itself. For example, suppose an interrupt is requested by device driver code, but is not immediately processed for some reason (e.g., device port delay). The interrupt handler associated with this interrupt may be executed later within a spin lock pair or after a shared variable access, and thus a race condition or a deadlock may occur. Our controllability module can be further extended to deal with such cases. For example, when an interrupt is triggered, the module can delay this interrupt by masking its interrupt enable register, and issue the interrupt after a certain event happens (e.g., shared variable access, spin lock is acquired). If there is no such event, the interrupt is issued on exiting the PuT.

In practice, when testing software components (e.g., device drivers and interrupt handlers), the first task that a test engineer must accomplish is to gain confidence that the software component is developed correctly. In our study, the analysis involves a test program, the interrupt handler that interacts with the device driver, and the device driver code. The key point here is that the tester focuses on a specific component and how it interacts with the rest of the components. If the focus changes to a different component, the same analysis can be applied to test the new component. As such, the proposed approach is not designed to test the entire system at once. Instead, it is more suitable for component testing.

In our current work, the test generation process was done manually (which is currently the norm in practice). Our study considers a test input to include input values and interrupt scheduling. However, there is no reason the approach could not also utilize input values created using existing test case generation approaches (such as dynamic symbolic execution [9, 42].) A problem with such approaches by themselves is that they generate large numbers of test cases with no methodology for judging system correctness beyond looking for crashes. Our approach provides more powerful, automated oracles, and thus should ultimately facilitate the use of larger numbers of automatically generated test cases.

6. Related Work

There are several techniques for testing embedded systems with a particular focus on interrupt related faults. As already noted, Higashi et al. [24] detect race conditions caused by interrupt handlers via a mechanism that causes interrupts to occur at all possible times. Their method and ours artificially amplify the frequency of interrupts to evaluate whether these interrupts can cause faults. However, our work has several advantages. First, by adding observability, we increase the power of fault detection while Higashi's method focuses on controllability. Second, instead of firing interrupts at all memory access instructions of a *PuT*, we issue interrupts only at shared variable accesses, which significantly reduces testing cost. Third, we adopt coverage criteria to cover all feasible shared variables in the *PuT* instead of using arbitrary inputs; this can help the program execute code regions that are more race-prone. Fourth, Higashi's method issues all interrupts during one program run. This may cause problems with fault masking and cascading errors. In contrast, we issue just one interrupt during a given program run. Fifth, Higashi's method does not consider situations in which interrupts cannot occur; however, our technique can determine whether it is possible to issue interrupts at runtime by observing hardware states, which further improves testing efficiency. Another implementation difference is that we built our framework on a virtual platform while their approach is built on an processor emulator.

In other work, Regehr et al. [38] use random testing to test Tiny OS applications. They propose a technique called restricted interrupt discipline (RID) to improve naive random testing (i.e., firing interrupts at random times) by eliminating aberrant interrupts. In our approach, however, interrupts are conditionally fired instead of randomly. Our evaluation has shown that conditionally fired interrupts increase the chances of revealing faults while reducing cost. Lai et al. [33] present a notation for modeling interrupt-driven nesC applications for testing purposes. They formulate two test adequacy criteria based on the notation. Their approach does not provide observability or controllability. In their approach, test cases are randomly selected from a test pool until coverage has been achieved. We believe that this process can be made more effective by adding controllability.

Static analysis techniques discover paths and regions in code that might be susceptible to concurrency faults (e.g., [19, 25, 46]). Techniques based on program state modeling and transitions (e.g., [16]) have been used to verify device drivers and kernels [5, 19]. There are also static analysis techniques used to verify embedded software with interrupts. Tan et al. [44] designs a type of annotation that can be used to detect OS concurrency faults related to interrupts. Their approach is based on statically analyzing comments and code. Brylow et al. [8] apply a model checker to check interrupt related real time properties such as interrupt latency. Schlich et al. [40] propose a technique called *interrupt handler reduction* to reduce the number of program locations at which an interrupt needs to be considered. The goal of this technique is to reduce program states in model checking. There are several drawbacks associated with static analysis techniques such as these. First, state explosion in static analysis may cause scalability problems. Second, static analysis can report false positives due to imprecise local information and infeasible paths. Third, as embedded systems are highly dependent on hardware, it is difficult for static analysis to annotate all operations on manipulated hardware bits; moreover, hardware events such as interrupts usually rely on several operations among different hardware bits.

Dynamic analysis tends to be more accurate than static analysis for detecting concurrency faults (see e.g., [28, 36]). Techniques that do not control thread interleavings (e.g., [39]) can miss faults that are caused by different interleavings. Moreover, existing dynamic techniques cannot leverage the scheduling policies for interrupts and main programs because such techniques do not consider priority based preemption. Controlling thread interleavings at runtime is a way to increase the chances of exposing faults. Sen et al. [41] first identify potential concurrency faults, and then control the underlying scheduler by inserting delays at context switch points. This technique, however, may not apply in our context due to different scheduling policies. (Hardware interrupts are asynchronous events generated from hardware, so they are not scheduled by kernel thread schedulers. For example, it is impossible to force shared variable accesses at the same time because an interrupt handler cannot be preempted by a normal program.) Other dynamic techniques such as interrupt tracing [22] are not designed to detect faults. Our goal is to utilize test cases to detect concurrency faults involving runtime execution of application and hardware interrupt service routine. Thus, we employ dynamic analysis.

Virtual platforms have been used to support tracing, replay, and debugging [1, 6, 12, 31, 37]; however, they have rarely been used to support testing. One notable example is work by Goh et al. [21]. They introduced a VM-based online testing approach to supplement off-line testing. With off-line testing, all possible test inputs may not be known ahead of time since embedded software systems are often influenced by external environments. Their work, however, did not consider the use of observability and controllability to enhance testing effectiveness. On the other hand, there have been some efforts to extend virtual platforms to provide greater observability in security domain [4, 14, 32]. However, these efforts did not utilize the additional observing power for testing.

7. Conclusion

The frequent use of interrupts for timing, sensing, and I/O processing in embedded software can cause concurrency faults to occur due to interactions between applications, device drivers, and interrupt handlers. This type of fault is considered by many practitioners to be among the most difficult to detect, isolate, and correct, in part because it can be sensitive to interleavings and often occurs without causing any observable incorrect output. In this work, we introduce *SimTester*, a framework that provides test engineers with the ability to precisely *control* execution events and *observe* runtime context at critical code locations. The framework is built on a commercial virtual platform that is commonly used as part of the hardware/software co-design process.

The main benefit of using virtual platforms is the ability to interrupt execution without affecting the states of the virtualized system. Furthermore, we can monitor function calls, variable values and system states, and manipulate memory and buses directly to make typically non-deterministic execution events more deterministic. To illustrate the effectiveness of SimTester, we use it to test software systems with two real-world concurrency faults, races and deadlocks, that were uncovered in the previous releases of Linux kernels. They are the result of untimely occurrences of interrupt at improperly synchronized code locations. We also apply SimTester to a number of seeded faults. Our evaluation clearly shows that our technique is effective in detecting faults that are unlikely to be detected in approaches that rely on observing incorrect outputs.

Acknowledgments

This work is supported in part by the National Science Foundation through awards CNS-0720757 and by the Air Force Office of Scientific Research through award FA9550-10-1-0406.

References

[1] L. Albertsson. Simulation-Based Debugging of Soft Real-Time Applications. In *Proceedings of the IEEE Real-Time Technology and Applications Symposium (RTAS)*, pages 107–108, Taipei, Taiwan, 2001.

[2] J. H. Andrews, L. C. Briand, and Y. Labiche. Is Mutation An Appropriate Tool for Testing Experiments? In *Proceedings of the International Conference on Software Engineering (ICSE)*, pages 402–411, 2005.

[3] Apache Software Foundation. Datarace on org.apache. catalina.loader.webappclassloader. https://issues.apache. org/bugzilla/show_bug.cgi?id=37458.

[4] K. Asrigo, L. Litty, and D. Lie. Using VMM-based Sensors to Monitor Honeypots. In *Proceedings of the 2nd International Conference on Virtual Execution Environments (VEE)*, pages 13–23, Ottawa, Ontario, Canada, 2006.

[5] T. Ball, E. Bounimova, B. Cook, V. Levin, J. Lichtenberg, C. McGarvey, B. Ondrusek, S. K. Rajamani, and A. Ustuner. Thorough Static Analysis of Device Drivers. In *Proceedings of the 1st ACM SIGOPS European Conference on Computer Systems (EuroSys)*, pages 73–85, Leuven, Belgium, 2006.

[6] S. Bhansali, W.-K. Chen, S. de Jong, A. Edwards, R. Murray, M. Drinić, D. Mihočka, and J. Chau. Framework for Instruction-level Tracing and Analysis of Program Executions. In *Proceedings of the 2nd International Conference on Virtual Execution Environments (VEE)*, pages 154–163, Ottawa, Ontario, Canada, 2006.

[7] M. D. Bond, K. E. Coons, and K. S. McKinley. PACER: Proportional Detection of Data Races. In *Proceedings of the ACM SIGPLAN Conference on Programming Language Design and Implementation (PLDI)*, pages 255–268, Toronto, Ontario, Canada, 2010.

[8] D. Brylow, N. Damgaard, and J. Palsberg. Static Checking of Interrupt-driven Software. In *Proceedings of the 23rd International Conference on Software Engineering (ICSE)*, pages 47–56, Toronto, Ontario, Canada, 2001.

[9] C. Cadar, D. Dunbar, and D. Engler. KLEE: Unassisted and Automatic Generation of High-Coverage Tests for Complex Systems Programs. In *Proceedings of the 8th USENIX conference on Operating Systems Design and Implementation (OSDI)*, pages 209–224, San Diego, California, 2008.

[10] Canonical Ltd. Launchpad: data-races-implementation sql crash. https://bugs.launchpad.net/f-4d-cb/+bug/516622.

[11] R. H. Carver and K.-C. Tai. Replay and Testing for Concurrent Programs. *IEEE Software*, 8:66–74, March 1991.

[12] M. Chang, E. Smith, R. Reitmaier, M. Bebenita, A. Gal, C. Wimmer, B. Eich, and M. Franz. Tracing for Web 3.0: Trace Compilation for the Next Generation Web Applications. In *Proceedings of the 2009 ACM SIGPLAN/SIGOPS International Conference on Virtual Execution Environments (VEE)*, pages 71–80, Washington, DC, USA, 2009.

[13] J. Chen and S. MacDonald. Testing Concurrent Programs Using Value Schedules. In *Proceedings of the Twenty-Second IEEE/ACM International Conference on Automated Software Engineering (ASE)*, pages 313–322, Atlanta, Georgia, USA, 2007.

[14] J. Chow, T. Garfinkel, and P. M. Chen. Decoupling dynamic program analysis from execution in virtual environments. In *USENIX 2008 Annual Technical Conference on Annual Technical Conference*, 2008.

[15] J. Corbet, A. Rubini, and G. Kroah-Hartman. *Linux Device Drivers, 3rd Edition*. O'Reilly and Associates, 2005.

[16] M. B. Dwyer and L. A. Clarke. Data Flow Analysis for Verifying Properties of Concurrent Programs. In *Proceedings of the 2nd ACM SIGSOFT Symposium on Foundations of Software Engineering (FSE)*, pages 62–75, New Orleans, Louisiana, 1994.

[17] EETIMES. Five top causes of nasty bugs. Web page. http://www.eetimes.com/design/embedded/4008917/Five-top-causes-of-nasty-embedded-software-bugs.

[18] J. Engblom. Virtutech device modeling language. White-Paper, 2009. http://www.virtutech.com/files/whitepapers/wp-dml-2009-03-30-letter.pdf.

[19] D. Engler, B. Chelf, A. Chou, and S. Hallem. Checking System Rules Using System-specific, Programmer-written Compiler Extensions. In *Proceedings of the 4th Symposium on Operating System Design & Implementation (OSDI)*, pages 1–16, San Diego, California, 2000.

[20] C. Flanagan and S. N. Freund. FastTrack: Efficient and Precise Dynamic Race Detection. In *Proceedings of the 2009 ACM SIGPLAN Conference on Programming language Design and Implementation (PLDI)*, pages 121–133, Dublin, Ireland, 2009.

[21] O. Goh and Y.-H. Lee. Schedulable Online Testing Framework for Real-time Embedded Applications in VM. In *Proceedings of the 2007 International Conference on Embedded and Ubiquitous Computing (EUC)*, pages 730–741, Taipei, Taiwan, 2007.

[22] G. Gracioli and S. Fischmeister. Tracing Interrupts in Embedded Software. In *Proceedings of the 2009 ACM SIGPLAN/SIGBED Conference on Languages, Compilers, and Tools for Embedded Systems (LCTES)*, pages 137–146, Dublin, Ireland, 2009.

[23] C. Haggstrom. *Detection of Memory Allocation Bugs on System Level*. PhD thesis, Umea University, Sweden, 2005. Adviser-Mikael Rannar.

[24] M. Higashi, T. Yamamoto, Y. Hayase, T. Ishio, and K. Inoue. An Effective Method to Control Interrupt Handler for Data Race Detection. In *Proceedings of the 5th Workshop on Automation of Software Test (AST)*, pages 79–86, Cape Town, South Africa, 2010.

[25] D. Hovemeyer and W. Pugh. Finding Concurrency Bugs in Java. In *In Proceedings of the PODC Workshop on Concurrency and Synchronization in Java Programs*, Newfoundland, Canada, 2004.

[26] I. Jackson. IRQ handling race and spurious IIR read in 8250.c. Web page. https://lkml.org/lkml/2009/3/12/379.

[27] I. van Lil. Serial: UART_BUG_TXEN race conditions. Web page. http://lkml.org/lkml/2006/6/28/81.

[28] P. Joshi, M. Naik, C.-S. Park, and K. Sen. CalFuzzer: An Extensible Active Testing Framework for Concurrent Programs. In *Proceedings of the 21st International Conference on Computer Aided Verification (CAV)*, pages 675–681, Grenoble, France, 2009.

[29] V. Kahlon, Y. Yang, S. Sankaranarayanan, and A. Gupta. Fast and Accurate Static Data-race Detection for Concurrent Programs. In *Proceedings of the 19th International Conference on Computer Aided Verification (CAV)*, pages 226–239, Berlin, Germany, 2007.

[30] Kernel Trap. deadlock in 3c59x driver. Web page. http://git.kernel.org/?p=linux/kernel/git/torvalds/linux-2.6.git;a=commit;h=4bf3631cdb012591667ab927fcd7719d92837833.

[31] T. Koju, S. Takada, and N. Doi. An Efficient and Generic Reversible Debugger using the Virtual Machine Based Approach. In *Proceedings of the 1st ACM/USENIX International Conference on Virtual Execution Environments (VEE)*, pages 79–88, Chicago, IL, 2005.

[32] K. Kourai and S. Chiba. HyperSpector: Virtual Distributed Monitoring Environments for Secure Intrusion Detection. In *Proceedings of the 1st ACM/USENIX International Conference on Virtual Execution Environments (VEE)*, pages 197–207, Chicago, IL, 2005.

[33] Z. Lai, S. C. Cheung, and W. K. Chan. Inter-context Control-flow and Data-flow Test Adequacy Criteria for nesC Applications. In *Proceedings of the International Symposium on Foundations of Software Engineering (FSE)*, pages 94–104, Atlanta, Georgia, 2008.

[34] Liang T. Chen. The Challenge of Race Conditions in Parallel Programming. http://developers.sun.com/solaris/articles/raceconditions.html.

[35] O. Lichtenstein and A. Pnueli. Checking that Finite State Concurrent Programs Satisfy their Linear Specification. In *Proceedings of the ACM SIGACT-SIGPLAN Symposium on Principles of Programming Languages (POPL)*, pages 97–107, New Orleans, Louisiana, 1985.

[36] C.-S. Park and K. Sen. Randomized Active Atomicity Violation Detection in Concurrent Programs. In *Proceedings of the 16th ACM SIGSOFT International Symposium on Foundations of Software Engineering (FSE)*, pages 135–145, Atlanta, Georgia, 2008.

[37] A. Pohle, B. Döbel, M. Roitzsch, and H. Härtig. Capability Wrangling Made Easy: Debugging on a Microkernel with Valgrind. In *Proceedings of the 6th ACM SIGPLAN/SIGOPS International Conference on Virtual Execution Environments (VEE)*, pages 3–12, Pittsburgh, Pennsylvania, USA, 2010.

[38] J. Regehr. Random Testing of Interrupt-driven Software. In *Proceedings of the 5th ACM International Conference on Embedded Software (EMSOFT)*, pages 290–298, Jersey City, NJ, USA, 2005.

[39] S. Savage, M. Burrows, G. Nelson, P. Sobalvarro, and T. Anderson. Eraser: A Dynamic Data Race Detector for Multithreaded Programs. *ACM Transactions on Computer Systems*, 15(4):391–411, 1997.

[40] B. Schlich, T. Noll, J. Brauer, and L. Brutschy. Reduction of Interrupt Handler Executions for Model Checking Embedded Software. In *Proceedings of the 5th international Haifa Verification Conference on Hardware and Software: Verification and Testing (HVC)*, pages 5–20, Haifa, Israel, 2011.

[41] K. Sen. Race Directed Random Testing of Concurrent Programs. In *Proceedings of the 2008 ACM SIGPLAN Conference on Programming Language Design and Implementation (PLDI)*, pages 11–21, Tucson, AZ, USA, 2008.

[42] K. Sen, D. Marinov, and G. Agha. CUTE: A Concolic Unit Testing Engine for C. In *Proceedings of the 13th ACM SIGSOFT International Symposium on Foundations of Software Engineering*, pages 263–272, Lisbon, Portugal, 2005.

[43] J. Takalo, J. Kaariainen, P. Parviainen, and T. Ihme. Challenges of Software-Hardware Codesign. White Paper, 2007. http://www.vtt.fi/inf/pdf/workingpapers/2008/W91.pdf.

[44] L. Tan, Y. Zhou, and Y. Padioleau. aComment: Mining Annotations from Comments and Code to Detect Interrupt Related Concurrency Bugs. In *Proceeding of the 33rd International Conference on Software Engineering (ICSE)*, pages 11–20, Waikiki, Honolulu, HI, USA, 2011.

[45] Wind River. Wind River Simics. Web-page, 2011. http://www.simics.net.

[46] J. W. Voung, R. Jhala, and S. Lerner. RELAY: Static Race Detection on Millions of Lines of Code. In *Proceedings of the the 6th joint meeting of the European Software Engineering Conference (ESEC) and the ACM SIGSOFT Symposium on Foundations of Software Engineering (FSE)*, pages 205–214, Dubrovnik, Croatia, 2007.

[47] T. Yu, A. Sung, W. Srisa-an, and G. Rothermel. Using Property-based Oracles when Testing Embedded System Applications. In *Proceedings of the Fourth International Conference on Software Testing, Verification and Validation (ICST)*, pages 100–109, Berlin, Germany, March 2011.

Swift: A Register-based JIT Compiler for Embedded JVMs

Yuan Zhang Min Yang Bo Zhou Zhemin Yang Weihua Zhang Binyu Zang
Parallel Processing Institute, Fudan University
{yuanxzhang, m_yang, bo-zhou, yangzhemin, zhangweihua, byzang}@fudan.edu.cn

Abstract

Code quality and compilation speed are two challenges to JIT compilers, while selective compilation is commonly used to trade-off these two issues. Meanwhile, with more and more Java applications running in mobile devices, selective compilation meets many problems. Since these applications always have flat execution profile and short live time, a lightweight JIT technique without losing code quality is extremely needed. However, the overhead of compiling stack-based Java bytecode to heterogeneous register-based machine code is significant in embedded devices. This paper presents a fast and effective JIT technique for mobile devices, building on a register-based Java bytecode format which is more similar to the underlying machine architecture.

Through a comprehensive study on the characteristics of Java applications, we observe that virtual registers used by more than 90% Java methods can be directly fulfilled by 11 physical registers. Based on this observation, this paper proposes *Swift*, a novel JIT compiler on register-based bytecode, which generates native code for RISC machines. After mapping virtual registers to physical registers, the code is generated efficiently by looking up a translation table. And the code quality is guaranteed by the static compiler which is used to generate register-based bytecode. Besides, we design two lightweight optimizations and an efficient code unloader to make *Swift* more suitable for embedded environment. As the prevalence of Android, a prototype of *Swift* is implemented upon DEX bytecode which is the official distribution format of Android applications.

Swift is evaluated with three benchmarks (SPECjvm98, EmbeddedCaffeineMark3 and JemBench2) on two different ARM SOCs: S3C6410 (armv6) and OMAP3530 (armv7). The results show that *Swift* achieves a speedup of 3.13 over the best-performing interpreter on the selected benchmarks. Compared with the state-of-the-art JIT compiler in Android, JITC-Droid, *Swift* achieves a speedup of 1.42.

Categories and Subject Descriptors D.3 [*Software*]: Programming Languages; D.3.4 [*Programming Languages*]: Processors—compilers, run-time environments, code generation

General Terms Performance, Language, Design

Keywords Register-based Bytecode, Just-In-Time Compiler, Embedded JVM, Android

VEE'12. March 3–4, 2012, London, England, UK.

1. Introduction

The widespread of Internet has given people access to information in an easier way, while the technology of mobile computing helps to achieve this on a level never experienced before. Mobile devices as simple as mobile phones and as complex as mobile internet devices with various network connections and all kinds of sensors (such as cameras, GPS, near-field communication and accelerometers, etc) are the current computing wave, competing heavily with desktops and laptops for market and popularity. As a widely anticipated open source operating system (OS) for mobile devices, Android runs on diverse devices, such as phones, tablet PCs, netbooks, etc. Taken Java's portability and its large community into account, Android OS and its applications are implemented in Java language. Programmers can easily develop powerful and rich applications for these kinds of devices without concerning their architectures and configurations.

To be machine-independent, Java is compiled into a portable instruction format called bytecode [18]. When Java is proposed by Sun, it mainly targets client applications running in the browser, so it uses a stack-based bytecode which is more compact, minimizing the consumption of network bandwidth. However, the mismatch between the stack-based architecture of Java virtual machine (JVM) and underlying register-based architecture commonly found in mobile devices introduces much overhead during just-in-time (JIT) compilation.

To reduce the compilation overhead of JIT, traditional JIT systems usually equip two compilers at least: a non-optimizing compiler which compiles all the methods without any optimizations or only few lightweight optimizations; an optimizing compiler which recompiles hot methods and performs heavy optimizations to boost performance. Due to the compilation overhead, the non-optimizing compiler usually uses a simple local register allocator or just mimics the behavior of virtual stack, sacrificing code quality. Meanwhile, the number of methods compiled by the optimizing compiler must be limited for its significant compilation overhead. When computing begins moving to embedded environment which is constrained by CPU cycles and power supply, a lightweight JIT technique without losing code quality is extremely needed.

In Android, a new register-based Java bytecode format, DEX [1], is firstly used to narrow the gap between bytecode format and machine instruction format. All instructions in DEX bytecode format are designed to directly operate on virtual registers. Although register-based bytecode becomes popular since the appearance of Android, it has been discussed many years ago. In [13], Davis et al. first propose a virtual register machine architecture for JVM and compare the standard Java stack-based bytecode with their proposed register-based bytecode. They find that the register-based format reduces the total instruction count by 34.88%, while increasing the bytecode size by 44.81%. Shi et al. [30] extend the prior work by implementing a register-based JVM and compare the performance of these two kinds of bytecode. They find that the register-based format reduces the execution time by 26.5% on a switch-based C interpreter [14, 15, 27]. Although JIT compilation techniques on stack-based bytecode is well studied, the research about constructing a register-based JIT is still blank. Actually, being much closer to Instruction Set Architecture (ISA) of physical machines, register-based bytecode creates an opportunity to improve the construction of JIT compiler on RISC processors. This paper focus on using register-based bytecode to design a lightweight JIT compiler without losing code quality.

Currently, Google has developed a JIT compiler (JITC-Droid) [11] in Android. JITC-Droid is very similar to the dynamic native optimization system proposed by Sullivan et al. [32] which works in two phases: *trace selection* and *trace compilation*. In JITC-Droid, a Java method is first executed by a very efficient interpreter which also detects the start points of hot traces by recording the execution counter at branch targets. When the execution counter exceeds a threshold, JITC-Droid enters the *trace selection* phase. The trace is selected by a special interpreter and composed of "non-control-flow" instructions. The *trace compilation* phase includes the following steps: CFG construction, SSA conversion, linear-scan register allocation, low IR construction and code generation. This process is very common in the traditional JIT compilers [12, 26, 31] which are proposed upon stack-based bytecode. After the trace is compiled, JITC-Droid will mark the start point of the trace so that the interpreter could immediately invoke the compiled code when the control flow transfers to this trace. Although JITC-Droid improves the performance a lot for some computational benchmarks against the best-performing interpreter in Android, it doesn't utilize the opportunity created by register-based bytecode. By exploiting the similarity between register-based bytecode and underlying register-based architectures commonly found in embedded processors, further performance gains can be expected.

Through a study on the characteristics of Java applications, we observe that virtual registers used by more than 90% Java methods can be directly fulfilled by physical registers. Based on this observation, this paper proposes *Swift*, a novel JIT compiler on register-based bytecode, which generates native code for RISC machines. After mapping virtual registers to physical registers, the code is generated efficiently by looking up a translation table. And the code quality is guaranteed by the static compiler which is used to generate register-based bytecode. Besides, we design two lightweight optimizations and an efficient code unloader to make *Swift* more suitable for embedded environment. As the prevalence of Android, a prototype of *Swift* is implemented upon DEX bytecode which is the official distribution format of Android applications.

Our proposed solution is better than traditional Just-In-Time compilers in the following two aspects. First, *Swift* can generate effective code online without extra effort, because register allocation and some optimizations are performed offline when compiling Java code to register-based bytecode. Second, our solution can compile all the methods executed without any prediction, because the translation is very fast. To the best of our knowledge, *Swift* is the first JIT compiler utilizing the opportunity created by register-based bytecode.

As the prevalence of Android, a prototype of *Swift* is implemented upon the generally accepted DEX bytecode. The major contributions of this paper are the following:

1. Through a study on the characteristics of Java methods, we show that register-based bytecode can be exploited to improve the construction of JIT compiler on RISC processors.
2. Based on the observation in the study, we propose a fast and effective Just-In-Time compiler called *Swift* specifically for register-based bytecode.
3. We implement a workable prototype of *Swift* for DEX bytecode in Dalvik Virtual Machine [10].
4. We evaluate *Swift* with three popular benchmarks on two platforms, including comparison with other two execution engines in Dalvik Virtual Machine.

The rest of the paper is organized as follows. Section 2 introduces register-based bytecode and illustrates our motivation. Section 3 describes our JIT system and its core components. Section 4 details the prototype of *Swift* for DEX bytecode, including two lightweight optimizations. In section 5, we evaluate *Swift* with three popular benchmarks on two ARM SOCs: S3C6410 (armv6) and OMAP3530 (armv7). The related work is discussed in Section 6. Section 7 concludes and makes some discussions.

2. Register-based Bytecode

In this section, we take DEX bytecode as an example to introduce register-based bytecode and compare it with traditional stack-based bytecode. Then through a study on Java method characteristics, we show the opportunity for JIT construction on register-based bytecode.

2.1 Bytecode Comparison

Designed to be machine independent, bytecode acts as an intermediate representation for managed languages. The original Java bytecode specified by Sun is stack-based. In this stack-based bytecode format, instructions operate on two sources of operands: *local area* and *virtual stack*. *Local area* is used to hold local variables of a Java method, while *virtual stack* is the place where computing occurs. Excluding the instructions interacting with VM, there are two kinds of instructions in this bytecode format: 1) data movement instruction which transfers data between *local area* and *virtual stack*; 2) computation instruction which fetches operands from the *virtual stack* and stores the result back to *virtual stack* according to the type of the instruction.

In Android, another kind of bytecode format called DEX bytecode is used to distribute Java applications. To run DEX bytecode, Google develops a Java virtual machine called Dalvik [10]. Different from the stack-based bytecode, DEX is based on virtual registers. The instructions in DEX can be grouped into two categories: 1)VM-related instructions which interact with virtual machine; 2)computation instructions which just compute on the virtual registers. There are about 232 instructions in DEX, and 43 of them are VM-related instructions. The remaining instructions are very simple instructions such as arithmetic instructions, logic instructions, etc.

Figure 1 shows an example of *sum* function and its corresponding bytecode in stack-based format and DEX format. From Figure 1, we can find that in stack-based bytecode, data are frequently transferred between *local area* and *virtual stack*, which is quite inefficient. By contrast, every instruction in DEX directly operates on virtual registers, eliminating unnecessary data movements.

As Android is widely accepted by hardware manufacturers, software companies and wireless operators, DEX is becoming more and more popular, especially in embedded devices. To be compatible with the stack-based bytecode which is the standard format for Java, Google develops a translation tool called ***dx***. It translates several *.class* files into one single *.dex* file. The translation process is showed in Figure 2. When allocating the virtual registers, ***dx*** use a graph-coloring algorithm with unlimited registers and the virtual registers are numbered from zero. To reduce the size of the *.dex* file, ***dx*** also compresses the *.dex* file by sharing a constant pool among all classes it handled.

In DEX, each method has its own virtual register set. The *sum* function showed in Figure 1 has 5 virtual registers and 3 of them

```
int sum(int start, int end){
    int sum = 0;
    for(; start < end; start ++)
        sum += start;
    return sum;
}
```

(a) *sum* function

```
000: iconst_0              //push const 0
001: istore_3              //pop 0 to v3(sum)
002: iload_1               //push v1(start)
003: iload_2               //push v2(end)
004: if_icmpgt 017         //compare start and end
007: iload_3               //push v3(sum)
008: iload_1               //push v1(start)
009: iadd                  //push (sum + start)
010: istore_3              //sum = sum + start
011: iinc     1, #1        //add v1(start) by 1
014: goto     002
017: iload_3               //push v3(sum)
018: ireturn               //return sum
```

(b) Stack-based Bytecode

```
000: const/4 v0, #0              //v0(sum) = 0
001: move v1, v3                 //v1 = v3(start)
002: if-ge v1, v4, 008           //test v1, v4(end)
004: add-int/2addr v0, v1        //v0 = v0 + v1
005: add-int/lit8 v1, v1, #1     //v1 = v1 + 1
007: goto 002
008: return v0                   //return sum
```

(c) DEX Instructions

Figure 1. Comparison of Stack-based bytecode and DEX bytecode in *sum* function.

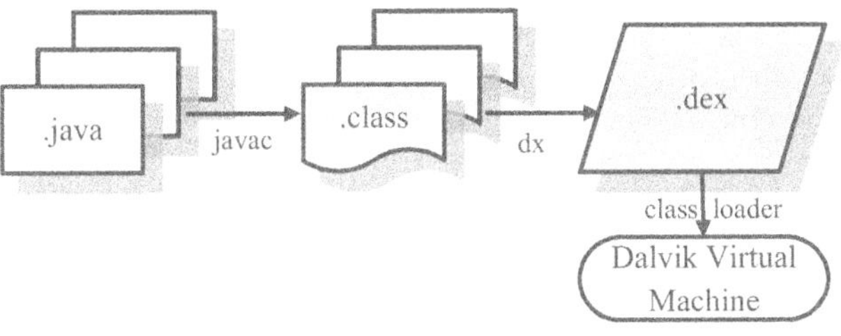

Figure 2. Transform several *.class* files to single *.dex* file.

are marked as *input registers*, ranging from v2 to v4. The remaining 2 registers are marked as *local register* used to store local variables ranging from v0 to v1. Through Figure 1, we find that the DEX instructions are very similar to machine instructions. We will show that this similarity can be exploited to construct a lightweight JIT compiler in the following.

2.2 Java Method Characteristics

The principle of separation logic is widely accepted today, especially in object-oriented programming languages, such as Java. In Java, programs are often divided into many packages, and each package is constructed by structured classes with inheritance. Each class is further divided into small methods to handles one specific logic. This loosely-coupled design makes Java program easy to extend. As a result, we can find that most Java methods are relatively simple. So we assume that a small amount of variables are enough for most Java methods to express their logic. To confirm this assumption, we design an experiment on Dalvik Virtual Machine.

Experimental Environment. The experiment is performed on OMAP3530 manufactured by Texas Instrument which has a 600MHz Cortex-A8 (armv7) CPU core with 16KB I-Cache, 16 KB D-Cache and 256KB L2 cache. We instrument the interpreter in Dalvik virtual machine to record all the Java methods executed. Dalvik runs in interpreter mode on 0xlab[1] Android 2.1 OS which is a customization for OMAP3530. To increase the reality of our experiment, we use six cases (*compress, jess, db, javac, mtrt, jack*)[2] in SPECjvm98 [4] with a problem size of 100 and six Android core applications (*system_server, app_process, input_method, calendar, setting, email*) to collect data. In register-based bytecode, virtual registers of a Java method are acted as variables of this method.

Observation. The *y-axis* in Figure 3 is the percentage of invoked methods which use no more virtual registers than the number specified by *x-axis*. We observe that more than 90% methods called in the experiment use no more than 11 virtual registers.

Motivation. Most embedded devices equip a RISC processor for its power efficiency, simple design and low price. And RISC processors often have many programmer-visible registers, for example there are 16 programmer-visible registers in ARM architecture and 32 programmer-visible registers in MIPS architecture. Excluding some special usage registers, there are still many registers available. Based on the observation above, we can conclude that this small amount of virtual register requirement can be easily satisfied with physical registers without performing any complex register allocation algorithm.

Besides, the homogeneity between register-based bytecode and RISC machine code eases the work of code selection. For example, we can find corresponding RISC instructions for 189 out of 232 DEX instructions. With the adequate amount of physical registers in RISC processors, we can easily allocate physical registers for all the virtual registers in most executed methods and machine code can be generated straightforwardly by replacing register-based bytecode with corresponding RISC instructions. The quality of the generated code is guaranteed, because the static compiler have performed a near-optimal register allocation and heavy optimizations when compiling Java code to register-based bytecode.

3. Register Mapping Translation

In this section, we presents our JIT compilation system for register-based bytecode. We begin this section with a high-level design issues that drive our work and then describe the architecture of *Swift*. The final part of this section details *Swift*'s two core components: *Register Mapping Table* and *Template-based Code Selector.*

3.1 Design Issues

To construct a lightweight JIT compiler with good quality for embedded JVMs, the design of *Swift* takes the following aspects into consideration:

- **Minimal Runtime Overhead.** JIT compilers always add additional burden to the applications. Unlike desktop application and server application, applications on embedded devices such as Android have a short lifecycle. As a embedded JIT compiler, *Swift* should feature lightweight compilation techniques, such as efficient register allocator and code selector to control its

[1] http://0xlab.org/

[2] *mpegaudio* is not included because ***dx*** fails to compile it's obfuscated bytecode to DEX.

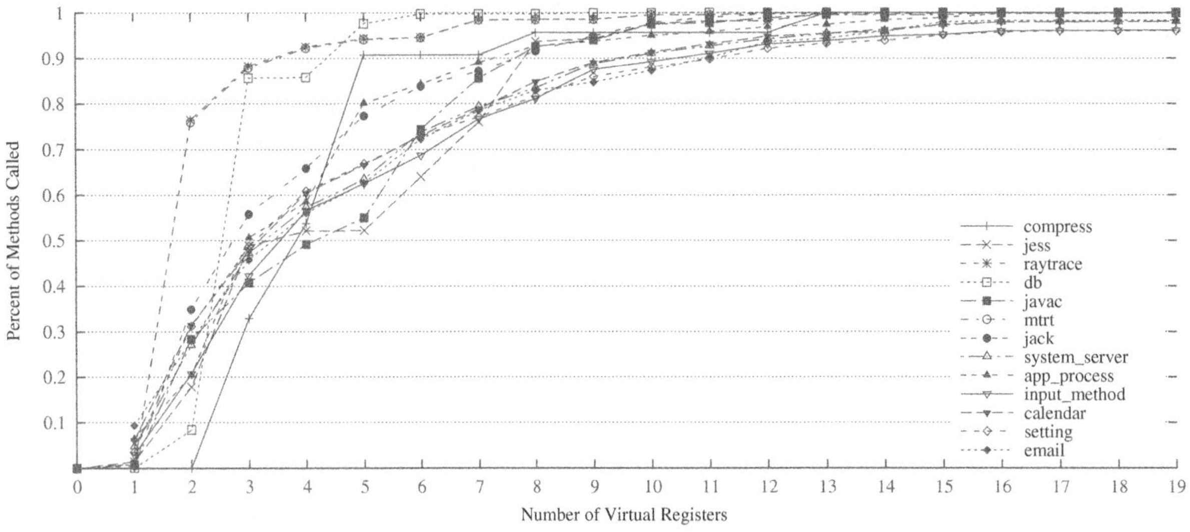

Figure 3. The percentage of invoked methods with varied number of virtual registers.

compilation overhead. Otherwise, the time used to compile bytecode can't be amortized.

- **Simple Design.** There are many architectures widely used in embedded devices, such as ARM, MIPS, etc. The design of a JIT compiler for embedded JVMs should be simple enough to minimize the efforts of porting it to other embedded architectures.
- **Moderate Code Size.** Current embedded systems such as Android encourage cooperation among multiple applications. Constrained by memory, the amount of applications running at the same time is also limited. While *Swift* has to use additional memory to store generated code, memory impact should also be taken into account.
- **Application portability.** Application portability is the most important issue in the design of managed execution environment. The design of *Swift* should not rely on any assumption about the application distribution format. So we don't consider annotation-assisted solutions [23, 24] or hybrid solutions which combines JIT compilation with Ahead-of-Time compilation [21, 33].

3.2 Swift Architecture

Like a non-optimizing compiler, *Swift* translates all methods executed except the *static class initializers* which are executed only once. To reduce the overhead of interpreting a method, *Swift* translates the method before it is executed. In *Swift* there is no specialized translator thread(s) and every method is translated by the thread which first executes it.

To prevent multiple threads from translating the same method which is very inefficient, a thread must acquire the lock of the method before translating it. The lock is represented by an integer and the acquire operation is implemented with atomic instructions. All the other threads must yield CPU if they attempt to translate a method whose lock is acquired by another thread.

Figure 4 depicts the architecture of *Swift*. As it shows, the translation process can be separated into two phases. The first phase is the local translation process, in which each thread translates the invoked method and stores the generated code in a thread-local code cache. In the second phase, the code in local cache is committed to a global shared code pool and the commit operation is protected by a global lock to avoid write contention.

Register allocation and code selection are two main parts in state-of-the-art JIT compiler [12, 26, 31]. Actually, in *Swift* the register allocator is quite straightforward, because physical registers are fixedly assigned to virtual registers by using a register-mapping algorithm. For code selection, *Swift* adopts a template-based translation technique which is lightweight enough for a Just-In-Time compiler. The code is generated within a single pass over the method's bytecode. Without performing any data-flow or control-flow analysis at runtime, the translation process is very fast.

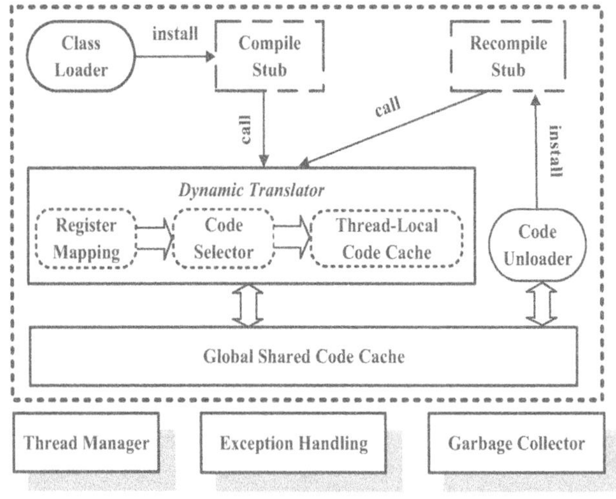

Figure 4. The architecture of *Swift*.

Like other JIT system, *Swift* must cache all the generated code for future use. As a result, the memory consumption of code cache is a critical problem on resource-constrained embedded devices. To reduce the code area, *Swift* features a code unloader which unloads generated code of unnecessary methods. A recompile stub is installed on the unloaded method to trigger recompilation before it is executed later. Besides, to support the execution of Java programs, *Swift* also need to cooperate with other VM modules, such as garbage collector (GC), etc.

3.3 Register Mapping Translator

As we find through the study on the characteristics of Java methods, more than 90% Java methods use no more than 11 virtual registers and these amount of registers can be easily satisfied by underlying RISC processors. Because ***dx*** performs a graph-coloring based algorithm to allocate virtual registers when translating *.class* files into a *.dex* file, it is unnecessary to perform additional complex allocation algorithm on DEX in *Swift*. Thus, a register mapping table is used per method, to record the static relations between virtual registers and physical registers.

Although the amount of free physical registers in the underlying processor is enough for most methods, there exists some large methods which use more virtual registers due to complex logic, bad programming habit, etc. *Swift* need to do special handling when translating these methods. To differentiate these two kinds of methods, we designate those methods whose virtual registers can be completely mapping to physical registers as *regular methods* and the remaining methods are designated as *irregular methods*.

Register Mapping Table. In DEX, virtual registers in a method are continuously numbered from zero, and the amount can be acquired in the method meta info from *.dex* file, so a register table can be constructed according to the register mapping algorithm before traversing DEX instructions. The register mapping algorithm should satisfy following rules and the detailed algorithm used in our prototype can be found in section 4.1:

1) In a *irregular method*, not all the virtual registers can be mapped to physical registers. Those virtual registers that hasn't been mapped are allocated in a continuous area in the corresponding stack frame of the function. This part of stack frame is called *spill area*.
2) In the scope of a method, the mapping from a virtual register to a physical register or *spill area location* is fixed and only determined by the method itself.
3) In every method, any physical register or *spill area location* should only be assigned to at most one virtual register. And every virtual register should have one corresponding physical register or *spill area location* even if it is not used by any DEX instruction[3].
4) In the translation of some DEX instructions such as VM-related instructions, temporary registers are needed due to their complex logic. In this situation, some physical registers (even the ones that have been assigned to some virtual registers) are selected as temporary registers. They are saved to the stack before the translation starts and restored after this DEX instruction is translated.

Template-based Code Selector. After mapping virtual registers to physical registers, machine code is generated by looking up a predefined translation template table indexed by DEX opcode. With this template table, the translator linearly traverses all the DEX instructions of the method and fills the local code cache. The translation can be finished in a single pass without complex logic, hence the translation is very fast.

The template table for *irregular methods* is different to the table for *regular methods*, because in *irregular methods* those virtual registers mapped to *spill area* need special handling when they are used in DEX instructions. To handle such a virtual register, we need to check whether it is a source register or a destination register. If it is a source register, a temporary register is allocated to store its value and used in the generated code of this DEX instruction. If it is a destination register, we just need to store the result to the corresponding *spill area*. Because the mapping from virtual registers to physical registers or *spill area* is fixed, the translation process is still very efficient.

4. Prototype of Swift

Based on the register mapping translator described above, we implement a prototype of *Swift* upon the generally accepted DEX bytecode. As ARM is the most popular architecture used in Android-powered devices, the implementation is built on ARM. However, our JIT technique is not restricted to ARM, it can be used in any other RISC processors, such as MIPS, SPARC. And more performance gains can be expected on these processors, because they have more registers than ARM. In this section, we detail this prototype, including an efficient code unloader and two lightweight optimizations.

4.1 Translator Implementation

On ARM platform, there are many kinds of instruction set supported in different ARM variants. *ARM instruction set* is a 32bits ISA that supported in all ARM variants. *Thumb instruction set* is a 16bits ISA which is more compact. Limited by the instruction width, Thumb instructions can't access all the registers and only part of them can support conditional execution. *Thumb2 instruction set* is an enhanced version of Thumb ISA and supported by armv6t2 and armv7. It is a mixed 16bits and 32bits ISA, so it is more powerful than Thumb ISA and more compact than ARM ISA.

Although Thumb2 ISA has obvious advantages, many chips applied in the market don't implement this ISA. To keep compatibility with all ARM variants while not harming performance, *Swift* chooses to generate ARM instructions. There are 16 programmer-visible registers designed in all ARM variants. Excluding three special purpose registers (*stack pointer register*, *link register* and *program counter register*), there are still 13 free registers(r0-r12) left for *Swift* to map virtual registers.

Regular Method. For every *regular method*, physical registers are assigned to virtual registers from r0 to r12. As other special usage registers, *link register* is not assigned to any virtual register. However, since *link register* is only used in *branch-with-link* instruction and saved in the method entry, we reuse it as temporary register.

```
DEX Instruction:
      000: const/4 v0, #0
      001: move v1, v3
      002: if-ge v1, v4, 008
      004: add-int/2addr v0, v1
      005: add-int/lit8 v1, v1, #1
      007: goto 002
      008: return v0
Generated ARM Code:
      0000: mov    r3, #0
      0004: mov    r4, r1
      0008: cmp    r4, r2
      000b: bge    001b
      0010: add    r3, r3, r4
      0014: add    r4, r4, #1
      0018: b 0008
      001b: //omit the complicated return logic here
```

Figure 5. Generated code of *sum* function.

Figure 5 shows the generated code slice of the *sum* function described in section 2.1. The logic of method entry and exit is

[3] The *sum* function described in section 2.1 has 5 virtual registers, but only 4 registers is used in its DEX instructions. This is because the *sum* function is an instance method, v2 register is used to store *this* reference although it is not used in any DEX instruction.

omitted from the figure, because they are not related to the translation algorithm. They are explained separately in the following. From Figure 5, we can conclude that the generated code is of good quality.

Irregular Method. For *regular methods*, *Swift* only allocates temporary registers for VM-related instructions. However, *irregular methods* even need temporary registers to translate computational instructions for handling the accesses to virtual registers that are mapped to *spill area*. *Link register* is still used as a temporary register for *irregular method*. And we find four temporary registers are enough for the translation of all the computational instructions in *irregular methods*, so three additional registers(r10-r12) are used as temporary registers. As a result, for every *irregular method*, physical registers are assigned to virtual registers from r0 to r9.

```
DEX Instruction:
    add-int/lit8 v15, v15, #int 1
Generated ARM Code:
    ldr r10,   [sp, #12]
    add r10,   r10, #1
    str r10,   [sp, #12]
```

Figure 6. Special handling of *spill area*.

Figure 6 shows the handling for accesses to those virtual registers allocated in *spill area*. The *add-int/lit8* DEX instruction also appears in the *sum* function described in section 2.1. The virtual register v15 is mapped into *spill area* with an offset of 12 relative to *stack pointer*. Before the add operation, a load instruction must be generated to load v15 to a temporary register and in this case, r10 is selected as the temporary register. After the add operation finishes, we need to store r10 to the mapped *spill area location* of v15, because its value has been changed since last load.

Register Mapping Algorithm. In DEX, virtual registers can be separated into two categories: *input virtual registers* which are used to store arguments of the method and *local virtual registers* which are used to store local variables. For any method, we first map *input virtual registers* to physical registers starting from r0, and then the *local virtual registers*. For example, in the *sum* function described in section 2.1, its *input virtual registers* v2-v4 are mapped to physical registers r0-r2 linearly, and *local virtual registers* v0-v1 are mapped to physical registers r3-r4 linearly. Those virtual registers that can not be mapped to physical registers are mapped to fixed *spill area locations*. This mapping algorithm is easy for caller to pass arguments because caller can determine the physical registers assigned to *input virtual registers* in callee before invocation.

Register allocator is critical to construct a fast and effective JIT compiler. In [22] Krall implements a simple register allocator for CACAO JavaVM. Through stack analysis, a register is allocated when a stack variable is pushed, and the register is recycled when the stack variable is poped. Local variables are always cached in registers. When the register is not enough, spill area is used. This strategy is simple but not effective, because it doesn't eliminate redundant data movements between stack variables and local variables. In LaTTe compiler[34], stack-based bytecode is first translated into pseudo RISC code with symbolic registers, and then register allocated to generate SPARC code. The register allocator use a linear-scan allocation algorithm with the local variable lookahead strategy. The authors think this is a good trade-off between quality and speed. Actually, the trade-off made by *Swift* is better than this one, because the register mapping table in *Swift* can be constructed with negligible overhead, and the quality is guaranteed by the static compiler which is used to compile Java source code to register-based bytecode.

4.2 Calling Convention

To support method invocation, *Swift* designs a convention between caller and callee to clarify their responsibilities.

1) **Caller, Before Call.** In Java, the size of return type is 8 bytes at most, so r0-r1 are used to pass return value in *Swift*. Before the invocation, caller must save *caller saved registers* and pass arguments to callee. The *caller saved registers* include r0-r1 as well as the physical argument registers in callee. The amount of *input virtual registers* in callee can be acquired from the *invoke* DEX instruction, so the physical argument registers in callee can be determined by caller according to the register mapping algorithm described previously.
2) **Callee, Method Entry.** In the method entry, callee must save *stack pointer register* and *link register* first and save *callee saved registers*. The *callee saved registers* include the physical registers assigned to *local virtual registers* in callee, excluding r0 and r1. Callee doesn't save r0-r1 because caller has saved them already.
3) **Callee, Method Exit.** Before callee returns, callee must restore *callee saved registers*, save return value to r0-r1, and restore *stack pointer register* and *link register*. Additionally, to cooperate with GC, callee also checks whether there is a GC suspend request.
4) **Caller, After Call.** After callee returns, caller must move r0-r1 to the correct result registers according to the DEX instruction and restores *caller saved registers*.

In this calling convention, responsibilities are clearly separated between caller and callee into 4 phases. There is no live registers across a method call, and we store floating point value in integer registers because DEX doesn't distinguish register types used to store floating point value and integer value..

During the method invocation, caller also need to resolve callee first according to different invoke types. In DEX, the callee of *virtual-call* or *interface-call* can only be resolved at invocation point due to the dynamic binding feature in Java. For these two type of calls, a runtime routine is called to resolve callee every time before invocation.

4.3 Code Unloading

Swift translates every method before it is executed, because the translation is very efficient. Although this translation strategy has little impact on the execution time, it increases the memory footprint, since the size of native code is much larger than that of its bytecode equivalent [36]. For embedded devices, this cost is significant, especially when memory is severely constrained.

Meanwhile, not all the translated methods are always needed after translation. As Zhang et al. [36] shows, for most Java workloads over 60% of methods are effectively live for less than 5% of the total time they are in the system. To reduce the size of code memory, *Swift* adaptively unloads the translated code. This is a compromise between the interpreter which doesn't store any code and JIT compiler which caches all the translated code. If an unloaded method is later invoked, *Swift* will also recompile it before invocation. Since our translation is very efficient, we could trade a few CPU cycles for memory space.

In [36, 37], Zhang et al. compares different unloading strategies including *Online eXhaustive profiling(OnX)*, *Online Sample-based profiling(OnS)*, *Offline exhaustive profiling(Off)*, and *No Profiling(NP)*. The first three strategies try to improve the efficiency of code unloading by finding the precise unloading candidates, while the *NP* strategy is too aggressive to unload a lot of methods that would be invoked in the near future. However, the *OnX* strategy and

OnS strategy suffer from increasing runtime overhead too much, and the *Off* strategy doesn't scale to all applications.

In *Swift*, we don't use a complex but maybe precise unloading strategies for the following considerations: 1) our JIT compiler is designed to be lightweight, a complex code unloader would make it too complicated; 2) a precise unloading strategy always needs exhaustive profiling which burdens the application; 3) the overhead of recompiling a method in *Swift* is quite low, so a precise unloading strategy seems not necessary. In *Swift*, code unloading is performed at GC point. To reduce the overhead of code unloading, it is only performed when the total code size exceeds a user-defined threshold. When GC thread enumerates the stack of every thread, it marks all the methods on the stack by increasing the counter of method. Any method which is observed unmarked twice is unloaded immediately. When a method is unloaded, all the memory resource related to it is released, and a recompile stub is installed. The impact of code unloading is evaluated in the next section.

4.4 Lightweight Optimizations

To further improve the performance of *Swift*, we also design two optimizations which are lightweight enough for embedded devices.

Optimization for *Irregular Method*. As described in section 4.1, physical registers are first mapped to *input virtual registers* and then the *local virtual registers* in *irregular methods*. When the physical registers are not enough for allocation, *spill area* is used. Any access to *spill area location* needs special handling as Figure 6 depicted. This mapping algorithm may be quite inefficient when *spill area locations* are frequently accessed.

To reduce the effect of this problem, we design a lightweight optimization to improve the previously mentioned register mapping algorithm for *irregular methods*. Firstly, a loop detection algorithm is used to detect all the loops in the method. Secondly, we order all the basic blocks according to their occurrences in loops. Finally, we map those virtual registers which are used in basic blocks with high loop occurrence to physical registers, and the remaining virtual registers are all mapped to *spill area*.

Optimization for *interface-call*. In Java, a class is allowed to inherit at most one class, so a *virtual-call* can be resolved by directly accessing the corresponding entry in object's vtable. However, a class is allowed to implement multiple interfaces, so we need to perform a linear search in all the interfaces the class implemented to resolve an *interface-call*. As a result, the overhead of an *interface-call* is quite larger than a *virtual-call*.

We use a class-test mechanism to reduce the overhead of an *interface-call*. When an *interface-call* is resolved, we record the class type of the object and the resolved callee in a cache near the call site. When this call is invoked again on the object with the same class type as the recorded class, then the callee can be directly fetched from the record. If the class type is mismatched, the callee info is resolved through the slow path. This optimization relies on the speculation that the object type of an *interface-call site* is always the same in most cases.

5. Evaluation

Previous sections describe our proposed JIT compiler which generates code by mapping virtual registers to physical register. This section shows our evaluation on it.

5.1 Experimental Environment

The evaluation is performed on two ARM SOCs: the first one is OMAP3530 manufactured by Texas Instrument which has a 600MHz Cortex-A8 (armv7) CPU core with 16KB I-Cache, 16 KB D-Cache and 256KB L2 cache; the second one is S3C6410 manufactured by Samsung which has a 800MHz ARM1176JZF-S (armv6) CPU core with 16KB I-Cache and 16 KB D-Cache (no L2 cache). The reason for including the armv6 based SOC is that there are quantities of armv6 based SOCs already applied in the market, although SOCs based on armv7 are very popular. This testbed configuration represents the main stream of ARM architecture.

Our prototype of *Swift* is developed on 0xlab Android 2.1 OS which is customized for OMAP3530. To the best of our knowledge, JITC-Droid is the only JIT compiler working on DEX bytecode, so *Swift* is compared with the best-performing interpreter and JITC-Droid in Android. To test the performance of interpreter and JITC-Droid, we patch 0xlab Android 2.1 with the source code of Android 2.3.4 fetched from the Android Open Source Project. We use the same source code to build executables for S3C6410 just by changing the building configuration.

For evaluation, three standard benchmarks (SPECjvm98 [4], EmbeddedCaffeineMark3 [2] and JemBench2 [28]) are used. Although the real workload Android applications, such as Angry Birds are the most appropriate to evaluate *Swift*, these applications are hard to measure quantitatively. According to the study in section 2.2, we believe these benchmarks can represent the real workload on Dalvik because they share the same feature exploited by *Swift*.

JemBench2 consists of kernel cases (*sieve*, *bubblesort*), real-world applications (*kfl*, *lift*, *udpip*), and parallel cases (*matrix multiplication*, *Nqueens*, *raytrace*, *AES*). EmbeddedCaffeineMark3 is a subset of the complete CaffeineMark suite, including the following cases: *sieve*, *loop*, *logic*,*string*, *float*, and *method*. SPECjvm98 is not aimed to run on embedded systems, but it provides large workloads for performance evaluation. It is used with a problem size of 100 and six cases (*compress*, *jess*, *db*, *javac*, *mtrt*, *jack*)[4].

5.2 Performance Evaluation

To evaluate the performance of *Swift*, experiments are performed on two SOCs with three benchmarks, and *Swift* is compared with the best-performing interpreter, JITC-Droid and *Swift* itself with the two optimizations described in section 4.4 disabled. We disable code unloading in *Swift* to collect performance data. The impact of code unloading is evaluated separately in the following. All the results are formatted as a ratio to the best-performing interpreter.

Figure 7 shows the performance results. As we expect, *Swift* gains an significant speedup on both SOCs for all the cases in the three benchmarks. Compared with the best performing interpreter, *Swift* gains an average speedup of 1.61, 4.18 and 4.74 on SPECjvm98, EmebeddedCaffeineMark3, and JemBench2 respectively. *Swift* also gains an average speedup of 1.42 over JITC-Droid. The impact of our proposed two lightweight optimizations is obvious. They achieve a further speedup of 1.11 and 1.05 when compared with the best-performing interpreter and JITC-Droid, respectively.

Swift acts better with SPECjvm98 on OMAP3530 than on S3C6410, because all the cases in SPECjvm98 exhibit a large memory footprint (large than 1GB) and OMAP3530 has a 256KB L2 cache while S3C6410 has no L2 cache. Compared with JITC-Droid, *Swift* has a higher speedup on S3C6410 than that on OMAP3530. This is because on S3C6410 JITC-Droid generates Thumb instructions which are less effective than ARM instructions used by *Swift*. Although this makes a little unfair for the comparison, huge engineer efforts are needed to perform an absolutely fair experiment. Actually the experiment on OMAP3530 is fair because on OMAP3530 JITC-Droid generates Thumb2 instructions which has the same ability as ARM instructions used by *Swift* and we can still find a significant speedup of Swift against JITC-Droid on OMAP3530 from figure 7.

[4] *mpegaudio* is not included because ***dx*** fails to compile it's obfuscated bytecode to DEX.

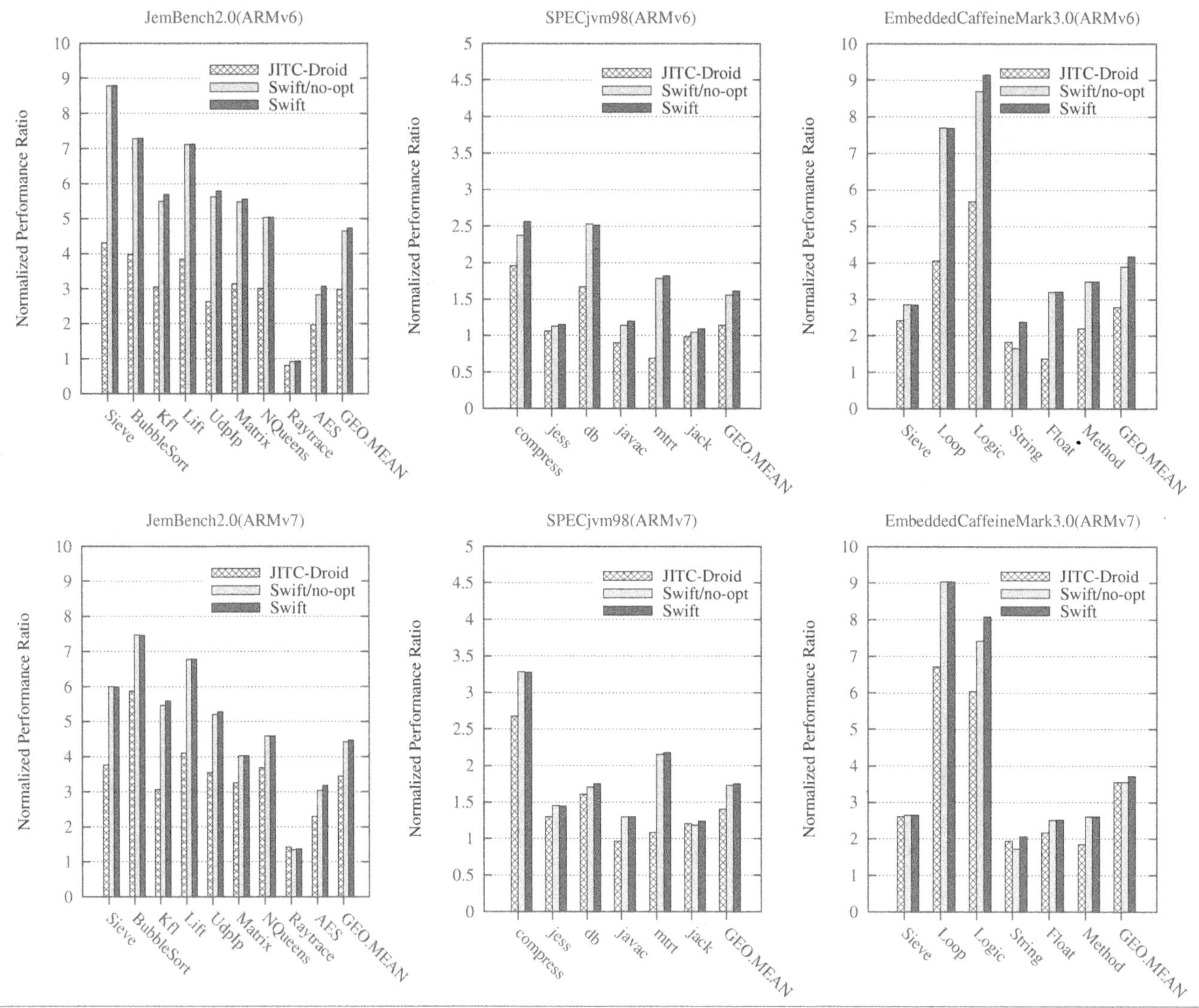

Figure 7. Normalized performance ratio of JITC-Droid and *Swift* to the best-performing interpreter in Dalvik. The results is showed in 6 diagrams of two SOCs and three benchmarks. A geometric mean ratio is presented last for each configuration.

Case	*Trans. Time(s)*	*Exec. Time(s)*	*Percent*
compress	0.117	91.170	0.128%
jess	0.185	77.924	0.237%
db	0.124	64.753	0.191%
javac	0.274	113.124	0.243%
mtrt	0.178	66.280	0.268%
jack	0.175	87.321	0.201%
ECM3	0.098	23.930	0.409%
JBench2	0.092	27.4	0.334%

Table 1. Translation Time of *Swift* for SPECjvm98, JemBench2, and EmebeddedCaffeineMark3 on OMAP3530.

Case	*Trans. Time(s)*	*Exec. Time(s)*	*Percent*
compress	0.257	109.167	0.236%
jess	0.850	85.913	0.990%
db	0.270	69.848	0.387%
javac	2.638	132.372	1.993%
mtrt	0.948	151.828	0.624%
jack	1.154	88.73	1.301%
ECM3	0.433	24.168	1.793%
JBench2	2.184	28.874	7.565%

Table 2. Translation Time of *JITC-Droid* for SPECjvm98, JemBench2, and EmebeddedCaffeineMark3 on OMAP3530.

Translation Time. Table 1 and table 2 shows the translation time of *Swift* and JITC-Droid on OMAP3530. The situation on S3C6410 is similar. Because the cases in JemBench2 and E-mebeddedCaffeineMark3 can't be measured individually, the w-hole benchmark's translation time is presented. *Swift* is configured to perform both optimizations described in section 4.4. For all the cases, *Swift* costs no more than 0.3 secs to translate all the executed Java methods. Translation time used by *Swift* occupies no more than 0.5% of the total execution time for every case. Compared to JITC-Droid, the translation time of Swift is less than 20% of the translation time of JITC-Droid in average. Considering the translation time of Swift and JITC-Droid both occupy a quite small part of the total execution time, the bigger performance gain of *Swift* is attributed to the better code quality. By exploiting the the similarity between register-based bytecode and RISC ISA, *Swift* is lightweight enough for resource-constrained devices.

5.3 Impact of Code Unloading

Table 3 shows the translated code size of *Swift* on OMAP3530 when code unloader is enabled and disabled. The translated code size on S3C6410 is similar. The evaluations in this section are all performed on OMAP3530 if not specially mentioned. The cases in JemBench2 and EmebeddedCaffeineMark3 can't be measured individually, so the whole benchmark's translated code size is presented. The two optimizations described in section 4.4 are not compatible with code unloader, so they are disabled in this experiment.

Case	*Unload On(KB)*	*Unload Off(KB)*	*Percent*
compress	122.442	313.229	39.1%
jess	154.969	549.314	28.2%
db	104.468	336.174	31.1%
javac	484.338	875.173	55.3%
mtrt	142.13	443.936	32.0%
jack	212.583	577.368	36.8%
ECM3	150.483	251.656	59.8%
JBench2	193.34	233.205	82.9%

Table 3. Translated code size of *Swift* for SPECjvm98, JemBench2, and EmebeddedCaffeineMark3 on OMAP3530. The code unloader is configured to unload code when the code size is larger than 200KB.

As the translated code size varies during the execution of the program, the average code size is used to represent the code size in the stable state. It is calculated by the following formula. In this formula, $code\_size_i$ is the size of code cache at the time t_i. The code size information is collected at every GC point.

$$average\_code\_size = \sum_{t_i=t_1}^{t_n} code\_size_i * (t_i - t_{i-1})/t_n$$

We can find that all the cases in SPECjvm98 exhibit a large code memory footprint due to the complex logic of these workloads, and our code unloader saves more than 40% code memory for each case. EmbeddedCaffeineMark3 and JemBench2 don't consume a large code area as SPECjvm98 and our code unloader doesn't save much space for them. In these two benchmarks, GC is not triggered frequently, and our code unloader is performed at GC point, so many translated methods exist too long in the code cache before being unloaded. This problem can be easily solved by adding a unloader trigger before committing local compiled code into the global code cache. As the GC pressure in EmbeddedCaffeineMark3 and JemBench2 is not high, the delay of code unloading doesn't have a significant impact on memory.

Impact on Performance. From Figure 8, we can find code unloading has little impact on performance for most cases and some cases even gain a further speedup on unloading, such as *udpip* in JemBench2 and *string* in EmbeddedCaffeineMark3. We can find some cases in SPECjvm98 have obvious performance degradation when enabling code unloading. This is due to the frequently recompilation of unloaded methods. For example, our collected data shows that in *javac* the translation time grows from 0.27 secs to 5.71 secs, and in *jack* the translation time grows from 0.15 secs to 1.97 secs. This overhead can be easily eliminated by caching unloaded method into the file system and loading back before the method is invoked later. Overall speaking, the impact of code unloading on performance is minor.

6. Related Work

The related work to this paper are divided into three parts: JIT construction, bytecode format and mobile code system.

State-of-the-art JITs. JIT is widely used in managed runtimes. There has been many Java Just-in-Time compilers for the desktop and server environment, such as Sun Hotspot [26], IBM J9 [31], Open Runtime Platform [12], etc. It has been studied extensively in compilation for dynamic scripting languages, such as PyPy [9] for Python, SPUR [7] and TraceMonkey [16] for JavaScript, and LuaJIT [35] for Lua. HotpathVM [17] and Maxpath [8] are JITs that target Java. HotpathVM introduces a tree-SSA representation for fast analysis and efficient enough for resource-constrained devices. Maxpath is a trace-JIT without an interpreter. It uses a method-based non-optimizing compiler to select hot trace and compiles the trace with an optimizing trace compiler. Maxpath achieves better performance than the original method-JIT. *Swift* can use the same technique in Maxpath to improve the performance. Guo et al.[19] study the soundness of traditional method-based optimizations on trace compilation (and vice versa), while Hiroshi et al.[20] describe their work of developing a trace-JIT by retrofitting a method-JIT. All the JITs described above are all based on stack-based bytecode.

Stack-based versus Register-based. The stack-based architecture and the register-based architecture are two counterparts in the design of machine instruction set architecture [25, 29]. As the most popular virtual machine, JVM uses a virtual stack architecture [18] for evaluating expressions, rather than the register architectures that are commonly used in real processors. In [13], Davis et al. first propose the virtual register machine architecture for JVM and compare the stack-based bytecode with the register-based bytecode. The result shows that the register-based format reduces the total instruction count by 34.88%, while increasing the bytecode size by 44.81%. Shi et al. [30] extend the previous work by implementing a register-based JVM and compare the performance of these two kinds of bytecode. They find that the register-based format reduces the execution time by 26.5% on a switch-based C interpreter [14, 15, 27]. Although JITC-Droid in Android works on register-based bytecode, it doesn't exploit the similarity between register-based bytecode and the underlying register-based architecture commonly found in physical machines, but acts like a traditional stack-based JIT compiler [12, 26, 31]. To the best of our knowledge, this paper is the first to concern the JIT construction with the insight of the opportunity created by register-based bytecode.

Mobile Code System. Mobile code is the program that can be shipped unchanged and executed on a heterogeneous collection of processors. Java was originally used as mobile code in browsers to support rich web applications. To enforce safety, traditional mobile code system sacrifices performance through abstract machine interpretation. In [5] Adl-Tabatabai et al. propose OmniVM, an efficient and universal mobile code system. OmniVM uses dynamic code generation to improve performance and software fault isolation to enforce safety. Although the instruction set in OmniVM is also register-based, it is quite different from register-based Java bytecode, such as DEX. First of all, OmniVM has limited (32) registers while the amount of registers in DEX is unlimited. Second, OmniVM only support several primitive types while DEX support complete type system of Java source code and opaque object layout. Third, DEX has many Java semantics, such as thread synchronization, exception handling, etc. Fourth, DEX has no separated floating-point registers while OmniVM has 16 special floating-point registers. From the perspective of intermediate representation level, OmniVM instructions set is much like a common hardware instruction set, and lower than Java bytecode. Observing the opportunity of register-based Java bytecode, *Swift* constructs a lightweight JIT compiler without sacrificing code quality.

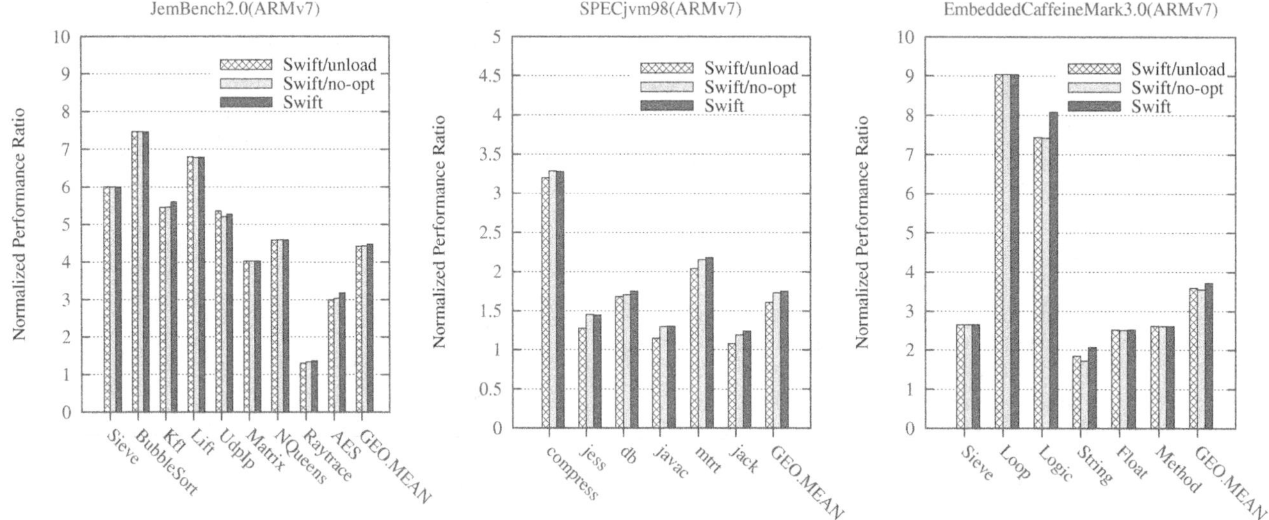

Figure 8. Performance impact of code unloading in *Swift* for JemBench2, SPECjvm98, and EmebeddedCaffeineMark3 on OMAP3530. The code unloader is configured to unload code when the code size is larger than 200KB.

7. Conclusions and Discussions

Since mobile computing becomes a new trend, JIT techniques for embedded JVMs attract more attention. However, JIT compilers suffer significant overhead when compiling stack-based Java bytecode to heterogeneous register-based machine code. This paper presents *Swift*, a fast and effective JIT compiler specifically for register-based bytecode. Taken the characteristics of Java methods and the similarity between register-based bytecode and RISC ISA into account, *Swift* proposes a new translation technique based on register mapping. The translation is very fast and code quality is guaranteed by the static compiler which is used to compile Java source code to register-based bytecode. The evaluation on two ARM SOCs shows the overall performance of *Swift* is competitive, indicating that *Swift* is promising.

Besides, our proposed compilation technique can be further optimized. To support all the ARM variants, current prototype of *Swift* generates ARM instructions which is not the best choice on armv7 architecture. Jazelle RCT [3] is a special processor mode, making small changes to the Thumb2 extended Thumb instruction set. These changes make the instruction set particularly suitable for dynamic code generation system in managed execution environments. It allows JIT compilers to generate smaller compiled code without impacting performance. By exploiting the Jazelle RCT instruction set, *Swift* can gain a further performance speedup with code size reduced. In section 6, we have discussed the possibility of combining Swift with a trace-based JIT. Swift can also be combined with mature staged/selective compilation technique. In such multiple-compiler system, Swift acts as a non-optimizing compiler which compiles all the methods before they are executed and heavy optimizations can be performed by another JIT compiler with a hot method detector. Possible optimizations include SIMD vectorization, method inline, etc. Targeting embedded devices, the detector should have high detection accuracy because the penalty of aggressively optimizing a false hot method is unacceptable and it should not add significant overhead to the application.

Discussion. Previous research [13, 30] has showed that register-based interpreter has performance advantages over stack-based interpreter. As a complement of previous research, our work has demonstrated that register-based bytecode also has advantages to construct a lightweight JIT with good performance. Besides, the register-based JIT proposed by our paper is not only applicable to embedded JVMs, but also can be used as the non-optimizing compiler in a staged/selective compiler system to reduce the startup time and boost normal applications with flat execution profile.

The good performance of our proposed translator shows that, the homogeneity between register-based bytecode and register-based architecture can be exploited to improve the performance of Just-In-Time compiler. We think register-based bytecode is a new responsibility division between online dynamic compiler and offline static compiler, and it is a good balance between Ahead-Of-Time compiler [6, 33] and Just-In-Time compiler which can enjoy good performance without losing portability. So register-based bytecode may be a better choice to distribute applications than stack-based bytecode, especially in embedded systems.

Acknowledgments

We would like to thank the anonymous reviewers for their helpful comments and feedback. This work was funded by Ministry of Industry and Information Technology of China under grant numbered 2009ZX01036-001-003.

References

[1] Dalvik executable format. http://source.android.com/tech/dalvik/dex-format.html.

[2] Embeddedcaffeinemark3.0. Pendragon Software Corporation.

[3] Jazelle rct technology. ARM Ltd., http://www.arm.com/products/processors/technologies/jazelle.php.

[4] Specjvm98. Standard Performance Evaluation Corporation.

[5] A.-R. Adl-Tabatabai, G. Langdale, S. Lucco, and R. Wahbe. Efficient and language-independent mobile programs. In *Proceedings of the ACM SIGPLAN 1996 conference on Programming language design and implementation*, PLDI '96, pages 127–136, New York, NY, USA, 1996. ACM.

[6] C. Badea, A. Nicolau, and A. V. Veidenbaum. A simplified java bytecode compilation system for resource-constrained embedded processors. In *Proceedings of the 2007 international conference on Compilers, architecture, and synthesis for embedded systems*, CASES '07, pages 218–228, New York, NY, USA, 2007. ACM.

[7] M. Bebenita, F. Brandner, M. Fahndrich, F. Logozzo, W. Schulte, N. Tillmann, and H. Venter. Spur: a trace-based jit compiler for cil. In *Proceedings of the ACM international conference on Object oriented programming systems languages and applications*, OOPSLA '10, pages 708–725, New York, NY, USA, 2010. ACM.

[8] M. Bebenita, M. Chang, G. Wagner, A. Gal, C. Wimmer, and M. Franz. Trace-based compilation in execution environments without interpreters. In *Proceedings of the 8th International Conference on the Principles and Practice of Programming in Java*, PPPJ '10, pages 59–68, New York, NY, USA, 2010. ACM.

[9] C. F. Bolz, A. Cuni, M. Fijalkowski, and A. Rigo. Tracing the meta-level: Pypy's tracing jit compiler. In *Proceedings of the 4th workshop on the Implementation, Compilation, Optimization of Object-Oriented Languages and Programming Systems*, ICOOOLPS '09, pages 18–25, New York, NY, USA, 2009. ACM.

[10] D. Bornstein. Dalvik vm internals. http://sites.google.com/site/io/dalvik-vm-internals.

[11] B. Cheng and B. Buzbee. A jit compiler for android's dalvik vm. http://www.google.com/events/io/2010/sessions/jit-compiler-androids-dalvik-vm.html.

[12] M. Cierniak, M. Eng, N. Glew, B. Lewis, and J. Stichnoth. The open runtime platform: a flexible high-performance managed runtime environment: Research articles. *Concurr. Comput. : Pract. Exper.*, 17:617–637, April 2005.

[13] B. Davis, A. Beatty, K. Casey, D. Gregg, and J. Waldron. The case for virtual register machines. In *Proceedings of the 2003 workshop on Interpreters, virtual machines and emulators*, IVME '03, pages 41–49, New York, NY, USA, 2003. ACM.

[14] M. A. Ertl and D. Gregg. Optimizing indirect branch prediction accuracy in virtual machine interpreters. In *Proceedings of the ACM SIGPLAN 2003 conference on Programming language design and implementation*, PLDI '03, pages 278–288, New York, NY, USA, 2003. ACM.

[15] M. A. Ertl and D. Gregg. The structure and performance of efficient interpreters. *Journal of Instruction-Level Parallelism*, 5:2003, 2003.

[16] A. Gal, B. Eich, M. Shaver, D. Anderson, D. Mandelin, M. R. Haghighat, B. Kaplan, G. Hoare, B. Zbarsky, J. Orendorff, J. Ruderman, E. W. Smith, R. Reitmaier, M. Bebenita, M. Chang, and M. Franz. Trace-based just-in-time type specialization for dynamic languages. In *Proceedings of the 2009 ACM SIGPLAN conference on Programming language design and implementation*, PLDI '09, pages 465–478, New York, NY, USA, 2009. ACM.

[17] A. Gal, C. W. Probst, and M. Franz. Hotpathvm: an effective jit compiler for resource-constrained devices. In *Proceedings of the 2nd international conference on Virtual execution environments*, VEE '06, pages 144–153, New York, NY, USA, 2006. ACM.

[18] J. Gosling. Java intermediate bytecodes. In *Papers from the 1995 ACM SIGPLAN workshop on Intermediate representations*, IR '95, pages 111–118, New York, NY, USA, 1995. ACM.

[19] S. Guo and J. Palsberg. The essence of compiling with traces. In *Proceedings of the 38th annual ACM SIGPLAN-SIGACT symposium on Principles of programming languages*, POPL '11, pages 563–574, New York, NY, USA, 2011. ACM.

[20] I. Hiroshi, H. Hiroshige, W. Peng, and N. Toshio. A trace-based java jit compiler retrofitted from a method-based compiler. In *Proceedings of the 8th annual IEEE/ACM international symposium on Code generation and optimization*, CGO '11, New York, NY, USA, 2011. ACM.

[21] D.-H. Jung, S.-M. Moon, and H.-S. Oh. Hybrid java compilation and optimization for digital tv software platform. In *Proceedings of the 8th annual IEEE/ACM international symposium on Code generation and optimization*, CGO '10, pages 73–81, New York, NY, USA, 2010. ACM.

[22] A. Krall. Efficient javavm just-in-time compilation. In *Proceedings of the 1998 International Conference on Parallel Architectures and Compilation Techniques*, PACT '98, pages 205–, Washington, DC, USA, 1998. IEEE Computer Society.

[23] C. Krintz and B. Calder. Using annotations to reduce dynamic optimization time. *SIGPLAN Not.*, 36:156–167, May 2001.

[24] C. Krintz and B. Calder. Using annotations to reduce dynamic optimization time. In *Proceedings of the ACM SIGPLAN 2001 conference on Programming language design and implementation*, PLDI '01, pages 156–167, New York, NY, USA, 2001. ACM.

[25] G. J. Myers. The case against stack-oriented instruction sets. *SIGARCH Comput. Archit. News*, 6:7–10, August 1977.

[26] M. Paleczny, C. Vick, and C. Click. The java hotspot server compiler. In *In USENIX Java Virtual Machine Research and Technology Symposium*, pages 1–12, 2001.

[27] T. H. Romer, D. Lee, G. M. Voelker, A. Wolman, W. A. Wong, J.-L. Baer, B. N. Bershad, and H. M. Levy. The structure and performance of interpreters. In *Proceedings of the seventh international conference on Architectural support for programming languages and operating systems*, ASPLOS-VII, pages 150–159, New York, NY, USA, 1996. ACM.

[28] M. Schoeberl, T. B. Preusser, and S. Uhrig. The embedded java benchmark suite jembench. In *Proceedings of the 8th International Workshop on Java Technologies for Real-Time and Embedded Systems*, JTRES '10, pages 120–127, New York, NY, USA, 2010. ACM.

[29] P. U. Schulthess and E. P. Mumprecht. Reply to the case against stack-oriented instruction sets. *SIGARCH Comput. Archit. News*, 6:24–27, December 1977.

[30] Y. Shi, D. Gregg, A. Beatty, and M. A. Ertl. Virtual machine showdown: stack versus registers. In *Proceedings of the 1st ACM/USENIX international conference on Virtual execution environments*, VEE '05, pages 153–163, New York, NY, USA, 2005. ACM.

[31] T. Suganuma, T. Ogasawara, M. Takeuchi, T. Yasue, M. Kawahito, K. Ishizaki, H. Komatsu, and T. Nakatani. Overview of the ibm java just-in-time compiler. *IBM Syst. J.*, 39:175–193, January 2000.

[32] G. T. Sullivan, D. L. Bruening, I. Baron, T. Garnett, and S. Amarasinghe. Dynamic native optimization of interpreters. In *Proceedings of the 2003 workshop on Interpreters, virtual machines and emulators*, IVME '03, pages 50–57, New York, NY, USA, 2003. ACM.

[33] C.-S. Wang, G. Perez, Y.-C. Chung, W.-C. Hsu, W.-K. Shih, and H.-R. Hsu. A method-based ahead-of-time compiler for android applications. In *Proceedings of the 14th international conference on Compilers, architectures and synthesis for embedded systems*, CASES '11, pages 15–24, New York, NY, USA, 2011. ACM.

[34] B.-S. Yang, S.-M. Moon, S. Park, J. Lee, S. Lee, J. Park, Y. C. Chung, S. Kim, K. Ebcioglu, and E. Altman. Latte: A java vm just-in-time compiler with fast and efficient register allocation. In *Proceedings of the 1999 International Conference on Parallel Architectures and Compilation Techniques*, PACT '99, pages 128–, Washington, DC, USA, 1999. IEEE Computer Society.

[35] A. Yermolovich, C. Wimmer, and M. Franz. Optimization of dynamic languages using hierarchical layering of virtual machines. In *Proceedings of the 5th symposium on Dynamic languages*, DLS '09, pages 79–88, New York, NY, USA, 2009. ACM.

[36] L. Zhang and C. Krintz. Adaptive code unloading for resource-constrained jvms. In *Proceedings of the 2004 ACM SIGPLAN/SIGBED conference on Languages, compilers, and tools for embedded systems*, LCTES '04, pages 155–164, New York, NY, USA, 2004. ACM.

[37] L. Zhang and C. Krintz. Profile-driven code unloading for resource-constrained jvms. In *Proceedings of the 3rd international symposium on Principles and practice of programming in Java*, PPPJ '04, pages 83–90. Trinity College Dublin, 2004.

Facilitating Inter-Application Interactions for OS-level Virtualization

Zhiyong Shan[†] Xin Wang[‡] Tzi-cker Chiueh[‡*] Xiaofeng Meng[†]
shanzhiyong@ruc.edu.cn xwang@ece.sunysb.edu chiueh@cs.sunysb.edu xfmeng@ruc.edu.cn
[†]Key Laboratory of Data Engineering and Knowledge Engineering (Renmin University of China), MOE
[‡]Stony Brook University
[*]Industrial Technology Research Institute

Abstract

OS-level virtualization generates a minimal start-up and run-time overhead on the host OS and thus suits applications that require both good isolation and high efficiency. However, multiple-member applications required for forming a system may need to occasionally communicate across this isolation barrier to cooperate with each other while they are separated in different VMs to isolate intrusion or fault. Such application scenarios are often critical to enterprise-class servers, HPC clusters and intrusion/fault-tolerant systems, etc. We make the first effort to support the inter-application interactions in an OS-level virtualization system without causing a significant compromise on VM isolation. We identify all interactive operations that impact inter-application interactions, including inter-process communications, application invocations, resource name transfers and application dependencies. We propose Shuttle, a novel approach for facilitating inter-application interactions within and across OS-level virtual machines. Our results demonstrate that Shuttle can correctly address all necessary inter-application interactions while providing good isolation capability to all sample applications on different versions of Windows OS.

Categories and Subject Descriptors
D.4.5 [**Operating Systems**]: Reliability; D.4.6 [**Operating Systems**]: Security and Protection

General Terms
Reliability, Security

Keywords
OS-Level Virtual Machines, Inter-application Interactions, Cross-VM Communications, Intrusion/Fault Isolation

1 Introduction

OS-level virtualization partitions the OS name space to form a number of separated Virtual Machines (VMs), i.e., containers. VMs on the same OS share a single OS kernel and the host environment, and each VM only preserves state changes within its local environment. Programs in a VM run as normal applications that directly use the host OS' system call interface and do not need to run on top of an intermediate hypervisor. Accordingly, such VMs have a minimal startup/shutdown cost, low resource requirement and high scalability. Thus OS-level virtualization is applicable for the applications that require both high performance and good isolation [23][28], including intrusion/fault toleration [6][28][29], server consolidation [19][27], high performance system [23][26], distributed hosting organizations like PlanetLab [5][23], as well as cloud computing in the future [3][23].

VEE'12, March 3–4, 2012, London, England, UK.

These system functions often involve a set of member applications. To isolate intrusion or fault, the member applications are distributed into different VMs. On the other hand, the member applications occasionally require inter-application interactions which are essential for their execution, thus communications across VM barriers are inevitable.

The challenge is how to correctly and accurately handle all necessary inter-application interactions while not significantly affecting the isolation effectiveness of virtualization. *Inter-application interactions* represent the operations between distinct applications, e.g., register, notify, request, reply, authenticate and launch. Depending on whether two involved applications are located in the same VM or the host space, inter-application interactions can be ascribed into three basic categories: cross-VM, intra-VM and intra-Host. Intra-Host interactions represent the original inter-application interactions in the host environment and thus do not depend on virtualization technology. Cross-VM interactions need to penetrate the VM boundaries which are normally forbidden by the virtualization mechanism. Cross-VM interactions can be further divided into two sub categories, VM-Host where two involved applications run inside a VM and in the host environment respectively, and VM-VM where two applications reside in two different VMs.

The VM-Host interactions apply to all forms of OS-level virtualization technologies due to their nature. As OS-level VMs co-located on a host share a single OS kernel and the host environment, in order to access the essential system services (e.g., authentication, application initialization) and resources (e.g., Windows registry) in the host environment, an application in a VM has to interact across the VM boundary with applications in the host environment. For example, on Linux VServer [13], an application running in a VM has to authenticate itself to processes *sshd* and *getty*, which are run in the host environment. Likewise, on FVM [28], an application in a VM needs to authenticate itself to a host-resident process *lsass*. Since the authentication operation violates the isolation principle, the virtualization mechanisms drop the request, which leads the application in a VM to be suspended.

The VM-VM interactions are needed for cooperating applications to interact with each other to achieve certain goals. For example, a high performance computing software may distribute a group of cooperative programs into different VMs [9][27] in order to isolate intrusion/fault/performance/function [28] or concurrently foster multiple instances of the same program in a single OS. However, the virtualization mechanism will prevent the required VM-VM conversations from being carried across VM boundaries. Applications running in separate VMs on a single OS might choose to exchange data using network communications to avoid penetrating through VM boundaries, but this would dramatically degrade the performance.

The intra-VM interactions are needed when two involved applications stay in the same VM and thus do not need to penetrate VM boundaries. However, improper startup sequence of the involved applications will cause the communications among them to fail. Accordingly, to prevent these failures, various types of OS-level virtualization platforms, e.g., Solaris Zones [20], Linux VServer [23] and FVM [28], invoke many unnecessary daemons or Windows services when booting and running a VM. This heavily slows down the booting procedure and increases the runtime overhead of a VM. As a result, it reduces the scalability of the OS-level virtualization technology, the main strength against the hardware-level virtualization [23][28]. Therefore, properly handling intra-VM interactions is necessary for improving the scalability of OS-level virtual machines.

In short, cross-VM and intra-VM interactions are often needed no matter what OS-level virtualization technology is used. Without a proper treatment, they will affect the running of the interaction-dependent applications and the scalability of OS-level VMs.

Moreover, as many interaction-dependent applications are important, it is necessary to enable their interactions efficiently. First, some of interaction-dependent applications are fundamental to the running of numerous other applications, for example, *RPCSS*, the RPC binding service; *PlugPlay*, the plug and play service; *NetDDE*, the distributed clipboard service. Second, some of interaction-dependent applications are critical to business organizations, such as web servers, database servers, high performance grid applications, transaction processing applications and enterprise-class applications. When exploiting the OS-level virtualization technology to consolidate servers or tolerate intrusion/fault, these interaction-dependent applications are deployed inside different VMs and need to communicate with other applications across the VM boundary or within a VM.

However, accurately identifying all possible inter-application interactions is not easy, as many applications are complex and their actual interactions vary across a wide range and are undocumented. Particularly on a commercial OS, as the OS and applications are close-sourced and most implementation details are kept confidential, identifying inter-application interactions poses a great challenge.

As far as we know, there is no scheme designed to systematically handle inter-application interactions in the literature. Existing papers concerning OS-level virtualization mostly focus on the general architecture of a specific type of OS-level virtualization [10][20][23][24][28], or exploit OS-level virtualization to consolidate servers[17][20], isolate intrusions [28][29] or build high performance systems [23], but never give a deep insight on the inter-application interactions. A few projects investigate how to improve cross-VM communications for hardware-level virtualization [6][9][27][30]. However, the cross-VM communications between hardware-level VMs only involve TCP/UDP-based network communications instead of inter-process communications that often occur across OS-level VMs, e.g., named pipe and event.

In this paper, we first investigate the interactive operations that affect the inter-application interactions using tracing and reverse-engineering skills. Based on the studies, we ascribe the interactive operations into four types: inter-process communications, application invocations, resource name transfers, and application dependencies. To address these issues, we design Shuttle, a novel approach that aims to facilitate all categories of inter-application

Table 1. Interactive operations affect certain inter-application interactions. Checks indicate the affected interactions.

Interactive Operations	Interaction Categories			
	Cross-VM		Intra-VM	Intra-Host
	VM-Host	VM-VM		
Inter-process communications	√	√	×	×
Application invocations	√	×	×	×
Name transfers	√	√	×	×
Application dependencies	×	×	√	×

interactions by intelligently handling four types of interactive operations while not leading to significant compromise of the isolation requirement of VMs. To demonstrate its effectiveness, we implemented Shuttle under the framework of Feather-weight Virtual Machine (FVM) [28] on different Windows platforms. The evaluations demonstrate that Shuttle can successfully support all tested Windows applications that depend on inter-application interactions with little impact on the VM isolation.

Shuttle is the first approach to handle inter-application interactions for OS-level virtualization. With this approach enforced, multiple instances of the RPCSS, Dcomlaunch, SQL Server and IIS can concurrently run on top of a single Windows OS, which are believed almost impossible previously [28]. As the approach depends little on a specific operating system or OS-level virtualization technology, we believe it can also be generalized and applicable to different types of OS or OS-level virtualization technology.

The paper is structured as follows. The next section introduces the results of our studies on inter-application interactions. The approaches to handling cross-VM and intra-VM inter-application interactions are described in Section 3 and 4 respectively. Section 5 presents the implementation of Shuttle on FVM. Section 6 evaluates the prototype with a group of Windows applications on different versions of Windows OS. Section 7 discusses the applicability of Shuttle techniques to virtualization on other types of OS. Section 8 compares this research with other related efforts in the literature. Section 9 concludes the work.

2 Study on Inter-Application Interactions

As most of the interactive applications are close-sourced, their internal implementation details, for example, the internal logic, kernel objects created, registry entries accessed, etc., are rarely documented and open to the public in the literature. In order to investigate the exact interactive operations, we have spent several months to dynamically trace and analyze their behaviors, and statically reverse-engineer their binaries. Concretely, we take three investigation methods. First, we trace the kernel-level and Windows API-level calls that an application invokes at run time in order to determine the set of resources an application accesses. Second, we use the tool ProcessExplorer[15] to find out the inter-application communication objects an application uses to interact with other applications. Last, we disassemble the application's binary code to identify all hard-coded resource names and API function calls that transfer the hard-coded resource names.

We conclude that there are basically four types of interactive operations affecting inter-application interactions. Without a proper treatment of these operations, the interactive applications would fail or behave abnormally. These operations are as follows:

- Inter-process communications carried between two applications through IPC (Inter-Process Communication)

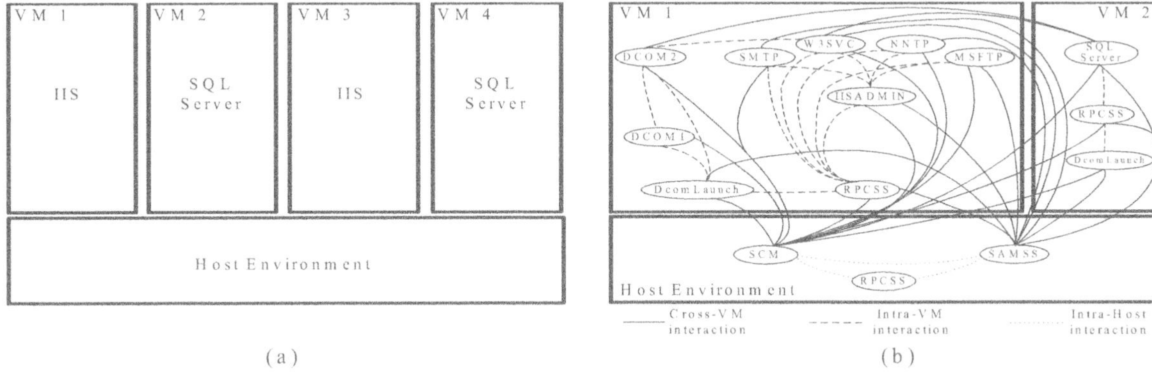

Figure 1. An illustration of inter-application interactions, running two groups of enterprise applications in different VMs on a single OS.

objects. Such operations include register, authenticate, request, reply, notify, exchanging data, etc.

- Application invocations where an application in the host starts other applications in a VM, which include daemons, Windows services, COM servers, etc.
- Name transfers needed for transferring resource names among applications running in different VMs. These names are hard-coded in application binaries and thus may escape the renaming mechanism of OS-level virtualization.
- Application dependencies when the running of an application (the *dependent application*) depends on the running of another application (the *master application*) in the same VM. The master application should run prior to the dependent application.

Table 1 summarizes our investigation results which associate the failures of inter-application interactions with the types of interactive operations. From the table, the former three types of operations might cause cross-VM interactions to fail while the last type might cause intra-VM interactions to fail. Further explanations of these results are presented in Section 3 and 4.

In order to better present the problems and our solutions, we perform a case study on a classical enterprise application in our lab using FVM [28]. We deploy two IIS servers and two SQL Servers in four distinct VMs on a single OS, as shown in Figure 1 (a). The two pairs of IIS and SQL Servers form two websites. Only with such a deployment, two instances of IIS or SQL Server can be separated without interfering with each other though they share a single OS kernel. Moreover, since each application is contained in a separate VM, the system constructed this way has the capability of intrusion/fault toleration. Similar deployments also can be found from Solaris Zones [20], OpenVZ [17] and Fido on Xen [6]. An alternative deployment scheme might place the two pairs of IIS and SQL servers into two VMs respectively. However, this setup not only can not completely avoid carrying out inter-application interactions cross-VM and intra-VM but also is not able to provide isolation as good as the former scheme.

Figure 1 (b) illustrates the detailed inter-application interactions across and within OS-level virtual machines, which only includes VM 1, VM 2 and the host. RPCSS is a fundamental Windows service on the Windows platform that provides RPC/COM/DCOM functions to other Windows services and applications, and is duplicated in each VM. Windows services are long-running programs that remain active without interacting with users, like daemons in a UNIX-style OS. Generally, there are about 100 services on Windows XP and nearly half of them depend on RPCSS. An IIS server consists of five Windows services: W3SVC service for web server, MSFTPSVC service for FTP server, SMTPSVC service for SMTP server, NNTPSVC service for network news server, as well as IISADMIN service for the management of IIS. DCOM1 and DCOM2 are a pair of DCOM servers started by DcomLaunch, which act as main and backup DCOM servers respectively. In Figure 1 (b), various specific inter-application interactions (e.g., register, notify, request, reply, launch and authenticate) among applications are represented by lines among them, which include cross-VM, intra-VM and intra-host interactions. The interactions among the applications are observed as a result of our efforts in tracing the process and performing reverse-engineering. However, due to these complex and hidden inter-application interactions, until now there is no public record showing a successful approach to making RPCSS or IIS run inside a VM.

3 Facilitating Cross-VM Interactions

3.1 Inter-Process Communications

According to the isolation principle of virtualization, the cross-VM inter-process communications should be strictly blocked although some applications may require interactions between each other. However, exceptions should be given to some essential cross-VM inter-process communications as shown in Figure 1 by solid lines. Hence, a carefully designed mechanism is required to facilitate these communications. To minimize the affection on VM isolation, the design should follow a principle: least penetration, which only allows least essential cross-VM communications.

3.1.1 Analyzing Cross-VM Inter-Process Communications

Corresponding to the Table 1, two categories of necessary cross-VM inter-process communications should not be blocked. One is the VM-Host communications between applications in a VM and the host environment, which possibly affect the VM-Host interactions. Such communications are often utilized by an application to get necessary services from core-applications, e.g., authentication and registration. The *core-applications* are the ones that provide system critical services to other applications, e.g., the Service Control Manager (SCM) on Windows, "launchd" on Mac OS and the "klogd"on Linux. They are actually the extensions of the OS kernel and closely tied with the kernel. They can not be duplicated in every VM and should stay in the host environment in order to be available to all VMs. Consequently this type of cross-VM communication is inevitable whenever an application inside a VM requests a system critical service.

The other is the VM-VM communications between applications in different VMs, which possibly affect the VM-VM interactions. In order to provide fault or intrusion isolation for individual applications, member applications belonging to the same system need to be placed in separate VMs [6][9][11][27][30]. Thus, the communications among these applications have to be carried across VM boundaries as exceptions to the basic isolation principle. For instance, storage systems (e.g., NetApp and EMC) may have a group of cooperative programs running in different VMs that need to communicate with each other. Similarly, a graphics rendering application in one VM may need to communicate with a display engine in another VM. Even routine inter-VM communications, such as file transfers or heartbeat messages may need to be performed frequently across the VM border.

Some of the VM-VM inter-process communications can be replaced by network communications, for example, using TCP/UDP communications to substitute named pipes. However, this will lead to a significant performance penalty [27] as the communication data need to go through the whole network stack twice in the same OS kernel. Therefore, facilitating VM-VM inter-process communications is indispensable not only for the successful running but also for better performance of cooperative programs.

Both categories of cross-VM inter-process communications are achieved via accessing Inter-Process Communications (IPC) objects, which have various types in an OS. For example, IPC objects in Windows include primitive ones (such as mutexes, events, timers, semaphores, and LPC) and higher-level ones (such as RPC and DCOM). Moreover, most actual IPCs between applications are undocumented and dynamic. Hence, it is difficult to thoroughly discover all the IPCs invoked by a running process, and decide which IPC should be confined within a VM and which IPC should not.

For the interaction-dependent applications that have well documented IPCs, one can manually give exceptions to permit the cross-VM communications to penetrate the boundaries of VMs. This is why existing OS-level virtualization technologies can successfully virtualize some interaction-dependent applications [23][28]. However, for the ones without documented IPCs, it is not feasible to manually identify all the cross-VM communications, especially for an ordinary user.

3.1.2 Handling Cross-VM Inter-Process Communications

In order to find a proper method to automatically handle cross-VM communications, we performed a study on the cross-VM IPC objects. The result shows that cross-VM IPC objects (e.g., named pipe, shared memory, mail slot, mutex, semaphore and socket) act at the server side of inter-application communications and hence must keep their names static to help the clients to locate them despite that the Id numbers of the objects are dynamic. For example, SQL Server prepares a pipe with static name "\Device\NamedPipe\sql\query" to wait for the connection request from local clients. In special situations, the name of an IPC object may partially change, i.e., with their name strings containing a number that changes over time. To address this issue, we can use a wildcard character * to stand for the variable number in the name string. In addition, a few special types of IPC objects might change names frequently, e.g., event. We can record the name of the receiver application rather than the name of the IPC object to help identify the IPC receiver.

Based on the study results, we devise our first Shuttle technique to leverage the names of cross-VM IPC objects to automate cross-VM communications. We employ *cross-VM endpoints* to point to the cross-VM IPC objects. A cross-VM endpoint in a VM is represented as $e=(n,i)$, where $e.n$ is the name of the corresponding cross-VM IPC object and $e.i$ is the Id of the VM containing the IPC object n. An IPC object is represented as $o=(n,t)$, where $o.n$ and $o.t$ represent the name and the type of the IPC object. The object type $o.t \in \{s,d\}$, where s means that the name of the object is static or contains a dynamic number, and d means that the name of the object is totally dynamic. An application is represented as $a=(n)$, where $a.n$ is the name of the application. A VM is represented as $v=\{i,O,E,A\}$, where $v.i$ is the Id, $v.O$ is the set of local IPC objects for intra-VM communications, $v.E$ is the set of endpoints for inter-VM communications, and $v.A$ is the set of applications of the VM. Accordingly, the logic to handle cross-VM communications can be formally described as follows:

$$
\begin{aligned}
& if((o_{r}.t = s \wedge (\exists o \in v.O, o_{r}.n = o.n)) \vee \\
& \quad (o_{r}.t = d \wedge (\exists a \in v.A, a_{r}.n = a.n))) \\
& \qquad DoIntraVMCommunication(o_{r}); \\
& else\ if((o_{r}.t = s \wedge (\exists e \in v.E, o_{r}.n \approx e.n)) \vee \\
& \qquad (o_{r}.t = d \wedge (\exists e \in v.E, a_{r}.n \approx e.n))) \\
& \qquad\quad DoCrossVMCommunication(e); \\
& \quad else \\
& \qquad DenyCrossVMCommunication(o_{r});
\end{aligned}
$$

When an application in a VM v requests to access an IPC object o_r of application a_r, we first determine whether the required communication is intra-VM by checking the local IPC object list and the application set of the VM. Then, we search for the IPC object name or the application name in the cross-VM endpoint list of the VM. If an endpoint is found, we can quickly locate the corresponding cross-VM IPC object that serves the communication. We deny all other communication requests according to the isolation principle of the virtualization mechanism. The operator $\approx$ represents that the two involved names are two instances of the same IPC object. For example, according to the renaming rule in many OS level virtualization technologies [20][28], a port named p will be renamed in VM1 as *p-VM1* while in VM2 as *p-VM2*, thus we say *p-VM1* $\approx$ *p-VM2*.

3.1.3 Generating Cross-VM Endpoints

The challenge of implementing the technique is how to recognize all cross-VM IPC objects from thousands of candidate ones in an OS and form the cross-VM endpoints in a VM. Based on our studies, the cross-VM IPC objects provided by a type of application are mostly stable rather than changing over time in order to wait for connection requests from other applications. When the cross-VM IPC object name is stable, the corresponding endpoint uses the name of the IPC object, otherwise uses the name of the application.

As manually discovering the cross-VM IPC objects is almost impossible, we develop a tool to complete this task automatically by monitoring and recording cross-VM IPCs. For every type of application, we only need to test it once and can use the result in various application scenarios with different deployments. To prevent potential security issues (e.g., the occurrence of some unexpected cross-VM communications), we run the application only in a secure environment and right after the system and applications are installed. Moreover, to thoroughly discover all cross-VM IPC objects of the tested application, we tried various possible running conditions during the test. When all possible conditions were tested and there were no new cross-VM IPC objects appear, we stopped the test for the application.

Given the set of cross-VM IPC objects of different types of applications, the set of endpoints associated with an application is the union of the endpoints provided by all master applications that the application depends on. An application depends on a master application as it has to access a cross-VM IPC object created by the master application. We say therefore that there is a cross-VM dependency between the dependent and master applications.

The cross-VM dependencies can be manually configured by users. The cross-VM dependencies between core-applications in the host and the applications in VMs are considered as default. Only the cross-VM dependencies between the cooperative applications running in different VMs require configuration. For example, if running a web server and a database server as a pair in two separate VMs on a single host, the administrator can configure a cross-VM dependency between the web server and database server.

However, when an application having a cross-VM IPC object runs multiple instances in different VMs, multiple instances of the cross-VM IPC object will confuse the applications which try to access one of them. Therefore, we introduce VM dependencies to address this issue. A *VM dependency* represents the cooperation between a dependent VM and a master VM. More specifically, an application running in the dependent VM will initiate a communication with the application running in the master VM. VM dependencies are generated by the following two rules:

First, when cooperating applications are deployed into different VMs, these VMs should have dependencies among them. For example, in Figure 1, as the IIS web servers and the SQL database servers are deployed in four VMs separately, the administrator should configure that VM 1 depends on VM 2 and VM 3 depends on VM 4 according to the existing cooperations. Second, the dependencies between the host and any VM are considered as default since applications in any VM require the services provided by the core-applications run in the host environment.

Taking into account the VM dependencies, the set of endpoints of a given application only contains the endpoints of the master applications running in the master VMs but not the ones running in other VMs. If a master application runs multiple instances in different VMs, only the endpoints of the instances in the master VMs are computed into the endpoint set rather than those from all VMs. Thus, the set of endpoints of a given VM is the union of the endpoints of all dependent applications running in the VM.

A question on our cross-VM communications technique is that the isolation offered by an OS-level VM might be compromised. There is actually a trade off between isolation and interaction. That is, virtual machines require isolation while interactive applications require cooperating with each other across VM boundaries. Hence, our technology follows the principle: least penetration, by only permitting the least necessary cross-VM communications. As presented above, this principle is followed by only allowing the communications between the applications that have predefined cross-VM dependencies and at the same time run in the VMs having predefined VM dependencies. This is in accordance with the basic principle of security protection: least privilege, which requires that every program of the system should operate using the least set of privileges necessary to complete the job [21].

3.2 Application Invocations

As shown in Table 1, cross-VM application invocations may cause some application failures. More specifically, some applications need to be cross-VM invocated by core-processes in the host environment, but the OS-level virtualization mechanism can not properly handle all of the cross-VM invocations, and thus such applications fail to be started inside VMs. Cross-VM invocations are inevitable as the core-applications responsible for launching such applications can not be virtualized, i.e., be duplicated in each VM. For example, all Windows services are started by SCM while SCM has to stay in the host as it is shared by all VMs and tightly

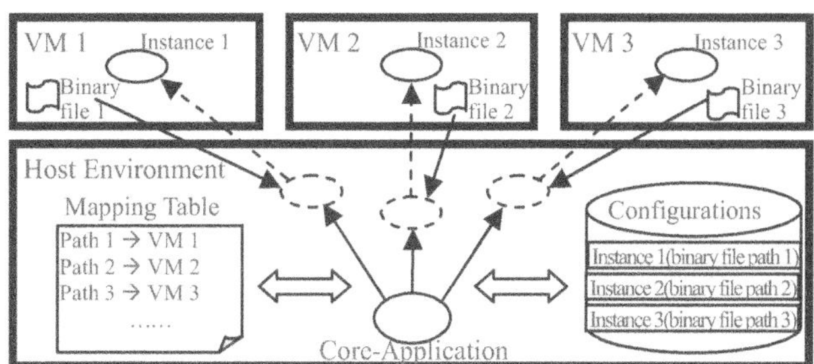

Figure 2. The mechanism for invocating applications cross-VM. It leverages a mapping table to help distribute multiple instances of the same application into multiple VMs.

related with the kernel. Linux, FreeBSD and Mac also have core-applications similar to SCM on Windows, e.g., init, getty and launchd, which are responsible for launching many daemons. Having tight relations with the kernel and providing shared services to many other applications, these core-applications are not allowed by the kernel to be duplicated in each VM. Hence, invocating applications cross-VM is also an issue for the OS-level VMs built on Linux, FreeBSD and Mac, e.g., Jails [10] and Linux VServer [23].

To handle cross-VM invocations, one can modify the application configuration database (e.g., Windows registry) or files to logically add a new instance of the application to be performed in a VM. Every time the core-application receives a request from a VM, it will fork a new process in the host, and then move the new process into the VM. However, as core-applications are not aware of the OS-level virtualization, it is difficult to decide which VM the new process should be moved into after the new process is generated. One can add extra information into the application configuration database to denote the VM that is requesting the new process. However, when multiple VMs simultaneously request to start the same application, we are still unable to correctly distribute multiple new processes into corresponding VMs.

To address this issue, we devise a novel mechanism that is illustrated in Figure 2. First, we prepare a distinct binary file for each application instance which is located in a distinct VM space, create a configuration entry containing the binary file path for each instance in the configuration database/file, and record the binary file path and the VM Id into the mapping table. Second, the core-application in the host environment starts a new process according to the corresponding configuration entry after receiving a startup request from a VM. Third, we intercept a new process and decide which VM the process should be placed into. The decision is made by searching the process' image file path in the mapping table so as to get the correct VM Id. Finally, we move the process from the host to the correct VM.

When starting an application from a VM the first time in response to a user request, Shuttle automatically prepares the binaries, registry entries and mapping table entry of the application. Specifically, when a user requests starting an application from a VM, Shuttle intercepts the request and checks whether the binaries and entries for the application running in the VM are prepared. If not, Shuttle prepares them and then forwards the request to the core application in the host to perform the start operation.

For example, an application CiSvc for indexing files has its image file at C:\WINNT\system32\cisvc.exe. To achieve cross-VM startup, we copy the file to the path C:\VMs\VM-Z\C\WINNT\system32\cisvc.exe that is within the space of VM Z, insert the path into a registry entry used to store the image path of an application to be cross-VM started, and record the path and VM Id Z into the mapping table. When starting a process of CiSvc, we determine the VM that the new process should belong to by searching the process' image path in the mapping table and getting VM Id Z, and then move the process into VM Z.

A special case for cross-VM invocation is that a few applications are in the form of DLL (Dynamic Link Library). A DLL-based application runs as a thread inside a host process instead of an independent process as normal applications do. For example, the DcomLaunch service is a DLL-based application running as a thread inside a generic Windows host process called *svchost*. However, our mechanism still can handle this special type of applications. That is, for a DLL-based application, we record the host process' image file path in the mapping table to recognize VM Id rather than the application's DLL file path, as the thread of the application and its host process always live together within the same VM. However, as multiple host processes with the same image file often foster different DLL-based applications, it is difficult to differentiate these applications' VM Ids based only on the host process' image file path. We found that, to launch a DLL-based application, the host process has to use an exclusive parameter to indicate the running of the application. Accordingly, we attach the parameter at the end of the host process' image file path in the mapping table in order to recognize the application. Thus, we can determine the VM Id by searching both the new process' parameter and image file path in the mapping table, in order to place the new process into the correct VM.

For example, the DLL-based application DcomLaunch runs inside a svchost process with a parameter "-k dcomlaunch". To achieve cross-VM startup, we record not only the host process' image file path and VM Id but also the parameter into the mapping table. When starting a svchost process, we first obtain the Id of the VM that the new process should belong to by searching the process' image path and parameter in the mapping table, and then move the process into the corresponding VM.

3.3 Resource Name Transfers

When an application in a VM performs a cross-VM communication, it might need to transfer resource names (e.g., the application's name) to the receiver application in another VM or in the host environment. In some situations, such names are hard-coded and originated from the application's binary without being renamed according to the rules that OS-level virtualizations often employ [20][28]. When multiple instances of the same application run in different VMs simultaneously send a hard-coded name to the same receiver application, unexpected conflicts or errors will cause the instances to fail.

For example, the RPCSS service on Windows is such an application with the hard-coded application name (i.e., "RPCSS"). In its binary, two hard-coded RPCSS service name strings are used as input arguments by the service management function *OpenServiceW()*. When the RPCSS is required to start in VM Z, it calls *OpenServiceW()* to send a request to the SCM process running in the host environment, using the hard-coded RPCSS name as a parameter. *OpenServiceW()* in turn communicates across VM boundaries with the SCM through a named pipe NtControlPipe. The SCM then checks whether the requested service name is valid and without conflict. If another instance of RPCSS is running in the host environment or in another VM, SCM will refuse the open service request from VM Z since the hard-coded RPCSS name is already registered in SCM. As a result, the RPCSS process in the VM Z will fail.

The basic reason is that, the original developers did not anticipate that a program may be replicated with multiple application names. They simply hard-coded a fixed application name in the program codes and used it as an argument in subsequent calls to Win32 API functions, which send the name across VM boundary through an IPC channel.

On further investigation, we find hard-coded resource names in binary files on other OS platforms, e.g., Linux and FreeBSD. As OS-level virtualization technologies often rely on resource renaming to separate VM spaces [20][28], this issue is not exclusive on Windows OS or FVM. However, existing OS-level virtualization technologies are not aware of this issue, let alone providing any solution.

A possible solution to this issue is to intercept the related API functions and change the parameters that are originated from hard-coded names following the virtualization rules. However, one can not intercept all the related API functions which use hard-coded names. If an application in a VM invokes a function that uses a hard-coded name but is not intercepted, the solution will not be able to rename the parameters.

A better solution is to intercept only IPC related system calls that have a limited number in an OS. Once capturing a resource name in its original form in an inter-process communication, Shuttle changes it following the renaming rules, e.g., appending a VM Id to the name. However, filtering the contents of the inter-process communications to find the names might significantly slow down the system as the communications are often frequent and contain a fair amount of content. Fortunately, Shuttle can differentiate cross-VM from intra-VM inter-process communications by checking the cross-VM endpoints as presented in Section 3.1. Thus, we can focus on the cross-VM inter-process communications. As they represent a very small fraction of the entire inter-process communications in a system, monitoring cross-VM inter-process communications only imposes little overhead on the system. Moreover, transferring hard-coded name across VM boundaries can be only pursued through IPC objects. Therefore, the monitoring of IPC in Shuttle is general and can be extended to apply in other type of OS.

In the previous example, Shuttle monitors the pipe NtControlPipe and changes the application name string that the RPCSS writes into the pipe. Then SCM will permit the open service request with the service name containing the VM Id, as the changed name will no longer conflict with those used in other RPCSS instances running in the host environment or other VMs.

4 Facilitating Intra-VM Interactions

Although intra-VM communications between applications are permitted by OS-level virtualization technology, incorrect startup sequence of the applications would cause an intra-VM communication to fail. This is due to the dependencies among applications in the same VM as shown in the Table 1. In other words, as some applications (say *dependent applications*) depend on the running of other applications (say *master applications*) in

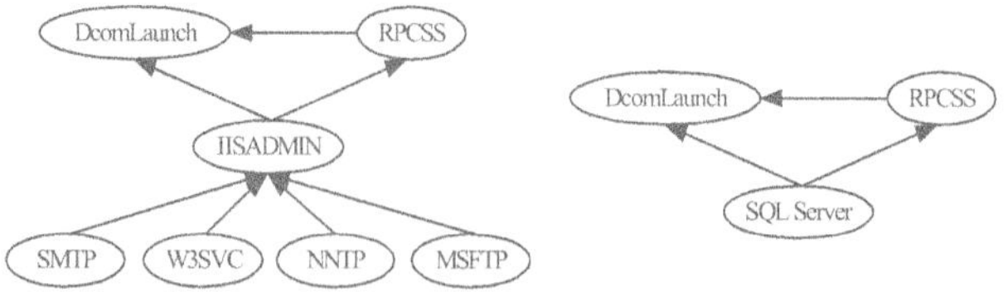

Figure 3. The intra-VM dependency graphs resulted from the enterprise application scenario in Figure 1.

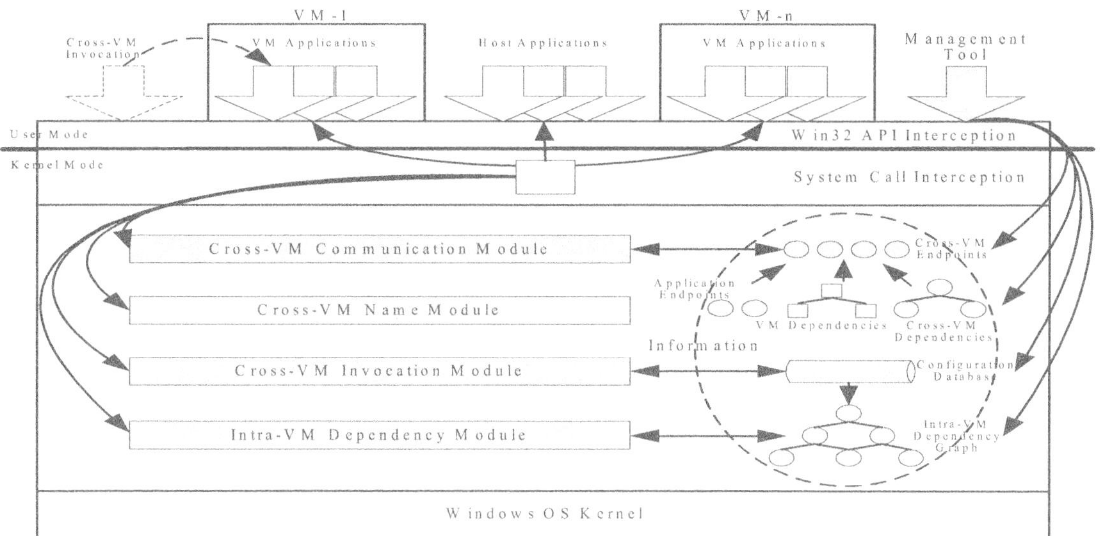

Figure 4. Shuttle architecture consists of four modules and six types of information in the kernel, as well as a management tool at the application level. The four modules handle the four types of interactive operations respectively based on the six types of information.

the same VM, the master applications should be started prior to the dependent ones.

This seems to be a standard OS design issue i.e., arranging for the startup scripts to start applications in the right order to satisfy their dependencies. However, to achieve VM scalability and thus increase the number of VMs that can be active concurrently on a single OS, OS-level virtualization has an extra high requirement on resolving this issue than that of a standard OS. That is, the solution of this issue should help to speed up the booting procedure or reduce system resource occupation of a VM to the minimum degree.

To avoid a possible application failure resulted from an intra-VM dependency, existing OS-level virtualization technologies [20][23][28] start many system applications that often serve as master applications when booting a VM through manual configuration, e.g., Linux daemons and Windows services. These applications then wait for the intra-VM communications initiated by other applications. This will significantly slow down the booting procedure of the VM and occupy extra system resources, e.g., CPU time and memory space. On the other hand, the system applications not being manually configured to start at the time of booting VM might later be required by some dependent applications, which thus causes unexpected failures of the dependent applications.

To address these issues, we propose a technique that starts master applications only on demand and stop master applications upon system idle, so that the master applications no longer slow down the VM booting procedure and unnecessarily occupy system resources at run time, as well as cause the failure of the dependent applications. This will improve the performance and scalability of OS-level virtualization technology.

As a core part, the technique uses an intra-VM dependency graph which can be represented as a set of vertices and a set of directed edges connecting the vertices. A vertex represents an application. An edge between two vertices represents a dependency between two applications. Based on the intra-VM dependency graphs, the start-on-demand and stop-on-idle policies can be specified as follows:

The start-on-demand policy starts a master application and increases it's referred count at the time a corresponding dependent application starts. The stop-on-idle policy decreases the referred count of a master application when a corresponding dependent application stops. Once the last dependent application of a master application stops, the policy stops the master application when it does not need to remain active.

The intra-VM dependency graph can be generated from application configuration files or database. For example, the registry entries `DependOnService` and `DependOnGroup` on Windows describe the dependencies between services and thus can be used to generate the graph. To automate the graph creation procedure, we develop a program to discover intra-VM dependencies among related applications by scanning the related entries in the Windows registry. As an example, Figure 3 (a) and (b) depict the intra-VM dependency graphs of the application scenario in Figure 1, which are generated by our program.

With these two policies enforced, an OS-level virtual machine does not need to start system applications at the booting time but only upon requests. Meanwhile, a VM does not need to foster the idle system applications. Accordingly, the overhead of booting and running an OS-level virtual machine can be significantly reduced, and the potential application failures incurred by the intra-VM dependencies can be avoided.

5 Shuttle Prototype

We have implemented Shuttle on FVM [28][29] to facilitate inter-application interactions within a VM or across VMs. Figure 4 shows the Shuttle architecture. All inter-application interactions, cross- and intra-VM, are captured by intercepting system calls in the kernel and Win32 APIs in Windows system libraries. Shuttle mainly intercepts system calls related to IPC, file, registry and process as they are often invoked for inter-application interactions. Some inter-application interactions that involve a few IPCs (e.g., message) and services can not be identified by intercepting system calls, we thus intercept the corresponding Win32 APIs.

To intercept the system calls, we modify the system call entry point in the *System Service Dispatch Table* (SSDT) within the

Table 2. Testing results of running interaction-dependent applications in VMs with the support of Shuttle. After addressing the interactive operations marked, all the applications can perform inside VMs and cooperate across VMs correctly.

Samples	Interactive Operations			
	Cross-VM Inter-Process Communications	Cross-VM Name Transfers	Cross-VM Application Invocations	Intra-VM Application Dependencies
RPCSS on Windows 2000	√	√	√	
IIS on Windows 2000	√	√	√	√
RPCSS on Windows XP	√	√	√	√
Dcomlaunch on Windows XP	√	√	√	
IIS on Windows XP	√	√	√	√
Mysql on Windows XP	√	√	√	√
Apache on Windows XP	√		√	
Tlntsvr on Windows XP	√		√	√
CiSvc on Windows XP	√		√	√
ImapiService on Windows XP	√	√	√	√
SQL Server on Windows XP	√	√	√	√
Ntsvcs on Windows XP	√	√	√	√
MS Word on Windows XP				√
MS PowerPoint on Windows XP				√
MS Excel on Windows XP				√
MS Office Assistant on XP				√
AutoCAD on Windows XP	√			√
Adobe installation on Windows XP	√			√
MS Office 2003 installation on XP	√			√
Regcmd installation on XP	√			√
StraceNT on Windows XP				√
ProcessMonitor on Windows XP				√

Table 5. Mapping table for cross-VM application invocations. Shuttle searches a new process' image file path within the table in order to get the corresponding VM Id, so that Shuttle can distribute the new process into the correct VM.

Binary file paths	VM Id
c:\fvms\VM1\C\WINNT\system32\inetsrv\inetinfo.exe (IIS)	1
c:\fvms\VM3\C\WINNT\system32\inetsrv\inetinfo.exe (IIS)	3
c:\fvms\VM2\C\PROGRA~1\MI6841~1\MSSQL\binn\sqlservr.exe (SQL Server)	2
c:\fvms\VM4\C\PROGRA~1\MI6841~1\MSSQL\binn\sqlservr.exe (SQL Server)	4
c:\fvms\VM1\C\WINNT\system32\svchost.exe -k rpcss (RPCSS)	1
c:\fvms\VM2\C\WINNT\system32\svchost.exe -k rpcss (RPCSS)	2
c:\fvms\VM3\C\WINNT\system32\svchost.exe -k rpcss (RPCSS)	3
c:\fvms\VM4\C\WINNT\system32\svchost.exe -k rpcss (RPCSS)	4
c:\fvms\VM1\C\WINNT \system32\svchost.exe -k DcomLaunch (DcomLaunch)	1
c:\fvms\VM2\C\WINNT \system32\svchost.exe -k DcomLaunch (DcomLaunch)	2
c:\fvms\VM3\C\WINNT \system32\svchost.exe -k DcomLaunch (DcomLaunch)	3
c:\fvms\VM4\C\WINNT \system32\svchost.exe -k DcomLaunch (DcomLaunch)	4

kernel. To intercept the Win32 APIs, we modify the library function entry point in the *Import Address Table* (IAT) of the application process. Shuttle adds and changes about 10k lines of code on FVM at both application level and kernel level.

The intercepted interaction requests are posted to four kernel modules to make decisions based on six types of information, which are presented as follows.

The Cross-VM Communication Module handles cross-VM inter-process communications based on the cross-VM endpoints.

Table 3. Endpoints for cross-VM inter-process communications. Every endpoint consists of the name of the cross-VM IPC object and the Id of the VM containing the object. The VM Ids listed on the right column indicate the VMs containing the corresponding endpoint.

Endpoints <IPC object name, Master VM Id>	VM Id
<\RPC Control\DNSResolver, 0>	1,2,3,4
<\RPC Control\ntsvcs, 0>	1,2,3,4
<\Device\NamedPipe\net\NtControlPipe*, 0>	1,2,3,4
<\Device\NamedPipe\ntsvcs, 0>	1,2,3,4
<\Device\NamedPipe\EVENTLOG, 0>	1,2,3,4
<\Device\NamedPipe\samr, 0>	1,2,3,4
<\Device\NamedPipe\sql\query, 2>	1
<\Device\NamedPipe\sql\query, 4>	3
<\BaseNamedObjects\DBWinMutex, 0>	1,2,3,4
<\BaseNamedObjects\RasPbFile, 0>	1,2,3,4
<\BaseNamedObjects\SHIMLIB_LOG_MUTEX, 0>	1,2,3,4
<\BaseNamedObjects\ShimCacheMutex, 0>	1,2,3,4
<\BaseNamedObjects__R_0000000000da_SMem__, 0>	1,2,3,4
<\BaseNamedObjects\DBWIN_BUFFER, 0>	1,2,3,4
<\BaseNamedObjects\ShimSharedMemory, 0>	1,2,3,4
<\BaseNamedObjects\ScmCreatedEvent, 0>	1,2,3,4
<\BaseNamedObjects\SvcctrlStartEvent_A3752DX, 0>	1,2,3,4
<\BaseNamedObjects\crypt32LogoffEvent, 0>	1,2,3,4
<\BaseNamedObjects\userenv: User Profile setup event, 0>	1,2,3,4
<\BaseNamedObjects\DINPUTWINMM, 0>	1,2,3,4
<\BaseNamedObjects\TESTMSSQLSERVER, 2>	1
<\BaseNamedObjects\TESTMSSQLSERVER, 4>	3
<\BaseNamedObjects\TESTMSSQLSERVER_MUTEX, 2>	1
<\BaseNamedObjects\TESTMSSQLSERVER_MUTEX, 4>	3
<\SECURITY\LSA_AUTHENTICATION_INITIALIZED, 0>	1,2,3,4

Table 4. Cross-VM names that are derived from hard-coded resource names and sent across VM boundaries by the corresponding applications, and in turn intercepted and renamed by Shuttle. Z indicates the Id of the VM that the corresponding applications live in.

Applications	Changed cross-VM names
RPCSS	RPCSS → RPCSS-vmZ
DcomLaunch	DcomLaunch → DcomLaunch-vmZ
IIS	W3SVC → W3SVC-vmZ
SQL Server	sqlservr → sqlservr-vmZ

The Cross-VM Name Module handles name transfers across VMs. It checks cross-VM IPCs to rename the hard-coded resource names derived from applications' binaries. The Cross-VM Invocation Module watches the processes that are cross-VM started and moves them into the corresponding VMs. Based on the intra-VM dependency graph, the Intra-VM Dependency Module suspends the processes to be started and starts their master applications first. It also monitors the processes to be stopped and requests to stop the master applications. For example, to stop a Windows service, Shuttle calls *ControlServiceEx()* with a control code SERVICE_CONTROL_STOP to request SCM to stop the service.

The six types of information used by the modules include cross-VM endpoints, cross-VM dependencies, VM dependencies, cross-VM endpoints of each type of application, intra-VM dependency graph and configuration database (i.e., Windows registry). We have five key data structures to represent the former five types of information. The cross-VM endpoints are generated by the Cross-VM Communication Module and management tool based on the cross-VM endpoints of each type of application, cross-VM dependencies and VM dependencies, using the method presented in Section 3.1. The intra-VM dependency graph is generated by the Intra-VM Dependency Module and management tool by scanning certain registry entries, e.g., `DependOnService` and `DependOnGroup`.

Shuttle was implemented in two different versions of Windows OS, i.e., Windows 2000 and Windows XP, as FVM was implemented in these two versions. We believe with minor changes Shuttle also can be implemented in a newer version of Windows, e.g., Vista, because the architecture of Shuttle does not contain technical details about specific version of Windows OS.

6 Evaluation

In this section, we present details on the experimental evaluations of our Shuttle prototype which consists of three parts. First, we investigate the effectiveness of Shuttle approach using a number of interaction-dependent applications and an enterprise application as the case to study. Second, we test whether Shuttle will cause a significant degradation of the isolation capability of an OS-level virtualization system. Third, we evaluate the performance overhead of our Shuttle prototype. The test-bed used in the evaluation consists of two machines. Machine A contains a Pentium-4 2.8GHz CPU with 1GB memory running both Windows 2K and XP and machine B contains an Intel Core 2 Duo 2GHz CPU with 2GB memory running both Windows 2K and XP. We installed FVM and Shuttle on both machines.

6.1 Effectiveness

The objective of the Shuttle approach is to facilitate inter-application interactions cross- and intra-VM so that the applications depending on these interactions can perform inside VMs without failures. To demonstrate the effectiveness of the Shuttle approach, we have run 22 interaction-dependent applications in the Shuttle prototype. Many of the sample applications have failed to perform inside a VM without the support of Shuttle so far, e.g., RPCSS, IIS, SQL Server, Ntsvcs, AutoCAD, Adobe installation and MS Office assistant. To sufficiently test all potential interferences among separate instances of the same application, each sample application at least runs three instances simultaneously on a single host. One instance runs in the host environment and the other two run in two different VMs respectively. Table 2 shows the evaluation results. Each row presents an application and the interactive operations appeared when running the application inside a VM. With these interactive operations resolved by Shuttle, all samples tested can successfully run three instances simultaneously on a single host.

Moreover, the sample applications running in VMs behaved correctly, which was verified as follows. RPCSS, Dcomlaunch and Ntsvcs were verified by the successful running of many other tested samples that depend on these three applications. IIS, Apache, Mysql and SQL Server were verified by building and operating websites. Tlntsvr was verified by supporting a telnet site. The installation programs were verified by the successful messages appeared at the end of installation procedures. StraceNT, Regcmd, CiSvc and ProcessMonitor were verified by checking whether they can work properly. The remaining samples were verified by opening and editing corresponding type of files.

As a case study, we further set up an enterprise application scenario that runs two pairs of web server and database server in four VMs respectively on a single Windows XP OS, as presented in Section 2. The applications worked properly and quickly. In the VMs, we performed various operations including browsing web pages, submitting web forms filled, downloading and uploading files. To handle some operations, the web servers cross-VM accessed the backend database server deployed in another VM. By calling the function *DbgPrint()* in the kernel and analyzing the results displayed with a debugging tool DbgView, we obtained the information used by Shuttle to handle the four types of operations that impact application interactions, which are presented as follows.

For cross-VM inter-process communications, the endpoints of every VM are listed in Table 3. In the table, all VMs have almost the same endpoints, except that VM 1 and 3 have more endpoints to access corresponding SQL Server in VM 2 and 4. The * character following the IPC object NtControlPipe indicates an arbitrary number that changes over time, as introduced in Section 3.1. The IPC objects DBWinMutex and DBWIN_BUFFER are specially generated by the DbgView for printing messages. The cross-VM names intercepted and changed are listed in Table 4. For the cross-VM application invocations, Table 5 presents the mapping table that records the binary file paths of the applications to be cross-VM started and their corresponding VM Ids. The intra-VM dependency graphs of all VMs are depicted in Figure 3 (a) and (b).

Therefore, Shuttle can successfully support all four types of interactive operations summarized in Table 1, which in turn supports all necessary cross-VM interactions.

6.2 Isolation

In order to evaluate the impact on the isolation capability of FVM caused by Shuttle, we prepared 19 pairs of small programs to test all possible forms of cross- and intra-VM operations. Each pair of programs is responsible for testing one type of Windows OS object, which consists of a client and a server. The testing results are shown in Table 6. The Intra-VM column indicates the results of the accesses from a client to a server both of which are placed within the same VM. All Intra-VM accesses are permitted. The VM-VM and VM-Host columns indicate the access results from a VM to another VM and from a VM to the host, which mostly are refused. In other words, cross-VM operations are correctly blocked and thus the VM isolation is preserved.

There are two exceptions in the table. One is at the rows for socket, which allows connect and send operations to cross VM boundary, because network communications should be permitted. The other is at the rows for file, registry and device, which allows read operations to be carried from a VM to the host. This is the result of the copy-on-write policy of FVM which aims to avoid duplicating a huge volume of OS objects from the host to each VM environment. However, this should not affect the isolation since any write result is saved separately within the corresponding VM. In addition, for many types of objects, e.g., event, we test open operation instead of read and write, because read and write operations need object handles that are obtained by open operations.

We also tested 30 more individual applications. Every application can smoothly run three instances simultaneously in two VMs and the host environment separately. The applications are as follows: Google Chrome, Windows command prompt, Internet Explorer, Microsoft Clip Organizer, MS Outlook Express, MS Messenger, mIRC, Visual C++, Firefox, Adobe Reader, Bitcomet, Foxmail, Windows Media Player, Putty SSH client, WinRAR, Skype, Windows FTP client, Beyond Compare, Source Insight, Calculator, Utility Manager, Notepad, Minesweeper, Hearts, WebBench Client, Winamp, Internet Backgammon, Diffutils Installation, Registry Commander, fvmsetup.

Moreover, our former test in Section 6.1 also shows that Shuttle can provide enough isolation even when facilitating cross-

Table 6. Testing results of the isolation capability of FVM enforced with Shuttle, which can correctly block general cross-VM interactions including both VM-VM and VM-Host interactions. × and √ represent blocked and allowed operations, respectively.

Objects	Operations	VM-VM	VM-Host	Intra-VM	Objects	Operations	VM-VM	VM-Host	Intra-VM
File/ Directory	Read	×	√	√	Service	Create	×	×	√
	Write	×	×	√		Open	×	×	√
	Create	×	×	√		Start	×	×	√
FileMapping	Open	×	×	√	Window	Find	×	×	√
Data Copy	Send	×	×	√	Mutant	Open	×	×	√
Registry	Read	×	√	√	Semaphore	Create	×	×	√
	Write	×	×	√		Open	×	×	√
	Create	×	×	√	Named Pipe	Read	×	×	√
RPC	Send	×	×	√		Write	×	×	√
Device	Read	×	√	√	Clipboard	Get Data	×	×	√
	Write	×	×	√		Set Data	×	×	√
	Create	×	×	√	Socket	Bind	×	×	√
Process	Open	×	×	√		Connect	√	√	√
Mailslot	Open	×	×	√		Send	√	√	√
Event	Open	×	×	√	Message	Send	×	×	√
COM	Request	×	×	√	Port	Connect	×	×	√
Timer	Open	×	×	√		Request	×	×	√

Table 7. Interception overhead of system calls and Win32 API functions. Compared with old FVM without Shuttle, the new FVM enforced with Shuttle adds less than 13.8% extra CPU cycles for file-related system calls, less than 10.5% for IPC-related system calls, and less than 1.8% for service related API functions.

System calls and Win32 API functions		Native (CPU Cycles)	FVM (CPU Cycles)		Shuttle (CPU Cycles)		Overhead (%)
File	NtCreateFile	334,492	401,931	(20%)	403,297	(21%)	0.3%
	NtOpenFile	167,620	216,895	(29%)	218,435	(30%)	0.7%
	NtCreateNamedPipeFile	183,574	223,960	(21%)	240,481	(31%)	7.4%
	NtCreateMailslotFile	40,790	42,015	(3%)	47,807	(17%)	13.8%
IPC	NtOpenSemaphore	30,234	64,286	(113%)	69,840	(131%)	8.6%
	NtCreatePort	37,241	72,309	(94%)	79,901	(115%)	10.5%
	NtOpenSection	38,134	72,742	(91%)	80,234	(110%)	10.3%
Service	StartService	2,166,808,231	2,166,819,311	(<0.1%)	2,166,818,157	(<0.1%)	<0.1%
	RegisterServiceCtrlHandlerEx	2,865,374	2,865,609	(<0.1%)	2,865,481	(<0.1%)	<0.1%
	QueryServiceStatusEx	2,011,945	2,011,960	(<0.1%)	2,011,959	(<0.1%)	<0.1%
	CreateService	8,264,623	8,406,775	(1.7%)	8,264,803	(<0.1%)	-1.7%
	OpenService	5,490,443	5,490,570	(<0.1%)	5,589,401	(1.8%)	1.8%

VM interactions, as multiple instances of the same application can simultaneously perform inside different VMs and the host.

In short, the three serials of testing results above show that, Shuttle can successfully offer isolation functionality while providing necessary exceptions for essential cross-VM interactions. The major reason lies in our principle of least penetration. That is, we only allow the cross-VM communications with specific IPC object names between predefined applications run in predefined VMs. Therefore, the chance of compromising the isolation of a VM is reduced to the minimum level.

6.3 Performance

In this section, we show the impact of Shuttle on the performance of virtualized applications and virtual machines. As the performance overhead of Shuttle results mainly from executing additional instructions when intercepting system calls and API functions, we measure specifically the interception overhead of the corresponding system calls and API functions. First we disable the FVM layer, run a group of applications natively in the host environment, and count the average number of CPU cycles spent in each system call and API function with the *rtdsc* instruction. Then, we enable the FVM layer without Shuttle, run the same applications in a VM and take the same measurements. Finally, we enable the FVM layer with Shuttle, run the same applications and take the same measurements. Each of the reported numbers shown in Table 7 is an average of the results of 100 runs on machine A running Windows 2K.

Table 7 shows the interception overheads in terms of CPU cycles of a set of intercepted system calls and Win32 API functions, including four file-related system calls, three IPC-related system calls and five service related API functions. The new FVM with Shuttle enforced takes up to 31% more CPU cycles than the native configuration for file-related system calls, up to 131% for IPC-related system calls and 1.8% for service related API functions. Although the per-system call overhead seems to be significant for IPC-related system calls, the end-to-end impact on the overall system performance is much smaller, because IPC-related system calls account for lower than 0.2% of all invoked system calls in our test applications. Moreover, compared with old FVM without Shuttle, the current implementation of the proposed Shuttle approach adds less than 13.8% extra CPU cycles for file-related system calls and less than 10.5% for IPC-related system calls. For most service related API functions, the new FVM is actually as fast as the old one or even slightly faster, because service names used in API functions do not need to be renamed when Shuttle is in place. From these results, we can conclude that the performance cost of Shuttle is quite acceptable.

7 Discussion

As Shuttle prototype is based on Windows OS, one might question whether it is applicable to the OS-level virtualization based on other OSes, e.g., Linux. First, the issues resolved by Shuttle should also appear in other OS-level virtualization systems, because they are irrelevant to specific OS or virtualization technique. As analyzed in Section 3.1.1, Section 3.2, Section 3.3 and Section 4, these issues are actually derived from the nature of OS-level virtualization or applications, and thus also occur in Linux-based virtualization systems. As some concrete examples, there is a list of programs that have problems with Linux-VServer [14]. Some of the problems correspond to the issues resolved in this paper, for example, the problem "OpenLDAP Startup" is caused by application dependency, "rndc" is caused by hard-coded name and "Links inside screen inside a V-Server" is caused by cross-VM invocation. The techniques in this paper should be useful when resolving these problems in Linux-VServer. Second, the shuttle solutions for these issues actually do not depend on specific OS, though we often use Windows OS as examples in order to present the techniques more clearly. Therefore, we believe Shuttle should be applicable to the OS-level virtualization systems on other OSes.

8 Related Work

As far as we know, there is no such a project that can successfully handle all types of inter-application interactions across and within OS-level VMs in the literature. There are three categories of projects close to our work.

The first category is OS-level virtualization projects that include FreeBSD Jail [10], Linux-VServer [23], Solaris Zones [20], Open VZ [24], FVM[28], Zap [16], PDS [1] and Cells [2] etc. These projects successfully partition a single OS environment into multiple VMs more extensively and efficiently. However, very limited efforts have been made on application interactions cross-VM and intra-VM, although they are required by many cooperative applications. FVM [28] hard-codes a few IPC object names as exceptions in its virtualization layer, so that it can partially support the cross-VM communications between applications in a VM and in the host environment. However, it can not flexibly support the types of cross-VM communications that are not hard-coded. Moreover, it can not support other types of interactive operations, e.g., cross-VM names and intra-VM dependencies. As a result, it is able to only virtualize a limited number of ordinary Windows services, whereas, it can not virtualize Windows system services such as RPCSS and ordinary Windows services that require complex inter-service interactions, e.g. IIS service group. To virtualize system services, we propose a service virtualization scheme in our former work [22]. In contrast, this paper focuses on inter-application interactions. As service virtualization also involves inter-application interactions, some issues might be similar. However, the resolutions to these issues are different. Moreover, the most important issue addressed in this paper is on VM-VM interactions, while it was not considered in our former work.

Zap [16] introduces pods, which are groups of processes that are provided a consistent, virtualized view of the system. Processes outside a pod can only interact with processes inside the pod using network communication and shared files instead of IPC. Shuttle provides a possible solution to facilitate inter-application interactions across pod boundary when pursuing a better performance. Cells [2] is a virtualization architecture for enabling multiple virtual smartphones to run simultaneously on the same physical cellphone. It sets up IPC sockets to facilitate communication between VM and the host. Shuttle, however, also address issues related to VM-VM communication, cross-VM invocation and transferring hard-coded names. These extended functions may allow Cells to work in more application scenarios.

The second category of projects similar to our work focuses on how to achieve inter-VM communications for a hardware-level virtualization system. For example, the Xen [4] platform enables applications to transparently communicate across VM boundaries using standard TCP/IP sockets and traversing the network communication path via Dom0. In order to improve the performance of cross-VM communications, XenSocket [30], IVC [9], XWay [11], XenLoop [27] and Fido [6] have exploited the inter-domain shared memory provided by the Xen hypervisor. However, these techniques in Xen intercepts outgoing network packets beneath the network layer, and thus can not handle the inter-process communication (IPC) in OS-level VM as most IPC data will not go beneath the network layer. Different from these projects, Shuttle focuses on facilitating IPCs between OS-level VMs. Moreover, it handles not only cross-VM communications but also cross-VM names and startups, as well as intra-VM dependencies, which are mainly resulted from the characteristic of OS-level virtualization when multiple VMs share the single OS kernel.

The third category of projects is library operating systems [7][8][12]. The idea is that the entire *personality* of the OS on which an application depends runs in its address space as a library. A recent project, Drawbridge [19], shows the library OS can offer better system security and more rapid independent evolution of OS components. As a structuring principle, Drawbridge identifies three categories of services in OS implementations: *hardware services*, *user services*, and *application services*. Then, it uses these service categories to drive the refactoring of Windows into the Drawbridge library OS. Drawbridge packages application services into the *library OS* and leaves user and hard-ware services in the *host OS*. The scheme of Shuttle to handle inter-process interactions across VM boundary can be useful to resolve the multi-process applications problem in Drawbridge.

9 Conclusion

Advances in OS-level virtualization technology have strengthened the isolation between VMs. However, many interaction-intensive applications require penetrating the isolation boundaries to cooperate with the applications in other VMs. In this paper, we make the first step towards supporting the application interactions in an OS-level virtualization system by facilitating four types of interactive operations, including cross-VM inter-process communications, cross-VM name transfers, cross-VM application invocations and intra-VM application dependencies. Specifically, we design a novel approach, Shuttle, that consists of four techniques, each of which intends to handle a corresponding interactive operations. As a result, a number of interaction-depending applications that can not run within a VM previously, e.g., RPCSS, IIS, can now run under the support of Shuttle. Empirical performance measurements on the prototype implementation of the proposed Shuttle approach show that the compromise on isolation are negligible and the additional performance overhead is rather minor, when compared with that of the original version of FVM.

Acknowledgement

We would like to thank our shepherd Galen Hunt and all the anonymous reviewers for their insightful comments and feedbacks. This work is supported by Natural Science Foundation of China under grants No. 60703103 and No. 60833005, US National Science Foundation under grants CNS-0751121, CNS-0751121 and CNS-0628093.

References

[1] B. Alpern, J. Auerbach, V. Bala, T. Frauenhofer, T. Mummert, and M. Pigott, "Pds: A virtual execution environment for software deployment," in *Proceedings of the 1st International Conference on Virtual Execution Environments*, 2005.

[2] J. Andrus, C. Dall, A. V. Hof, O. Laadan, and J. Nieh. Cells: a virtual mobile smartphone architecture. In *Proceedings of the Twenty-Third ACM Symposium on Operating Systems Principles* (SOSP '11). ACM, New York, NY, USA, 173-187.

[3] M. Armbrust, A. Fox, R. Griffith et al., Above the Clouds: A Berkeley View of Cloud Computing, Unversity of California, Berkeley, Berkeley, CA, 2009.

[4] P. Barham, B. Dragovic, K. Fraser, S. Hand, T. Harris, A. Ho, R. Neugebauer, I. Pratt, and A. Warfield. Xen and the art of virtualization. In *Proceedings of the 19th ACM Symposium on Operating Systems Principles*, pages 164–177. ACM Press, 2003.

[5] A. Bavier , M. Bowman , B. Chun , D. Culler , S. Karlin, S. Muir, L. Peterson, T. Roscoe, T. Spalink, M. Wawrzoniak, Operating system support for planetary-scale network services, *Proceedings of the 1st conference on Symposium on Networked Systems Design and Implementation*, p.19-19, March, 2004, California.

[6] A. Burtsev, K. Srinivasan, P. Radhakrishnan, L. N. Bairavasundaram, K. Voruganti, and G. R. Goodson, "Fido: Fast inter-virtual-machine communication for enterprise appliances," in *Proceedings of the USENIX Annual Technical Conference*, San Diego, USA, 2009.

[7] D. R. Cheriton and K. J. Duda. A Caching Model of Operating System Kernel Functionality. In *Proceedings of the 1st USENIX Symposium on Operating Systems Design and Implementation*, 1994.

[8] D. R. Engler, M. F. Kaashoek, and J. O'Toole, Jr.. 1995. Exokernel: an operating system architecture for application-level resource management. In *Proceedings of the fifteenth ACM symposium on Operating systems principles* (SOSP '95), Michael B. Jones (Ed.). ACM, New York, NY, USA, 251-266.

[9] W. Huang, M. Koop, Q. Gao, and D.K. Panda. Virtual machine aware communication libraries for high performance computing. In *Proceedings of SuperComputing*, Reno, NV, Nov. 2007.

[10] P.-H. Kamp and R. N. M. Watson. Jails: Confining the omnipotent root. In *Proceedings of the 2nd International SANE Conference*, 2000.

[11] K. Kim, C. Kim, S.-I. Jung, H.-S. Shin, and J.-S. Kim. Inter-domain socket communications supporting high performance and full binary compatibility on Xen. In *Proceedings of the fourth ACM International Conference on Virtual Execution Environments*, 2008.

[12] I. Leslie, D. McAuley, R. Black, T. Roscoe, P. Barham, D. Evers, R. Fairbairns, and E. Hyden. The Design and Implementation of an Operating System to Support Distributed Multimedia Applications. *IEEE Journal on Selected Areas In Communications, 14* (7), 1996.

[13] Linux VServer, http://linux-vserver.org/Documentation, 2010.

[14] Linux VServer, http://linux-vserver.org/Problematic_Programs, 2011

[15] Microsoft. Process Explorer. http://technet.microsoft.com/en-us/sysinternals/bb896653.aspx

[16] S. Osman, D. Subhraveti, G. Su, and J. Nieh. The Design and Implementation of Zap: A System for Migrating Computing Environments. In *Proceedings of the 5th USENIX Symposium on Operating Systems Design and Implementation (OSDI02)*, pages 361–376, Boston, MA, Dec 2002.

[17] P. Padala, X. Zhu, Z.Wang, S. Singhal, and K. Shin. Performance Evaluation of Virtualization Technologies for Server Consolidation. *Technical Report HPL-2007-59*, HP Labs, April 2007.

[18] PC Magazine, PC Magazine benchmarks, http://www.pcm-ag.com/encyclopedia_term/0,2542,t=WebBench&i=48947,00.asp

[19] D. E. Porter, S. Boyd-Wickizer, J. Howell, R. Olinsky, and G. C. Hunt. 2011. Rethinking the library OS from the top down. In *Proceedings of the sixteenth international conference on Architectural support for programming languages and operating systems* (ASPLOS '11). ACM, New York, NY, USA, 291-304.

[20] D. Price and A. Tucker. Solaris Zones: Operating system support for consolidating commercial workloads. In *Proceedings of the 18th Large Installation System Administration Conference* (LISA), USENIX, 2004.

[21] J.H. Saltzer and M.D. Schroeder. The protection of information in computer systems. In *Proceedings of the IEEE*, 63(9):1278-1308, September 1975.

[22] Z. Shan, T. Chiueh, and X. Wang. Virtualizing system and ordinary services in Windows-based OS-level virtual machines. In *Proceedings of the 2011 ACM Symposium on Applied Computing* (SAC '11). ACM, New York, NY, USA, 579-583.

[23] S. Soltesz , H. Pötzl , M. E. Fiuczynski, A. Bavier, L. Peterson, Container-based operating system virtualization: a scalable, high-performance alternative to hypervisors, In *Proceedings of the 2nd ACM SIGOPS/EuroSys European Conference on Computer Systems* 2007, March 21-23, 2007, Lisbon, Portugal.

[24] SWSoft, "OpenVZ - Server Virtualization," 2006, http://www.openvz.org/.

[25] VMware. Vmware products. http://www.vmware.com/products/home.html.

[26] P. Walters, V. Chaudhary, M. Cha, S. Guercio Jr., S. Gallo, "A Comparison of Virtualization Technologies for HPC," In *Proceedings of the 22nd International Conference on Advanced Information Networking and Applications* (aina 2008), pp.861-868.

[27] J. Wang, K.-L. Wright, and K. Gopalan. Xenloop: A transparent high performance inter-VM network loopback. In *Proceedings of the 17th International Symposium on High Performance Distributed Computing* (HPDC), 2008.

[28] Y. Yu, F. Guo, S. Nanda, L. Lam, T. Chiueh, ``A Feather-weight Virtual Machine for Windows Applications", in *Proceedings of the 2nd ACM/USENIX Conference on Virtual Execution Environments* (VEE'06), June 2006.

[29] Y. Yu, H. K. Govindarajan, L. Lam, T. Chiueh "Applications of Feather-Weight Virtual Machine", In *Proceedings of the ACM SIGPLAN/SIGOPS International Conference on Virtual Execution Environments* (VEE08), Seattle WA, March 2008.

[30] X. Zhang, S. McIntosh, P. Rohatgi, and J.L. Griffin. Xensocket: A high-throughput interdomain transport for virtual machines. In *Proceedings of Middleware*, 2007.

Enhancing TCP Throughput of Highly Available Virtual Machines via Speculative Communication

Balazs Gerofi
The University of Tokyo
bgerofi@il.is.s.u-tokyo.ac.jp

Yutaka Ishikawa
The University of Tokyo
ishikawa@is.s.u-tokyo.ac.jp

Abstract

Checkpoint-recovery based virtual machine (VM) replication is an attractive technique for accommodating VM installations with high-availability. It provides seamless failover for the entire software stack executed in the VM regardless the application or the underlying operating system (OS), it runs on commodity hardware, and it is inherently capable of dealing with shared memory non-determinism of symmetric multiprocessing (SMP) configurations. There have been several studies aiming at alleviating the overhead of replication, however, due to consistency requirements, network performance of the basic replication mechanism remains extremely poor.

In this paper we revisit the replication protocol and extend it with *speculative communication*. Speculative communication silently acknowledges TCP packets of the VM, enabling the guest's TCP stack to progress with transmission without exposing the messages to the clients before the corresponding execution state is checkpointed to the backup host. Furthermore, we propose *replication aware congestion control*, an extension to the guest's TCP stack that aggressively fills up the VMM's replication buffer so that speculative packets can be backed up and released earlier to the clients. We observe up to an order of magnitude improvement in bulk data transfer with speculative communication, and close to native VM network performance when replication awareness is enabled in the guest OS. We provide results of micro-, as well as application-level benchmarks.

Categories and Subject Descriptors C.4 [*Performance Of Systems*]: Fault-tolerance; D.4.5 [*Operating Systems*]: Reliability—Fault-tolerance, Checkpoint/restart

General Terms Design, Reliability, Performance

Keywords Virtualization; Hypervisor; Checkpoint; Recovery; Fault Tolerance

1. Introduction

With the recent increase in cloud computing's prevalence, the number of online services deployed over virtualized infrastructures, i.e., over Virtual Machines (VM), has experienced a tremendous growth. At the same time, the latest hardware trend of growing component number in current computing systems (e.g., datacenters, high-end computer clusters, etc.) renders hardware failures common place rather than exceptional [32]. Hence, designing software with fault-resilience in mind has become a major concern.

Replication at the Virtual Machine Monitor (VMM) layer is an attractive technique to ensure fault tolerance in virtualized environments, primarily, because it provides seamless failover for the entire software stack executed inside the virtual machine, regardless the application or the underlying operating system (OS).

There are currently two main approaches to primary-backup based replication of virtual machines. Log-replay records all input and non-deterministic events of the primary machine so that it can replay them deterministically on the backup node in case the primary machine fails [4], [25]. Although this solution provides high efficacy to uni-processor virtual machines, its adaption to virtual SMP environments, i.e., virtual machines with multiple virtual CPUs, is cumbersome, because it requires determining and reproducing the exact order in which CPU cores access the shared memory [24]. While virtual SMP environments are gaining increasing importance [20], it has been shown that log-replay imposes super-linear performance degradation with the increasing number of virtual CPUs on various workloads [11].

The other approach, checkpoint-recovery based replication, captures the entire execution state of the running VM at relatively high frequency in order to propagate changes to the backup machine almost instantly [6, 9, 12, 19, 35]. This solution, essentially, keeps the backup machine nearly up-to-date with the latest execution state of the primary machine so that the backup can take over the execution in case the primary fails [6]. One of the main strengths of checkpoint-recovery based replication is its inherent ability to tackle with multi-core configurations [12].

However, any fault tolerant system needs to ensure that the state from where an output message is sent will be recovered despite any future failure, which is commonly referred to as the *output commit* problem [27]. As a consequence of such requirement, output of the running VM needs to be held back, i.e., disk I/O and network traffic have to be buffered and can be released only after the backup machine acknowledged the corresponding update [6, 9, 19].

Several recent studies have explored the domain how to accelerate the failure free period of checkpoint-recovery based replication, focusing mainly on decreasing its computational overhead [12, 19, 35]. Communication performance, due to the consistency requirements mentioned above, remains notoriously poor [6]. Workloads, which require high-bandwidth TCP data transfer are particularly hurt, because TCP transmission is unable to progress as a result of the constant delay in acknowledgments from its peers.

In this paper we focus on the TCP communication performance of *replicated virtual machines*, i.e., virtual machines that are being replicated via checkpoint-recovery based replication. We make the following contributions:

VEE'12. March 3–4, 2012, London, England, UK.

- We revisit the basic replication protocol and extend it with *speculative communication*. Speculative communication fabricates and delivers speculative acknowledgments to the VM in response to its TCP packets so that the guest's TCP stack can progress with TCP transmission. In order to ensure consistency, speculative messages are not exposed to the client machines until the VM's corresponding execution state is checkpointed and the update is acknowledged by the backup host.
- We propose *replication aware congestion control*, an extension to the guest OS' TCP stack that aggressively fills up the replication buffer of the VMM so that speculative packets can be sent to the backup host and released earlier to the clients.
- Finally, a rigorous evaluation of the introduced mechanisms is given using two different interconnects, Gigabit Ethernet and Infiniband [1] (a high-performance interconnect that is gaining popularity also in data-centers) as the network for replication.

Experimental results show up to an order of magnitude improvement in bulk data transfer with speculative communication, and close to native network performance when replication awareness is enabled in the guest OS and replication is performed over Infiniband.

We begin with detailing the basic VM replication protocol in Section 2. Section 3 describes the design of our proposed mechanisms and Section 4 provides insight to the details of implementation. Experimental evaluation is given in Section 5. Section 6 surveys related work, Section 7 provides further discussion along with future plans, and finally, Section 8 concludes the paper.

2. Background and Motivation

This section provides an overview of the basic virtual machine replication protocol focusing in particular on communication aspects. It also motivates the need for further investigation how to improve communication performance.

2.1 Basic Replication Protocol

As mentioned above, checkpoint-recovery based replication of virtual machines is delivered by capturing snapshots of the running VM at relatively high frequency so that changes can be reflected to the backup machine almost instantly.

Between checkpoints the VM executes in log-dirty mode, i.e., write accessed pages are recorded so that when the checkpoint is taken only pages that were modified in the most recent execution phase need to be transferred, along with execution context of the virtual devices and vCPUs. One phase of dirty logging and transferring the corresponding changes is often called a *replication epoch* [6, 19, 35].

VM downtime during replication epochs, i.e., the period while the VM is stopped, can be eliminated almost entirely. Instead of leaving the VM paused and transferring the update synchronously, data can be buffered first and transferred in an asynchronous fashion (which we call the *basic asynchronous replication protocol* in the rest of this paper). This way the VM is stopped only for the buffering period, and execution of the next epoch can overlap the actual data transfer [6]. Copy-on-write (COW) can be used to omit VM downtime even while buffering the update [12].

When a failure occurs, the backup machine rolls back to the latest consistent state it received from the primary host and restarts the most recent replication epoch's execution phase. Since the execution path on the backup may be different (particularly, when multiple vCPUs access shared memory) than that executed on the primary machine, the primary machine's output, which may depend on such non-deterministic steps, have to be buffered and held back until the corresponding checkpoint is acknowledged by the backup.

This property of the replication protocol is consequence of the so-called *output commit* problem [27], which postulates that any fault tolerant system needs to ensure that the state from where a message is sent will be recovered despite any future failure.

2.2 TCP Communication

Transmission Control Protocol (TCP) is the most widely used network protocol for reliable data transfer over the Internet. TCP relies on acknowledgments to ensure data have been transferred entirely, and at the same time acknowledgments play a crucial role in adapting the transmission bandwidth to the properties of the underlying physical network.

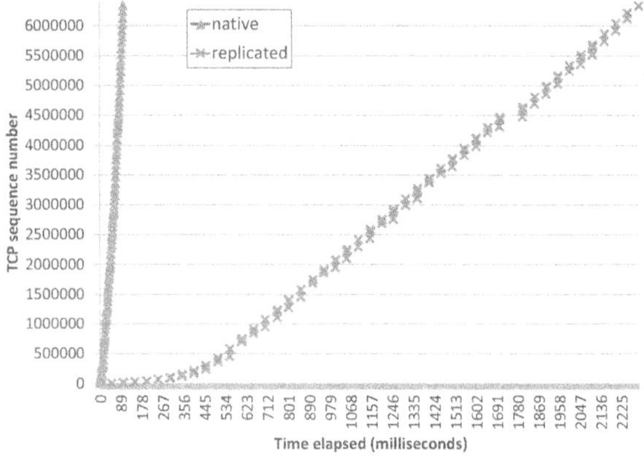

Figure 1. TCP bulk data transfer of the native and the replicated virtual machines. *Replication epoch length is set to 50 milliseconds in this experiment and Gigabit Ethernet is used as the underlying network between the VM and the client machine.*

Taking a closer look at how *output commit* affects the TCP performance reveals that the attainable network bandwidth is substantially lower compared to the native execution. Figure 1 demonstrates the difference between the native and the replicated virtual machine's TCP throughput, as recorded on the client side. The figure shows how TCP progresses with sequence numbers with respect to the time elapsed. One of the key observations is the grouped fashion of the transfer when replication is enabled. As seen, groups of packets appear approximately in every 50 milliseconds on the client machine, which is the length of the replication epoch in this experiment.

In each replication epoch the VM's TCP stack attempts to transmit a number of packets to the client, which are buffered and held back, i.e., delayed by the VMM (in order to guarantee output commit) until the end of the epoch. Consequently, acknowledgments of these packets are also delayed which prevents the VM's TCP stack to increase the congestion window at the same pace how the native execution would do. As a result of this quenched transmission, the VM's TCP stack believes the underlying network provides significantly lower bandwidth than it does in reality. In this experiment we obtain less than 6 MB/s TCP throughput from the replicated virtual machine, as opposed to the 110 MB/s of the native execution. In both scenarios, the physical link between the VM and the client machine was Gigabit Ethernet. Clearly, such degraded network performance is unacceptable for online services where clients expect reasonable bandwidth and short response times from the server machines.

3. Design

Motivated by the scenario presented above, this section discusses the idea of *speculative communication* and the role of *shadow sock-*

ets. Moreover, *replication aware congestion control*, a modification to the VM's TCP stack, which further improves attainable network bandwidth is also presented.

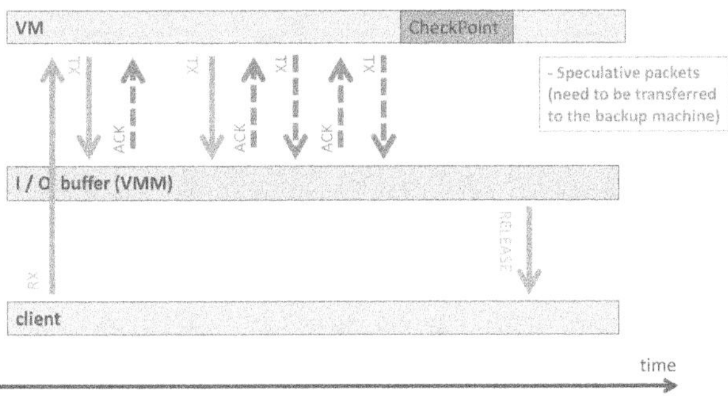

Figure 2. Speculative communication of replicated virtual machines. *Dashed arrows represent speculative acknowledgments of the VMM and speculative packets of the VM. Speculative communication allows the VM to progress with its TCP streams further than it can under the basic replication protocol. Speculative packets, however, need to be transferred to the backup host.*

3.1 Speculative Communication

The mechanism of *speculative communication* is shown in Figure 2. The basic idea is that instead of simply buffering network packets the VMM tracks established TCP connections and fabricates *speculative acknowledgments* that appear exactly the same as if the client sent them. The acknowledgments are submitted to the VM, which enables the VM's TCP stack to progress with data transfer and transmit more packets during the same period of time. In order to ensure consistency, the packets from the VM are not transferred immediately to the client machines, but are only buffered first, hence the name *speculative communication*. Once the corresponding checkpoint is acknowledged by the backup, the packets can be released. This mechanism allows the replicated VM to attain higher network throughput and better response times, however, it also opens up various questions and issues.

3.1.1 Determinism and Fault-Tolerance

One might be wondering whether or not allowing the VM to progress with its TCP streams breaks the conditions of fault tolerant execution. Since speculative packets are not exposed to the clients until the corresponding execution state's checkpoint is acknowledged by the backup machine, such packets do not depend on any non-deterministic steps of the VM that cannot be recovered in the future if a failure occurs. However, when a checkpoint is taken, the VM's TCP stack (encompassed by the execution context of the virtual machine) does represent a state where retransmission of these packets is already impossible, due to the fact that they have been acknowledged and the TCP stack has likely removed them from its retransmission queue. Consequently, the packets which are acknowledged by the VMM also need to be transferred to the backup machine so that they can be transmitted over the network again in case the primary machine fails. The main goal of speculative communication is to overlap the actual transfer on the network with the backup data transfer of the next epoch's speculative packets. (Note, that the replication takes place over a separate NIC.)

3.1.2 Correctness

Another issue is how buffered packets are released, i.e., actually transferred to the clients. TCP ensures that every single byte of a stream is received correctly (assuming no permanent error occurs on the network), and packets are retransmitted if they get lost or corrupted during the transfer. When the VMM acknowledges a TCP packet to the VM, the VM's TCP stack cannot be counted on for possible retransmissions any more, because it believes the packet reached its destination. Once data are buffered by the VMM, it becomes the VMM's responsibility to transfer that data properly and conforming to the TCP semantics. For this reason, the VMM maintains *shadow sockets* of each established TCP stream of the replicated VM. Shadow sockets ensure both necessary packet retransmissions and correct TCP congestion control of the speculative stream. The mechanism of shadow sockets, along with the necessary alternations to network packets of both incoming and outgoing traffic will be explained below.

3.2 Shadow Sockets

Shadow sockets play a central role in performing speculative communication. The VMM maintains a hash table of shadow sockets based on IP addresses and TCP port numbers of the given TCP flow. A simplified view of the shadow socket infrastructure is shown in Figure 3.

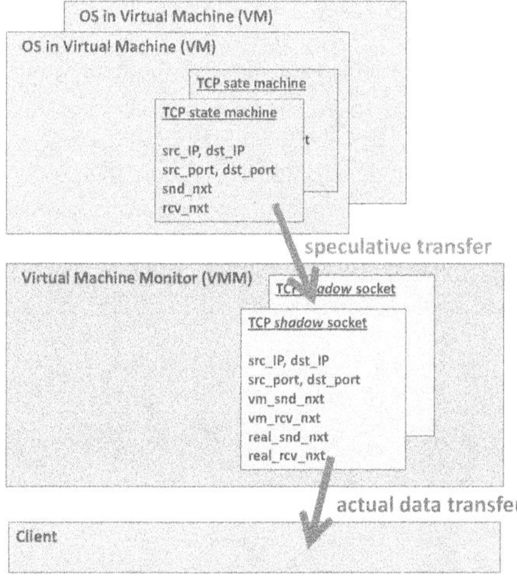

Figure 3. High-level overview of the shadow socket infrastructure. *Shadow sockets track TCP flows and perform speculative communication for the guest's TCP connections. They also are responsible for the actual data transfer to the client.*

Most importantly, a shadow socket stores information about the sequence numbers of a TCP stream, both from the point of view of the VM and the real network (i.e., the client). Essentially, speculative communication offloads the actual TCP transmission from the VM's TCP stack to the shadow socket of the VMM. Although data are transferred (during speculative communication) via TCP from the VM to the VMM, it is merely a memory copy, without any network transmission involved. The VMM stores the payload of the TCP packets from the VM and during packet release phase it transfers the data through the corresponding shadow socket. Since we utilize the Linux kernel's TCP stack to perform this task, as it will be detailed in Section 4, the actual TCP transmission over the network behaves entirely conforming to standard TCP semantics. In fact, it does so as if it was one of the host's non-virtualized TCP connections. It is also worth mentioning, that incoming traffic doesn't go through the shadow socket, but the payload is passed to the VM directly. However, special care has to be taken how incoming, outgoing and speculative packets are handled, which we describe in the next sections.

3.2.1 Connection Tracking

Our current implementation assumes that any TCP activity of the guest is initiated after the replication has been enabled. This makes TCP connection tracking slightly less complicated, because an established flow can be identified by the acknowledgment of the SYN-ACK packet. The VMM creates shadow sockets for any TCP flow once a SYN packet is identified (regardless if it originates from the VM or from the clients). When the connection enters the established state, the VMM starts performing speculative communication for the given flow.

Shadow sockets are destroyed in three possible scenarios. The most common ways are if both parties of the connection sent their respective FIN packets or if there is no activity on the flow for more than a user specified time interval. Besides these, RST flags can also indicate a connection break-down.

3.2.2 Traffic Handling

As shown in Figure 3, we use the same set of notations for TCP sequence numbers with the TCP protocol specification [31]. vm_snd_nxt denotes the next sequence number the guest OS sends, while vm_rcv_nxt is the next sequence number the VM expects on an incoming packet. Notice, that vm_snd_nxt, at the same time, is the highest valid ACK number the VM accepts. These values have to be updated according to the traffic to and from the VM. For example, when a TCP packet is sent by the VM, the corresponding shadow socket's vm_snd_nxt field has to be updated so that it stores the sequence number that equals to $seq + tcp\_length$ of the given packet. Similarly, vm_rcv_nxt will store the acknowledgment field of the outgoing packet, since by definition, that is the next sequence number the VM expects to receive. Looking at the sequence numbers of the actual TCP flow on the network, $real\_snd\_nxt$ represents the sequence number the shadow socket sends next, and $real\_rcv\_nxt$ is the next sequence number the VMM expects from the client.

The main source of complications with respect to incoming, outgoing and speculative packets is the fact that the VM's TCP stack can be ahead of the actual data transmission, due to speculative communication. Using the notations above, this means that effectively vm_snd_nxt is ahead of $real\_snd\_nxt$ when speculative communication is in action. This has several implications on how packets can be passed to and from the VM.

Speculative Acknowledgments. Speculative acknowledgments always contain vm_rcv_nxt as their sequence nr. and vm_snd_nxt as the acknowledgment. Essentially, they acknowledge the entire *in-flight* sequence interval of the VM, i.e., the sequence interval the VM believes currently resides on the network. There are two more important issues worth mentioning with regards to speculative acknowledgments.

First, it is infeasible to acknowledge every single outgoing packet of the VM one-by-one, because of the high frequency of packets during a high-bandwidth data transfer. For this reason we employ a similar technique that is widely used in TCP implementations, i.e., acknowledging smaller than maximum segment size (MSS) packets directly, but scheduling ACKs based on timers if packets with MSS size are frequent.

Second, while speculative packets are continuously transferred in the background to the backup machine (because they are part of the given epoch update), the VMM keeps track of the overall buffer size used and indicates to the VM once the buffer limit has been reached. The limit of the buffer is determined by the replication frequency and the available bandwidth between the primary and the backup machines. The VM is notified to stop transferring data by means of announcing zero window in the speculative acknowledgment. In order to resume data transfer, each shadow socket for which zero window has been announced is marked and an acknowledgment with non-zero window is sent in the beginning of the next replication epoch.

Incoming Traffic. When speculative communication is active, incoming packets cannot be passed directly to the VM's network stack, because the VM's TCP state machine may expect higher acknowledgments than that in the actual traffic on the network. This is due to the speculative acknowledgments the VMM submitted. Therefore, the ACK field in incoming packet's TCP header needs to be updated according to the shadow socket's vm_snd_nxt field. Otherwise, passing the packet would cause the VM to possibly discard it with the reason of invalid acknowledgment. Modifying the TCP header's ACK field also requires updating the TCP and IP checksums, which is performed by the VMM before passing the packet to the VM.

Outgoing Traffic. Special attention needs to be payed for outgoing packets from the VMM to the clients as well. Imagine a scenario where the client sends a packet to the VM which has non-zero payload. This will cause the VM to send an acknowledgment to the client, which is in turn buffered by the VMM. Instead of releasing this packet, the VMM needs to update the $real\_rcv\_nxt$ field of the shadow socket according to the ACK field of the packet's TCP header and send an acknowledgment with the correct sequence number, i.e., $real\_snd\_nxt$. Otherwise, the client TCP stack may receive packets that, on one hand, have sequence number ahead of the expected one (because $real\_snd\_nxt$ may be behind vm_snd_nxt), on the other hand, the client may believe that the original packet (with the payload) was lost on the network and retransmit packets unnecessarily.

3.3 Replication Aware Congestion Control

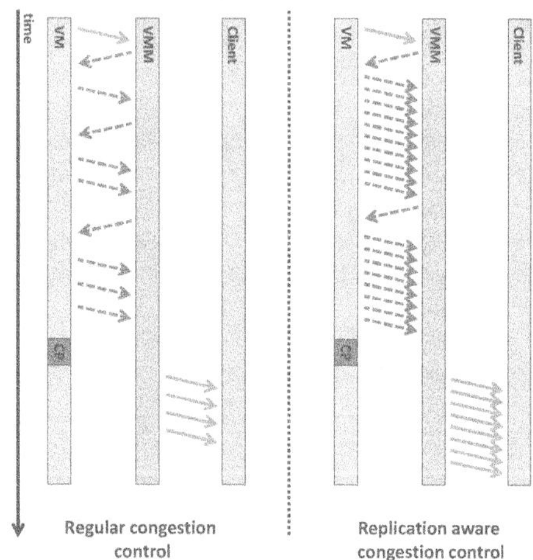

Figure 4. Replication aware TCP congestion control of the guest OS. *Replication aware congestion control aggressively transmits a large number of packets in order to fill up the replication buffer as soon as possible.*

As mentioned above, speculative communication essentially offloads the actual TCP transmission to the VMM's shadow sockets. However, since speculative packets have to be transferred to the backup machine first, the VMM should buffer speculative packets as fast as possible. There are two main factors that determine how fast the VM transfers packets to the VMM's buffer, the receive window size announced in the speculative acknowledgments and the congestion window size of the guest's TCP stack. Our first approach towards gathering as many packets as possible from the VM was to announce large receive window size (2MB in our current implementation) in the speculative acknowledgments.

Unfortunately, standard congestion window control algorithms (such as Vegas [3] or CUBIC [13]), which are widely used in operating systems' network stacks, are not designed for the conditions speculative communication promotes. On the other hand, congestion control policy in TCP stack implementations is often easy to alternate. Linux, for instance, provides a standard kernel interface to grow or shrink congestion window size in response to acknowledgments and different policies for congestion control can be easily implemented as loadable kernel modules.

Several prior studies have explored the idea to make the guest operating system aware of virtualization. In this paper we follow the same path, but we take the approach to the next level, where the guest OS is not only aware of virtualization, but also of high availability (i.e., it knows it runs in a replicated VM). In order to better cooperate with speculative communication we developed a very simple congestion control algorithm with a low slow start threshold followed immediately by a relatively large congestion window. Figure 4 indicates the difference between regular and replication aware congestion controls. Our congestion control algorithm aggressively transmits groups of packets together, filling up the speculative communication buffer much faster than operating under standard congestion window algorithms. In Section 5 we provide experimental results demonstrating the impact of this approach.

4. Implementation

We chose the Linux Kernel Virtual Machine (KVM) [17] as the platform of this study. KVM takes advantage of the hardware virtualization extensions so that it achieves nearly the same performance with the underlying physical machine.

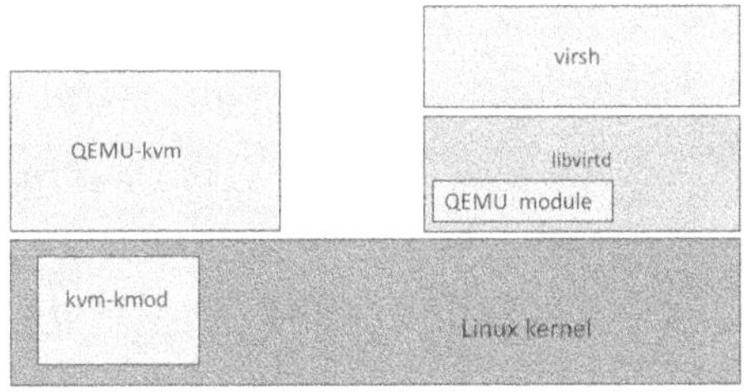

Figure 5. The Linux kernel virtual machine architecture.

Figure 5 depicts the high-level KVM architecture. The most important components are the *kvm* kernel module and *qemu-kvm*, a KVM tailored version of QEMU. On top of these, *libvirtd* is an often used facility for managing virtual machines, for which *virsh* provides a command line interface. A major advantage of the KVM architecture is the full availability of user-space tools in the QEMU process, such as threading or libraries. Similarly, the *kvm* kernel module can directly make use of any functionality provided by the Linux kernel, such as drivers or the TCP stack.

4.1 Replication Logic and Disk I/O Buffering

The replication logic is entirely implemented in *qemu-kvm*, leveraging a great amount of the live migration code.

For disk I/O buffering we modified the virtio driver of *qemu-kvm*. The disk I/O buffer behaves also as a hash table that operates on sector granularity so that read requests referring to sectors which are already buffered can be accessed consistently.

4.2 Speculative Communication and Shadow Sockets

Most of the speculative communication functionality is implemented in user-space, i.e., in the *qemu-kvm* process. Both incoming and outgoing packets are examined in the networking code of QEMU. Speculative packets are put on a *backup-queue* first, which is continuously processed by a background thread that transfers the packets to the backup machine. Packets that have been acknowledged are then put on the *transfer-queue*. However, the transfer-queue is only processed once the corresponding epoch's update is also acknowledged by the backup machine.

Shadow sockets, on the other hand, have components both in a user-space and in the Linux kernel. The user-space component is mainly responsible for tracking TCP flows from the VM's viewpoint (i.e., it takes care of vm_snd_nxt and vm_rcv_nxt) and handles speculative acknowledgments. Shadow sockets in *qemu-kvm* are created immediately once a SYN packet is detected and are maintained on a hash table so that a particular flow can be quickly identified. Kernel components are, however, only allocated when the connection enters the established state.

For the kernel-space component of shadow sockets we modified the *kvm* kernel module and extended it with special purpose *ioctl()* calls in order to create and close sockets, and also to perform write on them. Socket creation raises certain complications, because it requires imitating the steps of a connection establishment, without actually putting any packets onto the network. Nevertheless, for most of the functionalities of shadow sockets we directly leverage the underlying TCP implementation of the Linux kernel. This makes several things significantly easier. Because shadow sockets are identical to the non-virtualized TCP connections of the host, the Linux kernel completely exempts us from maintaining and identifying connections (such as hashing and looking up sockets for packets). It also handles the actual TCP transmission, and thus, we don't need to worry about packet retransmissions, congestion control, fairness among flows, and other aspects of the TCP protocol itself. We did need, however, an additional feature so that the rcv_nxt field of a TCP socket can be advanced from user-space in case it is dictated by an acknowledgment of the VM.

4.3 Replication Aware Congestion Control

Replication aware congestion control is a kernel module of the guest OS. The Linux kernel provides a standard interface for developing alternative congestion control algorithms in the form of implementing a *tcp_congestion_ops* structure and registering it via the *tcp_register_congestion_control()* function. The linux kernel adjusts the congestion window either according to the *slow start* algorithm or according to *congestion avoidance*. The slow start threshold (*ssthresh*) is used to determine whether to use slow start or congestion avoidance algorithms. A congestion control algorithm is allowed to specify *ssthresh* and once the threshold is reached, it can adjust the actual congestion window (*snd_cwnd*) in face of an ACK. We use a very low slow start threshold (*ssthresh* is set to 2), followed by a constant large congestion window (*snd_cwnd* is set to 1024).

4.4 Transactional Updates

Another particular issue worth mentioning is the transactional nature of updating the backup machine. When replication data are sent to the backup host, *qemu-kvm* cannot just read and apply the changes directly, because a failure during the update would leave the backup machine in an inconsistent state.

This implies that at the end of each replication epoch the backup machine needs to collect the updates first and then apply all changes together in a transactional fashion, only if all data were received successfully. Unfortunately, the network protocol of *qemu-kvm*'s live migration code doesn't support this by default.

For this reason we extended the *QEMUFile* object with a buffer and a flag that indicates that the file is in accumulating mode. The primary machine toggles this flag on the file corresponding to the backup connection and all subsequent writes are first buffered. We record the number of bytes to be transmitted and inform the backup machine in advance regarding the length of the update. It can then read the whole stream, store it in a buffer and toggle the backup file's flag to indicate that subsequent read operations issued by *qemu-kvm* should access the buffer instead of receiving data from the network.

5. Evaluation

In this section we present the evaluation of speculative communication and replication aware congestion control. We discuss bulk TCP throughput first, which is then followed by demonstration how application level performance is affected. We consider applications that are good candidates for deployment over virtualized infrastructures (i.e., in cloud computing environments) and for which high-availability is naturally expected.

5.1 Experimental Setup

Throughout our experiments the host machine of the replicated VM was equipped with a 4 cores Intel Xeon 2.2GHz CPU, with 2 hyperthreads per core (i.e., 8 hardware threads altogether), 6GBs of RAM and a 250GB SATA harddrive. The machine had two Intel 82546GB Gigabit Ethernet network interfaces. One of the physical network cards were bridged to the virtual machine and used for application traffic and the other was dedicated to the replication protocol for the experiments, when replication took place over Gigabit Ethernet. Moreover, a Mellanox MT26428 Infiniband QDR HCA was also present in both the primary and the backup hosts for the experiments utilizing Infiniband.

The host machines run Ubuntu server 9.10 on Linux kernel 2.6.37 and we used qemu-kvm 0.14.50 with kvm-kmod 2.6.37 as the basis of our implementation. For the virtual machines in each experiment we used the KVM virtio disk and network drivers. We do not present performance results on the native host machine, because in virtualized environments direct access to the underlying machines is normally not available. However, we had Intel's hardware MMU virtualization support, i.e. Extended Page Tables (EPT) enabled in all experiments. Unless stated otherwise, the VM had 1 GB of RAM allocated with memory ballooning support disabled.

5.2 TCP Throughput

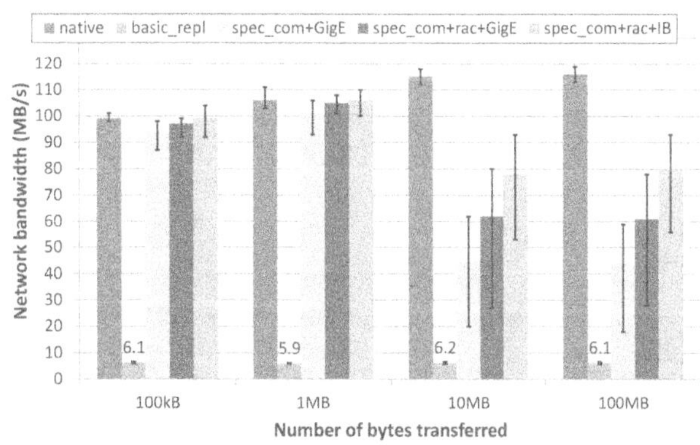

Figure 6. Bulk data transfer performance measured on the client machine. *The replication period is set to 50 milliseconds in this experiment.*

In our first experiment we measured the TCP network throughput from the virtual machine to a separate host. The VM and the client were connected through Gigabit Ethernet (i.e., theoretically the maximum throughput is around 120MB/s).

We ran the test under five different VM configurations, native virtual machine, VM replicated with the basic asynchronous replication protocol (see Section 2.1) over GigE, speculative communication enabled over GigE, speculative communication enabled over GigE with replication awareness in the guest kernel, and finally, speculative communication with replication aware congestion control in the guest, replicated over Infiniband. Replication period was set to 50 milliseconds, where replication was enabled. We used the *ttcp* utility [29] to perform these experiments. *ttcp* allows to define the number of bytes transferred over the link and we used four different scenarios, 100kB, 1MB, 10MB, and 100MB. Each experiment was executed multiple times and we report the average, the highest, and the lowest values (in form of error bars) we obtained. Figure 6 illustrates the results.

As seen, the native execution achieves up to 117MB/s, which is close to the maximum possible throughput of Gigabit Ethernet. Contrary, the throughput attained by the basic replication protocol is extremely low, approximately 6MB/s. Looking at the numbers for speculative communication, the figure reveals that speculative communication achieves near native network performance for short streams (100kB and 1MB), which is followed by a sudden drop in the performance settling around 40-50MB/s for longer transfers. Notice however, that speculative communication achieves up to 65MB/s throughput, which is an order of magnitude better performance compared to the basic replication protocol. Furthermore, replication awareness in the guest kernel further contributes up to 35% performance improvement compared to the only speculative communication case.

The sudden performance drop with longer streams is related to the replication period of the experiment. Because both 100kB and 1MB can be buffered under one replication epoch, the maximum achieved throughput is very close to the native execution, essentially, the transfer is merely double buffered. However, when the transfer spans multiple replication epochs (such as in case of the 10MB and 100MB transfers), speculative buffering is interrupted in every 50 milliseconds. Whereas replication aware congestion control in conjunction with Infiniband yields up to 95MB/s throughput even for longer streams, a similar tendency can be observed over Infiniband as well.

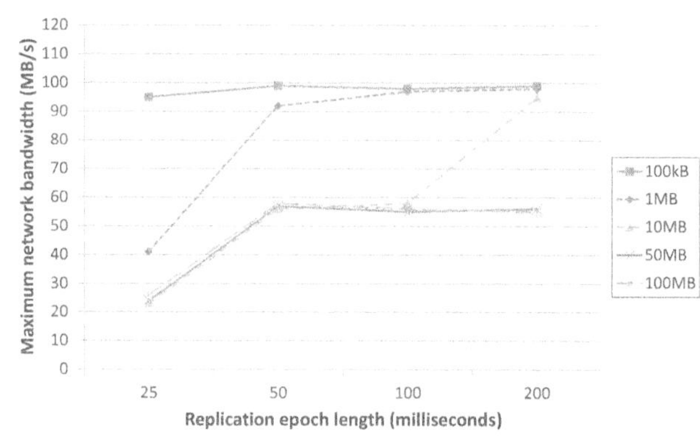

Figure 7. Bulk data transfer performance according to different stream sizes and replication epoch lengths. *Legend represents the number of bytes transferred. The experiments were executed over GigE, without replication aware congestion control in the guest OS.*

Another interesting observation is the relatively high deviation of the attainable bandwidth, especially for longer streams. We believe this is related to scheduling issues, similarly how related work describes it in case of TCP reception performance of virtualized environments [16].

In order to further investigate the bandwidth drop effect we ran additional tests with different replication epoch lengths for different stream sizes. These experiments were all executed over Gigabit Ethernet, without replication aware congestion control. Figure 7 shows the maximum bandwidth we could obtain for each combination. One of the key observations is the fact that streams with longer sizes perform worse, because they span through several replication epochs. As seen, in case of a 1MB stream the smallest replication buffer it fits was the one corresponding to 50 milliseconds epoch length, while the 10MB could only fit the 200 milliseconds one. It is also shown that enlarging the replication epoch length generally increases the attainable bandwidth, because longer epoch size means less frequent checkpoints, which in turn lowers the overhead of the replication itself.

In terms of network performance the basic replication protocol would favor shorter replication epochs, so that buffered packets can be released earlier, however, short replication epochs introduce higher computational overhead. The main strength of speculative communication is its ability to allow long replication epochs and reasonable network performance at the same time.

5.3 SPECweb 2005

The first application we investigated was SPECweb's Banking workload, which emulates an Internet personal banking web-site, where clients are accessing their accounts, making transactions, etc [14]. Requests are transmitted over SSL throughout the whole benchmark. The SPECweb configuration requires at least three machines for running the experiments. One of the server hosts is the actual SPECweb application server, which is accompanied by a backend machine. These were deployed in two VMs residing on two separate physical machines. On the application server we used Apache 2.2.11 with the default configuration the Ubuntu server distribution provides. Besides these, another machine was utilized for running the SPECweb client side scripts.

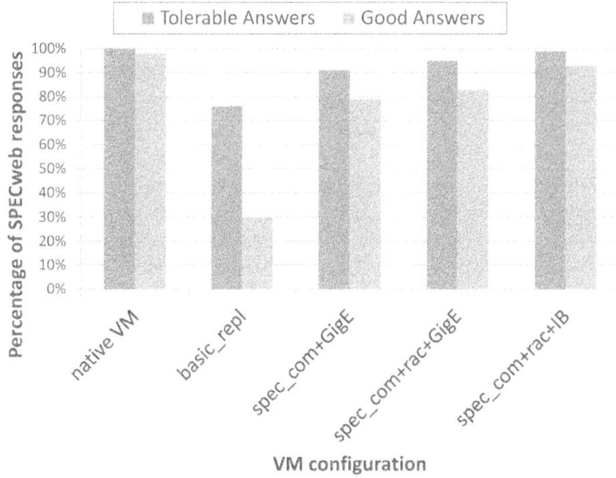

Figure 8. SPECweb2005 Banking results. *The replication period is set to 50 milliseconds and the number of simultaneous connections is 100.*

We replicated only the main SPECweb application server, for which another physical machine was utilized to serve as backup host. SPECweb reports two separate values for each experiment, the ratio of *good* and *tolerable* answers. First we tuned the SPECweb configuration so that 98% of the responses are categorized as *good* when executed on the native VM. In order to assess scalability aspects of the proposed improvements we set the number of simultaneous client connections to 100 in this setup. The same configuration was then used to measure the performance in case of the basic asynchronous replication over Gigabit Ethernet, speculative communication over GigE, speculative communication and replication aware congestion control over GigE, and finally, speculative communication with replication aware congestion control in the guest and replicated over Infiniband.

Figure 8 illustrates the ratio of answers we obtained from these experiments. As seen, the basic replication mechanism imposes substantial performance degradation, achieving only 30% of the *good* answers of the native execution. Webservers are good candidates for speculative communication, because a typical web interaction consists of a small request message which is then followed by a longer, bulk data transfer from the server process. Speculative communication allows the replicated server to possibly transmit the entire response into the VMMs buffer in one go, which can be transferred over the network during the next replication epoch, instead of spanning several epoch as it happens using the basic replication. We expected to see significant improvements due to this mechanism in case of SPECweb.

As the figure shows, speculative communication even over GigE yields 2.6X better performance in terms of *good* answers compared to the basic mechanism, achieving 80% of the native VM's performance. However, we do not observe significantly better performance when replication aware congestion control is enabled in the guest kernel. Further examination on SPECweb's attributes revealed that the average response size is approximately 50kB in this test, with the maximum size transfers not exceeding 150kB. Up to 150kB can be easily buffered even without replication aware congestion control, which explains why the two methods perform very similar in this benchmark.

Table 1. SPECweb Banking average response times (seconds)

Request Type	native VM	basic asynchr.	spec_com+ GigE	spec_com+ rac+IB
login	0.418	3.183	2.022	1.313
account_sum	0.105	2.356	1.389	0.720
check_detail	0.122	2.506	1.610	0.793
bill_pay	0.140	2.315	1.332	0.727
add_payee	0.129	1.820	0.960	0.473
payee_info	0.164	2.611	1.414	0.664
quick_pay	0.132	4.799	2.413	1.214
billpay_status	0.166	2.388	1.308	0.745
chg_profile	0.187	2.498	1.309	0.780
post_profile	0.107	2.412	1.328	0.888
req_checks	0.214	2.921	1.649	0.780
post_chk_order	0.157	2.392	1.156	0.607
req_xfer_form	0.179	2.089	1.238	0.687
post_fund_xfer	0.103	2.309	1.243	0.586
logout	0.139	1.845	0.822	0.522
check_image	0.016	0.827	0.382	0.179

Utilization of Infiniband, nevertheless, contributes another 13% increase in the attainable ratio of *good* answers, getting as close as 93% of the native execution. Infiniband provides significantly higher network bandwidth (up to 6X in our setup), which enables the backup machine to acknowledge a replication epoch's update in much shorter time. Consequently, the buffered reply can be also transferred with much smaller delay.

Table 1 provides further details on the average response time of each individual request types the benchmark consists of. As seen, the basic asynchronous replication renders the response times substantially longer than the native execution. Speculative communication alleviates the overhead with an average ratio of 57% shorter delay compared to the basic replication. We do not provide separate results for the replication aware congestion control case over GigE, because it's very close to the speculative communication only case. Infiniband, on the other hand, yields another 56% shorter delay in responses compared to the GigE case.

5.4 Hadoop

Hadoop [30] is an open-source implementation of the MapReduce (MR) [7] distributed data analysis tool, a framework often used in cloud computing environments. A Hadoop MR cluster consists of several worker nodes (called *TaskTrackers*) that are coordinated by a central entity, the *JobTracker*. While *TaskTrackers* may fail any time without bringing the entire job down, the failure of the *JobTracker* is fatal. Therefore, it is a good candidate for fault tolerant execution.

Our Hadoop cluster is relatively small scale, it consists of 16 worker nodes (i.e., TaskTrackers), each of them is a single vCPU VM with 1.2GB of RAM, residing on four different physical hosts equipped with Intel Xeon 2.2GHz Quad-core CPUs and 6GB of RAM. We used approximately 2GB of raw data on each node the as input. We evaluated the price of protecting the Hadoop master node via VM level replication through the MR/DB benchmark set [26]. MR/DB operates on random generated HTML data and it includes various common tasks that can be expressed either as SQL queries or as MapReduce computations, such as grep, select, aggregate and join.

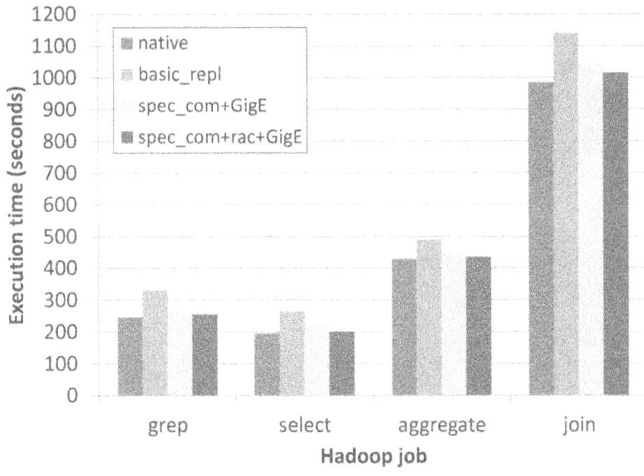

Figure 9. Hadoop MR/DB benchmark runtimes. *Experiments were run on a Hadoop cluster with 16 worker nodes and a separate master node protected via VM level replication.*

We ran four configurations for each benchmark, measuring execution running on native VM, basic asynchronous replication over GigE, speculative communication over GigE, and finally, speculative communication over GigE with replication aware congestion control enabled in the guest's kernel. We executed all tests five times and report the average values.

Figure 9 illustrates the results. As seen, the basic replication mechanism induces up to 34% overhead compared to the native execution, which is significant considering the scale of the system. Since the Hadoop JobTracker merely orchestrates the entire job, the protected VM's dominant action is communication rather than computation. Just as the case with webservers, the JobTracker is also a good candidate for speculative communication, because speculative communication prevents messages to span multiple replication epochs, which would otherwise slow down the entire communication. As the figure shows, speculative communication, even over Gigabit Ethernet, renders the overhead of replication between approximately 5% and 13%. With replication aware congestion control enabled in the guest's TCP stack, the overhead is further alleviated down to 3%, which is almost the same with the native execution. No experiments were run over Infiniband for these benchmarks.

6. Related Work

6.1 Virtual Machine Migration

Checkpoint-recovery based fault tolerance captures snapshots of the running VM at high frequency, often leveraging the live migration support of the underlying Virtual Machine Monitor (VMM). Thus, VM live migration is closely related to checkpoint-recovery based replication. Solutions, such as *Xen* [5], *KVM* [17], and *VMware's VMotion* [23] all provide the capability of live migrating VM instances. Pre-copy is the dominant approach to live VM migration [5, 23]. It initially transfers all memory pages then tracks and transfers dirty pages in subsequent iterations. When the amount of data transferred becomes small or the maximum number of iteration reached, the VM is suspended and finally, the remaining dirty pages and the VCPU context is moved to the destination machine. VM replication, on the other hand, leaves the VM running in pre-copy mode at all times so that dirty pages are logged and the entire execution state can be reflected to the backup node at the end of each replication epoch [6, 9].

Performance improvement to VM migration has been the focus of several prior studies. Xian et al. showed how data deduplication can be exploited to accelerate live migration [34], while *Microwiper* [10] proposed ordered propagation of dirty pages to transfer them according to their rewriting rates, reducing service downtime during the migration. High performance interconnects have also been used in the context of virtual machine migration, Huang et al. presented RDMA based migration over Infiniband [15],

6.2 Virtual Machine Replication

Bressoud and Schneider [4] introduced first the idea of hypervisor-based fault tolerance by executing the primary and the backup VMs in lockstep mode, i.e., logging all input and non-deterministic events of the primary machine and having them deterministically replayed on the backup node in case of failure. Whereas Bressoud and Schneider demonstrated this technique only for the HP PA-RISC processors VMware's recent work implements the same approach for x86 architecture [25]. These works, however, can handle only uni-processor environments. Deterministic-replay imposes strict restrictions on the underlying architecture and its adaption to multi-core CPU environment is cumbersome, because it requires determining and reproducing the exact order in which CPU cores access the shared memory.

In the context of deterministic (i.e. replayable) SMP execution, solutions on different abstraction levels have been proposed. *Flight Data Recorder* [33] is a hardware extension that enables deterministic replay for SMP environments, but it is unclear what degree of concurrency they can handle without significant performance degradation. Runtime system level solutions, such as *Respec* [18] and *CoreDet* [2] ensure deterministic execution of multi-threaded applications, but their main weakness compared to VM level solutions is the inability to provide fault tolerance for an entire software stack (including the operating system), which is encompassed by a virtual machine. *SMP-ReVirt* [11] exploits hardware page protection to detect and accurately replay sharing between virtual CPUs of a multi-core virtual machine, however, their experiments report superlinear slowdown with the increasing number of virtual CPUs.

Checkpoint-recovery based solutions such as *Remus* [6] and *Paratus* [9] can overcome the problem of multi-core execution by capturing the entire executions state of the VM and transferring it to the backup machine. Although most of the data transfer can be overlapped with speculative execution, transferring updates to the backup machine at very high frequency still comes with great performance overhead. *Kemari* [28] follows a similar approach to *Remus*, but instead of buffering output during speculative execution, it updates the backup machine each time before the VM omits an outside visible event.

Improving the performance of checkpoint-recovery based VM replication has become an active research area recently. Lu et al. [19] proposed fine-grained dirty region identification to reduce the amount of data transferred during each replication epoch, while Zhu et al. [35] improved the performance of log-dirty execution mode by reducing read- and predicting write-page faults. Gerofi et al. [12] utilized Infiniband RDMA for replicating multiprocessor virtual machines. All the above mentioned studies in the domain of checkpoint-recovery based VM replication, however, deal mostly with computational overhead. To the contrary, we focus on the communication aspect of highly available virtual machines.

6.3 Virtualized Network I/O

Alleviating the overhead of network device virtualization has been also an active research domain in recent years. Menon et al. proposed packet aggregation which reduces per-packet handling overhead between the guest and the VMM [21]. TwinDriver suggested tighter cooperation between the guest and the VMM by moving some of the functionalities of the network driver into the host [22]. Dong et al. proposed efficient interrupt coalescing for network I/O virtualization and virtual receive side scaling to effectively leverage multi-core processors [8]. The closest work resembling ours is vSnoop [16]. vSnoop offloads TCP acknowledgment handling to the VMM so that TCP reception performance doesn't suffer due to scheduling delays of virtual machines. The main difference between vSnoop and our work, is that vSnoop deals with TCP reception as opposed to TCP transmission, which eliminates the need of shadow sockets. Moreover, while our study also exploits the idea of offloading functionalities from the guest VM to the virtual machine monitor, we are focusing on improving network performance of virtualized environments with the additional feature of high availability.

7. Discussion and Future Directions

7.1 Scheduling and Epoch Length

We have already pointed out in Section 5.2 that one of the main strengths of speculative communication is the fact that high network throughput can be attained even with longer replication epochs. Generally, the longer the replication epochs are the smaller the overhead of the replication itself is. Therefore, as a general policy, one could enforce as long replication epochs as possible in order to minimize the overhead. However, under the basic replication protocol network I/O benefits from shorter epochs so that pending packets can be released earlier. As speculative communication opens up the way to prolong replication epochs but progress with network transmission at the same time, determining the optimal epoch length could be based on other aspects of the workload, such as the amount of dirtied memory pages, number of written disk I/O sectors, etc. In the future we intend to explore the idea of how workload adaptive checkpoint scheduling and speculative communication could interplay in an efficient manner, finding the optimal epoch lengths of the replication dynamically based on the workload executed in the VM.

7.2 Extended Replication Awareness

We have shown that making the congestion control algorithm of the guest's TCP stack replication aware yields significant improvements. Whereas this particular modification focuses solely on network performance, the guest's kernel could be further extended so that other aspects of the replication were also addressed.

General replication awareness in the guest kernel would open up various directions for further optimization. For example, if the guest kernel was aware of the checkpoint frequency (i.e., the exact time when the next checkpoint will be taken), it could schedule disk operations so that they are scattered among multiple checkpoints in a balanced way or even delay them according to other factors of the give epoch's update, such as dirtied memory pages.

A more pervasive approach of replication awareness in the guest's TCP stack would allow to transfer (i.e., buffer in the VMM) exactly the number of packets the replication buffer can handle, without having to announce zero window to indicate when the buffer is full. Furthermore, if the guest's TCP stack knew when the next checkpoint is going to be taken, it could simply transmit a large number of packets without expecting an acknowledgment until the next epoch, which would exempt us from having to transfer those packets to the backup machine, because the TCP stack would be aware of the fact that they are still not acknowledged.

8. Conclusions

Checkpoint-recovery based virtual machine replication is attractive, because it provides high availability for the entire software stack executed in the VM. Due to the output commit problem, however, network performance of the basic replication method is extremely poor.

In this paper we have revisited the replication protocol and extended it with *speculative communication*. Speculative communication enables the VM to progress with TCP transmission without exposing the messages to the client machines before the corresponding execution state is acknowledged by the backup host. We have introduced the notion of *shadow sockets*, which track TCP flows, perform speculative communication for the guest and effectively offload TCP transmission into the virtual machine monitor. Moreover, we have proposed *replication aware congestion control*, an extension to the guest's TCP stack that cooperates better with speculative communication. While we have focused on improving TCP transmission performance of replicated virtual machines, speculative communication is also applicable for TCP reception.

We have shown that speculative communication yields up to an order of magnitude better performance of bulk TCP transmission, and close to native network performance when replication aware congestion control is enabled in the guest's TCP stack and the replication is performed over Infiniband. We also presented measurements regarding the impact of speculative communication on applications, which naturally fit virtualized environments, and at the same time, require high-availability. SPECweb attains close to 80% of the native performance with speculative communication, and over 90% when replicated over Infiniband. We observe close to native performance with speculative communication of the Hadoop master node even when replication takes places over Gigabit Ethernet.

Acknowledgments

This work has been supported by the Core Research for Evolutional Science and Technology (CREST) project of the Japan Science and Technology Agency (JST).

References

[1] InfiniBand Trade Association. InfiniBand Architecture Specification, Release 1.2.

[2] T. Bergan, O. Anderson, J. Devietti, L. Ceze, and D. Grossman. CoreDet: a compiler and runtime system for deterministic multithreaded execution. In *Proceedings of the fifteenth edition of ASPLOS on Architectural support for programming languages and operating systems*, ASPLOS '10, pages 53–64. ACM, 2010. ISBN 978-1-60558-839-1.

[3] L. S. Brakmo and L. L. Peterson. TCP Vegas: End to End Congestion Avoidance on a Global Internet. *IEEE Journal on selected Areas in communications*, 13:1465–1480, 1995.

[4] T. Bressoud and F. B. Schneider. Hypervisor-based fault tolerance. In *Proceedings of the fifteenth ACM symposium on Operating systems principles*, SOSP '95, pages 1–11, New York, NY, USA, 1995. ACM. ISBN 0-89791-715-4.

[5] C. Clark, K. Fraser, S. Hand, J. G. Hansen, E. Jul, C. Limpach, I. Pratt, and A. Warfield. Live Migration of Virtual Machines. In *NSDI'05: Proceedings of the 2nd conference on Symposium on Networked Systems Design & Implementation*, pages 273–286, Berkeley, CA, USA, 2005. USENIX Association.

[6] B. Cully, G. Lefebvre, D. Meyer, M. Feeley, N. Hutchinson, and A. Warfield. Remus: high availability via asynchronous virtual machine replication. In *Proceedings of the 5th USENIX Symposium on Networked Systems Design and Implementation*, NSDI'08, pages 161–174, 2008. ISBN 111-999-5555-22-1.

[7] J. Dean and S. Ghemawat. MapReduce: simplified data processing on large clusters. *Commun. ACM*, 51:107–113, January 2008.

[8] Y. Dong, Y. Zhang, and G. Liao. Optimizing Network I/O Virtualization with Efficient Interrupt Coalescing and Virtual Receive Side Scaling. In *Proceedings of the 2011 IEEE International Conference on Cluster Computing*, CLUSTER '11, 2011.

[9] Y. Du and H. Yu. Paratus: Instantaneous Failover via Virtual Machine Replication. In *Proceedings of the 2009 Eighth International Conference on Grid and Cooperative Computing*, GCC '09, pages 307–312. IEEE Computer Society, 2009.

[10] Y. Du, H. Yu, G. Shi, J. Chen, and W. Zheng. Microwiper: Efficient Memory Propagation in Live Migration of Virtual Machines. In *Proceedings of the 2010 39th International Conference on Parallel Processing*, ICPP '10, pages 141–149, Washington, DC, USA, 2010. ISBN 978-0-7695-4156-3.

[11] G. W. Dunlap, D. G. Lucchetti, M. A. Fetterman, and P. M. Chen. Execution replay of multiprocessor virtual machines. In *Proceedings of the fourth ACM SIGPLAN/SIGOPS international conference on Virtual execution environments*, VEE '08, pages 121–130, 2008. ISBN 978-1-59593-796-4.

[12] B. Gerofi and Y. Ishikawa. RDMA based Replication of Multiprocessor Virtual Machines over High-Performance Interconnects. In *Proceedings of the 2011 IEEE International Conference on Cluster Computing*, CLUSTER '11, pages 35–44, 2011.

[13] S. Ha, I. Rhee, and L. Xu. CUBIC: a new TCP-friendly high-speed TCP variant. *SIGOPS Oper. Syst. Rev.*, 42:64–74, July 2008. ISSN 0163-5980.

[14] R. Hariharan and N. Sun. Workload Characterization of SPECweb2005. `http://www.spec.org/workshops/2006/papers/02_Workload_char_SPECweb2005_Final.pdf`, 2006.

[15] W. Huang, Q. Gao, J. Liu, and D. K. Panda. High performance virtual machine migration with RDMA over modern interconnects. In *Proceedings of the 2007 IEEE International Conference on Cluster Computing*, CLUSTER '07, pages 11–20, Washington, DC, USA, 2007. ISBN 978-1-4244-1387-4.

[16] A. Kangarlou, S. Gamage, R. R. Kompella, and D. Xu. vSnoop: Improving TCP Throughput in Virtualized Environments via Acknowledgement Offload. In *Proceedings of the 2010 ACM/IEEE International Conference for High Performance Computing, Networking, Storage and Analysis*, SC '10, pages 1–11, Washington, DC, USA, 2010. IEEE Computer Society.

[17] A. Kivity, Y. Kamay, D. Laor, U. Lublin, and A. Liguori. kvm: the Linux virtual machine monitor. In *Ottawa Linux Symposium*, pages 225–230, July 2007. URL `http://www.kernel.org/doc/ols/2007/ols2007v1-pages-225-230.pdf`.

[18] D. Lee, B. Wester, K. Veeraraghavan, S. Narayanasamy, P. M. Chen, and J. Flinn. Respec: efficient online multiprocessor replayvia speculation and external determinism. ASPLOS '10, pages 77–90. ACM, 2010. ISBN 978-1-60558-839-1.

[19] M. Lu and T. cker Chiueh. Fast memory state synchronization for virtualization-based fault tolerance. In *Dependable Systems Networks, 2009. DSN '09. IEEE/IFIP International Conference on*, pages 534 – 543, 2009.

[20] R. McDougall and J. Anderson. Virtualization performance: perspectives and challenges ahead. *SIGOPS Oper. Syst. Rev.*, 44:40–56, December 2010. ISSN 0163-5980.

[21] A. Menon, A. L. Cox, and W. Zwaenepoel. Optimizing network virtualization in Xen. In *Proceedings of the annual conference on USENIX '06 Annual Technical Conference*, pages 15–28, Berkeley, CA, USA, 2006. USENIX Association.

[22] A. Menon, S. Schubert, and W. Zwaenepoel. TwinDrivers: semi-automatic derivation of fast and safe hypervisor network drivers from guest OS drivers. In *Proceeding of the 14th international conference on Architectural support for programming languages and operating systems*, ASPLOS '09, pages 301–312, New York, NY, USA, 2009. ACM.

[23] M. Nelson, B. H. Lim, and G. Hutchins. Fast transparent migration for virtual machines. In *ATEC '05: Proceedings of the annual conference on USENIX Annual Technical Conference*, page 25, Berkeley, CA, USA, 2005. USENIX Association. URL `http://portal.acm.org/citation.cfm?id=1247360.1247385`.

[24] G. Pokam, C. Pereira, K. Danne, L. Yang, S. King, and J. Torellas. Hardware and Software Approaches for Deterministic Multi-Processor Replay of Concurrent Programs. In *Intel Technology Journal*, volume 13, issue 4, pages 20–41, 2009.

[25] D. J. Scales, M. Nelson, and G. Venkitachalam. The design of a practical system for fault-tolerant virtual machines. *SIGOPS Oper. Syst. Rev.*, 44:30–39, December 2010.

[26] M. Stonebraker, D. Abadi, D. J. DeWitt, S. Madden, E. Paulson, A. Pavlo, and A. Rasin. MapReduce and parallel DBMSs: friends or foes? *Commun. ACM*, 53:64–71, January 2010.

[27] Strom, R.E. and Bacon, D.F. and Yemini, S.A. Volatile logging in n-fault-tolerant distributed systems. In *Fault-Tolerant Computing, Eighteenth International Symposium on*, pages 44 –49, Jun 1988.

[28] Y. Tamura. Kemari: Virtual Machine Synchronization for Fault Tolerance using DomT. Technical report, NTT Cyber Space Labs, 2008.

[29] Test TCP (TTCP): Benchmarking Tool and Simple Network Traffic Generator. http://www.pcausa.com/Utilities/pcattcp.htm, 2010.

[30] A. TM. Hadoop. `http://hadoop.apache.org`.

[31] Transmission Control Protocol. Protocol Specification. `http://www.ietf.org/rfc/rfc793.txt`, 1981.

[32] K. V. Vishwanath and N. Nagappan. Characterizing cloud computing hardware reliability. In *Proceedings of the 1st ACM symposium on Cloud computing*, SoCC '10, pages 193–204, New York, NY, USA, 2010. ACM.

[33] M. Xu, R. Bodik, and M. D. Hill. A "flight data recorder" for enabling full-system multiprocessor deterministic replay. In *Proceedings of the 30th annual international symposium on Computer architecture*, ISCA '03, pages 122–135. ACM, 2003. ISBN 0-7695-1945-8.

[34] X. Zhang, Z. Huo, J. Ma, and D. Meng. Exploiting Data Deduplication to Accelerate Live Virtual Machine Migration. In *Cluster Computing (CLUSTER), 2010 IEEE International Conference on*, pages 88 –96, 2010.

[35] J. Zhu, W. Dong, Z. Jiang, X. Shi, Z. Xiao, and X. Li. Improving the Performance of Hypervisor-based Fault Tolerance. In *Parallel Distributed Processing (IPDPS), 2010 IEEE International Symposium on*, pages 1 –10, 2010.

SecondSite: Disaster Tolerance as a Service

Shriram Rajagopalan Brendan Cully Ryan O'Connor Andrew Warfield
Department of Computer Science, University of British Columbia
{rshriram, brendan, rjo, andy}@cs.ubc.ca

Abstract

This paper describes the design and implementation of SecondSite, a cloud-based service for disaster tolerance. SecondSite extends the Remus virtualization-based high availability system by allowing groups of virtual machines to be replicated across data centers over wide-area Internet links. The goal of the system is to commodify the property of availability, exposing it as a simple tick box when configuring a new virtual machine. To achieve this in the wide area, we have had to tackle the related issues of replication traffic bandwidth, reliable failure detection across geographic regions and traffic redirection over a wide-area network without compromising on transparency and consistency.

Categories and Subject Descriptors D.4.5 [*Operating Systems*]: Reliability—Backup procedures, Checkpoint/restart, Fault-tolerance

Keywords Wide Area Replication, Disaster Recovery

1. Introduction

Failures in the cloud are spectacular. In January 2010, Heroku, a Ruby-on-Rails application hosting company experienced the complete failure of their 22 virtual machines hosted on Amazon EC2. This outage, which was reportedly the result of a router failure, affected the 44,000 applications hosted on the site [7]. In May 2010, Amazon experienced four EC2 outages in a single week, the last of which resulted from a car crashing into a utility pole cutting power to a portion of the system [25]. Outages such as these are hardly limited to Amazon, who through the introduction of "availability zones", has taken steps to expose failure domains explicitly to customers so that applications may be designed to survive outages. However, while techniques to expose fate sharing and exposure to risk, such as Amazon's availability zones, help their customers engineer systems to survive failures, they are no panacea.

In April 2011, a "networking event" in the Virginia facility triggered a cascading failure in Amazon's Elastic Block Store (EBS), and resulted in a serious outage *across* multiple availability zones. An undisclosed number of virtual machines, including the hosts of a number of large, popular web-based applications, became unavailable for the initial twelve hours of the outage. Complete service was not restored for five days. Amazon published a detailed postmortem of the event, explaining that the outage stemmed from a series of bugs and unanticipated behaviors *in the failure recovery mechanisms* for EBS [37]. One of the concluding observations made in the document is that for the highest degree of availability, applications should be protected across multiple *regions*–geographically separate data center facilities that have a much lower degree of fate sharing than availability zones within the same data center.

The EBS failure is illustrative of the fact that while cloud computing environments are well maintained and professionally administered systems, they are not immune to outages. The postmortem, released less than a week after the outage itself, represents a surprisingly thorough and forthcoming explanation of the chain of events leading to failure. It also identifies a set of changes, to both software and administrative procedures, that will be taken to avoid repeating this sort of outage in the future. However, the failure severely impacted customers–even those who were making efforts to engineer their systems to be resistant to outages within the hosting environment–and left them without service for as many as five days. As such, the Virginia outage also demonstrates that while rare, outages are happening, and they are happening at scale. Even the skilled developers of mature Internet-based services face challenges in designing systems that handle these failures gracefully.

This paper describes ***SecondSite***, a high-availability and disaster tolerance service for virtual machines running in cloud environments. Based on the premise that implementing application- or OS-level fault tolerance is both difficult and expensive, we argue that facilities to enhance the availability of hosted software should be commodified, and offered as part of the hosting infrastructure. Just as spot markets [40] allow customers to receive a less reliable level of service at a cut rate, we argue that important workloads (and less sophisticated developers) would prefer a service that transparently provides a higher degree of availability. Using SecondSite, the owner of a hosted virtual machine may elect to have that VM's entire state continuously replicated to a backup image at an alternate geographic location. As with the Remus [11] system on which it is based, in the event of failure SecondSite allows the backup VM to take over in a completely transparent manner, requires no changes to OS or application code and exposes no failure to connected clients.

1.1 Failure Model

High-availability systems are typically complex: they require careful planning, complex integration with program logic, and ongoing maintenance as application code evolves over time. SecondSite makes two simplifying design decisions regarding its failure model that are intended to make it more practical for general purpose use.

Provide protection from fail-stop failures. Like Remus before it, SecondSite provides protection from fail-stop failures, the typical case in large-scale outages and disasters. The system provides transparent, continuous replication of a running VM to a passive backup host at another location. While fail-stop clearly includes destructive events such as fires and power outages, we also promote network failures to be fail-stop through the use of a watchdog that

VEE'12, March 3–4, 2012, London, England, UK.

	Local Area (Remus)	*Wide Area (SecondSite)*
Replication Link	Bonded Ethernet Interfaces	Routed IP connectivity over WAN
Replication Latency	Hundreds of microseconds	Tens of milliseconds
Failure Detection	Complete link failure of replication channel	Quorum among external vantage points
Network Relocation	Ethernet MAC (e.g. via ARP)	IP address (e.g. via BGP)

Table 1: Differences between the Local and Wide-Area Network.

automatically removes the active host from service in the case of network disconnection. This approach does not attempt to survive "wounded" applications experiencing partial failures as a result of overload, environmental problems, or bugs. However, it can help to maintain availability when a site is experiencing wide-area connectivity problems by transparently migrating to a better-connected backup during the network outage.

Protect the complete state of the running application. The failures for which SecondSite provides protection address concerns of *both* availability and durability. The established approach for disaster recovery in many environments today involves the asynchronous replication of storage. In the event of failure, storage-based disaster recovery systems (a) lose some amount of data and (b) require that the hosts reboot successfully from a crash-consistent image. In SecondSite, the disk image and complete running machine state are replicated, meaning that *no data* will be lost in the event of failure, and that reboots, with associated file system checks, are not required. This approach mitigates the risk associated with failures that may occur during restart on the backup host, such as problems checking the local (crash-consistent) file system.

In the next section, we characterize three challenges that we faced in evolving Remus to provide disaster tolerance as a service. The first of these concerns involve making replication work effectively over expensive and higher-latency wide-area links. The remaining two concerns address the network-related challenges of detecting failure and restoring service in an Internet, as opposed to local-area, environment. Many of the individual techniques described here have been used in other systems: the contribution of this work is to describe the development of an active disaster tolerant testbed that is currently deployed between two university data centers, approximately 260 kilometers apart. In addition to the architecture of the system, we describe several of the more painful corner cases that we experienced during development and deployment, and provide details of a continuous regression test suite that we use to validate and demonstrate confidence in the system to others.

2. Challenges of Wide-Area Disaster Tolerance

Remus [11] provides transparent high availability for unmodified OS and application software running within virtual machines on the Xen [4] hypervisor. Remus achieves this by employing checkpoint-based fault tolerance: during normal operation, incremental checkpoints of the entire VM state on the primary host are replicated to a backup host. These checkpoints are performed at a very high frequency (20-40 checkpoints/second) to enable fine grained recovery. On failure of the primary host, the VM at the backup host resumes execution from the latest completed checkpoint. The failover process is totally transparent to clients: the backup VM has the same IP address as the primary VM and, just as with live migration [9], the backup host issues a gratuitous ARP to ensure network packets going to the failed VM are automatically redirected to the backup VM as soon as it becomes available.

Remus checkpoints capture the entire state of the primary VM, which includes disk, memory, CPU and network device state. Checkpoint replication and acknowledgement is carefully pipelined and overlapped with execution to maintain low overhead, while still preserving consistency. The execution of the primary VM during each checkpoint interval is *speculative* until the interval has been checkpointed, since it will be lost if a failure occurs. Therefore, Remus uses output commit [29] to ensure that the external world sees a consistent view of the server's execution, despite failovers. More specifically, Remus queues and holds any outgoing network packets generated by the primary server until the completion of the next checkpoint, ensuring that unprotected speculative state is never exposed.

Output commit is also applied to isolate disk writes generated during a checkpoint interval. Writes received from the active server during an epoch are buffered and released to disk only after a checkpoint is complete. In the case of failure, Remus ensures that prior to resuming execution on the backup, all outstanding checkpointed writes have been written to disk and that any writes associated with speculative execution are discarded.

2.1 Challenges of Wide-Area Networks

Remus is designed for a LAN environment, and is intended to respond to the increased exposure to failure that results from consolidating many physical servers into virtual machines on a single host. In this environment, the failure of a single physical host carries elevated consequences, and Remus provided the ability to transparently recover from this class of failure by replicating state to a second physical server.

The environmental differences that face an availability system in moving from the local to the wide area are summarized in Table 1. First, the high bandwidth and low latency network of the local area is replaced with a typically lower bandwidth, and certainly higher latency IP connection between sites. As a consequence, the system must be more frugal with replication traffic, as networking resources are constrained and often also quite expensive.

A second difference is that Remus aims to survive any single, fail-stop physical failure. In Remus, replication traffic travelled over a dedicated point-to-point Ethernet link from the primary to the backup. This meant that Remus could survive the failure of any single physical component, even the loss of a replication NIC. In the wide area, the link between the active and backup hosts is often an IP route and may be lost even though the rest of the network remains available, requiring more careful consideration of failure notification. Finally, address relocation is considerably more challenging as a result of the need to alter upstream routing.

The remaining subsections discuss each of these three issues in more detail.

2.2 Bandwidth-Efficient Replication

Continuously replicating virtual machine checkpoints can require a lot of bandwidth. Depending on the frequency of checkpoint replication and the amount of state changed since the previous checkpoint, replication can easily consume up to 600 Mbps for memory intensive workloads. While a 1Gbps link supports this load, the cost of wide-area networking makes site-wide replication impractical at this rate. Furthermore, having multiple high-bandwidth streams share a single link can increase congestion and reduce the effective bandwidth of the link.

In previous work on optimizing Remus for databases [24], we faced similar challenges: database workloads can generate very large checkpoints to the point that even fast LAN links may become performance bottlenecks. We developed three main techniques to reduce checkpoint size and latency: *Commit Protection* relaxes output buffering of some network messages. *Read tracking* avoids replicating changes to the contents of memory where that state has previously been read from disk. Finally, *Checkpoint Compression* saves bandwidth by performing online compression of the replication stream.

2.3 Failure Detection

To ensure correct execution, it is very important that only one of the replicas is active at once. When the replicas lose contact with each other, we must ensure that the active replica has failed (or become globally unreachable). Remus deals with the problem of distinguishing between system failure and network partition by bonding together two physical NICs for the replication link, so that it will continue to operate even if a single NIC fails. This does not suffice across a WAN, where the connection between the primary and the backup is not necessarily under the control of the high-availability service provider.

Differentiating between network partition and host failure using only two hosts is not easy, and we do not attempt to do it. Instead, we rely on an arbitration service residing outside of the protected network. If the primary and backup hosts lose contact with each other, they attempt to contact the arbitrator to decide which of them should continue running. They will terminate if instructed to do so by the arbitrator, or if they cannot reach the arbitrator.

2.4 Failure Recovery

When a virtual machine is relocated, network traffic between it and its clients must take a different path. The transition between locations must have two properties to be effective: it must be *comprehensive* — as the VM is being recovered in a geographically distant location, traffic from all clients must be appropriately redirected to the new VM instance. Second, in order to maintain availability, it must also complete in a *timely* manner. In the LAN environment, these properties are easy to achieve: As both primary and backup hosts are on a common Ethernet network, relocation is not exposed to the IP layer beyond the use of ARP.

Unlike the LAN environment, wide-area migrations involve BGP updates to redirect IP traffic from one site to another. BGP convergence times are challenging to reason about and slow BGP convergence may result in considerably longer periods of unreachability for the backup host. Rather than attempting to tackle the general issue of convergence delays related to IP address migration in BGP our approach uses a specific, but realistic BGP configuration to provide failover: we configure the protected network on the active and backup sites in the same manner that dual-homed IP networks are configured to survive link or ISP failures. Our network configuration can be thought of as a dual-homed set up in which not only is the backup link is redundant, but so are the servers that they connect to.

3. SecondSite Design

SecondSite builds upon Remus and provides the same transparency and consistency guarantees. In a typical deployment, SecondSite runs on each physical host on the primary site, replicating all virtual machines (VM) running on that host across a WAN to a host on the backup site. Each VM is checkpointed independently.

When the primary site fails, the backup site performs the required network reconfiguration (e.g., BGP updates) and resumes the execution of all the protected virtual machines from their last consistent checkpoint. The failure and subsequent migration to a remote location is completely transparent to the VMs.

3.1 Reducing Replication Overhead

RemusDB [24] introduced a set of optimizations to address the large overheads of checkpoint-based HA for database applications. These optimizations addressed both latency and replication bandwidth, and thus can be very beneficial for disaster recovery. The following were the main optimizations introduced by RemusDB:

- **Checkpoint Compression** Using *Page Delta* compression [30, 34] and an LRU cache of previously dirtied pages, this technique reduces the size of a checkpoint dramatically. The observation here was that updates to memory were sparse but spread over a large working set.
- **Disk Read Tracking** Since the disk is kept synchronized by Remus during replication, pages read from the disk by Guest VM need not be included in the checkpoint as long as it is unmodified during the checkpoint. At the backup host, these pages are periodically read from disk into the backup VM's memory.
- **Commit Protection** Applications can dynamically override output commit through a `setsockopt()` option. The ability to dynamically switch a connection between buffered and unbuffered states, allows transactional workloads like OLTP to leverage consistency guarantees of Remus without incurring the latency overhead introduced by output buffering [29].

We have only used one of these techniques (checkpoint compression) in this work. The read tracking optimization was developed against the Remus disk replication module, which does not support resynchronization after failure. Preliminary investigation indicated that it would not produce large improvements for the workloads we examined (discussed in Section 4), and so we have not yet ported support to our new disk synchronization layer.

Commit protection can reduce client-perceived latency dramatically, but it requires understanding of the protected application and cannot simply be switched on. As a platform-level service, SecondSite aims for transparency for both the protected VMs and the service provider, and so we have only evaluated techniques that conform to that goal.

3.2 Failure Detection in SecondSite

In SecondSite, we only consider *fail-stop* failures. A node may suspect failure if the replication stream times out, but the failure of the replication link does not prove that the remote node itself has failed, or even that it has become unreachable to its clients. Incorrectly classifying link failure as node failure can lead to a *Split-Brain* scenario, where both primary and backup become active at the same time. Failure detection in distributed systems is a richly researched topic, with many possible approaches but no single perfect solution. Possible approaches include unreliable failure detectors [8], minimal synchrony [12] and partial synchrony [15]. Several variants of unreliable failure detectors have been proposed, such as heart beat [1, 2], adaptive timeouts [16], gossip-based detection [32], and so on. Such approaches assume partition tolerance, which SecondSite does not require.

SecondSite's failure detector requires the following properties:

- Quick detection — The failure detection logic contributes to the *service downtime*, as network packets from VMs are not released until a decision is made.
- No false positives — Incorrectly classifying a live site as dead leads to split brain situation and loss of data consistency.

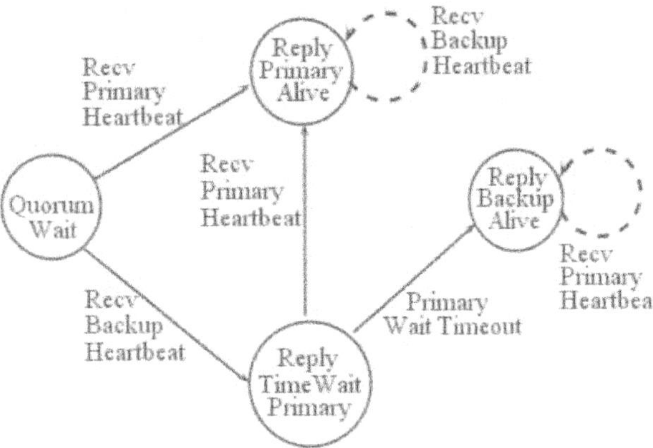

Figure 1: State Transitions of a Quorum Node

- Conservative failover — Network congestion can produce transient communication delays. Aggressively classifying such delays as failures and triggering recovery is expensive and could lead to reduced availability.

Quorum-based failure detection techniques can be used to achieve these requirements. There are several variants of the quorum technique. One simple technique is to use a *shared quorum disk*, where both nodes try to atomically reserve a disk partition (e.g. SCSI Reserve & Release). Such a solution is infeasible over a wide-area network. Another commonly used solution in WAN environments [41] is the *ping*-based approach. When the replication channel is broken, the backup site attempts to ping the primary site over a different network address. If the ping is successful, failover is avoided. This technique requires that there be at least two different routes between the primary and backup site, one to carry replication traffic and another for the ping test. This approach avoids requiring a third node by using distinct network interfaces to create a quorum. A third approach is to use quorum protocols [18] with one or more quorum nodes outside the WAN cluster acting as arbitrators.

Procedure 1 Quorum Logic at Primary Site

Require: $ReplicationTimeout == True$
  suspend VMs and stop replication
  result = SendHeartbeat(quorumNode)
  if result == PrimaryAlive **then** // *Link/Backup Failure*
    resume VMs
  else // *Failover happened*
    shutdown
  end if

Procedure 2 Quorum Logic at Backup Site

Require: $ReplicationTimeout == True$
  stop replication
  loop
    result = SendHeartbeat(quorumNode)
    if result == PrimaryAlive **then** // *Link Failure*
      shutdown
    else if result == TimeWaitPrimary **then**
      wait T secs for Primary to respond
    else if result == BackupAlive **then** // *Link/Primary failure*
      Issue BGP update to re-route network traffic
      resume VMs from latest checkpoint
    end if
  end loop

In SecondSite, we chose to use quorum server(s) to arbitrate during failure detection. We deployed a quorum web service in Google App Engine [39]. Figure 1 shows the state transitions of a quorum server used by SecondSite. The corresponding logic used by the primary and backup sites are illustrated in procedures 1 & 2 respectively. Using a quorum web service is just one example of how one could deploy a quorum service on the cloud cheaply. In fact, the quorum service we deployed consumed very little resources that it was well within the "daily free quota" offered by Google. When a failure is suspected by one node, a quorum is initiated. If the backup node initiates quorum first, it waits for a configurable time period for the primary node to make contact. The wait phase avoids unnecessary failovers caused by transient connectivity loss between the two nodes. While one quorum server is sufficient, to provide better redundancy one could deploy several quorum servers and use a simple majority quorum algorithm to decide which of the two nodes should be victimized in the event of network partition.

There are three failure scenarios to consider in our setup:

- **One Node Failure** Recovery succeeds with the help of quorum servers. If the surviving node is the backup node, failure recovery procedures are initiated.
- **Replication Link Failure** If a node obtains a quorum, it lives (or recovers). If not, it shuts down. It is thus possible that both nodes would shutdown if they fail to reach any quorum servers or the quorum nodes in any partition is insufficient to satisfy a majority. For services that cannot tolerate partitioned operation, this behavior ensures data consistency.
- **Quorum Node(s) Failure** Replication proceeds as usual.

Table 2 enumerates different failure scenarios, the quorum outcome and time to achieve the quorum (i.e. service downtime).

3.3 Failure Recovery

The dominant new challenge in recovering from failures in a wide-area environment is that of redirecting traffic: after failure detection determines that the backup site should step in, the IP addresses must be relocated as quickly as possible, between the two locations on the Internet. As Remus continues to perform output commit and the failure detection protocol ensures that at most one VM instance is ever active at a time, there is no possibility that open TCP sessions will ever move into an irrecoverable state due to mismatched sequence numbers. If IP advertisements change sufficiently quickly, failover will be almost completely transparent to clients; TCP sessions will remain open, and the only exposed aspect of failure will be the possibility of a small number of dropped packets during failover. To achieve this, SecondSite requires network support to quickly move IP addresses between the two sites.

Failing Component	*Quorum Outcome*	*Resolution Time (Service Downtime)*
Replication Link	Backup Shutdown	RTT to Quorum Service
Primary [+ Link]	failover to Backup	2 RTTs to Quorum Service + Quorum Timeout + Network Re-configuration
Backup [+ Link]	Primary survives	RTT to Quorum Service
Quorum Server	Replication continues	0
Primary + Quorum	Backup Shutdown	Service Failure (Manual Intervention)
Backup + Quorum	Primary Shutdown	Service Failure (Manual Intervention)
Link + Quorum	Primary & Backup Shutdown	Service Failure (Manual Intervention)

Table 2: Failure Scenarios and Down-times using Quorum Servers

The system achieves this by interacting with the Border Gateway Protocol (BGP) to influence Internet routing decisions.

BGP is a path vector protocol where every router selects the best route to destinations (IP address blocks) based on the routes advertised by neighboring routers. A BGP route advertisement for a given destination IP prefix contains the autonomous system numbers of all ASes it has traversed through, since originating from the AS responsible for that prefix. Route advertisements also have one or more attributes, that play a role in choosing the best possible route to a destination from a set of routes. Transitive attributes are passed on from one router to another, while non-transitive attributes are used to manipulate routing decisions between any two adjacent routers. When there are multiple routes to the same destination AS, the choice of the best route depends on the routing policies, AS path lengths and other attributes assigned to the route.

Figure 2 shows our routing architecture. We leverage BGP multi-homing to achieve failure recovery. On a high level, the system works as follows: the set of hosts being protected by SecondSite can be reached through two different Internet routes, one leading to the primary site and another to the backup site. Only the primary site's route is kept active (i.e. the best route) during normal operation. When a failover occurs, the backup site issues a new route advertisement that has preferable attributes to those of the existing preferred route. BGP route attribute manipulation enables us to influence the routing decisions made by upstream ASes.

An extensive measurement study done by Labovitz et al. [22] revealed that route updates from shorter to longer path lengths take longer time to converge compared to the converse case. As we are concerned with ensuring that reachability to the backup host be established as quickly as possible on failover, we have opted for a configuration in which a single upstream AS provides both links. We believe that this is realistic for many deployments, but also observe that the intuition from Labovitz et al. is that it is desirable to limit the number of ASes that advertisements need to propagate through to the greatest degree possible in order to reduce convergence times.

In practice, BGP multi-homing can be achieved in a number of ways. As examples, the following are some key attributes used to indicate route preferences:

- **Multiexit Discriminator (MED)**: When an AS has multiple entry points, the optional MED attribute can be used to provide a hint to neighbouring ASes about the preferred link for inbound traffic. As such, the MED attribute to switch inbound traffic from a primary to backup link. While MEDs are honored by current BGP implementations, they are non-transitive, i.e. a MED attribute received by an AS does not leave the AS. Thus, MED attribute based route manipulation only works in HA configurations that have a single upstream AS.
- **AS-path prepend**: AS-path prepending is a common way to influence BGP routing decisions of upstream routers. If there is no conflict with local routing policies, BGP routers generally select the route with the shortest path to a given destination prefix. Routers can be configured to indicate a reduced preference to the neighbouring ASes by advertising a longer AS-path for that prefix. AS-paths can be lengthened by prepending it one or more times with the router's AS number. AS-path prepending can be used as an HA mechanism for IP failover: The backup site advertises a longer path than the primary site for the IP prefix. On failover, it removes prepended entries to advertise a shorter path than the primary, resulting in a preferential route and so re-routing traffic to the backup site. This technique can be used even when there are multiple AS peerings at each site, however, the further upstream path adjustments have to travel in order to successfully redirect traffic, the more exposed the system will be to long convergence times and potential unreachability.
- **Communities and local preference**: A number of extensions have been added to BGP, largely with the intention of allowing ISPs to delegate a greater degree of control over routing decisions to their customers. BGP community and local preference attributes are two such extensions, and may be used in conjunction with AS-path prepending if the routing preferences should be visible beyond the ISP. The local preference attribute is used to influence routing decisions within an AS; routes with a higher local preference are favored over other routes. Communities allow collections of prefixes to be grouped and scoped together, and so act as a useful point of indirection to apply local preference updates.

  To influence routing decisions within the ISP, the client and the ISP agree to map certain BGP communities advertised by the client to local preferences within the ISP. This approach allows the client to use a private AS number, but will not propagate route changes beyond the ISP's AS without an analogous mapping of client BGP communities to ISP AS path prepends.

SecondSite uses BGP communities mapped to local preferences and AS path prepends, for failure recovery. The local preferences are used to influence routing decisions within our upstream AS. The community mappings to AS-path prepends influence routing decisions beyond our upstream AS. Both the primary and backup sites advertise a BGP route for a /24 CIDR block. All the protected VMs are assigned IP addresses from this block. The backup site's AS-path to the IP prefix is longer than the primary, as indicated in Figure 2, allowing the primary site to receive all network traffic for the VMs. When a failover is initiated, the backup site advertises a route with shorter AS-path and higher local preference, than the primary site. This causes traffic to flow to the backup site, once the routing update converges.

The approach that we have taken is hardly the only way to achieve route redirection with BGP. Other techniques, such as the use of more specific advertisements to redirect traffic are also possible. An earlier version of our system used this approach success-

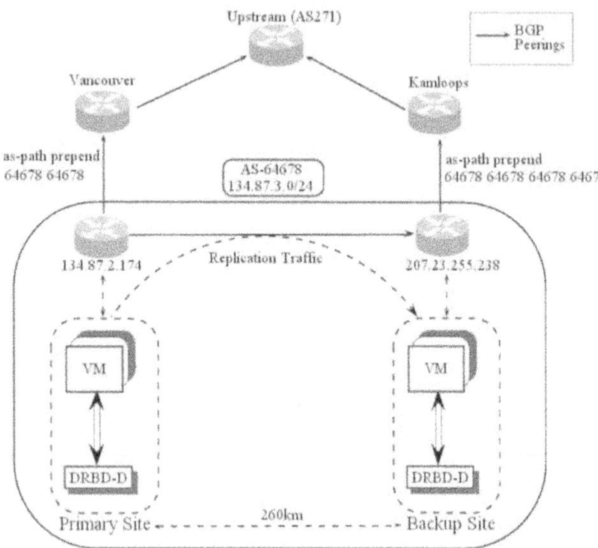

Figure 2: SecondSite setup over WAN

fully, but we were dissatisfied with the associated loss of IP address space that the technique required.

Further, BGP based IP multi-homing is not the only solution to transparently failover network connections. For example, in VPN based setups, routing reconfigurations could be done on the VPN concentrator [34], in order to maintain client connectivity during VM migration. Our concern with overlay network-based solutions such as these is that they often either introduced a single point of failure in the VPN concentrator, or led to situations in which traffic had to be routed through both active and passive sites during some classes of failure.

3.4 Seamless Failback

After a crashed primary site comes back online, in order to restart SecondSite, storage has to be resynchronized from backup to the primary site, without causing an outage to the VMs running in the backup site. Remus' storage replication driver, based on Xen's Blktap2 driver [36] does not provide a means for online resynchronization of storage. In order to understand the requirements of resynchronization, we turn the reader's attention towards the disk replication component of Remus.

Remus replicates disk writes asynchronously over the network to the backup site during a checkpoint interval. The backup site buffers in memory all writes received during a checkpoint. At the end of a checkpoint, primary site flushes any pending data in the socket and sends a *commit* message to the backup site. On reception of this message, the backup site sends an acknowledgement and then asynchronously flushes the buffered writes to disk. When the primary site fails during a checkpoint period, the backup site discards all buffered disk writes accumulated in that unfinished checkpoint.

A resynchronization module needs the following two functionalities:

- *Track blocks written by VMs at backup site after failover.* When the primary site is back online, these blocks have to be replicated from the backup to primary site, while the VMs continue performing i/o. This requires an online algorithm for dirty block tracking and resynchronization.
- *Discard writes made by primary site during the last unfinished checkpoint.* While it is easy for the backup site to compute these blocks from its checkpoint buffer and include them as part of dirty block resynchronization, it would be incomplete since replication is asynchronous. Only the primary site would have complete knowledge of blocks written before failure. This would necessitate the primary site to log the location of disk writes before doing the actual write. During resynchronization, the primary site would use the log to identify writes in the unfinished checkpoint prior to failure and overwrite them with data from the backup site.

DRBD [27] provides storage replication in asynchronous or synchronous mode with efficient *online resynchronization* functionality. Its *quick-sync* bitmap feature tracks writes done by a backup node after primary failure. Meanwhile, the primary node uses *activity logging* to keep track of active extents (4MB in size) during normal operation. It offers a variety of resynchronization options that suit SecondSite's needs. However, the current replication modes in DRBD do not support the checkpoint based asynchronous replication required by SecondSite. We modified DRBD to add a new Remus style replication protocol. DRBD is configured to perform a *one-way* resynchronization from backup to primary site, of all blocks indicated by the quick-sync bitmap at backup and activity log at primary.

During resynchronization period, the VMs at backup site continue to operate normally while the DRBD driver performs online storage resynchronization to bring the peer node up-to-date. Once the resynchronization is complete, SecondSite replication can be restarted very easily from either the primary site after live migrating the VMs back to it, or by reversing roles of primary and backup site.

4. Evaluation on a WAN Testbed

We have deployed SecondSite to provide continual protection for servers running in their home location at UBC in Vancouver, BC, backed up to a site 260 kilometers away at Thompson Rivers University in Kamloops, BC. The two sites are connected by a 1-Gigabit link with an average round trip time of 5ms. Figure 2 shows the topology of our configuration. The primary and backup servers are equipped with 8-core Intel Xeon processors and 16GB of RAM, and run Xen Linux 2.6.18-8 on Xen 4.0.0. SecondSite was configured to checkpoint the VMs on the primary host at 50ms epoch intervals, for a checkpoint frequency of 20 checkpoints per second.

4.1 Regression Tests

Using a high-latency routed link for replication applies stress to the checkpointing, failure detection and recovery systems that is not experienced over an Ethernet link. We felt the best way to validate our system was to run continuous regression tests under a real deployment between two distinct sites. The test suite consisted of a cluster of VMs (each with 512MB RAM and 1 vCPU) protected by SecondSite. The VMs ran synthetic workloads that stressed disk, memory and network subsystems, as described in Table 3. As they ran, we regularly triggered site failures. On failover, the test programs verified the integrity of their memory and files to ensure that data was not corrupted. When a crashed site came back online, its disks were resynchronized while online using DRBD. Once this phase completed, protection restarted with the recovered primary host acting as the new backup. The VMs continued to run their workload without interruption throughout this process.

Test Name	Workload	Test Goal
MemoryStress	Continuous malloc, dirty and free. Check integrity of allocated memory upon failover.	Trigger memory corruption bugs in compression logic.
PagetableStress	Parameterized fork bomb.	Trigger memory corruption bugs not caught by MemoryStress.
IOStress	Reads and writes on a large file in different I/O modes (buffered, direct).	Trigger bugs in disk replication logic.

Table 3: The Regression Test Suite

The regression test suite turned up some interesting corner cases:

Caching Pagetable Pages. Occasionally, the VM running the PagetableStress workload suffered fatal crashes in the guest kernel, pointing to random processes as the fault origin. Once it became evident that the crash was caused by memory corruption, we were able to trace the culprit to stale entries in the LRU page cache of the compression module. During live migration, a guest VM's pagetable pages are canonicalized before transmitting to target host, such that all references to the host's machine frames are replaced by their corresponding guest physical frames. On the receiving end, this process is reversed. The compression code only cached normal pages and transmitted pagetable pages as is, without updating the cache. Thus, when a normal page became a pagetable page, the cache ended up having a stale version of the page with the valid bit still set. When the page became a normal page again, a page delta would be taken against the wrong version of the page, resulting in memory corruption at the receiving end. Simply evicting the cache copy of the pagetable page fixed the issue.

Write after Write Race in Disk Replication. Write-heavy workloads sometimes experienced disk data corruption on failover. However, we could not reproduce the bug when we repeated the experiment several times on a different set of machines. We finally traced the problem to request re-ordering at the disk controller level. When the backup flushes a disk checkpoint, it simply queues up the writes to disk, merging the checkpoint flush with an ongoing one. When there are overlapping writes in adjacent checkpoint flushes, the disk does not guarantee the order of these writes. Inserting a *Disk I/O Barrier Request* at the end of every checkpoint flush fixed the issue.

4.2 Protecting a Cluster of VMs

Our goal in this section is to evaluate the cost and effectiveness of SecondSite in a production environment. To that end, we have provisioned an aggressive mix of macrobenchmark workloads on a single server and enable concurrent protection on all of them. Specifically, we have installed 2 web servers and 2 databases with different physical resource allocations onto a host with 8 physical CPUs. Domain-0 is configured with a vCPU for each physical CPU. Two VMs run the Apache web server with 1G of RAM and 2 vCPUs each, serving dynamic web pages. The *SPECweb 2005 Ecommerce benchmark* [43] is used to generate the web server workloads. The remaining two VMs run the MySQL Database Server, with 2G of RAM and 2 vCPUs each. The *DVD-Store OLTP benchmark* [42] is used to generate the database workloads. The VMs are assigned IP addresses from a */24* CIDR block that is protected by SecondSite using the BGP failover mechanism described earlier. Each workload has 100 concurrent clients accessing the services via their protected IP addresses. The benchmarks were run with 10 minutes of warm-up interval and 30 minutes of measurement. The OLTP benchmark's mean user think time was set to 10s. We present the benchmark results in terms of operations per minute, where the operation represents a database transaction for OLTP or an HTTP page request for SPECweb.

Figure 3 shows the throughput in terms of operations per minute observed by the clients over a 50 minute measurement period. A failure was injected at the primary site after 15 minutes of execution. With the quorum timeout set to 10 seconds, the backup site took 13 seconds to fully recover all the services and re-establish network connectivity.

Restarting HA. SecondSite takes advantage of DRBD to resynchronize storage with the recovering primary site, without interrupting the execution of VMs on the backup site. Once storage resynchronization completes, VM replication can be resumed from the backup site (now acting as primary) to the primary site (now acting as backup). If the primary site is the preferred home for the VMs, they may optionally be migrated back at this point.

After a 15 minute outage period, the primary host was brought online. Resynchronization of each VM's disk was initiated in parallel. Resynchronization took 52s to complete after which HA was restarted sequentially for each service, with the backup site now acting as the new primary. All VMs were fully protected after 88 seconds, with a constant time overhead of 20 seconds per VM to achieve steady state replication. The throughput increases after failover because the VMs are running in an unprotected mode, and therefore do not incur any checkpointing overhead. The drop in overall throughput starts during disk resynchronization period and settles back to pre-failure levels after all VMs are protected.

Disk Resynchronization. In order to restart HA for a VM, its disk has to be resynchronized with the recovered primary site. Our current recovery approach is to perform DRBD resynchronization of all VMs in parallel. This is a simple approach that is easy to validate and moves the system through recovery stages in lock step. However, it can produce contention on a shared physical disk that reduces the overall throughput of resynchronization. We have also experimented with resynchronizing VMs sequentially, so that each VM can be re-protected as soon as its individual synchronization is complete. This approach reduces the total resynchronization time and dramatically reduces the median unprotected window. In a test similar to the workload in Figure 3, the total resynchronization time is reduced from 37 seconds to 29 seconds, and median unprotected time falls from 23 seconds to 7 seconds.

4.3 DRBD Resynchronization Delays

Failback relies on DRBD to provide disk resynchronization, and cannot proceed until it completes. The time required for this process depends on the amount and locality of data written to disk while the VM is disconnected from its backup. To give an idea of the costs, Figure 4 presents the amount of data changed by the OLTP workload (a mixture of sequential and random I/O) as a function of the outage period, along with the time required to resynchronize the disk.

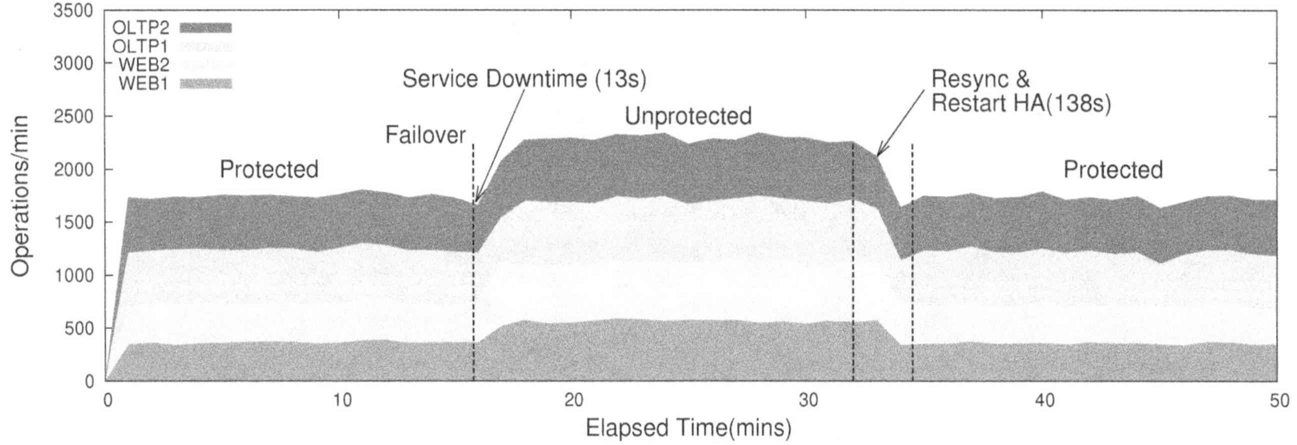

Figure 3: SecondSite Failover and Failback of a set of heterogeneous workloads.

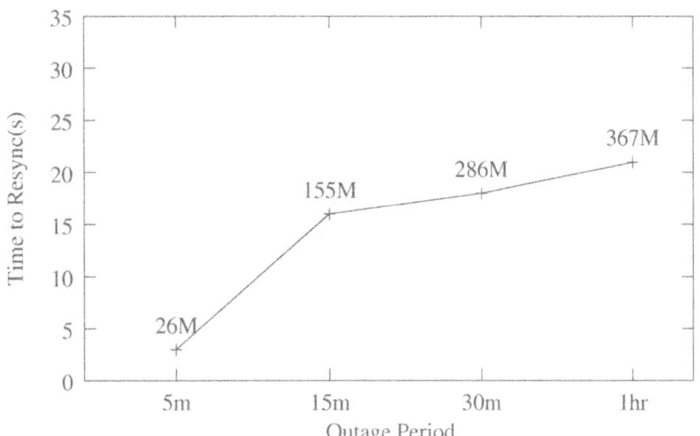

Figure 4: OLTP disk resynchronization costs

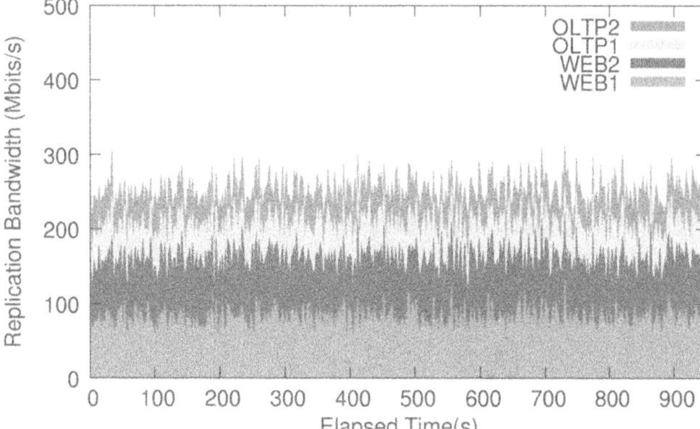

Figure 5: Replication Bandwidth Consumption before Failover (4 VMs x 100 Clients/VM)

Resource	Unprotected		Protected	
	Dom0	VMs	Dom0	VMs
CPU Usage (Primary)	1.1%	4.0%	12.0%	11.6%
			Dom0	VMs
CPU Usage (Backup)	–		8.4%	–
Replication Bandwidth	–		238.82 Mbps	

Table 4: Resource Consumption in a Multi-VM Environment

4.4 Resource Consumption & Throughput

Figure 5 shows the bandwidth consumption per VM when the entire site is protected by SecondSite. To get an idea of the CPU overhead incurred by SecondSite, we sampled the CPU utilization for all the domains on the physical host using the *xentop* [44] tool. All replication related overheads are accounted to Domain–0, while other VMs are executing. The CPU was sampled every 3 seconds over a one hour execution period. Xentop reports an additive percentage utilization over all physical cores. We normalize this value to 100% and report the CPU utilization of Domain–0 and aggregate CPU used by the four VMs in Table 4 for both unprotected and protected modes of operation. We also report the replication link bandwidth consumed by SecondSite during the one hour execution period in Table 4.

We also measure resources consumed by SecondSite (CPU and replication bandwidth) as a function of varying application loads. We vary the user's "think time" parameter of the OLTP workload, which in turn determines the number of requests/minute arriving at the server. We define three representative loads: High, Medium and Low, corresponding to think time values of 5s , 10s and 15s respectively. The aggregate CPU and network bandwidth consumed by Domain-0 are shown in Figure 6a and Figure 6b respectively.

4.5 Throughput vs Replication Latency

For a latency-sensitive workload like SPECweb, the throughput is limited by latency between the clients and the server. Our earlier work [11] examined the impact of network output buffering delay on SPECweb throughput, but did not examine the effects of replication link latency (there was none). In SecondSite, higher replication latencies result in longer times to commit the checkpoint at the backup site. Since the outgoing packets from the protected VM are buffered until the commit acknowledgement is received at the primary site, an increase in replication latency increases the protected server's response time. For workloads like SPECweb, this increased response time results in lower throughput, as illustrated in Figure 7.

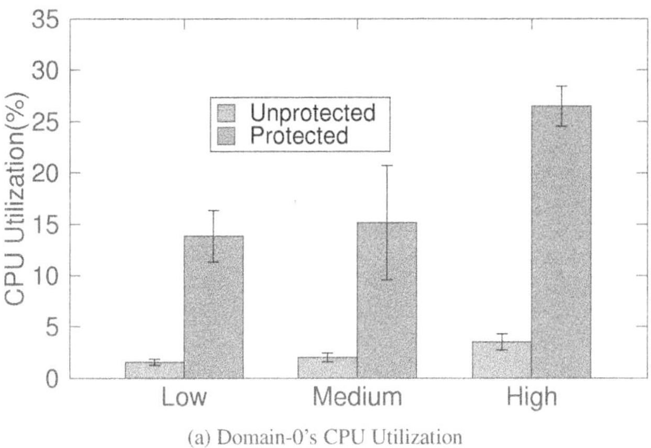

(a) Domain-0's CPU Utilization

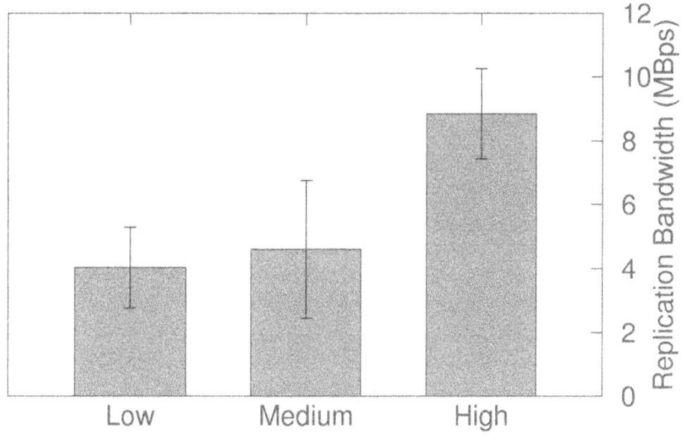

(b) Bandwidth usage on the ReplicationChannel

Figure 6: Cost of HA as a function of Application Load(OLTP Workload with 100 concurrent users).

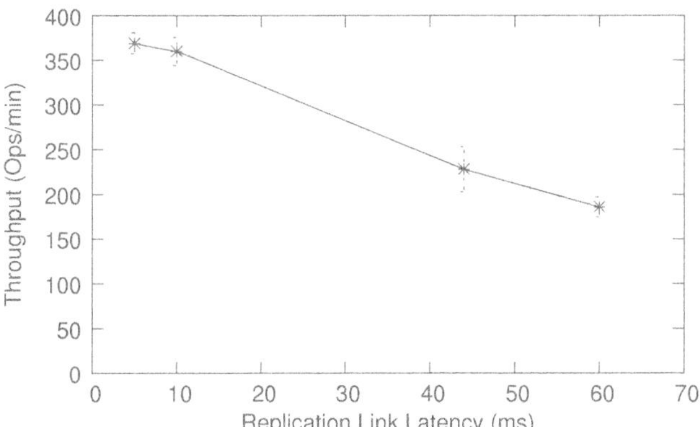

Figure 7: Impact of Replication Link Latency on Application Throughput (SPECweb with 100 Clients)

5. Related Work

5.1 Replication Overhead

Virtualization has been used to provide high availability for arbitrary applications running inside virtual machines, by replicating the entire virtual machine as it runs. Replication can be achieved either through event logging and execution replay or whole machine checkpointing. While event logging requires much less bandwidth than whole machine checkpointing, it is not guaranteed to be able to reproduce machine state unless execution can be made *deterministic*. Enforcing determinism on commodity hardware requires careful management of sources of non-determinism [6, 13], and becomes infeasibly expensive to enforce on shared-memory multiprocessor systems [3, 14, 35]. Respec [23] does provide deterministic execution recording and replay of multithreaded applications with good performance by lazily increasing the level of synchronization it enforces depending on whether it observes divergence during replay, but it requires intricate modifications to the operating system. It also requires re-execution to be performed on a different core of the same physical system, making it unsuitable for HA applications. For these reasons, the replay-based HA systems of which we are aware support only uniprocessor VMs [28]. SecondSite, like Remus [11] uses whole machine checkpointing, so it supports multiprocessor VMs.

Checkpoint-based replication builds on *live migration* [9] – the ability to migrate virtual machines from one physical host to another while they are running. The everRun VM [38] product, from Marathon Technologies, provides automated fault detection and failover for individual Windows VMs running over the Xen hypervisor. While it employs techniques similar to Remus, it is heavily tailored towards select Windows services like Exchange Server, SQL Server, etc. SecondSite on the other hand provides high availability through whole virtual machine replication with Xen [4] in an application and operating system agnostic manner, running over commodity hardware.

5.2 Minimizing Downtime

The established approach for disaster recovery in many environments today involves the synchronous or asynchronous replication of storage (e.g. SnapMirror [26], PipeCloud [33]). The Recovery Time Objective (RTO) and Recovery Point Objective (RPO) determines the degree of synchrony required and the overhead incurred during normal operation. Generally, some support is expected from the application level in order to restore the disk data to a consistent state.

Live migration has been successfully exploited by many systems to minimize *planned downtime*, when VMs are migrated across WAN. Storage migration over WAN has been explored by Bradford et. al [5] and Hirofuchi et. al [20]. Svärd et. al [30] evaluate the advantages of page delta compression for live migration for large enterprise class workloads.

CloudNet [34] demonstrated a viable cloud migration solution across data centers using storage migration, page delta compression and custom VPN concentrator components to maintain client connectivity during the migration. CloudNet primarily aims to tackle resource mobility and cloud burst scenarios for enterprise clouds. SecondSite could be integrated into CloudNet to achieve both dynamic resource pooling and fault tolerance across a WAN.

5.3 IP Migration across WAN

Harney et. al [19] use mobile IPv6 to solve the IP address migration issue. This system requires ISP network-level support for mobile IPv6 which is not yet widely available. Bradford et. al [5] propose the use of IP tunneling and dynamic DNS for maintaining network connectivity during live migration of a VM across WAN. Such a system is not resilient against site-wide failures or DNS caching at local proxies.

WOW [17] creates a VLAN on a P2P overlay network in which connectivity to the migrating virtual machine is maintained by forwarding it to the new destination. In WOW, the connectivity problem is restricted in scope to maintaining access only among peers of the P2P network. VIOLIN [21] uses a similar technique to create a VLAN on an overlay network, with software routers and switches to route traffic to appropriate nodes in the network. VIOLIN decouples the overlay virtual network from the underlying physical network, rendering changes in the underlying network topology transparent to the application. As with WOW, network transparency is only provided to participants in the overlay network

VM Turntable [31] explores the feasibility of long-haul live migration over WAN/MANs across two continents. Clients are required to establish IP Tunnels to the virtual machines and the network infrastructure at the destination takes care of reconfiguring the tunnel endpoint when the VM migrates across network domains. In contrast, SecondSite provides location transparency without requiring cooperation from clients.

6. Conclusion

Netflix weathered the April 2011 Amazon AWS outage with very little impact on its business [10]. Some key aspects of its cloud architecture include completely stateless services and NoSQL based data-stores that sacrifice consistency for availability and durability. SecondSite may not be a good choice for such stateless services. Building a scalable stateless e-commerce services like Netflix is *hard* and it requires an engineering skill that is generally not affordable by small and medium businesses. Application programmers use off-the-shelf solutions to rapidly develop and deploy web applications that often end up being stateful. We believe that SecondSite is a good fit for such applications as it eliminates the burden of maintaining consistency while adding high availability, transparent to the application.

Acknowledgments

We would like to thank Andree Toonk, Don McWilliam, Toby Wong, Michael Hrybyk and Marilyn Hay from BCnet and UBC IT for providing and supporting a WAN testbed for SecondSite. Andree in particular was invaluable in helping to explore how BGP could be configured to support failover. Thanks also to Cliff Harms and Brian Mackay at Thompson Rivers University for providing server hosting in Kamloops. Finally, we would like to thank the VEE reviewers for their insightful feedback and for accepting the paper for publication.

References

[1] M. K. Aguilera, W. Chen, and S. Toueg. Heartbeat: A timeout-free failure detector for quiescent reliable communication. Technical report, Ithaca, NY, USA, 1997.

[2] M. K. Aguilera, W. Chen, and S. Toueg. Using the heartbeat failure detector for quiescent reliable communication and consensus in partitionable networks. *Theor. Comput. Sci.*, 220:3–30, June 1999. ISSN 0304-3975.

[3] G. Altekar and I. Stoica. ODR: output-deterministic replay for multicore debugging. In *SOSP '09: Proceedings of the ACM SIGOPS 22nd symposium on Operating systems principles*, pages 193–206, New York, NY, USA, 2009. ACM. ISBN 978-1-60558-752-3.

[4] P. Barham, B. Dragovic, K. Fraser, S. Hand, T. Harris, A. Ho, R. Neugebauer, I. Pratt, and A. Warfield. Xen and the art of virtualization. In *SOSP '03: Proceedings of the nineteenth ACM symposium on Operating systems principles*, pages 164–177, New York, NY, USA, 2003. ACM Press. ISBN 1-58113-757-5.

[5] R. Bradford, E. Kotsovinos, A. Feldmann, and H. Schiöberg. Live wide-area migration of virtual machines including local persistent state. In *VEE '07: Proceedings of the 3rd international conference on Virtual execution environments*, pages 169–179, New York, NY, USA, 2007. ACM Press. ISBN 978-1-59593-630-1.

[6] T. C. Bressoud and F. B. Schneider. Hypervisor-based fault-tolerance. In *Proceedings of the Fifteenth ACM Symposium on Operating System Principles*, pages 1–11, December 1995.

[7] C. Brooks. Heroku learns the hard way from amazon ec2 outage. *SearchCloudComputing.com*, January 2010.

[8] T. D. Chandra and S. Toueg. Unreliable failure detectors for reliable distributed systems. *J. ACM*, 43:225–267, March 1996. ISSN 0004-5411. doi: http://doi.acm.org/10.1145/226643.226647.

[9] C. Clark, K. Fraser, S. Hand, J. G. Hansen, E. Jul, C. Limpach, I. Pratt, and A. Warfield. Live migration of virtual machines. In *Proceedings of the 2nd conference on Symposium on Networked Systems Design & Implementation*, Berkeley, CA, USA, 2005. USENIX Association.

[10] A. Cockroft, C. Hicks, and G. Orzell. Lessons Netflix Learned from the AWS Outage. http://techblog.netflix.com/2011/04/lessons-netflix-learned-from-aws-outage.html, April 2011.

[11] B. Cully, G. Lefebvre, D. Meyer, M. Feeley, N. Hutchinson, and A. Warfield. Remus: high availability via asynchronous virtual machine replication. In *NSDI'08: Proceedings of the 5th USENIX Symposium on Networked Systems Design and Implementation*, pages 161–174, Berkeley, CA, USA, 2008. USENIX Association. ISBN 111-999-5555-22-1.

[12] D. Dolev, C. Dwork, and L. Stockmeyer. On the minimal synchronism needed for distributed consensus. *J. ACM*, 34:77–97, January 1987. ISSN 0004-5411.

[13] G. W. Dunlap, S. T. King, S. Cinar, M. A. Basrai, and P. M. Chen. Revirt: Enabling intrusion analysis through virtual-machine logging and replay. In *Proceedings of the 5th Symposium on Operating Systems Design & Implementation (OSDI 2002)*, 2002.

[14] G. W. Dunlap, D. G. Lucchetti, M. A. Fetterman, and P. M. Chen. Execution replay of multiprocessor virtual machines. In *VEE '08: Proceedings of the fourth ACM SIGPLAN/SIGOPS international conference on Virtual execution environments*, pages 121–130, New York, NY, USA, 2008. ACM. ISBN 978-1-59593-796-4.

[15] C. Dwork, N. Lynch, and L. Stockmeyer. Consensus in the presence of partial synchrony. *J. ACM*, 35:288–323, April 1988. ISSN 0004-5411.

[16] C. Fetzer, M. Raynal, and F. Tronel. An adaptive failure detection protocol. In *Proceedings of the 2001 Pacific Rim International Symposium on Dependable Computing*, PRDC '01, pages 146–, Washington, DC, USA, 2001. IEEE Computer Society. ISBN 0-7695-1414-6.

[17] A. Ganguly, A. Agrawal, P. Boykin, and R. Figueiredo. WOW: Self-Organizing Wide Area Overlay Networks of Virtual Workstations. *High-Performance Distributed Computing, International Symposium on*, 0:30–42, 2006.

[18] D. K. Gifford. Weighted voting for replicated data. In *Proceedings of the seventh ACM symposium on Operating systems principles*, SOSP '79, pages 150–162, New York, NY, USA, 1979. ACM. ISBN 0-89791-009-5.

[19] E. Harney, S. Goasguen, J. Martin, M. Murphy, and M. Westall. The efficacy of live virtual machine migrations over the internet. In *Proceedings of the 2nd international workshop on Virtualization technology in distributed computing*, VTDC '07, pages 8:1–8:7, New York, NY, USA, 2007. ACM. ISBN 978-1-59593-897-8.

[20] T. Hirofuchi, H. Nakada, H. Ogawa, S. Itoh, and S. Sekiguchi. A live storage migration mechanism over wan and its performance evaluation. In *Proceedings of the 3rd international workshop on Virtualization technologies in distributed computing*, VTDC '09, pages 67–74, New York, NY, USA, 2009. ACM. ISBN 978-1-60558-580-2.

[21] X. Jiang and D. Xu. VIOLIN: Virtual Internetworking on Overlay Infrastructure. In *ISPA*, pages 937–946, 2004.

[22] C. Labovitz, A. Ahuja, A. Bose, and F. Jahanian. Delayed internet routing convergence. In *in Proc. ACM SIGCOMM*, pages 175–187, 2000.

[23] D. Lee, B. Wester, K. Veeraraghavan, S. Narayanasamy, P. M. Chen, and J. Flinn. Respec: efficient online multiprocessor replayvia speculation and external determinism. In *ASPLOS '10: Proceedings of the fifteenth edition of ASPLOS on Architectural support for programming languages and operating systems*, pages 77–90, New York, NY, USA, 2010. ACM. ISBN 978-1-60558-839-1.

[24] U. F. Minhas, S. Rajagopalan, B. Cully, A. Aboulnaga, K. Salem, and A. Warfield. Remusdb: Transparent high availability for database systems. *PVLDB*, 4(11):738–748, 2011.

[25] C. C. T. A. P. Outage. R. miller. *datacenterknowledge.com*, May 2010.

[26] R. H. Patterson, S. Manley, M. Federwisch, D. Hitz, S. Kleiman, and S. Owara. SnapMirror: File-System-Based Asynchronous Mirroring for Disaster Recovery. In *FAST '02: Proceedings of the 1st USENIX Conference on File and Storage Technologies*, page 9, Berkeley, CA, USA, 2002. USENIX Association.

[27] P. Reisner and L. Ellenberg. Drbd v8 – replicated storage with shared disk semantics. In *Proceedings of the 12th International Linux System Technology Conference*, October 2005.

[28] D. J. Scales, M. Nelson, and G. Venkitachalam. The design and evaluation of a practical system for fault-tolerant virtual machines. Technical Report VMWare-RT-2010-001, VMWare, Inc., Palo Alto, CA 94304, May 2010.

[29] R. Strom and S. Yemini. Optimistic recovery in distributed systems. *ACM Trans. Comput. Syst.*, 3(3), 1985.

[30] P. Svärd, B. Hudzia, J. Tordsson, and E. Elmroth. Evaluation of delta compression techniques for efficient live migration of large virtual machines. In *Proceedings of the 7th ACM SIGPLAN/SIGOPS international conference on Virtual execution environments*, VEE '11, pages 111–120, New York, NY, USA, 2011. ACM. ISBN 978-1-4503-0687-4.

[31] F. Travostino, P. Daspit, L. Gommans, C. Jog, C. de Laat, J. Mambretti, I. Monga, B. van Oudenaarde, S. Raghunath, and P. Y. Wang. Seamless live migration of virtual machines over the MAN/WAN. *Future Gener. Comput. Syst.*, 22:901–907, October 2006. ISSN 0167-739X. doi: 10.1016/j.future.2006.03.007.

[32] R. van Renesse, Y. Minsky, and M. Hayden. A gossip-style failure detection service. In *Proceedings of the IFIP International Conference on Distributed Systems Platforms and Open Distributed Processing*, Middleware '98, pages 55–70, London, UK, 1998. Springer-Verlag. ISBN 1-85233-088-0.

[33] T. Wood, H. A. Lagar-Cavilla, K. K. Ramakrishnan, P. Shenoy, and J. Van der Merwe. Pipecloud: using causality to overcome speed-of-light delays in cloud-based disaster recovery. In *Proceedings of the 2nd ACM Symposium on Cloud Computing*, SOCC '11, pages 17:1–17:13, New York, NY, USA, 2011. ACM. ISBN 978-1-4503-0976-9.

[34] T. Wood, K. K. Ramakrishnan, P. Shenoy, and J. van der Merwe. CloudNet: dynamic pooling of cloud resources by live WAN migration of virtual machines. In *Proceedings of the 7th ACM SIGPLAN/SIGOPS international conference on Virtual execution environments*, VEE '11, pages 121–132, New York, NY, USA, 2011. ACM. ISBN 978-1-4503-0687-4.

[35] M. Xu, R. Bodik, and M. D. Hill. A "flight data recorder" for enabling full-system multiprocessor deterministic replay. *SIGARCH Comput. Archit. News*, 31(2):122–135, 2003. ISSN 0163-5964.

[36] Xen Blktap2 Driver. http://wiki.xensource.com/xenwiki/blktap2 .

[37] Summary of the Amazon EC2 and Amazon RDS Service Disruption in the US East Region. http://aws.amazon.com/message/65648/ .

[38] Marathon Technologies: everRun DR. http://www.marathontechnologies.com/ .

[39] Google app engine. http://code.google.com/appengine/ .

[40] Amazon EC2 Spot Instances. http://aws.amazon.com/ec2/spot-instances/ .

[41] VMware KB: Configuring Split-Brain Avoidance in a WAN. http://kb.vmware.com/kb/1008606 .

[42] Dell DVD Store Database Test Suite. http://www.delltechcenter.com/page/DVD+Store .

[43] SPECweb2005. http://www.spec.org/web2005/ .

[44] Xentop. http://linux.die.net/man/1/xentop .

CompSC: Live Migration with Pass-through Devices

Zhenhao Pan
Tsinghua University
Beijing, China
frankpzh@gmail.com

Yaozu Dong
Intel Asia-Pacific Research and Development Ltd
No. 880 Zi Xing Rd, Shanghai, China
eddie.dong@intel.com

Yu Chen Lei Zhang Zhijiao Zhang
Tsinghua University
Beijing, China
{chyyuu,sosilent.lzh,acer.zhang}@gmail.com

Abstract

Live migration is one of the most important features of virtualization technology. With regard to recent virtualization techniques, performance of network I/O is critical. Current network I/O virtualization (e.g. Para-virtualized I/O, VMDq) has a significant performance gap with native network I/O. Pass-through network devices have near native performance, however, they have thus far prevented live migration. No existing methods solve the problem of live migration with pass-through devices perfectly.

In this paper, we propose CompSC: a solution of hardware state migration that will enable the live migration support of pass-through devices. We go on to apply CompSC to SR-IOV network interface controllers. We discuss the attributes of different hardware states in pass-through devices and migrate them with corresponding techniques. Our experiments show that CompSC enables live migration on an Intel 82599 VF with a throughput 282.66% higher than para-virtualized devices. In addition, service downtime during live migration is 42.9% less than para-virtualized devices.

Categories and Subject Descriptors D.4.4 [*Operating Systems*]: Communications Management—Network communication; D.4.5 [*Operating Systems*]: Reliability—Backup procedures

General Terms Design, Performance

Keywords Virtualization, Live migration, Pass-through device, SR-IOV

1. Introduction

Recently, virtualized systems have been experiencing dramatic growth. In data centers and cloud computing environments, for example, virtualization technology largely reduces hardware and resource costs [9, 18]. The virtual machine live migration technique [14] is considered as one of the most important features of virtualization [13]. It not only significantly increases the manageability of virtualized systems, but also enables several important virtualization usage models like fault tolerance [15, 28].

In such an environment, not only is the performance of CPU and memory virtualization a crucial component, but the performance of network I/O virtualization is also of upmost importance. In recent works, CPU and memory virtualization have been discussed in depth [8], and the performance with recent techniques is near native one [11, 31]. However, I/O device virtualization remains a great challenge, especially on network devices. Emulated network I/O [30] provides a complete emulation of the existing network interface controllers (NIC), and connects physical NICs together via a virtual bridge. Para-virtualized (PV) network I/O [3], which employs an optimized interface, has increased performance compared to emulated network I/O. Although recent efforts [23, 26, 29] largely improve the performance of PV network I/O, there still exists a significant performance gap with native network I/O [25, 26, 29] in addition to the burden of higher CPU overheads. Using pass-through I/O [7, 24], A.K.A direct I/O, a virtualized system can directly access physical devices without interceptions from the hypervisor, and thus is capable of providing near native performance. Single Root I/O Virtualization (SR-IOV) [16] is a modern specification proposed by PCI-SIG. This specification shows how PCIe devices can share a single root I/O device with several virtual machines. With the help of SR-IOV, one hardware device is able to provide a number of PCIe virtual functions to the hypervisor. By assigning these functions to virtual machines as pass-through devices, the performance and scalability of I/O virtualization can be considerably increased.

Nevertheless, pass-through I/O has limitations on virtual machine live migration. In pass-through I/O, the physical device is totally controlled by the virtual machine, and its internal states are not accessible by the hypervisor. If the internal states of the physical device are not migrated during a live migration, the device will stop working and the driver will likely crash. Several efforts have been made on enabling pass-through network I/O migration, such as the bonding driver solution [32] and Network Plug-in Architecture (NPA/NPIA) [2], but these methods all bypass the problem of hardware state migration by switching to either a PV device or an emulated device during the migration, and have similar short comings.

In this paper, we propose CompSC to address the problem of how to efficiently migrate the state of a hardware device and enable virtual machine live migration with pass-through NICs. We directly face and solve the challenge of hardware state migration. With an analysis on different kinds of hardware states, CompSC applies methods of state replay and self-emulation on pass-through devices. With few code changes on the device driver, CompSC achieves our objective of enabling live migration support for pass-through devices with minimal impact on run time performance as well as a minute time cost for hardware state migration.

We implemented CompSC on the Xen [11] platform, with the Intel 82576 SR-IOV NIC [19] and the Intel 82599 SR-IOV NIC [20]. In the evaluation section, we measured the performance impact of our method using micro benchmarks, scp, Netperf and SPECweb 2009 [4]. Our results show that CompSC enabled live

VEE'12, March 3–4, 2012, London, England, UK.

migration support on an Intel 82599 VF with a throughput 282.66% higher than PV network devices and 89.57% higher than VMDq. We also measured the service downtime during live migration; our solution had a 42.9% shorter downtime when compared to the PV network device.

Implementing and deploying CompSC is easy. A line count on code changes required by our implementation shows that CompSC needs little coding effort. After we implemented CompSC support on an Intel 82576 NIC, adding CompSC support on an Intel 82599 NIC only required two days time. Thus, we are convinced that CompSC can easily be deployed on a wide range of different NICs.

The remainder of this paper is structured as follows: Section 2 introduces the related work. Section 3 discusses the methods of migrating hardware states with different attributes. Section 4 describes the design of CompSC and the structure of the system. Section 5 describes how we implement CompSC on the Xen platform with an Intel 82576 NIC. Section 6 shows experimental results. Section 7 discusses the usage model of CompSC and we conclude in Section 8.

2. Related work

2.1 Migration

In the early years of distributed system research, process migration [27] was a hot topic. Process migration has many advantages, including processing power management, resource locality and fault resilience. However, process migration has suffered disadvantages with regards to implementation complexity and inflexibility. With the development of virtualization, the possibility of the live migration [14] of the whole operating system (OS) is now realizable and has in fact become a typical solution. In the study of Chen et al. [13], migration is considered as one of the most important features of virtualization. There are also studies that show further benefits of the live migration of virtual machines, including fault tolerance [15, 28] and trusted computing [12].

Live migration of virtual machines takes the advantage of the narrow and identical interface provided by the hypervisor. In the study by Christopher et al. [14], the process of live migration is divided into six stages:

1. Pre-Migration stage
2. Reservation stage
3. Iterative Pre-copy stage
4. Stop-and-copy stage
5. Commitment stage
6. Activation stage

Before the stop-and-copy stage, the virtual machine is running on the source host in the usual way. After the activation stage, the virtual machine runs on the destination host. The downtime (i.e. the time when the virtual machine is out of service) of the process consists of stop-and-copy and commitment stage. Downtime is one of the most important measurements of live migration.

There have been efforts on migration of the whole OS without virtualization as well. In a study of Michael et al. [22], issues and the solutions thereof for migration by OSs are discussed. Since OSs can be treated as a drivers of the whole machine, some of the issues raised by [22] are similar to ours.

2.2 SR-IOV

SR-IOV [16] is a new specification defined by PCI-SIG. The purpose of SR-IOV is to provide multiple PCI interfaces of one device in order to fit the usage model of directly-assigned/pass-through devices and provide increased performance. An SR-IOV device consists of one PF (physical function) and several VFs (virtual functions). The typical usage of an SR-IOV NIC on a virtual machine consists of using VFs as pass-through devices of virtual machines; the PF is used as a device of device domain or privileged domain, not only for networking, but also for VF management. On a PCI bus, a VF looks identical to an independent PCI device. Also, in virtual machines, pass-through VFs are equivalent to typical PCI NICs.

In today's cloud computing solutions, SR-IOV has been used in several NICs. In this paper, we use Intel 82576 and Intel 82599 NICs in our experiments, each of which support SR-IOV.

2.3 Similar works and technologies

There are several efforts on the topic of live migration with pass-through devices. In a study by Edwin et al. [32], the Linux Ethernet Bonding Driver [1] is used. In [32], a PV network device is used as the backup device of a pass-through device. Before the start of a live migration, the pass-through device is hot unplugged using an ACPI event. In this way, there is no need to worry about migrating the pass-through device. This method does not require any code changes on the virtual machine guest kernel, but has several disadvantages:

1. It only works with Linux guests.
2. It requires an additional PV network device. The physical device must be connected to the same Ethernet switch with the pass-through device. This may lead to additional hardware cost and resources costs.
3. The hot unplug event introduces another service downtime in our test. (Section 6.5)
4. After live migration, the driver clears every statistic register in the pass-through device, rendering the statistic function inaccurate or disabled.

In a similar work by Asim and Michael [21], a shadow driver is implemented to redirect network requests to a backup device during live migrations. Besides the flaws mentioned above, the method in [21] requires as many as 11K LOC (lines of code) changes on both the hypervisor and the guest kernel.

VMDq (Virtual Machine Device Queues) [5] is a technique proposed by Intel. The idea of VMDq is similar to SR-IOV, as both methods assign hardware resources to the virtual machine. In contrast to SR-IOV, however, VMDq also benefits from the PV network device. Unlike SR-IOV, which exposes a complete device interface to the virtual machine guest, VMDq only provides network queues to the virtual machine guest. With PV techniques like shared pages, VMDq avoids packet copying between the virtualized network queue and the physical network queue. VMDq provides faster performance than PV network devices and is still able to support live migration in a similar way. We elaborate the comparison of performance and downtime between VMDq and our solution in Section 6.5.

Network Plug-In Architecture (NPIA/NPA) [2] is an architecture raised by VMware and Intel that tries to solve the issues of pass-through device management and live migration. Instead of supporting all pass-through NICs, NPIA only focuses on SR-IOV [16] NICs. NPIA designs a shell/plug-in pair inside the kernel of the virtual machine. The shell provides a layer similar to a hardware abstraction layer, while the plug-in implements hardware communication under the shell. The plug-in can be plugged or unplugged during run time. To reduce the downtime during plug-in switches, an emulated network interface is used as a backup. By unplugging the plug-in, NPA can easily support live migration. Just like bonding driver solution, NPIA uses a software interface as backup device. Compared to the bonding driver solution, NPIA may need less time switching the pass-through device to the backup. One major drawback is that NPIA also needs to completely rewrite the network drivers, which might prevent NPA from being widely employed.

From the perspective of ReNIC [17], hardware extensions are proposed to solve the issues of SR-IOV network device live migration. ReNIC meets similar difficulties with us, and solves them using hardware way.

3. Approaches of hardware state migration

The core problem with live migration support of pass-through devices is the migration of hardware states. The whole of the pass-through devices are assigned to virtual machines, rendering them inaccessible to the hypervisor. In this section, we propose methods of solving this problem.

3.1 I/O registers migration

I/O registers are the main interface between hardware and software. Almost every visible state of a hardware device is exposed by various kinds of I/O registers. In modern PCI architectures, two kinds of I/O registers are used: Programmed I/O (PIO) and Memory-mapped I/O (MMIO). Reading/writing operations of PIO and MMIO are atomic, and the virtual machine will not be suspended during an I/O reading or I/O writing.

I/O registers are classified into different kinds according to the method of access. One of the most common kinds is read-write registers. If access to a read-write register does not lead to side effects, then the register can be simply migrated by the hypervisor. Other kinds of registers, such as read-only and read-clear registers, cannot be simply migrated by the hypervisor, however.

The access of certain registers may result in side effects. For example, modifying a NIC's TDT (Transmit descriptor tail) register may trigger packet transmission. Without the full knowledge of these registers, access of them by the hypervisor may cause unexpected behavior or device failure.

3.2 State replay

Hardware specifications describe every detail about the interface between the device and driver, and hardware behavior. Given knowledge of the past communications on the interface, the current state of the hardware can easily be deduced. It is assumed that the driver knows the past communications on the hardware-software interface as well as the hardware specification. In most cases, the driver is able to drive the destination hardware from an uninitialized state into some specified state by replaying a given set of past communications.

The idea of state replay consists of two stages: a recording stage, where driver must record every operation of the hardware on the source machine; and a replaying stage, where the driver reads past operations from a list, and commits them to the destination machine one by one.

In regards to state replay, driver complexity may be a problem. Because recording every past communication requires so much effort, driving the destination device may also need a significant number of code changes. Fortunately, with the knowledge of devices, many communications can be optimized. For example, the device driver may write a register many times. If the writing operation of the register brings no side effects, one does not need to record each operation. Instead, one can record only the last one, because it is only the last one that is valid in the hardware.

Another efficient optimization technique is to define operation sets(opset). Some drivers' implementations may consist of several device operations. Instead of recording every step of the drivers' work, the devices' operations are packed into operation sets. Figure 1 illustrates this optimization. In the figure, four operations `op1`, `op2`, `op3` and `op4` are packed into one opset `opset1`. With the assumption that a live migration will not happen inside operation sets, three states are safely omitted: `A`, `B` and `C`.

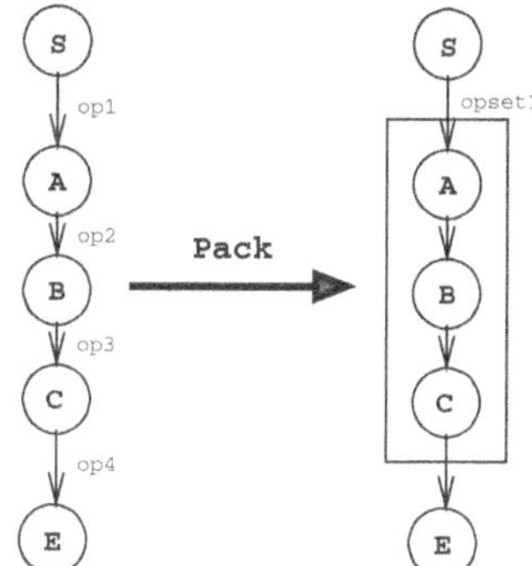

Figure 1. Packing device operations into an operation set

The opset optimization works especially well on NICs. With well-designed operation sets, the number of internal states of NICs can be largely reduced. In the case of VFs on the Intel 82576 NIC, i.e. the one used in our evaluation, all initializing and sending/receiving operations are packed into operation sets. The remaining states include only {uninitialized, up, and down} together with a collection of setting registers. In this kind of set up, only the latest operations on each setting register and whether or not the interface is up need to be tracked. In addition, the code for driving the destination hardware into the state of source hardware is significantly simplified by invoking existing initializing codes. In Section 6.6, we list the size of hardware states and past operations to be migrated for the Intel 82576 and Intel 82599 NICs.

Avoiding live migration inside an operation set needs a synchronizing method between the device driver and the hypervisor. A common question is whether or not this affects performance. The answer depends on the granularity of operation sets. If the driver makes an operation set that lasts for an extended period of time (e.g. several seconds), one can imagine that live migration may take a long time. Also problematic would be if the driver makes an operation set that can be invoked millions of times per second. With a set of well-defined operation sets, negative impacts on performance can be minimized. In Section 6.4, we prove that the performance deterioration in our implementation is negligible.

3.3 Self-emulation

Statistic registers of type read-only and read-clear commonly cannot be migrated through the software/hardware interface. The register that counts dropped packets in the NIC is an example. The only way to alter the register is to try to drop a packet. This is difficult, because to drop a packet would need cooperation with the external network. All existing solutions [2, 21, 32] do not cover this register. Instead, they perform device initialization after live migration, reset all statistic registers, and cause the statistic functions to become inaccurate or disabled.

Statistic registers often have mathematical attributes, e.g. monotonicity. After a live migration, one statistic register may have an incorrect value; the difference between its value and the correct value should be a constant. For example, let the count of dropped packets be 5 before live migration. After live migration, the same register on the destination hardware will be initialized to 0. After that, the value of register will always be smaller than the correct value by 5. If the value on the destination hardware is 2, the correct value will be 7. In the case of a read-clear register, the relationship is similar, with one notable difference: only the first access to a read-clear register will get an incorrect value after live migration.

With such a clear logic, the classic trap-and-emulation is chosen. In self-emulation, every access to a read-only or read-clear statistic register is intercepted by a self-emulation layer. In the layer, the correct value is calculated and returned to the caller. The self-emulation layer can be placed in any component on the access path of the register (e.g. the driver, the hypervisor). Figure 2 shows an example where the self-emulation layer is in the hypervisor.

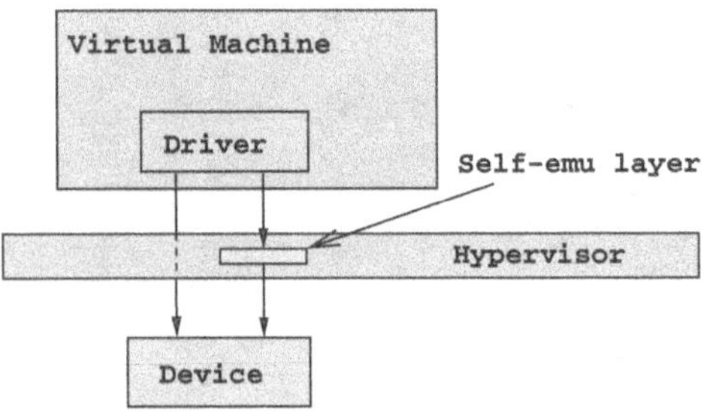

Figure 2. An example structure of self-emulation

3.4 Summary

I/O register migration is easy to perform, but the number of hardware states that support it are quite limited. State replay covers almost every hardware state, but demands extra code efforts in the driver. Statistic registers are hard to migrate, but can be covered by self-emulation. One practical approach for migration is to use the three of them in combination: use state replay for most hardware states, and use I/O register migration and self-emulation when possible.

We classify the states of the Intel 82576 VF as follows: configurations of rings such as RDBA (Receive Descriptor Base Address), TXDCTL (Transmit Descriptor Control) are migrated by I/O register migration; interrupt related registers and settings inside the Advanced Context Descriptor are migrated using state replay; and all statistic registers are covered by self-emulation. Using the prescribed methods in this way, the live migration of network devices in our experiment runs smoothly.

4. Design of CompSC

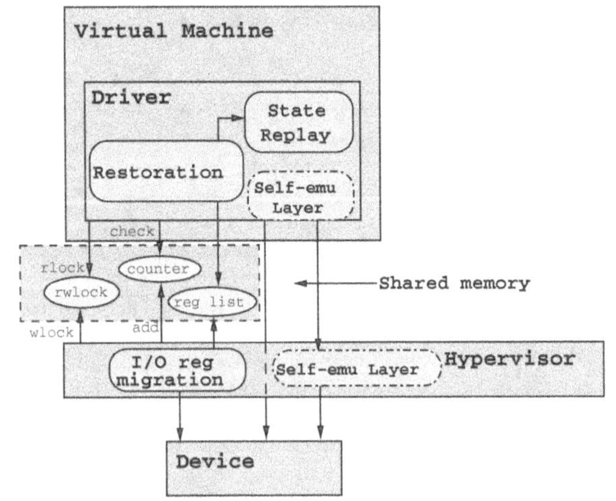

Figure 3. CompSC architecture

The architecture of CompSC is presented in Figure 3. The driver in the virtual machine is responsible for state replay and the hypervisor covers I/O register migration. A piece of shared memory between the hypervisor and the virtual machine is used for synchronization. Two self-emulation layers are provided in the driver and in the hypervisor.

Among the six stages of live migration [14], CompSC works inside the stop-and-copy stage and the activation stage. The usage of CompSC is intelligible: collecting the hardware states of the pass-through device at the stop-and-copy stage, and restoring them to the destination hardware at the activation stage. In addition, while collection is completed by different components (e.g. the hypervisor, the device driver, self-emulation layer), restoration is finished by the device driver only.

4.1 Synchronization

From the perspective of the device driver, live migration happens in a flash. After one context switch, the hardware suddenly turns into an uninitialized state. If there is anything that can indicate a live migration, it must be checked before every hardware access. If we use the state replay method and define several operation sets, the driver will never detect the disturbance of a live migration.

CompSC creates a shared memory area between the hypervisor and the virtual machine. An rwlock and a version counter are preserved in the memory area. The rwlock indicates the status of migration, and the counter records the number of live migrations that have occurred. When the stop-and-copy stage starts, the hypervisor tries to hold the write lock. In the activation stage, the hypervisor increases the version counter and releases the write lock. Conversely, the driver acquires the read lock before every hardware access. Once the lock is held, the driver checks the version counter to figure out whether a live migration has just occurred. If so, the restoration of the device driver will be invoked. In this way, the hardware is never accessed in an uninitialized state.

The logical meaning of the rwlock is as an indicator of who took over the hardware device. The device driver locks the read lock whenever it wants to access the hardware. After accessing is finished and the device state is taken over by the hypervisor for live migration, the driver unlocks the read lock. The hypervisor acquires the write lock before it touches the hardware device, after which the hardware device is taken over by the hypervisor.

We show that the cost of rwlock is relatively low. Intuitively, the lock will not be contended with as all the lock operations in the driver are read lock. The only costs during run time are the memory accesses and a little bit of cache pollution. In Section 6.4, we provide an evaluation on the costs of the rwlock.

4.2 Hardware state migration

CompSC performs the I/O register migration in a straightforward way. The hypervisor scans the list of registers on the network device and saves them into the shared memory area mentioned in Section 4.1. After a live migration, the driver inside the virtual machine is held responsible for restoration. Making as few least code changes as possible is one of CompSC's driving factors. In the design of CompSC, we try to prevent the hypervisor from having any device-specific knowledge. The hypervisor does not know the list of registers; it gets this list from the shared memory area, put there by the driver during the boot process.

State replay is completed by the device driver. The operation sets and hardware operations are protected by rwlock. Every time before the driver releases the read lock, it stores enough information of past operations or operation sets to achieve a successful restoration. In the restoration procedure, the device drives the destination hardware into the same state using the saved information.

The self-emulation layer can be put into the hypervisor or the device driver. A self-emulation layer in the hypervisor will trap all accesses to the emulated registers and return the correct value. A self-emulation layer in the driver will process the fetched value correct after the access as described in Section 3.3. The former needs only the list of emulated registers and leads to fewer code changes in the driver, but at the expense of degraded performance due to I/O interception. The latter gains less overhead, but produces much more code changes. CompSC provides both methods, and the driver is free to choose either. A detailed discussion of the overhead of I/O interception is described Section 6.2.

4.3 SR-IOV NIC Support

On an SR-IOV NIC, migration becomes slightly different. The PF in an SR-IOV NIC provides management interfaces with the VFs. In our environment (Intel 82576 and Intel 82599), the PF holds a subset of VF states such as MAC addresses. In this paper, we call them VF-in-PF states (the VF part of PF states). Some of VF-in-PF states can be accessed by the VF driver through the PF-VF mailbox [19] and can be migrated using state replay, but the remaining can only be accessed through PF registers by the PF driver. In order to cover all hardware states, CompSC also uses the state replay method on the PF driver. The PF driver records all hardware operations of the specified VF before migration and commits them to the destination machine later.

5. Implementation

We used Xen [11] as the base of our implementation on the 64-bit x86 architecture. For NICs, we used the Intel 82576 (an SR-IOV 1Gbps NIC), and the Intel 82599 (an SR-IOV 10Gbps NIC). The PF drivers and the VF drivers of the Intel 82576 and Intel 82599 were changed in our implementation, detailed in Section 5.1. Section 5.3 presents the self-emulation layer.

Xen provides functions in the hypervisor to access foreign guest domains' memory page, which allow for easy implementation of shared pages between the hypervisor and the device driver. Details are offered in Section 5.2.

5.1 Driver changes

In our experiment, CompSC is executed on Intel 82576 and Intel 82599 NICs, with corresponding VF drivers IGBVF and IXGBEVF, respectively. As mentioned in Section 4.1, the read lock of the rwlock is used to protect the hardware operations and operation sets we defined. As soon as the lock is acquired, the driver checks the migration counter and invokes a restoration procedure if a migration is detected.

Formally, we pack `igbvf_up` and `igbvf_down` in the igbvf driver, and `ixgbe_up` and `ixgbevf_down` in the ixgbevf driver as operation sets. All hardware operations and operation sets are protected by the read lock. Because most device states have a copy in the driver, the state replay needs few code changes. The restoration procedure conducts the following tasks: device initialization, saved register writing, and the restoration of all states using state replay.

5.2 Shared page and synchronization

Shared pages are allocated by the NIC driver. The driver allocates several continuous pages which are structured to contain three pieces of information:

- The rwlock and the version counter;
- The list of registers that should be saved in the migration;
- The list of counter registers that need the help of the self-emulation layer in the hypervisor.

After initialization, the GFN (guest frame number) of the first page is sent to the hypervisor. In our implementation, this number is sent by PF-VF communication. For non-SR-IOV NICs, this number can be sent by a high level communication using the TCP/IP protocol.

When a live migration starts, memory pages are transferred until the stop-and-copy stage [14], until the virtual machine is to be suspended. Right before suspending, the write lock of the rwlock is acquired by the hypervisor. In this way, the hypervisor seizes the control of the device hardware. After the virtual machine is suspended, the hypervisor accesses the shared pages, and saves all registers listed in them. The remaining part of live migration transpires on the backup machine. Before the hypervisor tries to resume the virtual machine, saved values of read-only and read-clear counter registers are sent to the self-emulation layer in the hypervisor.

The first time the driver acquires the read lock, the device restoration procedure is invoked. The driver does necessary initializations on the device and restores the state using information collected by the state replay and I/O register migration. When all of this is accomplished, device migration has successfully been achieved.

5.3 Self-emulation layer

Xen hypervisor provides functions for trapping memory accesses, and the self-emulation layer in the hypervisor is based on them. Every time the self-emulation layer receives a request to commit self-emulation on a list of registers, it places a mark on the page table of the register. All further access to these registers will be trapped and emulated. The emulation does the real MMIO and the layer returns the calculated value to the virtual machine. The granularity of this trapping mechanism in our implementation is one page. On 64-bit x86 architecture, this translates to 4 KB. It should be noted that this may lead to unnecessary trappings and performance impacts; we elaborate on this is in Section 6.4.

5.4 Pages dirtied by DMA

The process of live migration is highly dependent on dirty page tracking. Dirty page tracking is implemented with the help of page tables in the newest version of Xen. However, memory access by DMA cannot be tracked by page tables. Intel VT-d technology [7] provides I/O page tables, but it still cannot be used to track dirty pages.

Hardware cannot automatically mark a page as dirty after DMA memory access, but marking the page manually is effortless. All that is required is a memory write. In a typical NIC, hardware accesses descriptor rings and buffers by invoking DMA. After the hardware writes to anyone of them, an interrupt is sent to the driver in the virtual machine guest kernel. Because the driver knows all changes on the descriptor rings and buffers, it simply performs a series of dummy writes (read a byte and write it back) to mark the pages as dirty.

This method misses a few packets that have already been processed by the hardware but have yet to be processed by the driver. This may lead to packet duplication or missing. Fortunately, the amount of such packets is small enough that connections of reliable protocols like TCP connections will not be affected. Section 6.3 presents the details of these duplicated or missed packets.

5.5 Descriptor ring

During our implementation, we came across an issue with both Intel 82576 VF and Intel 82599 VF. The head registers of descriptor rings (either RX or TX) are read-only. Their values are owned by hardware, and writing any value except for 0 is not allowed (writing 0 is an initialization). Consequently, head registers should be restored using state replay. However, committing state replay on this register is not that easy. The only way of increasing head registers is trying to send/receive a packet. By putting dummy descriptors in the rings, altering head registers does not need cooperation with external network, but it costs thousands of MMIO writings.

One method of solving this is resetting everything in the rings. By freeing buffers in the rings and resetting the rings to be empty, the driver will work well with the device. But this method needs tens or hundreds of memory allocations and freeings. The time cost associated with this method may be a problem, especially when the device has a large ring.

Another idea to handle the head registers is shifting. Instead of restoring the value of head registers, we shifts the ring itself. During the restoration procedure, the driver shifts the RX and TX rings, and makes sure the position of each original head is at index 0. After that, the driver needs only to write a 0 on the head registers to make the rings work. In addition to this, the driver must save the offsets between the original rings and the shifted rings. Every time the head/tail registers or rings are accessed by the driver, the offsets are used to make sure the access is completed correctly.

In CompSC, we use the method of shifting. Shifting introduces additional operations to access to indices/rings, and thus consumes more CPU time in the driver. Section 6.4 measures this performance impact.

5.6 Implementation complexity

The CompSC needs modifications in the network driver. Among the common concerns about the practicality of deployment, the complexity of device code changes is the most critical. In Table 1, we depict the number of line code changes in our implementation on different components. The synchronization mechanism is common to every network driver capable of live migration. The number of common code changes is just 153 lines. In the IGBVF driver, only 344 lines of codes are added or modified, and in the IXGBEVF driver only 303 lines are added or modified. Even the CompSC architecture itself has a small number of code changes. 808 lines of code changes were committed in either the Xen hypervisor or Xen tools.

We claim that one can easily patch an existing device driver into a CompSC supported one. During our implementation, we first completed the CompSC support on Intel 82576 NIC and related experiments. Further efforts to add the CompSC support on Intel 82599 NIC only cost us two days. As a result, CompSC is easy and practical to deploy.

Table 1. Lines of code changes in the implementation

	Line of code
Xen hypervisor	362
Xen tools	446
VF driver(common)	153
IGBVF driver	344
IGB driver	215
IXGBEVF driver	303
IXGBE driver	233

6. Evaluation

In this section, we present the results of our experimental data that compare a system equipped with our implementation of CompSC to the original system (without CompSC); a system with PV network device; a system with the bonding driver solution; and finally a system using the VMDq technique. We first present a micro benchmark to measure the performance impact of the self-emulation layer in the hypervisor. In Section 6.3 we show our measurements of the number of duplicated or missed packet due to the DMA dirty page. With scp, Netperf and SPECweb2009 benchmarks, Section 6.4 presents a comparison of the run time performance between several situations including the original environment and our implementation. Section 6.5 illustrates the migration process using a timeline figure comparing CompSC, a PV network device, the VMDq technique, and the bonding driver solution. Finally, Section 6.6 lists the size of hardware states to migrate.

6.1 Benchmarks and environment

Our target application is virtualized web servers. As a result, in our evaluation, we focus on the throughput and the overall performance as web servers. We use the Netperf benchmark, perform file transferring using scp to measure the throughput of virtual machines, and use SPECweb2009 to evaluate web server performance.

The evaluation uses the following environment: two equivalent servers equipped with Intel Core i5 670 CPU (3.47 GHz, 4 cores), 4 GB memory, 1 TB hard disk, an Intel 82576 and an Intel 82599 NIC; one client machine for the SPECweb2009 client, running an Intel Core i3 540 CPU (3.07 GHz, 4 cores), 4 GB memory, 500 GB hard disk, one Intel 82578DC NIC and one Intel 82598 NIC. These three machines are connected using a 1 Gb Ethernet switch and a 10 Gb Ethernet switch. The virtual machine uses 4 virtual CPUs, 3 GB memory, and one VF of Intel 82576 NIC or Intel 82599 NIC, and is virtualized in HVM (Hardware-assisted Virtual Machine). The virtual machine also uses a PV network device in the tests with PV device.

6.2 Micro benchmark for self-emulation

In Section 3.2 we presented the idea of self-emulation, and discovered that the self-emulation approach has a trade-off between accuracy and performance. In this section, we measured the performance loss due to self-emulation. In our test, we accessed one of the counter registers 10,000 times. Using TSC register, we measured the total cost of CPU cycles and calculate its average. We ran our test in both the direct-access and intercepted scenarios. Table 2 contains the results.

Table 2. Micro benchmark for MMIO cost

MMIO direct	MMIO intercept
3911 cycles	11860 cycles

The results of our self-emulation test show that MMIO with interception needs an additional 7,949 cycles for `VMEnter/VMExit` and context switches. For low access frequencies, this overhead is negligible, but for high access frequencies, the overhead may become problematic. Next, we measure the access frequency of statistic registers on different workloads.

Table 3. Access rate of statistic registers

	Time	RX bytes	TX bytes	MMIO
Netperf	60.02 s	54.60 G	1.19 G	4.50/s
SPECweb	8015 s	8.55 G	294.68 G	4.50/s

Table 3 shows the access frequency of statistic registers. From these results, it can be seen that the frequency of statistic register access was a constant: 4.5 accesses, no matter which task was been executed, and no matter which of either RX or TX was heavier. A subsequent code check on the Linux kernel uncovered this behavior. The IGBVF driver used a watchdog with a 0.5 Hz frequency to observe the statistic registers, and the access frequency is expected to be a constant. At such a low frequency, the overhead of self-emulation is roughly 10.30 μs/s. With the consideration of cache and TLB, the overhead may be slightly more, but it can still be considered negligible.

6.3 Duplicated and missed packet due to unmarked dirty page

In Section 5.4, we presented the idea of marking pages dirtied by DMA, and claimed that the solution may cause packet loss and packet duplication. In this section, we measured the number of duplicated and missed packets under different workloads. A busy CPU leads to longer time in suspension, and a busy NIC increases the number of packets received/transmitted during migration. A straight-forward prediction is that the number of duplicated and missed packets may become larger while both the CPU and NIC are busy. In our measurements, the workload of scp and SPECweb were used, and the scenario when there is no workload is also considered.

Table 4. Duplicated and missed packet counts during live migration, using Intel 82576

	Dup	Miss
No workload	0	0
scp	0	0
SPECweb	0	3

The results in Table 4 show that our method worked perfectly both scenarios when there was no workload and also in scp; no packet loss or duplication occurred in either case. On the SPECweb workload, only 3 packets were lost, however, these abnormal behaviors did not break the TCP connection, and thus the service was kept alive during the migration.

6.4 Performance with workloads

In this section, the run time performance of CompSC is measured and compared to a bare system (without CompSC). CompSC adds a synchronization mechanism between the hypervisor and the driver, the performance impact of which was a vital concern to the design strategy of our solution. Our method of handling descriptor rings as described in Section 5.5 also has performance impact at run time. The self-emulation layer in the hypervisor also has performance overhead. Although in the test outlined in Section 6.2 concluded the measurable overhead is small, we still consider this factor in more detail this section. In Section 5.3 we described how the self-emulation layer in the hypervisor may perform unnecessary interceptions; because the layer is optional and only enabled after migration, we measured both cases with and without the layer enabled.

The first test ran a benchmark of Netperf and an scp workload with a CD image file `specweb2009.iso` of size 491.72 MB. In this test we measure the throughputs of the workload in three situations: original IGBVF driver (VF orig), IGBVF driver with CompSC (VF+comp), and IGBVF driver with CompSC and with the self-emulation layer enabled (VF+comp+int). Figure 4 illustrates the results. In the figure, we see that the throughput of three test cases were almost the same in the two different workloads. The CPU utilization in the figure shows that the VF+comp and VF+comp+int scenarios consume almost the same amount of CPU resources as the VF orig case. The only thing notable in the figure is that the throughput of scp on VF+comp+int was slightly less than that on VF orig and VF+comp. On the Netperf benchmark, the network was the bottleneck of the whole system while on the scp workload, it is the CPU that was the bottleneck. A CPU utilization near 100 percent shows a CPU bottleneck of a single-threaded workload. When the self-emulation layer in the hypervisor was enabled, more CPU resources get consumed and thus this scenario had a slightly lower performance compared to others.

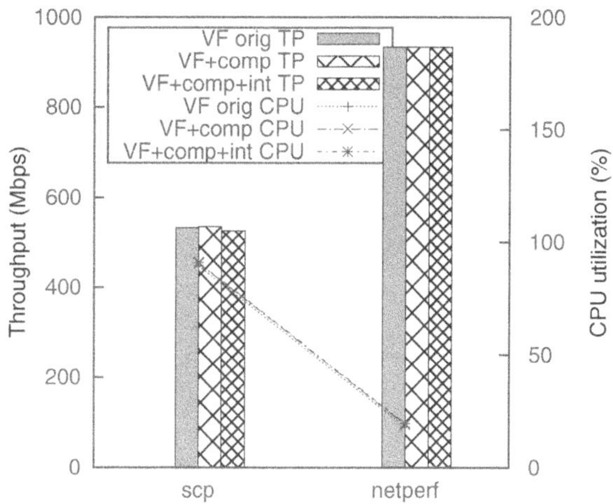

Figure 4. Throughput and CPU utilization by scp and Netperf on Intel 82576

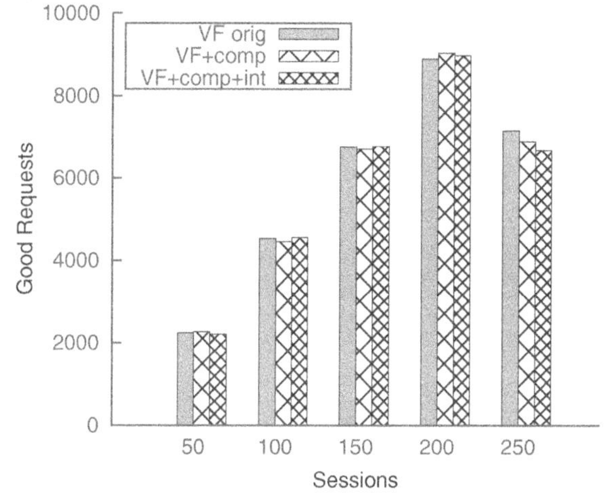

Figure 5. Good requests by SPECweb 2009 on Intel 82576

SPECweb 2009 is our real-world benchmark. In our evaluation, we configured and ran SPECweb 2009 with different pressures on the server in the virtual machine. We invoked the test with five different configurations: with 50, 100, 150, 200, and 250 concurrent sessions respectively. Tests with these configurations were run under three cases: using the original IGBVF driver (VF orig), the IGBVF driver with CompSC (VF+comp), and the IGBVF driver with CompSC and with the self-emulation layer enabled (VF+comp+int).

SPECweb 2009 classifies the requests based on response time into three types: good ones, tolerable ones, and failed ones. The good ones are requests which have a quick response, while the tolerable ones have a long but tolerable response. Failed ones have an intolerable response time or no response at all. In our test, we collected the number of good requests and present them in Figure 5.

The number of good requests increased in a linear fashion with the number of sessions, until we met a bottleneck at 250 sessions. To understand this bottleneck clearly, we also represent the average response time of requests in Figure 6. The average response times were comparable when the number of sessions was less than 250. On the test with 250 sessions, the response time grew by almost

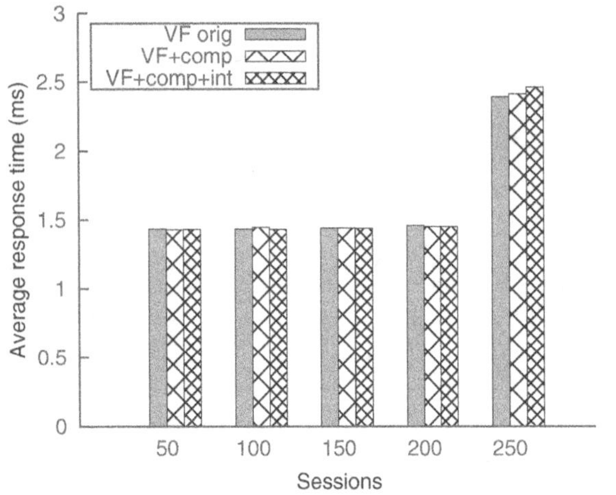

Figure 6. Average response time by SPECweb 2009 on Intel 82576

2/3 compared to previous sessions, which clearly indicates that the server was in a heavy workload.

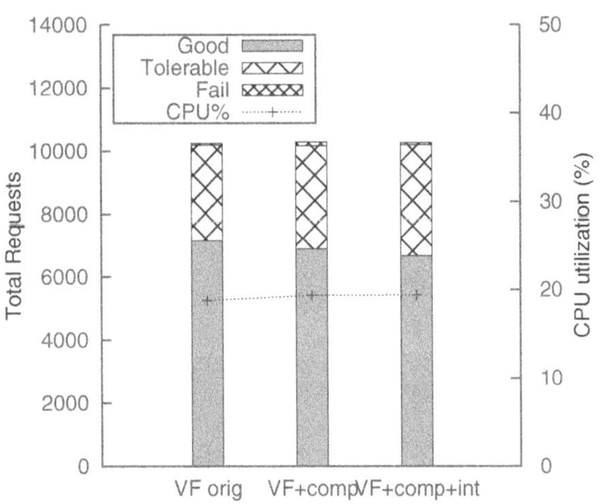

Figure 7. Performance and CPU utilization by SPECweb 2009 with 250 sessions on Intel 82576

Before reaching the bottleneck, no obvious differences present themselves in the three scenarios depicted in Figure 5 and Figure 6. This convinces us that the performance impact of our method under light workloads can be ignored. When the test approaches 250 sessions, VF+comp generated 3.74% fewer good requests than VF orig, and VF+comp+int generated 6.80% fewer good requests (in Figure 5). In regards to the measurement of average response time, VF+comp had a 0.75% higher response time and VF+comp+int had 2.88% higher response time when compared to VF orig (in Figure 6). To figure out why this is the case, we collected detailed performance data and CPU utilization results with the 250 sessions case in Figure 7.

The total requests handled by the server in the three scenarios were on the same horizontal line in Figure 7. The reason why VF+comp and VF+comp+int have fewer good requests is due to longer response time, in which case some of the requests were classified into tolerable requests. In other words, both the VF+comp and VF+comp+int cases had the same service capability, but had slightly longer response times. In the meantime, VF+comp and VF+comp+int consumed 0.59% and 0.64% more CPU than VF orig, respectively; this impact can also be considered as very small.

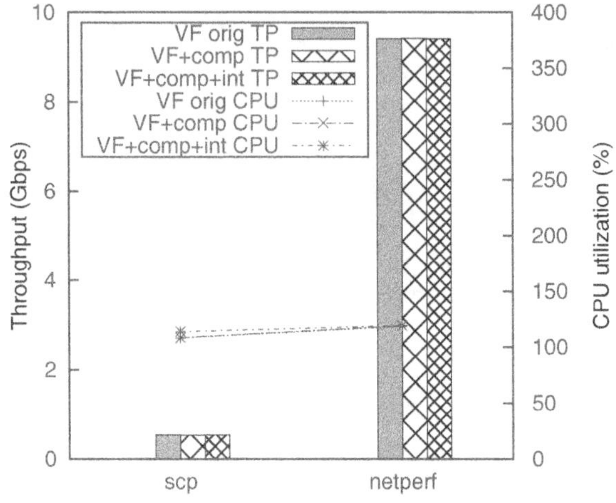

Figure 8. Throughput and CPU utilization by scp and Netperf on Intel 82599

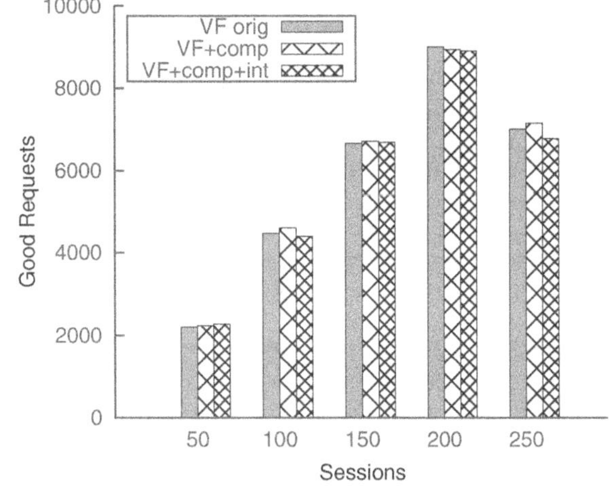

Figure 9. Good requests by SPECweb 2009 on Intel 82599

In order to evaluate the performance impact of CompSC on more challenging scenarios, we ran the Netperf tests, scp tests and SPECweb 2009 tests on an Intel 82599 VF with CompSC. As Figure 8 shows, the Intel 82599 VF was capable of more than 9.4 Gbps throughput on the Netperf tests, and CompSC had no detectable impact on throughput. In the scp tests, the Intel 82599 VF produced almost the same throughput as the Intel 82576 VF because the CPU was the bottleneck in scp tests. In the SPECweb2009 tests, the performance of the Intel 82599 VF was also comparable to the performance of the Intel 82576 VF. We can clearly see the bottleneck was reached at 250 sessions, and CompSC slightly degraded response time in a similar fashion to the Intel 82576 VF.

6.5 Service down time

In this section, we graphically illustrate the whole process of live migration. We treated the server as live if it had a positive throughput. To fulfill the throughput, we ran the Netperf benchmark during our test. The throughput on the Netperf client machine was recorded as data. In order to shorten migration time (mostly decided by the amount of memory), we modified the configuration of

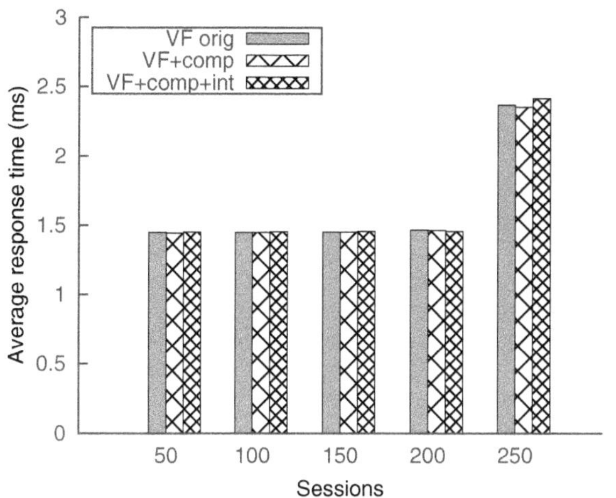

Figure 10. Average response time by SPECweb 2009 on Intel 82599

the virtual machine. In this test, the virtual machine was equipped with 1 GB of memory.

Figure 11 presents the throughput and CPU utilization during a live migration when using CompSC on an Intel 82576 VF, and Figure 12 presents the results with the PV device using an Intel 82576 PF as physical device. In the two figures, we first notice that the service downtime of CompSC was about 0.9s while the downtime of the PV device was about 1.4s. CompSC had a 35.7% shorter and better service downtime. It can also be seen that in PV device test, service was down shortly before the 1.4s downtime (On about 20.6s) and CPU utilization reached as high as 327%. The reason for this behavior is the suspension process of PV-on-HVM (Para-virtualization on Hardware-assisted Virtual Machine). The suspension on PV-on-HVM demanded the cooperation of drivers in the virtual machine. This cooperation consumed many CPU resources and caused a small period of service down. If we focus on CPU utilization, we notice that the CPU% lines on both figures have the same shape, and the line on Figure 12 is higher than the line on Figure 11. This fits our expectation. The pass-through device consumed less CPU resources than the PV device, which is the precise usage of pass-through devices.

We also have a test with regards to the bonding driver solution. Due to limitations of current Xen implementations, we only have a test for the bonding driver on a VF from the Intel 82576 and an emulated E1000 device as backup. Figure 13 shows the results of this test. The bonding driver solution had an extra service down at about 3s. Because the switching of the bonding driver took several milliseconds and caused packets to be lost. The shape of CPU utilization line is similar to that of the CompSC and PV device, but the throughput was much less. The performance of the emulated device was not as good as either the PV device or the pass-through device. In the figure, it can also be seen that the service downtime of bonding driver solution was about 1.2s.

In order to assess the performance benefit of SR-IOV, we evaluated the migration process of an Intel 82599 VF. Figure 14 depicts the results of our test on an Intel 82599 VF with CompSC solution. The shape of the CPU line and throughput line are almost the same as in Figure 11. Sometimes the throughput collapsed for a little while (less than 0.2s), because Dom0 and the guest were sharing the physical CPU, and a throughput of 10 Gbps was very challenging for our environment. The test results of PV device are shown in Figure 15. We used the PF Intel 82599 PF as the physical device of the PV device, however, the PV device could only achieve about 2.5 Gbps throughput. The Intel 82599 VF with CompSC achieved as much as a 282.66% higher throughput than the PV device. The impact on throughput occurred when the CPU utilization was higher than 200% (16s to 22s). In terms of downtime, the result these tests are similar to that of the Intel 82576 situations. The downtime of CompSC on the Intel 82599 VF was about 0.8s, which was 42.9% less than the downtime of the PV device, i.e. about 1.4s.

The test results of VMDq are presented in Figure 16. While VMDq support in Xen is currently abandoned, we found VMDq support on earlier version of Xen. Thus, in our VMDq tests, we used Xen 3.0 and Linux 2.6.18.8 with a PV guest virtual machine. We used an Intel 82598 NIC as the physical device of VMDq, because the Intel 82599 NIC is not supported in Linux 2.6.18.8. The migration time and downtime in the test was shorter than CompSC and PV scenarios due to the PV guest. The PV guest had advantages on migration, since the kernel of PV guest is modified for virtualization. The core issue of VMDq relates to throughput, which was about 5 Gbps. Although VMDq had larger throughput than the PV scenario, the throughput of the Intel 82599 VF with CompSC was 89.57% higher than VMDq.

6.6 Size of total hardware states and past communications

In Section 3.2, we mentioned that state replay may record large amounts of past communications, and introduced several optimizations in response. In this section, we list the amount of hardware states and past communications needed in our implementation with the Intel 82576 and Intel 82599 NIC.

Table 5. Size of total hardware states in our implementation

	Size (bytes)
States in IGBVF driver	88
VF-in-PF states in IGB driver	848
States in IXGBEVF driver	104
VF-in-PF states in IXGBE driver	326

According to Table 5, the total number of hardware states to be transferred during the migration is less than 1 kilobyte in both the IGBVF and IXGBEVF drivers. In a typical network environment, the network throughput is at least 100 Mbps. Consequently, the transmission cost of hardware states can safely be ignored.

7. Discussion

In this paper, we focus on the pass-through NIC, but in the design of CompSC, we focus on every pass-through device. While CompSC can be used for pass-through devices other than those in this work, not all devices might perform as this paper describes. One aspect that needs to be considered is the number of hardware states, which varies among different devices. In our evaluation, the number of hardware states of NIC is small, but some devices have tremendously large state capacities, such as graphic cards with large video memory. In modern graphic cards, video memory larger than 256 MB is quite common. With such devices, the transmission costs for device state is quite large and can have a large impact on the service downtime or even be a bottleneck. One potential solution would be to shut down some features of graphic cards such as 3D rendering before migration to reduce the total amount of the hardware states. Another aspect to be acknowledged is the cost for state replay. Since state replay only commits on invisible states, devices with many invisible states may have higher costs for state replay. Actually, IGBVF/IXGBEVF are examples of this phenomenon. Because the ring head register is invisible, the state replay may cost hundreds of MMIO. In our implementation, we use a method of shifting to avoid this large cost. The cost for state replay depends

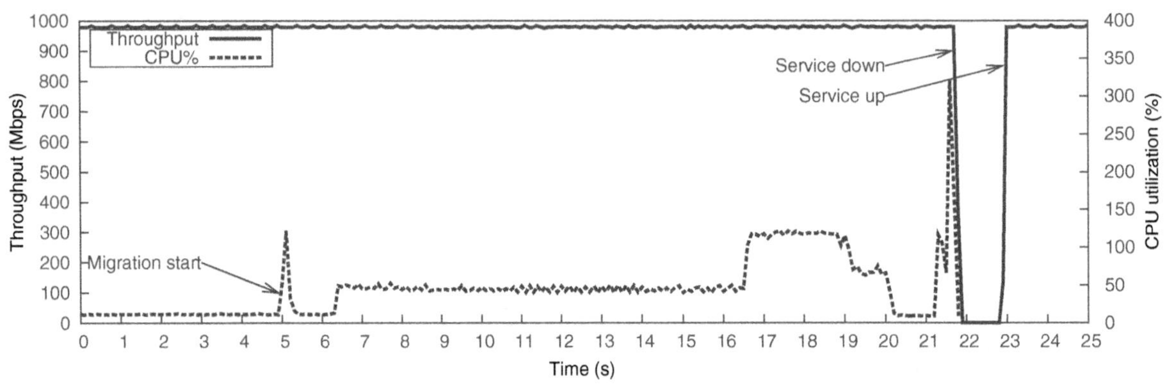

Figure 11. CompSC on Intel 82576: Throughput and CPU utilization during live migration

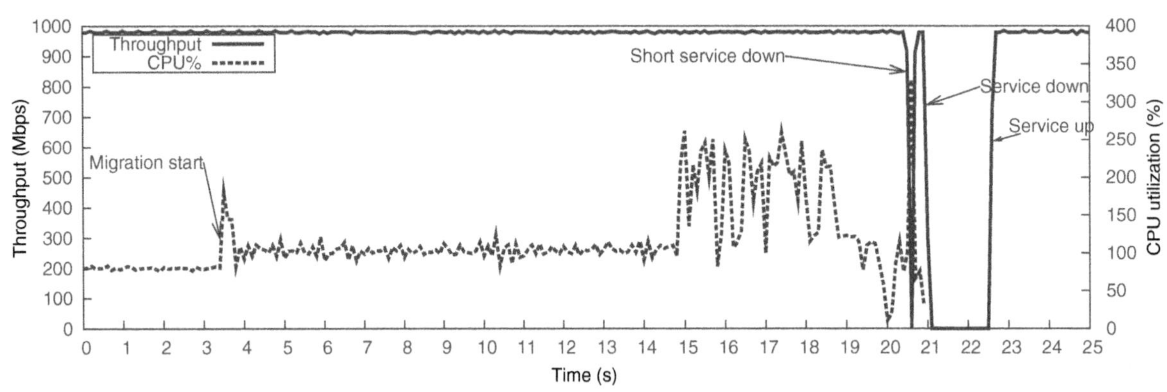

Figure 12. PV device on Intel 82576: Throughput and CPU utilization during live migration

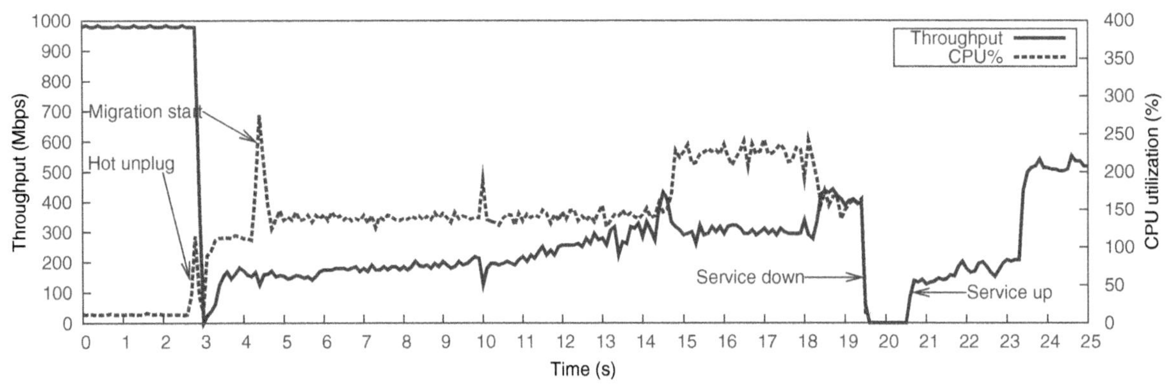

Figure 13. Bonding driver: Throughput and CPU utilization during live migration

on the hardware design of devices. Luckily, for most devices the cost for state replay is small because it is generally just the cost of device initialization.

CompSC can also be implemented on other hypervisors; no assumptions are made in this regard in the design of CompSC. The requirements for hypervisor of CompSC are: (1) Live migration support (2) Pass-through device support (3) Foreign page access. These features are common in today's hypervisors such as KVM [10] and VMware ESX [6]. Hopefully, the CompSC support of these hypervisors only need less than 1K LOC just like our implementation on Xen.

CompSC needs both driver changes and hypervisor changes. While this is somewhat of a limitation on deployment, CompSC does not need changes on virtual machine guest kernel, and the new driver is completely compatible with the original hypervisor and non-virtualized environments. In this respect, deployment is easy since one can safely use the new (CompSC) driver in old environments. Once the CompSC support of the hypervisor is settled, live migration is enabled. In terms of deployment, the bonding driver solution needs hypervisor changes, guest kernel changes, and a new guest driver. The convenience of the bonding driver solution is based on the fact that the Linux kernel already has the bonding

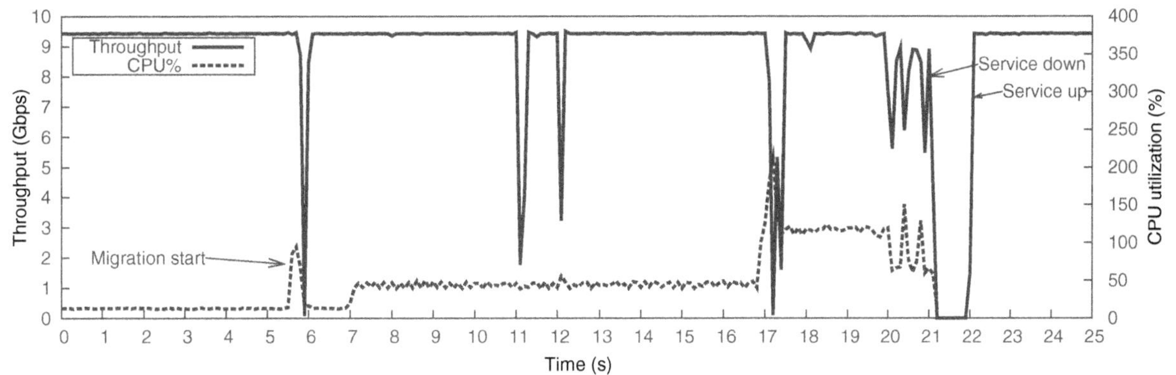

Figure 14. CompSC on Intel 82599: Throughput and CPU utilization during live migration

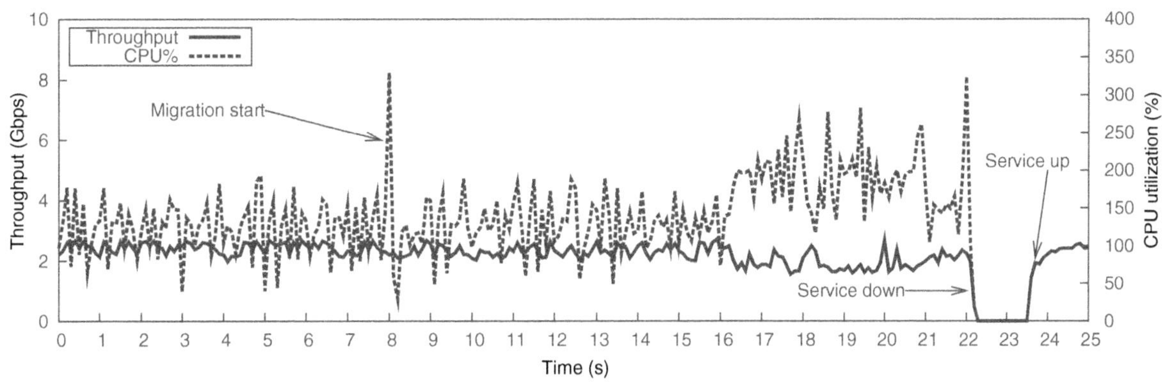

Figure 15. PV device on Intel 82599: Throughput and CPU utilization during live migration

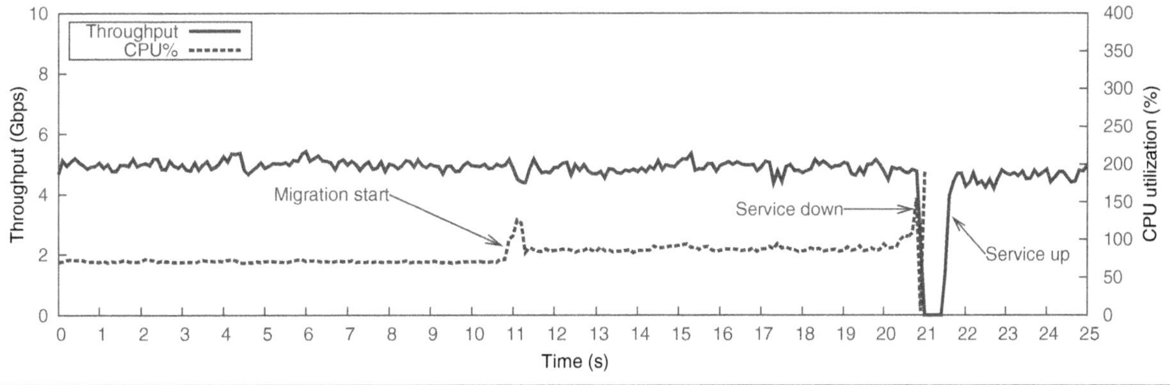

Figure 16. VMDq on Intel 82598: Throughput and CPU utilization during live migration

driver; the solution is hard to deploy on other OS such as Windows, however. NPIA needs hypervisor changes and a set of plug-in binaries. Compared to CompSC, every device NPIA supports has a brand new driver (plug-in binary). Furthermore, the new driver can only be used in NPIA environments. The VMDq solution is even worse: it needs hypervisor changes, guest kernel changes, and a pair of new drivers (A.K.A front-end driver and back-end driver). Overall, CompSC has deployment and usage advantages that outweigh these other solutions.

8. Conclusion

In this paper, we present CompSC: a solution of hardware state migration that achieves live migration support on pass-through network devices. With a synchronization mechanism between the device driver and the hypervisor, hardware is taken over by the hypervisor and hardware state saving is performed. Right after migration, the device driver restores the hardware state on the destination machine using knowledge of the device and saved states. Furthermore, a self-emulation layer inside the hypervisor is provided to ensure the accuracy of statistic registers.

With CompSC, the Intel 82599 VF enabled live migration support with a throughput 282.66% higher than PV network devices and 89.57% higher than VMDq. During live migration, the service downtime was 42.9% shorter than that of PV network devices. The performance impact of CompSC during run time is negligible. Lastly, CompSC needs minimal effort to implement and can easily be deployed on different NICs.

Acknowledgments

We would like to thank the anonymous reviewers for their comments and suggestions. We also would like to thank Ian Pratt for his insight in the paper. This work has been supported by National Natural Science Foundation of China under Grant No. 61170050 and Grant No. 60973143.

References

[1] Kvm and linux source. http://git.kernel.org/.

[2] Network plugin architecture discussion on lkml. http://kerneltrap.org/mailarchive/linux-kernel/2010/5/4/4565952.

[3] Paravirtops. http://wiki.xen.org/xenwiki/XenParavirtOps.

[4] Spec web 2009. http://www.spec.org/web2009/.

[5] Virtual machine device queues. http://www.intel.com/content/www/us/en/network-adapters/gigabit-network-adapters/io-acceleration-technology-vmdq.html.

[6] Vmware esx. http://www.vmware.com/products/vsphere/esxi-and-esx/index.htm.

[7] D. Abramson, J. Jackson, S. Muthrasanallur, G. Neiger, G. Regnier, R. Sankran, I. Schoinas, R. Uhlig, B. Vembu, and J. Weigert. Intel virtualization technology for directed i/o. *Intel Technology Journal*, 10, Aug 2006. http://www.intel.com/technology/itj/2006/v10i3/.

[8] K. Adams and O. Agesen. A comparison of software and hardware techniques for x86 virtualization. In *Proceedings of the 12th international conference on Architectural support for programming languages and operating systems*, ASPLOS-XII, pages 2–13, New York, NY, USA, 2006. ACM. ISBN 1-59593-451-0.

[9] M. Armbrust, A. Fox, R. Griffith, A. D. Joseph, R. Katz, A. Konwinski, G. Lee, D. Patterson, A. Rabkin, I. Stoica, and M. Zaharia. Above the clouds: A berkeley view of cloud computing. Technical report, Feb. 2009.

[10] K. Avi. Kvm : The linux virtual machine monitor. *Proceedings of the Ottawa Linux Symposium*, 2007.

[11] P. Barham, B. Dragovic, K. Fraser, S. Hand, T. Harris, A. Ho, R. Neugebauer, I. Pratt, and A. Warfield. Xen and the art of virtualization. *SIGOPS Oper. Syst. Rev.*, 37:164–177, October 2003. ISSN 0163-5980.

[12] S. Berger, R. Cceres, K. A. Goldman, R. Perez, R. Sailer, and L. Doorn. vtpm: Virtualizing the trusted platform module. In *In USENIX Security*, pages 305–320, 2006.

[13] P. M. Chen and B. D. Noble. When virtual is better than real. In *Proceedings of the Eighth Workshop on Hot Topics in Operating Systems*, pages 133–, Washington, DC, USA, 2001. IEEE Computer Society.

[14] C. Clark, K. Fraser, S. Hand, J. G. Hansen, E. Jul, C. Limpach, I. Pratt, and A. Warfield. Live migration of virtual machines. In *Proceedings of the 2nd conference on Symposium on Networked Systems Design & Implementation - Volume 2*, NSDI'05, pages 273–286, Berkeley, CA, USA, 2005. USENIX Association.

[15] B. Cully, G. Lefebvre, D. Meyer, M. Feeley, N. Hutchinson, and A. Warfield. Remus: High availability via asynchronous virtual machine replication. In *In Proc. NSDI*, 2008.

[16] Y. Dong, Z. Yu, and G. Rose. Sr-iov networking in xen: architecture, design and implementation. In *Proceedings of the First conference on I/O virtualization*, WIOV'08, pages 10–10, Berkeley, CA, USA, 2008. USENIX Association.

[17] Y. Dong, Y. Chen, Z. Pan, J. Dai, and Y. Jiang. Renic: Architecture extension to sr-iov network for efficient high availability replication. In *In Proceedings of the 7th International Conference on High Performance and Embedded Architectures and Compilers*, HiPEAC'12, 2012.

[18] W. Huang, J. Liu, B. Abali, and D. K. Panda. A case for high performance computing with virtual machines. In *Proceedings of the 20th annual international conference on Supercomputing*, ICS '06, pages 125–134, New York, NY, USA, 2006. ACM.

[19] *Intel 82576 Gigabit Ethernet Controller Datasheet*. Intel, . http://download.intel.com/design/network/datashts/82576_Datasheet.pdf.

[20] *Intel 82599 10 GbE Controller Datasheet*. Intel, . http://download.intel.com/design/network/datashts/82599_datasheet.pdf.

[21] A. Kadav and M. M. Swift. Live migration of direct-access devices. *SIGOPS Oper. Syst. Rev.*, 43:95–104, July 2009. ISSN 0163-5980.

[22] M. A. Kozuch, M. Kaminsky, and M. P. Ryan. Migration without virtualization. In *Proceedings of the 12th conference on Hot topics in operating systems*, HotOS'09, pages 10–10, Berkeley, CA, USA, 2009. USENIX Association.

[23] G. Liao, D. Guo, L. Bhuyan, and S. R. King. Software techniques to improve virtualized i/o performance on multi-core systems. In *Proceedings of the 4th ACM/IEEE Symposium on Architectures for Networking and Communications Systems*, ANCS '08, pages 161–170, New York, NY, USA, 2008. ACM. ISBN 978-1-60558-346-4.

[24] J. Liu, W. Huang, B. Abali, and D. K. Panda. High performance vmm-bypass i/o in virtual machines. In *Proceedings of the annual conference on USENIX '06 Annual Technical Conference*, pages 3–3, Berkeley, CA, USA, 2006. USENIX Association.

[25] A. Menon, J. R. Santos, Y. Turner, G. J. Janakiraman, and W. Zwaenepoel. Diagnosing performance overheads in the xen virtual machine environment. In *Proceedings of the 1st ACM/USENIX international conference on Virtual execution environments*, VEE '05, pages 13–23, New York, NY, USA, 2005. ACM.

[26] A. Menon, A. L. Cox, and W. Zwaenepoel. Optimizing network virtualization in xen. In *Proceedings of the annual conference on USENIX '06 Annual Technical Conference*, pages 2–2, Berkeley, CA, USA, 2006. USENIX Association.

[27] D. S. Milojicic, F. Douglis, Y. Paindaveine, R. Wheeler, and S. Zhou. Process migration. *ACM Computing Surveys*, 32:2000, 2000.

[28] A. B. Nagarajan and F. Mueller. Proactive fault tolerance for hpc with xen virtualization. In *In Proceedings of the 21st Annual International Conference on Supercomputing (ICS07*, pages 23–32. ACM Press, 2007.

[29] J. R. Santos, Y. Turner, G. Janakiraman, and I. Pratt. Bridging the gap between software and hardware techniques for i/o virtualization. In *USENIX 2008 Annual Technical Conference on Annual Technical Conference*, pages 29–42, Berkeley, CA, USA, 2008. USENIX Association.

[30] J. Sugerman, G. Venkitachalam, and B.-H. Lim. Virtualizing i/o devices on vmware workstation's hosted virtual machine monitor. In *Proceedings of the General Track: 2002 USENIX Annual Technical Conference*, pages 1–14, Berkeley, CA, USA, 2001. USENIX Association. ISBN 1-880446-09-X.

[31] C. A. Waldspurger. Memory resource management in vmware esx server. *SIGOPS Oper. Syst. Rev.*, 36:181–194, December 2002. ISSN 0163-5980.

[32] E. Zhai, G. D. Cummings, and Y. Dong. Live migration with pass-through device for linux vm. In *Ottawa Linux Symposium*, 2008.

libdft: Practical Dynamic Data Flow Tracking for Commodity Systems

Vasileios P. Kemerlis Georgios Portokalidis Kangkook Jee Angelos D. Keromytis

Network Security Lab
Department of Computer Science
Columbia University, New York, NY, USA
{vpk, porto, jikk, angelos}@cs.columbia.edu

Abstract

Dynamic data flow tracking (DFT) deals with tagging and tracking data of interest as they propagate during program execution. DFT has been repeatedly implemented by a variety of tools for numerous purposes, including protection from zero-day and cross-site scripting attacks, detection and prevention of information leaks, and for the analysis of legitimate and malicious software. We present libdft, a dynamic DFT framework that unlike previous work is at once *fast*, *reusable*, and works with *commodity software and hardware*. libdft provides an API for building DFT-enabled tools that work on unmodified binaries, running on common operating systems and hardware, thus facilitating research and rapid prototyping.

We explore different approaches for implementing the low-level aspects of instruction-level data tracking, introduce a more efficient and 64-bit capable shadow memory, and identify (and avoid) the common pitfalls responsible for the excessive performance overhead of previous studies. We evaluate libdft using real applications with large codebases like the Apache and MySQL servers, and the Firefox web browser. We also use a series of benchmarks and utilities to compare libdft with similar systems. Our results indicate that it performs at least as fast, if not faster, than previous solutions, and to the best of our knowledge, we are the first to evaluate the performance overhead of a fast dynamic DFT implementation in such depth. Finally, libdft is freely available as open source software.

Categories and Subject Descriptors D.2.5 [*Testing and Debugging*]: Monitors; D.2.13 [*Reusable Software*]: Reusable libraries

General Terms Design, Performance, Security

Keywords Data flow tracking, dynamic binary instrumentation, taint analysis, information leak detection, exploit prevention

VEE'12, March 3–4, 2012, London, England, UK.

1. Introduction

Dynamic data flow tracking (DFT), also referred to as information flow tracking, is a well known technique that deals with the tagging and tracking of "interesting" data as they propagate during program execution. DFT has many uses, such as analyzing malware behavior [21], hardening software against zero-day attacks (*e.g.,* buffer overflow, format string) [2, 18, 22], detecting and preventing information leaks [10, 31], and even debugging software misconfigurations [1]. From an architectural perspective, it has been integrated into full system emulators [5, 21] and virtual machine monitors [13, 17], retrofitted into unmodified binaries using dynamic binary instrumentation [22], and added to source codebases using source-to-source code transformations [28]. Proposals have also been made to implement it in hardware [8, 24, 26], but they had little appeal to hardware vendors.

Previous studies utilized DFT to investigate the applicability of the technique into a particular domain of interest, producing their own problem-specific and ad hoc implementations of software-based DFT that all suffer from one or more of the following issues: *high overhead*, *little reusability* (*i.e.,* they are problem specific), and *limited applicability* (*i.e.,* they are not readily applicable to existing commodity software). For instance, LIFT [22] and Minemu [2] use DFT to detect security attacks. While fast, they do not support multithreaded applications (the first by design). LIFT only works with 64-bit binaries, while Minemu only with 32-bit binaries, featuring a design that requires extensive modifications to support 64-bit architectures. More importantly, they focus on a single problem domain and cannot be easily modified for use in others.

More flexible and customizable implementations of fine-grained DFT have also failed to provide the research community with a practical and reusable DFT framework. For example, Dytan [6] focuses on presenting a configurable DFT tool that supports both data and control flow dependencies. Unfortunately, its versatility comes at a high price, even when running small programs with data flow dependencies alone (control flow dependencies further impact performance). For instance, Dytan reported a 30x slowdown when compressing with `gzip`, while LIFT reports less than 10x. Although the experiments may not be directly comparable, the significant disparity in performance suggests that the design of Dytan is not geared towards low overhead.

This paper argues that a practical dynamic DFT implementation needs to address all three problems listed above, and thus it should be concurrently *fast*, *reusable*, and *applicable to commodity hardware and software*. We introduce libdft, a meta-tool in the form of a shared library that implements dynamic DFT using Intel's Pin dynamic binary instrumentation framework [16]. libdft's performance is comparable or better than previous work, incurring slowdowns that range between 1.14x and 6.03x for command-line utilities, while it can also run large server applications like Apache and MySQL with an overhead ranging between 1.25x and 4.83x. In addition, it is versatile and reusable by providing an extensive API that can be used to implement DFT-powered tools. Finally, it runs on commodity systems. Our current implementation works with x86 binaries on Linux, while we plan to extend it to run on 64-bit architectures and the Windows operating system (OS). libdft introduces an efficient, 64-bit capable, shadow memory, which represented one of the most serious limitations of earlier works, as flat shadow memory structures imposed unmanageable memory space overheads on 64-bit systems, and dynamically managed structures introduce high performance penalties. More importantly, libdft supports multiprocess and multithreaded applications, by trading off memory for assurance against race conditions (see Section 7), and it does not require modifications to programs or the underlying OS.

The contributions of this paper can be summarized as follows:

- We discuss the design and implementation of a fast and reusable shared DFT library for commodity software. Specifically, we investigate and identify the underlying reasons responsible for the performance degradation incurred by previous DFT tools and present a design that minimizes it. We approach the problem from a systems perspective and attempt to answer the following questions: What are the performance boundaries of such a DFT tool? What practices need to be avoided by practitioners and system implementors? What is the source of the overhead? We also present a set of novel optimizations for further improving the performance of DFT.
- We evaluate the performance of libdft using real applications that include complex and large software such as the Apache and MySQL servers, and the Firefox web browser. libdft achieves performance similar, or better, than previous work, while being applicable to a broader set of software. Moreover, our extensive evaluation establishes a set of bounds regarding the performance of DFT. To the best of our knowledge, we are the first to perform such an extensive evaluation of a DFT framework.
- We present the development of a libdft-powered tool, namely libdft-DTA, to demonstrate the reusability of libdft as well as its capabilities. libdft-DTA performs dynamic taint analysis (DTA) to detect zero-day attacks similarly to TaintCheck [18], Eudaemon [20], and LIFT [22]. We show that our versatile API can be used for developing an otherwise complex tool in approximately 450 lines of C++ code.
- Our implementation is freely available as a shared library and can be used for developing tools that transparently (*i.e.*, without requiring any change on applications or the underlying OS) make use of DFT services. Developers can use the API provided to easily define data of interest, and then capture their use at arbitrary points. In this way, libdft facilitates research and rapid prototyping, by allowing potential users to focus on solving a particular problem (*e.g.*, detecting information leaks or application misconfigurations), rather than dealing with the elaborate details of an information flow tracking framework.

The remainder of this paper is organized as follows: Section 2 introduces DFT and discusses the differences between dynamic and static DFT approaches. We present libdft in Section 3 and elaborate on its implementation in Section 4. Section 5 discusses the use of libdft in various tools and presents its API through the creation of a DTA tool, which we evaluate along with libdft in Section 6. Section 7 examines the limitations of the current implementation, along with future considerations. Related work is presented in Section 8 and conclusions are in Section 9.

```
1: unsigned char csum = 0;
2:
3: bcount = read(fd, data, 1024);
4: while(bcount-- > 0)
5:     csum ^= *data++;
6:
7: write(fd, &csum, 1);
```

(a) Data flow dependency

```
1: int authorized = 0;
2:
3: bcount = read(fd, pass, 12);
4: MD5(pass, 12, phash);
5: if (strcmp(phash, stored_hash) == 0)
6:     authorized = 1;
7: return authorized;
```

(b) Control flow dependecy

Figure 1. Examples of code with data dependencies.

2. Data Flow Tracking

DFT has been a popular subject of research, primarily employed for enforcing safe information flow and identifying illegal data usage. In past work, it is frequently referred to as information flow tracking (IFT) [24] or taint analysis. This work defines DFT as: "the process of *accurately* tracking the flow of *selected* data throughout the execution of a program or system". This process is characterized by three aspects, which we will attempt to clarify with the help of the code-snippets shown in Figure 1.

Data sources Data sources are program or memory locations, where data of interest enter the system, usually after the execution of a function or system call. Data coming from these sources are tagged and tracked. For instance, if we define files as a source, the `read` call in Figure 1 would result in tagging `data` and `pass`.

Data tracking During program execution, tagged data are tracked as they are copied and altered by program instructions. Consider code snippet (a) in Figure 1, where `data` has already been tagged in line 3. The while loop that follows calculates a simple checksum (XOR all the bytes in `data`) and stores the result in `csum`. In this case, there is a data flow dependency between `csum` and `data`, since the former directly depends on the latter. On the other hand, `authorized` in (b) is indirectly affected by the value of `phash`, which in turn depends on `pass`. This is frequently called a control flow dependency, and in this work, we do not consider cases of implicit data flow that are in accordance with previous work on the subject [18, 24]. Dytan made provisions for conditionally handling such control-flow dependencies, but concluded that, while useful in certain domains, they frequently lead to an explosion in the amount of tagged data and to incorrect data dependencies [6]. Ongoing work seeks to address these issues [15].

Data sinks Data sinks are also program or memory locations, where one can check for the presence of tagged data, usually for inspecting or enforcing data flow. For instance, tagged data may not be allowed in certain memory areas and function arguments. Consider again the code-snippet (a) in Figure 1, where in line 7 `csum` is written to a file. If files are defined as data sinks, the use of `write` with `csum` can trigger a user-defined action.

Dynamic versus static DFT Performing DFT requires additional memory for the data tags. Also, the program itself needs to be extended with tag propagation logic, and data tagging and checking logic at the sources and sinks respectively. The additional code for that is frequently referred to as instrumentation code, and can be injected either statically (*e.g.*, during source code development and at compile/loading time), or dynamically using virtualization or dynamic binary instrumentation (DBI). Static systems apply DFT by recompiling software using a modified compiler [25], or a source-to-source transformation engine [28]. Conversely, the dynamic ones can be directly applied on unmodified binaries, including commercial off-the-shelf software [22, 27, 31]. In both cases, software needs to be extensively instrumented for associating data with some kind of tag and injecting logic that asserts tags at the sources, propagates them according to the data dependencies defined by the program semantics, and finally, inspecting the sinks for the presence of tagged data. Dynamic solutions, albeit being much slower than static ones, have the advantage of being immediately, and incrementally, applicable to already deployed software.

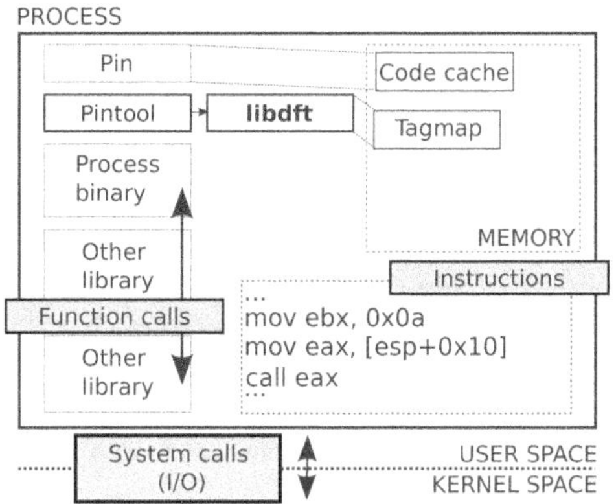

Figure 2. Process image of a binary running under libdft. The highlighted boxes describe possible data sources and sinks that can be used with libdft.

3. Design

We designed libdft for use with the Pin DBI framework to facilitate the creation of Pintools that employ dynamic DFT. Briefly, Pin consists of a virtual machine (VM) library, and an injector that attaches the VM in already running processes or new processes that launches itself. Pintools are shared libraries that employ Pin's extensive API to inspect and modify a binary at the instruction level. libdft is also a library, which can be used by Pintools to transparently apply fine-grained DFT on binaries running over Pin. More importantly, it provides its own API (presented in Section 5) that enables tool authors to easily customize libdft by specifying data sources and sinks, or even modify the tag propagation policy.

When a user attaches to an already running process, or launches a new one using a libdft-enabled Pintool, the injector first injects Pin's runtime and then passes control to the tool. There are three types of locations that a libdft-enabled tool can use as a data source or sink: *program instructions*, *function calls*, and *system calls*. It can "tap" these locations by installing callbacks that get invoked when a certain instruction is encountered, or when a certain function or system call is made. These user-defined callbacks drive the DFT process by tagging or un-tagging data, and monitoring or enforcing data flow. Figure 2 sketches the memory image of a process running under a libdft-enabled Pintool. The highlighted boxes mark the locations where the tool author can install callbacks. For instance, the user can tag the contents of the buffer returned by the `read` system call (as in the examples shown in Figure 1) and check whether the operands of indirect `call` instructions are tagged (*e.g.*, the `eax` register in Figure 2).

3.1 Data Tags

libdft stores data tags in a tagmap, which contains a process-wide data structure (shadow memory) for holding the tags of data stored in memory and a thread-specific structure that keeps tags for data residing in CPU registers. The format of the tags stored in the tagmap is determined by mainly two factors: (a) the granularity of the tagging, and (b) the size of the tags.

Tagging granularity In principle, we could tag data units as small as a single bit, or as larger contiguous chunks of memory. The former enables us to perform very fine-grained and accurate DFT, while using larger granularity means the data tracking will be coarser and more error prone. For instance, with page-level granularity, moving a single byte (tagged) into an untagged location will result into tagging the whole page that contains the destination, thus "polluting" adjacent data. However, choosing extremely fine-grained tagging comes at a significant cost, as more memory space is needed for storing the tags (*e.g.*, using bit-level tagging, 8 tags are necessary for a single byte and 32 for a 32-bit register). More importantly, the tag propagation logic becomes complicated, since data dependencies are also more intricate (*e.g.*, consider adding two 32-bit numbers that only have some of their bits tagged). libdft uses byte-level tagging granularity, since a byte is the smallest addressable chunk of memory in most architectures. Our choice allows us to offer sufficiently fine-grained tracking for most practical purposes and we believe that it strikes a balance between usability and performance [21].

Tag size Orthogonally to tagging granularity, larger tags are more versatile as they allow for different types of data to be tagged uniquely (*e.g.*, each byte could be tagged using a unique 32-bit number). Unfortunately, larger tags require complex propagation logic and more storage space. libdft offers two different tag sizes: (a) byte tags for associating up to 8 distinct values or *colors* to each tagged byte (every bit represents a different tag class), and (b) single-bit tags (*i.e.*, data are either tagged or not). The first allows for more sophisticated tracking and analysis tools, while the second enables tools that only need binary tags for conserving memory.

3.2 Tag Propagation

Tag propagation is accomplished using Pin's API to both instrument and analyze the target process. In Pin's terms, instrumentation refers to the task of inspecting the binary instructions of a program for determining what analysis routines should be inserted where. For instance, libdft inspects every program instruction that (loosely stated) moves or combines data to determine data dependencies. On the other hand, analysis refers to the actual routines, or code, being retrofitted to execute before, after, or instead of the original code. In our case, we inject analysis code implementing the tag propagation logic, based on the data dependencies observed during instrumentation.

The original code and libdft's analysis routines are translated by Pin's just-in-time (JIT) compiler for generating the code that will actually run. This occurs immediately before executing a code sequence for the first time, and the result is placed in a code cache (also depicted in Figure 2), so as to avoid repeating this process for the same code sequence. Our injected code executes before application instructions, tracking data as they are copied between registers, and between registers and memory, thus achieving fine-grained DFT. Pin's VM ensures that the target process runs entirely from within the code cache by interpreting all instructions that cannot be executed safely otherwise (*e.g.*, indirect branches). Moreover, a series of optimizations such as trace linking and register re-allocation are applied for improving performance [16].

Finally, libdft allows tools to modify the default tag propagation policy, by registering their own instrumentation callbacks via its API, for instructions of interest. This way tool authors can tailor the data tagging according to their needs, and cancel tag propagation in certain cases or track otherwise unhandled instructions.

3.3 Challenges for Fast Dynamic DFT

To keep libdft's overhead low, we carefully examined how DBI frameworks, such as Pin, work for identifying the development practices that should be avoided. Pin's overhead primarily depends on the size of the analysis code injected, but it can frequently be higher than anticipated due to the structure of the code itself. Specifically, the registers provided by the underlying architecture will be used to execute both application code, as well as code that implements the DFT logic, thus forcing the DBI framework to spill registers (*i.e.*, save their contents to memory and later restore them), whenever an analysis routine needs to utilize registers already allocated. Therefore, the more complex the code, the more registers have to be spilled.

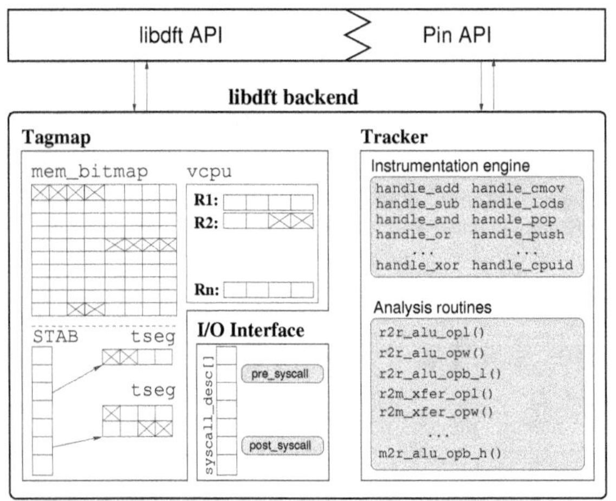

Figure 3. The architecture of libdft. The shaded components of I/O interface and tracker illustrate the instrumentation and analysis code that implements the DFT logic, whereas the x-marked regions on the tagmap indicate tagged bytes.

Additionally, certain types of instructions must be avoided due to certain side-effects. For instance, spilling the `EFLAGS` register in the x86 architecture is expensive in terms of processing cycles, and is performed by specialized instructions (`PUSHF, PUSHFD`). As a result, including instructions in analysis code that modify this register should be done sparingly. More importantly, test-and-branch operations have to be avoided altogether, since they result into non-inlined code. In particular, whenever a branch instruction is included in the DFT code, Pin's JIT engine will emit a function call to the corresponding analysis routine, rather than inline the code of the routine along with the instructions of the application. Imposing such limitations on the implementation of any dynamic DFT tool is a challenge. Our implementation takes into consideration these issues, in conjunction with Pin, to achieve good performance.

The design of libdft provides the foundation for a framework that satisfies all three properties listed in Section 1. By taking into consideration the limitations discussed above, we achieve low overhead. Moreover, the extensive API of libdft makes it reusable, as it enables users to customize it for use in various domains, such as security, privacy, program analysis, and debugging. Finally, the last property is satisfied through the use of a mature, rather than an experimental and feature-limited, DBI platform for providing the apparatus to realize DFT for a variety of popular systems (*e.g.*, x86 and x86-64 Linux and Windows OSs).

4. Implementation

We implemented libdft using Pin 2.9, which is currently available for Linux and Windows OSs. Our prototype works with unmodified multiprocess and multithreaded applications running on 32-bit x86 CPUs over Linux, but can be extended with moderate effort to operate on the x86-64 architecture and the Windows OS (we discuss future ports in Section 7). The main components of libdft are illustrated in Figure 3.

4.1 The Tagmap

The implementation of the *tagmap* plays a crucial role in the overall performance of libdft, since the injected DFT logic constantly operates on data tags.

4.1.1 Register Tags

We store the tags for all 8 general purpose registers (GPRs) of the x86 architecture in the `vcpu` structure, which is part of the tagmap (see Figure 3). Note that we tag and track only the registers that can be directly used by applications (like the GPRs). Registers such as the instruction pointer (`EIP`), `EFLAGS`, and segment registers, are not tagged or traced. Recall that according to our definition of DFT, we only track direct data flow dependencies, so it is safe to ignore `EFLAGS`. However, instructions that are executed conditionally, based on the contents of `EFLAGS`, are handled appropriately (*e.g.*, `CMOVcc`, `SETcc`). Moreover, floating point registers (`FPU`), as well as SSE registers (`XMM`, `MMX`), are currently ignored for the sake of simplicity. To support these registers in the future, we only need to enlarge `vcpu`.

The tagmap holds multiple `vcpu` structures, one for every thread of execution. Specifically, libdft captures the thread creation and thread termination events of an application and dynamically manages the number of `vcpu` structures. We locate the appropriate structure for each thread using its virtual id (*i.e.*, an incremental value starting from zero) that is assigned by Pin to every thread. In the case of bit-sized tags, we use one byte to hold the four 1-bit tags needed for every 32-bit GPR, so that the space overhead of `vcpu` is 8 bytes for each thread. Similarly, in case of byte-sized tags, we need 4 bytes for every 32-bit GPR, and hence the space overhead of `vcpu` becomes 32 bytes per thread.

4.1.2 Memory Tags

Bit-sized tags When libdft is configured to use bit-sized tags, it stores memory tags in a flat, fixed-size structure (see `mem_bitmap` in Figure 3) that holds one bit for each byte of process addressable memory. The total size of the virtual address space in x86 systems is 4GB (2^{32}), however the OS reserves part of that space for itself (*i.e.*, the kernel). The amount of space reserved for the kernel depends on the OS, with Linux usually adopting a 3G/1G memory split that leaves 3GB of address space for processes. In this case, we require 384MB to be contiguously reserved for the tagmap.

The memory tags of address *vaddr* can be obtained as follows: `tval = mem_bitmap[vaddr >> 3] & (MASK << (vaddr & 0x7)).` Specifically, we use the 29 most significant bits (MSBs) of *vaddr*, as byte index in `mem_bitmap`, for selecting a byte that contains the tags of *vaddr*. Then, we treat the 3 least significant bits of *vaddr* as bit offset within the previously acquired byte, and by setting `MASK` to 0x1 we obtain the tag bit for a single byte. Similarly, if `MASK` is 0x3, or 0xF, we obtain the tag bits for a word, or double word, respectively. The address space overhead imposed by `mem_bitmap` is 12.5%. Using a fixed-size structure instead of a dynamically managed one (*e.g.*, a page table-like one) allows us to avoid the penalties involved with managing and accessing it. Note that while on 32-bit systems the size of the tagmap is reasonable, flat bitmaps are not practical on 64-bit architectures. For instance, in x86-64 a flat bitmap would require 32TB.

Byte-sized tags When libdft is using byte-sized tags, it stores them in dynamically allocated tagmap segments (see `tseg` in Figure 3). Every time the application gets a new chunk of memory implicitly by performing an image load (*e.g.*, when loading a dynamic shared object), or explicitly by invoking a system call like `mmap`, `mremap`, `brk`, and `shmat`, libdft intercepts the event and allocates an equally sized contiguous memory region. For instance, if the application requests an anonymous mapping of 1MB using `mmap`, libdft will "shadow" the allocated region with a tagmap segment of 1MB, for storing the byte tags of the `mmap`-ed memory. More importantly, tagmap segments that correspond to shared memory chunks are also shared. Hence, two processes running under libdft can effectively share shadow memory. To the best of our knowledge, we are the first to implement such a tag sharing scheme.

We obtain information about memory areas mapped at load time, or before libdft was attached on the application, through the `proc` pseudo-filesystem (`/proc/<pid>/maps`). This way we acquire the location of the stack and other kernel-mapped memory objects, such as the vDSO and vsyscall pages, and allocate the respective tagmap segments accordingly. In order to deal with the implicit expansion of the stack, libdft pre-allocates a tagmap segment to cover the stack as if it expands to its maximum value, which can be obtained via `getrlimit(RLIMIT_STACK)`. However, the same is not necessary for thread stacks, since they are allocated explicitly using `mmap`.

During initialization, libdft allocates a segment translation table (`STAB`) for mapping virtual addresses to their corresponding bytes in tagmap segments. Since memory is given to processes in blocks that are multiples of page size, `STAB` entries correspond to page size areas. For each page, `STAB` stores an addend value, which is effectively a 32-bit offset that needs to be added to all memory addresses inside that page, for retrieving the respective tag metadata. Assuming again a 3G/1G memory split and 4KB pages, `STAB` requires 3MB (*i.e.,* one entry for each 4KB in the range 0x00000000 – 0xBFFFFFFF). Whenever we allocate or free a tagmap segment, we update the `STAB` structure accordingly. Moreover, we ensure that segments that match with adjacent memory pages are also adjacent. This not only allows dealing with memory accesses crossing segment boundaries (*e.g.,* unaligned multi-byte accesses that span two pages are valid in x86), but also enables us to use a simple operation to retrieve the tag for any memory address: `taddr = vaddr + STAB[vaddr >> 12]`. The 20 MSBs of $vaddr$ are used as index in `STAB` to get an addend value, which in turn added to $vaddr$ itself for obtaining the respective tag bytes.

Byte-sized tags let us tag data using 8 different colors, but incur a higher per-byte memory overhead. Additionally, dynamically managing the respective tagmap segments also introduces overhead. However, we proactively allocate tagmap segments whenever the application maps new memory, instead of lazily waiting until a tagmap segment is used, to avoid the penalties involved with using branching instructions in analysis routines.

4.2 Code Instrumentation and Analysis

The *tracker* is the core component of libdft that is in charge of instrumenting a program to retrofit the DFT logic. It consists of two parts, shown in Figure 3.

4.2.1 Instrumentation Engine

The instrumentation engine is responsible for inspecting program instructions to determine the analysis routine(s) that should be injected for each case. We use Pin's instrumentation API to inspect every instruction before it is translated by the JIT compiler. We first resolve the instruction type (*e.g.,* arithmetic, move, logic), and then we analyze its operands for determining their category (*i.e.,* register, memory address, or immediate) and length (byte, word, double word). After gathering this information, we use Pin to insert the appropriate analysis routine before each instruction.

The instrumentation code is invoked once for every sequence of instructions, and the result (*i.e.,* the original code and analysis routines) is placed into Pin's code cache. We exploit code caching, by handling the x86 ISA complexity during the instrumentation phase, and keeping the analysis routines compact and fast. Specifically, we move the elaborate logic of discovering data dependencies and handling each variant of the same dependency category into the instrumentation phase. This allows us to aggressively optimize the propagation code by injecting compact, category-specific, and fast code snippets before each instruction. Due to the complexity and inherent redundancy of the ISA, our instrumentation engine consists of ~3000 C++ lines of code (LOC).

4.2.2 Analysis Routines

The analysis routines contain the code that actually implements the DFT logic for each instruction. They are injected by the instrumentation engine before every instruction to assert, clear, and propagate tags, and unlike instrumentation code they execute more frequently (*i.e.,* the analysis code injected for a specific instruction, executes every time the instruction executes).

Carefully implementing these analysis routines is paramount for achieving good performance. For instance, while Pin tries to inline analysis code into the application's code, the use of branch instructions will cause it to insert a function call to the respective routines instead (recall that function calls require extra processing cycles). The same also stands for overly large analysis routines. *Interestingly, we observed that the number of instructions, excluding all types of jumps, which Pin can inline is ~20.*

For these reasons, we introduce two guidelines for the development of efficient tag propagation code: (i) tag propagation should be branch-less, and (ii) tagmap updates should be performed with a single assignment. Both of them serve the purpose of aiding the JIT process to inline the injected code and minimize register spilling. Our analysis routines are made up of ~2500 C LOC, and include only arithmetical, logical, and memory operations. Moreover, we force Pin to use the *fastcall* x86 calling convention, for making the DFT code faster and smaller (*i.e.,* the compiler will avoid emitting push, pop, or stack-based parameter loading instructions).

Tracking code can be classified in the following categories based on the corresponding instruction type (the numbers in parentheses indicate the total number of analysis routines we implemented for each class, which are necessary for capturing the semantics of different operand types and sizes):

- *ALU* (21): analysis routines for the most common x86 instructions that typically have 2 or 3 operands, such as `ADD`, `SUB`, `AND`, `XOR`, `DIV`, `IMUL`, and so forth. For such instructions, we take the *union* of the source and destination operand tags, and we store the result in the respective tags of the destination operand(s). Immediates are always considered untagged.
- *XFER* (20): this class includes data transfers from a register to another register (*r2r*), from a register to a memory location and vice-versa (*r2m* and *m2r*), as well as from one memory address to another (*m2m*). For this type of instructions the source operand tags are copied to the destination operand tags, and again, immediates are always considered untagged.
- *CLR* (6): certain fairly complex instructions always result in their operands being untagged. Examples of such instructions include `CPUID`, `SETxx`, *etc.* Similarly, x86 *idioms* used for "zeroing" a register (*e.g.,*`xor eax, eax` and `sub eax, eax`), also result in untagging their operands.
- *SPECIAL* (45): this class includes analysis routines for x86 instructions that cannot be handled effectively with the aforementioned primitives, such as `XCHG`, `CMPXCHG`, `XADD`, `LEA`, `MOVSX`, `MOVZX`, and `CWDE`. For instance, although `XADD` can be handled by instrumenting the instruction twice with the respective XFER routines (for exchanging the tag values of the operands), and once with the ALU routine that handles `ADD`, the code size expansion would be prohibitive. Thus, we choose to implement an optimized analysis routine, for minimizing the injected code and inflicting less pressure on the code cache. libdft has one special handler for each quirky x86 instruction.
- *FPU, MMX, SSE*: these are ignored by default, unless their result is stored into one of the GPRs, or to a memory location. In such cases, the destination is untagged.

```
-------------------[r2r_alu_opb_l]-------------------
threads_ctx[tid].vcpu.gpr[dst] |=
    threads_ctx[tid].vcpu.gpr[src] & VCPU_MASK8;
--------------------[r2m_alu_opw]--------------------
*((uint16_t *)(mem_bitmap + VIRT2BYTE(dst))) |=
    (threads_ctx[tid].vcpu.gpr[src] & VCPU_MASK16) <<
        VIRT2BIT(dst);
--------------------[m2r_alu_opl]--------------------
threads_ctx[tid].vcpu.gpr[dst] |=
    (*((uint16_t *)(mem_bitmap + VIRT2BYTE(src))) >>
-------------------[r2r_xfer_opb_l]------------------
threads_ctx[tid].vcpu.gpr[dst] =
    (threads_ctx[tid].vcpu.gpr[dst] & ~VCPU_MASK8) |
    (threads_ctx[tid].vcpu.gpr[src] & VCPU_MASK8);
--------------------[r2m_xfer_opw]-------------------
*((uint16_t *)(mem_bitmap + VIRT2BYTE(dst))) =
    (*((uint16_t *)(mem_bitmap + VIRT2BYTE(dst))) &
        ~(WORD_MASK << VIRT2BIT(dst))) |
    ((uint16_t)(threads_ctx[tid].vcpu.gpr[src] &
        VCPU_MASK16) << VIRT2BIT(dst));
--------------------[m2r_xfer_opl]-------------------
threads_ctx[tid].vcpu.gpr[dst] =
    (*((uint16_t *)(mem_bitmap + VIRT2BYTE(src))) >>
        VIRT2BIT(src)) & VCPU_MASK32;
```

Figure 4. Tag propagation code for various analysis routines when libdft is using bit-sized tags. The VIRT2BYTE macro is used for getting the byte offset of a specific address in mem_bitmap (it performs a bitwise right shift by 3), whereas VIRT2BIT gives the bit offset within the previously acquired byte.

```
-------------------[r2r_alu_opb_l]-------------------
*((uint8_t *)&threads_ctx[tid].vcpu.gpr[dst]) |=
    *((uint8_t *)&threads_ctx[tid].vcpu.gpr[src]);

--------------------[r2m_alu_opw]--------------------
*((uint16_t *)(dst + STAB[VIRT2STAB(dst)])) |=
    *((uint16_t *)&threads_ctx[tid].vcpu.gpr[src]);

--------------------[m2r_alu_opl]--------------------
threads_ctx[tid].vcpu.gpr[dst] |=
    *((uint32_t *)(src + STAB[VIRT2STAB(src)]));


-------------------[r2r_xfer_opb_l]------------------
*((uint8_t *)&threads_ctx[tid].vcpu.gpr[dst]) =
    *((uint8_t *)&threads_ctx[tid].vcpu.gpr[src]);

--------------------[r2m_xfer_opw]-------------------
*((uint16_t *)&threads_ctx[tid].vcpu.gpr[dst]) =
    *((uint16_t *)&threads_ctx[tid].vcpu.gpr[src]);

--------------------[m2r_xfer_opl]-------------------
threads_ctx[tid].vcpu.gpr[dst] =
    *((uint32_t *)(src + STAB[VIRT2STAB(src)]));
```

Figure 5. Code snippets for different analysis routines when libdft is using byte-sized tags. VIRT2STAB is a macro for obtaining the STAB index given a virtual address (it performs a bitwise right shift by 12).

Figures 4 and 5 show excerpts from different types of analysis routines in the case of bit- and byte-sized tags, respectively. Code snippets labeled as alu correspond to routines that instrument 2 operand instructions belonging to the ALU category. On the contrary, xfer indicates propagation code for instructions of the XFER category. The operand size (*i.e.*, 8-, 16-, 32-bit) is designated by the op{b, w, l} label suffix, while the r2r, r2m, and m2r prefix is used for specifying the operand type (register vs. memory).

In the case of byte-sized tags, achieving single assignment tagmap updates and branch-less tag propagation is relatively easy, due to the design of our shadow memory. Specifically, if both operands are registers, then we merely need to perform a copy or a bitwise OR operation, of the appropriate size, between the respective GPRs in the vcpu structure of the current thread. On the other hand, if one of the operands is a memory location, the effective address (*i.e.*, src or dst depending on the instrumented instruction) goes through STAB for getting the addend value that should be added to the address itself, in order to address the tag bytes from the corresponding tagmap segment (see Section 4.1.2). The final propagation is performed similarly to the previous case.

Note that when libdft is configured to use bit-sized tags, analysis routines tend to be larger and more elaborate. This is due to the pedantic bit operations that are required, since we cannot simply "move" separate bits between different tagmap locations. Hence, to avoid using branch instructions or multiple assignment statements, we resort in bit masks and bitwise operations.

4.3 I/O Interface

The *I/O Interface* is the component of libdft that handles the exchange of data between the kernel and the process through system calls. In particular, it consists of two small pieces of instrumentation code, namely the pre_syscall and post_syscall stubs, and a table of system call meta-information (syscall_desc[]), as illustrated in Figure 3. The syscall_desc table holds specific libdft-related information for all the 344 system calls of the Linux kernel (up to v2.6.39). For instance, it stores user-registered callbacks (for using a system call as a data source or sink), descriptors for the arguments of the call, or whether the system call writes data to user space memory.

When a system call is made by the application, the stubs are called upon entry and exit. If the user has registered a callback function for a specific system call (either for entering or exiting), it is invoked. Otherwise, the default behavior of the post_syscall stub is to untag the data being written/returned by the system call. The advantages of this approach are twofold. First, we enable the tool writer to hook specific I/O channels (*e.g.*, network I/O streams) and perform selective tagging. This way, the developer can customize libdft by using system calls as data sources and sinks. Second, we eliminate tag leaks by taking into consideration that some system calls write specific data to user-provided buffers. For example, consider gettimeofday that upon each call overwrites user space memory that corresponds to one, or two, struct timeval data structures. Such system calls always result in sanitizing (*i.e.*, untagging) the data being returned, unless the tool writer has installed a callback that selectively tags the returned data. Finally, hooking a function call is straightforward, and can be performed directly using libdft's and Pin's API.

4.4 Optimizations

4.4.1 Fast vcpu Access (fast_vcpu)

libdft initially stored the per-thread vcpu structure in a global array indexed by Pin's virtual thread id (see Section 4.1.1). However, we determined that this was not the most efficient structure for this purpose. Because the array can be concurrently accessed from multiple threads, proper locking is required to safely expand it when new threads are created. Moreover, retrieving the vcpu from an analysis routine demands extra instructions (*i.e.*, array lookup).

Instead, we can utilize Pin's scratch registers to store a pointer to the vcpu structure of each thread. Scratch registers are thread-specific, virtual registers used internally by Pin, but also available for use in Pintools. Each time a new thread is created, we allocate a new vcpu structure as before, but instead of adding it in an array, we save its address in such a register. Analysis routines are modified to receive the scratch register pointing to the vcpu as argument, with threads_ctx[tid].vcpu changed to thread_ctx->vcpu (see Figures 4 and 5). This approach demands more register spilling, but as we experimentally confirmed (see Section 6), the benefits from avoiding locking and an extra array indexing operation outweigh the spilling overhead.

4.4.2 Fast REP-prefixed Instructions (fast_rep)

Certain x86 instructions, such as MOVS, STOS, and LODS, can be executed repeatedly using the REP prefix. During instrumentation, Pin treats them as implicit loops containing the un-prefixed instruction to allow Pintools insert analysis routines that receive the correct effective address (EA) used on each repetition. This introduces overhead because the REP-prefixed instruction is transformed to a loop, and because tag propagating code is executed within the loop.

However, the effective address (EA) used on each repetition depends on the EA used on the previous repetition and the value of the DF bit in the EFLAGS register: $EA = EA_{prev} \pm \{1, 2, 4\}$. We exploit this observation to move part of the analysis code outside the loop. Particularly, we perform the expensive mapping of a memory address to its shadow memory address only on the first repetition. The analysis routine handling the first loop, in addition to performing the required address mapping and propagating tags, caches the translated shadow memory address. Afterward, the analysis routine handling the rest of the repetitions can use the cached address to perform tag propagation faster. Note that moving all the propagation logic before the loop frequently has adverse effects, such as causing Pin to use a function call instead of inlining.

4.4.3 Huge TLB (huge_tlb)

DFT logic constantly operates on data tags. Both when using bit- and byte-sized tags, the analysis routines continuously access the mem_bitmap and STAB structures respectively. As the tag propagation code is interleaved with application instructions, memory accesses are spread between application and shadow memory, thus leading to poor performance of the CPU's translation lookaside buffer (TLB). We attempt to alleviate the problem by utilizing the multiple page size feature on x86 architectures for reducing the misses in the TLB. Specifically, by allocating mem_bitmap and STAB using the MAP_HUGETLB option with mmap (only for Linux kernel versions $\geq$ 2.6.32), the allocation is performed using pages of 4MB in size[1], effectively reducing TLB "poisoning" due to accesses in libdft's tagmap (*i.e.,* fewer TLB misses due to memory accesses in mem_bitmap and STAB, as well as fewer evictions of process entries for serving tagmap page faults).

4.4.4 Tagmap Collapse (tmap_col)

When using byte-sized tags, the tagmap allocates a page of memory for every page used by the application, including pages used for the heap, the stack, libraries, and so forth. However, not all pages are assigned the same access rights. For instance, code segments are usually write-protected, and the same is also true for certain other types of data (*e.g.,* constants, immutable objects, special-purpose shared memory segments). Therefore, unless explicitly altered by a tool writer, the tags corresponding to such pages will always be constant. We observe that the DFT logic will never need to legitimately alter the tag(s) for such memory pages, since the code of the application cannot legitimately update them either.

We exploit this observation, and significantly reduce the memory overhead of tagmap, by collapsing segments that correspond to write-protected memory regions into a single, constant segment. In particular, we allocate a special page using mmap, namely a *zero* page for clean tags, and set the access bits of that page to PROT_READ, effectively disallowing all writes to it. When new write-protected pages are mapped/allocated by the application, we update the corresponding STAB entries with addend values that map to the zero page. Note that for this optimization we also need to explicitly handle the mprotect system call for dealing with write-protected pages that are later, or temporarily, mapped as writeable, and vice-versa.

[1] If Physical Address Extension (PAE) is enabled, the size of large pages is set to 2MB.

4.5 Memory Protection

Dynamic DFT is frequently used to analyze malware or enforce security, and in that context it is desirable to guarantee the integrity of libdft by protecting its memory similarly to a sandbox [12]. As shown in Figure 2, the same address space is used by the application, Pin that allocates memory to store its code cache, and libdft that allocates the tagmap. Since all of the above reside inside the same space, the tracked program could accidentally or intentionally corrupt Pin or libdft.

Our solution to the problem is inspired by the scheme proposed by Xu *et al.* [28], and relies on the premise that application code cannot execute natively without first being instrumented and analyzed by libdft. Since we instrument all memory accesses, an instruction that tries to write at memory address *vaddr* will be instrumented with the corresponding DFT logic, in order to assert or clear the respective tag(s) in tagmap. Therefore, by restricting access to specific blocks on the tagmap, we can prevent application code from accessing certain memory regions. In the case of bit-sized tags, we first enforce Pin to only use memory in a specific memory range (*e.g.,* in the lower 512MB, 0x00000000 – 0x20000000). Then, we proceed to protect the bits of mem_bitmap that correspond to that range (*e.g.,* the first 64MB). Whenever application code tries to access the lower 512MB of its virtual address space, the DFT analysis routines will access the protected blocks of the tagmap, leading to a memory violation error. However, note that the protected memory region cannot be arbitrary, and depends on the architecture's page size. Assuming a 4KB page size and 1-bit tags, both the beginning and ending of the protected memory range need to be aligned to 32K (8 bits per byte $\times$ 4KB page).

In the case of byte-sized tags, we allocate a *guard* page using mmap and set its access bits to PROT_NONE, effectively disallowing any access to it. During initialization, we set all STAB entries that correspond to unallocated memory pages to point to the guard page. From the application's perspective, Pin's and libdft's memory is always considered unallocated space. Hence, any access to these addresses will result in DFT logic operating on the guard page, leading again to a memory violation error. Note that by using libdft's API tool writers can register callback handlers for dealing with such violation errors.

5. Creating libdft-powered Tools

One of the most frequent incarnations of DFT has been dynamic taint analysis. DTA operates by tagging all data coming from the network as tainted, tracking their propagation, and alerting the user when they are used in a way that could compromise system integrity. In this case, the network is the source of "interesting" data, while instructions that are used to control a program's flow are the sinks. For the x86 architecture, these are jumps and function calls with non-immediate operands, as well as function returns. Attackers can manipulate the operands of such instructions, by exploiting various types of software memory errors, such as buffer overflows and format string vulnerabilities. They can then seize control of the program by redirecting execution to existing code (*e.g.,* return-to-libc, ROP [3]), or their own injected instructions.

In this section, we describe the design and implementation of a DTA tool, namely libdft-DTA, which we implemented in approximately 450 LOC in C++, using libdft with bit-sized tags and the API calls shown in Table 1. We only list part of the API used for the development of the tool, due to space considerations. First, libdft-DTA invokes libdft_init() for initializing libdft and allocating the tagmap. Next, it uses syscall_set_post() for registering a set of system call hooks to pinpoint untrusted data. Specifically, it monitors the socket API (*i.e.,* socket and accept) for identifying PF_{INET, INET6} socket descriptors. It also hooks

Function	Description
libdft_init()	Initialize the tagging engine
libdft_start()	Commence execution
libdft_die()	Detach from the application
ins_set_pre() ins_set_post() ins_set_clr()	Register instruction callbacks to be invoked before, after, or instead libdft's instrumentation
syscall_set_pre() syscall_set_post()	Hook a system call entry or return
tagmap_set{b,w,l}() tagmap_setn()	Tag {1, 2, 4} and n bytes of virtual memory

Table 1. Overview of libdft's API.

the dup, dup2, and fcntl system calls to ensure that duplicates of these descriptors are also tracked. Each time a system call of the read or receive family is invoked with a monitored descriptor as argument, the memory locations that store the network data are asserted using tagmap_setn(). libdft-DTA checks if tainted data are used in indirect control transfers (*i.e.,* loaded on EIP) using ins_set_post() with RET, JMP, and CALL instructions. In particular, it instruments them with a small code snippet that returns the tag markings of the instruction operands and target address (*i.e.,* branch target). If any of the two is tainted, execution halts with an informative message containing the offending instruction and the contents of EIP. In addition, for protecting against attacks that alter system call arguments, libdft-DTA also monitors the execve system call for tainted parameters.

Besides DTA, we have used libdft in other settings. Specifically, we used libdft for studying a set of optimization techniques that minimize the runtime slowdown of dynamic DFT, by combining dynamic and static analysis for separating program logic from tracking logic and eliminate needless tracking [14]. Our results not only indicate that libdft can be used as the apparatus for studying novel optimization methodologies, but also demonstrate the applicability of our framework to a different domain. Finally, colleagues that were given access to early versions of libdft used it for building Taint-Exchange [29], a generic cross-process and cross-host taint tracking tool that allows studying the interaction of distributed components, by multiplexing fine-grained taint information into I/O channels. Additional applications of libdft are in progress, which will help us validate and refine our API as needed.

6. Evaluation

We evaluated libdft using a variety of software including a web and database (DB) server, command-line and network utilities, a web browser, and the SPEC CPU2000 suite. Our aim is to quantify the performance of libdft, and establish a set of bounds for the various types of applications and software complexity. To the best of our knowledge, we are the first to evaluate the performance of a dynamic DFT framework in such depth. We also compare the performance of libdft with the results reported in selected related studies, and proceed to evaluate the effectiveness of the various optimizations and design decisions we took. We close this section with an evaluation of the performance and effectiveness of the libdft-powered DTA tool presented earlier.

The results presented throughout this section are mean values, calculated after running 10 repetitions of each experiment, while the reported confidence intervals correspond to 95%. Our testbed consisted of two identical hosts, equipped with two 2.66 GHz quad core Intel Xeon X5500 CPUs and 24GB of RAM each, running Linux (Debian "squeeze" with kernel version 2.6.32). The version of Pin used during the evaluation was 2.9 (build 39586). While conducting our experiments all hosts were idle.

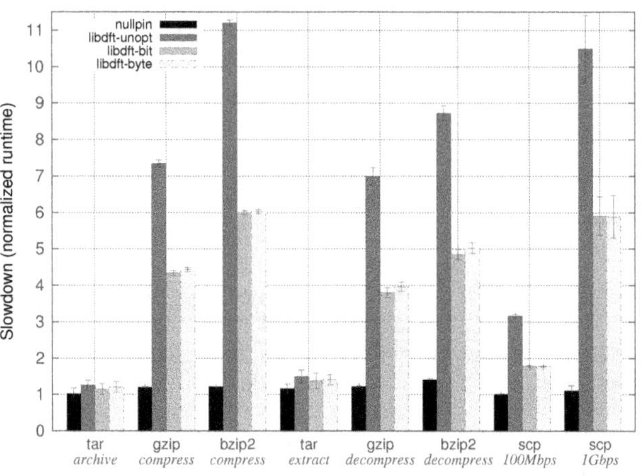

Figure 6. The slowdown imposed by Pin and libdft when running four common Unix command-line utilities.

6.1 Performance

We developed four simple Pintools to aid us in evaluating libdft. The first is *nullpin*, which essentially runs a process using Pin without any form of instrumentation or analysis. This tool measures the overhead imposed by Pin's runtime environment alone. The second and third, namely *libdft-{bit, byte}*, utilize libdft for applying DFT on the application being executed, and use bit-sized and byte-sized tags respectively. These tools measure the overhead of libdft when employing single assignment and branch-less propagation, plus the optimizations presented in Section 4.4. Finally, in order to demonstrate the efficacy of our design choices, we also evaluated *libdft-unopt*, which approximates the behavior of an unoptimized DFT framework. Specifically, it does not employ any optimization scheme and its analysis routines are not inlined, effectively resembling the impact of lax tag propagation.[2] Note that since the performance of libdft does not depend on the existence or amount of tagged data, none of our tools uses any of the API functions for customizing the applied DFT.

Utilities The goal of our first benchmark was to quantify the performance of libdft with commonly used Unix utilities. For this experiment, we used the GNU versions of tar, gzip, and bzip2, as well as scp from the OpenSSH package. We selected these applications because they represent different workloads. tar performs mostly I/O, while gzip and bzip2 are CPU-bound applications. In between, scp is both I/O driven and CPU intensive.

We run all the tools natively, and using our four tools, and measured their execution time with Unix time utility. We used tar for archiving and extracting a vanilla Linux kernel "tarball" (v2.6.35.6; ~400MB), whereas gzip and bzip2 were used for compressing and decompressing it respectively. For scp, we copied 1GB of randomly generated data over SSH, first over an 100Mbps link and then over an 1Gbps link. We present the results in Figure 6.

libdft-bit imposes a slowdown that ranges between 1.14x and 6x (average 3.65x), while libdft-byte ranges between 1.20x and 6.03x (average 3.72x). Pin alone imposes an 1.17x slowdown (this is Pin's baseline). Overall, the more CPU-bound an application is, the larger the impact of libdft. For instance, bzip2 is the most CPU intensive and tar the least, representing the worst and best performance of libdft. I/O operations have a positive effect on DFT. This is also confirmed by the overhead of scp over an 1Gbps link, which is higher when compared with the 100Mbps case.

[2] The body of the analysis routines used in libdft-unopt remains highly condensed, since they are the same routines that we use in libdft-{bit, byte}. Hence, the overhead measured with this tool gives a lower bound of an unoptimized DFT implementation.

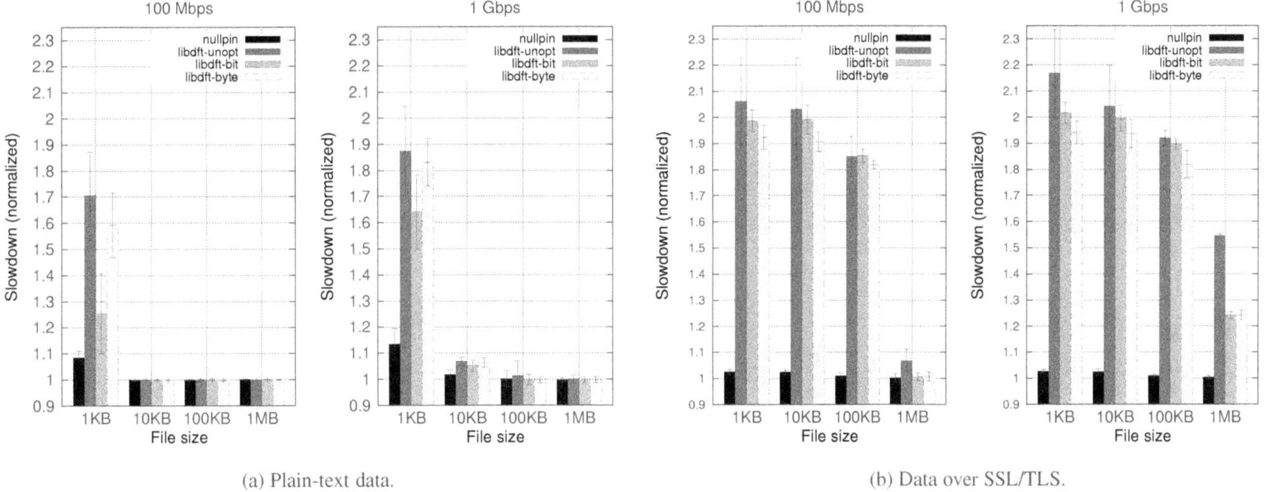

(a) Plain-text data.

(b) Data over SSL/TLS.

Figure 7. The slowdown incurred by Pin and libdft on the Apache web server when serving static HTML files of different sizes. We used Apache's benchmarking utility *ApacheBench (ab)* to measure the mean time per request for all four files, first over an 100Mbps link, and then over an 1Gbps link.

We surmise that nullpin and libdft perform worse when the limiting factor is not the I/O, because the respective latency hides the translation and tag propagation overhead. Indeed, when utilizing the 1Gbps link, the bottleneck shifts to the CPU, greatly reducing `scp`'s throughput. Also note that byte-sized tags impose an additional overhead of 1.9%, which stems from the management cost of the tagmap segments and memory shadowing (see Section 4.1.2). Compared with an unoptimized implementation, libdft with all our optimizations performs 3.64% to 46.37% faster.

Apache The second set of experiments calculates the performance slowdown of libdft when applied on larger and more complex software. Specifically, we investigate how libdft behaves when instrumenting the commonly used Apache web server. We used Apache v2.2.16 and configured it to pre-fork all the worker processes (pre-forking is a standard multiprocessing Apache module), in order to avoid high fluctuations in performance, due to Apache forking extra processes for handling the incoming requests at the beginning of our experiments. All other options were left to their default setting. We measured Apache's performance using its own utility `ab` and static HTML files of different size. In particular, we chose files with sizes of 1KB, 10KB, 100KB, and 1MB, and once again run the server natively and with our four tools. We also tested Apache over different network links, as well as with and without SSL/TLS encryption.

Figure 7(a) illustrates the results for running Apache, and transferring data in plaintext. We observe that as the size of the file being served increases, libdft's overhead diminishes. Similarly to our previous experiment, the time Apache spends performing I/O hides our overhead. As a result, libdft has negligible performance impact when Apache is serving files larger than 10KB at 100Mbps and 100KB at 1Gbps. In antithesis, libdft imposes an 1.25x/1.64x slowdown with 1KB files at 100Mbps/1Gbps when using bit-sized tags. The overhead of byte-sized tagging becomes more evident with smaller files because more requests are served by Apache, also increasing the number of `mmap` calls performed. This leads to higher tagmap management overhead, as segments need to be frequently allocated and freed. We anticipate that we can amortize this extra overhead by releasing segments more lazily, as we may have to re-allocate them soon after.

Figure 7(b) shows the results of conducting the same experiments, but this time using SSL/TLS encryption. We notice that libdft has larger impact when running on top of SSL. In the 100Mbps scenario, the slowdown becomes negligible only for files larger than 1MB, whereas at 1Gbps libdft imposes an 1.24x slowdown even with 1MB files. The reason behind this behavior is that the intensive cryptographic operations performed by SSL make the server CPU-bound.

Interestingly, libdft-byte performs 3% better (on average) than libdft-bit. In order to better understand this behavior, we analyzed the mix of the executed instructions and observed that serving a web page over SSL results in an increased number of XFER-type instrumentations, where one of the two operands is memory.[3] *Tag propagation code that corresponds to data transfers is more expensive in the case of bit-sized tags than the case of byte-sized tags.* This is because the body of the respective *r2m*, *m2r*, and *m2m* analysis routines contains more instructions, due to the elaborate bit operations that are necessary for asserting only specific bits in the tagmap (see Figure 4 and 5 in Section 4.2.2).

MySQL In Figure 8(a), we present the results from evaluating MySQL DB server. We used MySQL v5.1.49 and its own benchmark suite (`sql-bench`). The suite consists of four different tests, which assess the completion time of various DB operations like table creation and modification, data selection and insertion, *etc.* We notice that the average slowdown incurred by Pin's instrumentation alone is 1.64x, which is higher than the overhead observed when running smaller utilities (see Figure 6). The increased overhead is attributed to the significantly larger size of MySQL's codebase, which applies pressure on Pin's JIT compiler and code cache.

As far as libdft is concerned, the average slowdown on the five test suites was 3.36x when using byte-sized tags, and 3.55x when using bit-sized tags. Similarly to our previous experiments, libdft's overhead became more pronounced with more complex and CPU intensive tasks. In this case, the `test-insert` benchmark was the most exhaustive, involving table creations, random-ordered row insertions, duplicates checking, ordered selection, deletion, and so forth, and exhibited the largest slowdown (4.65x/4.83x). Note that libdft performs 5.65% faster when using byte-sized tags. Again,

[3] SSL makes heavy use of instructions like `MOVS`, `STOS`, `MOVSX`, and `MOVZX`.

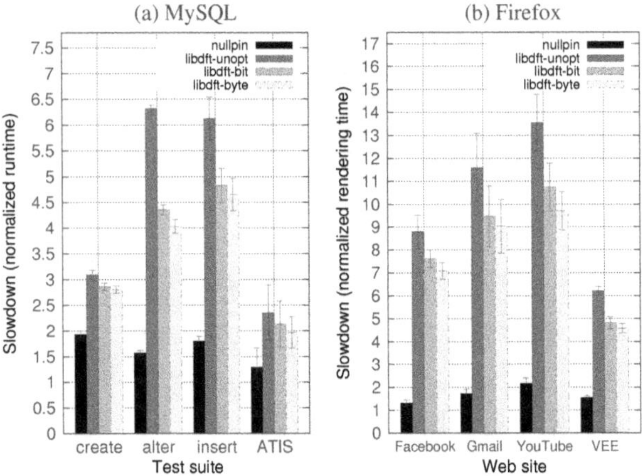

Figure 8. The overhead of Pin and libdft when running MySQL and Firefox. We employed MySQL's *sql-bench* benchmark suite, which measures table creation, data selection and insertion. Regarding Firefox, we accessed the 3 most popular web sites from Alexa's Top 500 and the VEE web site.

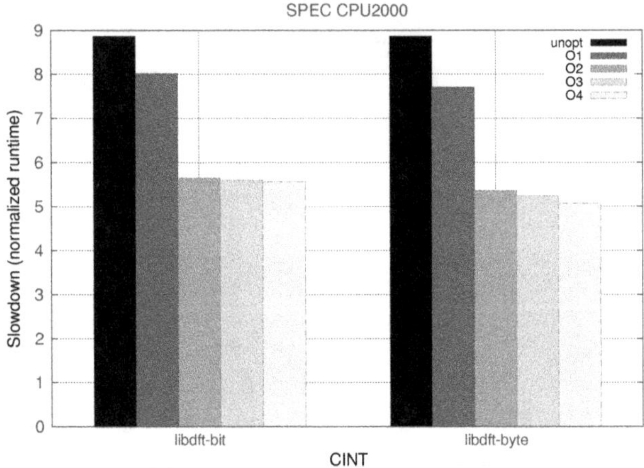

Figure 9. The impact of our optimizations when applied cumulatively on the SPEC CPU2000 benchmark: O1 (branch-less and single assignment tag propagation), O2 (O1 + `fast_vcpu`), O3 (O2 + `fast_rep`), O4 (O3 + `huge_tlb`).

we analyzed the instructions of MySQL and observed a significant amount of XFER-type tag propagation routines in the mix. Our combined set of optimizations reduces the runtime overhead by 20.58% – 24.83%.

Firefox After evaluating two of the most popular servers, we tested libdft with the Firefox web browser that has even larger and more complex codebase, and complements our evaluation of client-side software that started with the smaller utilities. We used Mozilla Firefox v3.6.18 to access the three most popular web sites according to Alexa's Top 500 (`http://www.alexa.com/topsites`), as well as the site of VEE, and measured the effect of libdft on rendering time. Figure 8(b) illustrates the results for this experiment. We see that the average slowdown under nullpin, libdft-bit, and libdft-byte, was 1.68x, 8.16x, and 7.06x respectively. The overhead is relatively low when accessing mostly static content web pages (VEE), while it increases significantly when accessing media-rich sites (YouTube), and sites that depend heavily on JavaScript (JS) like Gmail. Note that for Facebook and Gmail, we accessed and measured a real profile page and not the log in screen. The effect of optimizations ranges between 18.64% and 29.68%.

Next, we benchmarked the JS engine of Firefox using the Dromaeo test suite (`http://dromaeo.com/?recommended`). Dromaeo measures the speed of specific JS operations, so there is no I/O or network lag, as in the page loading benchmark. We observed that the slowdown incurred by both nullpin and libdft was considerably higher, with an average of 3.2x for nullpin, and 14.52x/13.9x for libdft-bit/libdft-byte respectively. While increased overhead was expected because this benchmark is also CPU-bound, the slowdown is significantly larger from previous CPU intensive experiments. *It seems that since JS is interpreted and subsequently "jitted" by the browser's runtime, it interferes with the translation and optimizations performed by Pin's JIT engine, thus leading to excessive runtime overheads.* In fact, this implies that significant overheads would emerge whenever DBI is combined with an interpreting runtime environment such as JS. Regardless, when using the browser to access common web sites, we do not suffer the performance decline observed in the Dromaeo benchmark.

6.2 Effectiveness of Optimizations

In order to quantify the impact of our set of optimizations presented in Section 4, we used the SPEC CPU2000 suite.

Application	Vulnerability	SecurityFocus ID
wu-ftpd v2.6.0	Format string	BID 1387
ATPhttpd v0.4	Stack overflow	BID 5215
WsMp3 v0.0.2	Heap corruption	BID 6240
ProFTPD v1.3.3	Stack overflow	BID 44562

Table 2. libdft-DTA successfully prevented the listed attacks.

Figure 9 shows the overhead of running the suite under the unoptimized version of libdft (libdft-unopt) normalized to native execution, and the improvement in performance contributed by each optimization as it is incorporated in our framework. Branch-less and single assignment tag propagation, denoted by O1, has a notable impact on the imposed overhead, reducing it by 10.65% when libdft uses bit-sized tags and 15.09% in case of byte-sized tags. This optimization captures the impact of our efforts for aggressively inlining the analysis routines implementing tag propagation. Optimization O2 (O1 + `fast_vcpu`) reduces running time by 29.45% and 30.34% for libdft-bit and libdft-byte respectively. Recall that `fast_vcpu` results in smaller and lock-free code. O3 and O4, which add `fast_rep` and `huge_tlb` respectively, offer marginally enhanced performance to libdft (*i.e.*, 0.8% and 0.6% with libdft-bit, and 2.17% and 3.15% with libdft-byte). This is because SPEC CPU2000 does not utilize large memory chunks, nor it contains a significant amount of REP-prefixed instructions.

6.3 The libdft-DTA Tool

The purpose of developing the libdft-DTA tool was not to provide a solid DTA solution, but to demonstrate that our API can be used to easily and quickly develop otherwise complex tools. Nevertheless, we tested its effectiveness using the set of exploits listed in Table 2. In all cases, it successfully detected and prevented the exploitation of the corresponding application. We also evaluated the performance of the tool using `scp`, Apache, and MySQL, and compare it with libdft's baseline performance. We observe that the additional overhead imposed by the tool is negligible ($\leq$ +7%) over the baseline overhead of DFT. While we cannot claim that all libdft-based tools will have such low additional overhead, our results demonstrate that libdft can be customized to implement problem-specific instances of DFT efficiently.

7. Limitations and Future Work

Thread safety As we discussed in Section 4.1.2, when libdft is configured to use bit-sized tags, it coalesces the tags of 8 consecutive byte memory locations into a single byte in mem_bitmap. However, since there is no synchronization among threads that update mem_bitmap in parallel, there may be a race condition. More specifically, in order to handle unaligned multi-byte memory accesses that are valid in x86, the analysis routines of libdft-bit implement the single assignment tag propagation scheme using 16-bit words (see Figure 4). Therefore, if more than one threads are concurrently updating memory locations that are less than 16 bytes apart, the respective analysis routines of libdft will operate on the same 16-bit word on tagmap, leading into clobbered results.

Although such cases are possible, our assumption is that they are very rare. An intuition that is also supported by the fact that compilers align most variables to 4 or even 8 bytes. During our experimental evaluation, we verified (by tracing memory accesses) that multithreaded applications like Firefox, MySQL, and Apache, do not access memory in such a way. Nevertheless, this was one of the reasons for implementing a shadowing scheme that supports larger tag sizes (byte-sized), which do not suffer from such issues.

Device control In Linux, device control is mostly performed using the system call ioctl. This call uses a command number that identifies the operation to be performed, and in certain cases the receiver in the kernel. While attempts have been made to apply a formula on this number, due to backward compatibility issues and programmer errors, actual ioctl numbers are many times arbitrary (interested readers are referred to ioctl_list(2)). Identifying individual ioctl calls is necessary to sanitize the memory locations where data are being read. While ioctl is not used by regular applications, later versions of libdft could utilize system call tracing tools, such as strace, for pinpointing ioctls.

Future considerations In the future, we plan to extend libdft to run on Windows OSs and 64-bit architectures. We expect that porting libdft to run on Windows will be straightforward. Currently, all of libdft's components, besides the system call part of the I/O interface, can be used "as is" with the Windows OS (the underlying ISA is the same). Note that although the Windows system calls are numerous, they are rarely used directly by developers. libdft needs to intercept them solely for sanitizing the data being read into the process. Also, porting our framework to work with 64-bit x86 architectures does not pose any significant challenges, but requires moderate engineering effort. Finally, we plan to further investigate the impact of the tmap_col and huge_tlb optimizations. Specifically, we seek to quantify the reduction in memory consumption of specific types of applications due to tagmap collapse, as well as identify cases where fewer TLB misses can speedup libdft.

8. Related Work

Dytan [6], Minemu [2], LIFT [22], and PTT [11], are previously proposed dynamic DFT systems that are highly related to libdft. Dytan is the most flexible tool, allowing users to customize its sources, sinks, and propagation policy, while it can also track data based on control-flow dependencies (see Section 2; Figure 1). Albeit flexible, it incurs high performance penalties. For instance, gzip executes 30x slower than running natively, even when implicit tracking is turned off. When the latter is utilized, gzip performs 50x slower, while it can also lead to taint explosion. That is, erroneously tracking large amounts of data, due to the imprecision of control-flow data dependencies [23].

In contrast, Minemu is the fastest tool, but it provides limited functionality. It uses an ad hoc emulator for the mere purpose of performing fast DTA, and cannot be configured for use in other domains without modifying the emulator itself. Moreover, it does not provide colored tags, nor it supports self-modifying code. More importantly, Minemu cannot be used "as-is" on 64-bit architectures, due to its shadow memory design and heavy reliance on SSE (XMM) registers. In particular, it exploits the XMM registers to avoid spilling GPRs during taint tracking. However, this optimization may not have the same benefits on x86-64, since SSE has become standard and Minemu will have to resort on XMM spilling.

LIFT is another low-overhead dynamic DFT system. Unlike libdft, it focuses on detecting attacks instead of providing an extensible framework. LIFT builds on the premise that programs frequently execute without tagged data, and as a result tag propagation can be omitted. Their approach involves activating data tracking, only when tagged data are loaded in one of the CPU registers. This optimization is orthogonal to libdft, which could also benefit from dynamically enabling and disabling data tracking. In practice, the speedup depends on the program at hand and how often it operates on tagged data. Note that with tracking always enabled, LIFT exhibits higher overhead than libdft when running the SPECint benchmark. Operation-wise, it only runs with x86-64 binaries, and it does not support multithreading by design.

PTT is different from the rest of the systems because it performs system-wide data tracking, and uses additional cores through parallelization to improve performance. Even though it is one of the fastest such systems, it still incurs significant overheads.

TaintCheck [18] was one of the first tools to utilize DTA, for protecting binary-only software from buffer overflow and other types of memory corruption attacks, entirely in software. TaintCheck incurs prohibitive slowdowns, which may cause an application to run up to 37x slower. Vigilante [7] utilizes DFT to generate self-certifying alerts (SCAs). These alerts accurately describe the network message that was used in a previously detected attack, and can be distributed to parties hosting vulnerable software without the need for a secure distribution channel, because they can be independently and securely certified by the receiving party. Vigilante relies on the possibility of capturing attacks on server honeypots that will generate the SCAs, and as such does not focus on performance.

Eudaemon [20] builds upon the Qemu user space emulator to allow one selectively apply taint analysis on a process (*e.g.*, when potentially harmful actions are taken, or the system is idle). It incurs an overhead of approximately 9x, which can be alleviated on long-running applications by selectively enabling or disabling DFT. TaintEraser [31] uses Pin to apply taint analysis on binaries for the purpose of identifying information leaks. Furthermore, it introduces the concept of "function shortcuts" to reduce the overhead. These shortcuts enable the native execution of frequently called functions, but need to be defined manually by the developer, reducing the portability and practicality of the system. libdft could also benefit by such shortcuts (*e.g.*, in prevalent libc functions).

Hardware implementations of DFT [8, 9, 24] have been proposed to evade the large penalties imposed by software-only implementations, but unfortunately they have had no appeal with hardware vendors. Implementations of DTA using virtual machines and emulators have been also proposed [5, 13, 21]. While these solutions have some practicality for malware analysis platforms and honeypots, they induce slowdowns that make them impractical on production systems.

Speck [19] increases the performance of security checks, like DTA, by decoupling the checks from application execution using process-level replaying and Pin. In this manner, DTA can be run parallel with the application, while the DTA itself can be also parallelized. Similarly, Aftersight [4] decouples VM execution from program analysis, offloading the task to a separate, or even remote, platform. HiStar [30] uses labels to tag and protect sensitive data. It is a new OS design, and its main focus is to protect the

OS from components that start exhibiting malicious behavior after being compromised. HiStar's data tracking is more coarse-grained than libdft's, and introduces major changes in the OS level.

9. Conclusions

We presented libdft, a practical dynamic DFT platform. Our goal is to facilitate future research by providing a framework that is at once *fast*, *reusable*, and applicable to *commodity software and hardware*. We also investigated the reasons that DFT tools based on DBI frameworks frequently perform badly, and presented the practices that need to be avoided by the authors of such tools. Our evaluation shows that libdft imposes low overhead, comparable to or faster than previous work. Its effect on web server throughput can be negligible when running over a 100Mbps network link and serving static HTML files, while even when switching to a 1Gbps link it never exceeds 2.04x. Moreover, we showed that performance depends on application CPU and I/O requirements. For instance, MySQL performs approximately 3.36x slower under libdft, while I/O intensive tools like `tar` sustain less than 1.14x overhead. We believe that libdft strikes a balance between usability and performance, incurring non prohibitive costs, even when running large and complex software like MySQL, Apache, and Firefox. Our implementation is freely available at: `http://www.cs.columbia.edu/~vpk/research/libdft/`

Acknowledgments

We thank Michalis Polychronakis, Dimitris Geneiatakis, and our shepherd, David Gregg, for providing comments on earlier drafts of this paper. This work was supported by DARPA, the US Air Force and the National Science Foundation through Contracts DARPA-FA8750-10-2-0253 and AFRL-FA8650-10-C-7024, and Grant CNS-09-14312, respectively, with additional support from Google and Intel Corp. Any opinions, findings, conclusions or recommendations expressed herein are those of the authors, and do not necessarily reflect those of the US Government, DARPA, the Air Force, NSF, Google or Intel.

References

[1] M. Attariyan and J. Flinn. Automating configuration troubleshooting with dynamic information flow analysis. In *Proc. of the* 9th *OSDI*, pages 237–250, 2010.

[2] E. Bosman, A. Slowinska, and H. Bos. Minemu: The World's Fastest Taint Tracker. In *Proc. of the* 14th *RAID*, pages 1–20, 2011.

[3] S. Checkoway, L. Davi, A. Dmitrienko, A.-R. Sadeghi, H. Shacham, and M. Winandy. Return-Oriented Programming without Returns. In *Proc. of the* 17th *CCS*, pages 559–572, 2010.

[4] J. Chow, T. Garfinkel, and P. M. Chen. Decoupling dynamic program analysis from execution in virtual environments. In *Proc. of the 2008 USENIX ATC*, pages 1–14.

[5] J. Chow, B. Pfaff, T. Garfinkel, K. Christopher, and M. Rosenblum. Understanding Data Lifetime via Whole System Simulation. In *Proc. of the* 13th *USENIX Security*, pages 321–336, 2004.

[6] J. Clause, W. Li, and A. Orso. Dytan: A Generic Dynamic Taint Analysis Framework. In *Proc. of the 2007 ISSTA*, pages 196–206.

[7] M. Costa, J. Crowcroft, M. Castro, A. Rowstron, L. Zhou, L. Zhang, and P. Barham. Vigilante: End-to-End Containment of Internet Worms. In *Proc. of the* 20th *SOSP*, pages 133–147, 2005.

[8] J. R. Crandall and F. T. Chong. Minos: Control Data Attack Prevention Orthogonal to Memory Model. In *Proc. of the* 37th *MICRO*, pages 221–232, 2004.

[9] M. Dalton, H. Kannan, and C. Kozyrakis. Real-World Buffer Overflow Protection for Userspace & Kernelspace. In *Proc. of the* 17th *USENIX Security*, pages 395–410, 2008.

[10] W. Enck, P. Gilbert, B.-G. Chun, L. P. Cox, J. Jung, P. McDaniel, and A. N. Sheth. TaintDroid: An Information-Flow Tracking System for Realtime Privacy Monitoring on Smartphones. In *Proc. of the* 9th *OSDI*, pages 393–407, 2010.

[11] A. Ermolinskiy, S. Katti, S. Shenker, L. Fowler, and M. McCauley. Towards Practical Taint Tracking. Technical Report UCB/EECS-2010-92, EECS Dept., University of California, Berkeley, USA, 2010.

[12] B. Ford and R. Cox. Vx32: Lightweight User-level Sandboxing on the x86. In *Proc. of the 2008 USENIX ATC*, pages 293–306.

[13] A. Ho, M. Fetterman, C. Clark, A. Warfield, and S. Hand. Practical Taint-based Protection using Demand Emulation. In *Proc. of the 2006 EuroSys*, pages 29–41.

[14] K. Jee, G. Portokalidis, V. P. Kemerlis, S. Ghosh, D. I. August, and A. D. Keromytis. A General Approach for Efficiently Accelerating Software-based Dynamic Data Flow Tracking on Commodity Hardware. In *Proc. of the* 19th *NDSS*, 2012.

[15] M. G. Kang, S. McCamant, P. Poosankam, and D. Song. DTA++: Dynamic Taint Analysis with Targeted Control-Flow Propagation. In *Proc. of the* 18th *NDSS*, 2011.

[16] C.-K. Luk, R. Cohn, R. Muth, H. Patil, A. Klauser, G. Lowney, S. Wallace, V. J. Reddi, and K. Hazelwood. Pin: Building Customized Program Analysis Tools with Dynamic Instrumentation. In *Proc. of the 2005 PLDI*, pages 190–200.

[17] A. C. Myers. JFlow: Practical Mostly-Static Information Flow Control. In *Proc. of the* 26th *POPL*, pages 228–241, 1999.

[18] J. Newsome and D. Song. Dynamic Taint Analysis for Automatic Detection, Analysis, and Signature Generation of Exploits on Commodity Software. In *Proc. of the* 12th *NDSS*, 2005.

[19] E. B. Nightingale, D. Peek, P. M. Chen, and J. Flinn. Parallelizing Security Checks on Commodity Hardware. In *Proc. of the* 13th *ASPLOS*, pages 308–318, 2008.

[20] G. Portokalidis and H. Bos. Eudaemon: Involuntary and On-Demand Emulation Against Zero-Day Exploits. In *Proc. of the 2008 EuroSys*, pages 287–299.

[21] G. Portokalidis, A. Slowinska, and H. Bos. Argos: an Emulator for Fingerprinting Zero-Day Attacks. In *Proc. of the 2006 EuroSys*, pages 15–27.

[22] F. Qin, C. Wang, Z. Li, H.-S. Kim, Y. Zhou, and Y. Wu. LIFT: A Low-Overhead Practical Information Flow Tracking System for Detecting Security Attacks. In *Proc. of the* 39th *MICRO*, pages 135–148, 2006.

[23] A. Slowinska and H. Bos. Pointless Tainting? Evaluating the Practicality of Pointer Tainting. In *Proc. of the 2009 EuroSys*, pages 61–74.

[24] G. E. Suh, J. W. Lee, D. Zhang, and S. Devadas. Secure Program Execution via Dynamic Information Flow Tracking. In *Proc. of the* 11th *ASPLOS*, pages 85–96, 2004.

[25] N. Vachharajani, M. J. Bridges, J. Chang, R. Rangan, G. Ottoni, J. A. Blome, G. A. Reis, M. Vachharajani, and D. I. August. RIFLE: An Architectural Framework for User-Centric Information-Flow Security. In *Proc. of the* 37th *MICRO*, pages 243–254, 2004.

[26] G. Venkataramani, I. Doudalis, Y. Solihin, and M. Prvulovic. Flexitaint: A Programmable Accelerator for Dynamic Taint Propagation. In *Proc. of the* 14th *HPCA*, pages 173–184, 2008.

[27] T. Wang, T. Wei, G. Gu, and W. Zou. TaintScope: A Checksum-Aware Directed Fuzzing Tool for Automatic Software Vulnerability Detection. In *Proc. of the* 31st *IEEE S&P*, pages 497–512, 2010.

[28] W. Xu, S. Bhatkar, and R. Sekar. Taint-Enhanced Policy Enforcement: A Practical Approach to Defeat a Wide Range of Attacks. In *Proc. of the* 15th *USENIX Security*, pages 121–136, 2006.

[29] A. Zavou, G. Portokalidis, and A. D. Keromytis. Taint-Exchange: A Generic System for Cross-process and Cross-host Taint Tracking. In *Proc. of the* 6th *IWSEC*, pages 113–128, 2011.

[30] N. Zeldovich, S. Boyd-Wickizer, E. Kohler, and D. Mazières. Making Information Flow Explicit in HiStar. In *Proc. of the* 7th *OSDI*, pages 263–278, 2006.

[31] D. Zhu, J. Jung, D. Song, T. Kohno, and D. Wetherall. TaintEraser: Protecting Sensitive Data Leaks Using Application-Level Taint Tracking. *SIGOPS Oper. Syst. Rev.*, 45(1):142–154, 2011.

Transparent Dynamic Instrumentation

Derek Bruening
Google, Inc.
bruening@google.com

Qin Zhao
Google, Inc
zhaoqin@google.com

Saman Amarasinghe
Massachusetts Institute of Technology
saman@csail.mit.edu

Abstract

Process virtualization provides a virtual execution environment within which an unmodified application can be monitored and controlled while it executes. The provided layer of control can be used for purposes ranging from sandboxing to compatibility to profiling. The additional operations required for this layer are performed clandestinely alongside regular program execution. Software dynamic instrumentation is one method for implementing process virtualization which dynamically instruments an application such that the application's code and the inserted code are interleaved together.

DynamoRIO is a process virtualization system implemented using software code cache techniques that allows users to build customized dynamic instrumentation tools. There are many challenges to building such a runtime system. One major obstacle is *transparency*. In order to support executing arbitrary applications, DynamoRIO must be fully transparent so that an application cannot distinguish between running inside the virtual environment and native execution. In addition, any desired extra operations for a particular tool must avoid interfering with the behavior of the application.

Transparency has historically been provided on an ad-hoc basis, as a reaction to observed problems in target applications. This paper identifies a necessary set of transparency requirements for running mainstream Windows and Linux applications. We discuss possible solutions to each transparency issue, evaluate tradeoffs between different choices, and identify cases where maintaining transparency is not practically solvable. We believe this will provide a guideline for better design and implementation of transparent dynamic instrumentation, as well as other similar process virtualization systems using software code caches.

Categories and Subject Descriptors D.3.4 [*Programming Languages*]: Processors – Optimization, Run-time environments

Keywords Process Virtualization, Dynamic Instrumentation, Transparency, Runtime System

1. Introduction

DynamoRIO [1] is a runtime code manipulation system that dynamically instruments an application such that the application's code and the inserted code are interleaved together. It provides a virtual execution environment within which arbitrary unmodified applications, even legacy software with no available source code, can be executed, monitored, and controlled. A software code cache is used to implement the virtual environment. The provided layer of control can be used for various purposes including security enforcement [14, 22], software debugging [8, 43], dynamic analysis [42, 45], and many others [40, 41, 44]. The additional operations are performed clandestinely alongside regular program execution.

First presented in 2001 [9], DynamoRIO evolved from a research project [6, 10] for dynamic optimization to the flagship product of a security company [22] and finally an open source project [1]. Presently it is being used to build tools like Dr. Memory [8] that run large applications including proprietary software on both Linux and Windows. There are many challenges to building such a system that supports executing arbitrary unmodified applications. The most critical challenge, however, is *transparency*: preventing a target application's native behavior from changing when running inside DynamoRIO.

1.1 Transparency Challenges

Many applications perform introspective operations such as reading function return addresses, iterating loaded modules, counting the number of threads, inspecting resource usage, etc. If DynamoRIO makes any modifications that violate the expected execution environment, in the best case the application's behavior will deviate slightly, but often it will crash. DynamoRIO must have its hands everywhere to maintain control, yet it must have such a delicate touch that the application cannot tell it is there. Table 1 shows a list of transparency requirements and specific applications that fail to run correctly when DynamoRIO does not preserve each given aspect of transparency.

In addition, DynamoRIO abstracts away the details of the underlying system and provides a simple interface for creating a custom tool, or *client* of the system, that is able to observe and modify a monitored application in a customized manner. In order to be widely usable, it must avoid imposing too many restrictions on clients: the client writer should not need to be a dynamic instrumentation expert and should be able to use traditional programming languages and libraries. Since standard libraries are not written to operate clandestinely, DynamoRIO must not only perform its own operations transparently but must also transform the client and its libraries such that they operate transparently within the monitored application.

Clearly, being transparent is critical in order to run a wide range of applications. While building *efficient* code manipulation (or instrumentation, translation, etc.) systems is a well-studied research topic [2, 6, 13, 15, 25, 32], we strongly believe that making the runtime environment *transparent* is the most important criterion for a successful system. To the best of our knowledge, this is the first paper that focuses on this critical issue.

Traditionally, transparency has been addressed on an ad-hoc basis. As there are no classifications or descriptions of transparency requirements, developers of a system only consider the need for any particular aspect of transparency when a target application starts

VEE'12, March 3–4, 2012, London, England, UK.

Category	Transparency requirement	Application(s) that fail if requirement is not met
Code	execute self-modifying code	Adobe Premiere
	execute code on the stack	MS Management Console
	execute dynamically generated code	Virtualdub, Java, .NET
Data	preserve beyond top of stack	MS Office
	support stack pointer not pointing at stack	Adobe Premiere
	preserve return address	Any application using COM
	hide from self-introspection	Mozilla
	preserve eflags across indirect branches	libc, code generated by Visual Studio compiler
Concurrency	support debugger threads	Visual Studio debugger
	separate system thread local storage slots from app	MS Exchange
Other	separate system libraries from app	Windows graphical applications
	separate system loader from app	Windows graphical applications
	deliver faults	MS Office
	separate system files from app	shells and daemons

Table 1. A list of transparency requirements in process virtualization systems and specific applications that fail to run correctly when each given requirement is not preserved. Section 6.1 elaborates on each of these examples.

misbehaving. In this work we attempt to change that by describing a necessary set of transparency requirements for running mainstream Windows and Linux applications. We believe this will provide a guideline for better design and implementation of future systems.

In this paper, we study the full spectrum of transparency challenges while building DynamoRIO. Our experiences have led us to formulate three *transparency guidelines* that should be followed when designing and implementing systems like DynamoRIO:

1. *Leave the application unchanged whenever possible.* Even when changes can lead to performance gains, in nearly every case such changes cause at least one application to fail. If correctness is a goal, design the system to perturb as little as possible.
2. *When changing the application is unavoidable, ensure the change is imperceivable to the application.* Some changes are unavoidable, in which case every effort should be made to hide the change from the application.
3. *Avoid resource usage conflicts.* Where possible, acquire resources directly from the operating system; if libraries must be used, fully isolate them from the application.

How these three guidelines are applied during the design and implementation of DynamoRIO are discussed throughout the rest of the paper.

1.2 Contributions

The contributions of this paper include:

- We identify three *transparency guidelines* for the design and implementation of transparent instrumentation systems.
- We enumerate and classify the full range of transparency issues.
- We discuss possible solutions to each issue, and evaluate tradeoffs between different choices.
- We identify cases where maintaining transparency is not practically solvable.
- We describe a necessary set of transparency requirements for running mainstream Windows and Linux applications.

We hope this paper can be used as a guide for building dynamic instrumentation tools and other similar process virtualization systems.

1.3 Paper Organization

The rest of the paper focuses on the transparency challenges of building a dynamic instrumentation system and is organized as follows: Section 2 describes the transparency issues when designing a dynamic instrumentation framework, while Section 3 discusses the implementation challenges of a transparent system. Section 4 describes the necessary transparency support for customized user components, and Section 5 discusses the limits of transparent systems. Section 6 evaluates the impact and tradeoffs of different solutions. Section 7 presents related work, and Section 8 concludes the paper.

2. Transparency in System Design

A key principle of designing transparent instrumentation is keeping as many aspects of the application as possible unchanged. This is *Guideline 1*, the first of our *transparency guidelines*. This applies to the original application binary, the application code, the application data, the number of threads, etc. If it is unavoidable to change something, the system should disguise the change to appear to the application as if it were unmodified (*Guideline 2*). In addition, to support arbitrary applications, DynamoRIO, or any similar system, cannot make any assumptions about a program's compilation, source code or annotation availability, stack or heap usage, or any of its dependences on the instruction set architecture or operating system. DynamoRIO can only assume the bare minimum architecture and operating system interfaces, and request resources directly from the operating system to avoid any resources usage conflicts (*Guideline 3*).

In this section, we categorize transparency issues into three groups: code transparency, data transparency, and concurrency transparency. We discuss each type of issue and possible solutions.

2.1 Code Transparency

Code transparency refers to the faithful reproduction of application behavior with respect to changes in or references to its code when executing in a process virtualization system. A process virtualization system implemented as a simulator or interpreter can control the program's execution via software interpretation without affecting its code, but the resulting runtime overhead is too high to run any large applications. Another approach is to use in-place modification of the application code to insert control and tool operations. In addition to presenting transparency challenges, this technique is unable to support the fine granularity of each individual instruc-

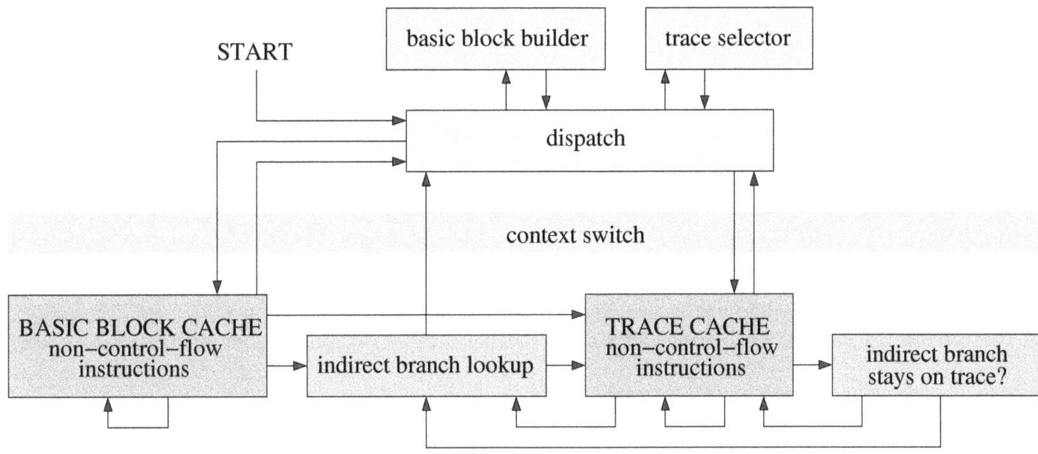

Figure 1. DynamoRIO system overview. A context switch separates the code cache (application state) from DynamoRIO code (system state); both execute in the same process and address space. Application code is copied into the two caches, with control transfers (shown by arrows in the figure) modified in order to retain control.

tion that DynamoRIO supports for its tools to control and manipulate a target program. In contrast to the two mentioned approaches, a software code cache can efficiently manipulate code and insert additional instructions without changing the original program. In addition to being used by DynamoRIO, code caches are also used by many similar systems including Pin [25], QEMU [5], and Valgrind [30].

2.1.1 Software Code Cache

Figure 1 shows the flow of control between the components of DynamoRIO and its code caches. When running an application, DynamoRIO copies the application code one *dynamic basic block* at a time into its basic block code cache and executes it there *in lieu of* the original code. A block that directly targets another block already resident in the cache is linked to that block to avoid the cost of returning to the DynamoRIO dispatcher. Frequently executed sequences of basic blocks are combined into *traces*, which are placed in a separate code cache. In the rest of the paper we will refer to both basic blocks and traces in code caches as code *fragments*. This software code cache and redirection complicates transparency, but no alternative approach provides sufficient flexibility and efficiency.

2.1.2 Application Address Transparency

When using a software code cache, although the application's code is copied into a cache, every address manipulated by the application must remain an original application address. DynamoRIO must translate indirect branch targets from application addresses to code cache addresses, and conversely if a code cache address is ever exposed to the application, DynamoRIO must translate it back to its original application address. The latter occurs when the operating system passes a machine context to a signal or exception handler. In that case both the faulting or interrupted address and the complete register state must be made to look like the signal or exception occurred natively, rather than inside the code cache where it actually occurred. Details of how to accomplish this will be discussed in Section 3.3.

2.1.3 Code Cache Consistency

DynamoRIO must ensure that each cached copy of application code is consistent with the original version in application memory. One common case where consistency is broken is unmapping of a file containing code (typically a shared library) from memory. As the application must make an explicit request to the kernel to accomplish the unmap, DynamoRIO need only monitor each system call that frees an area of the address space, and flush all cache fragments that contain pieces of code from that region.

The original code might also be modified via either self-modifying code or re-use of the memory region for dynamic code generation. DynamoRIO uses hardware page protection to detect such code modification by marking all regions that contain code in the code cache read-only, and keeping a list of all such regions. If such a region is written to, DynamoRIO traps the fault, flushes the code for that region from the code cache, removes the region from the list, marks the region as writable, and then re-executes the faulting write. Additionally, DynamoRIO intercepts Windows' `NtQueryVirtualMemory` system call and modifies the information it returns to pretend that areas it made read-only are in fact writable (*Guideline 2*). If the application changes the protection on a region DynamoRIO has marked read-only, it must update the information so that a later write fault will properly go to the application.

One complication with page protection occurs when the application requests output from a system call at an address that the virtualization system has made read-only. One solution, if all system call parameters are known, is to look for any output parameters that point at read-only pages and swap those pages to use sandboxing prior to invoking the system call.

Handling additional complications, including when the writing instruction and the target of a code modification are on the same page, are described elsewhere [7].

2.2 Data Transparency

Although the application code has been redirected to a code cache, application data can and should remain unchanged (*Guideline 1*).

2.2.1 Application State Preservation

Using a software code cache, the execution of application code is interleaved with the execution of DynamoRIO and the client's code. The application state must be preserved when execution exits the code cache to DynamoRIO and restored when it enters the cache. The application state to be saved includes the complete register state, conditional flags (`eflags` in IA-32), and floating-point state. If the system shares libraries with the application, per-library persistent state like `errno` in `libc` should also be saved. It is possible to reduce the overhead of each context switch by not preserving all of the state, e.g., not saving and restoring floating-point state when the intervening system code does not perform any floating-point operations. However, such optimizations must be careful to not cause any transparency violations. For example, early versions of DynamoRIO assumed that `XMM` registers were not used by its own code on the IA-32 architecture and did not preserve them on context switches. However, later implementations of `memset` and `strlen` from `gcc` and in the C library used by DynamoRIO and clients began to use register `xmm0`, violating the assumption and causing application crashes.

DynamoRIO simply copies the application code into the code cache with minimal modifications and performs a full context switch when execution transfers between the code cache and DynamoRIO. In contrast, Valgrind maintains virtual application state including the program counter and updates it after every operation translated from original application code. In other words, Valgrind emulates the application's execution while natively executing Valgrind's own code, while DynamoRIO natively executes either one or the other, context switching between the runtime system and the application process. By minimizing the number of context switches via linking code fragments in code caches, the approach adopted by DynamoRIO incurs much lower runtime overhead than Valgrind's approach.

2.2.2 Stack Transparency

DynamoRIO uses a private stack and never touches the application's stack (*Guideline 1*).

It is tempting to assume that the space beyond the top of the application stack is not accessed and can be used for scratch space by a dynamic instrumentation system. For instance, HDTrans [36] spills registers to the application stack. However, some applications do access data beyond the top the stack. For example, Microsoft Office has code that stores data on the top of the stack, moves the stack pointer to the previous location, and then accesses the data. Additionally, some hand-crafted code uses the stack pointer as a general-purpose register, in which case one cannot even assume that the memory pointed at by the stack pointer is safe to access.

Another tempting way to use the application stack is using code cache addresses as return addresses instead of the original application return addresses [20], which allows an instrumentation system to use `ret` instructions directly and avoid any translation cost on function returns. However, this violates application address transparency (Section 2.1.2). Many applications examine their stack. For example, position-independent code obtains the current program counter by making a call to the next instruction and then popping the return address. The system can do pattern matching on this and other common ways the return address is read in order to get many applications to work, but even some of the SPEC 2000 CPU benchmarks [38], like `perlbmk`, read the return address in too many different ways to detect easily. Moreover, the return address replacement makes it difficult to construct a call stack from the application stack, and causes problems when debugging the application.

2.2.3 Heap Transparency

Memory allocated by DynamoRIO must be separate from that used by the application, for two reasons. First, the memory allocated for DynamoRIO should not interfere with the data layout of the application or with application memory bugs, e.g., heap buffer overflows. Additionally, sharing heap allocation routines with the application violates *Guideline 3*. Most heap allocation routines are thread-safe but not re-entrant (Section 3.1) and are thus not safe to call by DynamoRIO. Instead, DynamoRIO obtains its memory directly from system calls and parcels it out internally with a custom memory manager.

2.2.4 Self-Introspection Transparency

Many applications perform various introspective operations: iterating over loaded libraries, counting the number of threads, inspecting resource usage, etc. For instance, Linux's process information pseudo-file system (`/proc`) allows users or applications to inspect the status of a process, including memory maps, file usage, and other information. DynamoRIO intercepts system calls that query information and modifies the results returned to the application in order to hide DynamoRIO's presence. Section 3.2 discusses particular system calls that must be intercepted.

2.3 Concurrency Transparency

Multi-threaded applications have their own transparency issues beyond the code and data transparency discussed so far.

2.3.1 Thread Transparency

There are several options to map multi-threaded application execution onto the runtime environment. DynamoRIO uses application threads as system threads and creates no new threads, which avoids interfering with applications that monitor all threads in the process. DynamoRIO code is executed by application threads, with a context switch to separate its state from application state. Each application thread has its own separate DynamoRIO state and stack.

Using a separate system thread per application thread can be more transparent by truly separating contexts, in particular Thread-Local Storage (TLS), and avoiding having to handle application threads suspending threads that are executing in system code. However, it can also reduce application scalability in applications with hundreds or thousands of threads by doubling the number of threads. In addition, the communication and synchronization between an application thread and its system thread might cause performance problems. It is also possible to multiplex all application threads onto one single system thread, but this arrangement is unlikely to be performant enough. For example, Valgrind serializes all threads' execution, which incurs significant slowdown.

2.3.2 Synchronization Transparency

Sharing locks with the application can cause many problems and should be avoided (*Guideline 3*). Concurrency is challenging enough to get right in a single body of code where protocols can be agreed upon and code changed to match them. When dealing with an arbitrary application, the only viable solution, adopted by DynamoRIO, is to avoid acquiring locks that the application also acquires. Similarly, DynamoRIO must worry about application threads sharing system routines and locks, and cannot allow an application thread to suspend another thread that is inside a non-re-entrant system routine or holding a system lock.

Even without sharing locks, the application and system may still interfere with each other and cause deadlock. For example, if one application thread is waiting for an application lock to be released by another thread, which is blocked on acquiring a system lock held by the first thread, neither thread can make forward progress. To prevent such deadlocks, DynamoRIO's solution is to enforce that no DynamoRIO lock can be held when a thread is executing application code inside the code cache.

2.3.3 Memory Ordering Transparency

If a dynamic instrumentation system modifies application memory accesses, or re-orders application instructions, it could cause a change in behavior with respect to the order of memory references seen across threads. Without any particular tool running on top of it, a dynamic instrumentation system should avoid such changes. DynamoRIO does not make these types of modifications. If a tool decides to do so, it can choose accept the consequences as a trade-off.

Additionally, reading another thread's memory could result in behavior that differs from native execution, due to timing differences. The only application memory locations that need to be read by DynamoRIO are indirect branch targets and certain system call arguments on Windows where arguments are stored in memory. This minimal memory interaction results in minimal interference and does not add any races. Thus, in a race-free application, the dynamic instrumentation system will also be race-free. In an application with races, the behavior when running under the dynamic instrumentation system will contain a valid ordering that can occur natively, though it may not be the behavior that is seen most often natively due to timing changes. This may be unavoidable. Section 5.1 discusses related challenges.

3. Transparency in System Implementation

Beyond the design issues, there are many additional challenges when actually implementing a dynamic instrumentation system like DynamoRIO. Ideally, DynamoRIO's resources should be completely disjoint from the application's. However, that is not possible when DynamoRIO is executing inside the same process as the application. DynamoRIO must do its best to avoid conflicts (*Guideline 3*).

3.1 Library Transparency

Sharing libraries with the application can cause problems with re-entrancy and corruption of persistent state like error codes. DynamoRIO code can execute at arbitrary points in the middle of application code. If both the application and DynamoRIO use the same non-re-entrant library routine, DynamoRIO might call the routine while the application is inside it, causing incorrect behavior. For example, if the system calls *malloc* while the application is inside that same routine, *malloc*'s global state may be in an inconsistent state. If a library routine acquires locks, deadlock can easily occur even though the routine is thread-safe.

To avoid the problems described above, early versions of DynamoRIO took the following approach: (*i*) preserve persistent library state (e.g., `errno`) on each context switch; (*ii*) only use re-entrant library routines, implementing separate versions of non-trivial routines like `vsnprintf` when necessary; and (*iii*) request resources such as memory and files only from system calls and never from user libraries.

The current implementation of DynamoRIO loads a separate copy of application libraries for its own use and use by clients, to avoid conflicts with the application. However, duplicating libraries does not solve all of the problems. Some routines may still conflict with the application on resource usage, such as `malloc` requesting memory via the `brk` system call, which must be redirected to DynamoRIO's own routines.

Another example is Thread Local Storage (TLS) access. In 64-bit Linux on the AMD64 architecture, TLS is accessed via the `fs` register. If executed unchanged, the two sets of libraries must use the same `fs` register and its value must be swapped to maintain transparency. An alternative approach taken by DynamoRIO is to mangle each application TLS access to not use a segment register, avoiding the expensive swapping.

3.2 System Calls

DynamoRIO must understand and handle system calls properly for two reasons: (*i*) it must execute raw system calls itself to request resources, and (*ii*) it must monitor certain system calls made by the application in order to maintain system state and to enforce transparency.

The system call interface on Linux and most operating systems is a standard mechanism for requesting services (Figure 2a). However, on Windows, the documented method of interacting with the operating system is not via system calls but instead through an application programming interface (the *Win32 API*) built with user libraries on top of the system call interface (Figure 2b). Experience from early versions of DynamoRIO tells us that using the Win32 API interface causes numerous transparency issues including problems described in Section 3.1. The system call interface (Figure 2c) must be used, rather than the API layer, which, unfortunately, binds DynamoRIO to an undocumented interface that may change without notice in future versions of Windows.

DynamoRIO can fully control every process action in user mode, but usually has little control over kernel mode actions. It must intercept and monitor application system calls and modify them if necessary. For example, DynamoRIO must intercept and redirect any `sigaction` system call invoked by the application to avoid losing control on signal delivery. As discussed in Section 2.1.3, DynamoRIO must monitor all system calls that free memory regions and flush all cache fragments accordingly to keep the code cache consistent. These calls include `munmap` and `mremap` on Linux and `NtUnmapViewOfSection`, `NtFreeVirtualMemory`, and `NtFreeUserPhysicalPages` on Windows. Additionally, the Windows system call `NtGetContextThread` enables one thread to obtain the context of another thread. DynamoRIO must intercept this call and translate the returned context (see Section 3.3) so that the target thread appears to be executing natively instead of in the code cache. System calls like thread and process creation should also be monitored so the system can maintain control over all execution.

Furthermore, DynamoRIO must hide itself from introspection. For example, on Windows, applications can iterate over all loaded shared libraries using the system call `NtQueryVirtualMemory` [28] to traverse each region of memory and the routine `GetModuleFileName` to find out if a library is present. DynamoRIO detects such queries to its own addresses and modifies the returned data to make the application think that there is no library there. This trick is required to correctly run certain applications, such as `Mozilla`, which install hooks in loaded libraries.

For application queries to Linux's process information pseudo-file system (`/proc`), it is possible to replace the contents of each file (e.g., `/proc/self/maps`) with custom content by monitoring file access system calls. By doing so, we can create the illusion that the application is executing natively. DynamoRIO currently does not implement this feature as we have not seen any problems caused by real applications accessing `/proc`.

3.3 Context Translation

When handling exceptions and signals, DynamoRIO must translate every machine context that the operating system passes to the application, to pretend that the context originated in application code rather than the code cache.

Systems like Valgrind that emulate the application state can simply hand the emulated machine context to the application because that state is always up-to-date. This comes at a performance cost, however, that we consider too high. In DynamoRIO, if the interrupting event requiring translation can be delayed, e.g., on receiving a timer alarm signal on Linux, DynamoRIO will delay the translation until a controlled point outside of the code cache where the application state is easily obtained. For such cases, the delayed event will still occur at a point it might have occurred natively. Otherwise, context translation takes several steps for events that are not

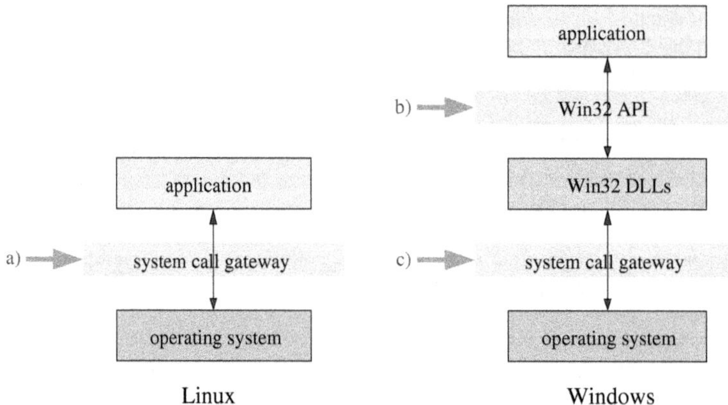

Figure 2. On Linux, the system call interface is the documented method of interacting with the operating system, as shown on the left. On Windows, however, a layer of user libraries makes up the Win32 API, which is the documented interface, while the system call layer is undocumented.

delayable, each bringing the code cache context closer to the state it would contain natively.

The first step is translating the program counter from the code cache to its corresponding application address. One translation method is to store a mapping table for each cache fragment. DynamoRIO's preferred approach, to save memory, is to re-create the cache fragment from application code, and then correlate the code cache address to the recreated cache fragment to obtain the appropriate application address. DynamoRIO rebuilds the cache fragment as though it were encountering new code, making sure to store the original address of each instruction. It then re-applies any instrumentation (this method only works for deterministic instrumentation: a table must be used otherwise). Finally, DynamoRIO walks through the reproduction and the cache fragment in lockstep, until it reaches the target point in the cache fragment. The application address pointed at by the corresponding instruction in the reconstructed cache fragment is the program counter translation.

The second step is ensuring that the registers contain the proper values. In the absence of code transformations, only inserted code for indirect branches by DynamoRIO causes problems here (the load of the indirect branch target could fail, requiring context translation). In this case several registers must have their application values restored to complete the translation. How to recreate registers in the presence of other code transformations is discussed in Section 4.2.

3.4 Error Transparency

Application errors under DynamoRIO must occur as they would natively. There are real-world cases of applications that access invalid memory natively, handle the exception, and carry on. Without error transparency such applications would not work properly. When an error is passed to the application, it must be made to look like it occurred natively, which requires context translation (Section 3.3) and necessary kernel emulation.

An illegal instruction or a jump to invalid memory should not cause DynamoRIO's decoder to crash — rather, the error must be propagated back to the application. The best solution is to have the decoder suppress the exception and stop the basic block construction prior to the faulting instruction. Only if a new basic block is requested whose first instruction faults should it be delivered to the application. This also makes it easier to pass the proper machine context to the application, since the start of a basic block is a clean checkpoint of the application state. To implement error handling for decoding, checking every memory reference prior to accessing it is too expensive. A fault-handling solution is used instead, with a flag set to indicate whether the fault happened while decoding a basic block.

Supporting precise synchronous interrupts in the presence of code modification is challenging. DynamoRIO currently does not do this in every case. As an example, it transforms a far call into a push of the `cs` segment selector, a separate push of the return address, and then a jump. If there is an exception on the selector push or the jump, DynamoRIO need do nothing special. However, if the return address push faults (due to stack overflow, e.g.), the segment selector push should be undone. When executed natively the processor makes the whole sequence atomic. DynamoRIO must emulate this behavior in its fault handler. Today, DynamoRIO does undo the stack pointer adjustment of the selector push, but does not restore the stack value to its prior state. Unlike many transparency corner cases, this one is extreme enough to be ignored for mainstream applications. Systems that perform more aggressive optimizations than DynamoRIO often require hardware support to provide precise interrupts efficiently [18, 23].

Because DynamoRIO uses page protection for code cache consistency, it must distinguish write faults due to its page protection changes from those that would occur natively. When DynamoRIO receives a write fault targeting an area of memory that the application thinks is writable, that fault is guaranteed to belong to DynamoRIO, with all other faults routed to the application.

Error transparency overlaps with heap transparency (Section 2.2.3), stack transparency (stack overflows and underflows, Section 2.2.2), address space transparency (application writes targeting DynamoRIO data, Section 5.2), and context translation (translating contexts presented to application error handlers, Section 3.3).

Error transparency also relates to security vulnerabilities. Many security attacks take advantage of abstraction differences between software conventions and underlying platform enforcement. For example, the classic stack buffer overflow overwrites the return address on the stack. A security attack should work under a dynamic instrumentation system as well as it does natively. Often, address space shifts (see Section 5.2) thwart attacks. These observations lead to the idea of deliberately violating transparency in a tool in order to block security attacks [22].

3.5 Debugging Transparency

A debugger should be able to attach to a process under DynamoRIO's control just like it would natively. This is a reason for

DynamoRIO to not rely on debugging interfaces to control the target application, as only one debugger can be attached to a process at a time. Many debuggers also inject a thread into the debuggee process in order to efficiently access its address space. DynamoRIO would need to identify this thread as a debugger thread, and let it run natively, for full debugging transparency. DynamoRIO currently runs the thread under its control, but most debuggers work fine with DynamoRIO, including `gdb` [19] and the Debugging Tools for Windows [27].

The first transparency guideline serves us well when interacting with a debugger. Stack transparency and data transparency make debugging the application nearly identical to debugging it when running natively, including call stacks. The main difference is, of course, that the program counter and sometimes register values are different. One solution taken by Chaperon, a runtime memory error detector that ships with Insure++ [31], is to modify a debugger like `gdb` to automatically translate the machine context (or at least the program counter) from the code cache to the original application code location.

4. Client Transparency

DynamoRIO is designed to be a general dynamic instrumentation system that supports building custom tools via plug-ins called *clients*. Clients can insert custom instrumentation and execute arbitrary code, including calling standard libraries that can conflict with the application, adding new challenges to transparency enforcement. This section discusses those issues.

4.1 Instrumentation Control

The client writer may not be an expert in transparency, and the client's added instrumentation might have unintended effects on the application's semantics. Similar to Pin and Valgrind, DynamoRIO provides an interface to insert clean calls to C or C++ code, in which operations can be performed. Unlike those other systems, however, DynamoRIO additionally exposes the application's instruction list prior to emitting it into the code cache so that the client can manipulate the application code directly at the granularity of individual instructions and operands. This gives the client more flexibility and power to control the code, allowing for highly efficient instrumentation. However, it leaves the responsibility for transparency in the user's hands.

4.2 State Preservation and Reconstruction

Translating the machine context for an exception or signal handler in the presence of arbitrary client code transformations can become complex. Because DynamoRIO allows the client to manipulate the code directly, it is very difficult for DynamoRIO to recreate the application state by itself. To solve this problem, in the first step of context translation (Section 3.3) DynamoRIO calls on the client to repeat its instrumentation while reconstructing the code fragment. Similarly, DynamoRIO also asks the client for help in the second step to recreate the application register state. This solution only works if the client instrumentation is deterministic. For non-deterministic instrumentation, DynamoRIO stores a mapping table for each code fragment to support state reconstruction.

4.3 Library Usage

If the client calls utility functions from application libraries, the system will encounter the issues discussed in Section 3.1. DynamoRIO uses a custom loader to load separate copies of libraries to avoid sharing libraries with the application. In addition, DynamoRIO exports for client use the methods and resources that it uses itself for better transparency, including memory allocation, reading and writing files, and many others.

4.4 Sideline Threads

The client may want to create new threads to take advantage of multi-core systems for *sideline* computation. DynamoRIO should prevent the application from seeing client threads (Section 3.2) and avoid interfering with applications that monitor all threads in the process. DynamoRIO's client threads on Linux are created in a separate thread group with a separate process identifier from the application, providing isolation from signal delivery, itimers, and introspection.

An instrumentation system should also provide appropriate synchronization to support sideline threads interacting with application threads. DynamoRIO currently only supports simple mutual exclusion locks.

5. Limitations

The further we push transparency, the more difficult it is to implement, while at the same time fewer applications require it. It is challenging and costly to handle all of the corner cases, and many can be ignored if we only want to execute simple programs like the SPEC CPU2006 [39] benchmarks. Yet, for nearly every corner case, there exists an application that depends on it.

We would like to provide *absolute* transparency so that the application cannot distinguish between running inside DynamoRIO and native execution. However, this may not be attainable for some aspects of execution. In this section, we will discuss the limits of transparency in dynamic instrumentation.

5.1 Timing Transparency

Timing transparency is difficult to achieve as it brings efficiency into the transparency equation. The overhead of DynamoRIO is not easy to hide.

Changing the timing of multi-threaded applications can uncover behavior that does not normally happen natively. An example is Microsoft's Removable Storage service, in which under certain timing circumstances when run under DynamoRIO one thread unloads a shared library while another thread returns control to the library *after* it is unloaded. This is not strictly speaking a transparency violation, as the error *could* have occurred without DynamoRIO. Some of these timing violations might also occur natively if some other modification altered the timing, e.g., executing on a different processor.

Another timing related issue is time interrupt transparency. The application may use time interrupts for timeouts or polling. Running in DynamoRIO, the application may experience problems in code that is sensitive to time changes. In addition, the client might use time interrupts for profiling. DynamoRIO must multiplex the client and application uses of the single underlying interrupt system.

5.2 Address Space Transparency

An application bug that accesses invalid memory and generates an exception should do the same thing under DynamoRIO, even if DynamoRIO has allocated its own memory at that location. If the access is a memory write, we can use page protection to detect any inadvertent (or malicious) writes to DynamoRIO memory by the application. DynamoRIO uses this scheme in the context of building a secure execution environment [22]. However, this approach does not work if the access is a memory read, as at least one memory region used by DynamoRIO must be readable throughout the execution, viz., the software code cache. The general solution would be to monitor every application memory access, which would cause prohibitive runtime overhead.

It is also possible for an application to request memory from a specific address that happens to be used by the instrumentation system. To support this, the system should be able to relocate its own memory and make room for the application's request.

5.3 Resource Limitations

Because the instrumentation system and the application are running in the same process, they share the resources of that process. Thus, any resource limit is a potential source of transparency violations if the resource usage reaches its limit earlier than it would if the application were running natively. For example, Memcheck [33], a memory checking tool built on top of Valgrind, is unable to run certain benchmarks when compiled 32-bit. The *434.zeusmp* benchmark from SPEC CPU2006 [39] contains a 1GB data segment, which is too large for Memcheck to handle [29], for all versions of Memcheck including the most recent version (3.7.0) as of the time of this writing.

In 32-bit architectures where only 4GB or less virtual address space is available, a memory-intensive application may work well natively but crash due to failure to allocate memory when running in a virtual environment. In 64-bit architectures, using up the entire address space is less likely to happen. However, DynamoRIO only requests memory from the first 2GB of the address space, which may cause contention with application memory usage in that range. A memory request might fail if both the application and DynamoRIO keep requesting memory from the same region.

5.4 Client Limitations

We would like to allow a client to modify the application instruction stream in any way it chooses, but unfortunately it may violate transparency. If a client violates transparency, there is often little that DynamoRIO can do about it (though it may be the desired effect for some clients). Application correctness may fail with no chance for recovery. For example, a client that seriously changes basic block control flow can disrupt DynamoRIO's trace creation. DynamoRIO does not disallow this, but it cautions clients to perform dramatic changes to basic block control flow at their own risk.

5.5 Other Limitations

Some types of transparency violations are exceedingly difficult to avoid or disguise. For example, in order to maintain control across callbacks on Windows and system calls that use `sysenter` on Linux, DynamoRIO must modify certain application code to which control is transferred directly by the kernel. The application can read that code and discover whether it is running in DynamoRIO, which can only be prevented by monitoring every memory access.

Another transparency issue is memory modification from another process. One process can change memory in another process via system calls (`NtWriteVirtualMemory` on Windows or `ptrace` on Linux). A kernel module could help here to detect cross-process modifications.

6. Experimental Results

In this section we evaluate the performance impact of several transparency choices made in DynamoRIO. By measuring the tradeoff between correctness and performance, we can understand the cost of a system being fully transparent. We first discuss real application code that violates tempting transparency assumptions.

6.1 Commercial Evaluation

In many cases, performance can be improved for several benchmarks by violating transparency, but the resulting system fails to run all applications. Real-world examples abound, as shown in Table 1. In this section we elaborate on the examples from that table, beginning with code transparency. If true self-modifying code is not handled, Adobe Premiere will not operate correctly as it contains self-modifying code, making this not some never-seen corner case, but actual behavior in a real-world, mainstream application.

```
<generate "ret $0x4" on the stack>
...
104a4: lea    0xc(%ebp), %esp
104a7: popa
104a8: jmp    *-0x28(%esp)
<the jmp target is on the stack:>
 fd04: ret    $0x4
```

Figure 3. Generated code executed beyond the top of the stack in some versions of Microsoft Office.

Further examples of code transparency corner cases are seen in several Windows applications, including versions of the Microsoft Management Console, that execute code on the stack. This code typically takes the form of small trampolines used to create closures for nested functions. As the stack unwinds and is re-extended, these trampolines can be replaced with other trampolines, resulting in different code at the same address. A system that is unable to correctly execute such generated code in memory areas that can be re-used for different code will be unable to run these real-world programs. Similar trampolines are also generated by `gcc` on Linux, and on the heap in other programs.

Large applications such as Microsoft Office contain dynamic languages that generate code during initialization and other normal execution sequences. Another instance of dynamically-generated code comes from applications that store code on disk in a packed format and unpack it at runtime. Virtualdub is an example of a packed application.

Moving on to data transparency, some versions of Microsoft Office contain instances of data being read beyond the top of the stack. In some cases this data is actually code. In one scenario, a return instruction is generated on the stack, the stack pointer is incremented, and then control is transferred to the instruction which is now beyond the top of the stack. Figure 3 shows the code sequence for this. Any system that uses the stack for scratch space runs the risk of breaking transparency for Office.

In addition to containing self-modifying code, Adobe Premiere also contains optimized loops that use the stack pointer as a general-purpose register. Again, any system that assumes it can safely access memory pointed at by the stack pointer may not operate correctly on this mainstream commercial software.

Further examples of data transparency corner cases include glue code used for COM software which manipulates return addresses placed on the stack. Any system that does not preserve the original return addresses will have trouble with COM. Any system that does not hide itself from applications that examine their own address space and loaded libraries may fail to run Mozilla software. A final data transparency example considers condition flags: as will be discussed in Section 6.3, if condition flags are not preserved across indirect branches, even the SPEC CPU benchmarks compiled with the Microsoft compiler will fail.

Regarding concurrency transparency, some Windows applications, including Microsoft Exchange, use a large number of thread-local storage slots and can conflict with a process virtualization system. If Windows thread-local fields are not isolated from client libraries, graphical Windows applications will execute incorrectly, in many cases displaying incorrect pixels and crashing. Other examples of transparency corner cases include applications, like Microsoft Office, that recover from faults as part of normal execution.

Throughout our transparency discussions we have shown which aspects of transparency are necessary by presenting examples of applications whose correctness depends on each aspect. To evaluate

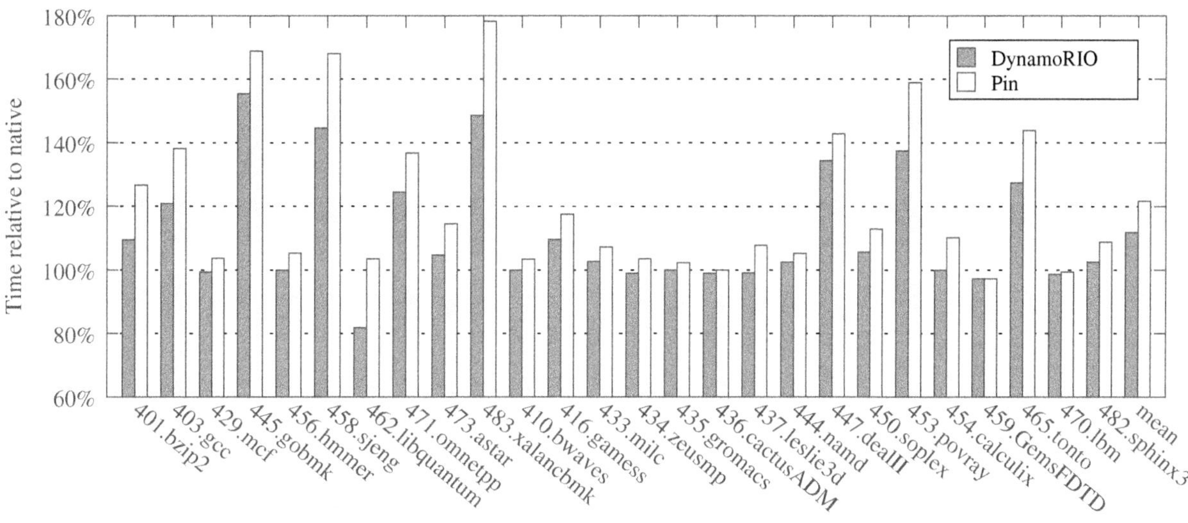

Figure 4. Performance of DynamoRIO and Pin relative to native execution on the SPEC CPU2006 benchmarks compiled as 64-bit.

whether our list of issues is sufficient, we relate our experiences with DynamoRIO in a commercial venture. DynamoRIO was used by Determina in a security product that was installed on tens of thousands of customer machines. When there were application failures, in most cases they were due to resource saturation or clear violations of normal programming practices such as overwriting or patching another application's library entry points (*hooking*) that created problems for many other use cases. We found no additional transparency violations.

6.2 Performance Evaluation

We evaluate the performance of SPEC CPU2006 [39] [1] running in DynamoRIO and Pin. We collected our results on a machine with 8-core Intel Xeon X7550 2 GHz processors, 18M L3 Cache, and 128 GB RAM running 64-bit Linux 2.6.32. We compiled the benchmarks as 64-bit applications. Figure 4 shows the relative performance impact over native execution. The average slowdown of the DynamoRIO base system is merely 11% where Pin has a 21% slowdown. Both systems keep their overhead reasonably low while providing enough transparency to run large applications.

6.3 Application State Transparency

Indirect branch handling is a major source of runtime overhead when executing an application under DynamoRIO. The original single application instruction turns into a lookup routine to locate the correct target code cache fragment. DynamoRIO has tried many ways to minimize overhead without violating transparency, including inlining the lookup routine to avoid a full context switch, using the fastest available method (`lahf` and `seto` on IA-32) to preserve the `eflags` condition flags, and analyzing the code to avoid restoring `eflags` if they are dead in the target.

One experiment we tried that violates transparency in order to gain performance is to simply assume that we do not need to preserve `eflags` across indirect branches. However, we found code in *libc-2.7.so*, shown in Figure 5, that breaks the assumption and causes nearly every application to crash. We instead tried preserving `eflags` over all but `ret` instructions and did manage to run all of our benchmarks. Figure 6 shows the resulting performance

[1] We omit the three benchmarks `400.perlbench`, `464.h264ref`, and `481.wrf` as they fail to run natively.

```
63a3a: lea    0x41(%rip),%rdx # 63a82
...
63a59: lea    -0x21(%rbp),%rax
63a5d: test   %rdi,%rdi
63a60: jmpq   *%rdx
...
63a82: je     63b58
```

Figure 5. An example of code that uses `eflags` across indirect branches.

impact: an average 3%, and as high as 16% on individual benchmarks, performance improvement. However, we found code in several benchmarks in SPEC CPU2000 [38] compiled with Visual C++ 6.0 on Windows, including `vpr` and `eon`, and some versions of large applications like Word and Photoshop, that clearly uses `eflags` across `ret` as follows:

```
call 0x50881d8e
je   0x508eeac7
```

The experiment above shows an example of the tradeoff between performance and transparency: typically one comes at the cost of the other.

7. Related Work

Software virtual machines like Connectix VirtualPC [17], VMWare [12], and Xen [4] perform dynamic binary manipulation, and are able to execute entire operating systems and their workloads. In contrast, process virtualization's goal is to build tools that operate on a single application in a lightweight manner for use on commodity, production platforms. A process virtualization system executes *on top of* the operating system. Perhaps counterintuitively, the technology of building a full system virtualization tool is not sufficient to build a process virtualization tool, which has a completely different set of challenges. When operating on top of the operating system, one must *transparently* operate within the confines of the operating system, intercepting its transfers of control and handling its threads, all the while pretending that one is

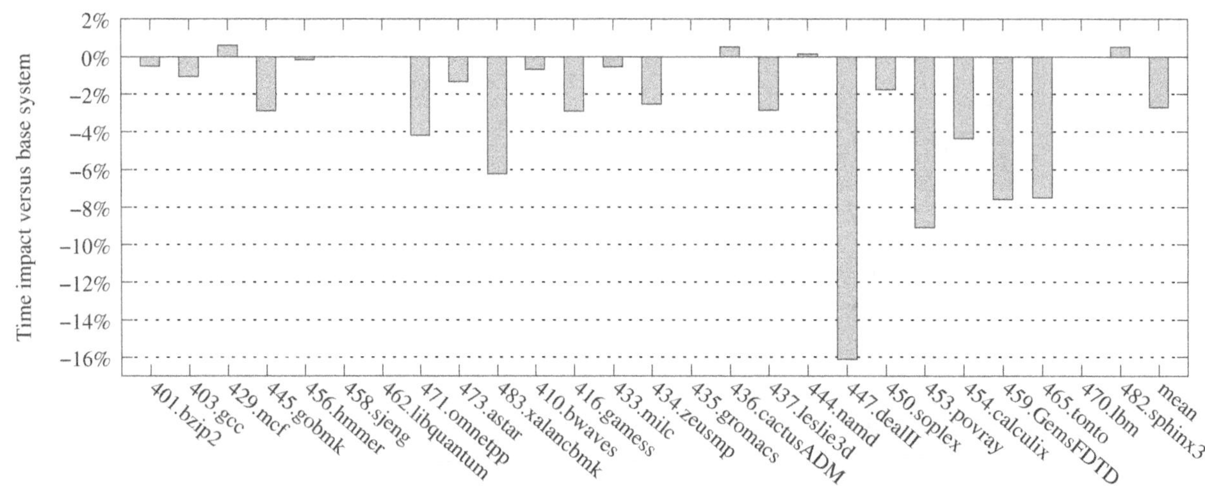

Figure 6. Performance impact of not preserving `eflags` across `ret` instructions.

not occupying the application's address space to avoid interfering with its behavior.

Dynamic instrumentation systems like Pin [25] and Valgrind [30] are implemented with software code caches in a similar manner to DynamoRIO. Other systems like Dyninst [11], Detours [21], and Vulcan [37] modify the original application code in memory by inserting trampolines, which suffer from transparency problems. Additionally, extensive modification of the code quickly becomes unwieldy through these mechanisms, especially in the face of variable-length IA-32 instructions.

Dynamic translators translate from one instruction set to another at runtime, making them similar to instruction set emulators. They include Aries [46] for PA-RISC to IA-64, Walkabout [15] for IA-32 to SPARC, IA32 EL [3] for IA-32 to IA-64, Dynamite [35] for IA-32 to MIPS, and many others including QEMU [5] and HDTrans [36]. Having different host and guest architectures, dynamic translation faces some cross target execution challenges that dynamic instrumentation does not have. For example, an instruction in the source ISA might not have an equivalent corresponding instruction in the target ISA. The host and guest architecture could have different endian-ness. Moreover, misaligned address accesses might cause memory faults on one architecture but not on the other, which adds new challenges to dynamic translation. On the other hand, dynamic translation across architectures often has less pressure for performance and transparency as there is no local native comparison.

Previous work has discussed some aspects of transparency: Pin for Windows [34] discusses transparency issues of Windows system call interception; Shade [16] and Daisy [18] discuss timing and error transparency; Tdb [24] discusses debugging transparency; and Strata [32] uses non-transparent code cache return addresses for performance improvement, accepting the loss of transparency. Machine contexts for signal handlers are translated to their native values in Dynamo [2]. Mojo [13] translates the program counter back to its native value for exception handlers. The transparency of CPU emulators with respect to corner cases of the instruction set has also been explored [26].

To best of our knowledge, there is no prior work that discusses the full range of transparency issues in the design and implementation of a dynamic instrumentation system.

8. Conclusion

DynamoRIO is a powerful runtime code manipulation system that provides a virtual execution environment within which an unmodified application can be monitored and controlled while it executes. *Transparency* is one major challenge when building such a system. Unlike SPEC CPU and other relatively simple benchmarks, many commercial applications rely on a pristine execution environment and a precise ABI. In order to run all of these applications, DynamoRIO must be fully transparent and cannot ignore seemingly obscure corner cases. In this paper, we identified a necessary set of transparency requirements for running mainstream Windows and Linux applications. We discussed possible solutions to each issue, evaluated tradeoffs between different choices, and identified cases where maintaining transparency is not practically achievable. We hope this paper can be used as a guide for building transparent dynamic instrumentation tools and other similar process virtualization systems.

References

[1] DynamoRIO dynamic instrumentation tool platform, Feb. 2009. `http://dynamorio.org/`.

[2] V. Bala, E. Duesterwald, and S. Banerjia. Dynamo: A transparent runtime optimization system. In *Proceedings of the ACM SIGPLAN Conference on Programming Language Design and Implementation (PLDI '00)*, pages 1–12, June 2000.

[3] L. Baraz, T. Devor, O. Etzion, S. Goldenberg, A. Skaletsky, Y. Wang, and Y. Zemach. IA-32 Execution Layer: a two-phase dynamic translator designed to support IA-32 applications on Itanium-based systems. In *36th International Symposium on Microarchitecture*, 2003.

[4] P. Barham, B. Dragovic, K. Fraser, S. Hand, T. Harris, A. Ho, R. Neugebauery, I. Pratt, and A. Warfield. Xen and the art of virtualization. In *Proceedings of the 19th ACM Symposium on Operating System Principles (SOSP '03)*, pages 164–177, Oct. 2003.

[5] F. Bellard. QEMU, a Fast and Portable Dynamic Translator. In *USENIX Annual Technical Conference*. USENIX Association, 2005.

[6] D. Bruening. *Efficient, Transparent, and Comprehensive Runtime Code Manipulation*. PhD thesis, M.I.T., Sept. 2004.

[7] D. Bruening and S. Amarasinghe. Maintaining consistency and bounding capacity of software code caches. In *Proceedings of the International Symposium on Code Generation and Optimization (CGO '05)*, pages 74–85, Mar. 2005.

[8] D. Bruening and Q. Zhao. Practical memory checking with Dr. Memory. In *The International Symposium on Code Generation and Optimization*, Chamonix, France, Apr 2011.

[9] D. Bruening, E. Duesterwald, and S. Amarasinghe. Design and implementation of a dynamic optimization framework for Windows. In *Proceedings of the 4th ACM Workshop on Feedback-Directed and Dynamic Optimization (FDDO-4)*, pages 19–30, Dec. 2001.

[10] D. Bruening, T. Garnett, and S. Amarasinghe. An infrastructure for adaptive dynamic optimization. In *Proceedings of the International Symposium on Code Generation and Optimization (CGO '03)*, pages 265–275, Mar. 2003.

[11] B. R. Buck and J. Hollingsworth. An API for runtime code patching. *Journal of High Performance Computing Applications*, 14(4):317–329, Winter 2000.

[12] E. Bugnion, S. Devine, and M. Rosenblum. Disco: Running commodity operating systems on scalable multiprocessors. In *Proceedings of the 16th ACM Symposium on Operating System Principles (SOSP '97)*, pages 143–156, Oct. 1997.

[13] W. Chen, S. Lerner, R. Chaiken, and D. M. Gillies. Mojo: A dynamic optimization system. In *Proceedings of the 3rd ACM Workshop on Feedback-Directed and Dynamic Optimization (FDDO-3)*, pages 81–90, Dec. 2000.

[14] W. Cheng, Q. Zhao, B. Yu, and S. Hiroshige. Tainttrace: Efficient flow tracing with dynamic binary rewriting. In *Proceedings of the Proceedings of the 11th IEEE Symposium on Computers and Communications (ISCC '06)*, pages 749–754, 2006.

[15] C. Cifuentes, B. Lewis, and D. Ung. Walkabout – a retargetable dynamic binary translation framework. In *Proceedings of the 4th Workshop on Binary Translation*, Sept. 2002.

[16] R. F. Cmelik and D. Keppel. Shade: A fast instruction-set simulator for execution profiling. Technical Report UWCSE 93-06-06, University of Washington, June 1993.

[17] Connectix. Virtual PC. `http://www.microsoft.com/windows/virtualpc/default.mspx`.

[18] K. Ebcioglu and E. Altman. DAISY: Dynamic compilation for 100% architectural compatibility. In *Proceedings of the 24th International Symposium on Computer Architecture (ISCA '97)*, pages 26–37, June 1997.

[19] GDB. The GNU Project Debugger. `http://www.gnu.org/software/gdb/gdb.html`.

[20] J. D. Hiser, D. Williams, W. Hu, J. W. Davidson, J. Mars, and B. R. Childers. Evaluating indirect branch handling mechanisms in software dynamic translation systems. In *Proceedings of the International Symposium on Code Generation and Optimization*, CGO '07, pages 61–73, Washington, DC, USA, 2007. IEEE Computer Society.

[21] G. Hunt and D. Brubacher. Detours: Binary interception of win32 functions. In *Proceedings of the USENIX Windows NT Workshop*, pages 135–144, July 1999.

[22] V. Kiriansky, D. Bruening, and S. Amarasinghe. Secure execution via program shepherding. In *Proceedings of the 11th USENIX Security Symposium*, pages 191–206, Aug. 2002.

[23] A. Klaiber. The technology behind Crusoe processors. Transmeta Corporation, Jan. 2000. `http://www.transmeta.com/crusoe/download/pdf/crusoetechwp.pdf`.

[24] N. Kumar, B. Childers, and M. L. Soffa. Tdb: A source level debugger for dynamically translated programs. In *the Sixth International Symposium on Automated And Analysis-Driven Debugging (AADEBUG)*, 2005.

[25] C.-K. Luk, R. Cohn, R. Muth, H. Patil, A. Klauser, G. Lowney, S. Wallace, V. J. Reddi, and K. Hazelwood. Pin: Building customized program analysis tools with dynamic instrumentation. In *Proceedings of the ACM SIGPLAN Conference on Programming Language Design and Implementation (PLDI '05)*, pages 190–200, June 2005.

[26] L. Martignoni, R. Paleari, G. F. Roglia, and D. Bruschi. Testing CPU emulators. In *Proceedings of the 2009 International Conference on Software Testing and Analysis (ISSTA)*, pages 261–272. ACM, July 2009. Chicago, Illinois, USA.

[27] Microsoft Debugging Tools for Windows. `http://www.microsoft.com/whdc/devtools/debugging/default.mspx`.

[28] G. Nebbett. *Windows NT/2000 Native API Reference*. Macmillan Technical Publishing, Indianapolis, IN, 2000.

[29] N. Nethercote. Spec2006 zeusmp and dealII on Valgrind 3.3.0, 2008. (These failures are still present in version 3.7.0.) `http://article.gmane.org/gmane.comp.debugging.valgrind/7947/match=spec2006`.

[30] N. Nethercote and J. Seward. Valgrind: A framework for heavyweight dynamic binary instrumentation. In *Proceedings of the ACM SIGPLAN Conference on Programming Language Design and Implementation (PLDI '07)*, pages 89–100, June 2007.

[31] Parasoft. Insure++. `http://www.parasoft.com/jsp/products/insure.jsp?itemId=63`.

[32] K. Scott, N. Kumar, S. Velusamy, B. Childers, J. Davidson, and M. L. Soffa. Reconfigurable and retargetable software dynamic translation. In *Proceedings of the International Symposium on Code Generation and Optimization (CGO '03)*, pages 36–47, Mar. 2003.

[33] J. Seward and N. Nethercote. Using Valgrind to detect undefined value errors with bit-precision. In *Proceedings of the USENIX Annual Technical Conference*, pages 2–2, 2005.

[34] A. Skaletsky, T. Devor, N. Chachmon, R. Cohn, K. Hazelwood, V. Vladimirov, and M. Bach. Dynamic program analysis of microsoft windows applications. In *International Symposium on Performance Analysis of Software and Systems (ISPASS)*, 2010.

[35] J. Souloglou. *A Framework for Dynamic Binary Translation*. PhD thesis, University of Manchester, 1996.

[36] S. Sridhar, J. S. Shapiro, E. Northup, and P. P. Bungale. HDTrans: An open source, low-level dynamic instrumentation system. In *Proceedings of the 2nd International Conference on Virtual Execution Environments (VEE '06)*, pages 175–185, New York, NY, USA, 2006. ACM Press.

[37] A. Srivastava, A. Edwards, and H. Vo. Vulcan: Binary transformation in a distributed environment. Technical Report MSR-TR-2001-50, Microsoft Research, Apr. 2001.

[38] Standard Performance Evaluation Corporation. SPEC CPU2000 benchmark suite, 2000. `http://www.spec.org/osg/cpu2000/`.

[39] Standard Performance Evaluation Corporation. SPEC CPU2006 benchmark suite, 2006. `http://www.spec.org/osg/cpu2006/`.

[40] Q. Zhao, J. E. Sim, L. Rudolph, and W. Wong. Dep: Detailed execution profile. In *International Conference on Parallel Architectures and Compilation Techniques*, Seattle, WA, Sep 2006.

[41] Q. Zhao, R. Rabbah, S. Amarasinghe, L. Rudolph, and W.-F. Wong. Ubiquitous memory introspection. In *International Symposium on Code Generation and Optimization*, San Jose, CA, Mar 2007.

[42] Q. Zhao, I. Cutcutache, and W.-F. Wong. Pipa: Pipelined profiling and analysis on multi-core systems. In *The International Symposium on Code Generation and Optimization*, Boston, MA, Apr 2008.

[43] Q. Zhao, R. M. Rabbah, S. P. Amarasinghe, L. Rudolph, and W.-F. Wong. How to do a million watchpoints: Efficient debugging using dynamic instrumentation. In *Proceedings of the 17th International Conference on Compiler Construction (CC '08)*, pages 147–162, 2008.

[44] Q. Zhao, D. Bruening, and S. Amarasinghe. Umbra: Efficient and scalable memory shadowing. In *The International Symposium on Code Generation and Optimization*, Toronto, Canada, Apr 2010.

[45] Q. Zhao, D. Koh, S. Raza, D. Bruening, W.-F. Wong, and S. Amarasinghe. Dynamic cache contention detection in multi-threaded applications. In *The International Conference on Virtual Execution Environments*, Newport Beach, CA, Mar 2011.

[46] C. Zheng and C. Thompson. PA-RISC to IA-64: Transparent execution, no recompilation. *IEEE Computer*, 33(3):47–53, Mar. 2000.

Execution Mining

Geoffrey Lefebvre Brendan Cully Christopher Head Mark Spear
Norm Hutchinson Mike Feeley Andrew Warfield
Department of Computer Science, University of British Columbia
{geoffrey, brendan, chead, mspear, norm, feeley, andy}@cs.ubc.ca

Abstract

Operating systems represent large pieces of complex software that are carefully tested and broadly deployed. Despite this, developers frequently have little more than their source code to understand how they behave. This static representation of a system results in limited insight into execution dynamics, such as what code is important, how data flows through a system, or how threads interact with one another. We describe Tralfamadore, a system that preserves complete traces of machine execution as an artifact that can be queried and analyzed with a library of simple, reusable operators, making it easy to develop and run new dynamic analyses. We demonstrate the benefits of this approach with several example applications, including a novel unified source and execution browser.

Categories and Subject Descriptors D.2.5 [*Software Engineering*]: Testing and Debugging—Tracing, Diagnostics

General Terms Design, Experimentation, Measurement, Performance

Keywords Binary Analysis, Offline Analysis, Virtual Machine, Semantic Gap

1. Introduction

> *"The creatures were friendly, and they could see in four dimensions. They pitied Earthlings for being able to see only three. They had many wonderful things to teach Earthlings about time."*
>
> –A description of the Tralfamadorians from Kurt Vonnegut's "Slaughterhouse Five" [35]

Execution is fleeting. As each moment of execution is lost to the past, an important opportunity to understand a system's behavior may be lost as well. In addition to the complexity that is inherent in operating system code, developers are often hamstrung by a lack of useful tools to assist in understanding how source behaves in practice. Where tools such as debuggers, profilers and leak detectors are available at all, they operate on only a glimpse of execution, either as a point in time or as a predetermined summary. These tools are "stuck in time", and must anticipate or recreate any execution scenario they seek to examine. Execution behavior that is not anticipated before it occurs can not be examined.

VEE'12, March 3–4, 2012, London, England, UK.

The lack of insight into how an operating system actually behaves when it runs presents a major challenge to both novice and experienced developers: code bases for these systems are large, and control flow through a system – whether it has to do with servicing a system call or delivering a received packet to the appropriate application – frequently spans large numbers of source files and is indirected through function pointers and across multiple execution contexts. A view of program source alone does not provide an intuition for where common execution paths are, which regions of code are particularly performance sensitive, or how data structures such as packets or block requests move across subsystems.

In this paper, we explore the idea that detailed, CPU-level traces of system execution can usefully enable analysis on execution as a whole, as opposed to execution in the moment. Rather than considering dynamic analysis as a "one-off" task that is performed against a running system, we propose performing repeated analysis against a persistent trace instance that may be kept and analyzed over a long period of time and by multiple users.

We describe the design and implementation of *Tralfamadore*, an offline dynamic analysis tool that borrows ideas from streaming databases [30] to treat a single execution trace as a shared resource that may be used by a community of developers to understand program behaviour. Tralfamadore explores the opportunities that exist where large reference executions, such as regression test suites or samples of production execution environments, are treated as archival recordings. Our system provides tools to map the low-level details of these recordings up to the source-level semantics used by developers. This approach allows the cost of analysis to be amortized over many users and related queries, making considerably more complex forms of analysis practical.

In this manner, Tralfamadore allows developers to better understand the execution dynamics of the software they are working on: they may explore sweeping queries, like "*show me a histogram of all parameters ever passed to this function,*" "*summarize all execution stacks that have ever invoked this line of code,*" or "*summarize the path through the kernel taken by all received UDP packets,*" in order to quickly get a sense of how complex system code behaves. Furthermore, as the analyses performed by the system are based on the composition of an extensible set of analysis operators, we demonstrate how new analyses can be written, often without requiring a low-level understanding of the nuances of a specific architecture or instruction set.

Our work can be viewed as an extension of recent results that decouple dynamic analysis from live execution [10, 27]. However, rather than simply running traditional analysis against a system recording, we explore the broader set of analyses that are possible across the entirety of an execution trace, and tackle some of the consequent challenges, such as indexing execution for efficient query evaluation. Tralfamadore allows the developer to engage in a dialogue with a system's execution, bridging the gap between the *intention* expressed in the source code and the *experience* of actual execution.

2. Goals

Tralfamadore aims to allow developers to understand large, complicated code bases that are difficult to analyze with existing tools. This problem produced four specific design goals for our tool:

2.1 Treat Execution as an Artifact

Traditional dynamic analysis frameworks such as Pin [20] or Valgrind [24] are *online* tools, meaning that they analyze a program as it executes. In Tralfamadore, the execution of the system being analyzed is first recorded and stored persistently, and all analyses are performed afterwards on this static data set. Tralfamadore analyzes executions as opposed to analyzing programs as they execute.

Running dynamic analyses against a static data set has multiple advantages, such as enabling new analyses not foreseen at the time of recording. This approach allows for repeated analysis over the same execution, providing consistency between each run, an important asset for developers using dynamic analysis in the cyclical process of understanding or debugging complex pieces of code such as an operating system kernel. Another advantage is that analyses are no longer "stuck in time" and can freely navigate execution by arbitrarily going back in time or jumping ahead. Analyses themselves are also easier to debug; their deterministic behaviour simplifies the task of validating whether an error in the analysis has been fixed or not. An offline approach also helps alleviate the "observer" effect. Although recording may affect the behaviour of the system, once an interesting behaviour has been captured, this behaviour is guaranteed to manifest for all analyses however intrusive they may be.

2.2 Support Whole-System Analysis

A motivation of our system is to help developers understand behavior that occurs at any layer of the software stack. In this paper we focus on kernel execution, but Tralfamadore is able to record the execution of entire systems. As the OS kernel is typically the most privileged, lowest-level software installed on a system, this goal leads to a number of requirements:

First, the traces should be *comprehensive*, meaning that it should be possible to record the execution of an entire system, including the execution of its operating system kernel and of all its applications. Traces should be captured at the hardware level, underneath the operating system, to ensure a complete visibility of the system's execution. In this paper we focus on kernel execution, but Tralfamadore is able to record the execution of entire systems.

Second, to capture the execution of unmodified systems requires recording execution *transparently* without explicitly changing the target system. Further, being transparent requires Tralfamadore to handle dynamically generated and self-modifying code without the need to be explicitly notified by the system being recorded.

Third, the information recorded should be *complete*, meaning that the recording should contain sufficient information for analyses to inspect the register and memory state of the system at an instruction granularity. Section 4.2 describes how Tralfamadore records execution and provides more details on how it meets these three requirements.

2.3 Bridge the Semantic Gap

Doing dynamic program analysis on an executing binary inherently introduces a *semantic gap*. On one side, the CPU executes a stream of instructions which update the state of the processor and memory, and on the other side, developers expect to be able to reason about a running program at the level of source code. This semantic gap makes developing new analyses challenging. An analysis writer needs to understand many low-level aspects of execution, such as how arguments are passed on function calls, or how memory is allocated from the heap. This effort can be considerable, and requires domain expertise over the instruction set, application binary interface (ABI), etc. This gap widens with operating system code, which does not provide standardized and stable programming interfaces such as POSIX or the C standard library.

```
int deliver_skb(struct sk_buff *skb,
      struct packet_type *pt,
      struct net_device *dev)
{
  atomic_inc(&skb->users);
  return pt->func(skb, skb->dev, pt, dev);
}
```

Figure 1. Packet delivery via type-specific function pointer from the protocol table

Unfortunately, existing dynamic analysis frameworks force analysis writers to constantly reinvent the wheel; low-level aspects of execution must be re-learned for every new analysis. A good example of this problem is Valgrind [24], which includes two different race detectors, and to which engineers at Google recently added a third one.[1] Although all three detectors differ in the algorithm used to identify races, they each reimplement instrumentation to extract the same information (lock acquisition/release, accesses to heap memory). The required instrumentation is orthogonal to the analysis used and could be shared across implementations if Valgrind made it easy to do so.

2.4 Provide Interactive Results

Finally, as the previous goals lead to a system that performs deep and complex analysis over large volumes of execution data there is a risk that analysis may take a long time to complete. Tralfamadore aims to enable highly interactive exploration of trace data, and so we desire that the system provide interactive results so that developers can get answers as quickly as possible. To achieve this, Tralfamadore provides mechanisms to generate trace indices that subsequent analyses can use to only read the relevant portions of a trace. Many analyses end up reading a small fraction ($< 1\%$) of the trace. The Tralfamadore framework is based on a dataflow model that is well suited to produce results in an online manner. Analyses can return partial results as soon as they are available. This is advantageous for analyses that take a long time to complete because they need to read a substantial fraction of the trace. All the analyses described in this paper can return partial results within seconds, although some of them take much longer to complete.

3. An Example: Linux Networking

The Linux network stack is an illustrative example of the challenges faced by developers in understanding unfamiliar code. This code base has a number of features that contribute to the difficulty of understanding it.

First, it is very large. According to SLOCCount[2], there are 342,536 lines of code in the net subdirectory of the Linux kernel (version 2.6.24). Restricting our attention to the most relevant subcomponents (ipv4, netfilter, core, sched, and ethernet) reduces the count to 113,110 lines. Second, it spans all the layers of kernel abstractions from system calls through device drivers. Third, it uses dynamic control flow techniques that are challenging for static tools to understand, such as function pointers (Figure 1 shows one ex-

[1] http://code.google.com/p/data-race-test/wiki/ThreadSanitizer

[2] http://www.dwheeler.com/sloccount/

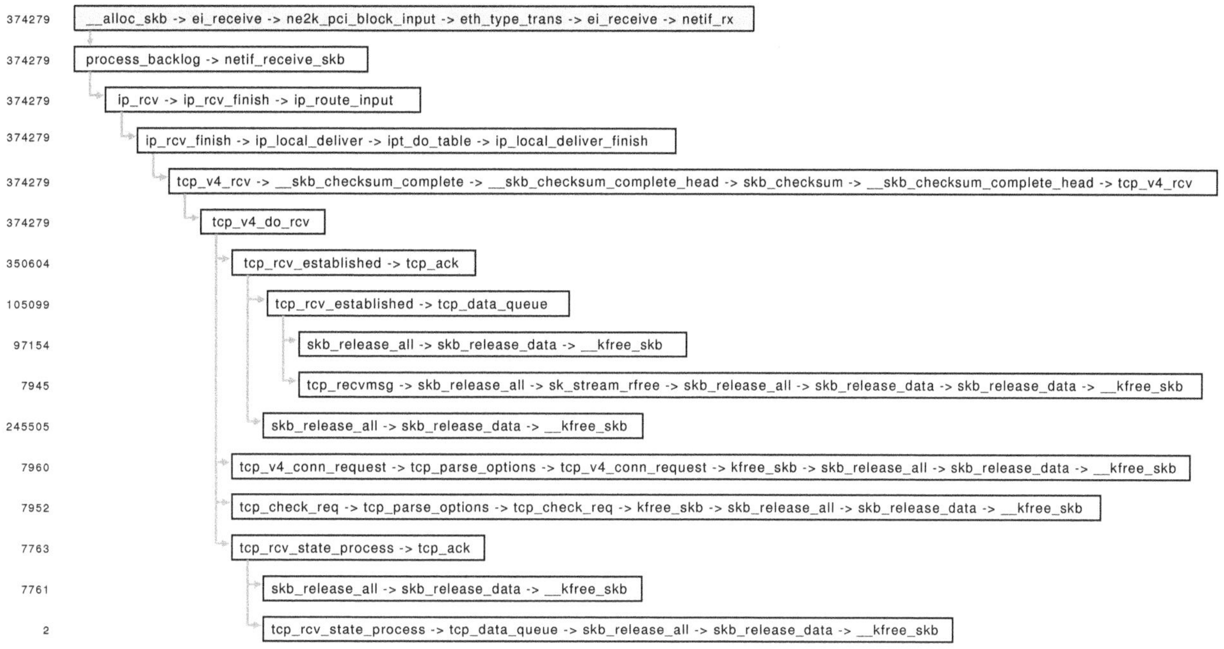

374279 __alloc_skb -> ei_receive -> ne2k_pci_block_input -> eth_type_trans -> ei_receive -> netif_rx
374279 process_backlog -> netif_receive_skb
374279 ip_rcv -> ip_rcv_finish -> ip_route_input
374279 ip_rcv_finish -> ip_local_deliver -> ipt_do_table -> ip_local_deliver_finish
374279 tcp_v4_rcv -> __skb_checksum_complete -> __skb_checksum_complete_head -> skb_checksum -> __skb_checksum_complete_head -> tcp_v4_rcv
374279 tcp_v4_do_rcv
350604 tcp_rcv_established -> tcp_ack
105099 tcp_rcv_established -> tcp_data_queue
97154 skb_release_all -> skb_release_data -> __kfree_skb
7945 tcp_recvmsg -> skb_release_all -> sk_stream_rfree -> skb_release_all -> skb_release_data -> skb_release_data -> __kfree_skb
245505 skb_release_all -> skb_release_data -> __kfree_skb
7960 tcp_v4_conn_request -> tcp_parse_options -> tcp_v4_conn_request -> kfree_skb -> skb_release_all -> skb_release_data -> __kfree_skb
7952 tcp_check_req -> tcp_parse_options -> tcp_check_req -> kfree_skb -> skb_release_all -> skb_release_data -> __kfree_skb
7763 tcp_rcv_state_process -> tcp_ack
7761 skb_release_all -> skb_release_data -> __kfree_skb
2 tcp_rcv_state_process -> tcp_data_queue -> skb_release_all -> skb_release_data -> __kfree_skb

Figure 4. TCP packet receive

```
int netif_rx(struct sk_buff *skb)
{
  struct softnet_data *q;
  q = &__get_cpu_var(softnet_data);
  __get_cpu_var(netdev_rx_stat).total++;
  __skb_queue_tail(&q->input_pkt_queue, skb);
  return NET_RX_SUCCESS;
}

int process_backlog(..., int quota)
{
  struct softnet_data *q;
  q = &__get_cpu_var(softnet_data);

  do {
    struct sk_buff *skb;
    skb = __skb_dequeue(&q->input_pkt_queue);
    netif_receive_skb(skb);
  } while (++work < quota);

  return work;
}
```

Figure 2. Top/bottom half network processing

ample of this, the packet delivery function, which dispatches the packet through a type-specific function pointer). Fourth, the functionality of the network stack is split in accordance with the standard Linux top/bottom driver architecture: the "top half" executes in interrupt context, which must complete as quickly as possible. It simply receives a packet from a device driver and queues it. Actual packet processing (the "bottom half") is deferred until interrupts have been serviced. Figure 2 shows the code used by network card interrupt handlers to queue received packets and the processing function that runs asynchronously to dequeue packets to push them up the protocol stack. This causes standard call-flow analysis to be unable to capture the end-to-end processing of packets from arrival to final delivery.

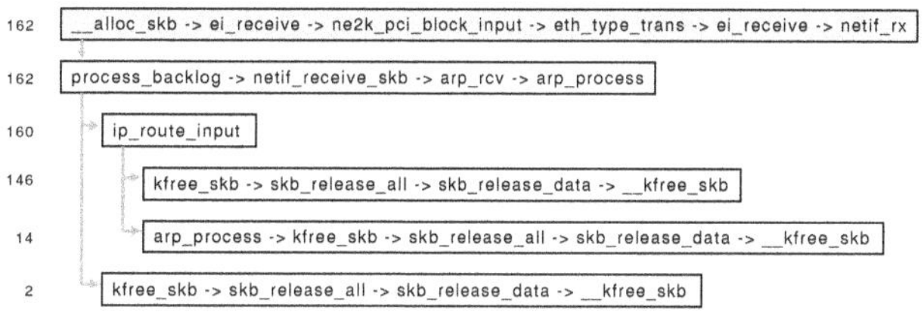

162 __alloc_skb -> ei_receive -> ne2k_pci_block_input -> eth_type_trans -> ei_receive -> netif_rx
162 process_backlog -> netif_receive_skb -> arp_rcv -> arp_process
160 ip_route_input
146 kfree_skb -> skb_release_all -> skb_release_data -> __kfree_skb
14 arp_process -> kfree_skb -> skb_release_all -> skb_release_data -> __kfree_skb
2 kfree_skb -> skb_release_all -> skb_release_data -> __kfree_skb

Figure 3. ARP packet lifetime through the network stack

Static analysis tools that perform call flow analysis cannot deal with this level of indirection, but even if they could, constructing a static call graph only tells part of the story. A large portion of system code is there to handle errors and rare corner cases. Static analysis cannot guide a developer to concentrate on the important or most commonly used functionality of the network stack, nor can it identify unused or outlying code paths.

The network stack is inherently data-driven and has a single data structure (the packet) at its core. Developers who want to understand the stack typically want to begin with understanding how a specific subset of packets flow through it. What if a developer could point to a function in the source code and ask, "Where are packets processed by this function coming from and where are they going to?" The answer to this question for the function `arp_rcv` is illustrated in Figure 3 which shows a tree produced by our tool of the functions that access every packet which passes through `arp_rcv`, from its allocation to is eventual release. Function names in the first, shaded text box are executed in device interrupt context, while subsequent processing occurs in a `soft_irq`. Numbers to the left of the figure indicate the number of packets that take the indicated path through the code. Looking at the figure, the developer can quickly learn that packets are allocated by the function `__alloc_skb`, are operated on at the ARP level primarily by the function `arp_process`, and are eventually freed by `__kfree_skb`.

Having understood this simple flow for ARP packets, the developer might then ask about packets processed by another function, perhaps for a more complex protocol such as TCP. The flow of packets going through the function `tcp_v4_do_rcv` is shown in Figure 4. The graph is much larger, representing the increased complexity of TCP processing relative to ARP.

The figures in this section were generated from a trace of a virtual machine running the Apache web server on Linux. The data used to generate these figures is obtained with a new analysis we have dubbed *Heap Slicing* which we describe in Section 5.4, after we have explained the overall architecture of our platform.

4. The Trace Analysis Engine

Figure 5 illustrates the Tralfamadore architecture. Analysis starts with an execution trace, which is captured at the virtual machine level and stored as a database which the analysis engine uses to answer queries. User queries are constructed out of simple modules under a dataflow model similar to network packet processing engines such as Click [16] and Bro [28]. In this paradigm, data is processed by single-function components, which are called *operators* in Tralfamadore. These operators are connected as a DAG, where each operator consumes a stream of records from one or more upstream operators and produces a stream of records for downstream operators. Data traverses the graph of operators, *flowing* from the leaves to the root of the tree.

Tralfamadore analyses execute by parsing the trace into a *stream* of records called *annotations* corresponding to the execution of machine-level instructions and the occurrence of events such as interrupts or page faults. The stream is passed through an analysis-specific configuration of operators that progressively augment the stream with semantically richer annotations corresponding to higher-level events such as function calls, lock uses, or heap allocations. Analyses can be expressed succinctly in terms of higher level annotations instead of dealing directly with a CPU-level trace.

The current implementation of the Tralfamadore analysis engine consists of approximately 5000 lines of C code and 12000 lines of OCaml code. The C language is used to implement performance critical code such as the trace parser and the instruction disassembler. All of the operators and analyses are written in OCaml. OCaml is a garbage-collected, statically typed functional language with imperative and object-oriented features. We choose OCaml because many of its features such as variant types and pattern matching map naturally to the tasks accomplished by Tralfamadore operators.

4.1 Primitives

Operators are the main functional abstraction in Tralfamadore. Each operator is designed to recognize specific patterns in the stream corresponding to the occurrence of events and produce annotations that describe these events. The type of an operator is solely defined by the annotations it produces. This encapsulation makes it easy to replace the implementation of an operator with a different one.

Annotations are the basic unit of information in the system. They are typed and parameterized, and operators are able to define new annotations that they will produce for downstream operators. Annotations are logically timestamped to provide an ordering between annotations which is needed when merging multiple annotation streams. The trace parser operator reads the raw trace on disk and produces *basic block* and *event* annotations, which are the most basic form of annotations used in the system. Section 5 describes some of the current stream operators and the annotations that they use. We are actively developing new operators in order to provide support for other operating systems and the analysis of user-level applications.

A **stream**, then, is an interface across which operators may send and receive sequences of annotations. As mentioned above, the flow of annotations in the system is driven by a "pull" from the sink operator in the DAG rather than a "push" from the trace itself. This allows operators to elect to work with specific, small regions of the trace. The programmatic idiom for streams in our system is that of an infinite lazy list, whose contents are materialized on demand.

4.2 Tracing

Almost all operators consume annotations from other operators in order to produce semantically richer annotations. The most important exception is the *trace operator*, which consumes the trace itself to produce annotations representing changes to the state of the system at the (virtual) hardware level. The trace is captured by running the target system on a modified version of QEMU [5]. QEMU is a fast whole-machine emulator that uses dynamic binary translation to emulate a guest instruction set architecture on a (possibly different) host architecture. QEMU breaks guest instructions into a series of RISC-like micro-operations which are fed into a code generator to produce native code that executes directly on the host. We made straightforward additions to these micro-operations to log their changes to emulated guest state as they execute. The resulting log is a faithful recording of every change to guest state, detailed enough that the exact state of the machine at any point in its execution can be recreated later. The modifications we have made to support trace generation are based on QEMU version 0.9.1 and consist of approximately 2200 lines of C code.

In order to support arbitrary analyses, the execution trace must record every change to the state of the machine as it runs. This includes every instruction executed, every exception, every interrupt, and all changes to register and memory, whether due to instructions or I/O.

```
c01373e8 sti                 EFL=00000206
c01373e9 nop 0x0(%eax,%eax,1)
E[20,0000,c01373f1]          STL[cd903f74]=206 STL[cd903f70]=60
                             STL[cd903f6c]=c01373f1 R[ESP]=cd903f6c
                             S[CS]=0060,00000000,ffffffff,00cf9a00
                             BR=c010859c EFL=00000006
c010859c push $0xffffffff STL[cd903f68]=ffffffff R[ESP]=cd903f68
c010859e jmp 0xc0108ddc      BR=c0108ddc
c0108ddc cld                 EFL=00000006
c0108ddd push %fs            STL[cd903f64]=000000d8 R[ESP]=cd903f64
c0108ddf push %es            STL[cd903f60]=0000007b R[ESP]=cd903f60
c0108de0 push %ds            STL[cd903f5c]=0000007b R[ESP]=cd903f5c
c0108de1 push %eax           STL[cd903f58]=00b77000 R[ESP]=cd903f58
...
c0108de7 push %ebx           STL[cd903f40]=00000002 R[ESP]=cd903f40
c0108de8 mov $0x7b,%edx      R[EDX]=0000007b
c0108ded mov %edx,%ds        S[DS]=007b,00000000,ffffffff,00cff300
```

Figure 6. Trace sample.

Figure 6 is a concrete example of the level of detail captured by our trace collector. At the start of the section, the CPU program counter is at `0xc01373e8`, which contains the `sti` instruction that causes interrupt delivery to be enabled (setting bit 9 of the `EFLAGS` register). Upon execution of this instruction, an interrupt (`0x20`, the timer interrupt) is immediately delivered. As part of interrupt delivery, the CPU saves essential state on the stack, disables interrupt delivery, and branches to an interrupt dispatch function. The dispatcher saves register values on the stack to free the registers for use by the interrupt handler it is about to call.

As is probably apparent from Figure 6, this approach produces an enormous amount of trace data, and slows execution significantly (see Section 7 for details). For a system like ours, which is designed as a developer tool and in which a single trace can be reused for large numbers of analyses, the benefits can be worth the costs. For applications that demand less overhead during execution (e.g., debugging, security, or forensics), it is possible to re-

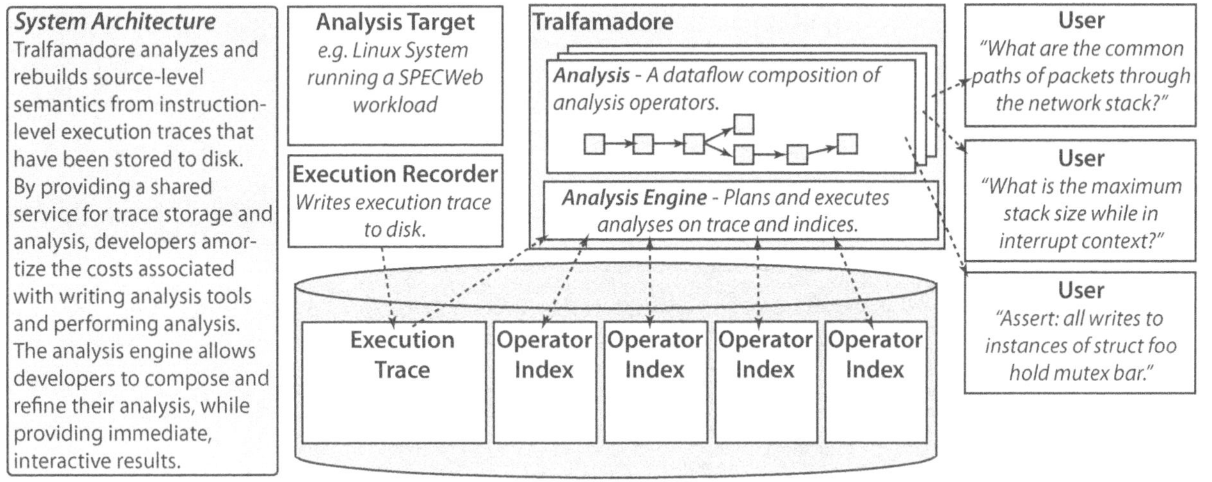

Figure 5. Tralfamadore Architecture

duce recording cost by separating it from trace generation, using deterministic virtual machine record and replay [11]. These logs are small, and recording them imposes only modest performance costs. As an event log, the recording contains very little information about execution, making it unsuitable for direct analysis. However, it provides enough information to regenerate the entire execution history in a subsequent, offline replay phase during which the full execution trace can be produced [38]. We are currently working on adding support for deterministic record/replay in QEMU and in Xen. Our goal is to be able to record execution in Xen and replay it in QEMU, similarily to Aftersight [10], to generate traces.

4.3 Trace Analysis

Figure 7 illustrates how operators gradually reconstruct execution semantics when streaming a CPU-level trace through the configuration of operators shown in Figure 8. The left hand side of Figure 7 shows an excerpt of raw trace containing basic block (BBlk) annotations. These annotations are generated by the *Trace Parser* operator. The stream passes through the *Invoke* operator which augments the stream with *Invoke* and *Return* annotations corresponding to function calls and return statements. A third operator (*Alloc*), uses the *Invoke* annotations to identify calls to `__kmalloc()`, and further augments the stream with heap allocation annotations. The *Alloc* annotation shown on the right hand side indicates the allocation of a block of 1024 bytes at address `0xdfcc5800`. Subsequent operators interested in heap allocations do not need to be concerned with identifying calls to `__kmalloc()`, but can simply use the *Alloc* annotation directly without knowing how it was generated.

In addition to gradually bridging the semantic gap, the dataflow architecture encourages the design of analysis that are *composable* and *reusable*. Composable means that analyses can be easily structured as a combination of simple single-function operators. This design also makes it easy to reuse these operators across multiple analyses, saving developers from the burden of constantly having to re-understand low-level aspects of execution.

4.4 Caching and Indexing

Many analyses only need to look at small portions of the trace to extract the information they need. A good example is extracting the value of an argument for all calls to a specific function. It is sufficient to revisit the trace at all call sites and inspect the register or memory state to extract the argument values. Analyses could execute much faster if they had the ability to only read the relevant portions of a trace.

```
BBlk(2):
c01b0623: mov  $0x000000d0  -> %edx : R[edx]=000000d0
c01b0628: call 0xfffe7228 %esp -> %esp (%esp) : ST32[f755bea4]=c01b062d
          R[esp]=f755bea4 BR=c0197850
                                   Invoke (__kmalloc, 0xf755bea4)
BBlk(8):
c0197850: sub  $0x1c %esp -> %esp : R[esp]=f755be88
c0197853: cmp  %eax $0x00000800:
c0197858: mov  %ebx -> 0xc(%esp): ST32[f755be94]=ff
c019785c: mov  %esi -> 0x10(%esp): ST32[f755be98]=100
c0197860: mov  %edi -> 0x14(%esp): ST32[f755be9c]=f755bf0cc0197864:
          mov %ebp->0x18(%esp): ST32[f755bea0]=dfda0600
c0197868: mov  %edx -> 0x8(%esp) : ST32[f755be90]=d0
c019786c: jcc  0x00000099 : FL=00000287
...
BBlk(7):
c01978ce: mov  %ebx  -> %eax : R[eax]=dfcc5800
c01978d0: mov  0xc(%esp) -> %ebx : LD32[f755be94]=ff R[ebx]=000000ff
c01978d4: mov  0x10(%esp) -> %esi : LD32[f755be98]=100 R[esi]=00000100
c01978d8: mov  0x14(%esp) -> %edi : LD32[f755be9c]=f755bf0c R[edi]=f755bf0c
c01978dc: mov  0x18(%esp) -> %ebp : LD32[f755bea0]=dfda0600 R[ebp]=dfda0600
c01978e0: add  $0x1c %esp -> %esp : R[esp]=f755bea4
c01978e3: ret  %esp (%esp) -> %esp : LD32[f755bea4]=c01b062d R[esp]=f755bea8
          BR=c01b062d FL=00000292
                                   Return (0xf755bea4)
                                              Alloc (0xdfcc5800, 1024)
```

Figure 7. Reconstruction of execution semantics using progressively higher-level annotations.

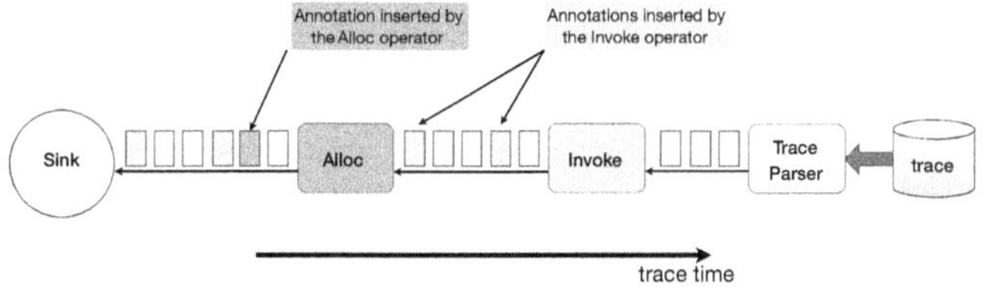

Figure 8. Operator configuration.

To efficiently support this sort of analysis, Tralfamadore operators can be configured to create persistent caches of the annotations they generate. Subsequent analyses can use cached annotations as indices to map annotations or annotation attributes to interesting positions in the trace. These positions can be used as starting points to examine a trace, or used to identify interesting slices of a trace, such as the range of a trace where a specific thread was running. Operators that support this mechanism export a query interface that lets analyses instantiate an operator that will produce the subset of annotations matching the query. This is conceptually similar to

Operator	Description
Trace Parser	Parses the raw trace file. Produces: ***BBlk****(pc, instructions, side effects)*, ***Event****(vector, error code, pc, side effects)*
Context	Identifies independent contexts of execution (threads, interrupts). Depends: ***BBlk****(side effect =* `store[TSS.esp0]` | *mnemonic =* `sysenter` | `iret` | ...*)*, ***Event**** Produces: ***Context****(act id, stack addr,* `Entry` | `Exit` | `Switch`*)*
Invoke	Identifies function call and return points. Depends: ***BBlk****(pc = function addr* | *instr.mnemonic =* `ret`*)* Produces: ***Invoke****(pc, stack pointer)*, ***Return****(stack pointer)*
Alloc	Tracks the allocation and release of objects on the heap. Depends: ***Context****, ***Invoke****, Produces: ***Alloc****(ptr, size, pc)*, ***Release****(ptr)*
MemTrace	Tracks memory access. Depends: ***BBlk****(side effect =* `load[*]` | `store[*]`*)* Produces: ***MemTrace****(pc, address, access size,* `R` | `W`*)*
HeapTrace	Tracks accesses to objects allocated on the heap. Depends: ***MemTrace****, ***Alloc**** Produces: ***HeapTrace****(pc, ptr, offsetm access size,* `R` | `W`*)*

Table 1. Some of the current library of streaming operators available in Tralfamadore.

a *select* operation in a relational database where a subset of the rows—those that match the selection criteria—are returned.

5. Operator Library

Whole-system analysis faces unique challenges in mapping CPU-level execution to source-level semantics. Our approach provides a framework in which new analyses can be composed from existing operators that refine low level trace annotations into progressively higher-level semantics. While our focus with the system to date has been in studying the Linux operating system on x86 hardware, we have also begun work on Windows support, as well as user-level analysis. Extending the system in these directions is largely a matter of developing new operators. Tralfamadore currently hosts a library of about twenty operators, a subset of which are described in Table 1.

Operators are intended to be standalone sections of code that embed a specific aspect of analysis. Lower-level operators include detailed knowledge about the hardware and how it is used by the OS, while higher-level operators encode details about how the OS behaves, for instance with regard to its heap management. The remainder of this section describes three of the more complex of the fundamental operators in additional detail.

5.1 Execution Contexts

One of the primary responsibilities of an operating system is to schedule independent threads of execution onto shared physical CPUs. Since the trace is a record of instructions at the CPU level, these threads of control will appear to be arbitrarily interleaved. Yet many modes of analysis (the simplest is call flow extraction) operate on single execution flows. Therefore, we provide a *Context* operator for demultiplexing the trace. Tracking contexts in operating systems kernels is challenging, due to the asynchronous, interrupt-driven environment in which they operate: a flow of execution may be suspended and resumed for a number of reasons, including explicit context switches, interrupts (which may be nested), and exceptions. Identifying these transitions requires an understanding of both the physical architecture and how a given OS uses that architecture in its implementation. Specifically, the *Context* operator needs to track three things: the start and end of interrupt and fault handlers, system calls, and the occurrence of context switches from one thread to another.

The execution of interrupt and exception handlers (including system calls that use software interrupts to enter the kernel) can be identified by Event annotations in the trace. At these points, the current flow of execution is suspended and control jumps to an event handler. An *iret* instruction marks the end of handler execution and the resumption of the original execution context. System calls may also be invoked through fast entry instructions that do not generate events; their boundaries are identified as pairs of *sysenter/sysexit* Instruction annotations in the stream.

There are multiple ways to identify software execution contexts, with different trade-offs. In order to pair a thread resumed by the operating system scheduler with its previously suspended execution the *Context* operator needs a mechanism to identify each thread in the system. One simple way to do this would be to track the invocation of the operating system stack switching routine such as `__switch_to` on Linux, using its argument to identify threads. We currently use a more generic approach (that works for both Linux and Windows) which is to track updates to the esp0 field of the Task State Segment (TSS). This field indicates the base address of the kernel stack for the task about to run. This address uniquely identifies a thread over its lifetime and thus serves as a suitable context identifier.

The *Context* operator tags each flow by emitting an annotation whenever a flow of execution is suspended or resumed (whether due to a software context switch or a hardware interrupt). The first attribute of the annotation is an activation ID that uniquely identifies a flow (such as the invocation of a system call or interrupt handler) over its lifetime. The second attribute is the base address of the kernel stack, which can be used to group all system calls executed by the same thread.

To deal with nested interrupts, the operator maintains a stack of live activations for each thread it has seen. When an interrupt occurs, the operator emits an annotation with a new activation ID and pushes that ID on the stack. When the handler terminates, the operator pops its stack and emits an annotation with the ID of the resumed activation. Similarly, on a software context switch, the operator emits an annotation indicating the activation and stack address of the resumed thread.

Analyses using annotations from the *Context* operator require no specific knowledge of Linux or the x86 architecture. They may simply use the annotations to identify the regions of trace that comprise a single activation or thread of execution.

5.2 Invocations

The Invoke operator produces annotations that simplify the tracking of call flow for downstream operators; compiler optimizations such as tail call elimination can make this challenging. The operator produces two annotations: *Invoke* and *Return*. The *Invoke* annotation includes the function being called and the value of the stack pointer at the time of the call. The *Return* annotation includes the value of the stack pointer just before the return address is consumed by a `ret` instruction. The stack pointer can be used as a key to pair matching function calls and returns. In the case of tail call optimization where a single `ret` instruction will unwind multiple calls, a *Return* annotation will match more than one *Invoke* annotation.

Inline functions cannot be tracked in this way, since they are not explicitly called. We do, however, provide limited support (restricted to control flow) for inline functions based on debugging information.

5.3 Allocations

The *Alloc* operator tracks the allocation of objects on the heap and issues annotations whenever an object is allocated or freed. It contains domain-specific knowledge of the allocation functions being used. The allocation annotation contains the address of the object, its size and the address of the caller to the allocation function.

The biggest difficulty with tracking allocations is that with most allocators the parameters used to determine the size — either the size itself or a pointer to a memory pool — are passed on invocation, but the pointer to the object is only available on return. The *Alloc* operator takes advantage of the stack pointer matching provided by the *Invoke* operator's annotations to match the object with its size.

5.4 Putting It Together: Heap Slicing

The figures in Section 3 were generated by extracting *heap slices* from a trace of a virtual machine running the Apache web server on Linux. Heap slicing is a new analysis that extracts the set of statements that have touched a set of heap objects between their allocation and release. It produces a representation of where and how these objects are used throughout their lifetime.

The goals of heap slicing are different than with program slicing [4, 36], a program analysis technique which extracts program statements that have affected the value of a variable at a specific point in a program. This set of statements, called a program slice, helps developers focus on the relevant portion of a program when trying to understand how and why a variable holds a certain value. The goal of heap slicing is more holistic as it is to provide a view of how an entire data-driven subsystem operates at runtime.

The inputs to heap slicing are a function and one of its arguments which should be a pointer to a heap object. The analysis executes in two passes over a trace. In the first pass, the value of the pointer is extracted at all points in time where the function is called. This pass uses the function index to only visit relevant call sites, skipping most of the trace. The (timestamp, pointer) tuples extracted in this first pass are cross-referenced with a heap allocation index to determine the allocation and release time for each pointer/heap object.

In the second pass, for every object, the analysis scans the trace from allocation to release to extract all accesses to the object throughout its lifetime. The result is an access trace for each object. The results are forwarded to the frontend where they are summarized in a tree, similar to the ones shown in Figure 3 and 4, where each access trace is inserted from the root down using longest prefix matching. The root of the tree corresponds to the allocation function and the leaf nodes are deallocation functions. A given analysis can produce more than one graph if the objects were allocated by more than one function.

This two pass approach is only possible with an offline framework such as Tralfamadore where multiple analyses or analysis passes can execute over the same persisted execution. From an execution point of view, the analysis effectively goes back in time from the point in time where the selected function is called to the point where the object is allocated. Heap slicing could be implemented in an online manner but such an implementation would be highly inefficient for two reasons. First, the analysis, unaware of where objects are allocated and released, would need to examine the entire execution. Analysis built with Tralfamadore can leverage indices to only look at sections of trace containing live objects. Second, it would have to track memory accesses to all heap objects, and then discard objects that were never manipulated by the function of interest. Tralfamadore only needs to track accesses to the set of objects that will actually be part of the slice, reducing the overhead of the analysis.

```
1  module HeapTraceOp  = struct
2
3   (* This operator acts as a filter,
4      removing all annotations not part of an object heap trace. *)
5
6   let rec next st () =
7     (* Pull the next annotation from the upstream operator *)
8     let a = st.m.M2Op.next () in
9     match a.Annot.attr with
10    | 'Alloc alloc -> (
11      st.live_obj <- add_to_live_obj st.live_obj alloc;
12      a
13    )
14    | 'Release rel -> (
15      st.live_obj <- del_from_live_obj st.live_obj rel;
16      if live_obj_is_empty st.live_obj then (
17        (* If there is no live obj, seek to the next allocation. *)
18        try st.m.M2Op.seek_1 () with EOF -> ()
19      );
20      a
21    )
22    | 'MemTrace mt -> (
23      (* If this memtrace annotation corresponds to an access to a live
24         heap object, produce a heap trace annotation. *)
25      try
26        (* Find the allocation matching the access *)
27        let alloc = find_in_live_obj st.live_obj mt.MemTrace.addr in
28        let off = Guest32.sub addr alloc.Alloc.base in
29        'HeapTrace { base = alloc.Alloc.base; off = off;
30                     sz = mt.MemTrace.sz; access = mt.MemTrace.access }
31      with Not_found -> next st ()
32    | _ -> next st ()
33
34  ...
35
36  end
```

Figure 9. HeapTrace operator.

Figure 9 shows the core of the *HeapTrace* operator which extracts the object access traces, skipping sections of trace without live objects. This example shows how an operator reuses existing operators to compose a new analysis. The operator writer needs not to be concerned with specific knowledge of the Linux kernel heap allocation functions or which x86 instruction touches memory. This knowledge is abstracted away by using the *Alloc* and *Release* annotations (Line 10 and 14 respectively) produced by the *Alloc* operator, and the *Memtrace* annotations (Line 22) produced by the *MemTrace* operator.

6. Example Applications

Tralfamadore preserves a complete execution as a data set in order to make it possible to explore it interactively in the same way that developers interrogate source repositories. To support this usage, and to demonstrate the types of analyses that Tralfamadore facilitates, we have built several applications on the platform. In this section, we present our prototype execution browser, which integrates interactive execution queries directly into a conventional source code browser using a simple and intuitive interface. We follow this with a series of more complex applications that highlight the development advantages of our data-driven processing architecture, in which simple pipelines of reusable operators combine to produce powerful analyses.

6.1 Understanding Execution

Reasonably simple applications of static analysis are often used to assist developers in navigating large bases of source code. Editors have "tag" facilities, and often also allow developers to use a search facility that is tied to a language-specific parser in order to find things like the declaration of a specific variable or the definition

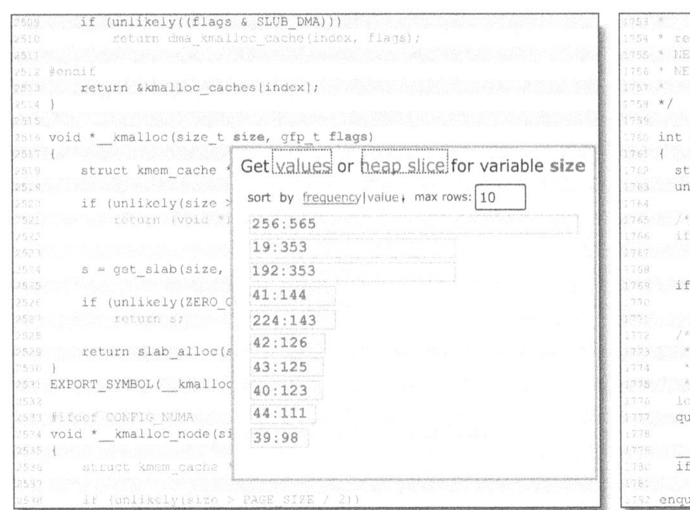

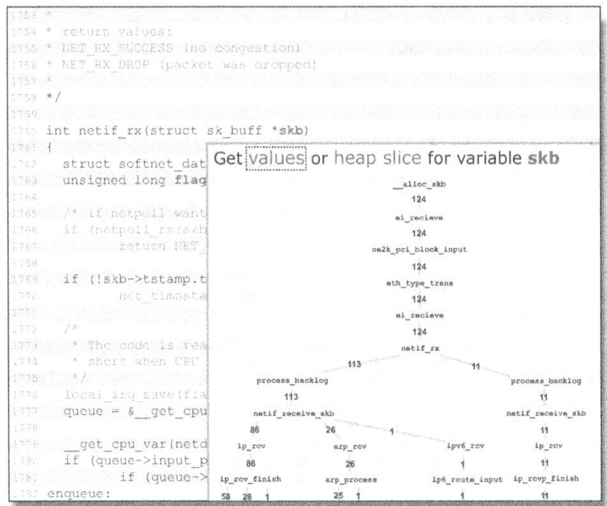

Figure 10. Live data value and heap slice analyses from the source understanding tool. (Section 6.1)

of some function. Dynamic techniques have also been applied to help developers understand how source behaves under execution by exposing details such as profiling and coverage information. With Tralfamadore, we felt that a significantly more powerful tool could be provided for understanding program execution. We have developed a web-based source navigator that maps interactive analysis tools directly onto the source code.

In a previous paper [18], we described an early prototype of this source navigator that maps binary trace information into source-level call and control flow graphs. With this initial support, a function in source can be annotated with a graph that shows the specific unique control flow paths that travel through it, and allows developers to choose between focusing on the common case, outliers, or unexecuted code, depending on their interest.

Figure 10 shows the interface provided by our source understanding tool for two new data-oriented analyses. From the source browser, a developer may select a function parameter and request a histogram of the values of that parameter across all calls to the function, or, in the case of pointers to heap objects, they may generate a data flow graph that summarizes all accesses to the set of objects passed to that function. Partial results are streamed into the browser over AJAX as soon as they become available, and the result set is continuously updated as the query is processed.

6.1.1 Argument value distribution

The left-hand side of Figure 10 shows an online query in which a user browsing the source to the Linux `__kmalloc` memory allocator has become curious about the size of allocation requests observed during a trace. She clicks on the `size` argument to the function and is presented with a pop-up window in which she can select from one of two variable queries. In this case, she chooses the *values* option. Immediately, a histogram appears showing the sizes observed in the trace. At the point seen in the figure, the query has been running for 1 second and shows that the most commonly requested object size so far is 256 bytes.

6.1.2 Heap Slicing

On the right of Figure 10 is a screen capture of a heap slicing query in progress (figures in Section 3 were generated by this tool and adjusted for presentation). In this case, the user has clicked on the `skb` parameter of the `netif_rx` function and chosen the *heap slicing* option. The heap slice of all packets passing through `netif_rx` begins to form, stabilizing within a few seconds.

This example extends recent work in visualizing data flow in systems code [23], by allowing the dynamic and *interactive* mapping of arbitrary objects in source to a graph illustrating the use of all instances of that object in actual execution. In the future, we hope to extend this tool to allow users to navigate execution by iteratively following this sort of graph across both control flow and data flow representations of execution.

6.2 Retroactive Assertions

The use of assertions is common practice when attempting to debug, understand, or otherwise validate assumptions about the way that a system is behaving. Unfortunately, they typically must be made *a priori*, either by compiling assert statements into source or inserting dynamic probes prior to running a system. VAssert [2] partly solves this problem by allowing assertions on applications running in a virtual machine to be validated during replay, but while they allow the evaluations of assertions to be deferred, the assertions themselves are no more powerful. We now consider the use of Tralfamadore to validate *retroactive assertions* that would be very difficult to write in the traditional style.

6.2.1 Ownership Violation

For simplicity and scalability, applications desire to use as little locking as possible. In Linux, for example, many functions assume that their objects are never accessed in interrupt context. They may use runtime assertions[3] to catch some violations, but it is difficult to be assured that all possible accesses have been guarded.

Tralfamadore makes it straightforward to validate whether such an assumption holds throughout the duration of a trace, and can additionally produce a detailed report about the violation. Here we present a simple *ownership* assertion that detects whenever an object is accessed by contexts other than the one in which it was allocated, which may be checked against all instances of a given object type within the trace. The algorithm is a refinement of the heap slicing algorithm presented in Section 6.1.2: Each object's lifetime is looked up from the allocation index, and the moment of allocation is then cross-referenced with the context index to identify the *allocation context*. The trace can then be scanned linearly from the time of allocation to the point where the object is freed. Whenever the object is touched, the *accessor context* is recorded. If the set of accessor contexts contains multiple

[3] BUG_ON(in_interrupt());

elements, then an ownership violation has occurred. If a violation is detected, a subsequent query can retrieve the necessary information to produce a graph showing the exact sequence of accesses that produced the violation overlayed with the control flow of both the *owner* and *violator*. Figure 11 shows a portion of the report produced by a test case we created, in which an *owner* thread creates an object, and a *violator* running as a timer interrupt handler accesses it. The sequence on the left is an abridged call trace of the owner context, and the one on the right is the call trace of the violator context. The chain of arrows between the two represents the sequence of accesses, including the violating access.

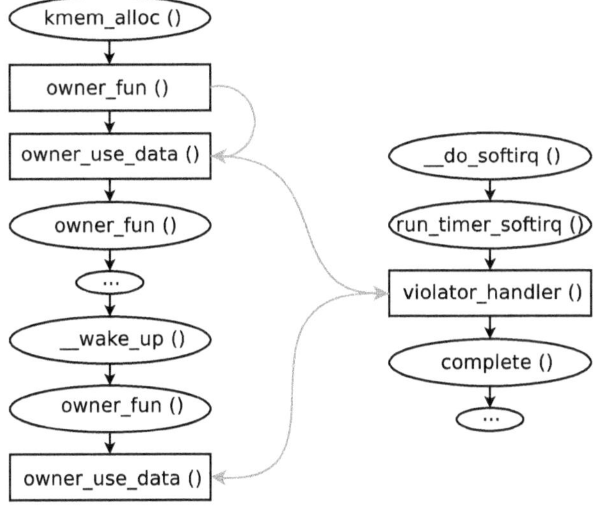

Figure 11. Ownership violation example

6.2.2 Stack Usage

Stack space in the kernel is at a premium: each thread of each process needs its own stack, and the address space is small. For this reason, Linux includes a compilation option to use 4K stacks instead of the default 8K. Unfortunately, stack usage is a highly dynamic property, depending on a combination of control and data (for example, a recursive function's stack usage can vary wildly depending on input). And so while the developers believe that 4K should suffice, and that it would allow many more threads, the default remains at 8K. The kernel developers are washing their hands of the problem, leaving it to the end user to decide whether to take the chance of stack corruption in exchange for better scalability, with no good idea of even how likely that corruption may be.

If the target workload is run under Tralfamadore, the actual amount of stack used can be easily measured. We constructed a simple query that measures the amount of stack in use whenever it changes. Running it on the `kernel` workload described in Section 7 produces the usage distribution shown in Figure 12. This reveals the exact moment at which the stack reaches its largest point (in this case, the maximum size of 2960 bytes was reached 14 times). A query for the call stack at that point returns the stack shown in Figure 13, showing that the cause of the high stack usage was a network interrupt being handled while the kernel was deep in the processing of a *sys_write* system call. Further inspection revealed that all 14 occurrences were at this location, due to the interrupt handler repeatedly processing a backlog of packets. This easily reveals the motivation for the decision of the Linux developers to enable a separate interrupt stack frame when the 4K stack option is enabled.

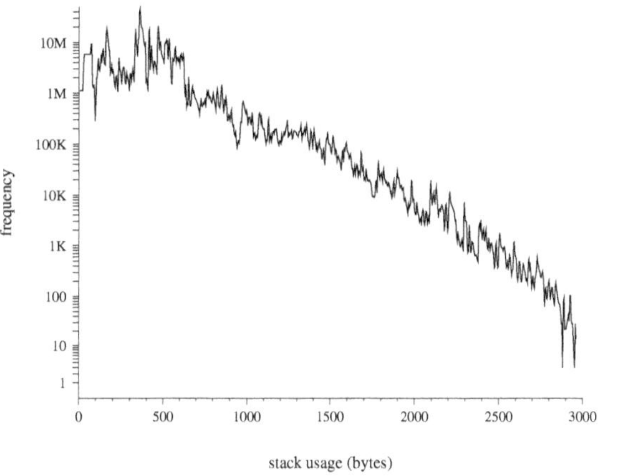

Figure 12. Distribution of stack sizes

```
sysenter_past_esp/sys_write/vfs_write/do_sync_write/
ext3_file_write/generic_file_aio_write/
__generic_file_aio_write_nolock/generic_file_buffered_write/
ext3_write_begin/block_write_begin/__block_prepare_write/
ext3_get_block/ext3_get_blocks_handle/ext3_new_blocks/
__ext3_journal_get_write_access/journal_get_write_access/
do_get_write_access/__get_free_pages/__alloc_pages/
get_page_from_freelist/common_interrupt/do_IRQ/irq_exit/
do_softirq/__do_softirq/net_rx_action/process_backlog/
netif_receive_skb/ip_rcv/ip_rcv_finish/ip_local_deliver/
ip_local_deliver_finish/tcp_v4_rcv/tcp_v4_do_rcv/
tcp_rcv_established/__tcp_push_pending_frames/tcp_transmit_skb/
ip_queue_xmit/ip_output/ip_finish_output/dev_queue_xmit/
__qdisc_run/pfifo_fast_dequeue
```

Figure 13. Maximum stack depth seen (kernel compile).

7. Evaluation

Tralfamadore approaches dynamic analysis in a manner that is dramatically different from previous systems and in which tools may access any point in execution history at any time. This comes with a cost: large amounts of fine-grained trace data must be collected, stored, and processed. In this section, we evaluate the practicality of this approach. First, we measure the overhead of taking and storing raw trace data. We then evaluate the cost of generating and storing trace indices used to speed up queries, and the degree to which they improve the speed and efficiency of various queries. We conclude with a consideration of the class of analyses for which Tralfamadore is currently suited and discuss how it might be evolved to serve a broader set of use cases.

7.1 Overheads of Trace Capture and Storage

Table 2 shows the overheads of trace collection for four different example workloads. *Kernel* is a minimal build of the Linux kernel which balances CPU and I/O, and exercises a variety of kernel services. *OS Boot* traces a virtual machine as it boots. *Postmark* is a standard file system benchmark. Finally, *apache* is a trace of 30 minutes of activity totalling 7981 requests on our departmental web server.

Each workload was run natively, then under virtualization using QEMU 0.9.1 and VMware Workstation 7.0, with and without tracing activated. The host was a 2.5GHz quad-core Xeon server with 16GB of RAM and a 1 TB 7200rpm SATA2 hard drive. Table 2 shows the effects of virtualization and tracing on total workload execution time, as well as the sizes of the traces produced (*Apache* measures request latency rather than total time, since the workload is bursty). QEMU traces are generated using the modifications described in Section 4.2, whereas VMware traces are event logs created using its deterministic logging feature. We include both the

	Native Linux	Qemu Base	Qemu Tracing	Log Size (Kernel)	Log Size (All)	VMware Base	VMware Tracing	Log Size (All)
Kernel	89 sec	1569 sec	7459 sec	101.64 GB	1991.01 GB	87 sec	88 sec	0.002 GB
OS Boot	38 sec	153 sec	549 sec	66.43 GB	128.31 GB	25 sec	31 sec	0.022 GB
Postmark	152 sec	332 sec	523 sec	274.54 GB	297.40 GB	237 sec	310 sec	0.014 GB
Apache	6.17ms	49.98ms	144.34ms	74.63 GB	80.06 GB	10.55ms	26.41ms	0.18 GB

Table 2. Tracing overheads for various workloads.

full size of the trace and the portion of it which represents kernel activity; the analyses we evaluate operate on the kernel component of the trace alone.

The storage requirements and workload performance overhead of direct tracing are high. However, both could be mitigated by using deterministic record-replay to capture execution, and expanding the log into a trace on demand [38]. The VMware columns in Table 2 show the considerable degree by which recording costs could be realistically reduced.

File	Size	Ratio
raw trace	101.6 GB	100%
Invoke index	2.2 GB	2.20%
Context index	324 MB	0.32%
Alloc index	12 MB	0.01%

Table 3. Index size relative to trace size (kernel).

Workload	Query	% trace (large)	% trace (small)
Postmark	Heap Slicing	0.01%	0.00%
	Arguments	0.23%	0.00%
Kernel	Heap Slicing	1.25%	0.02%
	Arguments	0.17%	0.06%
Apache	Heap Slicing	37.5%	0.01%
	Arguments	0.25%	0.00%

Table 4. Amount of trace read when using indices.

7.1.1 Indexing Performance

As shown in Table 2, the full trace grows very rapidly, to the point that scanning it directly can take considerable time. Fortunately, many trace operators only need to see a small amount of the trace, and can make use of indices to read only the relevant sections. Table 3 shows the relative size of the index to the trace for the most used operators in our operator library. As this table demonstrates, the size of the index is generally inversely proportional to the degree of semantic information it provides. This results from the fact that higher-level operators consume filtered information from the operators below them.

The cost of analysis is determined largely by the amount of physical trace that must be read. Table 4 measures the benefit of using indices in terms of the percentage of trace that an analysis must examine when the relevant indices are available (without indices, it would be necessary to read the entire trace). For each of the workloads described at the start of this section, we ran two heap slicing analyses and two argument value extraction queries. The large heap slicing analysis examines every TCP packet passing through the `tcp_v4_rcv` function, while the small only examines (relatively infrequent) ARP packets passing through `arp_rcv`. Similarly, the two functions chosen for argument value extraction were the common `kmem_cache_alloc`, which is involved in most object allocations, and the relatively rare `mmap_region`. Because the heap slicing analysis must scan the physical trace from the time an object of interest is allocated until it is freed, and because in the Apache workload there is almost always a live TCP packet, the heap slicing query consumed a large amount of physical trace even when indexed. Every other query consumed a tiny fraction of the total trace, completing quickly.

7.1.2 Evaluation Summary

In our current prototype, there is no denying that traces are large and slow to generate. But the premise of Tralfamadore is to decouple trace generation from analysis, and we find that having done so, analysis itself performs well. Because Tralfamadore can aggressively reuse trace data, we are relatively unconcerned with the space required to store it. We also believe that trace-based analysis makes it much easier to develop new analyses, since they can be written in the author's choice of language and with a full complement of libraries, and that being able to freely seek within a trace allows a more natural style of query expression. Furthermore, persistent traces allow users to break the expensive and delicate cycle of hypothesis, instrumentation, execution, and analysis which is generally used for query refinement.

However, it is clear that the ability to collect and analyze traces more easily and with lower overhead would make the techniques described in this paper apply to a broader range of problems. As discussed in Section 4.2, a natural optimization would be to use deterministic logging during the recording phase. The full log could then be treated as a cache that could be regenerated when necessary using replay. We believe that this approach would allow operators to rapidly create the data needed to populate their indices. From this point, some analyses could proceed largely based on the contents of their indices, and use replay to materialize only the relevant regions of the complete trace, on demand. Such an approach could facilitate the processing of much larger amounts of trace.

8. Related Work

As described in Section 2.2, the traces recorded with Tralfamadore are complete, meaning that analyses based on these traces have access to the register and memory state on every instruction boundary. This section compares Tralfamadore with other frameworks that provide access to the same level of information. This includes traditional dynamic binary instrumentation (DBI) frameworks such as Pin [20], and replay based frameworks such as Aftersight [10].

Aftersight [10] proposes to decouple dynamic analysis from execution by using deterministic record-replay to efficiently record the execution of virtual machine and replay this execution in an whole-system emulator (QEMU). Like Tralfamadore, Aftersight supports whole-system or kernel-level offline analyses, but does not provide an instrumentation API, forcing users to directly embed their instrumentation and analysis into QEMU's micro-operations.

SimOS [32] explores the idea of using a machine simulator to study the execution of entire systems. Similar to Tralfamadore, SimOS proposes the use of annotations to capture events at a higher semantic level. As with Tralfamadore, annotations can be recursive (annotations can be built from other annotations).

SimOS can operate in two modes: emulation mode which uses dynamic binary translation and accurate mode which executes the system under a cycle-accurate simulator. Analyses performed in emulation mode execute in an online manner, and do not provide the benefits of offline analysis. Analyses performed in accurate mode may be repeatable if the simulation is deterministic but the overheads in this mode are much higher than with Tralfamadore, ranging between 180 and 6400× for a uniprocessor simulation [31].

Although analyses built with SimOS are composable, SimOS does not address the issue of reusability. Also, SimOS does not support indices to efficiently navigate execution, and therefore does not provide mechanisms such as annotation caching to deal with stateful analyses, as described in Section 4.4.

Traditional binary instrumentation frameworks are fundamentally different than Tralfamadore. These are online tools and are "stuck in time." They are limited to analyzing a program as it executes instead of analyzing an execution. Dynamic binary instrumentation frameworks such as Pin [20] and Valgrind [24] use process-level dynamic binary translation to add instrumentation to a program as it executes. Because both the analysis and the target program execute in the same address space, analysis writers are forced to use clever techniques to avoid clashing with the target program. This technique does not require explicit modifications to the program being analyzed but it is not completely transparent because it may cause memory conflicts between the program being analyzed and the analysis.

These tools are unable to instrument and analyze the execution of operating system code. PinOS [7] addresses this issue by extending Pin with the ability to do whole-system analysis. Because it uses virtualization, most of the instrumentation framework sits outside of the system being analyzed but the instrumentation code and data still need to be embedded within the system, potentially causing memory clashes as with Pin and Valgrind.

JIFL [25] proposes to embed a DBI within the Linux kernel. This approach allows adding arbitrary dynamic instrumentation to the Linux kernel but requires the operating system to be explicitly modified to add support for a just-in-time compiler.

Nirvana [6] is a user-level offline dynamic analysis framework based on a variant of record-replay. Instead of explicitly logging all the external inputs and non-deterministic events, Nirvana captures this information implicitly by logging the complete register state after kernel-to-user transitions and non-deterministic instructions such as `rdtsc`, and logging all values read from memory by the processor while executing.

Nirvana provides an instrumentation API but, unlike Tralfamadore, it does not support capturing and analyzing the execution of operating system code. Nirvana can record and analyze unmodified programs, but it is not completely transparent. Like Pin and Valgrind, the Nirvana execution recorder is embedded in the address space of the program being recorded, which can cause memory conflicts. PinPlay [27] extends Pin to support replay-based offline analysis in a manner similar to Nirvana, and uses a software-simulated cache coherency protocol to deterministically replay the execution of a process on a multi-processor machine. PinPlay provides the same level of transparency as Pin.

Bitblaze [33] is an online whole-system binary analysis framework based on QEMU. Like Tralfamadore and Aftersight, Bitblaze analyzes execution at the processor level which provides a transparent approach to dynamic analysis, and support for the analysis of operating system code. Because Bitblaze is an online framework, it is also "stuck in time" and can only analyze programs as they execute.

Time-travelling virtual machines [15] use deterministic replay to allow a debugger attached to a Linux kernel to step execution backwards as well as forwards. VMware Workstation now includes a record-replay facility [38] that can be used for replay debugging [3] of recorded software. Time-travelling virtual machines support the offline analysis of operating systems but the interface provided to analyze execution is limited to debugging contexts (e.g., breakpoints, watchpoints, etc.)

Omniscient debugging [1, 8, 19, 29] is an approach to debugging where the execution of a program is stored and indexed using techniques borrowed from program slicing [36], allowing debugging to work "backwards in time." All existing implementations of omniscient debugging are limited to user-space programs and provide an interface limited to debugging.

Whole Execution Traces (WET) [39] is a generic trace format with the same completeness properties as traces collected with Tralfamadore. WET traces embed control and data flow information in the trace to provide efficient backward navigation. This information could be added to the Tralfamadore trace format to simplify going backward to get register and memory definitions.

8.1 Deterministic Record-Replay

As discussed in Section 4.2, it is possible to use deterministic virtual machine record-replay to capture a lightweight event log of a running system, which can be reconstituted into a full trace during a later replay phase [38]. Tralfamadore could use this complimentary technique to reduce the overhead on execution incurred by the trace collection facility. The overhead of this approach are very low for single core systems. Recording multicore execution is substantially more challenging due to the need to capture memory races. The overhead can be substantial for workloads that exhibit a large amount of shared memory communication. Fortunately, deterministic record-replay for multicore is an active area of research and recent work both at the software [26, 34], and at the hardware [13, 22, 37] level aim to address this issue. Just as in the single processor case, these emerging techniques will be usable to generate detailed traces of multicore workloads.

8.2 Offline and Whole-System Analyses

TaintBochs [9] uses a mix of online taint tracking and offline trace-based analysis to study the lifetime of sensitive information such as passwords. TaintBochs uses a modified version of the Bochs emulator [17] to record traces that contain all writes to memory and all updates to a specific subset of registers. One could use Tralfamadore to also implement the taint propagation offline, using a recorded execution to experiment with different taint propagation policies.

Dataflow tomography [23] proposes the use of whole-system taint tracking as a tool to understand complex computer systems. This project is complementary to Tralfamadore, meaning that Tralfamadore could be used to implement the various taint policies described in the paper. Using Tralfamadore would have provided the authors with the benefits of deterministic analysis, in addition to using a high-level language instead of dealing directly with QEMU's dynamic binary translation engine.

Introvirt [14] proposes to use virtual machine deterministic replay to retroactively detect the presence of an intrusion. Introvirt is the original source of inspiration for the idea of retroactive assertions described in Section 6.2. While Introvirt checks are expressed at the source level, Tralfamadore retroactive assertions are written as binary analyses and can validate assertions difficult to express at the source level such as detecting a stack overflow.

8.3 Querying Execution

Several projects have explored the notion of querying program execution, either by providing an explicit query interface to the end user or using machine learning to discover execution patterns. Two recent projects from the programming languages community, relational queries over program traces [12], and the program query language PQL [21], have proposed query interfaces to allow developers to search for interesting aspects of program behavior. The scalable omniscient debugging project [29] also explored query interfaces to assist in navigation. A suitable query interface would be an excellent tool for interacting with traced execution. These query languages are designed around specific language runtimes and are not designed to query operating system execution. They operate at a higher level and rely on runtime information provided by the operating system or the language runtime. Tralfamadore analyses execution at the hardware level below the operating system and needs to explicitly reconstruct this information.

9. Conclusions and Future Work

We believe that developers (especially kernel developers) would benefit greatly from being able to explore actual program execution as easily as they can navigate source. To that end, we have built a platform for recording execution of an entire machine as a persistent object, and facilities for easily constructing complex and powerful dynamic analyses from a library of simple, reusable components. We have demonstrated several applications of this system, including an interactive source-level execution browser with interfaces for both control and data flow, and a variety of retroactive assertions against the behavior of an executing system.

The overheads associated with our approach seem high compared to traditional dynamic analysis, but they can be amortized over large numbers of queries. Additionally, trace-based analysis avoids the difficulties of reproducing machine state when performing cyclical analysis, and provides a much richer and more convenient environment for writing interactive dynamic analysis tools. Our evaluation has demonstrated that it is practical to capture and analyze complete traces of kernel activity for reasonable periods of time, including workloads such as kernel compilation, OS boots, and samples of server workloads. Further, once recorded, it is possible to perform highly interactive analyses of these workloads, often receiving complex answers about a control and data flow within a matter of seconds.

Tralfamadore is still in its infancy. While the system already represents a considerable effort, spanning four years and contributions from a group of six graduate students, many challenges remain. We are in the process of releasing a hosted version of the system that allows developers to analyze current and historical versions of the Linux kernel. To address performance challenges and scale, the system is being extended to parallelize and dispatch analysis to a cluster of physical hosts. Once this framework is in place, we hope to explore how Tralfamadore can be used to compare execution across multiple versions of software, which we hope will aid in identifying and diagnosing performance challenges and helping developers to reproduce and identify root-causes for software failures.

Acknowledgments

We thank the VEE reviewers for their insightful feedback and for accepting the paper for publication. We also thank many of our peers, including Paul Barham, Herbert Bos, Steve Gribble, Steven Hand, Rebecca Isaacs, and Timothy Roscoe, for being supportive and encouraging over the course of this work. We acknowledge the graduate students in CS538W 2010 ("Execution Mining") for suffering through project assignments on an early version of the system and helping to find and fix bugs.

As some previous reviewers have pointed out, the Tralfamadore project has involved quite a bit of *engineering*: while many of the techniques used by "Tralf" are well understood, tying together the necessary pieces to perform trace collection, parsing, instruction analysis, as well as source-level interactions through DWARF and symbol files involved a lot more effort than we imagined at the beginning of the project, despite considerable experience in underestimating such things!

References

[1] C/C++ trace-based debugger based on chronicle and eclipse. http://code.google.com/p/chronomancer/.

[2] Vassert programming guide. http://www.vmware.com/pdf/ws65_vassert_programming.pdf.

[3] Replay debugging on linux. http://www.vmware.com/pdf/ws7_replay_linux_technote.pdf.

[4] H. Agrawal and J. R. Horgan. Dynamic program slicing. In *PLDI '90*.

[5] F. Bellard. QEMU, a fast and portable dynamic translator. In *USENIX Annual Technical Conference*, 2005.

[6] S. Bhansali, W.-K. Chen, S. de Jong, A. Edwards, R. Murray, M. Drinić, D. Mihočka, and J. Chau. Framework for instruction-level tracing and analysis of program executions. In *VEE '06*.

[7] P. P. Bungale and C.-K. Luk. Pinos: a programmable framework for whole-system dynamic instrumentation. In *Virtual execution environments*, 2007. ISBN 978-1-59593-630-1.

[8] J.-D. Choi, B. P. Miller, and R. H. B. Netzer. Techniques for debugging parallel programs with flowback analysis. *ACM Transactions on Programming Languages and Systems*, 13, 1991. URL http://doi.acm.org/10.1145/115372.115324.

[9] J. Chow, B. Pfaff, T. Garfinkel, K. Christopher, and M. Rosenblum. Understanding data lifetime via whole system simulation. In *USENIX Security Symposium*, 2004. URL http://portal.acm.org/citation.cfm?id=1251375.1251397.

[10] J. Chow, T. Garfinkel, and P. M. Chen. Decoupling dynamic program analysis from execution in virtual environments. In *USENIX Annual Technical Conference*, 2008.

[11] G. W. Dunlap, S. T. King, S. Cinar, M. A. Basrai, and P. M. Chen. Revirt: enabling intrusion analysis through virtual-machine logging and replay. In *Operating Systems Design and Implementation*, 2002.

[12] S. Goldsmith, R. O'Callahan, and A. Aiken. Relational queries over program traces. In *Object-Oriented Programming, Systems, Languages, and Applications*, 2005.

[13] D. R. Hower and M. D. Hill. Rerun: Exploiting episodes for lightweight memory race recording. In *International Symposium on Computer Architecture*, 2008. URL http://dx.doi.org/10.1109/ISCA.2008.26.

[14] A. Joshi, S. T. King, G. W. Dunlap, and P. M. Chen. Detecting past and present intrusions through vulnerability-specific predicates. In *Symposium on Operating Systems Principles*, 2005. URL http://doi.acm.org/10.1145/1095810.1095820.

[15] S. T. King, G. W. Dunlap, and P. M. Chen. Debugging operating systems with time-traveling virtual machines. In *USENIX Annual Technical Conference*, 2005.

[16] E. Kohler, R. Morris, B. Chen, J. Jannotti, and F. M. Kaashoek. The Click modular router. *ACM Transactions on Computer Systems*, 2000.

[17] K. P. Lawton. Bochs: A portable PC emulator for unix/x. *Linux Journal*. ISSN 1075-3583.

[18] G. Lefebvre, B. Cully, M. J. Feeley, N. C. Hutchinson, and A. Warfield. Tralfamadore: Unifying source code and execution experience (short paper). In *EuroSys*, 2009.

[19] B. Lewis. Debugging backwards in time. In *Workshop on Automated Debugging*, 2003.

[20] C.-K. Luk, R. Cohn, R. Muth, H. Patil, A. Klauser, G. Lowney, S. Wallace, V. J. Reddi, and K. Hazelwood. Pin: building customized program analysis tools with dynamic instrumentation. In *Programming Language Design and Implementation*, 2005.

[21] M. Martin, B. Livshits, and M. S. Lam. Finding application errors and security flaws using pql: a program query language. In *Object-Oriented Programming, Systems, Languages, and Applications*, 2005.

[22] P. Montesinos, L. Ceze, and J. Torrellas. DeLorean: Recording and deterministically replaying shared-memory multiprocessor execution efficiently. In *International Symposium on Computer Architecture*, 2008. URL http://dx.doi.org/10.1109/ISCA.2008.36.

[23] S. Mysore, B. Mazloom, B. Agrawal, and T. Sherwood. Understanding and visualizing full systems with data flow tomography. In *Architectural Support for Programming Languages and Operating Systems*, 2008.

[24] N. Nethercote and J. Seward. Valgrind: a framework for heavyweight dynamic binary instrumentation. In *Programming Language Design and Implementation*, 2007.

[25] M. Olszewski, K. Mierle, A. Czajkowski, and A. D. Brown. JIT instrumentation: a novel approach to dynamically instrument operating systems. In *EuroSys*, 2007. URL http://doi.acm.org/10.1145/1272996.1273000.

[26] S. Park, Y. Zhou, W. Xiong, Z. Yin, R. Kaushik, K. H. Lee, and S. Lu. PRES: probabilistic replay with execution sketching on multiprocessors. In *Proceedings of the ACM SIGOPS 22nd symposium on Operating systems principles*, SOSP '09, pages 177–192, New York, NY, USA, 2009. ACM. ISBN 978-1-60558-752-3. doi: http://doi.acm.org/10.1145/1629575.1629593. URL http://doi.acm.org/10.1145/1629575.1629593.

[27] H. Patil, C. Pereira, M. Stallcup, G. Lueck, and J. Cownie. PinPlay: a framework for deterministic replay and reproducible analysis of parallel programs. In *Code Generation and Optimization*, 2010. URL http://doi.acm.org/10.1145/1772954.1772958.

[28] V. Paxson. Bro: a system for detecting network intruders in real-time. *Computer Networks*, 31(23–24), 1999.

[29] G. Pothier, E. Tanter, and J. Piquer. Scalable omniscient debugging. In *Object-Oriented Programming, Systems, Languages, and Applications*, 2007.

[30] F. Reiss, K. Stockinger, K. Wu, A. Shoshani, and J. M. Hellerstein. Enabling real-time querying of live and historical stream data. In *Scientific and Statistical Database Management*, 2007.

[31] M. Rosenblum, S. A. Herrod, E. Witchel, and A. Gupta. Complete computer system simulation: The SimOS approach. *IEEE Parallel and Distributed Technology*, 3, 1995. URL http://dx.doi.org/10.1109/88.473612.

[32] M. Rosenblum, E. Bugnion, S. Devine, and S. A. Herrod. Using the SimOS machine simulator to study complex computer systems. *ACM Transactions on Modeling and Computer Simulation*, 7, 1997. URL http://doi.acm.org/10.1145/244804.244807.

[33] D. Song, D. Brumley, H. Yin, J. Caballero, I. Jager, M. G. Kang, Z. Liang, N. James, P. Poosankam, and P. Saxena. BitBlaze: A new approach to computer security via binary analysis. In *International Conference on Information Systems Security*, 2008. doi: http://dx.doi.org/10.1007/978-3-540-89862-7_1. URL http://dx.doi.org/10.1007/978-3-540-89862-7_1.

[34] K. Veeraraghavan, D. Lee, B. Wester, J. Ouyang, P. M. Chen, J. Flinn, and S. Narayanasamy. DoublePlay: parallelizing sequential logging and replay. In *Proceedings of the sixteenth international conference on Architectural support for programming languages and operating systems*, ASPLOS '11, pages 15–26, New York, NY, USA, 2011. ACM. ISBN 978-1-4503-0266-1. doi: http://doi.acm.org/10.1145/1950365.1950370. URL http://doi.acm.org/10.1145/1950365.1950370.

[35] K. Vonnegut. *Slaughterhouse Five*. Delacorte, 1969. ISBN 0-385-31208-3.

[36] M. Weiser. Program slicing. In *International Conference on Software Engineering*, 1981.

[37] M. Xu, R. Bodik, and M. D. Hill. A "flight data recorder" for enabling full-system multiprocessor deterministic replay. In *International Symposium on Computer Architecture*, 2003.

[38] M. Xu, V. Malyugin, J. Sheldon, G. Venkitachalam, and B. Weissman. Retrace: Collecting execution trace with virtual machine deterministic replay. In *Modeling, Benchmarking and Simulation*, 2007.

[39] X. Zhang and R. Gupta. Whole execution traces and their applications. *ACM Transactions on Architecture and Code Optimization*, 2, 2005. URL http://doi.acm.org/10.1145/1089008.1089012.

DDGacc: Boosting Dynamic DDG-based Binary Optimizations through Specialized Hardware Support

Demos Pavlou[†,1] Enric Gibert Fernando Latorre Antonio Gonzalez[†]

Intel Barcelona Research Center (IBRC) - Intel Labs

[†]Department of Computer Architecture, Universitat Politècnica de Catalunya

{demos.pavlou, enric.gibert.codina, fernando.latorre, antonio.gonzalez}@intel.com

Abstract

Dynamic Binary Translators (DBT) and Dynamic Binary Optimization (DBO) by software are used widely for several reasons including performance, design simplification and virtualization. However, the software layer in such systems introduces non-negligible overheads which affect performance and user experience. Hence, reducing DBT/DBO overheads is of paramount importance. In addition, reduced overheads have interesting collateral effects in the rest of the software layer, such as allowing optimizations to be applied earlier. A cost-effective solution to this problem is to provide hardware support to speed up the primitives of the software layer, paying special attention to automate DBT/DBO mechanisms and leave the heuristics to the software, which is more flexible.

In this work, we have characterized the overheads of a DBO system using DynamoRIO implementing several basic optimizations. We have seen that the computation of the Data Dependence Graph (DDG) accounts for 5%-10% of the execution time. For this reason, we propose to add hardware support for this task in the form of a new functional unit, called DDGacc, which is integrated in a conventional pipeline processor and is operated through new ISA instructions. Our evaluation shows that DDGacc reduces the cost of computing the DDG by 32x, which reduces overall execution time by 5%-10% on average and up to 18% for applications where the DBO optimizes large code footprints.

Categories and Subject Descriptors B.8.2 [*Hardware*]: Performance and Reliability—Performance Analysis and Design Aids

General Terms Algorithms, Design, Performance

Keywords Co-designed processors; hardware acceleration; dynamic binary optimization; start-up overhead.

1. Introduction

Dynamic Binary Translation (DBT) and Dynamic Binary Optimization (DBO) by software are related techniques that have been applied (and will still be applied) for a long time for portability, backward compatibility, performance, design simplification, and virtualization, among others. DBT and DBO can be applied at different levels [22], ranging from user-level virtual machines (DynamoRIO [5], Dynamo [3], Intel's IA-32 Execution Layer [4], Java Virtual Machines [12]) to whole system virtual machines (co-designed virtual machines like Transmeta Crusoe [11], Daisy [7], BOA [18], etc.). In all these types of virtual machines a software layer (henceforth, the optimizer) is responsible to dynamically analyse code generated for a specific source ISA and translate it to a target ISA by applying several transformations and/or optimizations (the source and target ISAs may be the same). The resulting translated/optimized version of the code is often cached for reuse in a code cache.

The software layer incurs overheads since the processor spends a non-negligible amount of cycles in the dynamic process of transforming a piece of code into another, which does not allow the emulated program or system to make progress. Such overheads impact directly the overall performance of the system. However, overall performance is not the only important metric. For example, although overall overheads may be small once an application has been executed, start-up or reactive overheads may not. Start-up overheads refer to the overheads that are paid until the system reaches the steady state, where the vast majority of the executed code comes from the translated/optimized code cache. On the other hand, reactive overheads are caused by re-translation and re-optimization of regions of code that have been evicted from the translation cache, especially in the case of a multiprogrammed environment with shared translation cache. Start-up and reactive overheads are related and have an impact on another important metric: responsiveness, which in turn, affects user experience [10]. Thus, reducing the DBT/DBO overheads is of paramount importance. Furthermore, reducing the overheads has interesting collateral effects in the design of the optimizer, such as: (i) optimizations may be applied earlier or eagerly, (ii) more expensive optimizations that were discarded previously may now be applied, (iii) simpler code cache management algorithms may be employed, among others.

A key observation of DBT/DBO systems is that the software layer goes through a set of common primitives despite the level at which it operates. In that respect, the optimizer will among other things: (i) profile the code in order to detect hot regions, (ii) build regions, (iii) decode instructions, (iv) optimize regions, (v) code scheduling, (vi) code caching etc. Note that the aforementioned tasks do not need to be executed necessarily in this strict order.

In this work we characterized the overheads of a DBT/DBO system that performs several basic optimizations. From our study, we have observed that building the Data Dependence Graph (DDG) is among the most costly operations. The primary sources of overhead in a DBT/DBO system are instruction decoding, software profiling

[1] The presented work was completed while Demos Pavlou was a Research assistant at Universitat Politécnica de Catalunya.

VEE'12, March 3–4, 2012, London, England, UK.

and code cache. Hu et al. [10] attack the problem of instruction decoding, Merten et al. [15] propose hardware to do profiling and Hazelwood et al. [8] propose effective code cache management algorithms. In this paper, we propose to use specific hardware support to reduce the costs of building the DDG. We believe that providing specialized hardware to speedup the optimizer is the most effective solution. This is especially true in system virtual machines, in which the software layer is always executed regardless of the host applications being emulated/optimized.

In this paper, we define and evaluate DDGacc, a new functional unit, which enhances the process of computing the DDG. Computing the DDG is mainly necessary for performing a good instruction scheduling algorithm. Although we envision DDGacc to be more useful in system virtual machines, it is generic enough to be applied to a user virtual machine as well (it is mainly a matter of making the interface visible to the user). In addition, we have paid special attention to devote specialized hardware to automatize the DBT/DBO mechanisms, and leave the DBT/DBO policies to the optimizer. In this respect, the proposed hardware computes the DDG, while the heuristics to perform good instruction scheduling are left to the software layer. This is the key in order to be able to evolve/improve the optimizer over time and/or provide different optimizer configurations to different customers.

In particular, we have extended DynamoRIO with a client that applies a set of optimizations whenever a hot region is detected and a trace is created. This set consists of an algorithm for the creation of the DDG, dead code removal (DCR) and redundant load elimination (RLE). We measured the overheads introduced by such optimizations and we observed that approximately 5%-10% of the total time was spent on optimizing hot regions. The most costly optimization was the creation of the DDG which accounted for 32% of the optimization overhead. To tackle this, we propose and evaluate a hardware accelerator that provides support for the software DBO for building the DDG. Our studies show that the cost of the algorithm is reduced by 32x, using an in order processor. This is translated into an average improvement between 5% and 10% on average depending on the optimization threshold.

The rest of the paper is organized as follows. Section 2 presents the experimental framework used throughout the paper. In section 3 the overheads of the baseline DBO are exposed and characterized. The hardware accelerator we propose is presented in section 4. DDGacc is evaluated in section 5. In section 6, we discuss related work and concluding remarks are given in section 7.

2. Experimental framework

In this section we describe the DBO infrastructure we used for our studies as well as our evaluation methodology.

2.1 DBO Infrastructure

As mentioned before, we envision DDGacc to be used mainly by co-designed VMs. However, to the best of our knowledge, there is not a single public and extensible tool to perform research on co-designed VMs. Since the proposed solution can also be used by user-level VMs, we have used DynamoRIO [5], a state-of-the-art x86 user-level binary analyzer to conduct our experiments. DynamoRIO is a dynamic instrumentation tool that allows runtime code manipulation on any part of the program. It provides an interface for building dynamic tools that can be used for optimization among others. It is in fact a process VM which takes control of the application and translates basic block by basic block at the beginning. When a basic block is determined to be hot, meaning it reached a predefined threshold, a trace is generated by packing together several BBs based on the profiling information gathered during the so far execution. Traces are single-entry multiple-exit code sequences. Translated basic blocks and traces are cached in a code cache for reuse.

Table 1. Benchmarks

Benchmark	Input Size
SPEC CPU2006	Ref
Gnome Calculator	Application Start
OpenOffice Writer	Application Start
OpenOffice Calc	Application Start

For our study, we implemented a tool that applies optimizations whenever a new trace is created. Specifically, we first create the data dependence graph (DDG) and do some preparation for memory aliasing by analyzing load and store instructions. Then, we apply dead code removal (DCR) and redundant load elimination (RLE). DCR and RLE are quite traditional algorithms in the context of DBO since their overhead is small and can give significant performance benefits when applied to large regions such as the traces. On the other hand, the creation of the DDG introduces high overhead because of its complexity and large data structures that are traversed during the creation. Critical optimizations though, like instruction scheduling and hoisting, depend on the DDG creation for their effectiveness. The implemented algorithm is based on [16].

2.2 Evaluation methodology

For the evaluation of the overheads of the DBO we used the functional model of Simics to collect execution traces. The emulated machine uses an x86 processor based on Pentium4 and runs Fedora Core 5. The linux process tracker provided by Simics was used to isolate the dynamic instruction stream of the selected application (the application running under the control of DynamoRIO) and we used hooks in order to mark the code sections of interest and be able to distinguish them in the dynamic stream.

For this evaluation we picked two different types of application suites that cover the two scenarios a dynamic binary optimizer typically faces. On the one hand, we selected SPEC CPU2006 [1] suite as an example of applications with small number of static instructions with respect to the number of executed dynamic instructions (30.3M dynamic/static). Dynamic binary optimizers are very effective on these applications because any overhead produced on the optimization of a static instruction is easily amortized since this instruction is executed very often. On the other hand, we picked GnomeCalculator, OpenOffice Writer and Calc as an example of applications with large number of static instructions with respect to the dynamic number of executed instructions. This latter scenario is complex for dynamic binary optimizers because overheads spent on optimizing static instructions are sometimes not amortized incurring in poor performance. The set of applications is summarized by Table 1.

For all the benchmarks, the first 300 million instructions are being ignored in order to avoid completely the initialization phase of DynamoRIO, as well as some of the applications initialization routines. Then, we split the execution of each application into chunks of 1 billion instructions and we generate a trace for the odd chunks so that we can analyze the behavior of DynamoRIO for different phases of the applications. In total we collect the traces for 5 1-billion instruction chunks for each benchmark covering in total the first 9 billion instruction of the application.

For the timing evaluation, we implemented an x86 trace simulator which assumes a simple in-order processor. The configuration used is summarized in Table 2. We assume a perfect instruction cache due to constraints in the simulation infrastructure. The cache structures and the branch predictor used are based on the ones provided with SimpleScalar [2].

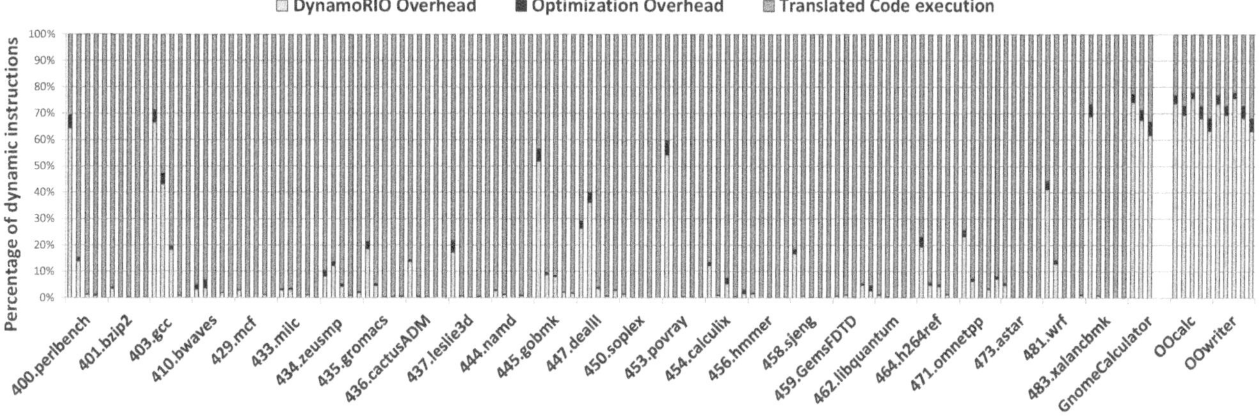

Figure 1. Dynamic instruction breakdown including DynamoRIO overhead. Each application has 5 assosiated bars, one for each 1 billion instruction chunk.

Table 2. Timing simulator configuration

Issue Width	2
Issue Queue Entries	16
Address Calculation Units	1
Simple Arithmetic Units	2
Complex Arithmetic Units	2
Branch Predictor	2K entries correlating
BTB	256 entries, 4-way
L1 Data Cache	64KB, 64B block size 4-way
L1 Data Cache latency	1 cycle
L2 Cache	512KB, 128B block size 8-way
L2 Cache latency	10 cycles
DTLB	256 entries 8-way
DTLB miss penalty	100 cycles
Memory latency	100 cycles

3. Overhead characterization

In this section we discuss the dynamic instruction breakdown of the benchmarks under DynamoRIO with the optimizing tool.

A complete breakdown is shown in Figure 1. Each bar represents one of the selected 1 billion dynamic instruction chunks. The instructions are grouped into three main categories. The first one is "DynamoRIO overhead" and it includes the process of creating basic blocks and traces, as well as the management of the code caches and the client tool. This overhead is quite big due to the fact that DynamoRIO is implemented as a generic tool that provides a rich interface to enable the user to build his/her own client. Such overheads are dominated by the insertion of callouts/trampolines, and a rather complex instruction decoding and representation in a generic and flexible intermediate language. The second one is "Optimization overhead" which includes all the instructions that correspond to the optimization process. Notice that a more detailed breakdown is presented later for this category since it is our main focus. Finally, the category "Translated code execution" represents the instructions executed from the code cache.

It is interesting to notice that most of the SPEC CPU2006 benchmarks share the same characteristics as expected. The biggest overhead is encountered at the beginning of the application, specifically in the first chunk and sometimes the second. This is justified by the high repetition of a kernel loop. Over time, the overhead introduced by the DBO is amortized.

In contradiction, for large applications like GnomeCalculator, OOcalc and OOwriter, the DBO incurs high overhead throughout the whole execution. This kind of applications have abundant static code which exceeds the optimizations threshold, while the reuse of the code is not enough to completely hide the overhead. Furthermore, as commented before, overall performance is not the only important metric, as responsiveness is often as important, which signifies the need for more efficient translation/optimization.

In the context of this paper, we are more interested in the overhead introduced by the optimizer alone. As mentioned before, the bar labeled "DynamoRIO overhead" is quite big due to the flexible nature of its design. This is so because the version of DynamoRIO we are using (the one that is publicly available with its full source code) is more an instrumentation tool than a DBO itself. Such overheads would be totally removed if we strip out such instrumentation features, as we have observed in other DBO tools such as Strata [21]. For example, since the source and guest ISAs are the same (x86), during the basic block translation phase, only partial decoding is necessary in order to distinguish branches and collect their targets. In contrast, in the presence of an instrumentation client DynamoRIO is doing a full decoding in order to facilitate code manipulation by the client. Thus, from this point forward we do not account for the DynamoRIO component in our study, as this overhead does not exist on pure DBO infrastructures. Ignoring this part of the overhead does not restrict our study since we are mainly concentrating on the overhead of the optimizing part of the VM with respect to the application's code execution.

3.1 The real view of the optimizer overheads

Consider Figure 2 which presents the breakdown of the optimizer and the translated code. The top bar shows the instructions that correspond to translated code. The second bar shows the instructions of the two basic optimizations; RLE and DCR. The third bar shows the instructions for the memory aliasing preparation and the fourth bar represents the instructions corresponding to the DDG. Finally, some other sources of overhead like the initialization phase of the optimizations are shown with the bottom bar.

A general observation is that the optimization overheads for most of the SPEC CPU2006 applications are negligible, especially after the first billion of instructions. This can be justified by the fact that 10% of static instructions are responsible for 90% of the execution and static instruction reuse is huge. There are though some

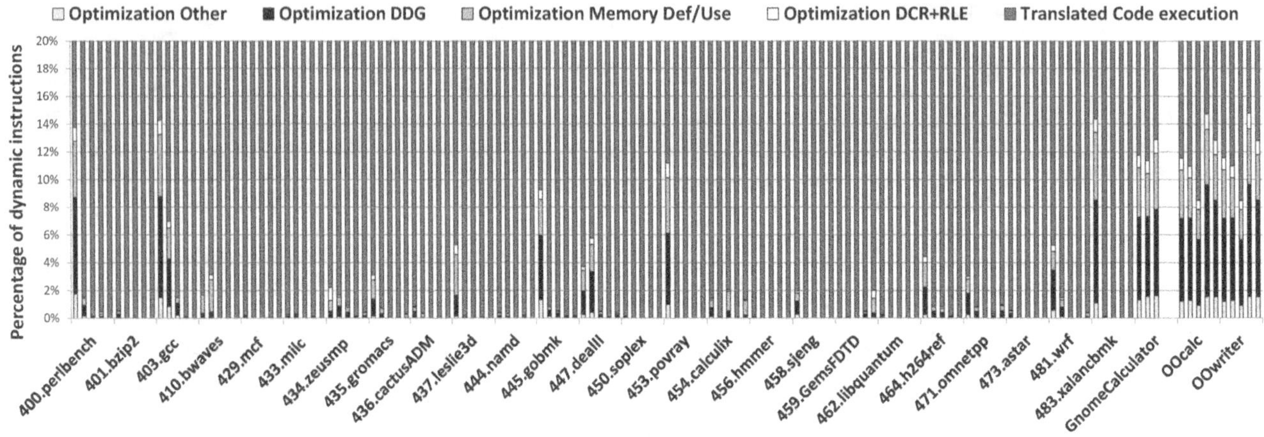

Figure 2. Dynamic instruction breakdown of optimizer and executed application. The Y axis maximum is at 20%. The rest 80% accounts for Translated Code execution. Each application has 5 assosiated bars, one for each 1 billion instruction chunk.

exceptions like 403.gcc where the execution is not concentrated in a few loops alone. This leads to the generation and optimization of more traces. Moreover, the overall overheads are low since the default threshold for creating a trace in DynamoRIO is at 50 executions, which gives a good balance between the amount of traces and coverage.

As it can be seen, applications with low static footprint are more tolerant to DBO overheads because they are amortized by the high repetition of the optimized code. However, DBO overheads for applications with large ratio between static and dynamic instructions are significant leading to poor performance and low response time.

Studying the breakdown in detail, we noticed that the DDG is the most costly part accounting on average for 6% of the dynamic instruction stream where DBO has high activity. An interesting difference is that for applications with low static to dynamic ratio, the proportional part of the DDG varies from 1% to 6% whereas on applications with high ratio the overhead varies from 5% to 7% across all the traces.

While such overhead could be avoided by a DBO that targets an out-of-order processor, computing the DDG is a key component for a DBO that targets in-order or VLIW processors, like Crusoe or Efficeon. The use of the DDG enables the implementation of more efficient and fruitful algorithms for optimizations like instruction scheduling and register allocation which are quite important for final performance. For instance, it has been shown that instruction scheduling is a key DBO component to enhance the quality of the generated code [6].

4. Reducing the overheads

Providing hardware support to speed up the execution of DBT/DBO primitives is the most efficient solution to reduce its overhead, since the runtime of the VM is always executed regardless of the emulated/translated application. However it is important to devote hardware to enhance the mechanisms of the primitives, leaving the execution of the heuristics to the software, which has more flexibility.

Moreover, one of the purposes of DBO is to provide maximum performance on simple processors like in-order processors so that we sustain good performance at a very low power [11]. For this reason, although hardware hooks are natural solutions to overcome DBO overheads, these HW enhancements should be simple enough so that we do not lose the power advantage of using a simple processor.

```
readOps[]
writeOps[]
for each insn i {
    readOps[i] = extract insn read operands
    writeOps[i] = extract insn write operands
}

for each insn i {
     for each readOp in readOp[i]
         if(readOp defined in trace)
             add flow dependence from last definition
     for each writeOp in writeOp[i]
         if(writeOp defined in trace)
             add output dependence from last definition
         if(writeOp used in trace)
             add anti dependence from last uses
     Update register uses with readOp[i]
     Update register definitions with writeOp[i]
}
```

Figure 3. Pseudo code of the DBO's module that creates the DDG

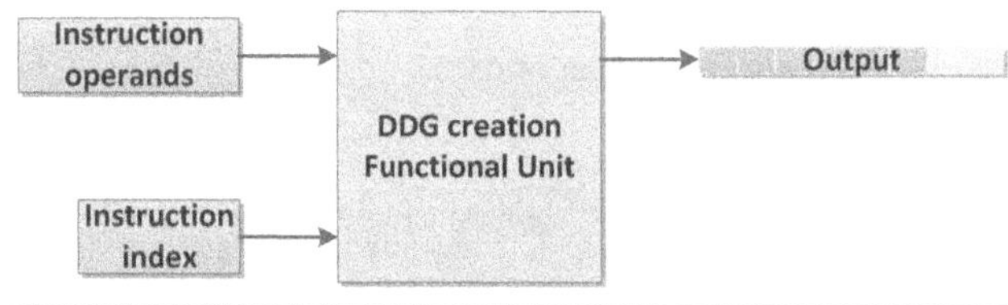

Figure 4. DDG functional unit block diagram

In this section we describe the proposed hardware support for the creation of the DDG. We take a top down approach in describing our proposal. First we discuss the software-only implementation in order to derive the basic components that are necessary for the execution of the algorithm. Such software-only implementation is our baseline. Then, we describe the proposed hardware support, its interface, and we demonstrate its functionality through an example. Finally, we explain how the functional unit can be integrated in a conventional pipelined processor.

4.1 Software-only implementation

As mentioned in section 2 the DDG creation algorithm is based on the one described in [16]. The DDG stores all the flow dependences (RAW), anti-dependences (WAR) and output dependences (WAW)

based on the register definitions and uses of the instructions belonging to a trace. All the memory operations are considered to be dependent between them, meaning that they must execute in order. We may also add hardware in our future work to perform memory disambiguation and be more aggressive with memory dependences. The pseudo code of the part of the DynamoRIO tool that implements the software-only algorithm is shown in Figure 3. The first loop traverses the instructions to extract the read and write register operands to some custom structures in order to avoid the extensive use of DynamoRIO API and increase data locality. The second loop traverses the operands that are read or written and according to the definition and use state of each register from the previous instructions, dependences are added to the graph. The actual implementation, in our case, is more complicated since there are several corner cases due to the x86 particularities that need to be taken in to account. One such case is register aliasing. For example eax, ax, al, ah are all the same register but when al or ah are defined the rest of the register remains unchanged. The def/use state consists of an array with an entry for each architectural register that holds the last definition of that register and the uses corresponding to it.

4.2 Proposed solution

As shown in section 3, the creation of the DDG is the most costly primitive compared to the rest of the optimizer. In order to improve the efficiency of the DBO we propose a functional unit, called *DDGacc*, that could be easily integrated in the processor pipeline. Such a functional unit will work in a similar manner as the software implementation, meaning that the DDG is going to be built incrementally. The block diagram of the *DDGacc* is depicted in Figure 4. The input to the FU is the operands of one instruction and the index of the instruction inside the corresponding trace. The input will be given by means of a new ISA instruction. The output will be the indexes of the instructions from which the input instruction has dependences from.

In more detail, the input of the accelerator is a 32-bit value that describes a single instruction. Its fields are shown in Figure 5(a). The first part is composed by all the register operands of the instruction, either explicit or implicit. Seven bits are used to represent a register id (Reg1, Reg2 and Reg3) and two extra to determine if the register is read, write, read/write by the instruction or not used (invalid). Note that due to particularities of the x86 ISA, an instruction can have more than one destination register (e.g. `xchg` and `pop`) which deems necessary to mark all the registers with the two extra bits. Moreover, a single bit is used to designate if the instruction is a memory read (load) and another if it is a memory write (store). Finally, two extra bits are used to designate whether the `EFLAGS` register is modified or read following the same definition as Reg Type field. Adding up, the inputs consist of 31 bits which is convenient since a general purpose 32bit register can be used to carry the input. Note that if the target architecture provides 64bit registers, more detail can be provided to the functional unit, e.g. separation of the `EFLAGS` in three groups and/or the input traces can be larger than 256 instructions.

The output of the functional unit is depicted in Figure 5(b). Each element contains the index of the instruction from which the input has flow or output dependence. Since we limit our traces to 256 instructions, 8 bits are sufficient to encode the index of any instruction in the trace. For each register operand specified in the input, one flow dependence field is pre-assigned in the output. For example if there is flow dependence due to Reg1 then the index of the instruction defining Reg1 will be written into the Reg1 output field. The fourth and fifth fields (MemW, MemR) are used for flow dependences due to memory operations. Finally, the last two elements are used to track output dependences. Note that the last element can also be used for output dependences due to the `EFLAGS` register, since instructions that define two registers at the same time like `xchg` do not modify the `EFLAGS`.

4.3 DDGacc operations

The DDGacc will be operated by means of new ISA instructions. Specifically two new instructions are required. The first one is an instruction that will initialize all the internal structures of the accelerator in order to be prepared for the creation of a new DDG. The instruction is named ***ddgReset***.

The actual dependence calculation will be instructed using the second ISA instruction called ***ddgAppend*** which has the format: `ddgAppend m64, Rin`.

The instruction is similar to a store instruction where m64 is the memory position where the output of the functional unit will be stored. The address is described by [DDGBase@+insnIndex] where DDGBase@ is the beginning address of the output array, which can be held in a general purpose register, and insnIndex is an offset computed by the functional unit which is internally incremented each time ***ddgAppend*** instruction is executed. The input is given by `Rin` which is a general purpose register with values as described previously. The instruction operates like a conventional store with the only difference that the data will be taken directly from the functional unit by means of forwarding the output value directly to the store buffer just like a normal `add mem, reg`.

As an example, consider the implementation of the DDG algorithm depicted in Figure 6(a) and compare it to that in Figure 3. The basic difference from the software-only algorithm is that the dependences and the tracking of the definitions of the registers are done by a single instruction that will instruct the functional unit to handle them. In the example given in Figure 6(b) we apply the algorithm on a sample trace of 3 instructions. Concerning the input, the first instruction defines and uses register ebx, hence the first register is marked read/write. Moreover the add instruction modifies the `EFLAGS` register. The second instruction defines `eax` and reads register `ebx`. The last instruction stores the value of `eax` to the address contained by `ebx`, therefore the write memory field is marked with 1. As for the output, the first instruction has no dependences since it is the first in the trace. The second instruction depends on the first one because it uses `ebx`. The last instruction depends on both previous since it uses the two defined registers.

4.4 DDGacc implementation

The functional unit design is depicted in Figure 7. Due to space constraints, we do not describe here the detailed implementation. We refer the reader to a technical report [19] for further details.

The proposed accelerator contains a small memory structure, called LDRF that keeps track of the last definition of each register. Each line of the structure has size of 8 bits, since the maximum index number encountered is 255, and 92 lines are needed to store the index of the defining instruction for each register. In total, the memory needed to handle the registers is 92 Bytes plus 92 valid bits. The lastMemoryW, lastMemoryR and the lastEFLAGSW keep track of the last instruction that was a memory write, a memory read and that modified the EFLAGS register respectively, increasing the total memory requirements to 116 Bytes.

The LDRF is indexed by the 3 register IDs given from the input. Three read ports are needed to get the last definition of all registers in parallel and two write ports to update the last definition of up to two registers in parallel. One valid bit for each entry designates whether this operand was defined by an instruction in the trace under consideration. The output of LDRF for each register is the 8 bit identifier of the defining instruction along with the valid bit (total 9 bits). The memory cells for the last memory write, read and EFLAGS definition also follow this concept. The outputs of the LDRF and the other memory cells are directly connected to their

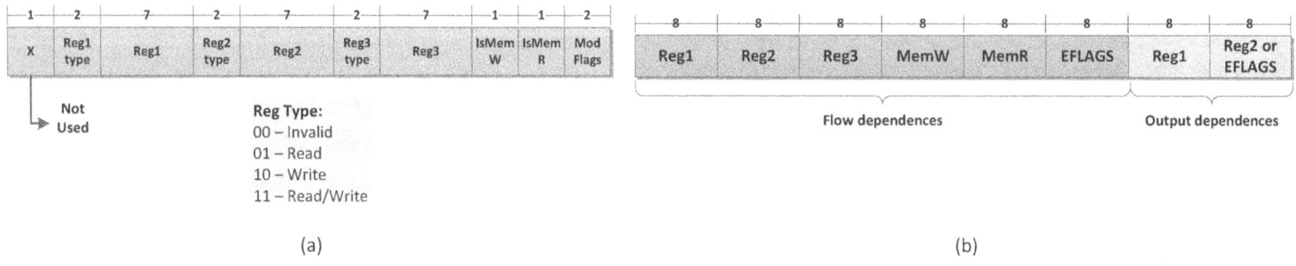

Figure 5. (a) Input of the accelerator consisting of the register operands and (b) Output of the accelerator consisting of the indexes of the instructions that there is dependence from

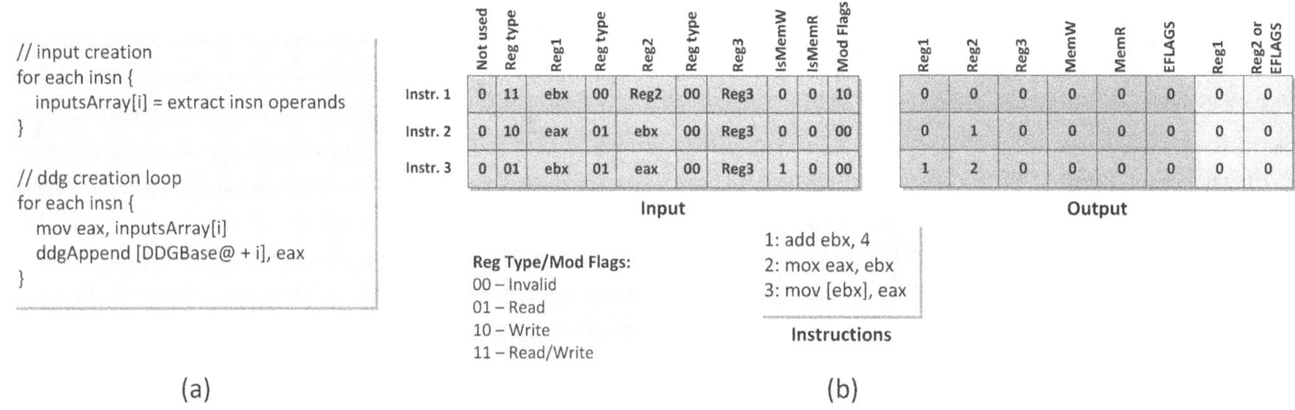

	Not used	Reg type	Reg1	Reg type	Reg2	Reg type	Reg3	IsMemW	IsMemR	Mod Flags
Instr. 1	0	11	ebx	00	Reg2	00	Reg3	0	0	10
Instr. 2	0	10	eax	01	ebx	00	Reg3	0	0	00
Instr. 3	0	01	ebx	01	eax	00	Reg3	1	0	00

Reg1	Reg2	Reg3	MemW	MemR	EFLAGS	Reg1	Reg2 or EFLAGS
0	0	0	0	0	0	0	0
0	1	0	0	0	0	0	0
1	2	0	0	0	0	0	0

Figure 6. (a) HW/SW co-designed implementation of DDG algorithm. (b) Example of operation on instructions

respective output slots that will be written to memory. The final outcome depends on the different control bits from the input.

Internally to the functional unit, a two-step process is necessary for it to operate correctly: read and update. In the first step, the values from the LRDF and the other memory cells are read and the output is prepared. On the second step, the defined operands have to be updated with the index of the current instruction.

We have identified that the LDRF structure is the critical path of the proposed functional unit, which can be implemented as a 3-read and 2-write direct-mapped cache. We have calculated the access time and the area of LDRF using CACTI [24] assuming 32nm technology.

The access time for such small cache is 0.19ns. Since the tag and the data are accessed in parallel, we can safely assume that this access time is an upper bound for the access time of the LDRF. In reality, the LDRF access time will be less. Assuming a cycle time of 0.33ns (3 GHz) then both steps (read and update) can be done in two cycles. Finally, the area required for this structure is 0.003495 mm2.

Regarding the LDRF initialization with the ddgReset instruction, in order to minimize the penalty of initializing the LDRF, the valid bits can be gang-cleared as explained in [14]. The latency of this instruction will be one cycle.

Another issue is whether the memory kept in the functional unit should be part of the architectural state. The state of LDRF and the rest of memory cells are vital for the correctness of the output. The answer depends on how these instructions are going to be used. If an algorithm using these instructions is implemented as a part of the DBO in a co-designed virtual machine, the state is not necessary to be part of the architectural state as long as the VM guarantees that the algorithm cannot be interrupted. On the other hand, if the instructions are used in the context of a software-only DBO, complete execution is not guaranteed. Hence, in this case the state of the LRDF and the other memory cells has to be part of the architectural state.

The parameters used for the description of DDGacc are targeted towards x86 ISA, due to our evaluation infrastructure. We would like to point out that use of the functional unit is not limited by any manner just to x86 ISA. In fact, the changes that are necessary for retargeting are very few and it could be also enhanced for providing more information with the output if the ISA supports for example 128bit stores.

5. Evaluation

This section is organized in two parts. In the first part we present and discuss the evaluation results of our proposal against the baseline software-only DBO. For the timing evaluation, we selected the chunks in which more traces were generated and optimized. We present results for a total of 24 chunks of 1 billion instructions. For the second part, we show the effectiveness of the accelerator when the threshold for generating and optimizing traces is lower. For all the experiments, the latency of the accelerator is assumed to be 2 cycles as explained in the implementation section. However, it is worthy to note that results obtained with larger latencies show that the proposed solution is extremely tolerant to latency.

In this paper we concentrate on reducing the introduced overheads of the optimization sequence rather than evaluating the performance gains from applying different optimizations. As such, we do not present results comparing the performance of the application executed under the DBO against native execution.

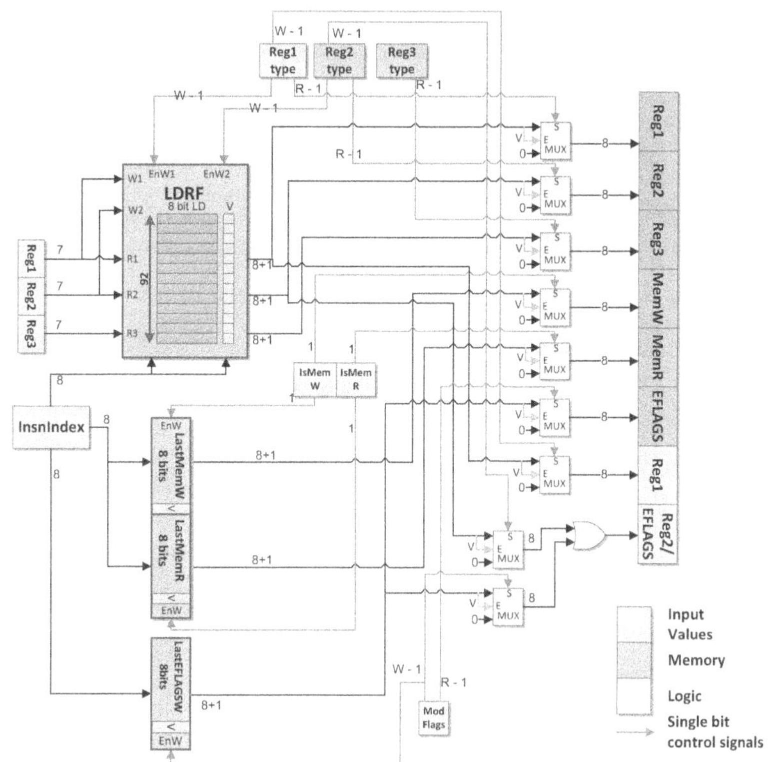

Figure 7. DDGacc implementation

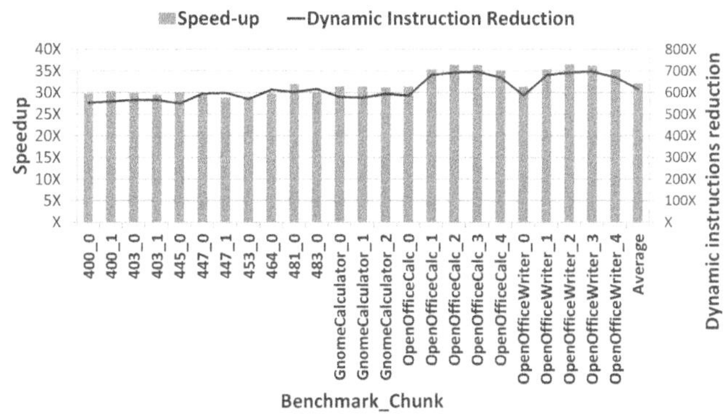

Figure 8. Speedup of the HW/SW co-designed DDG against the software-only implementation and the reduction of the dynamic instructions

5.1 Evaluation against the baseline

Figure 8 shows the speedup of the hw/sw co-designed algorithm to compute the DDG against the software-only implementation. Moreover, on the secondary axis we show the reduction of the dynamic instructions corresponding to the DDG creation. On average, the speedup is 32x while the dynamic instruction reduction is 615x. These big benefits can be understood by comparing the software only algorithm presented in Figure 3 to the proposed hardware/software algorithm shown in Figure 6(a)

However, there are several reasons why a 600x reduction in the number of dynamic instructions is not translated into a 600x reduction in number of cycles. First of all is that we assume a perfect instruction cache, which means that the reduction of instruction cache accesses due to less dynamic instructions is not reflected in our results. Cycle reduction results would be better if an instruction cache were modeled, as the software-only baseline would perform worse. As mentioned before, not being able to model an instruction cache is a caveat of our infrastructure.

Moreover, we use fixed addresses for the memory locations of the input array and the DDG array for the hw/sw algorithm. This results in an increased miss rate on the L1 D$ compared to the software-only algorithm, in which locality is exploited. This reduces the performance benefits. This is also a caveat of our research infrastructure.

Concerning the variation of the speedup and the dynamic instruction reduction among the different chunks (speedups ranging from 28x to 36x and reductions from 550x to 696x), the cost of calculating the dependences of a static instruction, with the software algorithm, is not constant. The cost varies with respect to the type of the instruction, the number of register operands (explicit and implicit) as well as the type of the register. For example the cost of an instruction that is using an aliased register (e.g. eax) is higher since all the "sub-registers" must be taken into consideration. On the other hand, the hardware accelerator is handling the aliasing through its normal functionality.

Figure 9 shows the execution time of both implementations normalized to that of the baseline. The bar labeled as SW refers to the software only implementation and the bar labeled HW/SW refers to our proposal. The total execution time is divided into three regions. The first one stands for the optimization overhead excluding the DDG generation (blue bar) which is represented by the second region (red bar). The third one is the time spent executing instructions from the translation cache (green bar). The software only implementation of the DDG algorithm accounts for 4.6% of the total execution time on average and for 32% of the optimization time. The overhead varies from 1%, for traces with

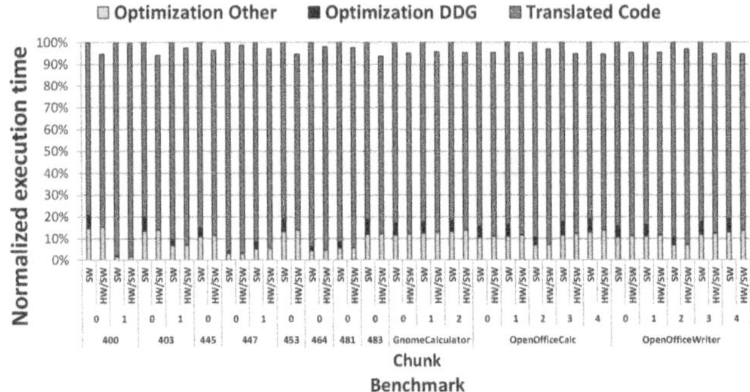

Figure 9. Normalized execution time breakdown of the baseline DBO and the DBO using the hw/sw co-designed DDG creation

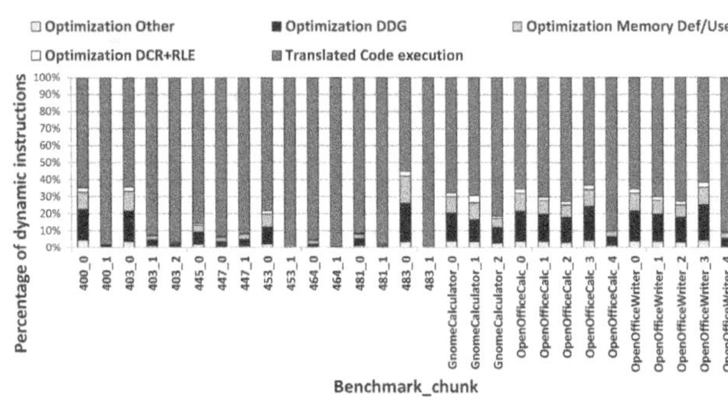

Figure 11. Dynamic instruction breakdown of the selected chunks when optimizing at the threshold of 10

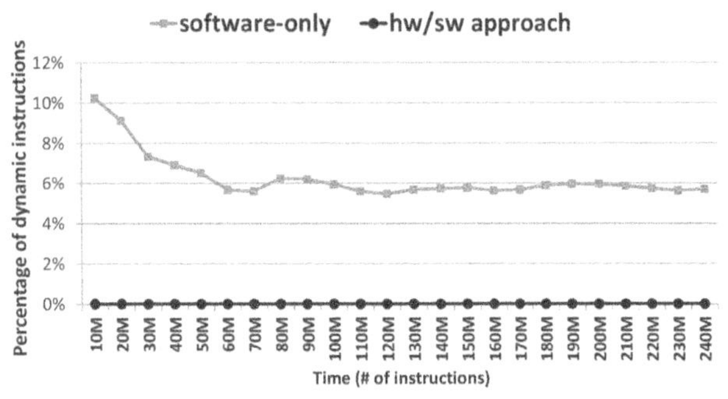

Figure 10. DDG activity over time

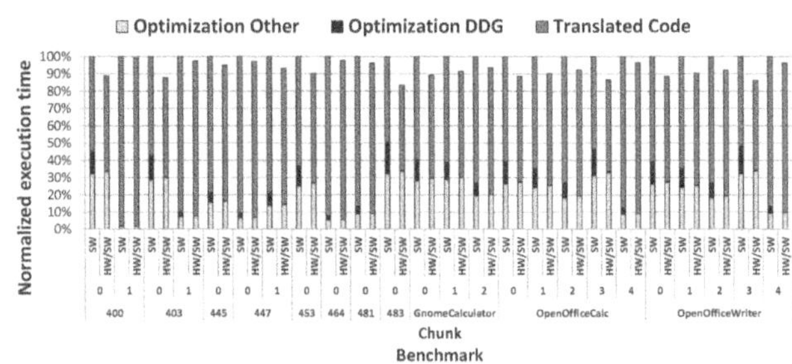

Figure 12. Normalized execution time of the baseline DBO with threshold of 10 and the DBO using the hw/sw co-designed DDG creation

low DBO activity like 447.0, to 7% for traces with high DBO activity like OOWriter.4. While the dynamic instructions of the DDG are higher than the rest of the optimizations, the fact that in the software version data locality is well exploited, the execution time is lower.

Using the hardware functional unit for the creation of the DDG, improves the execution time significantly. The section that corresponds to DDG is reduced to 0.1% of the execution time across all traces which is almost negligible. The total execution time is reduced by an average of 4.6% due to this reduction, while on the traces with high activity of the DBO the benefits are up to 7%.

The direct benefit from this improvement is that the overhead introduced from the optimizer is reduced by approximately 27%. The execution time gained could be used to apply some other complex optimization which will be using the DDG or as a raw decrease of execution time. We believe that this improvement is of high importance in the context of co-designed VMs, since the impact of the overhead is significant not only at the beginning of the execution of a process, but throughout its life since evictions from the code cache can result in re-translation and re-optimization of regions of code.

In addition, there are side effects due to this reduction. The 615x reduction of dynamic instructions results to fewer accesses to the instruction and data caches. We observed 417x reduction of data cache accesses. Moreover, this reduction of instructions results in less energy consumption since fewer instructions need to be executed.

Finally, Figure 10 shows the optimizer activity over time with respect to the DDG creation. In particular the y-axis shows the accumulated ratio of dynamic instructions executed to compute the DDG with respect to the rest of the instructions over time (the x-axis is the 1 billion instruction chunk divided into sub-chunks of 10M instructions each). We present the results for the first chunk of the application GnomeCalculator as an example. As the applications progresses with its execution, less code is being optimized, which means that the overheads devoted to compute the DDG are lower. The line of the software-only approach shows this clearly with an initial overhead of 10% which is reduced to 6% towards the end of the chunk. Although the hw/sw approach has the same trend, the introduced overheads are negligible which makes our approach very intriguing.

5.2 Applying the optimizations earlier

Following our initial claim that using the functional unit will reduce the overhead of the DDG creation algorithm to a point that it can be applied earlier, we reduced the threshold at which traces are being generated from 50 repetitions to 10. Of course this means that more traces will be generated and optimized, resulting to higher overhead, but optimizing the instructions earlier would also imply higher performance and better response time.

The breakdown of the dynamic instruction stream for the 24 selected chunks is depicted in Figure 11. In general the overhead is increased because of the increase of the optimizer's activity, which for some applications is significant, e.g. for the real applications where it doubles. Regarding to SPEC applications, for some of them like 400 and 403 it is increased significantly as well. On the other hand, applications like 464 and 481 where the overheads where quite low with a threshold of 50, there is no substantial increase of the overhead since the amount of static code optimized is almost the same. In these cases, code is optimized earlier with a lower threshold which is the desired effect.

Considering execution time, the breakdown is depicted in Figure 12. The software implementation of the DDG accounts for 8%

of the execution time on average for the SPEC applications and 12% for the real applications with a maximum reaching 18%. For the global picture, overhead can be as high as 50% of the execution time. Such extreme overhead is what is preventing early optimization.

With the use of DGGacc, the DDG creation overhead is reduced to 0.2% of the total execution time, providing a global speedup of 8% for the SPEC applications and 12% for the real applications. The overhead is again reduced by approximately 27%. Such improvement is more significant in raw numbers than when optimizing at the threshold of 50 since it allows for the DDG creation to be applied as early as possible without introducing additional overheads.

The ramification of such low execution time requirements is that not only the optimization can be applied earlier at the beginning, but it can also be applied earlier when a hot region is evicted from the code cache in the case where it is shared by several threads. Earlier optimization will allow the application to reach a steady state earlier which will result in more repeated executions of the optimized code. This in turn will allow for the overhead to be amortized earlier and the performance benefits to be observed as soon as possible.

6. Related work

Some of the most characteristic examples of process level VMs are Dynamo [3], DynamoRIO [5] and IA-32 execution layer [4]. All of them employ different techniques to reduce the overall overheads and guarantee that the application will reach the steady state as fast as possible. For example DynamoRIO and IA-32 EL start with basic block translation, while Dynamo starts with interpretation. Different heuristics are used to construct larger regions as early as they can afford. The common ground among the three though, is that they apply only simple, low-cost optimizations in order to minimize the overhead impacts. Our proposal offers a viable example that hardware acceleration could in fact enable more complex optimizations in these systems.

In the field of co-designed VMs, where the DBO is part of the hardware platform, the most representative example is Transmeta's Crusoe [11] where the Code Morphing Software [6] is translating x86 instructions to a VLIW instruction set. Other examples are the DAISY/BOA [7, 18] projects from IBM. Both of them apply a set of low cost optimizations in order to increase the ILP and take advantage of their underlying VLIW architectures. There is no report of any hardware accelerators for their optimizations.

Characteristic examples of hardware only optimizers are rePLay [17] and PARROT [20]. Both of them implement an optimization pipeline which operates on the ìops generated during the execution of x86 code. rePLay focuses on performance gains while PARROT is giving special attention to power awareness. The major drawback of hardware-only implementation of optimizations is that the mechanism and the heuristics assumed are hardcoded. In contrast, our proposal is providing hardware support for the primitive of the optimization but leaves the heuristics to the software which has more flexibility.

Adore [13] and Trident [25] also use hardware support for dynamic optimization. Specifically, Adore uses hardware performance counters to collect samples for profiling and when it detects a hot region a second thread is invoked to generate and optimize the hot region. Trident works in a similar manner while utilizing multiple helper threads, hardware events and simultaneous multithreading to amortize the introduced overhead.

There are several other proposals (either software or hardware) that focus on speeding up basic actions of the DBT/DBO. Instruction decoding was attacked by [10]. Hardware based profiling was proposed by [15]. Effective code cache management algorithms were proposed by [8] and by [23]. The implementation of Strata, a retargetable and reconfigurable software dynamic same-ISA translator is described in [21] and techniques for reducing the overhead of indirect branches is proposed in [9]. Other tasks such as interpretation, trace chaining etc. are discussed in [22].

7. Conclusions

DBO overheads may turn into poor performance and slow response time for applications with large static code. Reducing the overheads of the software layer (the optimizer) in a DBT/DBO system impacts overall performance and user experience. Furthermore, reduced overheads have interesting collateral effects that may affect the design of other optimizer components, such as applying optimizations earlier or eagerly, among others. For all these reasons, we propose to provide hardware support to speed up the mechanisms of DBT/DBO primitives as a solution, leaving the heuristics to the software, which has greater flexibility.

In this paper, we have characterized the overheads of a DBO system based on DynamoRIO, implementing several basic optimizations, and we have identified the biggest sources of overheads. We have observed that the construction of the Data Dependence Graph (DDG), a crucial primitive to enable other optimizations such as instruction scheduling, accounts for 5%-10% of the execution time.

Hence, we have proposed hardware support to accelerate this part. DDGacc is integrated in a conventional pipelined processor as a regular functional unit that is operated by two new ISA instructions. We have provided a detailed description of DDGacc, its interface and how software can use it. After that, we have compared the performance of the proposed hardware/software solution against a software-only implementation, and we have observed that the cost to compute the DDG is reduced by 600x in number of dynamic instructions and 32x in number of cycles. This is translated on an overall improvement of the system of 5%-10% on average, depending on the optimization threshold. Moreover, this technique provides up to 18% for applications with large static code footprint.

Acknowledgments

The presented work was partially supported by the Generalitat de Catalunya under grant 2009SGR1250, the Spanish Ministry of Education and Science under contracts TIN2007-61763 and TIN2010-18368, and Intel Corporation. Demos Pavlou was partially funded by the Generalitat de Catalunya under an FI-AGAUR grant.

References

[1] Standard Performance Evaluation Corporation. SPEC CPU2006 Benchmarks. URL `http://www.spec.org/cpu2006/`.

[2] T. Austin, E. Larson, and D. Ernst. Simplescalar: an infrastructure for computer system modeling. *Computer*, 35(2):59 –67, feb 2002. ISSN 0018-9162. doi: 10.1109/2.982917.

[3] V. Bala, E. Duesterwald, and S. Banerjia. Dynamo: a transparent dynamic optimization system. In *PLDI '00: Proceedings of the ACM SIGPLAN 2000 conference on Programming language design and implementation*, pages 1–12, New York, NY, USA, 2000. ACM. ISBN 1-58113-199-2. doi: http://doi.acm.org/10.1145/349299.349303.

[4] L. Baraz, T. Devor, O. Etzion, S. Goldenberg, A. Skaletsky, Y. Wang, and Y. Zemach. Ia-32 execution layer: a two-phase dynamic translator designed to support ia-32 applications on itanium®-based systems. In *MICRO 36: Proceedings of the 36th annual IEEE/ACM International Symposium on Microarchitecture*, page 191, Washington, DC, USA, 2003. IEEE Computer Society. ISBN 0-7695-2043-X.

[5] D. Bruening, T. Garnett, and S. Amarasinghe. An infrastructure for adaptive dynamic optimization. In *CGO '03: Proceedings of the international symposium on Code generation and optimization*, pages 265–

275, Washington, DC, USA, 2003. IEEE Computer Society. ISBN 0-7695-1913-X.

[6] J. C. Dehnert, B. K. Grant, J. P. Banning, R. Johnson, T. Kistler, A. Klaiber, and J. Mattson. The Transmeta Code Morphing™ Software: using speculation, recovery, and adaptive retranslation to address real-life challenges. In *CGO '03: Proceedings of the international symposium on Code generation and optimization*, pages 15–24, Washington, DC, USA, 2003. IEEE Computer Society. ISBN 0-7695-1913-X.

[7] K. Ebcioğlu and E. R. Altman. Daisy: dynamic compilation for 100% architectural compatibility. *SIGARCH Comput. Archit. News*, 25(2):26–37, 1997. ISSN 0163-5964. doi: http://doi.acm.org/10.1145/384286.264126.

[8] K. Hazelwood and M. D. Smith. Managing bounded code caches in dynamic binary optimization systems. *ACM Trans. Archit. Code Optim.*, 3:263–294, September 2006. ISSN 1544-3566. doi: http://doi.acm.org/10.1145/1162690.1162692. URL `http://doi.acm.org/10.1145/1162690.1162692`.

[9] J. D. Hiser, D. Williams, W. Hu, J. W. Davidson, J. Mars, and B. R. Childers. Evaluating Indirect Branch Handling Mechanisms in Software Dynamic Translation Systems. In *CGO '07: Proceedings of the International Symposium on Code Generation and Optimization*, pages 61–73, Washington, DC, USA, 2007. IEEE Computer Society. ISBN 0-7695-2764-7. doi: http://dx.doi.org/10.1109/CGO.2007.10.

[10] S. Hu and J. E. Smith. Reducing startup time in co-designed virtual machines. In *ISCA '06: Proceedings of the 33rd annual international symposium on Computer Architecture*, pages 277–288, Washington, DC, USA, 2006. IEEE Computer Society. ISBN 0-7695-2608-X. doi: http://dx.doi.org/10.1109/ISCA.2006.33.

[11] A. Klaiber. The Technology Behind the Crusoe Processors. White paper, January 2000.

[12] T. Lindholm and F. Yellin. *Java Virtual Machine Specification*. Addison-Wesley Longman Publishing Co., Inc., Boston, MA, USA, 1999. ISBN 0201432943.

[13] J. Lu, H. Chen, R. Fu, W.-C. Hsu, B. Othmer, P.-C. Yew, and D.-Y. Chen. The performance of runtime data cache prefetching in a dynamic optimization system. In *Proceedings of the 36th annual IEEE/ACM International Symposium on Microarchitecture*, MICRO 36, pages 180–, Washington, DC, USA, 2003. IEEE Computer Society. ISBN 0-7695-2043-X. URL `http://dl.acm.org/citation.cfm?id=956417.956549`.

[14] J. F. Martínez, J. Renau, M. C. Huang, M. Prvulovic, and J. Torrellas. Cherry: checkpointed early resource recycling in out-of-order microprocessors. In *MICRO 35: Proceedings of the 35th annual ACM/IEEE international symposium on Microarchitecture*, pages 3–14, Los Alamitos, CA, USA, 2002. IEEE Computer Society Press. ISBN 0-7695-1859-1.

[15] M. C. Merten, A. R. Trick, E. M. Nystrom, R. D. Barnes, and W.-m. W. Hmu. A hardware mechanism for dynamic extraction and relayout of program hot spots. In *Proceedings of the 27th annual international symposium on Computer architecture*, ISCA '00, pages 59–70, New York, NY, USA, 2000. ACM. ISBN 1-58113-232-8. doi: http://doi.acm.org/10.1145/339647.339655. URL `http://doi.acm.org/10.1145/339647.339655`.

[16] S. S. Muchnick. *Advanced compiler design and implementation*. Morgan Kaufmann Publishers Inc., San Francisco, CA, USA, 1997. ISBN 1-55860-320-4.

[17] S. Patel and S. Lumetta. rePLay: A hardware framework for dynamic optimization. *Computers, IEEE Transactions on*, 50(6):590–608, Jun 2001. ISSN 0018-9340. doi: 10.1109/12.931895.

[18] S. S. Paul, P. Ledak, J. Leblanc, S. Kosonocky, M. Gschwind, J. Fritts, A. Bright, E. Altman, and C. Agricola. Boa: Targeting multi-gigahertz with binary translation. In *In Proc. of the 1999 Workshop on Binary Translation, IEEE Computer Society Technical Committee on Computer Architecture Newsletter*, pages 2–11, 1999.

[19] D. Pavlou, E. Gibert, F. Latorre, and A. Gonzalez. Improving Dynamic Binary Optimizers Efficiency through Specific Hardware Support. Technical Report UPC-DAC-RR-ARCO-2009-11, Universitat Politecnica de Catalunya, Department of Computer Architecture, September 2009.

[20] R. Rosner, Y. Almog, M. Moffie, N. Schwartz, and A. Mendelson. Power awareness through selective dynamically optimized traces. In *Computer Architecture, 2004. Proceedings. 31st Annual International Symposium on*, pages 162–173, June 2004. doi: 10.1109/ISCA.2004.1310772.

[21] K. Scott, N. Kumar, S. Velusamy, B. Childers, J. W. Davidson, and M. L. Soffa. Retargetable and reconfigurable software dynamic translation. In *CGO '03: Proceedings of the International Symposium on Code Generation and Optimization*, pages 36–47, Washington, DC, USA, 2003. IEEE Computer Society. ISBN 0-7695-1913-X.

[22] J. Smith and R. Nair. *Virtual Machines: Versatile Platforms for Systems and Processes (The Morgan Kaufmann Series in Computer Architecture and Design)*. Morgan Kaufmann Publishers Inc., San Francisco, CA, USA, 2005. ISBN 1558609105.

[23] W. Srisa-an, M. B. Cohen, Y. Shang, and M. Soundararaj. A self-adjusting code cache manager to balance start-up time and memory usage. In *Proceedings of the 8th annual IEEE/ACM international symposium on Code generation and optimization*, CGO '10, pages 82–91, New York, NY, USA, 2010. ACM. ISBN 978-1-60558-635-9. doi: http://doi.acm.org/10.1145/1772954.1772968. URL `http://doi.acm.org/10.1145/1772954.1772968`.

[24] S. Wilton and N. Jouppi. Cacti: an enhanced cache access and cycle time model. *Solid-State Circuits, IEEE Journal of*, 31(5):677–688, May 1996. ISSN 0018-9200. doi: 10.1109/4.509850.

[25] W. Zhang, B. Calder, and D. M. Tullsen. An event-driven multithreaded dynamic optimization framework. In *Proceedings of the 14th International Conference on Parallel Architectures and Compilation Techniques*, PACT '05, pages 87–98, Washington, DC, USA, 2005. IEEE Computer Society. ISBN 0-7695-2429-X. doi: http://dx.doi.org/10.1109/PACT.2005.7. URL `http://dx.doi.org/10.1109/PACT.2005.7`.

Adding Dynamically-Typed Language Support to a Statically-Typed Language Compiler: Performance Evaluation, Analysis, and Tradeoffs

Kazuaki Ishizaki[+], Priya Nagpurkar[*], Takeshi Ogasawara[+], David Edelsohn[*], Jose Castanos[*], Toshio Nakatani[+]

[+]IBM Research – Tokyo

[*]IBM Thomas J. Watson Research Center

kiszk@acm.org

Abstract

Applications written in dynamically typed scripting languages are increasingly popular for Web software development. Even on the server side, programmers are using dynamically typed scripting languages such as Ruby and Python to build complex applications quickly. As the number and complexity of dynamically typed scripting language applications grows, optimizing their performance is becoming important. Some of the best performing compilers and optimizers for dynamically typed scripting languages are developed entirely from scratch and target a specific language. This approach is not scalable, given the variety of dynamically typed scripting languages, and the effort involved in developing and maintaining separate infrastructures for each. In this paper, we evaluate the feasibility of adapting and extending an existing production-quality method-based Just-In-Time (JIT) compiler for a language with dynamic types. Our goal is to identify the challenges and shortcomings with the current infrastructure, and to propose and evaluate runtime techniques and optimizations that can be incorporated into a common optimization infrastructure for static and dynamic languages.

We discuss three extensions to the compiler to support dynamically typed languages: (1) simplification of control flow graphs, (2) mapping of memory locations to stack-allocated variables, and (3) reduction of runtime overhead using language semantics. We also propose four new optimizations for Python in (2) and (3). These extensions are effective in reduction of compiler working memory and improvement of runtime performance. We present a detailed performance evaluation of our approach for Python, finding an overall improvement of 1.69x on average (up to 2.74x) over our JIT compiler without any optimization for dynamically typed languages and Python.

Categories and Subject Descriptors D.3.4 [**Programming Languages**]: Processors – Compilers, optimization, run-time environment

General Terms Performance, Languages.

Keywords Just-In-Time compiler; dynamically typed language; Python

1. Introduction

Dynamically typed scripting languages (called scripting languages) such as PHP, Python, Ruby, and JavaScript are becoming increasingly popular due to high productivity and ease of programming that they enable. These languages have been especially successful for Web applications [29, 33]. Flexibility provided by dynamic types, meta-programming features, high-level data structures, interoperability with other languages, and a rich set of frameworks and libraries such as Ruby on Rails [31] all contribute to high productivity.

Unfortunately, the same flexibility that makes these languages popular with programmers also makes optimization and efficient code generation challenging. As the use of these languages grows, optimizing their performance is increasingly important. Although the original and commonly used implementations of most dynamically typed scripting languages are interpreters with relatively poor performance, several optimization approaches ranging from interpreter and runtime techniques to Just-In-Time (JIT) compilation have been proposed [7, 15, 24, 44]. Of course, neither the dynamic languages nor their optimization techniques are new. For example, those optimizations, which were originally proposed for Self as early as 1989 [10, 11], have been successfully applied to modern scripting languages [6, 7, 15, 48].

This paper describes how we adapt an existing method-based JIT compiler, originally designed for a statically typed language, to work with a dynamically typed language. This approach leverages existing optimizations in a production quality JIT compiler [26, 27] and allows compiler writers to quickly create a compiler for a new language, thereby reducing the costs associated with developing and maintaining a new JIT compiler. The Open Source Unladen Swallow (Python) [44], Rubinius (Ruby) [30], and Tamarin with LLVM [36] projects also used similar approaches, using the Open Source LLVM compiler infrastructure [21] as an optimizer and native code generator. However, this approach has not been systematically evaluated in existing literature.

We show that, not surprisingly, the naïve approach to translate a dynamically typed language to an intermediate representation (IR) of an existing compiler only yields a small improvement. We identify three main performance-inhibiting issues in this naïve translation. The first issue is the generation of complex control flow graphs. The second is the generation of many memory accesses in the heap area. The last is the generation of calls to generic runtime helpers. We introduce a new technique to address each of these three issues: (1) to simplify CFGs by introducing new IR opcodes for exceptions and garbage collection (GC) related operations, (2) to map frequently accessed stack operands and local variables of a dynamically-typed language to stack-allocated variables, and (3) to replace the generic helper calls with helper calls optimized for a particular type that is inferred using dynamic profiling. In addition, we also propose three new optimizations to enable mapping of the operand stack of the original language to stack-allocated variables and to cache and pre-compute the built-in functions. Our experimental results show that these techniques and optimizations are effective. In particular, technique (1) is effective in reducing working memory at compilation time. Technique (2) shows 1.18x performance improvement, and technique (3) shows 1.26x performance improvement.

We choose Python as our initial target language due to our interest in server-side workloads. In addition to leveraging the JIT compiler, maintaining compatibility with the original, commonly-used Python (called CPython) interpreter [28] is central to our design. This is because CPython has many useful libraries that are closely linked to the internal objects of the CPython runtime. In summary, our approach couples the CPython interpreter with the production JIT compiler with preserving the compatibility with these useful libraries.

There are some design choices to implement a JIT compiler for a new dynamically typed language. Here we discuss two choices. One is whether we generate native code from the dynamically typed language bytecode or from other bytecode such as Java bytecode translated by Jython [39]. The latest Jython generates Java bytecode from Python source file or bytecode, but this leads to the loss of semantic information in the original Python. For example, the Java JIT compiler cannot recognize the Java bytecode sequence corresponding to an attribute access in Python. Because the JIT compiler misses optimization opportunities at the Python language level, the performance is not good for many of the benchmarks. Thus, we choose to generate native code directly from the dynamically typed language bytecode. Although SPUR [5] takes a similar approach, its compiler to generate CIL is carefully designed with its trace JIT to achieve excellent performance. The other design choice is whether we write a new JIT compiler for every dynamically typed language or we reuse the existing JIT compiler. There are several JIT compilers [6, 7, 22, 48] that are newly developed. They achieve excellent performance since they are designed for the target language. On the other hand, it is not easy to extend them to other languages. One exception is PyPy [7] that is trying to support other languages. From an engineering effort perspective, it would be desirable to design an extensible compiler framework that supports multiple languages without compromising on performance. This is the interesting and challenging research issue that we will address since the limited number of implementations [5, 7, 30, 36, 44] adopted this approach.

The contributions of this paper are as follows:

- Three methods to effectively extend a compiler designed for a statically typed language to a dynamically typed language: (1) simplify control flow graphs, (2) map memory locations to stack-allocated variables, and (3) reduce runtime overhead using target language semantics (Sections 6.2, 6.3, and 6.4).
- Three new optimizations for (2) and (3) in Python: (a) Mapping of the operand stack to stack-allocated variables to enable existing optimizations, (b) caching results of the isinstance() built-in function, and (c) pre-computation of the hasattr() built-in function to reduce the runtime overhead (Sections 7.1, 7.2, and 7.3).
- Performance evaluation of our approach implemented on the production IBM JIT compiler [26] using programs from the publicly available Unladen Swallow benchmarks [40] showing average performance improvement of 1.76x (up to 2.67x) over the CPython interpreter, compared to a 1.34x performance improvement without any optimizations that will be described in Sections 6 and 7 (Section 8.1).
- Detailed evaluation of optimizations, which yields an overall improvement of 1.69x on average (up to 2.74x) against without any optimization, for adapting a compiler for a statically typed language (Section 8.2).

The paper is organized as follows: Related work is discussed in Section 2. We show the motivation and highlight the problem that we address in Section 3. Then, we give a brief overview of the dynamically typed language we focus on, viz. Python, especially of the aspects that are relevant to our work in Section 4. Section 5 gives an overview of our JIT compiler, followed by a description of our adaptation techniques in Section 6 and optimizations for CPython in Section 7. Then, Section 8 evaluates effectiveness of techniques in Section 6 and 7. Section 9 concludes this paper.

2. Related Work

Dynamically typed, object-oriented programming languages have a long history from Smalltalk and Self [14, 10] to more recent languages like Python, Ruby, PHP, ActionScript, and JavaScript. *Self* pioneered the development of many important optimizations, specialization, and performance adaptation techniques in its research environment. Recently, we have seen a surge of interest in improving dynamically typed language performance via JIT compilation and VM improvements. We focus on related work in the JIT compilation space.

2.1 Python

Although CPython is the most widely used Python implementation today, there are several projects in industry and academia that seek to improve Python performance via compilation.

The most recent one and the closest to our work is the Unladen Swallow compiler [44] led by Google. Unladen Swallow attaches a JIT compiler based on LLVM [21] to CPython and selectively compiles Python methods at runtime. It has not been active recently. Given the similarity of our approaches, we have included comparisons with Unladen Swallow in our evaluations and descriptions, where applicable.

PyPy [7] implements the Python language in an interpreter written in a restricted, statically typed subset of Python called RPython [2]. The PyPy JIT compiler is a trace JIT compiler that traces through PyPy's runtime layers. As the interpreter written in RPython runs, traces of the IR to which RPython is translated are collected and compiled. This approach of tracing through the runtime lends itself well to specialization as the collected traces capture type information. The runtime is completely different from CPython's runtime that we used, and is highly optimized for PyPy [8]. For example, its runtime is annotated for PyPy's optimizers [8] and tuned for PyPy [34]. Maps [9] are used for dictionaries while CPython uses a closed hash table. We do not compare the performance with PyPy in this paper.

Jython [39] and IronPython [18] convert Python to the Java and CLR/.NET world. A Python application running under Jython or IronPython becomes a pure Java or .Net application. It then relies on the Java or .Net JIT compiler to perform optimizations without knowledge of the original, dynamically typed language. However, with the loss of semantic information from the original dynamically typed language, the JIT compiler is not as effective. The performance of both systems with JIT compilers lags behind CPython for many of the benchmarks that we analyzed.

To eliminate complications of implementing dynamically typed languages on top of a Java virtual machine (JVM), Da Vinci Machine Project [38] proposes extensions to the JVM. For example, invokedynamic bytecode has been added, which make method invocations simple in the absence of static type information. Our approach uses typical compiler IR instead of using Java bytecode.

2.2 Method-based Compilers for other dynamically typed languages

Both method-based and trace-based compilation have also been explored in compilers for dynamically typed languages other than Python. Besides Unladen Swallow (Python), other major method-based dynamically typed language compilers are V8 [48] (JavaScript), JägerMonkey [6] (JavaScript), Rubinius [30] (Ruby), Tamarin with LLVM [36] (ActionScript), and P9 [37] (PHP).

V8 is one of the fastest JavaScript engines. The use of hidden classes, which is similar to maps in Self, speeds up name-based attribute lookup in JavaScript. Large performance improvements also come from a careful redesign of the runtime, such as the use of tagged pointer representation for numeric objects and the use of a better garbage collector. Our design goal of maintaining compatibility with CPython makes similar modifications difficult. In contrast to our approach, V8 uses its VM and a custom JIT to compile JavaScript methods.

JägerMonkey is a hybrid JIT compiler that combines benefits of method-based and trace-based compilation for JavaScript. It focuses on optimizations specifically targeted at dynamic languages, such as polymorphic inline caching. Rubinius and Tamarin use an approach similar to Unladen Swallow and leverage LLVM to compile Ruby or ActionScript code to machine code at runtime. P9 is a method-based JIT for PHP that is also based on Testarossa. To the best of our knowledge, these approaches have not been described or analyzed in detail, especially in terms of the compiler infrastructure and optimizations that they implement.

2.3 Trace-based compilation for dynamically typed languages

The major trace JITs for dynamically typed languages today are TraceMonkey [15] (JavaScript) and SPUR [5] (JavaScript), LuaJIT [22] (Lua), and PyPy (Python). Trace compilation is appealing for dynamically typed languages due to ease of type concretization, and faster and simpler compilation due to simple trace topologies.

TraceMonkey and LuaJIT compile traces formed out of the target language bytecode. As such, the JIT can optimize the code using knowledge of the language semantics captured in the trace. TraceMonkey, for instance, supports very aggressive type specialization and unboxing optimizations. LuaJIT performs redundancy elimination and folding optimizations on Lua bytecode. In contrast, SPUR and PyPy form traces by tracing through the runtime of the target, dynamically typed language. For instance, SPUR compiles traces formed out of Common Intermediate Language (CIL) instead of JavaScript bytecodes. As such, the optimizer can optimize any dynamically typed language that is implemented on top of CIL, thus offering a scalable approach to support many dynamically typed languages.

Yermolovich et al. [49] devised an approach that an interpreter of a dynamic language (guest VM) and running it on top of an optimizing trace-based virtual machine (host VM). This is very similar to PyPy. In this approach, the host VM compiles traces to machine code without implementing a custom JIT compiler for the guest VM.

3. Problem

We reuse the existing components in the compiler as much as possible to easily apply traditional optimizations to dynamically typed languages. These components are designed to operate on the IR for statically-typed languages such as Java. We can naïvely translate higher-level bytecode of a dynamically typed language into an IR, in which the IR is almost a series of invocations of the bytecode handlers of the dynamically typed language interpreter. This translation is simple, however, it leads to the following two problems that inhibit optimizations:

1. IR explosion: the large number of IR instructions with complex control flow to execute a single bytecode for the dynamically typed language.
2. Loss of semantics: the loss of the semantics when the original dynamically typed language is translated to the IR of a statically typed language.

With Problem 1, the large working memory required and complexity due to IR explosion often limits optimizations. The handler of each bytecode in dynamically typed languages contains complicated control flow in many cases. There are three reasons: One is untyped operands -- the bytecode can take objects of any type as the input operands. The interpreter tests the types for the operand objects and chooses the code that is specific to the types, which can execute the operation on the specific types. Second is error checking and exception handling -- most of the bytecodes in dynamically typed languages potentially throw exceptions. One of the reasons for this is that operations for some combinations of types in operands are not defined. Therefore, the interpreter checks whether an exception is thrown whenever each bytecode handler of a dynamically typed language is executed. Third is the reference counting garbage collection (GC). For example, PHP and CPython use this form of GC. In reference counting GC, the interpreter decrements the reference count of the objects when they are no longer used, and reclaims them if the reference count reaches zero.

With Problem 2, a compiler cannot use the semantics of the original bytecode of a dynamically typed language for optimizations since the IR that the compiler uses does not retain this information. For example, the code for reference counting is represented in the IR as a sequence of instructions that decrement of a value at a given memory address, test the value, branch conditionally to a function. It is not easy to infer the original semantics from the sequence. Retaining the original semantics would offer more opportunities for applying advanced optimizations.

Figure 1 shows an example of a Python program and the corresponding CPython bytecode. **Figure 2** shows an example of naïve translation of BINARY_ADD CPython bytecode at idx 6 in **Figure** 1. The iaload instruction gets an address value from a memory location specified by an address in the operand. The aiadd instruction calculates a new address by adding an integer to an address. The "if igt 0, t1, L2" jumps to L2 if the integer t1 equals 0. The iastore instruction puts an address value in a memory location specified by an address in the operand. The "acall @PyNumber_add" calls a polymorphic runtime helper for an add operation for any type combinations of two operands. The "vcall @DecRef" reclaims an object given by an argument.

```
g = 1.2
class sample(object):
  i = 0.1
  def foo(self, a):
    global g
    t = a + g
    return t + self.i
```

```
# idx  opcode        operand     comment
  0    LOAD_FAST     1 (a)
  3    LOAD_GLOBAL   0 (g)
  6    BINARY_ADD
  7    STORE_FAST    2 (t)
 10    LOAD_FAST     2 (t)
 13    LOAD_FAST     0 (self)
 16    LOAD_ATTR     1 (i)
 19    BINARY_ADD
 20    RETURN_VALUE
```

Figure 1. An example Python program and CPython bytecode for a method foo

```
                                     // osp is operand stack ptr.
L0: w   = iaload [osp - 4]           // 1.
    osp = aiadd osp, -4              // w = POP()
    v   = iaload [osp - 4]           // v = POP()
    osp = aiadd, osp, -4
                                     // 2. and 3.
    x   = acall @PyNumber_Add, w, v // types should be checked
                                     // in @PyNumber_Add
                                     // 4.
    t1 =  iaload [w + #obj_refcnt]// Decrement referece count
    t1 =  t1 - 1                     // for w
          iaload [w + #obj_refcnt] = t1
          ifigt 0, t1, L2
L1:       vcall @DecRef, w
L2: t2 =  iaload [v + #obj_refcnt]// Decrement reference count
    t2 =  t2 - 1                     // for v
          iaload [v + #obj_refcnt] = t2
          ifigt 0, t2, L4
L3:       vcall @DecRef, v
L4:       iastore [osp + 0] = x      // 5.
                                     // PUSH(x)
    osp = aiadd osp, 4
                                     // 6.
          ifaneq x, 0, L6            // if (x == NULL) {

L5: vcall @throwException            //   throwException()
L6:                                  // }
```

Figure 2. The naïve IR sequence for a BINARY_ADD bytecode at idx 6 in Figure 1

```
L0:
t1 =  s1                           // load from stack-allocated variable
                                   // for operand stack[1]
t0 =  s0                           // load from stack-allocated variable
                                   // for operand stack[0]
t2 =  acall @PyAdd_Float_Float, t1,t0 // Add specialized for two floats
                                   // types should be checked in it
      ReferenceCount t1, -1 // Decrement ref. count in t1
      ReferenceCount t0, -1 // Decrement ref. count in t0
s0 =  t2                           // store t2 to stack-allocated variable
                                   // for operand stack[0]
      ExceptionCheck t2            // Check whether an exception happened
```

Figure 3. The optimized IR sequence for a BINARY_ADD bytecode at idx 6 in Figure 1

```
a0 =  iaload [PyFrameObject+0]  // get an argument (self) from PythonFrame
                                // and put into stack-allocated variable
a1 =  iaload [PyFrameObject+4]  // get an argument (a) from PythonFrame
                                // and put into stack-allocated variable
s0 =  a1
      ReferenceCount s0, 1      // Increment reference count in s0
i =   iaload [PyCode+invalid]   // load flag whether code is valid
      SideExit      i           // if i is 1, bail out an interpreter
s1 =  1.2
      ReferenceCount s1, 1      // Increment reference count in s1
t =   acall @PyAdd_Float_Float, s0,s1
      ReferenceCount s1, -1
      ReferenceCount s0, -1
      ExceptionCheck t
a2 =  t
s0 =  a2
      ReferenceCount s0, 1
s1 =  a0
      ReferenceCount s1, 1
t =   acall @PyGetAttr_Offset, s1, 0 // Get a value of attribute i
                                // (profiled offset=0)
      ReferenceCount s1, -1
      ExceptionCheck t
t =   acall @PyAdd_Float_Float, s0, t
      ReferenceCount t, -1
      ReferenceCount s0, -1
      ExceptionCheck t
      iastore [PyFrameObject+0] = a0 // write back to the PythonFrame
      iastore [PyFrameObject+4] = a1 // write back to the PythonFrame
      iastore [PyFrameObject+8] = a2 // write back to the PythonFrame
      return t
```

Figure 4. The optimized IR sequence for the program in Figure 1

Figure 3 shows an IR sequence for the BINARY_ADD that we will generate to achieve better performance by applying optimizations. Compared to **Figure** 1, there are some improvements: the number of BBs is reduced, operations for operand stack are simple, and a runtime helper for is specialized. **Figure 4** shows an IR sequence for the program in **Figure** 1 that we will generate by applying optimizations.

4. The Python Language

This section provides a short introduction to the Python language, and its popular implementation, the CPython environment, to support the explanation of our approaches and optimizations that will be presented in Sections 6 and 7.

4.1 Overview

Python is a general purpose high-level, object-oriented programming language for rapid programming that supports several dynamic features for dynamic typing, dynamic objects, reflection, and dynamic code [17].

With dynamic typing, variables in Python are not associated with a fixed type, but take the type of the object assigned to them in a program. Without static type inference, internal representations in Python are type generic and defer concretizing abstract operations until runtime, This means a statement 'a = b + c' could describe integer addition, string concatenation, or whatever semantics are chosen for a user-defined object.

For dynamic objects, Python programs do not contain type declarations of fields and methods (referred to collectively as *attributes*) in a class. Also, objects can change their classes, class hierarchies can be changed, the existing attributes can be modified or deleted, and new attributes can be added to an object or class after its creation or definition. Although Python is an object-oriented language, Python cannot assume a fixed object structure at compile time.

Reflection refers to the use of meta-object facilities, such as obtaining an attribute, setting an attribute, invoking a method, and inspecting an object or its class using a name determined at runtime. Dynamic code creation in Python allows a program to construct and execute code at runtime.

4.2 Semantics

The reference implementation of Python is CPython although there are several other implementations for the Python language. This implementation is an intentionally simple interpreter written in the C language.

On a call to a Python function, the CPython interpreter creates a PyFrameObject that contains the complete environment needed to execute the function, including a reference to the bytecode sequence, the stack operands, and local variables. The VM steps through this bytecode sequence executing each bytecode. **Figure** 5 shows examples of bytecode handlers for the LOAD_FAST, LOAD_CONST, and BINARY_ADD instructions.

In comparison to a standard Java bytecode interpreter, the CPython interpreter executes many machine instructions per bytecode and has a fairly complex control flow.

The rest of this section describes several types of CPython bytecode instructions.

```
PyObject *x, *v, *w, **TOS;
...
switch (opcode) {
  case LOAD_FAST:
    x = GETLOCAL(oparg);
    Py_INCREF(x);     // increment x's reference count
    PUSH(x);          // *TOS++ = x
    if (x == NULL) { throwException(); }
    break;
  case LOAD_CONST:
    x = PyTuple_GetItem(CONSTS, oparg);
    Py_INCREF(x);
    PUSH(x);          // *TOS++ = x
    break;
  case BINARY_ADD:
    w = POP();        // w = *--TOS
    v = POP();        // v = *--TOS
    x = PyNumber_Add(v, w);
    Py_DECREF(v);     // decrement v's reference count
    Py_DECREF(w);     // decrement w's reference count
    PUSH(x);          // *TOS++ = x
    if (x == NULL) { throwException(); }
    break;
  ...
}
```

Figure 5. Bytecode instruction handlers for LOAD_FAST, LOAD_CONST, and BINARY_ADD in CPython

4.2.1 Built-ins and function calls

There are two types of function calls in Python: invocations of functions written in Python and invocations of functions written in another language such as C. For Python, a function invocation allocates and initializes the PyFrameObject, which includes a reference to the bytecode sequence, the stack operands, and local variables, and passes the arguments of Python. For C, a function invocation uses an indirect function call at the C level.

4.2.2 Local variables

There are slots for local variables in the PyFrameObject. A local variable can be accessed with a fixed offset from the local variable's slot. Therefore, a local variable can be accessed by LOAD_FAST and STORE_FAST bytecode instructions faster than an attribute.

4.2.3 Attributes and global variables

Access to attributes and global variables are frequent in Python programs, which reference variables by name. Due to the dynamic nature of Python, at runtime they are resolved each time they are referenced by their names, in contrast to static languages such as Java that resolve each of them only once. For example, the LOAD_ATTR (for object attribute) and LOAD_GLOBAL (for global variables or built-in) handle these resolutions with lookups in dictionaries (hash tables) using the name as a key. These resolutions also involve indirect function calls, since the exact procedure depends on the object type, and this adds overhead [24].

4.2.4 Reference counting GC

The Python language does not explicitly specify a particular algorithm for GC. CPython uses a reference counting GC [13]. In addition, a mark-and-sweep GC is invoked periodically to reclaim objects that have cyclic references.

For the reference counting GC, **Figure** 5 shows that instruction handlers control the increments and decrements of the reference count of an object with Py_INCREF() and Py_DECREF().

4.2.5 Exceptions

Most of the CPython bytecode instructions are potentially excepting instructions (PEIs). This is because they create an object for a result or they involve a complex or user-defined operation, any of which may throw an exception. In contrast with bytecode for static typed languages such as Java, most instructions are not PEIs. This is because they do not create an object for a result and usually perform a few simple operations.

4.2.6 Operand stack

Java bytecode maintains a stability property for the operand stack of the Java VM, so called *Gosling property*: the stack level at a given bytecode index always is the same regardless of the execution path used to arrive there [16]. CPython bytecode almost maintains the same stability except for one case. This exceptional case causes a problem that will be described in detail in Section 7.1.

4.2.7 Generic operations

Generic operations are ordinary operations such as 'NOT', '+', '+=', or 'a[1]'. These operations are untyped. When the operands are popped from the operand stack of the original VM of a dynamically typed language, the types are determined and based on the combination of types, the actual operation is performed. If both types are integer, arithmetic integer addition is invoked and the result is stored in an object.

5. Overview of Our JIT Compiler

Figure 6 shows an overview of our Python runtime system. The boxes in white are the same as the CPython runtime without our extensions. The boxes in grey are new components introduced by our runtime. As shown in the figure, we extended both the existing CPython virtual machine (VM) and the JIT compiler. The JIT compiler has a profiler and exports the API functions that update the profile repository to the CPython VM. The interpreter also collects type information and branch histories and stores them in the profile repository that we implemented. When the interpreter identifies a frequently executed method, the JIT compiler is invoked and compiles this method to native code, which is then executed.

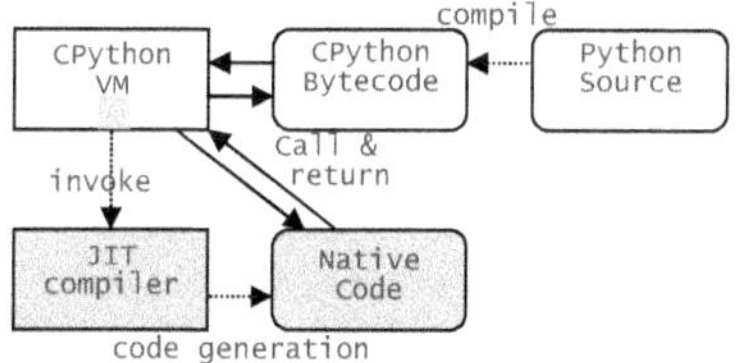

Figure 6. Overview of our Python runtime system

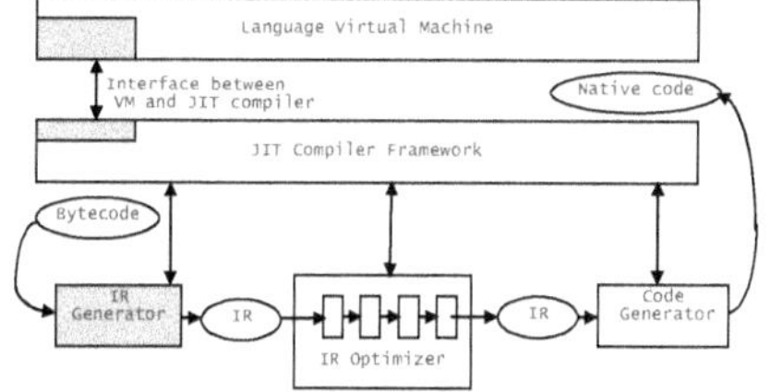

Figure 7. Overview of the our JIT compiler

We developed our JIT compiler by reusing the production-grade IBM J9/TR Java VM and the JIT compiler [26]. It supports Java 6, which does not support invokedynamic bytecode. Our JIT compiler is a method-based JIT compiler that consists of three customizable components, for intermediate representation (IR) generation, IR optimization, and native code generation as shown in **Figure** 7. The boxes in grey are new components for our JIT compiler for a dynamically typed language. Features that are described in Sections 6 and 7 are implemented in the IR generator and optimizer phases. From a high level view, we developed a new IR generator that translates a sequence of dynamically typed language bytecodes into our IR and a new set of optimizations for a dynamically typed language while maintaining our JIT compiler infrastructure for standard optimizations and code generation.

When compiling a method, the new IR generator walks through the method's CPython bytecodes to generate the IR while applying optimizations for dynamic languages, such as type specialization. Each IR instruction has explicit type information such as iadd (the add operation for integers). An object is represented as a structure, and is referred to using an address type. The new IR generator does not use any Java bytecode.

Our JIT compiler supports a variety of optimization levels, which trade optimization complexity against speed. At the hot optimization level that we used in this paper, our JIT compiler performs about a hundred optimization phases including copy propagation, constant propagation, dead code elimination, common sub-expression elimination, redundant exception check elimination, and global register allocation [25].

The code generator performs register allocation and instruction scheduling, and generates the specified machine instructions.

6. Adapting a Compiler to a dynamically typed language

This section describes the main techniques that we employed to adapt an existing compiler designed for a statically typed language to support a dynamically typed language. The goal of this section is to build the simple IR sequence, which the existing compiler can easily apply optimizations to, as shown in **Figure 3**.

We classify these techniques into four categories:

1. Representation of Python operations and objects in an IR for statically typed languages such as our IR.
2. Control flow graphs (CFGs) simplification.
3. Mapping memory locations to stack-allocated variables.
4. Reducing runtime overhead from the dynamic nature of the code.

The rest of this section describes each category implemented in detail.

6.1 Representation in IR for statically typed languages

We already presented the loss of semantics problem in IR for statically typed languages in Section 3.

We want to preserve the semantics of the user program without it being obfuscated by a naive translation of the code in the interpreter. For this purpose, when we translate a CPython bytecode instruction to our IR sequence, we use two policies.

- Represent memory operations such as accesses to the operand stack and the object of the dynamically typed language explicitly. The motivation for this policy is that standard compiler optimizations such as common subexpression elimination can be subsequently applied.
- Represent a step that has a large number of instructions such as a generic addition using one IR opcode. This opcode exposes more higher-level semantic information to the compiler than is available from individual low-level operations. Later, this opcode can be optimized using a specialized version.

6.2 Simplifying CFGs

This section looks at the complexity of the naively translated CFG and describes how we simplify the CFG.

In **Figure 2**, we show that naively translating one BINARY_ADD instruction generates seven basic blocks (BBs) in our IR sequence. The sources of these new BBs are an exception check and the handling of the reference counting GC.

The rest of this section describes how to reduce the number of BBs. This is effective in reducing the size of the working memory, while at the same time it also is effective at increasing the opportunities to apply optimizations because the number of instructions within each BB is increased.

6.2.1 Exceptions

We apply the factored CFG technique [12] to reduce the number of BBs in our IR sequence. The factored CFG creates a BB including several potentially excepting instructions (PEIs), which is represented by an ExceptionCheck opcode, and factored edges to connect with destination BBs for the exceptions. This approach was effective in reducing of the number of BBs for Java bytecode.

This is even more effective for dynamically typed languages that have many PEIs in their bytecode sequences. This is because several types of exceptions appear in the bytecode handler such as LOAD_FAST and BINARY_ADD as shown in **Figure** 5. Unlike our approach, Unladen Swallow relies on LLVM and explicitly represents the exception edges in its CFG as standard edges [44].

6.2.2 Reference counting GC

To represent operations for the reference counting GC, we defined a new ReferenceCount opcode in our IR, as shown in **Figure 3**, which increments or decrements the object targeted by a reference. In addition, when the reference count reaches zero, the object is reclaimed [19]. This notation avoids the introduction of new BBs. [19] uses this notation to simply the optimization of reference count operations. We also use this notation to reduce the number of BBs for simplification of CFGs. Unladen Swallow compiles a reference counting operation as an inlineable LLVM bitcode function, later exposing those actions in the LLVM IR [44].

6.3 Mapping memory locations to stack-allocated variables

It is important to map a memory location that is accesses by indirect load and store instructions to a stack-allocated variable. This mechanism leads to more optimization opportunities because, when a complier applies a dataflow optimization, it easily can pass the dataflow information for the variable properties along with the stack-allocated variables. In general, it is not easy for a compiler to pass the information about memory locations that may be aliased with other memory references.

We used two optimizations to map to stack-allocated variables. One is to map the operand stack and the other is to map local variables of a Python program. Because we apply these optimizations to the limited two types of indirect memory accesses, we can identify memory alias information and pre-calculate the size of stack allocation at compilation time.

6.3.1 Operand stack

It is important to map the operand stack of the original language to stack-allocated variables and to eliminate push and pop operations for the operands to reduce overhead of memory accesses.

Many VMs (including the Java VM) use a stack architecture for portability and smaller code size. For example, in Java bytecode, it is straightforward to map from stack operand locations to stack-allocated variable numbers [32]. This is because Java bytecode always maintains the stability property for the operand stack: the height of the stack operand is constant for a given bytecode index regardless of the previous execution path. This allows the compiler to conveniently assign one stack-allocated variable to each level of the operand stack.

Although CPython bytecode almost maintains this property, there are some exceptional cases. We devised an optimization to handle the exceptional cases, which will be described in Section 7.1.

6.3.2 Local variables

This optimization allows a compiler to map a local variable of a Python program to a stack-allocated variable instead of a slot in PyFrameObject during the execution of the compiled code. To implement this optimization, the compiled code copies arguments into stack-allocated variables in the method prolog, and copies the values in stack-allocated variables into local variable slots on the PyFrameObject in the method epilog.

In Python, the locals() built-in and sys._getframe().f_locals attribute can put the values of local variables into a dictionary. When these are executed, our runtime should put the values of the local variables from the stack-allocated variables into the dictionary to enable reflection on a frame object.

6.4 Reducing runtime overhead

This section describes optimizations to reduce runtime overhead by exploiting knowledge of the dynamically typed language and its implementation. All of the optimizations use the profile information that is collected during interpreted execution.

6.4.1 Attributes

This optimization reduces the cost of searching dictionaries for the LOAD_ATTR and STORE_ATTR instructions described in Section 4.2.3. The LOAD_ATTR and STORE_ATTR naively look in two dictionaries, the method resolution order (MRO) dictionary in the class object and the instance dictionary in the receiver object. The MRO determines the actual attributes in a class hierarchy with multiple inheritances by using the C3 algorithm [4]. The LOAD_ATTR and STORE_ATTR operations are given a receive object and an attribute name. At run time, this instruction introduces four lookups of the MRO directory and one lookup for the instance directory in the worst case. Our optimization reduces these overheads by combining the following two approaches. Unlike us, Unladen Swallow used the first one.

To address the MRO dictionary overhead, an optimization looks up the MRO dictionary using the profiled type at compilation time and generates the code using the result [42]. The MRO dictionary is rarely modified after being constructed [17]. If the types of the receiver and the cached descriptor are changed or if the class hierarchy and the MRO are changed, the pre-lookup result is invalidated.

To address the instance dictionary overhead, an optimization caches the associated entry in the instance dictionary at each access site by a LOAD_ATTR or STORE_ATTR instruction. The compiled code at each access site has a tuple of a version number and an offset that are collected by our profiler in the interpreter. We added a version number to each dictionary. The version number of a dictionary is incremented when the dictionary is rehashed or its entry is deleted. CPython implements an instance dictionary using a closed hash table. Thus, an offset can point out each entry in the dictionary. If the version number at an access site is equal to the number of the instance dictionary, the compiled code gets a value in the entry pointed by the offset without the comparison with the key of the entry. It can largely eliminate the lookup overhead.

6.4.2 Global variables

This optimization reduces the cost of looking up dictionaries for the LOAD_GLOBAL instruction described in Section 4.2.3. LOAD_GLOBAL looks in one or two dictionaries. To address the overhead of name-based dictionary lookup, an optimization searches the dictionaries for a variable at compilation time and speculatively uses the results as constants [46].

In many applications, it is observed that global variables are updated at the startup of an application and rarely updated after the startup [17]. Based on this assumption, after the interpreter executes methods during the startup, the compiler speculatively uses the constant value. If STORE_GLOBAL instruction updates the global variable, and modifies the immediate value, the speculation is invalid. When the speculation is invalid, the entire compiled version of the method is invalidated. This is accomplished by checking the condition at the method entry and prior to LOAD_GLOBAL instructions. If the condition is not satisfied, the execution bails out an interpreter.

In addition, in Python, after a module is loaded, it is also rarely updated. Therefore, the compiler generates a constant load using the value at compilation time to load the module with the IMPORT_NAME instruction. After the compilation, the compiled code for this method will also be invalidated if the VM modified by Unladen Swallow detects an update of global variables [45].

In addition to Unladen Swallow, our JIT compiler recompiles without this speculation when the method is invoked again after invalidation. This yields relatively good performance, even if the speculation fails.

6.4.3 Specialization

This optimization reduces the path length by removing unnecessary and expensive checks and indirections. This optimization generates calls to a runtime helper that prepares both specialized implementation and generic implementation, similar to the implementation in Unladen Swallow [43], as shown in **Figure** 8. The specialized implementation for the specific type is generated if this operation is executed with mostly monomorphic types as indicated by the profiler. For example, arithmetic, logical, and comparison operators are guarded based on a particular type such as float, and fast implementations are used. If the guard is not satisfied, the generic implementation for polymorphic types is executed.

```
PyObject *PyAdd_Float_Float(PyObject *o1, PyObject *o2){
  if (o1->type == PyFloat && o2->type == PyFloat) {
    // specialized implementation for float
    float f = o1->float_value + o2->float_value;
    r = PyObject_fromFloat(f); // allocate object
  } else {
    // generic implementation
    r = PyGeneric_Add(o1, o2);
  }
  return r;
}
```

Figure 8. A runtime helper of a BINARY_ADD specialized for float

Our JIT compiler exploits more opportunities for specialization than Unladen Swallow. We apply specialization to unary operations for integer or float, binary operations for a pair of integers, floats, or float and integer, compare operations for a pair of integers or floats, getting an item for str, unicode, list, tuple, or dict, setting an item for list, slice operations for str, unicode, list, or tuple, and unpacking a sequence for list or tuple.

Similarly, many built-in functions incur considerable overhead to perform a very small amount of work. While a built-in function can be overridden by a global name as shown in Section 6.4.2, this rarely occurs in practice. By applying appropriate guards to ensure it has not been changed by the user, the built-in function can be specialized to reduce the overhead. For example, there is a len()

built-in function that returns the number of elements in an given object, for str, unicode, list, tuple, and dict types in Unladen Swallow [41].

6.5 Application to other dynamically typed languages

Our approach directly generates compiler IR from the bytecode of the original dynamically typed language. Our JIT compiler will generate native code from the generated IR. The specialization is based on runtime helpers already prepared by the compiler. Another approach is the dynamic language runtime (DLR) [23] that dynamically generates an abstract syntax tree (AST) from the source file of the original dynamically typed language. Then, the AST generates a compiler's IR, and a JIT compiler will generate native code from the IR. DLR prepared flexible framework for generating the AST. The specialization is based on polymorophic inline cache that automatically updates a target method for an operation such as add.

Our approach generates a subroutine-threaded code, and then replaces unoptimized subroutines with optimized routines. Since we can reuse subroutines in a bytecode handler in the original VM for a dynamically typed language as unoptimized subroutines, it is easy to attach the JIT compiler to the original VM. If we prepare an IR generator and a specialization optimizer for a new dynamically typed language, we would implement a JIT compiler for the language.

7. Optimizations for CPython

This section focuses on teaching the JIT compiler deeper CPython-specific semantics to better understand the potential gains while Section 6 presented optimizations that can be applied (with implementation modifications) to a broad range of dynamically typed language environments.

For this exercise we chose two operations that have a high cost in CPython: operand stack and built-ins (more specifically isinstance() built-in and hasattr() built-in).

7.1 Operand stack

We devised a new optimization to always map the operand stack to stack-allocated variables and to eliminate push and pop operations for operands in the CPython bytecode. Our optimization retains compatibility with CPython bytecode observable behavior, while the previous approach, followed by Unladen Swallow [47], is not compatible.

The stability property described in Section 6.3.1 allows a compiler to straightforwardly map from stack operand locations to stack-allocated variable numbers with the analysis [1]. This is because the height of the stack operand is constant for a given bytecode index regardless of the previous execution path. However, CPython bytecodes, such as the END_FINALLY instruction, violate this property in the finally clause in two cases: when an exception is thrown and when a break or continue statement is executed. In the following, for the sake of brevity, we will explain the case of a continue statement.

An example of a continue is shown in **Figure 9**. At bcindex 30, two stack levels of the operand stack can be selected along the two execution path as shown in **Figure 10** (b). The stack level is one if no continue statement was executed from the index 21. The object Py_None shows no break or continue was executed from the index 13. The stack level is two if the CONTINUE_LOOP instruction, which corresponds to a continue statement, was executed. In this case, one object shows the next index, 3, will be executed after executing the END_FINALLY instruction at bcindex 30. The other object is for CONTINUE and indicates that execution came from the CONTINUE_LOOP. The operand stack level differs in the two execution paths.

To solve this problem, our JIT compiler performs an analysis that removes the object for the next index from the operand stack. The compiler can avoid pushing the object for the next index onto the operand stack by generating a conditional branch that goes to bcindex 3 if the stack top is CONTINUE at the END_FINALLY. Below are the steps to generate this code.

1. Make a work stack structure whose entry has {type, depth, bytecode index} empty, and set 0 to the nest_depth variable.
2. Walk the bytecode sequence of CPython in reverse post order.
3. If a SETUP_LOOP instruction is found, increment nest_depth by 1; else
4. If a CONTINUE_LOOP instruction is found, push {nest_depth, CONTINUE, next index (operand of CONTINUE_LOOP)} onto the work stack and generate code that pushes CONTINUE onto the top of the operand stack; else
5. If an END_FINALLY instruction is found, scan the work stack. If the current nest_depth is equal to the value in the depth field at the entry of the work stack and the value of the type field of this entry is CONTINUE, then generate the next code, and pop this entry and decrement nest_depth by 1.; else go to 2.

```
if (operand_stack[top] == CONTINUE)
  goto next_index // go to index 3 in Figure 7
```

Unladen Swallow solves this problem by changing the CPython bytecode sequence and runtime to ensure the stability property described in Section 6.3.1 [47]. This approach sacrifices compatibility with an existing CPython bytecode file. For example, the CPython bytecode file that Unladen Swallow generates will not work in the CPython runtime environment. Our new approach retains compatibility with the existing CPython bytecode files.

```
class test(object):
  def foo(self, a):
    while 1:
      try:
        if a:
          continue
      finally:
        i = 0
```

```
# idx opcode            operand
3  0 SETUP_LOOP         31 (to 34)

4  3 SETUP_FINALLY      18 (to 24)

5  6 LOAD_FAST          1 (a)
   9 JUMP_IF_FALSE      7 (to 19)
  12 POP_TOP

6 13 CONTINUE_LOOP      3
  16 JUMP_FORWARD       1 (to 20)
  19 POP_TOP
  20 POP_BLOCK
  21 LOAD_CONST         0 (None)

8 24 LOAD_CONST         1 (0)
  27 STORE_FAST         2 (i)
  30 END_FINALLY
  31 JUMP_ABSOLUTE      3
  34 LOAD_CONST         0 (None)
  37 RETURN_VALUE
```

Figure 9. The example program and bytecode for END_FINALLY

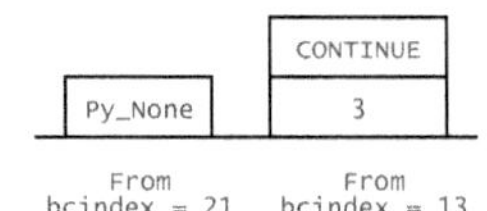

Figure 10. The operand stack levels at the finally clause (bcindex=30)

7.2 isinstance() built-in

We devised a new optimization to reduce the large overhead of the isinstance() built-in function. Python provides the isinstance() built-in function to check if an object is an instance of a given class. Many object-oriented programs switch tasks depending on the type of an object. For such programs, it is critical to reduce the overhead of instance checks for higher performance [27, 35].

We found that a function call to isinstance() requires about 7 times more time than the relatively slow LOAD_GLOBAL instruction. The large cost of isinstance() is due to the cost of the function call. It is difficult to reduce this overhead by inlining the built-in function into a Python method because CPython and the built-in functions are written in C and the built-in functions rely on the internal structures of CPython.

To reduce the cost of instance checks, caching the results of instance check has been proposed for Java [27, 35] to avoid calling functions written in C. Caching the results of instance checks in Python poses a challenge. In Python, class unloading is frequent, and the classes and the class hierarchy can change at runtime. Therefore, we must check whether or not the cache results are valid.

Our optimization consists of a profiling phase and a JIT compilation phase. The profiling phase collects the information and constructs the caches. The JIT compiler generates the code that returns result to be stored in the caches. When the classes that are profiled or that are used to construct the caches are modified during the execution of the program, we need to invalidate both the profile information and the code that uses the caches.

When isinstance() is called, our profiler collects information about (a) the call site of the built-in function, (b) the tested object's class, (c) the target class, (d) the result of the instance check, and (e) the frequency.

The JIT compiler uses the profile information to optimize the instance checks. If a bytecode includes a call site for isinstance() with a record in the profile repository, the JIT compiler translates the call into an InstanceCheck IR instruction. This instruction is translated into guard code and the instructions that look up the cache entries at a later phase. The guard code validates the cached class information before using it by ensuring that each of the cached classes is not unloaded and is not modified.

7.3 hasattr() built-in

We devised a new optimization to reduce the runtime overhead for the hasattr() built-in function. This built-in has two arguments: a Python object and an attribute name. This built-in examines whether an object has an attribute matched by a name. Our profiles show that hasattr() is almost always called with a constant second argument. If the profiled type of the first argument is one of known built-in types, the compiler can check whether or not the name, which is given as a constant in the second argument, exists and create code to return true or false. This check at compile time uses the same mechanism as the LOAD_ATTR described in Section 6.4.1 . At runtime, the constant can be used if the type guard succeeds.

We also modified CPython so that hasattr() does not rely on exception handling. The exception handling significantly increases the cost of hasattr() if the attribute is not found. To eliminate the cost of exception handling, we created a specialized path that returns False when the attribute is not found.

8. Performance Evaluation

We evaluated the optimizations described in Sections 6 and 7 on two 2.93-GHz Intel Xeon X5670 processor and we present these result in this section. The turbo boost feature in the CPU cores was disabled. The system has 24GB of memory and runs the RedHat Enterprise Linux 5.5 OS. We used the Unladen Swallow compiler [44] at revision 1167 for the Unladen Swallow data presented in this section, and used the 'hot' optimization level of our JIT compiler. CPython 2.6.4, the python interpreter that we used as a baseline, was built to exploit the computed-goto extension of GCC because Unladen Swallow and our JIT compiler also exploit this extension. CPython 2.6.4, our JIT compiler, and Unladen Swallow were all built using GCC/G++ 4.4. Both JIT compilers generate binary code for the IA-32 architecture.

We evaluated the performance of nine programs from the Unladen Swallow benchmark suite [40] as shown in Table 1. The Unladen Swallow benchmark suite was created by Google for the Unladen Swallow project. It consists of a variety of python programs, some of which are based on real applications, and is currently considered the de facto standard by the python community. All benchmarks are singled-threaded programs. The relatively small benchmarks float, nbody, nqueens, pystone, and richards each have less than 400 lines of source code. The larger, more realistic benchmarks like django, rietveld, spambayes rely on popular python frameworks or libraries, as line of source code is shown in the most right-hand column. We target long running web applications and ignore the effect of compilation on performance by modifying the number of warm-up iterations. Although we have not yet tuned our JIT compiler for compilation time, it can be improved by tuning the adaptive compilation mechanism [3] and by using concurrent compilation [20]. Our runtime calls the JIT compiler when the hotness counter for a method reaches 10,000. The counter is incremented at method entries and loop back edges. For each result, we report the average of 50 runs (with the exception of 250 runs for float because it runs for a much shorter time compared to the other benchmarks) along with a 95% confidence interval.

Table 1. Description of the Unladen Swallow Benchmarks

name	Description	Lines of source code app./library
float	floating point-heavy benchmark originally used by Factor	51 / 0
nbody	the N-body Shootout benchmark	107 / 0
nqueen	small solver for the N-Queens problem	54 / 0
pystone	the classic dhrystone benchmark	214 / 0
richards	the classic Richards benchmark	303 / 0
django	Django template to build a 150x150-cell HTML table	36 / 72727
rietveld	Django template that the Rietveld code review application uses	85 / 88820
spam-bayes	a scanned mailbox through a SpamBayes ham/spam classifier	37 / 48902
slow-spitfire	Spitfire template system to build a 1000x1000-cell HTML table without Psyco	56 / 4569

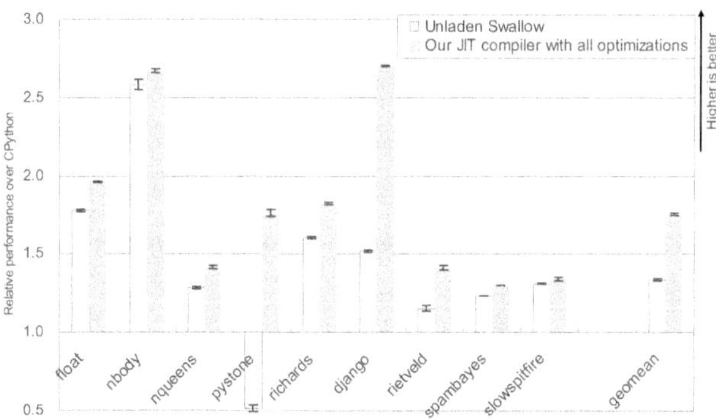

Figure 11. Performance comparisons between CPython, Unladen Swallow, our JIT compiler

8.1 Performance of the Unladen Swallow benchmarks

Figure 11 compares the performance of our JIT compiler with CPython and Unladen Swalow. Our JIT compiler and Unladen Swallow are built on top of CPython. Our JIT compiler improves the performance by 1.76x on average over CPython. We observed that larger performance improvements for nbody and django are 2.74x and 2.67x, respectively. On an average, our JIT compiler shows an additional 1.42x performance improvement over the 1.34x improvement of Unladen Swallow relative to CPython. This additional benefit is the highest for django, where our JIT compiler is 1.78x faster than Unladen Swallow. The optimization for the isinstance() built-in achieves large performance improvement in django. For Unladen Swallow, the performance of pystone is degraded by the overhead of invalidating code due to frequent updates of global variables.

8.2 Effectiveness of optimizations

This subsection investigates effectiveness of optimizations that we described in Sections 6 and 7. To confirm the overall effectiveness of the optimizations for dynamically typed languages described in Sections 6 and 7, **Figure 12** compares the performance of our JIT compiler with and without all of the optimizations. They improve the performance by 1.69x on average. The performance improvements for nbody and django are 2.74x and 2.60x. The runs of pystone and rietveld failed due to working memory overflow during method compilation without our optimizations.

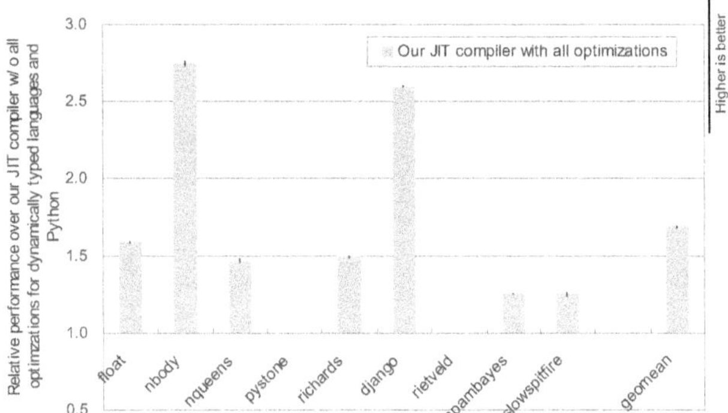

Figure 12. Performance comparisons between our JIT compiler w/ and w/o any optimizations for dynamically typed languages

Table 2. Descriptions of the Unladen Swallow Benchmarks

Category	Optimization	Section	Novelty compared to Unladen Swallow
Simplify CFGs	Exceptions	6.2.1	New
	Reference counting GC	6.2.2	Same
Map memory locations	Operand stack	6.3.1 and 7.1	New
	Local variables	6.3.2	Same
Reduce runtime overhead	Specialization	6.4.3	Incremental
	Hasattr	7.3	New
	Atttributes	6.4.1	New
	Global variables	6.4.2	Incremental
	Isinstance	7.2	New

We categorized all of the optimizations into three categories: Simplify CFG, map memory locations, and reduce runtime overhead. Table 2 shows the each category and includes the optimizations and section number of its description. We also include a column to compare the difference between our optimizations and those of Unladen Swallow. While two of the optimizations are the same, to the best of our knowledge, they have not been evaluated before.

Figure 13 shows the benefit of optimizations in different categories by selectively enabling optimizations in three categories. The graph shows the relative performance improvements of our JIT compiler compared to the JIT compiler when disabling the specified optimizations. The simplify CFGs optimization shows a 1.17x performance improvement. In particular, the performance improvement for nbody is 2.25x. Because this optimization increases the number of IR opcodes in a BB by avoiding the introduction of new BBs, optimizations for intra-BB are effectively applied. More importantly, without simplifying CFGs, the compilations of pybench and rietveld failed due to insufficient working memory, confirming that it is important to reduce the size of the IR. Therefore, we make it a mandatory optimization. Mapping memory locations shows a 1.26x performance improvement on average. In particular, this is effective for django because the specialization for built-in functions cannot be used due to the difficulty identifying such functions without this optimization. Reducing the runtime overhead yielded a 1.39x performance improvement on average. In particular, this is effective for nbody and django. Other optimizations, which are not possible when enabling only some optimizations, become possible when several optimizations are used at the same time.

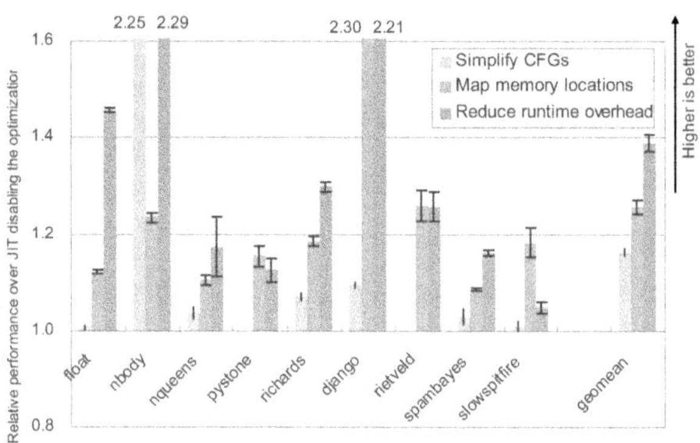

Figure 13. Performance improvements of each category

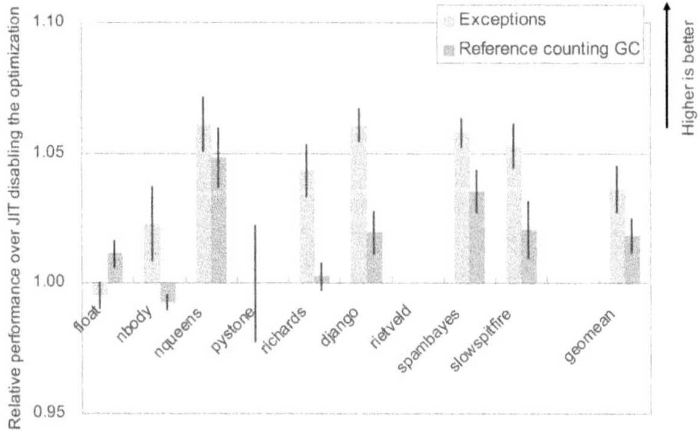

Figure 14. Performance improvements of each optimization to simply CFGs

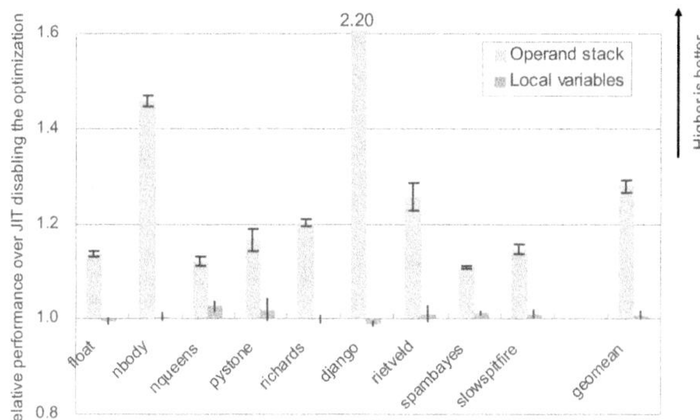

Figure 15. Performance improvements of each optimization to map stack-allocated variables

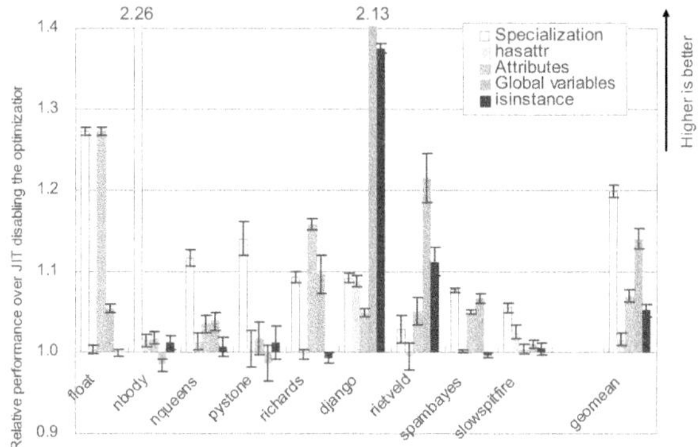

Figure 16. Performance improvements of each optimization to reduce runtime overhead

For further insight, we measured the effectiveness of individual optimizations in each category. **Figure 14** shows the effectiveness of the two optimizations for simplifying CFGs. For rietveld, both optimizations are needed to compile the program. **Figure 15** shows the effectiveness of the two optimizations described for mapping stack-allocated variables. The operand stack improves the performance by 1.28x on average. In particular, it is effective for django. Again, this is because the precise analysis for stack operand is necessary to identify a built-in function and apply other optimizations. The local variables are less effective for these programs. Currently Unladen Swallow and our JIT compiler do not fully exploit stack-allocated variables. For example, a primitive value such as int or float in an object is not allocated into the stack-allocated variable while a primitive operation such as add can be specialized using the type information. If a compiler could allocate primitive values into the stack-allocated variable, this optimization would be more effective.

Figure 16 shows the effectiveness of the five optimizations in reducing the runtime overhead. Specialization improves the performance by 1.20x on average. In particular, it is effective for nbody. This is because a hot method in nbody includes binary floating point operations that can be specialized. For float, it is also effective. However, the hot method includes square root functions that were not specialized and take more time. Hasattr improves the performance of django by 1.09x. Attribute improves the performance of float by 1.28x and richard by 1.16x. They frequently access a fixed number of attributes in the hot method. Thus, the fastest path is frequently executed. Global variables improve the performance of django by 2.13x and rietveld by 1.22x. In django, a method that executes the IMPORT_NAME instruction is frequently executed, and the imported module is not modified [45]. This optimization is also a prerequisite for the isinstance optimization. When this is disabled, the isinstance optimization is also disabled. Isinstance improves the performance of django by 1.38x. In this program, the isinstance() built-in function is very frequently called.

9. Conclusion

We presented an approach to improving the performance of dynamically typed scripting languages like Python along with a thorough evaluation of the techniques and optimizations we proposed. Our approach was based on leveraging an existing production quality compiler designed for a statically typed language to minimize development and maintenance costs. We presented three methods to effectively extend the compiler with support for dynamically typed languages: simplifying control flow graphs, mapping memory locations to stack-allocated variables, and reducing runtime overhead using language semantics. We showed a 1.69x performance improvement on average by using these three methods. We also analyzed the effectiveness of each optimization in these three categories.

In future work we plan to investigate how to effectively adopt optimizations implemented in trace-based JIT compilers, such as load-store forwarding, unboxing, and minimizing reference counting operations. In addition, we plan to identify more complex execution paths, such as regions, as a compilation unit. This approach will also benefit from using an existing method-based compiler capable of applying optimizations to complex CFGs.

References

[1] Agesen, O., Detlefs, D., and Moss, J. E. Garbage collection and local variable type-precision and liveness in Java virtual machines. In Proceedings of the ACM SIGPLAN 1998 conference on Programming language design and implementation, pp.269-279, 1998.

[2] Ancona, D., Ancona, M., Cuni, A., and Matsakis, N. D. RPython: a step towards reconciling dynamically and statically typed OO languages. In Proceedings of the 2007 Symposium on Dynamic Languages, pp.53-64, 2007.

[3] Arnold, M., Fink S. J., Grove, D., Hind, M., and Sweeney, P. F. A Survey of Adaptive Optimization in Virtual Machines. In Proceedings of the IEEE, 93(2), 2005.

[4] Barrett, K., Cassels, B., Haahr, P., Moon, D. A., Playford, K., and Withington, P. T. A monotonic superclass linearization for Dylan. In Proceedings of the ACM international Conference on Object-Oriented Programming, Systems, Languages, and Applications, pp.69-82, 1996.

[5] Bebenita, M., Brandner, F., Fahndrich, M., Logozzo, F., Schulte, W., Tillmann, N., and Venter, H. SPUR: a trace-based JIT compiler for CIL. In Proceedings of the ACM international Conference on Object Oriented Programming Systems Languages and Applications, pp.708-725, 2010.

[6] Bebenita, M., Brandner, F., Fahndrich, M., Logozzo, F., Schulte, W., Tillmann, N., and Venter, H. Mozilla Foundation, https://wiki.mozilla.org/JaegerMonkey/.

[7] Bolz, C., Cuni, A., Fijalkowski, M., and Rigo, A. Tracing the Meta-Level: PyPy's Tracing JIT Compiler. In Proceedings of the 4th workshop on the Implementation, Compilation, Optimization of Object-Oriented Languages and Programming Systems, pp.18-25, 2009.

[8] Bolz, C., Cuni, A., Fijalkowski, M., Leuschel, M., Rigo, A., and Pedroni, S. Runtime Feedback in a Meta-Tracing JIT for Efficient Dynamic Languages, In Proceedings of the 6th workshop on the Implementation, Compilation, Optimization of Object-Oriented Languages and Programming Systems, 2011.

[9] Chambers, C. and Ungar, D. and Lee, E. An efficient implementation of SELF a dynamically-typed object-oriented language based on prototypes, In Proceedings of the ACM international Conference on Object Oriented Programming Systems Languages and Applications, pp.49-70, 1989.

[10] Chambers, C. and Ungar, D. Customization: optimizing compiler technology for self, a dynamically-typed object-oriented programming language. In Proceedings of the ACM SIGPLAN Conference on Programming language design and implementation, pp.146-160, 1989.

[11] Chambers, C., Ungar, D., and Lee. E. An efficient implementation of SELF a dynamically-typed object-oriented language based on prototypes. In the ACM international Conference proceedings on Object-oriented programming systems, languages and applications. pp.49-70, 1989.

[12] Choi, J.-D., Grove, D., Hind, M., and Sarkar, V. Efficient and precise modeling of exceptions for the analysis of Java programs. In Proceedings of the 1999 ACM SIGPLAN-SIGSOFT workshop on Program analysis for software tools and engineering, pp.21-31, 1999.

[13] Christopher, T. W. Reference count garbage collection. Software-Practice and Experience, 14(6), pp.503-507, 1984.

[14] Deutsch, L. P. and Schiffman, A. M. Efficient implementation of the smalltalk-80 system. In Proceedings of the 11th ACM SIGACT-SIGPLAN Symposium on Principles of Programming Languages., pp.297-302, 1984.

[15] Gal, A., Eich, A., *et al.* Trace-based just-in-time type specialization for dynamic languages. In Proceedings of the ACM SIGPLAN Conference on Programming Language Design and Implementation, pp.465-478, 2009.

[16] Gosling, J. Java intermediate bytecodes: ACM SIGPLAN workshop on intermediate representations, pp.111-118, 1995.

[17] Holkner, A. and Harland, J. Evaluating the dynamic behaviour of Python applications. In Proceedings of the Thirty-Second Australasian Conference on Computer Science - Volume 91, pp.19-28, 2009.

[18] IronPython, http://ironpython.net/.

[19] Joisha, P. G. Compiler optimizations for nondeferred reference: counting garbage collection. In Proceedings of the 5th international symposium on Memory management. pp.150-161, 2006.

[20] Kulkarni, P. A. JIT compilation policy for modern machines, In Proceedings of the ACM international conference on Object oriented programming systems languages and applications, pp.773-788, 2011.

[21] Lattner, C. and Adve, V. LLVM: A Compilation Framework for Lifelong Program Analysis & Transformation. In Proceedings of the international Symposium on Code Generation and Optimization: Feedback-Directed and Runtime Optimization, pp.75-86, 2004.

[22] LuaJIT roadmap 2008, http://lua-users.org/lists/lua-l/2008-02/msg00051.html.

[23] Microsoft corporation. Dynamic Language Runtime, http://dlr.codeplex.com/

[24] Mostafa, N., Krintz, C., Cascaval, C., Edelsohn, D., Nagpurkar, P., Wu, P. Understanding the Potential of Interpreter-based Optimizations for Python, UCSB Technical Report 2010-14, 2010.

[25] Muchnick, S. S. Advanced Compiler Design and Implementation. Morgan Kaufmann Publishers Inc., 1998.

[26] N. Grcevski, A. Kielstra, K. Stoodley, M. G. Stoodley, and V. Sundaresan. Java just-in-time compiler and virtual machine improvements for server and middleware applications. In Proceedings of the 3rd Virtual Machine Research and Technology Symposium, pp.151-162. 2004.

[27] Paleczny, M., Vick, C., and Click. C. The java hotspot server compiler. In Proceedings of the Symposium on Java Virtual Machine Research and Technology Symposium, pp.1-12, 2001.

[28] Python Programming Language, http://www.python.org/

[29] Rossum, G. van. http://mail.python.org/pipermail/python-dev/2006-December/070323.html.

[30] Rubinius, http://rubini.us/

[31] Ruby on Rails, http://rubyonrails.org/

[32] Shi, Y., Gregg, D., Beatty, A., and Ertl, M. A. Virtual machine showdown: stack versus registers. In Proceedings of the 1st ACM/USENIX international Conference on Virtual Execution Environments, pp.153-163, 2005.

[33] Shire, B. PHP and Facebook, http://blog.facebook.com/blog.php?post=2356432130

[34] Speeding up JSON encoding in PyPy, http://morepypy.blogspot.com/2011/10/speeding-up-json-encoding-in-pypy.html.

[35] Suganuma, T., Ogasawara, T., Takeuchi, M., Yasue, T., Kawahito, M., Ishizaki, K., Komatsu, H., and Nakatani, T. Overview of the IBM Java just-in-time compiler. IBM System Journal, 39(1), pp.175-193, 2000.

[36] Tamarin on LLVM - More Numbers, http://www.masonchang.com/blog/2011/4/21/tamarin-on-llvm-more-numbers.html

[37] Tatsubori, M., Tozawa, A., Suzumura, T., Trent, S., and Onodera, T. Evaluation of a just-in-time compiler retrofitted for PHP. In Proceedings of the 6th ACM SIGPLAN/SIGOPS international Conference on Virtual Execution Environments, pp.121-132, 2010.

[38] The Da Vinci Machine Project, http://openjdk.java.net/projects/mlvm/.

[39] The Jython Project, http://www.jython.org/Project/.

[40] Unladen Swallow Benchmarks, http://code.google.com/p/unladen-swallow/wiki/Benchmarks/.

[41] Unladen Swallow, Change log, http://code.google.com/p/unladen-swallow/source/detail?r=1102.

[42] Unladen Swallow, Change log, http://code.google.com/p/unladen-swallow/source/detail?r=923.

[43] Unladen Swallow, Change log, http://code.google.com/p/unladen-swallow/source/detail?r=957.

[44] Unladen Swallow, http://code.google.com/p/unladen-swallow/.

[45] Unladen Swallow, Optimize IMPORT_NAME, http://codereview.appspot.com/217052

[46] Unladen Swallow, Optimize LOAD_GLOBAL, http://codereview.appspot.com/109043

[47] Using tracing to jump out of a loop causes the Python object stack to overflow, http://code.google.com/p/unladen-Swallow/issues/detail?id=91

[48] V8 JavaScript Engine. http://code.google.com/p/v8/.

[49] Yermolovich, A., Wimmer, C., and Franz, M. Optimization of dynamic languages using hierarchical layering of virtual machines, In Proceedings of the 5th symposium on Dynamic languages, pp. 79-88, 2009.

Unpicking The Knot: Teasing Apart VM/Application Interdependencies

Yi Lin
Australian National University
Yi.Lin@anu.edu.au

Stephen M. Blackburn
Australian National University
Steve.Blackburn@anu.edu.au

Daniel Frampton
Australian National University
Daniel.Frampton@anu.edu.au

Abstract

Flexible and efficient runtime design requires an understanding of the dependencies among the components internal to the runtime and those between the application and the runtime. These dependencies are frequently unclear. This problem exists in all runtime design, and is most vivid in a metacircular runtime — one that is implemented in terms of itself. Metacircularity blurs boundaries between application and runtime implementation, making it harder to understand and make guarantees about overall system behavior, affecting isolation, security, and resource management, as well as reducing opportunities for optimization. Our goal is to shed new light on VM interdependencies, helping all VM designers understand these dependencies and thereby engineer better runtimes.

We explore these issues in the context of a high-performance Java-in-Java virtual machine. Our approach is to identify and instrument transition points into and within the runtime, which allows us to establish a dynamic execution context. Our contributions are: 1) implementing and measuring a system that dynamically maintains execution context with very low overhead, 2) demonstrating that such a framework can be used to improve the software engineering of an existing runtime, and 3) analyzing the behavior and runtime characteristics of our runtime across a wide range of benchmarks. Our solution provides clarity about execution state and allowable transitions, making it easier to develop, debug, and understand managed runtimes.

Categories and Subject Descriptors D.3.4 [*Programming Languages*]: Processors—Run-time environments

General Terms Languages, Design, Measurement

Keywords Metacircular, Virtual Machine, Isolation, Dependency

1. Introduction

The engineering of a high performance managed runtime is a major undertaking. The competing goals of correctness, completeness, performance, robustness, agility and flexibility sit in tension. In this paper we explore the interdependencies among the components internal to a managed runtime and those between the application and the runtime. We do so in a metacircular runtime — a context where these interdependencies are particularly important and particularly hard to tease out. The challenge of cleanly and correctly identifying and designing for these dependencies is key to runtime design and perhaps the greatest impediment to wider use of metacircularity.

VEE'12, March 3–4, 2012, London, England, UK.

Metacircular runtimes are implemented in the same language that they target, an approach which can bring software engineering and performance benefits, intriguing technical challenges, and a satisfying sense of closure. The intellectual appeal of metacircular managed runtimes is therefore unsurprising. We don't see metacircularity as a meaningful end in runtime design and there are few, if any examples of the approach being commercially successful. However, we are convinced of the value of using a high-level language to build a high performance runtime [6, 10]. When the target language is also a good candidate for runtime implementation, metacircularity is the logical outcome. One outcome of this paper is a teasing out of the benefits of metacircularity from its shortcomings. Another outcome is that our findings allow us to make significant improvements to an existing metacircular JVM and shed light on an element of runtime design relevant to implementers of future runtimes, metacircular or not. Because it acutely demonstrates the problem of identifying runtime interdependencies, the context throughout the remainder of this paper is a metacircular runtime.

Metacircularity can have three obvious benefits. First, the strengths of the target language are brought to bear on the implementation. In the case where the target is a strongly typed high level language, the software engineering benefits may be clear, particularly where the high level language is capable of efficiently expressing low-level semantics [10]. Second, the impedance mismatch between implementation and target languages is removed. This problem is most clear at performance-critical boundaries between the runtime and the application, such as in the hot paths of barriers and allocation sequences [3]. Finally, a metacircular runtime 'eats its own dogfood'. This means that the implementers are particularly motivated towards correctness and performance because their implementation has a circular dependency on those properties. Successful cases of metacircular runtimes include Singularity in C# [11], Jikes RVM/Squawk/Maxine/JNode in Java [1, 14, 16, 18], PyPy in Python [15], Klein VM in Self [19], etc.

Despite this academic success, we know of no commercially successful metacircular runtimes. One explanation might be the performance overheads that one associates with high level languages, due to garbage collection, dynamic compilation, etc. However, Alpern et al. note that Jikes RVM achieved 95% the performance of its then commercial counterpart, the IBM 1.3.0 DK JVM, on the SPECjvm98 benchmarks on Linux/IA32 [2]. Indeed, metacircularity has the attraction of potential performance benefits:

- *Aggressive inlining and optimization:* Runtime code can be directly inlined into the application context, and optimizations applied across the resulting integrated code.
- *Seamless library downcalls into runtime:* No cross-language bridge is needed for library downcalls, which provides more inlining and optimization opportunities.

However, while these benefits flow from addressing the target-host impedance mismatch, they also blur the relationship between the application and runtime. The application, language library and runtime components do not have a crisply defined boundary within the runtime, and are heavily mixed together. So it is generally not possible to tell, dynamically, whether a thread is executing code on behalf of application or the runtime. This absence of runtime/application isolation is the metacircular runtime's dirty laundry, manifest in issues such as security and resource management.

Resource management is one conspicuous manifestation of the lack of isolation that comes with metacircularity. In general it is impossible to know whether an object is allocated by the runtime or by the application because they both allocate to the same heap. A single allocation site (within a standard library, for example), may allocate objects on behalf of the application and the runtime without distinction. Thus class objects, class metadata, code, compiler detritus, and other generic objects used by the runtime are intermixed with application allocations. As a consequence, it is hard to know what the real footprint of the application is, and it is hard to know what the adverse locality effect is of this intermingling. Ogata et al. reported that in the IBM J9 JVM, a conventional JVM written in C/C++, non-Java memory usage can account for more than the Java heap in over half of the DaCapo benchmarks [12]. We use our framework to conduct a similar experiment with Jikes RVM, and find that the runtime/application breakdown in our system is similar. As an average of ten DaCapo benchmarks, 56.6% of memory is used by runtime allocated objects, with only 43.4% of memory consumed by application objects. Thus the Java heap footprint of a benchmark running on a runtime such as Jikes RVM is significantly overstated.

Security can also suffer when isolation is diminished and boundaries are blurred. Consider, by contrast, the boundary between the system and user spaces in an operating system, which are crisply and rigorously defined. Generally within a runtime there are many instances of code that should be considered as privileged. When the execution context of such privileged code is ill-defined security is compromised. This downside to metacircular runtimes is a significant inhibitor to commercial uptake. During the development of the Moxie project, leading developers were polled, and the issue of application/runtime isolation was rated as one of the most pressing issues confronting metacircular runtime design [8].

In this paper we first propose an efficient framework for creating efficient and clean runtime/application isolation and extend it to distinguish among multiple runtime sub-components such as the compiler, garbage collector, classloader, etc. We examine the Jikes RVM code base and identify 41 calls into the runtime. We take the model further by introducing a well-defined concept of *runtime services* code; statically identifiable code that is executed by the application on behalf of the runtime, and is typically inlined and optimized by the compiler. This approach minimizes points where execution context cannot be inferred statically. We have implemented this framework in Jikes RVM, and present preliminary performance numbers that show that it can be implemented at virtually no overhead. We give examples of the mechanism we use to analyze allocation patterns across the application and runtime components. Finally, we argue that the isolation and clarity from using this framework carries with it software engineering benefits, including enhanced modularity within the runtime.

The contributions of this paper are: 1) a critique of metacircularity that identifies lack of isolation and blurred boundaries as blockers to more widespread uptake of metacircularity, 2) a concrete implementation of a new very low overhead framework that reintroduces isolation without forsaking the benefits of metacircularity, 3) a quantitative analysis of Jikes RVM's behavior that was not possible without our framework, and 4) insight into how these lessons can be applied to existing and future runtime implementations, whether they are metacircular or not.

2. Tracking Execution Context

Our goal is to better understand the dependencies and dynamic execution behavior of a managed runtime. In particular we want to remove contextual ambiguity, which arises because of the interactions and dependencies between components. This problem is particularly acute in a metacircular setting, because metacircular runtimes are *reentrant*: while servicing a request from the application the runtime may need to re-enter itself. For example, while performing a classloading operation, the runtime may need support from the memory manager to allocate objects. In that example, what the memory manager sees as the 'application' is in fact the classloader, another part of the runtime. In the absence of dynamic context to inform it, the memory manager is not aware of the fact that it is being called by another part of the runtime.

We attack the issue of contextual ambiguity directly by dynamically maintaining an explicit *execution context* for each thread in the runtime. We define execution contexts as holding the current runtime request being executed (e.g., classloading or compilation). This state allows us to:

1. Realize context-specific policies, such as using different heaps according to the *dynamic* context of the allocation. For example, the compiler could use a separate, dedicated, memory management policy.
2. Explicitly assert that certain code may only be executed from within certain dynamic context(s), improving isolation and security, and making it easier to understand the code.
3. Relate behavior to contexts. For example, establishing how often a given library function is dynamically called from within different runtime components or by the user application. Such information could guide optimizations or structural improvements to the runtime design.

Transition Points In order to track execution context, we identify and annotate *transition* points. These points are comprised of *runtime downcalls* (DCs): transitions from the 'application' to the runtime; and *runtime service calls* (SCs): intra-runtime requests where the responsibility for execution is transferred to another service. In a metacircular runtime, the 'application' may in fact be the runtime itself, so intra-runtime transitions may be due to either downcalls or service calls. We analyzed the Jikes RVM code base and annotated all calls that constitute a transition. A simplified depiction of the context transition graph for Jikes RVM is illustrated in Figure 1(a).

Limiting Interdependencies While dependencies between runtime components are an essential property of a managed runtime (in particular in the metacircular case), infinite regress is not. It follows that certain transitions are permissible whilst others are not. As an example, it is fine for the compiler to trigger a garbage collection, but it is not correct for the garbage collector to recursively trigger a garbage collection. So while intra-runtime transitions are permissible, we require that the graph of these context transitions be acyclic. This helps to curtail dependencies within the runtime, and is of particular value in dealing with metacircularity. In general, this corresponds to disallowing individual features or services from (transitively) requiring access to the feature or service they implement.

Selecting Contexts We broaden the definition of execution contexts from the binary *application/runtime* divide, to include a number of key components of the runtime as discrete contexts, such as *memory management*, *class loading*, etc. This refinement allows us to differentiate an acyclic downcall from the classloader to the memory manager from a cyclic call from the classloader to itself or from the memory manager to itself. Figure 1(b) exposes the intra-runtime dependencies that were elided from Figure 1(a). Only sub-

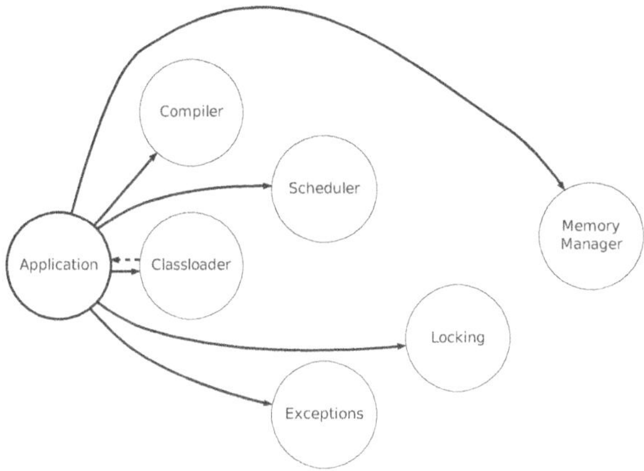

(a) Transitions from the application

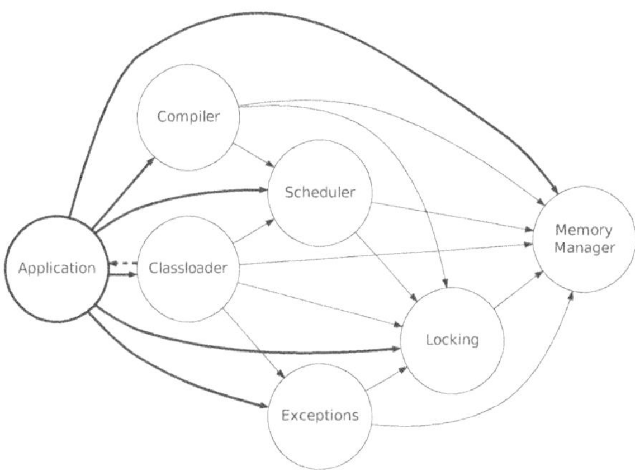

(b) All context transitions, including metacircular edges. Moving from left to right, subsystems exhibit fewer and fewer dependencies.

Figure 1. A simplified depiction of dynamic context transitions in Jikes RVM.

stantive transitions are tracked. There also exist 'lightweight', superficial, transitions which are not tracked for pragmatic reasons and therefore do not register as transitions, as we discuss below.

Upcalls Managed runtimes often require upcalls from the runtime back to the application. For example, a downcall to the classloader may eventually lead to an upcall to the application to execute a class initializer (illustrated in Figure 1 as a dashed line). The upcall may in turn lead to a downcall, creating a cycle. The possibility of generating cycles this way is a property of the runtime specification, independent of the runtime implementation, and is therefore outside the scope of this paper. However, our approach must accommodate upcalls. To achieve this, we include an explicit transition of execution context when an upcall is made, and we discount upcall edges when checking for cycles in the graph of context transitions. Upcalls in effect amount to a break in the graph of metacircular context transitions.

Lightweight Transitions In addition to the 'substantive' transitions discussed above, there also exist lightweight transitions which we pragmatically do not track. Examples of these may include SCs such as accessor methods within the classloader which are used by the compiler or garbage collector to identify field offsets, or DCs such as the fast path of an allocation sequence or write barrier. In the absence of a context transition, the dynamic context remains that of the calling context (e.g. the compiler) although the code falls within the static domain of the callee context (e.g. the classloader). In a non-metacircular case, the code for a lightweight DC is easy to identify because it will be written in the target language (e.g. Java) or perhaps in inlined assembler. However in a metacircular case there is no language transition so the transition point for the lightweight DC is ambiguous. To remove this ambiguity, we explicitly identify and annotate such code with a `@RuntimeService` annotation, which facilitates static checking whilst still supporting this common optimization.

Precise Transition Placement In practice, a transition between components, in particular from the application to the runtime, may manifest as a relatively lengthy call chain, inviting the question of where to draw the line and declare the transition point. For example, a request for memory when allocating a new object will typically start with a frequently taken *fast path*, and only fall through to a *slow path* in the uncommon case. In both metacircular and non-metacircular runtimes, the fast path is typically inlined into the application code by the compiler, while the call to the slow path is kept out of line. In this case we can argue that the fast-path constitutes a lightweight DC with the substantive DC only beginning at the call to the slow path. In a non-metacircular runtime, a natural choice may be the inevitable language boundary between the supported language (Java) and implementation language (C++), which most likely occurs at the call to the slow path. In a metacircular runtime the language transition does not exist, forcing the implementer to make a decision in each case. Our approach, when given a choice, was to select the first out-of-line call as the point of the DC. We reason that this allows us to trigger transitions as close to the application as possible whilst ensuring transitions do not occur too frequently, which would lead to unacceptable overheads.

3. Implementation

We now describe an implementation of our framework for efficiently tracking execution context. Concretely, the implementation involves two steps: 1) additions to the runtime that provide the mechanisms for efficiently identifying and tracking context transitions, and 2) modifications to the runtime to identify all transition points (DCs and SCs).

3.1 Supporting Mechanisms

We create two annotations, `@RuntimeDownCall` and `@RuntimeServiceCall`, to allow us to cleanly identify and differentiate DCs and SCs within the runtime. Figure 2(a) illustrates how `@RuntimeDownCall` annotation is used to identify `Object.wait()` as a downcall. The compiler then expands the annotated method to include context switching calls, as illustrated in Figure 2(b). Figure 3 illustrates context switch methods that track the execution context for each thread, and may optionally implement assertions to ensure only legal context transitions occur.

Assertion of execution context. We use two basic techniques to assert the current execution state, helping with both finding transition points and making runtime development easier. First, we implement an `@AssertExecutionState` annotation that may be applied at the granularity of a class or method, which asserts that the code covered by the scope of the assertion is only executed within a specified set of execution contexts. Thus, if there exists a class that may only ever be called within the context of garbage collection, such an assertion will ensure that this restriction is enforced. Second, we automatically inject assertions into user code at run time to ensure that such code is only executed in an 'application' context.

```
@RuntimeDownCall(Context.Scheduler)
public void Object.wait() {
    /* Original code */
}
```

(a) Annotating `Object.wait()` as a DC

```
public void Object.wait() {
  int old = switchContextTo(Context.Scheduler);
  try {
    /* Original code */
  } finally {
    switchContextBack(old);
  }
}
```

(b) The same code after expansion by the compiler

Figure 2. An example transition point, Java's `Object.wait()`.

```
class VMThread {
  /* Current execution context */
  int executionContext;
  /* Change context and return previous context */
  int switchContextTo(int newContext) {
    int oldContext = executionContext;
    /* Assert that transition is valid */
    executionContext = newContext;
    return oldContext;
  }
  /* Change back the context */
  void switchContextBack(int oldContext) {
    executionContext = oldContext;
  }
  ...
```

Figure 3. `VMThread` support for dynamic execution context.

Newly created threads are assigned an initial execution context based on the type of thread being created. For threads that exist within the runtime, such as the compiler thread, we set their initial execution context appropriately.

3.2 Finding Transition Points

We identified transition points iteratively. First we identified major runtime contexts such as the garbage collector, scheduler, etc, and found all transitions into each context. We resolved whether a transition was a DC (from the 'application' to the runtime) or an SC (intra-runtime requests), and marked it with corresponding annotation. For example, Figure 2(a) illustrates a downcall to the `Scheduler` context. We then enforced the acyclic limitation on interdependencies, and further refined context selection. We chose the set of contexts to reflect the structure of the runtime and to maintain the invariant that no transition point is called from within the context it targets.

We also made extensive use of assertions, which we added to code whose context we knew unambiguously. For example, an assertion of garbage collection state that is placed unambiguously within the garbage collector would fail if a transition point into the garbage collector had been overlooked. By following the stack trace from the failed assertion we were able to identify the missing transition point. We repeated this process until we found all transition points. During this process we identified small sections of code within the gray area where execution context is ambiguous. Our identification of these ambiguous areas led to us refactoring the runtime to remove such ambiguities, as we discuss in Section 4.

Transition Point Class	Count
MemoryManager	8
Scheduler	8
Classloader	6
StackTrace	6
Compiler	4
Exception	3
Locking	2
Reflection	2
YieldPoint	1
NewArrayArray	1
Total	**41**

Table 1. Transition Point classes and counts for Jikes RVM.

Table 1 summarizes the transition points we found in Jikes RVM, and their groupings. In all, we identified 41 transition points grouped into 10 classes. We implemented a simple tool that generates a state transition diagram, which allows us to visualize all state transitions. This tool was used to automatically generate Figure 1. Note from this figure that the memory manager can be reached directly from the application, and also via a chain through the classloader, exceptions, and locking, but never from itself. This graph highlights the fact that the memory manager is written in a restricted style which ensures that it does not generate downcalls to any of the other subsystems of the runtime.

4. Design Implications and Lessons

The act of making context and context transitions crisp and explicit encouraged us to rethink elements of the runtime design. In our case this resulted in some minor refactoring and explicit annotations with the consequence that the static code context more closely matches the dynamic execution context. Such changes improved the VM we target and we imagine that the patterns we applied will be relevant to other VMs, whether or not they are metacircular.

In Section 2 we introduced an annotation, `@RuntimeService`, to statically identify contexts where lightweight service calls are executed by the caller on behalf of the callee's context. When we systematically applied this annotation throughout Jikes RVM, it highlighted the fact that ambiguity between contexts, including those between the application and runtime code are re-enforced by the structure and software engineering of the runtime. We now describe how we refactored code to better reflect execution context boundaries.

Inter-class refactoring. Where possible, we moved all lightweight SCs out of their original context into distinctly named packages. By better reflecting the dynamic contexts in the structure of the runtime, this restructuring avoided a large number of unnecessary transition points. It also became straightforward to assert the correct context in the majority of the codebase, since it was largely cleansed of ambiguous code, making the static to dynamic context mapping straightforward in many cases.

Figure 4 illustrates our refactoring with the example of a bump pointer allocator. Figure 4(a) shows the fast path of the allocator, which is executed by the application on behalf of the memory manager. The code is in a distinct package for runtime services and

```java
1  package org.jikesrvm.runtime.services.mm
2
3  @RuntimeService
4  public class BumpPointer {
5    Address cursor;
6    Address limit;
7    BumpPointerSpace global;
8
9    @Inline
10   public Address alloc(int bytes) {
11     Address start = cursor;
12     Address end = start.plus(bytes);
13     if (end.GT(limit))
14       return global.allocSlow(this, bytes);
15     cursor = end;
16     return start;
17   }
18 }
```

(a) Fast path of bump pointer allocator; an example of a runtime service.

```java
package org.mmtk.util.alloc

public class BumpPointerSpace {

  @NoInline
  @RuntimeDownCall(Context.MemoryManager)
  public Address allocSlow(BumpPointer allocator,
                           int bytes) {
    Extent blockSize = getBlockSize(bytes);
    Address start = acquire(blocksize);
    if (start.isZero()) {
      return Address.zero();
    }
    allocator.cursor = start;
    allocator.limit = start.plus(blockSize);
    return allocator.alloc(bytes);
  }

  ...
}
```

(b) Slow path of bump pointer allocator in the memory manager.

Figure 4. Refactored bump pointer allocation code.

the class is annotated with `@RuntimeService`. When a local pool of memory is exhausted (in line 14), the fast path falls through to a slow path. This call is a transition point, a fact reflected by the call into the memory manager proper to a method annotated with a `@RuntimeDownCall` annotation (Figure 4(b)).

Our refactoring also brings the metacircular runtime closer to a non-metacircular runtime, where the impedance matching service code is explicitly identified and exposed. The change also makes it easier to consider hosting another language.

Intra-class refactoring. We found that it was not always practical or desirable to factor runtime services into separate classes and packages. Figure 5 contains an example of the intra-class refactoring that was applied to the classloader. The classloader we use represents classes with `RVMClass` instances. These contain metadata and simple methods to inspect that data in addition to heavy-weight operations such as those to support loading and resolving classes. A number of services, such as `isResolved()`, are typically inlined by the compiler into the application code. These cases are lightweight DCs because they are executed by the application on behalf of the runtime. In this circumstance, insisting on separating them into separate classes would not achieve our software engineering goals, and would only serve to complicate the structure of the runtime. Instead we place `@RuntimeService` annotations on these inspection methods. This solution does not provide all the benefits of separate classes, but allows stronger isolation and clarity.

```java
public class RVMClass {
  private byte state;  //current class-loading stage

  ...

  @RuntimeService
  @Inline
  public boolean isResolved() {
    return state >= CLASS_RESOLVED;
  }

  @RuntimeService
  @Inline
  public synchronized void resolve() {
    if (isResolved()) return;
    if (superClass != null) superClass.resolve();
    for (RVMClass interface : declaredInterfaces)
      interface.resolve();

    resolveInternal();
  }

  @RuntimeDownCall(Context.Classloader)
  public synchronized void resolveInternal() {
    /* heavyweight resolving code */

    state = CLASS_RESOLVED;
  }
}
```

Figure 5. Intra-class refactoring of runtime services: `RVMClass`.

5. Results

We now present results for several experiments we conducted using our framework. In the first experiment we measure the performance impact of our refactoring and our framework for tracking dynamic execution context, showing that the overhead of each is negligible. In the second experiment we use the framework to analyze the behavior of Jikes RVM, measuring the distribution of transitions, as well as a break-down of the time spent in each execution context. In the third experiment we analyze Jikes RVM's memory management behavior, showing that different contexts exhibit different behavior, and that on average around half the memory footprint is due to the runtime.

5.1 Methodology

Our implementation is based on Jikes RVM [1] release 3.1.1 +hg r10393. All experiments use a *production* build: the default high-performance configuration which has debugging assertions turned off, builds code with an aggressive optimizing compiler, and utilizes a high-performance generational Immix garbage collector [5]. For performance measurements we run each benchmark 10 times (10 invocations) and report the average time for the 5th iteration (steady state performance). We also report 95% confidence intervals for the average using Student's t-distribution.

We draw our benchmarks from the DaCapo [7] and SPECjvm98 [17] benchmark suites. We use benchmarks from both the 2006-10-MR2 and 9.12 Bach releases of DaCapo to enlarge our suite and because some 9.12 benchmarks do not run on Jikes RVM.

Performance measurements were conducted using a six-core AMD Phenom II X6 1055T with 3MB of L2 cache running at 2.8GHz, and 4GB of RAM. The machine was running the Ubuntu 10.04.01 LTS server distribution with a 64-bit (x86_64) 2.6.32-24 Linux kernel.

5.2 Framework and Refactoring Overhead

We start by examining the performance overhead of the design changes we made to support the framework (as described in Section 4) and the overhead of dynamically tracking execution con-

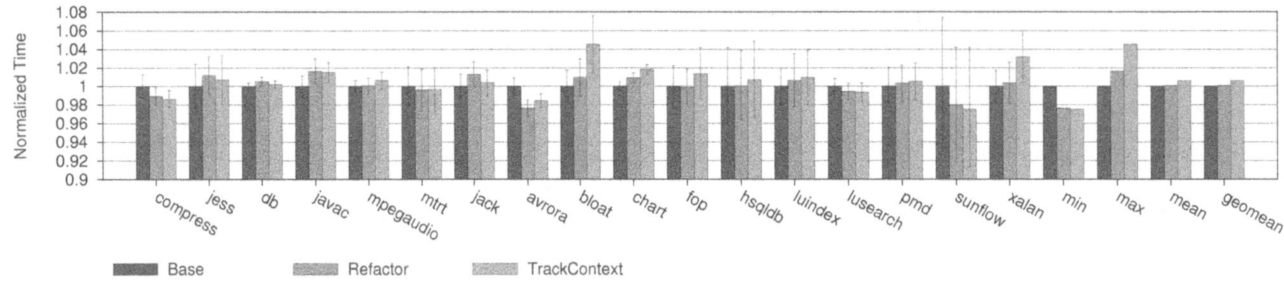

Figure 6. Performance overhead of our refactoring and the mechanism for tracking dynamic execution context.

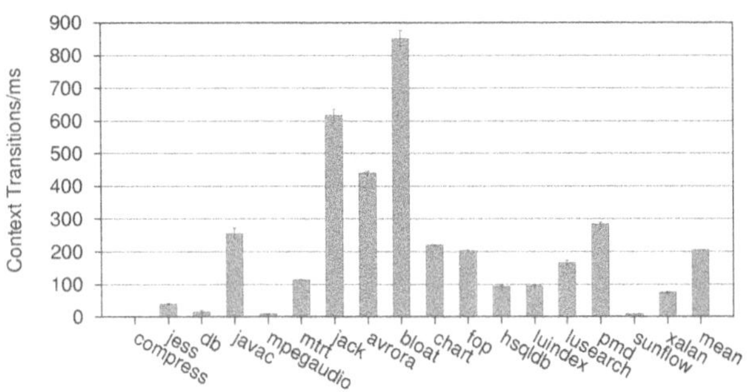

Figure 7. Dynamic transition frequency (transitions per millisecond).

text in a moderate (4× minimum) heap. Figure 6 shows the performance impact due to the refactoring (red) and then the refactoring with dynamic context tracing (green), both relative to an unmodified Jikes RVM configuration (blue).

RuntimeServices refactoring. We did not anticipate any significant overhead due to our refactoring, and Figure 6 shows that this is generally true, with an average overhead of 0.1%, which is well within the noise. Individual benchmarks range from 2.4% speedup to a 1.6% slowdown.

Tracking execution context. Our TrackContext configuration performs on average 0.6% worse than the Base system. Again, these values are very small compared to the noise, suggesting that on average tracking context incurs a negligible overhead. There are two benchmarks, bloat and xalan, that exhibit slightly higher overheads (4.5 and 3.2% respectively) although it is worth noting that the confidence intervals for these benchmarks are also among the largest. In summary, these results show that across a wide selection of benchmarks our execution context tracking incurs minimal overhead.

5.3 Context Transition Analysis

We now use our framework to analyze dynamic context transitions using instrumented versions of our framework. We count both the overall frequency of transitions, and the distribution across individual transition points for each benchmark. We also count the CPU time executing each context to help understand where time is spent during execution.

Execution frequency The frequency of transitions will have a direct impact on the overhead of our system. Figure 7 shows the transition frequency for each benchmark, measured in invocations per millisecond. We see a wide range of values, from 850 calls per millisecond for bloat, to less than 10 per millisecond for compress, mpegaudio and sunflow. Note that these low-frequency benchmarks are kernel-based benchmarks, and that two of the three are from the older SPECjvm98 benchmark suite. On average, the frequency is 205 transitions/ms.

In general, we expect benchmarks with more frequent transitions to incur a greater overhead. However, comparing Figures 7 and 6 shows no clear relationship. As an example, avrora has an invocation frequency more than 30× that of db, but avrora speeds up, while db slows down. This indicates that the overhead of changing execution state is small, and being obscured by other factors. We believe these effects are due to interactions with the optimizing compiler. Injecting code may affect inlining decisions, and may more significantly affect methods which have greater register pressure.

Distribution of executed transition points. Table 2 shows the most frequently executed transition points, both on average and for individual benchmarks. By far the most frequently executed transitions occur at `Lock.lock` and `Lock.unlock`, which support the implementation of Java's **`synchronized`** keyword. Note that the frequency of lock and unlock calls in Table 2 do not match. This is primarily due to the use of a biased locking protocol. When an object is first locked, a DC is required for the first thread to obtain the bias for the lock, which then allows that thread to continue to lock and unlock that object within a lightweight DC, assuming no contention occurs.

Although allocations and generational write barrier invocations are very frequent, heavyweight DCs related to these operations are uncommon because they only occur during (rarer) slow path invocations. This shows the benefit of using lightweight DCs for the fast path. If heavyweight DCs were used on the write barrier fast path, they would account for over a third of all transitions on average.

Time spent in execution contexts. Table 3 shows the CPU cycles spent in each execution context when running a single iteration for each benchmark (i.e. startup, rather than steady state). Each result is the fraction of total CPU time spent in each context (including the application context and runtime contexts). We measure cycles for all threads in the system, which includes applications threads as well as runtime threads (e.g, garbage collection and adaptive compilation threads) which never directly run application code but still contribute to overall execution time.

Table 3 shows that for most benchmarks the vast majority of time is spent performing application work. However, for some benchmarks, time spent in the runtime can be significant, in particular for avrora which spends more than half of all of its cycles executing slow paths for synchronization primitives (e.g., wait, notify, lock, and unlock). On average, nearly 13% of cycles are spent performing compilation, and nearly 10% of cycles can be attributed to synchronization/scheduling operations. Garbage collection and

rank	transition point	mean	cumulative mean	compress	jess	db	javac	mpegaudio	mtrt	jack	avrora	bloat	chart	fop	hsqldb	luindex	lusearch	pmd	sunflow	xalan
1	`Lock.lock`	44.09	44.09	37.20	42.31	55.02	61.29	37.86	15.50	64.38	44.96	84.59	7.41	69.03	50.35	42.31	38.51	30.33	18.56	50.02
2	`Lock.unlock`	21.06	65.15	21.89	21.32	30.97	29.39	22.14	8.16	6.79	26.74	0.65	3.97	12.22	44.04	33.32	21.07	27.94	12.01	35.39
3	`Scheduler.yieldpoint`	5.75	70.90	18.45	6.18	4.26	1.14	20.75	6.67	0.67	2.16	0.68	2.04	1.29	1.64	3.08	1.92	1.90	22.38	2.56
4	`MM.addFinalizer`	5.74	76.64	2.32	3.33	0.34	0.62	2.02	28.56	0.13	0.22	4.28	41.19	3.35	0.06	7.01	0.25	1.35	0.16	2.42
5	`UPCALL.invokeFinalize`	5.64	82.28	1.73	3.25	0.25	0.46	1.87	28.49	0.12	0.21	4.27	41.14	3.11	0.04	6.90	0.20	1.33	0.11	2.38
6	`MM.allocSlowInline`	4.27	86.55	2.33	13.40	2.73	1.04	3.69	6.39	1.09	0.51	0.93	1.95	1.14	1.39	1.74	5.99	2.10	23.15	3.02
7	`Exception.deliverException`	3.95	90.50	0.28	0.39	0.06	2.51	0.30	0.11	26.09	0.01	0.01	0.10	1.92	0.05	0.06	15.20	19.87	0.07	0.15
8	`MM.addReferenceCandidate`	2.18	92.68	8.03	4.41	2.41	0.43	5.06	2.48	0.34	0.28	0.12	1.16	3.91	0.89	2.89	0.36	1.88	1.67	0.71
9	`StackTrace.<init>`	1.73	94.40	0.14	0.20	0.03	2.49	0.15	0.05	0.02		0.01	0.09	1.70	0.03	0.04	15.44	8.26	0.05	0.64
10	`Runtime.newArrayArray`	1.10	95.50		0.17			0.04					0.02						18.40	
11	`Scheduler.wait`	1.08	96.58	1.00	0.14	0.17	0.03	0.58	0.16	0.01	15.53	0.01	0.02	0.02	0.04	0.07	0.05	0.04	0.51	0.06
12	`Reflection.invoke`	1.07	97.65	2.37	1.73	2.50	0.15	1.77	1.69	0.08	0.10	4.29	0.20	0.47	0.22	0.33	0.29	0.26	0.48	1.19
13	`Scheduler.notifyAll`	0.82	98.47	1.17	0.26	0.19	0.13	1.13	0.31	0.02	8.77	0.01	0.04	0.03	0.07	0.55	0.07	0.07	1.02	0.11
14	`Compiler.compile`	0.39	98.86	0.98	0.84	0.32	0.11	0.93	0.44	0.06	0.08	0.04	0.16	0.78	0.18	0.54	0.06	0.43	0.50	0.22
15	`StackTrace.getClassFromStack`	0.20	99.06	0.01	0.06			0.01					0.04				0.01	2.96		0.35
16	`MM.allocSlowOOL`	0.17	99.24	0.69	0.32	0.21	0.04	0.48	0.32	0.03	0.02	0.01	0.04	0.14	0.08	0.19	0.03	0.11	0.17	0.06
17	`WriteBarrier.DequeAlloc`	0.17	99.41	0.20	0.38	0.09	0.05	0.13	0.15	0.06	0.16	0.04	0.10	0.05	0.38	0.14	0.22	0.38	0.18	0.20
18	`WriteBarrier.DequeEnqueue`	0.17	99.58	0.20	0.38	0.08	0.05	0.12	0.14	0.06	0.16	0.04	0.10	0.05	0.38	0.14	0.22	0.38	0.18	0.20
19	`Classloader.resolve`	0.11	99.69	0.26	0.27	0.10	0.02	0.26	0.10	0.02	0.02	0.01	0.06	0.24	0.04	0.19	0.03	0.13	0.10	0.05
20	`Classloader.instantiate`	0.10	99.79	0.26	0.27	0.10	0.02	0.26	0.10	0.02	0.02	0.01	0.04	0.23	0.04	0.11	0.01	0.10	0.10	0.05

Table 2. Distribution across individual transition points, showing the 20 most frequently executed on average. Each number indicates the percentage of total transitions for that benchmark that were of the given type.

Benchmark	Application (%)	Runtime (%)					
		Classloader	Compiler	Garbage Collector	Memory Manager	Scheduler /Lock	Other
compress	91.78	0.15	0.99	2.14	1.29	2.39	1.27
jess	58.51	0.93	18.73	8.34	6.31	4.64	2.53
db	85.65	0.17	5.23	3.56	1.21	2.98	1.19
javac	56.75	0.62	15.49	10.86	2.66	9.81	3.27
mpegaudio	84.16	0.32	8.28	1.76	0.74	3.30	1.43
mtrt	74.56	0.38	8.31	6.60	3.67	3.79	2.68
jack	56.01	0.41	12.78	7.62	4.05	10.90	1.88
avrora	30.78	0.27	8.83	1.76	0.85	57.08	0.43
bloat	43.93	0.34	30.51	7.75	3.37	11.93	2.16
chart	63.31	0.90	14.84	8.82	4.96	3.99	3.17
fop	65.46	3.76	10.10	7.09	3.12	7.41	2.82
hsqldb	41.94	1.14	26.54	13.29	3.04	12.65	1.40
luindex	69.17	1.50	14.09	5.32	2.59	5.56	1.75
lusearch	55.42	0.31	10.54	7.02	12.81	7.66	4.90
pmd	56.93	2.65	9.86	6.63	3.56	9.62	7.93
sunflow	88.53	0.25	2.35	1.34	2.73	3.88	0.91
xalan	63.99	0.87	17.49	5.74	3.67	6.59	1.62
min	30.78	0.15	0.99	1.34	0.74	2.39	0.43
max	91.78	3.76	30.51	13.29	12.81	57.08	7.93
mean	**63.93**	**0.88**	**12.65**	**6.21**	**3.57**	**9.66**	**2.43**

Table 3. CPU cycles spent in each execution context.

other memory management operations (such as slow path allocation) account for a further 10% of execution on average.

5.4 Memory Management Behavior

One of the motivations for this work was isolating application and runtime behaviors, allowing new analyses and optimizations. The behavior of different contexts are typically conflated, in particular when analyzing a metacircular runtime such as Jikes RVM. In this experiment we examine the memory management behavior of the runtime and applications separately. Specifically, we explore allocation volume, nursery survival rate, and heap footprint. These experiments were run using a 2.5× minimum heap size.

Object Allocation To understand object allocation patterns, we collect allocation information by instrumenting the allocation fast path and tagging each object as it is allocated. Because many execution contexts allocate very little (or not at all) we use a *logarithmic* scale, and only show those contexts that make a significant contribution, aggregating the rest into an 'Other Runtime' category.

Figure 8 shows the fraction of total allocation attributed to each execution context. It is clear that application allocation dominates, although it does vary significantly between benchmarks (not shown in the figure). The most active context is the *compiler*, followed by *booting* and *classloader*. In all the benchmarks, the compiler allocates more than all other runtime contexts combined, and in 13 of the 17 benchmarks, more than 10× that of the rest of the runtime.

Survival Ratios Object lifetime patterns help guide memory management policies. If different runtime contexts exhibit significantly different lifetime patterns, there may be an opportunity to apply context-specific memory management optimizations. Here we measure the fraction of data that survives the first nursery collection after allocation. To measure survival rate for each context, we tag the current execution context in the header of each object at allocation time and count the total number of bytes allocated in each context. Then during collection we count the bytes that survive the collection, and express this as a ratio of the total bytes allocated in that context. The experiment is imperfect because a nursery col-

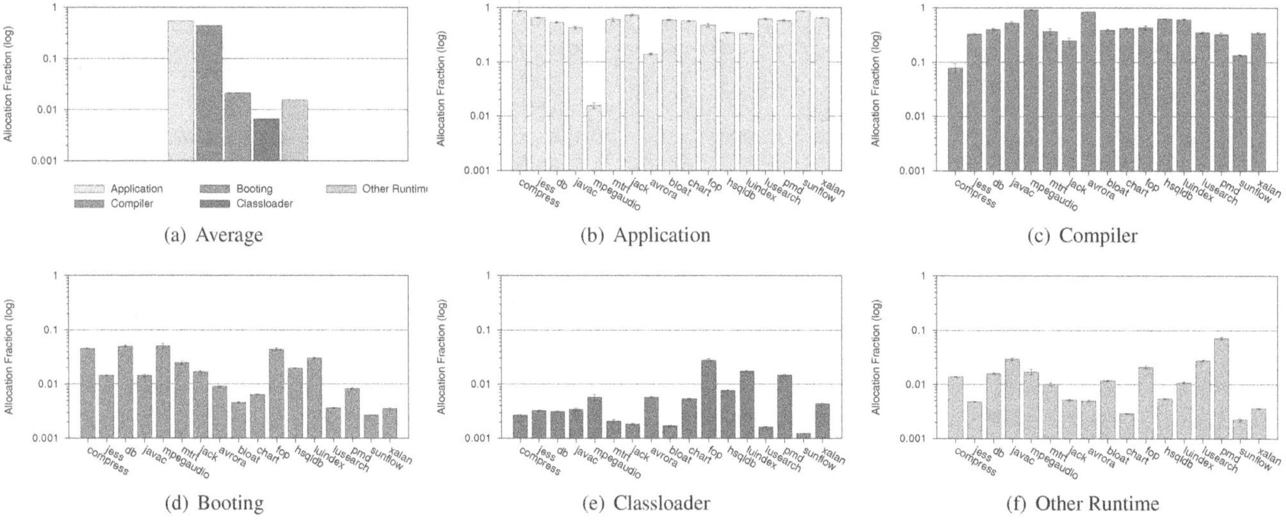

Figure 8. Fraction of total allocation attributed to execution contexts.

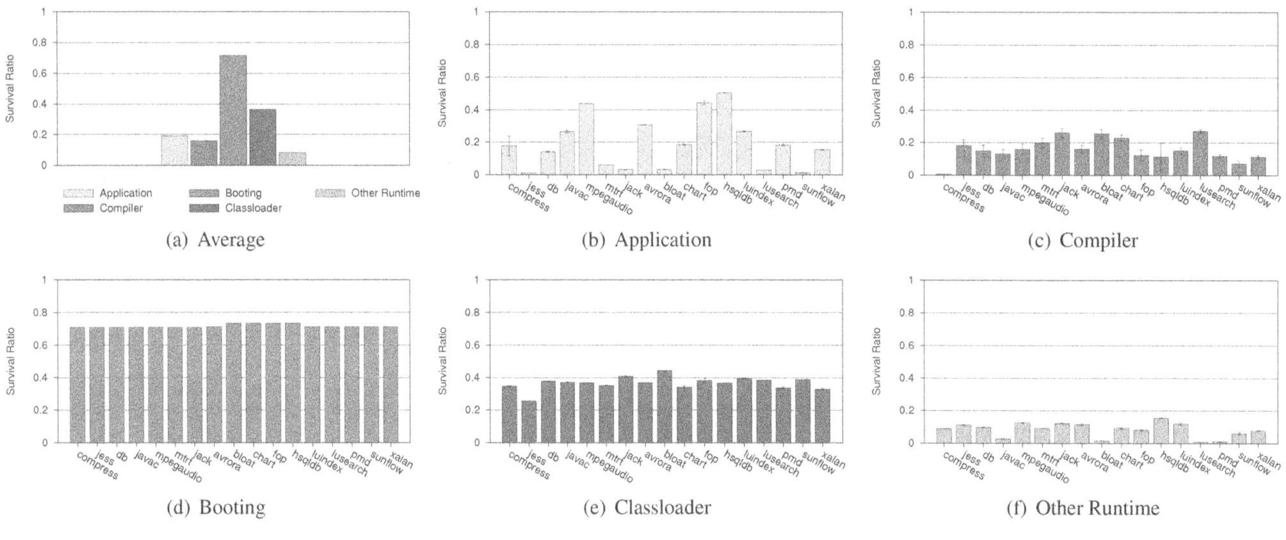

Figure 9. Nursery survival characteristics for objects allocated by execution contexts.

lection is triggered based on total allocation, not allocation per context, but the results still provide interesting insights. Figure 9 shows the result of this experiment. The *booting* and *classloader* contexts show consistently high survival rates. In comparsion, the survival rate for the *compiler* is consistently low, with less than 20% of data surviving the first nursery collection in 12 of the 17 benchmarks.

These experiments show that while allocation behavior between applications varies, allocation in runtime contexts follows a more regular pattern. The compiler context allocates more memory than all other runtime contexts combined for every benchmark, and also shows a consistently low survival rate, averaging just 16.4%. The other allocation-intensive contexts are the classloader and runtime booting procedure, which have stable and high survival ratios.

Heap Footprint Our framework allows us to easily determine the objects allocated by the runtime. This is generally difficult in a metacircular runtime because application and runtime objects are mixed together in a single heap. In our preliminary study we allocate runtime objects into a different region of memory based on the dynamic execution state. Then at garbage collection time, we can measure the live size of the respective heaps to determine the memory footprint for the application and the runtime separately.

Figure 10 shows that in more than half of the benchmarks the memory footprint of the runtime is larger than that of the application. Ogata et al. make a similar observation for the IBM J9 runtime, which is not metacircular [12].

5.5 Summary

These results show that a framework such as ours can disambiguate dynamic execution context at very low overhead, and can also be used to both understand and improve the implementation of managed runtimes.

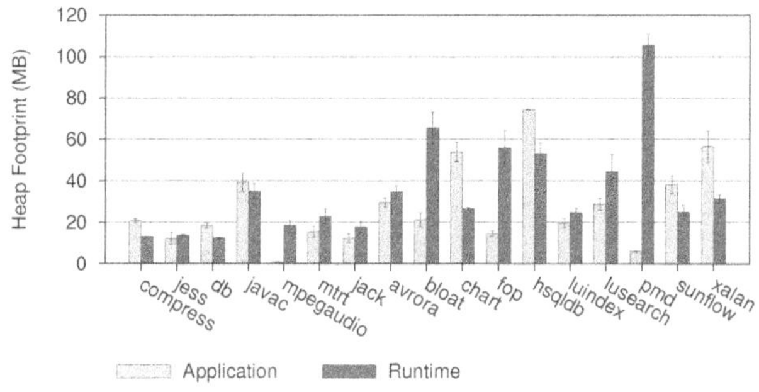

Figure 10. Memory footprint for application and runtime allocated objects.

6. Related work

We categorize related work in two parts: 1) the state of the art for metacircular runtimes, for which ambiguous context is one of the major problems, and 2) approaches to improve isolation within runtimes more broadly.

6.1 Metacircular VMs

There is a long history of metacircular runtimes, tracing back to LISP in the 1960s. In some languages, metacircular implementations are in the mainstream (e.g., LISP and Smalltalk). For others, in particular Java, metacircular implementations have been more of a sideshow to commonly used production runtimes, despite a long thread of interest: the first Java-in-Java runtime was created not long after Java's initial introduction.

Jikes RVM (formerly known as Jalapeño) was the first high-performance metacircular runtime written in Java [1]. Besides a small amount of C code used to boot the runtime and act as an OS interface layer, Jikes RVM is entirely implemented in Java, and once built can execute without the support of a host JVM. Jikes RVM largely ignores matters of application/runtime isolation in its design. While Jikes RVM generally identifies methods that have calls injected by the compiler (one type of downcall from the application into runtime) this convention is not enforced by the runtime. Our implementation is based on the most recent release of Jikes RVM.

Moxie was designed to be a platform for developing production-quality JVMs and performing research into new JVM designs and technologies [8]. Moxie is metacircular, and targets portability, clean bootstrap, debugging and systems programming. The importance of VM/application isolation was recognized early in the Moxie design process. Moxie set a goal of having all transitions from application to JVM services explicit (similar to an operating system trap). As part of this process, Moxie developed a quite different bootstrap model to that used in Jikes RVM, and its *hosted-target* execution model was an important step towards strong VM/Application isolation [8]. Unfortunately, the Moxie VM was never publicly released.

Maxine is, like Moxie, a research platform for next generation Java runtimes [18]. Maxine is metacircular, and is built on principles of modularity and configurability. Maxine provides dedicated replacement mechanisms for important components, including the compiler, garbage collector, and object model. To our knowledge, Maxine does not particularly address the issue of application/runtime ambiguity that arises due to metacircularity and which is the focus of our work.

Ovm is a research JVM that particularly targets realtime applications. [13]. Ovm provides the basic components of a managed runtime, each of which is written almost entirely in Java. Ovm is designed as a general framework to support different object models. Ovm's intermediate intermediate representation, OvmIR reduces some of the ambiguity between the runtime and target language. However, this approach does not serve as a common solution to the context ambiguity and isolation problem that arises from metacircularity, which is our focus in this paper.

6.2 Prior Work in VM Isolation

Other work has focused on the issue of isolation in the context of managed runtimes more broadly, motivated by other concerns such as security and inter-application isolation.

KaffeOS [4] is a Java runtime system designed to implement isolation and resource management boundaries between different applications in a single runtime based on the Kaffe VM. KaffeOS is not metacircular, but is closely related to our work because isolation between different contexts is a primary goal of KaffeOS. In KaffeOS, to support application isolation, limited VM/application isolation is also required. KaffeOS uses a *red line* metaphor [9] to divide 'user mode' and 'kernel mode' contexts. This 'red line' metaphor is similar to our dynamic switching, but there are also some important differences, due to the non-metacircular nature of KaffeOS. First, the kernel in KaffeOS is written in C while the other parts are written in Java, thus a clear cross-language boundary indicates parts of the 'red line' between the runtime and application. Also, the metaphor does not translate well to the metacircular setting, because the metacircular runtime is *reentrant*: during execution a 'red line' could be crossed multiple times. We analyze this problem in detail and propose a clean approach for maintaining a more appropriate runtime state for a metacircular runtime. In addition, our approach to maintaining context has a low overhead, while the isolation used by KaffeOS is more heavyweight, with an 11% overhead.

7. Conclusion

The dependencies between the application and the runtime that supports it–and between the components of the runtime itself–are critical elements of runtime design, yet are often unclear. We examine the problem of these dependencies in the context of a metacircular runtime, where the boundaries between the application and individual runtime components are particularly unclear. We demonstrate a low overhead framework that allows us to clearly identify the dynamic execution context within the runtime, and show how this has led to software engineering improvements in the JVM we use.

Our approach is to restructure and annotate the runtime to transparently reflect context transitions. To do this, we: 1) introduce transition point annotations that allow the runtime to maintain a clear dynamic execution context within the metacircular runtime with very low overhead, 2) use the explicit identification of transition points to drive a restructuring of an existing runtime to substantially reduce structural context ambiguity, and 3) use our framework to analyze behavior and runtime characteristics of a metacircular runtime across a wide range of benchmarks.

Although our implementation is developed in the context of a particular runtime, the principles we apply are more general. In particular, we hope that our insights and analysis may help runtime developers think more clearly about the various contexts that constitute a VM and their relationship. We hope that by substantially reducing ambiguity, this work will make metacircular designs more tenable for the next generation of managed runtimes.

References

[1] B. Alpern, C. R. Attanasio, A. Cocchi, D. Lieber, S. Smith, T. Ngo, J. J. Barton, S. F. Hummel, J. C. Sheperd, and M. Mergen. Implementing Jalapeño in Java. In *Proceedings of the 14th ACM SIGPLAN*

Conference on Object-Oriented Programming, Systems, Languages, and Applications, OOPSLA '99, pages 314–324. ACM, 1999.

[2] B. Alpern, M. Butrico, A. Cocchi, J. Dolby, S. Fink, D. Grove, and T. Ngo. Experiences Porting the Jikes RVM to Linux/IA32. In *Proceedings of the 2nd Java(TM) Virtual Machine Research and Technology Symposium*, JVM '02, pages 51–64. USENIX Association, 2002.

[3] Apache. DRLVM – Dynamic Runtime Layer Virtual Machine. `http://harmony.apache.org/subcomponents/drlvm/`.

[4] G. Back, W. C. Hsieh, and J. Lepreau. Processes in KaffeOS: Isolation, Resource Management, and Sharing in Java. In *In Proceedings of the 4th Symposium on Operating Systems Design and Implementation*, OSDI 2000, pages 333–346, 2000.

[5] S. M. Blackburn and K. S. McKinley. Immix: A Mark-Region Garbage Collector with Space Efficiency, Fast Collection, and Mutator Performance. In *Proceedings of the 2008 ACM SIGPLAN conference on Programming Language Design and Implementation*, PLDI '08, pages 22–32. ACM, 2008.

[6] S. M. Blackburn, P. Cheng, and K. S. McKinley. Oil and Water? High Performance Garbage Collection in Java with MMTk. In *Proceedings of the 26th International Conference on Software Engineering*, ICSE '04, pages 137–146. IEEE Computer Society, 2004.

[7] S. M. Blackburn, R. Garner, C. Hoffmann, A. M. Khang, K. S. McKinley, R. Bentzur, A. Diwan, D. Feinberg, D. Frampton, S. Z. Guyer, M. Hirzel, A. Hosking, M. Jump, H. Lee, J. E. B. Moss, A. Phansalkar, D. Stefanović, T. VanDrunen, D. von Dincklage, and B. Wiedermann. The DaCapo Benchmarks: Java Benchmarking Development and Analysis. In *Proceedings of the 21st annual ACM SIGPLAN Conference on Object-Oriented Programming Systems, Languages, and Applications*, OOPSLA '06, pages 169–190. ACM, 2006.

[8] S. M. Blackburn, S. I. Salishev, M. Danilov, O. A. Mokhovikov, A. A. Nashatyrev, P. A. Novodvorsky, V. I. Bogdanov, X. F. Li, and D. Ushakov. The Moxie JVM experience. Technical Report TR-CS-08-01, Australian National University, Department of Computer Science, May 2008.

[9] D. R. Cheriton and K. J. Duda. A Caching Model of Operating System Kernel Functionality. In *In Proceedings of the First Symposium on Operating Systems Design and Implementation*, pages 179–193. USENIX Association, 1994.

[10] D. Frampton, S. M. Blackburn, P. Cheng, R. J. Garner, D. Grove, J. E. B. Moss, and S. I. Salishev. Demystifying Magic: High-level Low-level Programming. In *Proceedings of the 2009 ACM SIGPLAN/SIGOPS international conference on Virtual execution environments*, VEE '09, pages 81–90. ACM, 2009.

[11] G. Hunt, J. Larus, M. Abadi, M. Aiken, P. Barham, M. Fähndrich, C. Hawblitzel, O. Hodson, S. Levi, N. Murphy, B. Steensgaard, D. Tarditi, T. Wobber, and B. Zill. An overview of the Singularity project. Technical Report MSR-TR-2005-135, Microsoft Research, 2005.

[12] K. Ogata, D. Mikurube, K. Kawachiya, S. Trent, and T. Onodera. A Study of Java's non-Java Memory. In *Proceedings of the ACM International Conference on Object Oriented Programming Systems Languages and Applications*, OOPSLA '10, pages 191–204. ACM, 2010.

[13] K. Palacz, J. Baker, C. Flack, C. Grothoff, H. Yamauchi, and J. Vitek. Engineering a Common Intermediate Representation for the Ovm Framework. *Science of Computer Programming*, 57:357–378, September 2005.

[14] E. Prangsma. Why Java is practical for modern operating systems, 2005. Presentation only. See `http://www.jnode.org`.

[15] A. Rigo and S. Pedroni. PyPy's Approach to Virtual Machine Construction. In *Companion to the 21st ACM SIGPLAN Symposium on Object-Oriented Programming Systems, Languages, and Applications*, OOPSLA '06, pages 944–953. ACM, 2006.

[16] D. Simon, C. Cifuentes, D. Cleal, J. Daniels, and D. White. Java on the Bare Metal of Wireless Sensor Devices: The Squawk Java Virtual Machine. In *Proceedings of the 2nd International Conference on Virtual Execution Environments*, VEE '06, pages 78–88. ACM, 2006.

[17] Standard Performance Evaluation Corporation. Specjvm98. `http://www.spec.org/jvm98/`.

[18] Sun Microsystems. Maxine Research Project. `http://research.sun.com/projects/maxine/`.

[19] D. Ungar, A. Spitz, and A. Ausch. Constructing a Metacircular Virtual Machine in an Exploratory Programming Environment. In *Companion to the 20th annual ACM SIGPLAN Conference on Object-Oriented Programming, Systems, Languages, and Applications*, OOPSLA '05, pages 11–20. ACM, 2005.

Block Storage Virtualization with Commodity Secure Digital Cards

Harvey Tuch Cyprien Laplace Kenneth C. Barr Bi Wu *

VMware, Inc.

{htuch, claplace, kbarr}@vmware.com, bi.wu@duke.edu

Abstract

Smartphones, tablets and other mobile platforms typically accommodate bulk data storage with low-cost, FAT-formatted Secure Digital cards. When one uses a mobile device to run a full-system virtual machine (VM), there can be a mismatch between 1) the VM's I/O mixture, security and reliability requirements and 2) the properties of the storage media available for VM block storage and checkpoint images. To resolve this mismatch, this paper presents a new VM disk image format called the Logging Block Store (LBS). After motivating the need for a new format, LBS is described in detail with experimental results demonstrating its efficacy. As a result of this work, recommendations are made for future optimizations throughout the stack that may simplify and improve the performance of storage virtualization systems on mobile platforms.

Categories and Subject Descriptors D.4.2 [*Operating Systems*]: Storage Management

General Terms Design, Performance, Reliability, Security

Keywords Virtualization, Log Structured File System, Secure Digital card (SD card)

1. Introduction

We are presently at a crossover point, at which the volume of smartphones sold each year has surpassed PC sales [31]. Mobile devices will, within a brief period of time, become the dominant end user computing platform. As a result, mobile devices are fast becoming a first-class concern amongst enterprises who face the task of managing a heterogeneous fleet of phones and tablets.

VMware's Mobile Virtualization Platform (MVP) provides an enterprise mobile device management solution, multiplexing two phone personas, a work and a home phone, on a single device via system virtualization. A Bring Your Own Device (BYOD) model is facilitated, in which an employee is given the freedom to select his own device and provision it with a virtual machine (VM) containing the work environment. The hypervisor and on-device management components enable the VM to be managed remotely by the enterprise, while the home environment remains under the complete control of the employee.

The MVP hypervisor is based on a hosted architecture, similar to that of VMware Workstation [28] and Fusion, in which the host provides the home environment and the guest provides the enterprise environment. The virtual machine monitor (VMM) is provisioned from an app store prior to the installation and launch of the enterprise VM. Further motivation for and details of this system structure are provided by [3].

This hypervisor deployment scenario introduces several constraints on storage virtualization:

- *Hardware diversity*. Since devices are selected by employees, MVP must support a wide array of phones, with different storage devices and filesystems. We focus on the variety of Android devices in this paper, but many of the details at the hardware and hypervisor level are common across mobile platforms.
- *Non-perturbation*. Introducing the hypervisor and VM should not cause the user to lose any existing data or require the technical sophistication involved in reformatting or repartitioning storage media.
- *Reliability*. Not all storage is journaled or logged, yet power on the phone may be lost at any time due to battery depletion. VM corruption should not be possible in the event of power loss or a host crash.
- *Security*. The backing store and checkpoint files for the work VM, residing on host filesystems, must be protected from malicious host applications.

Android devices typically offer two types of storage to applications:

- *Internal*. Internal NAND flash memory or embedded MultiMediaCard/Secure Digital (eMMC/eSD) chips are constrained in size due to cost and power consumption. Today, capacities typically range between 256 MB and 16 GB. The system kernel, middleware and libraries reside on internal storage as well as application code and some application data.
- *External*. Small form factor Secure Digital (microSD) cards are standard and provide removable mass storage (up to 32 GB) for application data. Secure Digital Extended Capacity (SDXC) cards will support up to 2 TB capacities in the future. SD card storage benefits from the economies of semiconductor scaling and supply after a smartphone has been shipped and purchased.

The storage footprint for a typical guest, 3 GB or higher, can easily exceed the available space on internal storage for some devices. In order to achieve broad support, the VM backing storage and checkpoint files need to be placed on external microSD cards.

* Bi Wu is a graduate student at Duke University. This research was performed while he was an intern at VMware.

VEE'12, March 3–4, 2012, London, England, UK.

SD cards are optimized for cost, compatibility and the I/O mixture expected from the transfer of large sequential files such as MP3s, photos and videos. As a result, they are formatted with the FAT filesystem and have simple flash translation layer (FTL) controllers (utilizing a minimum of costly SRAM) that perform extremely poorly with small random writes [1, 6]. The I/O mixture from the guest is far less sequential than that of the media workloads that SD cards are intended for. In addition, FAT does not support Unix permissions and does not provide robustness guarantees in the event of a host upset. Users cannot be expected to reformat the SD card due to the non-perturbation requirement. These challenges motivate a new VM backing store and checkpoint storage system capable of meeting the constraints outlined above while performing the bulk of storage on FAT-formatted microSD cards.

Our contributions in this paper are as follows:

- An empirical characterization of the unique storage characteristics of SD cards and Android VM workloads.
- A storage architecture and block storage format, which we refer to as the *logging block store* (LBS), capable of providing the desired impedance matching between our enterprise VMs and low cost consumer-grade SD card storage.
- Experimental evaluation of LBS and a performance characterization.
- Potential optimizations at other levels of the I/O stack capable of improving VM performance if adopted in mobile platforms.

While the individual techniques we employ in LBS are familiar, to the best of our knowledge this is the first system to combine them to bridge the gap between the high performance/reliability/security requirements of a VM and the characteristics of the low-cost solid state storage on mobile devices.

In the rest of the paper, we first show how device performance characteristics (Section 2) and virtual machine workload characteristics (Section 3) motivate the design of LBS. This is followed by the design and implementation details for LBS in Section 4 and evaluation in Section 5. The paper concludes with suggested optimizations in Section 6, related work in Section 7 and future directions in Section 8.

2. SD card performance characteristics

An SD card is composed of NAND devices, providing the raw storage media, organized by an FTL into a logical block structure that is exported across an SD card bus connector. The FTL performs wear leveling, error detection and the remapping of bad blocks. The limiting storage performance characteristics are hence dictated by the FTL, NAND read/write/erase times and page/erase block organization. For cost reasons, the FTLs are optimized for simplicity of implementation and minimization of SRAM, distinguishing SD cards from their richer cousins, solid state disks, which have more significant resources available for the FTL. The random access property of NAND is as a result constrained by the FTL, with the internal data structures utilized by simple FTLs being optimized for sequential write patterns and coarse block operations [6].

SD cards are rated by speed classes, e.g. Class 2, Class 10, indicating the expected minimum sequential I/O bandwidth (MB/s) in the presence of zero fragmentation [26]. Unfortunately, this rating provides no guarantee of random or fragmented I/O performance. We present some illustrative examples of these characteristics below, gathered on a HTC Nexus One smartphone by a synthetic tool, *sdperf*, designed to characterize SD cards. *sdperf* opens a file or raw block device and performs read or write I/O of specific sizes to the target file. Sequential, strided, partitioned and random patterns are supported.

Manufacturer	Capacity	Class	Alloc. unit	FAT cluster
SanDisk™	4GB	4	4MB	32KB
SanDisk™(WP7)	8GB	4	4MB	32KB
Kingston™	4GB	4	4MB	32KB
ADATA™	8GB	6	4MB	32KB
PNY™	16GB	10	4MB	32KB

Table 1. SD card details.

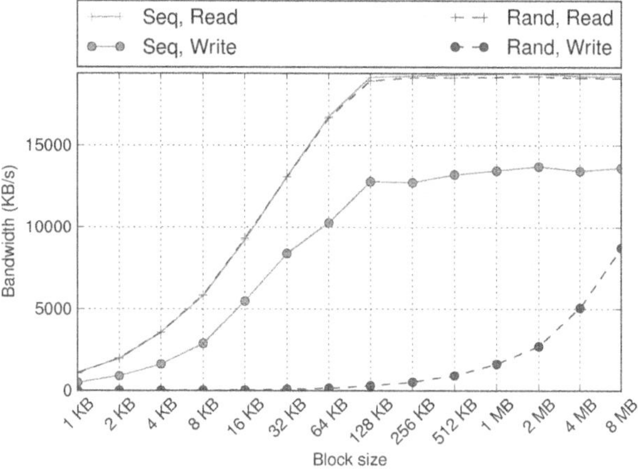

Figure 1. 8 GB ADATA Class 6 SD card I/O bandwidth as a function of block size and I/O ordering.

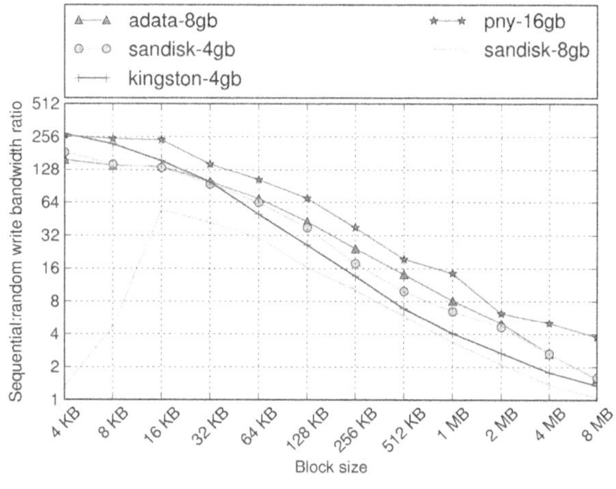

Figure 2. Sequential:random write bandwidth ratio as a function of block size.

Below we describe the results of various I/O read/write patterns within a preallocated 128 MB file, intended to be representative of a VM disk image file. The page cache layer in the Linux kernel was bypassed with `O_DIRECT` to avoid interference. Five SD cards from different manufacturers and with different speed class ratings were analyzed; card specific details are provided in Table 1. The 8 GB SanDisk card packaging was labeled as being Windows Phone 7 compliant, indicating potential improved support for random read/write operations [29].

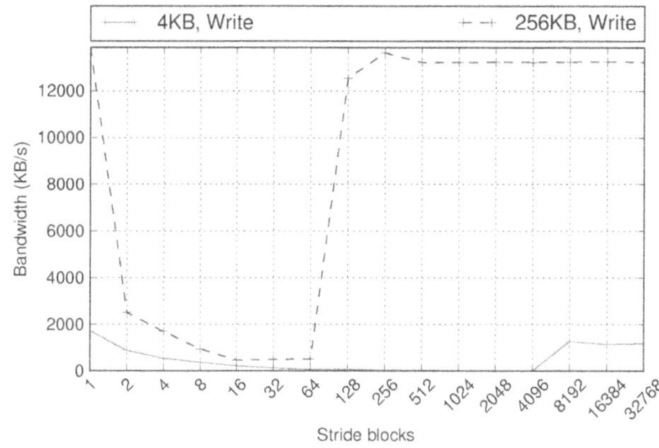

Figure 3. 8 GB ADATA Class 6 SD card write bandwidth as a function of inter-write stride distance and block size.

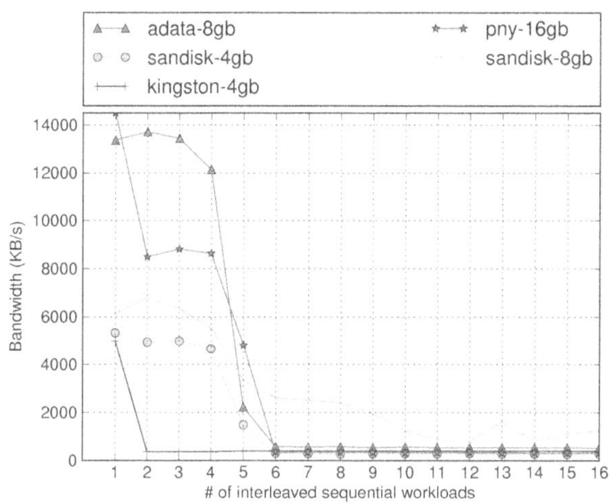

Figure 4. Write bandwidth as a function of the number of interleaved sequential workloads, separated by 2 AU, at 256 KB block size.

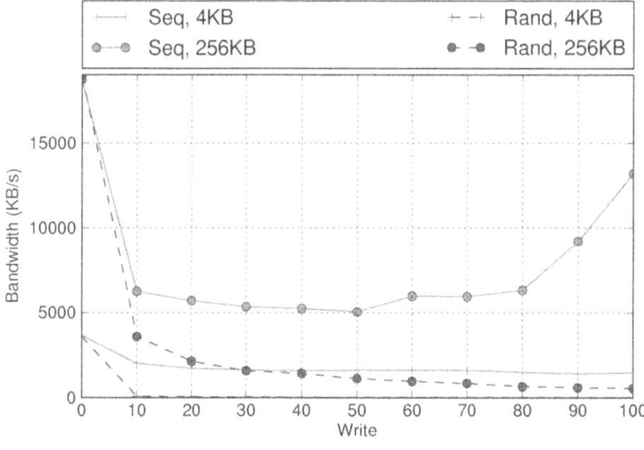

Figure 5. 8 GB ADATA Class 6 SD card I/O bandwidth as a function of write percentage in I/O mixture and I/O ordering.

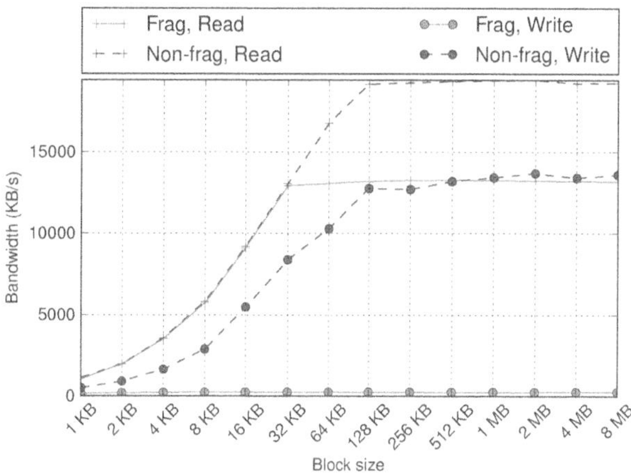

Figure 6. 8 GB ADATA Class 6 SD card sequential I/O bandwidth as a function of block size and fragmentation.

Figure 1 provides the observed I/O bandwidth as a function of the block size and access pattern on the 8 GB Class 6 ADATA SD card. There is little difference in these examples between sequential and random read performance, but a marked distinction on writes, in particular at small block sizes. Figure 2 provides the sequential-to-random write performance ratio for all five cards. A similar random write penalty can be observed across the tested cards, with the exception of the 8 GB SanDisk. The card exhibited comparable sequential and random write performance at 4 KB block sizes but behaved similarly otherwise to its peers past 16 KB. We use the 8 GB ADATA card as a running example in the rest of the paper since its key characteristics are similar to other cards we have examined.

The penalty for a non-sequential write is not uniform, it depends to some extent on the location and distance between the two writes, as well as the history of previous writes. Figure 3 provides the write bandwidth at the 4 KB and 256 KB block sizes when a stride takes place between writes. At stride of 1 block, we have the sequential case and performance drops until writes are an *allocation unit* (AU) apart. The AU is a logical unit provided by the SD card at which erase operations are preferred and speed class calculations performed. For a given card it has a fixed size, dictated by the NAND erase block size and card internal organization (4 MB for the card in the figure). Writes at a smaller granularity can involve a read-modify-write operation. When the stride becomes sufficiently large, we might expect to see a change in performance when once again only a single AU is in use, as strides wrap around at the file size, 128 MB. A performance improvement occurs earlier however, at 32 MB, likely due to an FTL implementation that supports efficient interleaving of writes to multiple AUs as long as sequentiality is maintained within each stream [19]. This effect is visible in Figure 4, where we simulate interleaved sequential writers, with the writes occurring at a distance of 2 AU. Several of the cards show good performance with up to four sequential writers. The PNY card is best with a single writer, but supports 2-4 writers with mid-range performance. The Kingston card supports only a single writer. While it may be tempting to exploit these patterns, they are card and distance specific: with only 5 cards we were able to identify 3 behaviors. We assume the non-sequential write penalty to be high for the rest of this paper, since we are aiming to provide a portable solution where the SD card is unknown.

Even a small number of write accesses in an I/O mixture can drive overall performance towards the write performance curve, as indicated in Figure 5, where write accesses were inserted at random

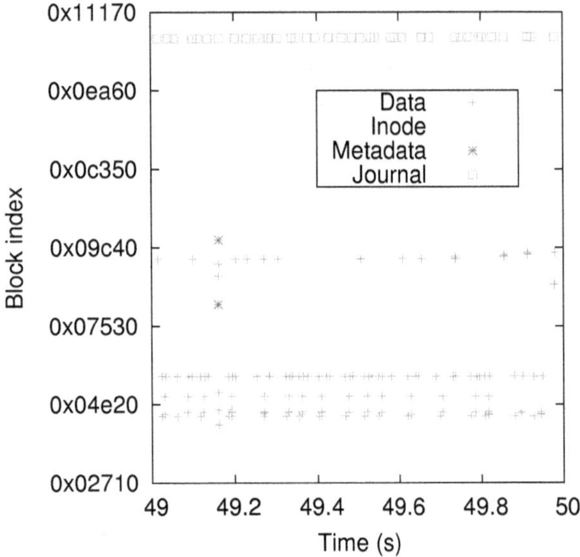

Figure 7. 1 second sample of browsing session writes on ext3.

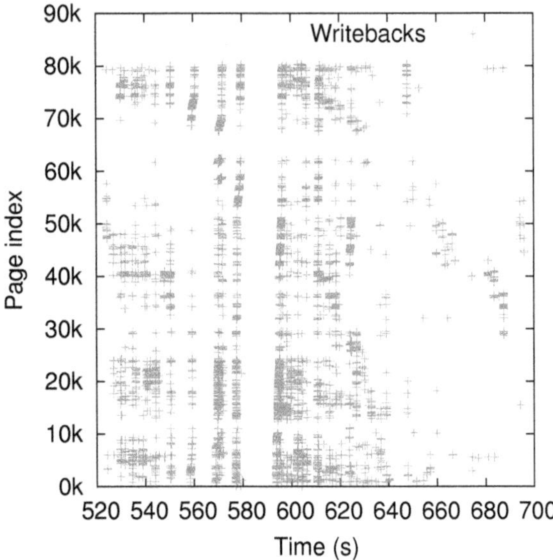

Figure 8. 180 second sample of background cold page writebacks of a large space of guest physical memory.

in the I/O mixture at differing percentages. Beyond 10% there is little difference between a mixed and pure write workload.

Fragmentation within an AU will result in a decrease in sequential write performance. In the above experiments, the image file had zero measured fragmentation, with logically contiguous blocks placed on contiguous FAT clusters. Figure 6 presents a comparison of sequential I/O performance in the non-fragmented and worst case fragmentation cases. Worst case fragmentation here is simulated by placing files of 1 MB in size until the card is filled, and then releasing a single FAT cluster from each file prior to image file allocation. This results in the image file being spread across the maximum number of AUs. The curves representing performance of sequential I/O on a non-fragmented filesystem are the same as those in Figure 1. When the file system is severely fragmented, data is only contiguous within a 32 KB FAT cluster, so read performance is limited by the speed of 32 KB reads. Sequential write performance devolves to that of 32 KB random writes.

Beyond the above observations, there are implementation details that apply to specific cards. For example, the initial blocks backing the file allocation table are optimized for the smaller, non-sequential writes that occur in the region [16]. These card specific details are also not relied upon in the LBS design presented in Section 4.

3. Virtual machine I/O mixture

The I/O mixture from the perspective of the host is non-sequential for three reasons in our system: guest filesystem design, opportunistic checkpointing and application behavior.

The guest uses ext3 and FAT filesystems over paravirtualized block storage devices. With the simpler FAT filesystem, non-sequentiality can arise from application access patterns and fragmentation. The journaling ext3 filesystem introduces additional non-sequential writes, jumping between ordinary data and the journal. Figure 7 shows a sample of a block write trace to an ext3 partition during an Android 2.2 web browsing session. Non-sequential writes can be observed as the application accesses four different regions of data (the four "stripes" below 0x09c40). Access to metadata, inodes and the journal interrupt data access with additional non-sequentiality.

MVP also supports virtual machine checkpointing. It is possible to save all virtual machine state on the host storage and to restore it later. A virtual machine's state is composed of the following parts:

- The *virtual platform*, including CPU registers and virtual device state (approximately 200 KB).
- The *storage*, maintained in persistent images by the paravirtualized block storage devices.
- The *memory*, which may require $\geq$ 512 MB of data to be written on checkpoint.

Of these components, saving the VM's large memory dominates the space and time required to save a checkpoint. To shorten the duration of checkpoint creation, unused memory is written to persistent storage proactively in the background. An adapted Clock-Pro [14] working set estimation algorithm is used to select blocks to write. Cold blocks are preferred with the assumption that they are the least likely to change prior to explicit checkpoint creation time. Unfortunately, this working set driven selection often leads to non-sequential ordering of page writebacks, as shown in the sample given in Figure 8.

Application behavior in the presence of the guest buffer cache introduces another source of non-sequential I/O. We examined several mobile workloads by generating traces of their I/O (details of the tracing procedure are given in Section 5).

1. **Android Boot**. The initial boot of an Android OS. The trace ends when Android issues its BOOT_COMPLETED intent. A considerable number of writes occur during Android's optimization of application bytecode.
2. **Contacts Database**. Import 2000 contacts into the Android Contacts application. Search for and delete 40 contacts.
3. **Mail Client**. Use the Android Mail 2.2.1 client to access an IMAP mailbox. The mailbox is 24 MB and contains 356 messages and 3 folders with lengths and attachments generated by the SPECmail2009 benchmark [27] initialization script to reflect size distributions of a large corporation.
4. **Slideshow**. Browse through 52 NASA images [18] using the Astro file browser [17]. Astro creates thumbnails and scales

Name	Writable	Filesystem	Description
/system		squashfs	Android binaries
/data	x	ext3	user-installed programs and data
/cache	x	ext3	cache space used by Android
/sdcard	x	FAT	SD card for multi-media files
/flex		squashfs	enterprise customizations

Table 2. Disk partitions in the Android guest under test.

photos from their original size to fit on the device's 800x480 pixel screen.

5. **Web Browsing**. A one second sample of web browsing activity using the Android 2.2 browser.

The Android guest that produced the traces has 5 partitions as shown in Table 2. Note that squashfs partitions are not writable and are managed by flat files in our implementation rather than LBS.

The traces stress the partitions in different ways. Table 3 describe the characteristics of each trace. Unaccessed partitions are elided from the tables. While some partitions are lightly used or not accessed at all during the workload, we see that workloads such as the Contacts Database and Email Client are dominated by small writes to the data partition.

Recall from Section 2 that random workloads with a write percentage as little as 10% can perform as slowly as if 100% of their I/Os were writes. In the case of the Contacts Database and Email Client workloads, the high percentage of writes to /data — with 12%-17% of these writes being non-sequential — is cause for concern and motivates a virtualization layer that will transform the workload into large sequential writes. In most of our traces, the number of barrier commands per I/O is low, but the email trace stands out with 33% of its I/O commands being barriers. To achieve consistency, barriers force the contents of any buffers to be flushed to the disk which inhibits the ability to batch commands into large, fast I/O operations.

The table also shows that except in the case of Android Boot, write activity consists mostly of small (no larger than 4 KB), less efficient I/O. Read activity is more likely to contain larger I/O commands which should perform well if not interspersed with writes.

4. Logging block store (LBS)

We observed in Section 2 and Section 3 a mismatch with the underlying SD card characteristics and the guest Android VM and checkpoint I/O mixture. There are also two additional challenges facing a storage virtualization and checkpointing solution employing commodity SD cards on a hosted hypervisor:

- *Security*. The VM image and checkpoint files stored on the SD card must be protected from malicious host applications. On Android, any application which has been granted permission to access the SD card may access any file. This permissiveness stems from the lack of access control in the FAT filesystem.
- *Reliability*. A VM on a mobile device executes in a hostile physical environment in which power may be lost due to battery exhaustion, a phone being dropped or the host kernel crashing. The FAT filesystem does not provide any resiliency against data loss in such events.

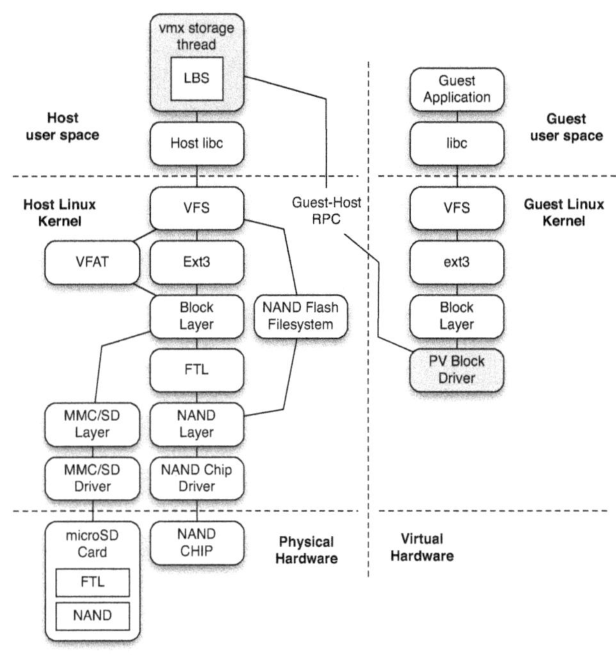

Figure 9. MVP storage architecture.

In this section we present a VM image format that addresses the performance, security and reliability problems described above. We call this image format the *logging block store* (LBS).

As an illustration of the role LBS plays in the MVP hypervisor, consider the various layers in both the guest and host storage stacks shown in Figure 9. The guest kernel contains a paravirtualized block storage driver, providing the *front-end* of the virtual device. The driver is responsible for communicating requests in the kernel's block request queue with a thread executing in host user space, residing in a process known as the `vmx`. The storage virtualization *back-end* is implemented with standard POSIX file operations on host filesystems residing on both internal and external storage. LBS is the component responsible for the back-end virtualization in the `vmx` storage thread.

4.1 LBS format

As suggested by its name, LBS is a log structured file format intended to represent VM disk images at the block granularity. The log structure allows us to bridge the gap between the non-sequential I/O mixture observed in Section 3 and the SD card performance characteristics described in Section 2.

An LBS image is split between a data file, with suffix `.lbsd`, and a meta-data file, suffixed `.lbsm`. We locate the data file on the FAT filesystem backed by the SD card due to its significant size and place the meta-data file on internal storage, since it is a fraction of the size of its data counterpart and is able to enjoy the security and robustness benefits of the location. Figure 10 illustrates the layout of the respective LBS backing files.

The data file consists of a number of fixed sized *blocks* (1 KB) organized into fixed size *clusters* (256 KB). We refer to the block index in the data file as the *physical block number* (PBN). The *logical block number* (LBN) refers to the index of a 1 KB block inside the VM disk image being represented via LBS. A page mapping table is maintained by LBS in the `vmx` process to translate between LBN and PBN. Clusters exist for the purpose of garbage collection (GC) and ensuring that contiguous sequential runs of

partition	read size (KB)	read count	read I/O Sizes (KB) 1	read I/O Sizes (KB) ≤ 4	read I/O Sizes (KB) > 4	read skip %	write size (KB)	write count	write I/O Sizes (KB) 1	write I/O Sizes (KB) ≤ 4	write I/O Sizes (KB) > 4	write skip %	write %	barrier %
Android Boot														
`/system`	18562	1275	21	39	1215	0	0	0	0	0	0	NA	0	0
`/data`	28	24	24	0	0	41	16468	1204	120	43	1041	1	98	2
`/cache`	11	7	7	0	0	27	18	9	7	1	1	19	56	6
`/flex`	29	6	3	1	2	7	0	0	0	0	0	NA	0	0
Contacts Database														
`/system`	763	64	8	6	50	1	0	0	0	0	0	NA	0	0
`/data`	855	83	32	21	30	4	55281	21048	15414	3348	2286	17	100	4
Email Client														
`/system`	6218	511	80	26	405	1	0	0	0	0	0	NA	0	0
`/data`	2473	191	53	51	87	3	52100	16668	10520	2595	3553	12	99	33
`/sdcard`	6	3	2	1	0	17	112	97	90	7	0	43	97	0
Slideshow														
`/system`	5664	449	55	23	371	1	0	0	0	0	0	NA	0	0
`/data`	500	82	27	23	32	8	6452	659	173	73	413	2	89	10
`/sdcard`	38	18	14	2	2	22	13701	1883	1407	197	279	6	99	0
Browsing														
`/data`	43895	1662	313	228	1121	1	12609	3512	2149	542	821	10	68	18

Table 3. Characteristics of I/O traces (read/write breakdown). The size of the trace is expressed in KB and as a count of total operations. A rough classification of I/O sizes is provided in which each column is exclusive of adjacent columns. "Skip" is a measure of sequentiality: the number of block accesses that are not adjacent to a previous access. A skip percentage of 100 represents a completely non-sequential workload; a skip percentage of 0 is completely sequential. Write and barrier percentages are relative to the total number of I/O operations per-partition.

blocks exist to speedup writes. Writes always append to the end of the current *active* cluster, with GC maintaining a pool of free clusters to provide when the active cluster is full. Read operations first map from LBN to the current PBN for the logical block, using the page mapping table, prior to reading from the data file.

To minimize write latency and increase the size of sequential writes, LBS employs a write buffer. The write buffer is flushed on guest barrier operations and when it is full. Significant performance improvements are possible by write buffering when operating at the sequential write performance plateau, which occurs at 128 KB in Figure 1 — the write buffer size we employ is 256 KB.

Both the guest and host kernels maintain a page cache. When a file is read by a guest application, the data of that file are cached by the guest kernel, and the same data would ordinarily be cached by the host kernel. To avoid this double caching, the `vmx` storage thread uses the `O_DIRECT` flag when opening the `.lbsd` file, instructing the host kernel to avoid using the page cache for this file.

The meta-data file is an append-only log of meta-data and barrier entries. On each guest write, an entry is appended to the meta-data file, reflecting changes to the LBN→PBN mapping. When the guest kernel issues barriers, a barrier entry is appended, as described in Section 4.2. Meta-data entries are run-length encoded and zero blocks are optimized in both data and meta-data files. At the end of each meta-data entry is a series of fields providing block checksums and timestamps for non-zero blocks; Section 4.2 and Section 4.3 provide further details.

The meta-data file is not garbage collected online. Instead, when the VM image is opened, or when its size reaches a fixed limit, we perform an offline, atomic sweep to eliminate stale entries.

The in-memory LBN→PBN structures require 12 MB per 1 GB of logical block space. While we do not face the severe memory constraints that exist in other systems, for example FTLs on SD cards, it is wasteful and unnecessary to maintain the entire set of structures in memory at all time. Instead, they are placed in a `mmap`ed file located in internal storage, allowing the host kernel's existing page cache writeback and eviction mechanisms to manage the portions of the meta-data mapping structures that are maintained in memory and those on flash, based on the working set behavior of LBS. This has similarities to DFTL [11] page map caching and by placing the backing file on internal storage, we separate the competing data and meta-data I/O streams, conferring a performance advantage analogous to the HAT FTL scheme [12].

LBS data files are fully allocated on the FAT at creation, preventing further fragmentation once initialized. This is intended to alleviate the fragmentation penalty discussed in Section 2.

4.2 Reliability

There are several modes by which VM storage could possibly fail and which we wish to mitigate against:

- When a host crashes, due to battery depletion, software bugs or other causes:

  [CRASH-META] Corruption of the filesystem meta-data on which the `.lbsd`/`.lbsm` files reside during write operations.

  [CRASH-DATA] Corruption of the filesystem data on which the `.lbsd`/`.lbsm` files reside during write operations.

  [BUFFER-LOSS] Loss of write buffers in either main memory or on the flash controller. Buffers may be partially written back (in any order) at crash time.

- When a NAND device fails:

  [MEDIA-FAIL] Media failure and/or corruption in the internal or external NAND devices at the page or erase block granularity.

As a hosted hypervisor we rely on the guarantees provided by the underlying filesystems for *[CRASH-META]*. Internal storage is typically formatted with some log structured filesystem, such as YAFFS or JFFS2, which provides robustness for the `.lbsm` meta-data files. We accept as a fundamental limitation that possible FAT allocation table corruption presents an unmitigated point-of-failure for the data file.

[CRASH-DATA] is detectable through the use of checksums on both the LBS data and meta-data. Each data block has a 32 bit Fletcher checksum [9] or SHA-256 checksum computed when

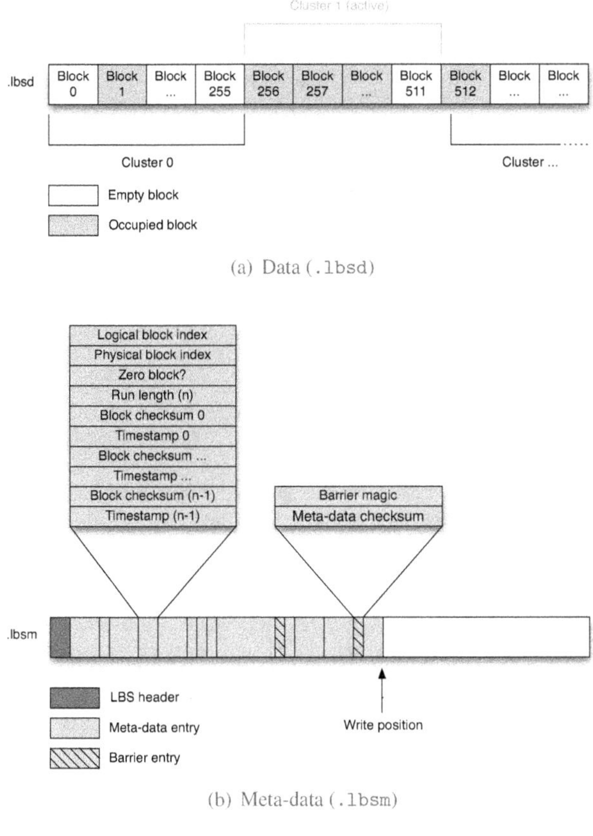

(a) Data (.lbsd)

(b) Meta-data (.lbsm)

Figure 10. LBS file formats.

written and the checksum is stored in the corresponding meta-data entry. Barrier entries in the meta-data are written whenever the journaled guest ext3 filesystem issues a barrier, and contain a Fletcher-32 checksum of the meta-data entries since the last barrier entry. In this way, if a missing terminating barrier or corruption of the LBS meta-data is detected, it is possible to rollback to the last barrier while maintaining the expected guest barrier semantics during recovery.

The LBS implementation ensures that internal write buffers are flushed and that `fsync/fdatasync` calls are made on first the `.lbsd` and then the `.lbsm` on a guest issued barrier operation to manage *[BUFFER-LOSS]*.

When meta-data GC is performed, there is a possibility of failure occurring due to a host crash. To reduce the likelihood of this occurring, we write to a secondary meta-data file `.lbsm2`, and only when the GC is complete is an atomic `rename` system call issued.

While there already exist error detection mechanisms within the FTLs for both internal and external storage, the checksums provide an additional mechanism to detect *[MEDIA-FAIL]*. This is particularly useful when a malicious attacker may freely modify blocks in the `.lbsd`, producing symptoms similar to media failure from the point-of-view of LBS while being undetectable from the point-of-view of the FTL, which regards the modification as a legitimate write operation. This attack is further detailed in the next section.

It is a significant challenge to test and validate the failure paths of a storage virtualization stack, since the failure modes we expect are rare and unlikely to appear under normal conditions. The resilience of the LBS design and implementation to the failure modes described above has been validated with in-situ model checking techniques, similar to Yang et al [33] but applied at the block storage device level instead of filesystems. The LBS implementation was recompiled and linked against a `ptrace`-based test harness instead of the `vmx`. The test harness provided a means to simulate an adversarial environment, for example by injecting system call failures or partially corrupting uncommitted data during a simulated crash. A number of serious implementation bugs were corrected with the results provided by this technique and confidence in correctness gained at both design and implementation level.

4.3 Security

We have derived a threat model capturing the concerns of MVP's users based on discussions with enterprises, carriers and OEMs. There are two classes of attacks that are widely seen as being the most relevant to a virtual phone:

- *Physical attacks*. Here we are primarily concerned with the confidentiality of data if a phone or SD card is lost or stolen. This is also known as confidentiality of *data-at-rest*.
- *Malicious host applications*. Malware may attempt to compromise the confidentiality or integrity of the VM image by exploiting weaknesses in the host OS security model, either while the VM is running or when it is suspended.

The LBS data file is encrypted at block granularity with an XTS-AES cipher. If an SD card or phone is stolen, there is no plain text on the storage media available to an attacker. The key is located on the protected internal storage and has the same confidentiality guarantees that exist for the Android application keystore.

Malicious host applications are a significant concern on Android if relying on the SD card for storage. Since the SD card is FAT formatted, the standard Unix permission model that Android uses to sandbox applications is limited by the lack of ownership and group information support in the filesystem. The XTS-AES cipher provides some reprieve from this threat, since malicious host applications may not learn the contents of the LBS data file, but does not directly protect against *replay* and *randomization* attacks. Replay attacks occur when a legitimate encrypted block from the past is reintroduced in the LBS data file by a malicious application, causing the guest behavior to be influenced by the contents of the injected block. The attacker does not need to know the plain text contents of the block, simply the associated guest behavior that was previously observed. Randomization attacks occur when a block is intentionally corrupted, e.g. fuzzed, leading to guest applications or the kernel behaving outside the usual control envelope where they depend on the contents of a block.

To combat replay and randomization attacks, we maintain a timestamp and checksum respectively in the LBS meta-data. The timestamp refers to a logical clock maintained by LBS, incremented after each write. The checksum selection is configurable and may be either a Fletcher-32 or truncated SHA-256 hash, allowing for a tradeoff to be made between the cheap to compute but not cryptographically strong Fletcher checksum and the more expensive SHA-256, depending on policy. In both cases, the checksum is applied to the plain text block contents prior to XTS-AES and the resulting checksum is hidden from the malicious host application, being located in the LBS meta-data, protected by Unix permissions on the more full featured YAFFS or JFFS2 used for internal storage. Hence, when attempting a randomization attack, the attacker is limited by a lack of knowledge of the checksummed block contents.

4.4 Garbage collection

Cluster garbage collection (GC) takes place in a thread separate from the main storage virtualization backend thread. GC starts when the number of free clusters drops below a low watermark and stops when the number of free clusters climbs back up above a high watermark. The watermarks hence provide GC control hysteresis.

The GC thread selects clusters to free based on heuristics that take into account the "emptiness" of a cluster, i.e. the number of unoccupied blocks. Occupied blocks from selected clusters are arranged in a queue and their contents are loaded in the background into memory. When enough data exists to complete the current active cluster, the preloaded blocks are extracted from the queue and written to the active cluster. The LBS data file is overprovisioned with space, e.g. the number of physical blocks allocated might be 112% of the logical blocks, to ensure that even a full guest image maintains adequate space for performant GC.

It is desirable to minimize the number of non-sequential jumps in the write position, even when write buffering and achieving sequential access within a cluster. We have found that the simple occupancy heuristic mentioned above results in the freeing of non-contiguous physical clusters over time, resulting in free clusters scattered around the data file. One solution to this problem is to combine additional heuristics using a scoring for each cluster, and garbage collect contiguous occupied clusters that have the highest score. The current scoring function has four weighted components:

- *[EMPTINESS]* The number of unoccupied blocks divided by blocks-per-cluster. A cluster with more free blocks is valued higher.
- *[LEFT EMPTY]* An award to clusters whose left sibling is empty because we want as many contiguous free clusters as possible. We assume that most I/O is ascending, so the right sibling is likely to be considered in the future; without this component, we might not otherwise examine the left sibling.
- *[OUTLIER CORRECTION]* An award provided to those clusters which have an abnormally high amount of occupied blocks compared to the clusters around them. Outlier clusters can be favored by treating them as if they are almost as empty as their surrounding clusters. Reclaiming an unusually full cluster in the midst of many empty clusters can extend the length of a contiguous series of clusters.
- *[WRITE POSITION]* A boost in score is given to the cluster next to the cluster currently being written. This promotes contiguous writes.

The components are equally weighted for the experiments in this paper, but an improved scoring function may exist in which component weight is dependent on the amount of free space for GC in the file. The more free space we have, the more important *[WRITE POSITION]* and *[LEFT EMPTY]* become. When there is little free space available for GC (typically below 25%), *[EMPTINESS]* starts to dominate the other factors.

The storage virtualization stack supports the propagation of guest TRIM commands. These are leveraged within LBS to assist GC by providing a more precise view of block status. More details can be found in Section 6.2.

5. Evaluation

This section describes the experiments used to quantify LBS performance. The benefits of LBS are shown with both synthetic and trace-based tests. The costs of write amplification, integrity checking and encryption are measured and discussed.

5.1 Experimental setup

Both synthetic and realistic, user-centric tests were used to characterize the performance of LBS. All experiments were conducted on an HTC Nexus One phone. The Nexus One contains a 1 GHz Qualcomm Snapdragon chipset and 512 MB of DRAM [10]. The phone ran an aftermarket version of Android 2.3 (Gingerbread) called CyanogenMod 7.1.

device ID	the partition accessed by this I/O
R/W	flag indicating whether this I/O is a read or a write
fragment	position in scatter-gather list
offset	location on disk
length	number of bytes accessed
barrier	flag indicating that this record represents a barrier request

Table 4. Trace record

The synthetic test is *sdperf* from Section 2. For realistic and repeatable results of the storage behavior of mobile applications, we wrote a trace-driven execution tool called *blksim*. We first gather an I/O trace using the guest block device driver during the use of an application. A trace record contains the fields shown in Table 4.

To replay the trace, *blksim* opens a raw block device in the guest with the `O_DIRECT` flag. Using a raw device removes filesystem effects. `O_DIRECT` removes the effect of the guest OS buffer cache and ensures that the virtualized device is presented with the same stream of I/O that was captured in the trace. Prior to enabling performance measurement, the trace is read into memory to create one command stream for each disk partition represented in the trace; this prevents the I/O required to read the trace from impacting the measured portion of the experiment.

Each partition's command stream is then applied to the device, one at a time. Reads and writes are emulated with `pread` and `pwrite`. A custom `ioctl` is used to provide end-to-end barrier semantics in the guest by blocking the guest *blksim* thread until the host has completed the `fsync` to the physical device.

We use the workloads described in Section 3 with one change: the Android Boot and Slideshow workloads were expanded by repeating each five times to produce a longer-running trace to magnify any performance differences and reduce variance.

5.2 Benefit of LBS

The results of the *sdperf* test with the 8 GB ADATA Class 6 SD card are shown in Figure 11. We compare LBS to a simpler "flat" VM image format which does not buffer I/O and uses a straight-through mapping of virtual disk blocks to physical disk blocks in the VM image. The graph presents the ratio between bandwidth achieved with both file formats. Garbage collection was not triggered during the experiments.

Like Figure 1, the upper graph shows the similarity of sequential and random reads. The performance difference between flat and LBS is due to encryption, integrity checking and indirection. It suggests that flat VM image formats are a better choice for read-only partitions, especially with larger block sizes.

When writes are present, performance will be closer to that shown in the lower graph. Here we see regions in which LBS has advantages for SD cards. For small writes ($\leq$ 32 KB), the LBS write buffer allows it to exceed the bandwidth achieved with a simple flat file — even for sequential writes — by making fewer, faster large I/Os to the SD card. For all tested block sizes, LBS outperforms the flat file for random writes. This is due to both the write buffering present in LBS and its ability, due to its log-based structure, to transform a stream of random writes into a sequential stream more suited for the SD card.

The benefit of LBS over a flat file can also be seen in the *blksim* results shown in Figure 12. Each workload was repeated three times for each set of filesystem options. The average of the three runs is normalized to the runtime of a flat virtual disk. We show a cluster

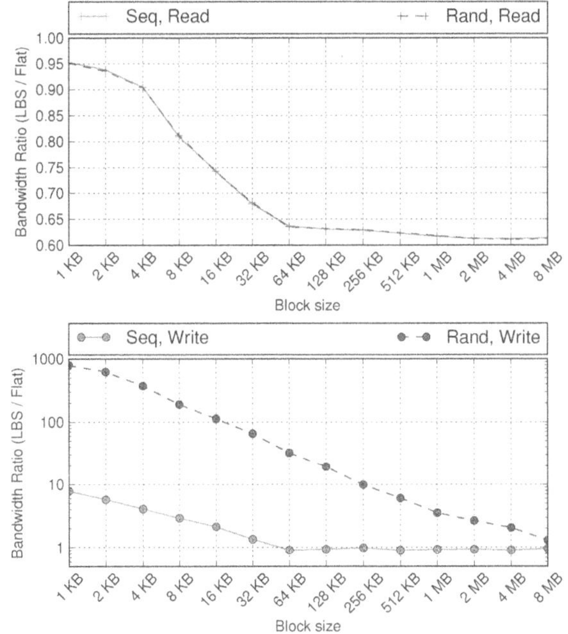

Figure 11. 8 GB ADATA Class 6 SD card I/O bandwidth: Ratio between LBS and Flat file format.

of bars for each partition that had non-negligible traffic. 160 MB was set aside to provide LBS with sufficient free blocks such that garbage collection does not occur; the impact of garbage collection is shown in Section 5.3.

Recall that the Contact Database workload is almost completely small writes with little sequentiality and a relatively small number of barriers. Thus, it exhibits a dramatic 17× improvement over the flat virtual disk due to LBS transforming the I/O into large, sequential writes. The other write-heavy workloads benefit as well. The email workload is nearly 5× faster with LBS than it is with a flat file; the reason it is not better may be due to it having the highest percentage of barriers within its I/O trace. Each barrier forces a flush of the LBS write buffer, and smaller writes are less efficient.

5.3 Write amplification

As described in Section 4.4, a garbage collection thread runs when space is low to provide free clusters for future writes. While this causes additional write operations to occur, their cost can be mitigated for two reasons. First, if no other write activity is required, the additional writes can occur in the background. Second, the writes will be to contiguous blocks which are relatively inexpensive on SD cards.

In Table 5, we show this *write amplification* due to LBS for the two workloads that triggered garbage collection. The table aggregates the writes from all of the virtual disk partitions. In this context, we ignore the effect of hardware-level writes that may occur depending on the implementation of the SD card's flash translation layer. Column 1 lists the number of 1 KB writes generated by the guest block driver. Note that these writes have been filtered by the guest OS buffer cache at the time of trace capture.

Column 2 shows the number of writes that actually occur, measured in units of both 1 KB blocks and 256 KB LBS clusters. These counts were gathered by setting aside 100% of the virtual disk's space as a buffer for the garbage collector so that the workload never triggers the GC threshold, and no GC writes occur. A small

trace	requested writes	LBS writes without GC	LBS writes with GC
Contacts	219124 blocks	219124 blocks 855 clusters	223593 blocks, 873 clusters (802 contiguous)
Email	216057 blocks	215972 blocks 843 clusters	220160 blocks 860 clusters (813 contiguous)

Table 5. Software-level write amplification due to garbage collection. 12% additional storage used for garbage collection.

reduction in writes occurs in the Email Client workload due to overwriting stale data in the LBS write buffer.

Column 3 reflects both the reduction in writes due to buffering and the write amplification due to garbage collection (the LBS data file had 12% extra space for GC). While the number of blocks that must be written has increased, recall that blocks belong to larger clusters, many of which are contiguous. The large size and high contiguity make LBS efficient.

5.4 Cost of encryption and integrity checking

Figure 12 also shows how encryption and integrity checking affect performance. The cost of encryption varies for each trace from as little as 2% for the Email Client workload, with its high barrier percentage, to as much as 35% for Android Boot. The relative cost of encryption increases as block size increases. For larger blocks, fixed I/O overhead represents a smaller fraction of overall time, and encryption overhead (which is proportional to block size) has a greater relative impact. Investigating the use of hardware encryption offload engines is left as future work.

As mentioned in Section 4.2, data blocks can be protected by the fast Fletcher checksum or a slower-to-compute, cryptographically strong SHA-256 checksum. The incremental cost of integrity checking with Fletcher-32 ranges from 1%–6%. Unfortunately, cryptographic hashes such as SHA-256 are relatively expensive to compute on each block. Using a C implementation of Fletcher-32 and the standard Android 2.2 OpenSSL implementation on a Nexus One device (in ARM assembly language), the following throughput figures (with 1KB block sizes) represent the speed at which memory contents can be checksummed. SHA-256 requires nearly 7.7× longer than Fletcher-32 to process data in these tests.

SHA-1	46.83 MB/s
SHA-256	31.26 MB/s
Fletcher (32 bits)	240.81 MB/s

Corporate policies may demand cryptographically strong hash algorithms such as SHA-256. In our tests, *sdperf* results were degraded by approximately 4–8% for block sizes less than 4 KB when SHA-256 was used instead of Fletcher-32. Overhead of the more expensive hash function increases with larger I/O as the cost of computation becomes a larger portion of the total I/O cost. While this is non-negligible, even the worst-case *sdperf* result (17% reduction in bandwidth for 256 KB reads, 13% reduction for writes) is much better than the 7.7× slowdown observed in memory-only tests.

6. Optimizing the mobile I/O stack

LBS effectively bridges the gap between the available storage media characteristics and VM I/O requirements. Enhancements in the guest, host and SD card have potential to further improve LBS performance and/or simplify the VM image format. These optimizations may prove beneficial even on non-virtualized systems.

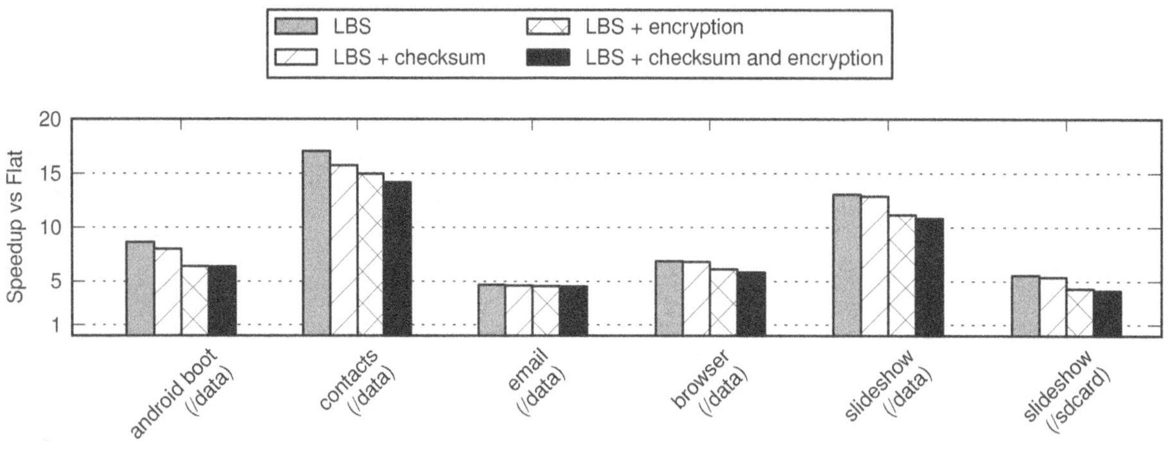

Figure 12. Performance of I/O traces without garbage collection.

6.1 Guest

The sequential vs. random and block size write asymmetry may also be addressed at the filesystem level in the guest, rather than with the block storage virtualization layer, with a suitable guest log structured filesystem. The YAFFS and JFFS families of flash filesystems employ a log structure and appear natural candidates on Android. Beyond scalability concerns, the chief drawback in a virtualized setting is the increased complexity at the guest-VMM surface, where a device model capable of emulating NAND devices is required, since these filesystems leverage the spare area associated with pages in NAND. MVP currently presents a simple paravirtualized block device to the kernel's block layer, minimizing both guest driver and VMM complexity and overhead. In addition, such filesystems are optimized for direct NAND control and some translation will be required to bridge between the FTL-abstracted NAND on the SD card and the virtual NAND devices. Other Linux log structured filesystems, e.g. LogFS and NILFS, are experimental as of 2.6.35 and are unsuitable for enterprise VMs as a result.

A stable implementation of a Linux log structured filesystem operating on the block layer will open up the possibility of deployment within MVP guests, lessening the need for the log structure of LBS, but not the security and reliability aspects. The guest memory working set behavior and resulting checkpoint subsystem writebacks cannot be modified as simply as the filesystem, since these are properties of the application and kernel and not under our control. As a result, the host filesystem is still presented with a non-sequential I/O stream, and a system such as LBS will continue to be advantageous for VM checkpointing on SD cards — even if a log structured filesystem is in use in the guest.

6.2 Host

The fundamental assumption guiding a hosted mobile hypervisor architecture is that the host OS and hardware are the purview of OEMs, silicon and mobile OS vendors. Below we provide several suggestions for these entities that should prove beneficial for VMs or applications that make extensive use of the SD card:

- As mentioned in Section 4, the LBS data files are allocated on the FAT filesystem at initialization time, reducing fragmentation and ensuring availability of space at runtime. This is a slow operation for large images: since FAT does not support sparse files or extents, space must be reserved by allocating each block of the file (e.g., with zeroes). MVP provides a host kernel patch that allocates filesystem structures for an LBS file and omits the block zeroing. OEMs may optionally apply this patch to improve the speed of VM provisioning.
- Similar to the guest in Section 6.1, formatting the host's SD card with alternate filesystems could lessen the requirements on the virtualization layer in terms of I/O reordering, security and reliability. This would come at the cost of limiting the inter-operability of the SD card with other devices expecting a FAT filesystem or via USB mass storage. In addition, SD card FTLs are optimized for FAT and the use of other filesystems will require careful tuning [5] (or cooperation from SD card manufacturers to design hardware to suit a new filesystem standard).

  There is also a trend towards the use of eSD/eMMC chips on recent phones for internal storage. These devices share the problems of microSD cards discussed above, with the exception that they can use a custom filesystem and often employ ext3/ext4. The relationship between these filesystems, the more general I/O mixture from Android applications and middleware and the FTLs on the devices is an interesting area for exploration.
- SD card access control granularity can be improved without modifying the filesystem, for example by the use of loopback mounted encrypted images on the SD card with `dm-crypt` [24], with mounts restricted to specific applications or capabilities. This approach has been supported for read-only application code since Android 2.2, but not for application data, which is where the VM images are located. In addition, integrity checking is currently lacking from solutions based around these mechanisms on the Android and Linux platforms.
- The TRIM command for solid-state disks provides a means to detect when a block is no longer in use. TRIM commands are supported by LBS, which marks given blocks as free in the meta-data. This can reduce the garbage collector overhead and increases the write bandwidth.

  An example of where we greatly benefit from TRIM in LBS GC is the interaction between memory ballooning [30], used to balance memory between the host and guest, and the checkpoint subsystem's continuous writeback. It is common for the balloon to release large amounts of guest memory, which translates directly to the discarding of the released pages from the checkpoint image.

SD cards support erase operations which are natural candidates for the translation of TRIM or discard commands. This would enable the SD card's FTL to also reduce its garbage collection overhead. Unfortunately, the FAT filesystem does not provide a means for applications like the `vmx` to convey this information. Appropriate user-level primitives would assist here.

- Section 5.2 and Section 5.4 demonstrate the non-negligible cost of hashing and encryption in software. Mobile SoCs include dedicated cryptographic engines [2], however these are not exposed at user-level on Linux. A standard API providing access to these features would make practical their adoption in LBS when the setup and invocation costs are outweighed by the offloading advantage.

  Another area that hardware security features could assist is in key storage. As mentioned earlier, the LBS AES key is only as secure as the host application keystore, which is typically protected by file permissions only. The hardware based secure storage functionality offered on some SoCs [2] could provide further protection for keys, but again there is no standardized means to access this at the application level today which hinders a portable implementation.

6.3 SD card

FTLs with support for a VM or general purpose workload I/O mixture are another way to attack the mismatch LBS solves. An example of such cards are Windows Phone 7 compliant cards [29], such as the 8 GB SanDisk in Section 2, where small random writes are not penalized. However, the batching achieved by the LBS write buffer may still prove beneficial, since it amortizes the kernel context switch, host controller and SD card communication costs.

SD cards can include a small protected area for DRM-style device use [23], however this is not a general purpose secure storage mechanism and is not exported in a standard way to user-level applications. If SD cards were to provide hardware encrypted partitions, similar to some secure USB keys [13], then data-at-rest confidentiality can be guaranteed for the VM without the need for interposition at the VM layer. Protection from malicious host applications will still require effective access control at the operating system level, i.e. a generally accessible FAT partition requires encryption in the `vmx` before the data hits the filesystems.

7. Related work

The performance characteristics of many SD cards are studied by Bergmann and the Linaro Project [5, 16]. In addition to the observations in Section 2 regarding the disadvantage of non-sequentiality in write patterns at small block sizes, they delve into reverse engineered internal FTL characteristics. While the Linaro effort is focused on understanding these characteristics to motivate kernel changes to better support SD cards, we demonstrate application level optimizations, above the FAT layer, instead and apply them to the VM backing store domain.

Bouganim et al [7] present a benchmarking methodology for block addressed flash memory devices. Our performance characterization in Section 2 is similar in nature to a subset of the microbenchmarks they describe, targeted at the filesystem level instead of block layer. We also chose to focus on bandwidth instead of latency, since we found this both easier to measure and throughput to be a more important consideration than individual I/O latency for operations such as checkpoint suspend and resume.

While performance modeling and system optimization for SSDs has been extensively studied, e.g. [1, 8, 21, 25], SD cards have received comparably little attention in the literature, perhaps as a result of their assumed role as ancillary media stores rather than devices backing key workloads such as databases and virtual machines. Some studies have included examples of related low cost consumer storage in the form of Compact Flash (CF) cards [19] and USB flash drives [6, 7], but without publicly available SD card implementation details, it is unclear whether this related work can be applied to a given SD card.

Log structured filesystems were proposed to address the I/O bottleneck caused by fast CPU and slow disks [22]. While the original work focused on mechanical disks, the same relative penalty exists for mobile devices using commercial SD cards. The use of a log structured filesystems to improve performance on flash memory has been studied in the Cloudburst project [4]. LBS shares several of the same goals as Cloudburst, but the works differ in that LBS focuses on NAND flash rather than NOR flash. The Cloudburst virtual disk was implemented between the filesystem and the physical media, directly interfacing with NOR flash chips. LBS is a different sort of virtual disk: one that exists between a VM's virtualized media and a host filesystem. Log structured filesystems have also been employed on flash media for wear leveling and reliability [32], LBS already benefits from the wear leveling provided by an SD card's FTL but is required to add missing reliability features. DFS [15] utilizes features of a log structured FTL with large virtual address space and crash recovery support, implemented as a kernel device driver for FusionIO drives, to simplify flash filesystem implementation. The tradeoff between performance and memory use was explored by NANDFS [35], LBS delegates this decision to the kernel's page cache layer.

The concept of *reading* VM checkpoint images sequentially is discussed in a paper on fast restore [34]. In this work, the ability to quickly restore a VM is aided by sequential placement on disk of memory that is not necessarily contiguous. Work on fast checkpointing of VMs trades checkpoint speed for potential slowdown during restore due to random placement of memory blocks on disk [20]. Our work focuses on quickly *writing* checkpoints to disk, but it shares the desire to enable sequential placement of disk blocks despite memory access patterns that are not necessarily sequential.

8. Conclusion

The storage virtualization layer in a mobile hypervisor needs to take into account the performance, security and reliability characteristics of the host devices and filesystems providing bulk storage. In this paper we have presented the motivation, design, implementation and performance evaluation for a block storage virtualization layer capable of matching an Android VM's I/O mixture with these characteristics of commodity SD cards and the FAT filesystem. SD cards, while not designed with the use case in mind, are capable of effectively supporting a storage virtualization backend with such a layer. Going forward, there are many avenues presented in Section 6 for VMware, OEMs, silicon vendors, mobile operating systems and the systems research community to explore in further enhancing VM and general purpose storage I/O on low cost commodity devices, an area that has to date been under-explored.

Acknowledgments

The authors would like to thank Craig Newell for his direction; Prashanth Bungale, Viktor Gyuris, Andrew Isaacson, Priti Mishra and Ian Wienand for their careful reviews; and our managers for permitting us to spend time on this paper.

References

[1] Nitin Agrawal, Vijayan Prabhakaran, Ted Wobber, John D. Davis, Mark Manasse, and Rina Panigrahy. Design tradeoffs for SSD performance. In *USENIX Annual Technical Conference*, June 2008.

[2] Jerome Azema and Gilles Fayad. *M-Shield^{TM} Mobile Security Technology: making wireless secure*. Texas Instruments, February 2008.

[3] Ken Barr, Prashanth Bungale, Stephen Deasy, Viktor Gyuris, Perry Hung, Craig Newell, Harvey Tuch, and Bruno Zoppis. The VMware Mobile Virtualization Platform: is that a hypervisor in your pocket? *SIGOPS Operating Systems Review*, 44:124–135, December 2010.

[4] Gretta Bartels and Timothy Mann. Cloudburst: A compressing, log-structured virtual disk for flash memory. Technical Report 2001-001, Compaq Systems Research Center, February 2001.

[5] Arnd Bergmann. Optimizing Linux with cheap flash drives. *Linux Weekly News*, February 2011. URL: `http://lwn.net/Articles/428584/` [visited September 2011].

[6] Andrew Birrell, Michael Isard, Chuck Thacker, and Ted Wobber. A design for high-performance flash disks. *SIGOPS Operating Systems Review*, 41(2):88–93, April 2007.

[7] Luc Bouganim, B. Jónsson, and Philippe Bonnet. uFLIP: Understanding flash IO patterns. In *Conference on Innovative Data Systems Research*, January 2009.

[8] Kaoutar El Maghraoui, Gokul Kandiraju, Joefon Jann, and Pratap Pattnaik. Modeling and simulating flash based solid-state disks for operating systems. In *WOSP/SIPEW International Conference on Performance Engineering*, January 2010.

[9] John G. Fletcher. An arithmetic checksum for serial transmissions. *IEEE Transactions on Communications*, 30(1):247 – 252, January 1982.

[10] Google, Inc. Nexus One [online]. URL: `http://www.google.com/phone/detail/nexus-one` [visited October 2011].

[11] Aayush Gupta, Youngjae Kim, and Bhuvan Urgaonkar. DFTL: A flash translation layer employing demand-based selective caching of page-level address mappings. In *International Conference on Architectural Support for Programming Languages and Operating Systems*, March 2009.

[12] Yang Hu, Hong Jiang, Dan Feng, Lei Tian, Shuping Zhang, Jingning Liu, Wei Tong, Yi Qin, and Liuzheng Wang. Achieving page-mapping FTL performance at block-mapping FTL cost by hiding address translation. In *IEEE Symposium on Massive Storage Systems and Technologies*, May 2010.

[13] IronKey. *IronKey Basic S200 datasheet*, 2009.

[14] Song Jiang, Feng Chen, and Xiaodong Zhang. CLOCK-Pro: An effective improvement of the CLOCK replacement. In *USENIX Annual Technical Conference*, April 2005.

[15] William K. Josephson, Lars A. Bongo, Kai Li, and David Flynn. DFS: A file system for virtualized flash storage. *ACM Transactions on Storage*, 6:14:1–14:25, September 2010.

[16] Linaro. Flash card survey [online]. URL: `https://wiki.linaro.org/WorkingGroups/Kernel/Projects/FlashCardSurvey` [visited September 2011].

[17] Metago. ASTRO File Manager version 2.5.2 [online]. URL: `http://market.android.com/details?id=com.metago.astro` [visited August 2011].

[18] NASA. *Ornamentation* photographs [online]. December 2010. URL: `http://www.flickr.com/photos/nasacommons/sets/72157625514008231/` [visited October 2011].

[19] Suman Nath and Phillip B. Gibbons. Online maintenance of very large random samples on flash storage. *The VLDB Journal*, 19:67–90, February 2010.

[20] Eunbyung Park, Bernhard Egger, and Jaejin Lee. Fast and space efficient virtual machine checkpointing. In *ACM SIGPLAN/SIGOPS International Conference on Virtual Execution Environments*, March 2011.

[21] Abhishek Rajimwale, Vijayan Prabhakaran, and John D. Davis. Block management in solid-state devices. In *USENIX Annual Technical Conference*, June 2009.

[22] Mendel Rosenblum and John K. Ousterhout. The design and implementation of a log-structured file system. In *ACM Symposium on Operating Systems Principles*, October 1991.

[23] SanDisk. *SanDisk SD Card Product Manual*, 2.2 edition, November 2004. Document No. 80-13-00169.

[24] Christophe Saout. dm-crypt: a device-mapper crypto target [online]. URL: `http://www.saout.de/misc/dm-crypt/` [visited October 2011].

[25] Mohit Saxena and Michael M. Swift. FlashVM: virtual memory management on flash. In *USENIX Annual Technical Conference*, June 2010.

[26] SD Group (Panasonic, SanDisk, Toshiba) and SD Card Association. *SD Specifications Part 1. Physical Layer. Simplified Specification. Version 3.01*, May 2010.

[27] Standard Performance Evaluation Corporation. SPECmail2009, March 2009. URL: `http://www.spec.org/mail2009/`.

[28] Jeremy Sugerman, Ganesh Venkitachalam, and Beng-Hong Lim. Virtualizing I/O devices on VMware Workstation's hosted virtual machine monitor. In *USENIX Annual Technical Conference*, June 2001.

[29] Microsoft Support. Windows Phone 7 Secure Digital Card limitations [online]. URL: `http://support.microsoft.com/kb/2450831` [visited October 2011].

[30] C. Waldspurger. Memory resource management in VMware ESX Server. In *Symposium on Operating Systems Design and Implementation*. USENIX, December 2002.

[31] Seth Weintraub. Industry first: Smartphones pass PCs in sales [online]. Feb. 2011. URL: `http://tech.fortune.cnn.com/2011/02/07/idc-smartphone-shipment-numbers-passed-pc-in-q4-2010/` [visited October 2011].

[32] David Woodhouse. JFFS: The journaling flash file system. In *Ottawa Linux Symposium*, July 2001.

[33] Junfeng Yang, Paul Twohey, Dawson Engler, and Madanlal Musuvathi. Using model checking to find serious file system errors. *ACM Transactions on Computer Systems*, 24:393–423, November 2006.

[34] Irene Zhang, Alex Garthwaite, Yury Baskakov, and Kenneth C. Barr. Fast restore of checkpointed memory using working set estimation. In *ACM SIGPLAN/SIGOPS International Conference on Virtual Execution Environments*, March 2011.

[35] Aviad Zuck, Ohad Barzilay, and Sivan Toledo. NANDFS: a flexible flash file system for ram-constrained systems. In *ACM International Conference on Embedded Software*, October 2009.

Replacement Attacks Against VM-protected Applications

Sudeep Ghosh Jason Hiser Jack W. Davidson

{sudeep, hiser, jwd}@virginia.edu

Department of Computer Science, University of Virginia, Charlottesville, VA-22903, USA.

Abstract

Process-level virtualization is increasingly being used to enhance the security of software applications from reverse engineering and unauthorized modification (called *software protection*). Process-level virtual machines (PVMs) can safeguard the application code at run time and hamper the adversary's ability to launch dynamic attacks on the application. This dynamic protection, combined with its flexibility, ease in handling legacy systems and low performance overhead, has made process-level virtualization a popular approach for providing software protection. While there has been much research on using process-level virtualization to provide such protection, there has been less research on attacks against PVM-protected software. In this paper, we describe an attack on applications protected using process-level virtualization, called a replacement attack. In a replacement attack, the adversary replaces the protecting PVM with an attack VM thereby rendering the application vulnerable to analysis and modification. We present a general description of the replacement attack methodology and two attack implementations against a protected application using freely available tools. The generality and simplicity of replacement attacks demonstrates that there is a strong need to develop techniques that meld applications more tightly to the protecting PVM to prevent such attacks.

Categories and Subject Descriptors D.3.4 [*Programming languages*]: Processors – Run-time Environments; D.4.6 [*Operating Systems*]: Security and Protection

General Terms Security

Keywords Software protection, Process-level virtualization, Dynamic binary translation, Code obfuscation, Reverse engineering, Software tamper resistance.

1. Introduction

Process-level virtualization is a versatile and powerful technique that addresses a wide range of system challenges. It has been increasingly used to deliver solutions in the area of software protection (i.e., mechanisms that protect software applications from reverse-engineering attacks and tamper) [1, 20]. A number of commercial products have been designed to provide software protection via process-level virtualization such as VMProtect [51], Code Virtualizer [37], Themida [36]. A number of computer gaming software applications employ the StarForce virtualization system for copy protection and anti-reverse engineering [48]. Recently, malicious agents have used this protection technique to design state-of-the-art malware that can evade current detection systems [41]. There are several reasons why PVMs are popular amongst security researchers for enhancing software protection.

- Process-level virtualization provides a platform for enhanced run-time security. Attackers are increasingly using dynamic techniques to attack software (e.g., running applications under a debugger or a simulator) [5]. PVMs allow run-time monitoring and checking of the code being executed, making them an excellent tool for devising dynamic protection schemes [38]. PVMs can also mutate the application code as it is running (e.g., changing code and data locations, replacing instructions with semantically equivalent instructions, etc.), hampering iterative attacks [20].
- It is advantageous to have the protection techniques closely integrated with the application, yet keep the implementations separate. This modular approach enables easier testing and debugging of the system, and it allows legacy systems to be retrofitted with new protections without the need for modification and recompilation. PVMs can be used to provide such a flexible capability.
- Static protection schemes can be strengthened when the application is run under a PVM. For example, encryption is a useful technique that hampers static analysis of programs. Because the encrypted code cannot be run directly on commodity processors, the software decryption of the application code becomes a point of vulnerability. For example, schemes which decrypt the application in bulk are susceptible to dynamic analysis techniques [5], whereas decryption at a lower granularity (e.g., functions) can suffer from high overhead [9, 29]. In contrast, executing encrypted applications under the control of a PVM has been shown to have a better performance-security tradeoff [27]. The PVM incurs low information leakage, with the addition of a small performance overhead [20]. Another example is the improvement of the robustness of integrity checks that are located in the application. When run under a PVM, these integrity checks never execute from their original location, instead, they can be invoked from randomized locations in memory [20]. This randomization makes it harder for the attacker to locate and disable the checks.

Considering their increasing use in program protection, it is important to assess the security of process-level virtualization as a whole. The existence of any weaknesses in the PVM or its interaction with the application can seriously undermine any protection mechanism that relies on process-level virtualization.

VEE'12, March 3–4, 2012, London, England, UK.

This work presents a generic attack methodology, called a replacement attack, that targets applications protected using process-level virtualization. The basic premise behind this attack strategy is that the PVM is not anchored sufficiently to the execution environment, and can be replaced by the attacker at run time. Using a replacement attack, the attacker can effectively remove any dynamic protection technique actuated by process-level virtualization and proceed to analyze the application at run time. Some of the contributions of this work are listed below.

- This paper describes replacement attacks, a novel attack methodology targeted towards virtualized applications (i.e., applications that run under the mediation of a process-level virtual machine), that seeks to render the protective PVM ineffective. A replacement attack can be used against any application that is run under the mediation of a process-level virtual machine. The goal of a replacement attack is the circumvention of the dynamic protections driven by PVMs, thereby making dynamic analysis easier.
- Our analysis shows that existing protection schemes, such as software checksumming guards (proposed by Chang et al. [10]), fail to adequately protect virtualized applications from this class of attack.
- We present a comprehensive two-part case study describing the replacement attack methodology. The first part of this study describes the creation of a protected, virtualized application, and then how an attacker can easily replace the protective PVM. We describe two prototypes of the replacement attack using easily available, free-to-use tools. The first involves replacing the protective PVM with an attack PVM (i.e., a PVM without any protections). The second prototype involves running the application on a modified simulator which circumvents the protective PVM and simulates the application directly. These examples demonstrate the feasibility and effectiveness of replacement attacks on non-trivial applications.
- We then discuss the implications of the replacement attack in the second part of our case study. It involves examining dynamic attacks on unprotected applications, PVM-protected applications, and applications subjected to the replacement attack. Our results show that the replacement attack renders the application completely vulnerable to run-time analysis and subsequent tamper.
- This research demonstrates that process-level virtualization currently fails to provide adequate protection to applications. Techniques that tightly bind PVMs with the protected applications are needed to thoroughly realize the protective capabilities of PVMs.

The remainder of the paper is organized as follows. Section 2 provides background on process-level virtualization. The protection model for a virtualized application is described in Section 3. Section 4 describes the attacker's capabilities and goals. Section 5 gives a high-level overview of the dynamic replacement attack. Section 6 uses a case study to describe the details of the protection mechanisms and how a dynamic attack circumvents them to leave an application vulnerable. Section 7 discusses the impact of this methodology with respect to reverse engineering. Section 8 explores some of the requirements to mount a successful attack. Section 9 describes some of the past work in the field of software tamper resistance, and finally, Section 10 presents the conclusions.

2. Process-level Virtualization

A software application is a sequence of instructions that execute on a particular computing system. Virtualization is a software layer that encapsulates the application and its associated platform from the native computing system, allowing the application to execute on different platforms. Virtualization has been used to overcome the barriers imposed by new hardware [17, 39], or to improve security [7, 19, 30]. Formally, virtualization involves the construction of an isomorphism that maps a virtual system (called the *guest*) onto the native system (called the *host*). It is the responsibility of the virtual machine to run the application compiled for the guest (called the *guest application*) on the host system. Some of the necessary tasks include converting the guest application's instructions to run on the host, and mediating communication between the application and the host platform. Virtualization can be done at the system level (i.e., operating system), or at the process level (a single application).

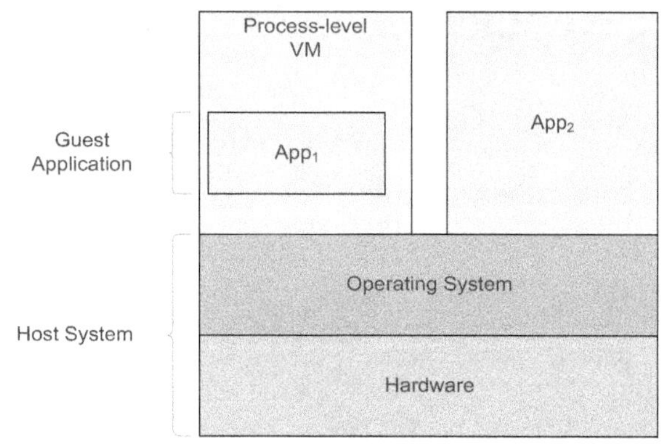

Figure 1. High-level overview of process-level virtualization. The guest application runs under the mediation of the process-level VM, giving an outward appearance of a process that is native to the underlying platform.

Figure 1 illustrates a typical process-level virtual machine environment, where the guest application runs under the control of the PVM, giving it the outward appearance of a native host process. This work focuses exclusively on process-level virtualization and its weaknesses with respect to software protection.

During program startup, the PVM assumes control and starts decoding the application's instructions in program order. The decoded instructions are then used to invoke appropriate handling routines, which interpret the instructions on the host. As such, the PVM can regularly monitor the application code being executed on the host system, and serve as a platform for applying protection schemes dynamically.

3. Software Protection Model

This section describes the importance of software protection techniques and illustrates the general protection model in the context of a virtualized application.

Software applications often perform critical tasks in a wide variety of fields, such as banking, transportation and medical systems. Any unauthorized modification to such critical software systems can lead to extensive disruption of services and potential losses in terms of life and property. Therefore, it is important to protect software applications from malicious modification. We define the entity whose goal is to preserve the integrity of the software application as the *defender*. To achieve his goals, the defender uses different protection schemes to protect the critical functionality of the software. Numerous such techniques have been proposed to safeguard software, which can broadly be divided into static tech-

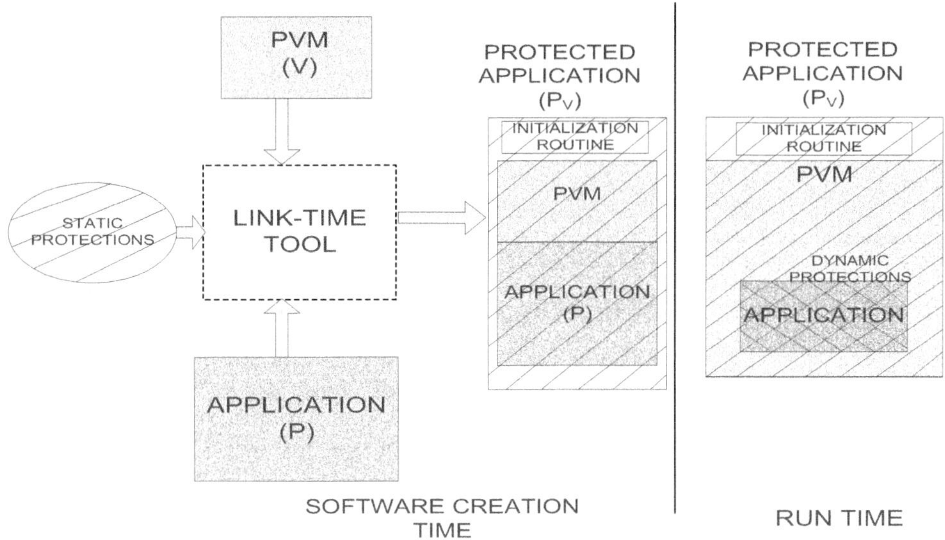

Figure 2. A high-level overview of the protected software creation process. A link-time tool is used to assemble the application code, libraries and the PVM code and apply various protection mechanisms, to create a protected binary. At run time, the application runs under the control of the protective PVM.

niques (which protect the on-disk binary from analysis), and dynamic techniques (which protect the software while it is running).

Static protections protect the on-disk binary from analysis and modification. A number of powerful static protection techniques have been proposed in recent years [13, 14, 32, 52]. For example, opaque predicates are a common technique that aid in program obfuscation [14]. An opaque predicate is a construct with *true/false* outcome. The opaqueness of these predicates is attributed to the fact that, it is hard to reverse engineer their values from the on-disk binary using static techniques. These constructs are utilized in obfuscating control-flow information. Code encryption is another useful technique against static analysis [9]. Figure 2 illustrates the creation of the virtualized application which is protected by such techniques. At software creation time, the defender packages the protective VM with the guest application P, along with its software libraries using a link-time rewriting tool. The tool then applies various protection schemes to the virtualized application P_V. Once the protection techniques are applied, the rewriting tool outputs the protected binary, as shown in Figure 2.

Static techniques alone fail to provide adequate protection. As we describe in Section 4, attackers are increasingly using run-time techniques to analyze applications. To protect against such attacks, a few solutions have been proposed which involve changing program code as it runs, to create a shifting attack target (e.g., dynamic instruction rewriting [28], and edit scripts [35]). Another solution involves packaging a process-level VM with the application, that protects the run time from analysis and generic attack [1, 20, 51], as shown in the right side of Figure 2. The application is modified such that, at program start up, the PVM is initialized and control is transfered to it. Subsequently, the application runs under the control of the PVM, rather than directly on the native platform. The code for invoking the PVM is stored in the *initialization routine* of the virtualized application. There are different techniques to create these initialization routines (e.g., in Executable and Linking Format (ELF) files, these routines can be placed in the `.init` section [54]. The MacOS binary format, Mach-O, contains the `__DATA,__mod_init_func` section for placing class constructors [2]).

A PVM's ability to monitor the guest application's code makes it a suitable platform for dynamic protection. As the PVM is virtualizing the guest application, it can check to make sure the code has not been modified, and introduce schemes to obfuscate the code. The PVM can be used to apply protection schemes on a *per-run* basis, creating a different attack surface every time the application is run [20]. Such a scheme makes it difficult to launch automated attacks on the application. PVMs have been shown to increase the effectiveness of existing protection techniques as well. For example, code encryption schemes are often vulnerable due to coarse levels of decryption at run time [5]. PVMs facilitate just-in-time, on-demand code decryption [20]. Only those instructions of P which are scheduled to be executed, get decrypted. After execution, the instructions can be re-encrypted. Therefore, P is never fully decrypted at any point during execution.

4. Attack Model

Once the software application is deployed, it may be subjected to various attacks. The attacker is defined as the entity that seeks to affect a software's functionality or misappropriate critical information from it. To achieve their goal, the attacker has to initially analyze the software and obtain a level of understanding of its operation. Using this derived knowledge, the attacker can then proceed to disable the protection scheme.

The attacker's goals have been aided by recent advances in reverse engineering technology, which have led to the availability of powerful tools for analyzing software. There are two types of analysis tools: *static analysis* tools that collect information about a program by studying its binary but without executing it (e.g., disassemblers and decompilers), and *dynamic analysis* tools that collect information from program runs (e.g., debuggers, simulators, dynamic analysis frameworks, and emulators [18, 34, 55]). In particular, the development and availability of dynamic tools has strengthened the attacker's capabilities because many static protec-

Term	Notation	Definition
Guest Application	P	The software application
Protective PVM	V	A process-level virtual machine that has been configured to apply various protection techniques at run time.
Virtualized application	P_V	Software application consisting of the P packaged together with a protective PVM.
Entry function	EP	The function in the VM code which initiates the process of application virtualization. To mount a successful attack, the attacker has to locate this function.
Attack PVM	M	A process-level VM that can aid the attacker in analyzing P.
Code Introspection Framework	CIF	An introspection framework capable of monitoring and instrumenting the code being executed.

Table 1. Glossary of the terminology used in this paper.

tion techniques are susceptible to run-time analysis [5]. Using these tools, the attacker attempts to obtain information necessary to carry out the intended attack. The attack described in the next section enables use of such tools on PVM-protected applications.

The terminology used in this paper is summarized in Table 1.

5. Replacement Attack

This section describes an attack methodology that targets software applications protected by process-level virtualization. The goal of this attack methodology involves replacing the protective PVM, rendering P_V vulnerable to analysis. The attacker can then use some of the tools described in Section 4 to obtain relevant information.

This methodology targets the surface of the application that is most vulnerable to attack (i.e., when protections are at their weakest). More specifically, this attack methodology targets the application just after start up (when static protections are not as effective), but before the PVM assumes control and begins applying protections to the application. If successful, the attack disengages the protective PVM and disables the run-time protections.

To craft a successful replacement attack against PVM-protected applications, certain requirements need to be met:

- The attacker must be able to locate the entry function (EP) of the protective PVM in P_V. The entry function is defined as the function of the PVM which initiates software virtualization. The entry function often takes the starting address location of P's code as an argument.
- The attacker must be aware of the guest application's instruction set architecture. The code of the guest application P, is typically obscured using a secret ISA or encryption. To analyze and run P after the protective PVM has been disabled, the attacker needs to be cognizant of the ISA, which involves either analyzing and understanding the secret ISA, or extracting the key from the binary.

Section 8 discusses these requirements in more detail, including heuristics that the attacker can employ to obtain the required information.

The attack occurs in two stages. In the first stage, the attack PVM has to be extended to decode the protected application, which involves understanding the guest ISA. If the ISA is encrypted, the decryption keys and algorithms must also be obtained and used to further extend the attack PVM by including the decrytion algorithm and keys. Details on deciphering the guest application's ISA are given in Section 8.2.

Figure 3 illustrates the second stage of the attack on P_V. In Figure 3(a), the attacker invokes P_V, under a *code introspection framework* (CIF), observing instructions as they execute. Well known examples of CIFs include Pin [33] and QEMU [3]. The attacker modifies the CIF to locate the call to the entry function of the protective PVM.

The initialization routine then proceeds to prepare the PVM's internal structures. As the entry function of the protective PVM is invoked, the CIF intercepts this call and extracts the start address, depicted in Figure 3(b). Details on identifying the PVM's entry function are given in Section 8.1

The CIF then proceeds to load and initialize the attack PVM, shown in Figure 3(c). The CIF then invokes this attack PVM with P's start address which has been extracted from the initial call.

Thus, P now runs under the mediation of the attack PVM (shown in Figure 3(d)). The protective PVM is circumvented and fails to provide dynamic protection to P. The attack PVM can be used to perform tasks that helps the attacker understand P (e.g., dump information, identify function locations, trace instructions, etc.).

In Section 6, we describe two proof-of-concept implementations that use the approach just described. The first prototype makes use of a widely used CIF, Pin, to replace the protective PVM with an attack PVM and execute the guest application. The second uses a modified architectural simulator, which performs code introspection as well as virtualization.

6. Case Study

This section provides a comprehensive case study of the replacement attack methodology. It describes, Strata, the protective virtual machine, and the creation of the protected application, P_V. The target application was chosen from the integer benchmarks of the SPEC CPU2000 suite. The benchmarks were selected as examples of typical applications and they are commonly used to measure run-time performance. These benchmarks range from a few thousands lines of code to hundreds of thousands of lines, and perform various tasks. Thus, these benchmarks present a wide range of code size and functionality to validate our ideas. For the purposes of this discussion, we focus on the *256.bzip2* benchmark as the target guest application, P. *256.bzip2* is a modified version of the bzip compression program, designed to evaluate CPU performance. All our tests were carried out on the Intel x86 32-bit platform running Linux OS. All the components were initially compiled using *gcc*.

6.1 Dynamic binary translation

Section 2 gave a high-level overview of process-level virtualization. Although process-level virtualization systems are complex in nature, they are all variations of the *decode-dispatch* approach [46]. *Decode-dispatch* systems consists of a main loop that iterates through three phases for every guest application instruction: *decode, dispatch* and *execute*. The decode phase fetches the opcode for the instruction. The dispatch phase uses this information to invoke appropriate handling routines. The execute phase then fetches the operands and proceeds to invoke the corresponding

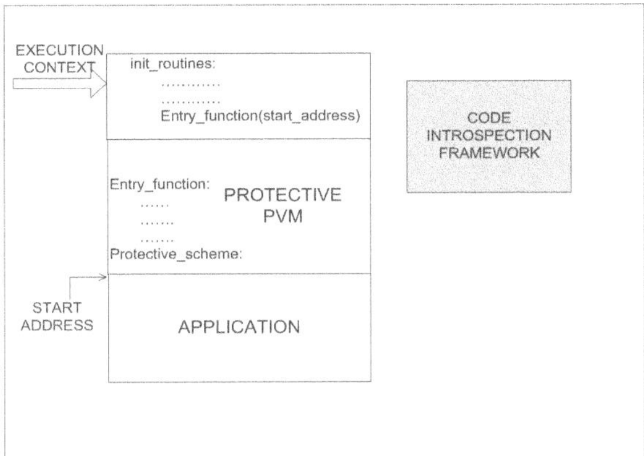

(a) The virtualized application, P_V, is run under an introspection framework.

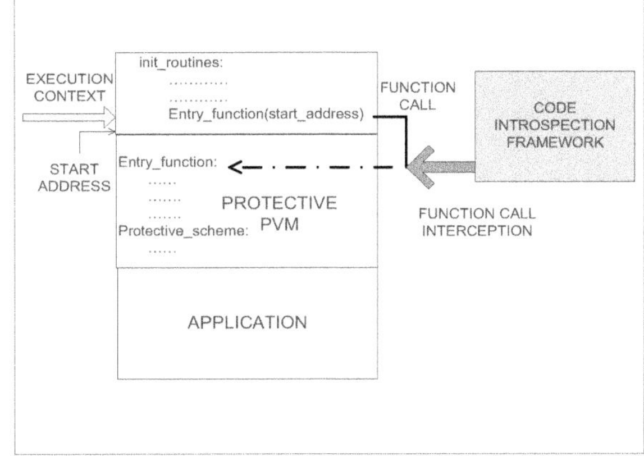

(b) The CIF intercepts the call to the entry function of the protective PVM.

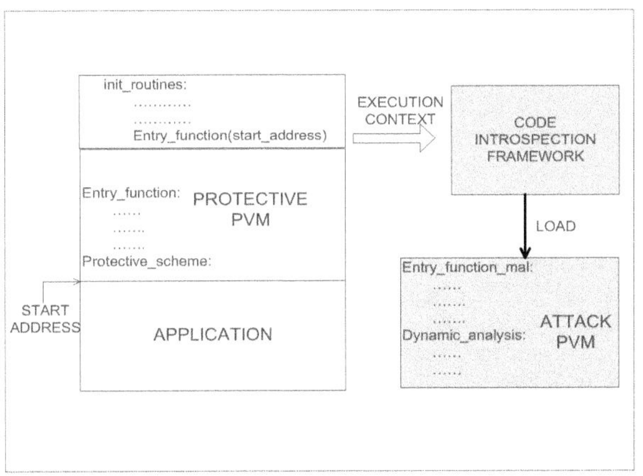

(c) The CIF proceeds to load an attack PVM.

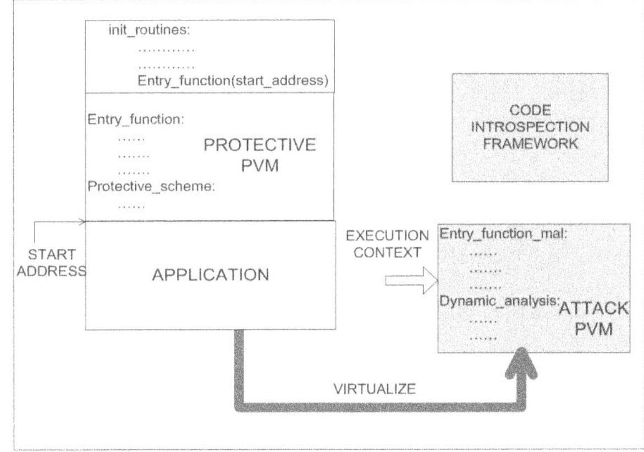

(d) Control is then transferred to the entry function of the attack PVM, which proceeds to run P without any dynamic protections.

Figure 3. Steps illustrating the attack methodology on virtualized applications.

handling routine implemented on the host. Performance overhead can become an issue with *decode-dispatch* systems in their basic form. One of the requirements of using virtualization as a platform for security is low run-time overhead. This case study focuses on process-level virtualization based on *dynamic binary translation* [45], which involves performing just-in-time, on-demand conversion of guest application code blocks into executable instructions for the host machine and caching them for subsequent use. A number of efficient, low-overhead dynamic binary translation tools have been created, including DynamoRIO [7], HDTrans [47], Pin [33], PTLSim [55], and Strata [43].

The protective PVM in our case study is implemented using the Strata binary translator [42, 43]. Figure 4 illustrates the mechanism of Strata and the dynamic protection techniques. At program start up, Strata gains control of execution, saves the current execution context (i.e., current PC, register values, conditional codes, etc.), and starts fetching, decoding and translating instructions from the P's start address. This process continues until an end-of-translation condition is satisfied. The translator restores context and proceeds to transfer control to the newly translated block. After the block completes execution, control transfers back to the translator, and it begins translation at the next address.

The translated code blocks, instead of being disposed of after execution, are cached in memory (called the code cache) [7]. Strata initially searches the cache before attempting translation. If the block is found, control will be directed to the cached block. This process of caching significantly reduces the cost of translation. Numerous other techniques have also been proposed for reducing performance overhead of binary translators [24, 25].

Strata is configured to enhance run-time security. For example, during translation, it introduces dead code of random size in the virtualized code blocks. Thus, the layout of the code cache will be different for each program run. This technique makes it harder to launch automated attacks, since the actual location of the translated code varies from run-to-run.

The code cache is also reinforced to hamper analysis [20]. One such reinforcement technique is periodic cache flushing, in which the translated code is deleted from the cache at regular intervals. All the code cache snapshots must be collated to reconstruct the whole application. Strata can use code metamorphosis [6] so that the same application blocks are translated into different forms after each flush. Flushing also ensures that translated code reappears at different locations during execution. Such dynamism makes it harder to locate and remove protections.

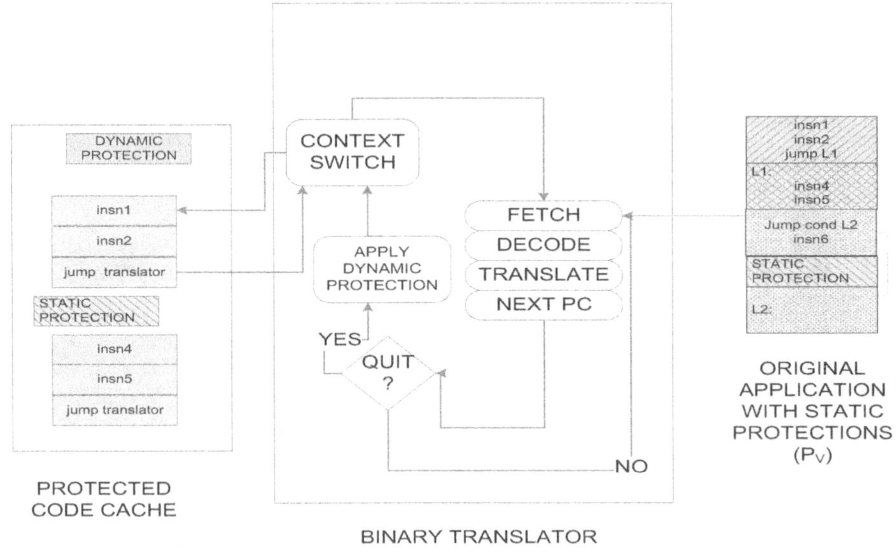

Figure 4. Strata Virtual Machine modified to apply dynamic protections.

6.2 Protected software creation

The protected virtualized application was created using a link-time binary rewriting tool, *Diablo* [16]. Diablo reads in all the object files and libraries constituting the application and creates an internal representation. It provides an API to modify and augment this representation. The modified representation can then be written out as an executable file. We modified Diablo to apply several protection techniques to the application. For example, *checksumming guards*[1] are placed in code regions for both *256.bzip2* and Strata. At run time, the guards present in *256.bzip2* safeguard Strata and vice versa, creating a cyclical level of verification. Diablo was also adapted to interleave the code of the PVM and the guest application, making static analysis harder. Figure 5(a) shows the layout of the virtualized application's binary after normal compilation and linking. A knowledgeable adversary could possibly analyze and identify the individual code regions and extract useful information. Therefore, during linking, Diablo shuffles code blocks of *256.bzip2* with Strata's code blocks using random permutation, resulting in a layout depicted in Figure 5(b). Dissecting the permuted code using static mechanisms is equivalent to the problem of separating code from data, which is unsolvable in the general case [26]. The application code blocks were encrypted using AES.

6.3 Attack implementations

This section describes two implementations of the attack methodology that renders the application, P, vulnerable to analysis and subsequent attack based on information obtained from that analysis. The first proof-of-concept uses a dynamic instrumentation framework (Pin) to replace Strata with an attack PVM (built using HDTrans that we extended to perform AES decryption). The second implementation uses an architectural simulator, PTLsim [55], as both the code introspection framework and the attack PVM. While we use these particular tools to demonstrate the methodology, any similar tools would suffice.

[1] A checksumming guard is a small sequence of instructions that verifies at run time that the checksum over a range of the application's instructions matches the checksum calculated during software creation [10]

6.3.1 Attack using a dynamic binary translator

This prototype uses Intel's run-time binary instrumentation framework, Pin [33], to replace Strata with another binary translator, HDTrans [47]. Pin offers a rich API to dynamically inspect and modify the instrumented application's original instructions. The instrumentation functionality is implemented in a module called a Pintool. At run time, the Pin framework takes as input the Pintool and the target software, and performs the necessary instrumentation.

Because the protected application is encrypted, we must first locate the decryption routine in the protective PVM and extend the attack VM to use the same algorithm. The cryptographic primitives are located in the PVM which is not as strongly protected as the application, enabling easier analysis. Techniques have been proposed which can automatically infer these cryptographic primitives from binary code [8, 21, 31]. These schemes involve profiling the virtualized application and analyzing the trace to locate the cryptographic primitives. We successfully used Gröbert's technique to identify the underlying algorithm (AES) and extracted the key [21]. HDTrans was subsequently modified to use AES decryption on the application code blocks prior to translation. Section 8.2 describes techniques that can be used to obtain cryptographic information in greater detail.

The Pintool, which implements the attack, operates as follows: It starts by loading and starting execution of the protected application. As execution proceeds, the Pintool watches for the entry point function of the protective PVM. In the case of Strata, the call to entry point function is preceded by the following code sequence:

```
pop %eax
sub 0x1c, %esp
pusha
pushf
push %eax ; contains application start address
push <address>  ; return address
jmp <address>   ; jump to entry point function
```

When the entry point function is invoked, the Pintool extracts the application's start address from its argument list. It then dynamically loads the extended HDTrans, proceeds to initialize HDTrans,

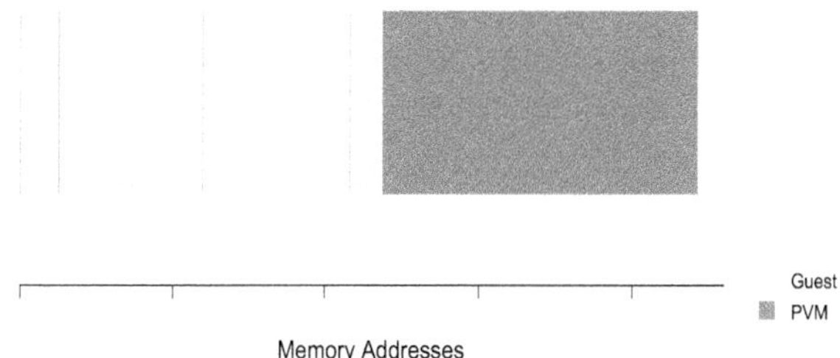

(a) Layout of the code regions of the virtualized application, as produced by standard compilation process. The PVM and P's code regions are clearly distinct.

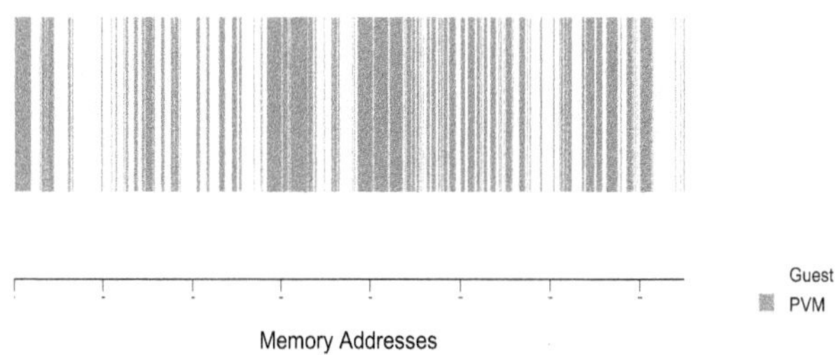

(b) Layout of the code regions after the instruction blocks have been shuffled.

Figure 5. Layout of the text section of the virtualized *256.bzip2* application. The code blocks from the VM and the application have been randomly interleaved, making static separation harder.

and transfers the application start address to HDTrans. Thus, HDTrans takes control of the protected application and Strata never executes. The application can now be analyzed in any number of ways. We modified HDTrans to dump all the executed instructions to disk.

The attack essentially disables checksumming guards from verifying code integrity. Guards located in Strata are never invoked, whereas guards present in P continue to verify the integrity of P and Strata which remain unchanged. At this point, P's code is available for analysis.

6.3.2 Attack using an architectural simulator

The second prototype for the attack uses the PTLSim architectural simulator [55]. In this implementation, PTLSim acts as the instrumentation framework as well as the attack PVM. PTLsim models a modern superscalar Intel x86 compatible processor core along with the complete cache hierarchy, memory subsystem and supporting hardware devices. It models all the major components of a modern out-of-order processor, including the various pipeline stages, functional units and register set. PTLsim supports the full x86-64 instruction set along with all the extensions (SSE, SSSE, etc.). More details of the simulator can be found in the user's manual.

The Intel x86 ISA is a two-operand CISC ISA, however PTLSim does not simulate these instructions directly. Instead, each x86 instruction is first translated into a series of RISC-like micro-operations (`uops`). To further improve efficiency, PTLSim maintains a local cache containing the program ordered translated `uop` sequence for the previously decoded basic blocks in the program.

The attack proceeds as follows: The cryptographic primitives are obtained as in Section 6.3.1, and PTLSim is extended to decrypt instructions after fetching them from memory. At load time, PTLSim initializes its internal data structures and reads in P_V's binary file. The fetch stage of PTLSim accesses instructions from the memory address pointed to by its program counter, called the Virtual Program Counter (VPC). We modified the fetch stage to check for the instruction sequence (illustrated previously in Section 6.3.1) denoting Strata's entry function. Once the fetch stage recognizes the entry function, the simulator retrieves its arguments, which contain the start address of the application code. The simulator then discards its current instruction, waits for the pipeline to empty, and then proceeds to fetch instructions from the retrieved application start address. The simulator decrypts the instruction using the extracted key before decoding it into its constituent `uops`. In this way, Strata never executes and PTLSim is able to fetch and simulate P's instructions directly.

As with the previous prototype, checksumming guards fail to provide adequate protection. The guards only check the original code, which is never executed. We can analyze P in PTLSim's local cache and modify it, if desired.

7. Implications of the Attack

This section discusses how the VM-replacement methodology facilitates analysis and reverse engineering of PVM-protected applications. The first step of any attack involves obtaining a basic understanding of the application. Useful information in program understanding and analysis is the control flow graph (CFG). The CFG obtained from the on-disk binary contains the superset of all possible paths through the program. Obtaining the CFG from the binary in the presence of static protections can be computationally very expensive [49]. As such, attackers have increasingly focused on run-time techniques to obtain the CFG. Although CFGs obtained dynamically can be incomplete, they still provide the attacker with useful information about the application. PVMs provide protection by making dynamic CFG construction and analysis highly resource- and time-intensive tasks. Therefore, to successfully reverse engineer the application, the protective PVM must be replaced using the methodology discussed in this work.

To demonstrate this point, we studied dynamic reverse engineering schemes that have been shown to be successful in attacking software [34, 50], and compared their effectiveness in the presence of a protective PVM. Typically, these techniques involve instrumenting the protected application to obtain the instruction trace. The trace is analyzed to identify individual basic blocks. Consequently, control flow analysis is performed to obtain the dynamic CFG of the application. The attacker then performs profiling of various structures, such as basic blocks and procedure calls, to isolate relevant portions of the code. For example, Madou et al. used basic block execution frequency and in-degree of functions to identify a watermarking function [34]. Similarly, Udupa et al. used edge profiling to identify and remove unnecessary edges from the static CFG [50].

To show that the protective PVM must be replaced, we explored the applicability of such profiling techniques on three different runtime scenarios:

- The application executing without any protections (No protection).
- The application executing in the presence of a protective PVM (Protected).

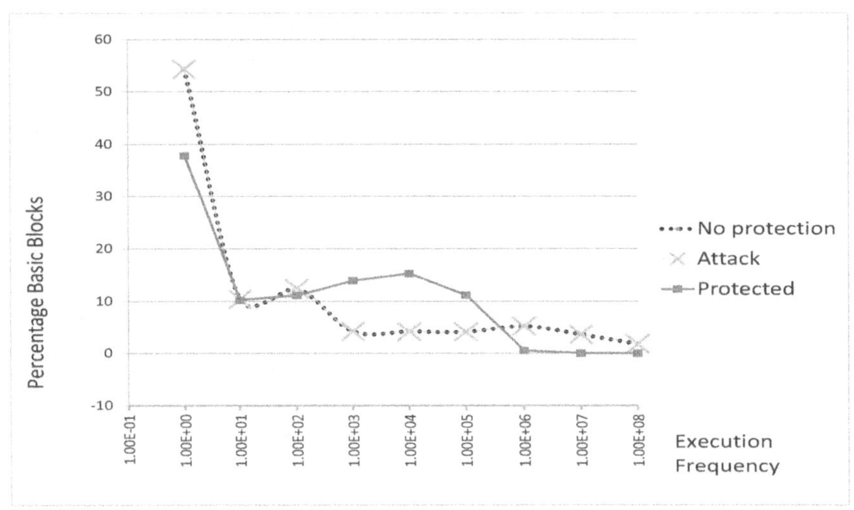

Figure 6. Execution frequencies for the application blocks under the 3 run-time scenarios (No protection, Protected, and Attack). The periodic flushing and retranslation of the application's code blocks by the protective VM drastically changes the execution frequency characteristics. Under the control of the VM, blocks no longer execute at very high frequencies (10^7), instead substantially more blocks execute at intermediate rates (10^3 and 10^5), forcing the attacker to expand their search space. Replacing the protective VM restores the original execution characteristics.

- The protected application that has been subjected to a PVM-replacement attack, i.e., the application is running under the control of a compromised PVM (Attack).

To facilitate collection of application code blocks that have been virtualized, the application was run under an instrumentation framework in all three scenarios. In the following discussion, we refer to such blocks as *dynamic blocks*. The dynamic blocks are identified based on their starting virtual address. The protective PVM was also modified to generate the mapping between on-disk application code blocks and translated blocks. This modification was performed only for the purposes of this study and would not typically be available to the attacker. The goal of this study was to demonstrate that the replacement methodology exposes the original run-time characteristics of the application that have been obfuscated by the PVM, facilitating program analysis and understanding.

We began by comparing instruction trace generation and block analysis across the three scenarios. On comparison, we observed that packaging a protective PVM with the application makes analysis of the dynamic trace and CFG generation much harder. First, the periodic flushing and retranslation of application code increased the number of individual basic blocks manifold. In the case study involving *256.bzip2*, the number of dynamic code blocks increased from around 3.7K for the unprotected run, to more than 160K when the application was subjected to PVM protection. Similarly, the number of distinct CFG edges rose from 6.4K to 290K. Although a large number of these dynamic blocks originate from the same application blocks, the PVM can employ techniques such as code polymorphism, instruction rescheduling and dead-code insertion to make code blocks appear diverse [6]. Thus, the attacker would have to perform control and data flow analysis on a much larger instruction trace. Employing the replacement attack enables the attacker to obtain the original instructions from the application and reduces the search space significantly.

The periodic flushing and randomization of the VM's code cache alter a number of dynamic characteristics of the application, such as block execution frequency, and in and out degrees of the CFG nodes. Figure 6 shows the execution frequency of the dynamic blocks in the three scenarios. When the application was run with no protections, we observed that there were a few code blocks which execute very frequently (of the order 10^7). An attacker would initially focus on reverse engineering these blocks, as they are on the hot paths of the application. Madou et al. used this heuristic to locate the watermarking function [34]. Running the application under the control of a protective PVM obfuscates such blocks due to periodically flushing and retranslation to different locations. The execution frequency for the protected application show that there are no longer blocks which execute as frequently (i.e., no blocks with an execution frequency over 10^7). Instead, there are now more code blocks executing at a lower frequency (e.g., between 10^2 and 10^5). For example, 15% of the blocks execute at least 10^4 times when running under the control of a protective PVM, as compared to just 4% in the unprotected run. Thus, there are no obvious candidate blocks where the attacker could initiate analysis. The attacker will have to increase the search space to find the hot paths for the application.

The PVM also provides misleading information to the attacker. In the three scenarios mentioned above, we ranked all the code blocks based on their execution frequency. Rank 1 was assigned to the most frequently executing block. Table 2 shows the top-ten most frequently executing blocks when the application is run without any protections. Traditionally, an attacker would focus on analyzing these blocks first. Column 2 displays the ranking of these blocks when the application is run under the control of the PVM. For example, the most frequently executing application block in the unprotected run, appears at the 121st position when the application is run under the protective PVM. Thus, the PVM is able to reorder the blocks based on execution frequency. We observed

Application Address	Rank (No Protection)	Rank (Protected)	Rank (Attack)
0x8048830	1	121	1
0x804ac3c	2	45	2
0x804ae1b	3	13	3
0x80507d4	4	9	4
0x80507d9	5	173	5
0x80507c0	6	18	6
0x80507fa	7	29	7
0x805082c	8	351	8
0x8050810	9	139	9
0x804a750	10	779	10

Table 2. Original application addresses of the top-10 most frequently executing blocks in the unprotected run, with their corresponding rank when run under the protection of a PVM. The standard deviation for these blocks in the protected run comes to 239, indicating a very high degree of variability. Consequently, more effort will be required to locate the blocks. A successful replacement attack restores the rankings.

Application Address	Rank (No Protection)	Rank (Protected)	Rank (Attack)
0x804bec0	162	1	162
0x804ae21	17	2	17
0x804ac74	36	3	36
0x804bed3	21	4	21
0x804a7a0	42	5	42
0x804abaf	164	6	164
0x804a81a	88	7	88
0x804a99b	126	8	126
0x80507d4	4	9	4
0x804a7ca	63	10	63

Table 3. Original application addresses of the top 10 most frequently executing blocks when the application is run under the protection of the PVM, along with their corresponding rank when the application runs unprotected, and when it is subjected to the replacement attack.

similar reordering when rankings were based on the in degree of the code blocks. As indicated by column 4 in Table 2, replacing the protective PVM restores the original dynamic properties of the application. Table 3 shows the list of the ten most frequently executed blocks when the application is run under the protection of the PVM, along with their corresponding ranks in the unprotected run. Therefore, this study shows that frequency analysis is not useful to the attacker in the presence of virtualization. The critical information (in this case, the ranking based on frequency) is dispersed by the protective PVM, making it difficult for the adversary to locate and exploit it.

Finally, the constant shifting of code for the application makes it difficult to detect the execution location. We ran the PVM-protected application ten times and observed that application blocks were translated to different code cache addresses each time. Therefore, even if the adversary is able to identify critical code (i.e., the address of a relevant function) in the on-disk binary, that information is of no use at run time since there is no *a priori* knowledge about the final location of the translated code. For example, in Madou et al.'s case study, once the watermarking function was determined; the application was run under the control of a debugger and the control flow changed to circumvent the function using breakpoints. This technique will not work in the presence of a protective PVM, as code is repositioned continually. Thus, to effectively analyze the application under a debugger, the PVM has to be replaced.

Therefore, PVMs have the potential to provide strong protection against dynamic analysis on software applications. PVMs can greatly increase the search space for the attacker, provide misleading run-time information and continuously relocate critical code, making dynamic analysis exceedingly difficult to accomplish. There has been research which aims to reverse engineer PVM-protected applications, by identifying code belonging to the VM in the execution trace [15, 44]. However, such methodologies usually involve performing complex analysis on the trace information and are targeted towards applications which are typically small in size (i.e., a few hundred instructions e.g., malware). These methodologies fail to provide satisfying results when applied to VM-protected applications as they are unable to process the complex data and control flow typically associated with large applications. Thus, the replacement attack methodology is pivotal to the success of reverse engineering PVM-protected applications. Once the protective PVM has been replaced, the application can be analyzed and its true characteristics studied without any obstruction.

8. Discussion

Section 6 described two implementations of an attack that seeks to remove the protective PVM from a virtualized application, P_V. Both implementations were crafted using freely-available tools, and resulted in the guest application, P, running with the added protections disabled. Checksumming guards inserted into P_V failed to prevent the replacement. To successfully orchestrate the attack, some prior information about P_V is required. In this section, we discuss some heuristics the attacker can use to determine this information.

8.1 Determining PVM entry function

To launch a successful attack, the location of the entry function to the protective PVM must be determined. The attack PVM intercepts any calls to this function, as one of the arguments consists of the start address to P. To obtain this location, the attacker can inspect P_V for distinctive instruction sequences that indicate the location of the entry function.

For example, as we described in Section 6.1, prior to initialization, the PVM saves the current application's context. Upon initialization, the PVM restores the application's context. On 32-bit Intel x86 platforms, the instructions `pusha` and `pushf` are commonly used by dynamic translators to save state. Section 6.3.1 displayed the instruction sequence used by Strata to save state, which contains these two instructions. Dynamo-RIO and HDTrans also use these instructions to store register and flag values prior to initiating translation[2]. Investigation into the C benchmarks of the SPEC CPU2000 suite, compiled using standard flags, revealed that none of the application binaries contained these instructions. Consequently, an adversary can use the presence of these instructions to help identify potential entry points into the PVM. Because of the unique actions of the PVM, simple examination of these potential entry points can determine the actual entry point.

The attacker can also use information flow analysis to determine the entry point of a PVM. Most compilers place code and data in separate sections in the binary file. Data-read accesses into the code section are likely to be from the PVM. Thus, using taint analysis on this data and backtracing where the data location was

[2] We were not able to verify the use of these instructions in Pin as its source code is not publicly available.

determined will enable the attacker to determine the entry function of the PVM. Since the PVM initialization typically occurs very early, the attacker will only have to analyze a smaller amount of code to determine the entry function. This code is not subjected to any dynamism, making analysis easier.

8.2 Determining the ISA of the guest application

Another requirement to use a replacement attack is the identification of the ISA of the guest application, P. Traditionally, P's code has been protected by obscurity [1, 51] or encryption [20]. The attacker has to analyze the on-disk binary to obtain information required for determining the ISA, which is then used to configure the attack PVM. This section discusses some heuristics that the attacker can utilize to obtain the relevant information.

Rolles et al. have done extensive work in investigating ISAs used by obfuscation tools such as VMProtect and Themida [41]. The semantics of the ISA are not released to the public, providing security through obscurity. At the time protections are applied, P's instructions are converted to a custom ISA chosen from a set of template ISAs, which is then interpreted at run time by a PVM designed specifically for that ISA. These ISAs are RISC-like, lacking many of the complex features of traditional ISAs like Intel x86. Since these tools derive the final ISA from a template, the instruction sequences of two different protected binaries will have many similarities. This fact makes the analysis of the syntax and semantics more tractable. Further, parts of the x86 instruction set such as the SIMD instructions are not virtualized by VMProtect.

The guest ISA can also be protected via encryption. Manually analyzing and reverse-engineering cryptographic keys and routines can be an arduous task. Recently, researchers have designed techniques that facilitate automatic identification and extraction of cryptographic routines. Gröbert et al. have presented a novel approach to identify cryptographic routines and keys in an encrypted program [21]. Their techniques involves profiling the application and applying heuristics to detect the cryptographic operations. Some of the heuristics proposed by the authors include excessive use of arithmetic functions, loops and investigating the data flow between intermediate variables across multiple runs. This technique is able to identify common encryption algorithms, such as AES and DES, and extracts the key as well.

Even if the application is protected by a proprietary encryption algorithm, researchers have devised techniques to isolate and extract this information from the binary. Caballero et al. have designed a technique to automatically identify code fragments from executable files, so that they are self-contained and can be reused by external code (called *binary code reutilization*) [8]. They successfully applied this technique to identify and extract cryptographic routines from a set of malware files. Similary, Leder et al. examined data in-flow and out-flow in memory buffers, to isolate cryptographic functions [31]. Therefore, such identification techniques can be applied to the protective PVM to obtain the decryption routines, and consequently, used to configure the attack PVM.

Decryption key management is also an issue for the protective PVM. The attacker can use dynamic analysis techniques to extract the decryption key. Halderman et al. point out that modern DRAMS retain their contents for a significant amount of time and an attacker could locate and exploit these keys to analyze encrypted data [22]. Skype is a popular VoIP tool which uses encryption as a tool to hamper static analysis. Biondi et al. were able to decipher Skype's code by obtaining its decryption key from memory [5]. Techniques, such as white-box cryptography, were proposed to improve key management in encrypted systems [12]. However, researchers have since developed solutions to extract the key from such systems [4]. Once the key is available, deciphering the encrypted ISA is straightforward regardless of the the strength of the encryption algorithm.

Therefore, obscuring the ISA fails to adequately protect the guest application from analysis. Previous work has shown that the attacker can analyze such ISAs using reasonable time and effort [5, 41]. Once the the ISA is known, the attacker can successfully replace the protective PVM.

9. Related Work

Software systems are increasingly being used to control critical systems. As such, much research has been performed in the area of software security. A number of techniques have been devised to hamper static analysis of applications. Linn et al. described novel techniques to defeat disassembly of code [32]. Wang et al. proposed using indirect branches to obfuscate the control flow of the application [53]. Chang et al. explored the idea of using a network of self-verifying checksumming code, called guards, to maintain the integrity of code [10]. Collberg et al. studied various techniques to obscure code [13, 14]. However, most of these techniques can be overcome using dynamic analysis. Researchers have also investigated using run-time techniques to obscure code, including using self-modifying code to obfuscate instructions [28]. Code encryption is also useful technique to hamper analysis. The code can be decrypted by hardware (i.e., a secure co-processor) [56], which can add substantially to the costs. Software decryption is less expensive solution [9], but is vulnerable to dynamic analysis.

Software virtualization is an active area of research with implications in software security, both at the system level and at the process level. Process-level virtual machines, such as Pin [33], Strata [43] and HDTrans [47], have been used code optimization [7], instrumentation [33], and in particular, security [20, 23, 40].

Researchers have used process-level virtualization to improve the resistance of code to analysis, both to improve the security of programs [1, 20] and more recently, to obfuscate malicious software, like viruses, trojans, etc. (called *malware*). Commercial PVMs have been created recently, such as VMProtect [51], Themida [36], with a special focus on program security. and Code Virtualizer [37]. These tools follow the conventional interpretation model [46] and use obscure ISAs to protect applications from analysis.

There has been recent work aimed at deobfuscating malware protected by virtual machines. Coogan et al. have developed a scheme which focuses on identifying the flow of values to system call instructions used by the malware, thereby obviating the need to analyze VM instructions [15]. However, their scheme does not produce encouraging results when applied to complex applications. Sharif et al. have also devised techniques to automatically reverse engineer malware that is obfuscated by such PVMs [44]. Although their goals are somewhat similar to this work, there are marked differences. The authors target their work towards software (typically malware) that is transformed to random ISA's and then interpreted on-the-fly at run time. In their model, the PVM does not generate native code but dispatches application instructions to appropriate handler routines (e.g., using a switch table). In particular, their work is targeting applications which do not have a performance constraint, which is often true of malware. The authors state that their techniques do not apply to programs protected by binary translation systems due to the complex run-time behavior of such systems. Their work is based on the assumption that the interpreters do not perform any dynamic transformations or generate new code, making control and data flow analysis easier to perform on the generated trace. Finally, their approach is focused towards reverse engineering malware code, which is typically smaller in size (of the order of a few thousands lines of code). Our attack focuses on real applications that are protected by PVMs. The proof-of-concept prototypes have been tested on real-life applications, consisting of hundreds of thousands of lines of code.

System-level virtual machines have been utilized to provide secure solutions as well. The Terra system implements a trusted virtual machine monitor which can be used to create closed-box platforms where the developer can tailor the software stack to meet security requirements [19]. However, it requires hardware support to validate the software stack. Chen et al. discuss Overshadow, a system that cryptographically isolates an application inside a VMM from the guest OS it is running on. This system offers another layer of tamper resistance, even in the case of total OS compromise [11].

10. Conclusions

Process-level virtual machines (PVMs) are increasingly being used to safeguard applications from reverse engineering. PVMs can continuously transform code during execution, as well as introduce new protection techniques. This scenario makes it hard for the adversary to analyze and understand the application. Traditionally, the virtualization layer has always been decoupled from the guest application. In this paper, we have presented a novel attack scheme that replaces the protective PVM packaged with an application at run time, leaving it vulnerable to analysis. This attack methodology is successful due to the lack of strong dynamic coupling between the application and the protective PVM instance. Our methodology illustrates that this lack of dynamic cohesion leads to serious shortcomings when used in software protection. We described an extensive case study analyzing the protection mechanisms in a real VM-protected application and discussed two prototypes of this attack constructed using freely available tools. The results from this work show that there is an urgent need to reassess the protection properties of PVMs, and to develop techniques that can thwart this attack methodology.

Acknowledgments

This research is supported by National Science Foundation grants CNS-00716446 and CCF-0811689 and the Air Force Research Laboratory (AFRL) under contract FA8650-10-C-7025. The views and conclusions contained herein are those of the authors and should not be interpreted as necessarily representing the official policies or endorsements, either expressed or implied, of the AFRL or the U.S. Government.

References

[1] ANCKAERT, B., JAKUBOWSKI, M., AND VENKATESAN, R. Proteus: virtualization for diversified tamper-resistance. In *DRM '06: Proceedings of the ACM Workshop on Digital Rights Management* (New York, NY, USA, 2006), ACM Press, pp. 47–58.

[2] APPLE. Mac OS X ABI Mach-o file format reference, 2009.

[3] BELLARD, F. QEMU, a fast and portable dynamic translator. In *ATEC'05: Proceedings of the USENIX Annual Technical Conference* (Berkeley, CA, USA, 2005), USENIX Association, pp. 41–41.

[4] BILLET, O., GILBERT, H., AND ECH-CHATBI, C. Cryptanalysis of a white box AES implementation. In *Selected Areas in Cryptography* (Hiedelberg, 2004), Springer-Verlag, pp. 227–240.

[5] BIONDI, P., AND FABRICE, D. Silver needle in the skype. In *Black Hat Europe* (Amsterdam, the Netherlands, 2006).

[6] BORELLO, J.-M., AND MÈ, L. Code obfuscation techniques for metamorphic viruses. *Journal in Computer Virology 4* (2008), 211–220. 10.1007/s11416-008-0084-2.

[7] BRUENING, D., GARNETT, T., AND AMARASINGHE, S. An infrastructure for adaptive dynamic optimization. In *CGO '03: Proceedings of the IEEE/ACM International Symposium on Code Generation and Optimization* (Los Alamitos, CA, USA, 2003), IEEE Computer Society, pp. 265–275.

[8] CABALLERO, J., JOHNSON, N. M., MCCAMANT, S., AND SONG, D. Binary code extraction and interface identification for security applications. In *NDSS '10: Proceedings of the Network and Distributed System Security Symposium* (2010), The Internet Society.

[9] CAPPAERT, J., PRENEEL, B., ANCKAERT, B., MADOU, M., AND DE BOSSCHERE, K. Towards tamper resistant code encryption: practice and experience. In *ISPEC'08: Proceedings of the 4th International Conference on Information Security Practice and Experience* (Berlin, Heidelberg, 2008), Springer-Verlag, pp. 86–100.

[10] CHANG, H., AND ATALLAH, M. Protecting software code by guards. In *Proceedings of the ACM Workshop on Security and Privacy in Digital Rights Management* (2000), pp. 160–175.

[11] CHEN, X., GARFINKEL, T., LEWIS, E. C., SUBRAHMANYAM, P., WALDSPURGER, C. A., BONEH, D., DWOSKIN, J., AND PORTS, D. R. Overshadow: a virtualization-based approach to retrofitting protection in commodity operating systems. In *ASPLOS XIII: Proceedings of the 13th International Conference on Architectural Support for Programming Languages and Operating Systems* (New York, NY, USA, 2008), ACM Press, pp. 2–13.

[12] CHOW, S., EISEN, P. A., JOHNSON, H., AND OORSCHOT, P. C. V. White-box cryptography and an AES implementation. In *SAC '02: Revised Papers from the 9th Annual International Workshop on Selected Areas in Cryptography* (London, UK, 2003), Springer-Verlag, pp. 250–270.

[13] COLLBERG, C., THOMBORSON, C., AND LOW, D. A taxonomy of obfuscating transformations. *University of Auckland Technical Report* (1997), 170.

[14] COLLBERG, C., THOMBORSON, C., AND LOW, D. Manufacturing cheap, resilient and stealthy opaque constructs. In *POPL'98:Proceedings of the 25th ACM SIGPLAN-SIGACT Symposium on Principles of Programming Languages* (New York, NY, USA, 1998), ACM Press, pp. 184–196.

[15] COOGAN, K., LU, G., AND DEBRAY, S. Deobfuscating virtualization-obfuscated software: A semantics-based approach. *CCS '11: Proceedings of the ACM Conference on Computer and Communications Security* (October 2011). To appear.

[16] DE BUS, B., DE SUTTER, B., VAN PUT, L., CHANET, D., AND DE BOSSCHERE, K. Link-time optimization of ARM binaries. In *LCTES'04: Proceedings of the 2004 ACM SIGPLAN/SIGBED Conference on Languages, Compilers, and Tools for Embedded Systems* (Washington D.C., U.S.A, 7 2004), ACM Press, pp. 211–220.

[17] DEHNERT, J. C., GRANT, B. K., BANNING, J. P., JOHNSON, R., KISTLER, T., KLAIBER, A., AND MATTSON, J. The Transmeta code morphing software: using speculation, recovery, and adaptive retranslation to address real-life challenges. In *CGO'03: Proceedings of the International Symposium on Code Generation and Optimization* (Washington, DC, USA, 2003), IEEE Computer Society, pp. 15–24.

[18] EAGLE, C. *The IDA Pro Book: The Unofficial Guide to the World's Most Popular Disassembler*. No Starch Press, San Francisco, CA, USA, 2008.

[19] GARFINKEL, T., PFAFF, B., CHOW, J., ROSENBLUM, M., AND BONEH, D. Terra: a virtual machine-based platform for trusted computing. In *SOSP'03: Proceedings of the 19th ACM Symposium on Operating Systems Principles* (New York, NY, USA, 2003), ACM Press, pp. 193–206.

[20] GHOSH, S., HISER, J. D., AND DAVIDSON, J. W. A secure and robust approach to software tamper resistance. In *IH '10: Proceedings of the 12th International Conference on Information Hiding* (Berlin, Heidelberg, 2010), Springer-Verlag, pp. 33–47.

[21] GRÖBERT, F., WILLEMS, C., AND HOLZ, T. Automatic identification of cryptographic primitives in binary programs. In *RAID '11: Proceedings of the 14th International Symposium on Recent Advances in Intrusion Detection* (London, UK, 2011), Springer-Verlag, pp. 45–65.

[22] HALDERMAN, J. A., SCHOEN, S. D., HENINGER, N., CLARKSON, W., PAUL, W., CALANDRINO, J. A., FELDMAN, A. J., APPELBAUM, J., AND FELTEN, E. W. Lest we remember: cold-boot attacks on encryption keys, May 2009.

[23] HISER, J. D., COLEMAN, C. L., CO, M., AND DAVIDSON, J. W. Meds: The memory error detection system. In *ESSoS '09: Proceedings of the 1st International Symposium on Engineering Secure Software and Systems* (Berlin, Heidelberg, 2009), Springer-Verlag, pp. 164–179.

[24] HISER, J. D., WILLIAMS, D., FILIPI, A., DAVIDSON, J. W., AND CHILDERS, B. R. Evaluating fragment construction policies for SDT systems. In *VEE '06: Proceedings of the 2nd International Conference on Virtual Execution Environments* (New York, NY, USA, 2006), ACM Press, pp. 122–132.

[25] HISER, J. D., WILLIAMS, D., HU, W., DAVIDSON, J. W., MARS, J., AND CHILDERS, B. R. Evaluating indirect branch handling mechanisms in software dynamic translation systems. In *CGO'07: Proceedings of the International Symposium on Code Generation and Optimization* (Washington, DC, USA, 2007), IEEE Computer Society, pp. 61–73.

[26] HORSPOOL, R. N., AND MAROVAC, N. An approach to the problem of detranslation of computer programs. *Computer Journal 23*, 3 (1980), 223–229.

[27] HU, W., HISER, J. D., WILLIAMS, D., FILIPI, A., DAVIDSON, J. W., EVANS, D., KNIGHT, J. C., NGUYEN-TUONG, A., AND ROWANHILL, J. Secure and practical defense against code-injection attacks using software dynamic translation. In *Proceedings of the 2nd International Conference on Virtual Execution Environments* (New York, NY, USA, 2006), ACM Press, pp. 2–12.

[28] KANZAKI, Y., MONDEN, A., NAKAMURA, M., AND MATSUMOTO, K.-I. Exploiting self-modification mechanism for program protection. In *COMPSAC'03: Proceedings of the 27th Annual International Conference on Computer Software and Applications* (Washington, DC, USA, 2003), IEEE Computer Society, pp. 170–176.

[29] KC, G. S., KEROMYTIS, A. D., AND PREVELAKIS, V. Countering code-injection attacks with instruction-set randomization. In *CCS '03: Proceedings of the 10th ACM Conference on Computer and Communications Security* (New York, NY, USA, 2003), ACM Press, pp. 272–280.

[30] KIRIANSKY, V., BRUENING, D., AND AMARASINGHE, S. P. Secure execution via program shepherding. In *USENIX'02: Proceedings of the 11th USENIX Security Symposium* (Berkeley, CA, USA, 2002), USENIX Association, pp. 191–206.

[31] LEDER, F., MARTINI, P., AND WICHMANN, A. Finding and extracting crypto routines from malware. In *Proceedings of the IEEE 28th International Performance Computing and Communications Conference (IPCCC)* (Washington, DC,USA, December 2009), IEEE, pp. 394 - 401.

[32] LINN, C., AND DEBRAY, S. Obfuscation of executable code to improve resistance to static disassembly. In *CCS'03: Proceedings of the 10th ACM Conference on Computer and Communications Security (CCS)* (Washington D.C., U.S.A, 2003), ACM Press, pp. 290–299.

[33] LUK, C.-K., COHN, R., MUTH, R., PATIL, H., KLAUSER, A., LOWNEY, G., WALLACE, S., REDDI, V. J., AND HAZELWOOD, K. Pin: building customized program analysis tools with dynamic instrumentation. In *PLDI '05: Proceedings of the 2005 ACM SIGPLAN Conference on Programming Language Design and Implementation* (New York, NY, USA, 2005), ACM Press, pp. 190–200.

[34] MADOU, M., ANCKAERT, B., DE SUTTER, B., AND DE BOSSCHERE, K. Hybrid static-dynamic attacks against software protection mechanisms. In *DRM '05: Proceedings of the 5th ACM workshop on Digital Rights Management* (New York, NY, USA, 2005), ACM Press, pp. 75–82.

[35] MADOU, M., ANCKAERT, B., MOSELEY, P., DEBRAY, S., DE SUTTER, B., AND DE BOSSCHERE, K. Software protection through dynamic code mutation. In *The 6th International Workshop on Information Security Applications (WISA 2005)* (August 2005), vol. LNCS, Springer Verlag.

[36] OREANS TECHNOLOGIES. Themida. `http://oreans.com/themida.php`, 2009.

[37] OREONS TECHNOLOGY. Codevirtualizer. `http://oreans.com/codevirtualizer.php`, 2009.

[38] PAYER, M., AND GROSS, T. R. Fine-grained user-space security through virtualization. In *VEE'11: Proceedings of the 7th ACM SIGPLAN/SIGOPS International Conference on Virtual Execution Environments* (New York, NY, USA, 2011), ACM Press, pp. 157–168.

[39] POPEK, G. J., AND GOLDBERG, R. P. Formal requirements for virtualizable third generation architectures. *Communications of the ACM 17* (July 1974), 412–421.

[40] PORTOKALIDIS, G., AND KEROMYTIS, A. D. Fast and practical instruction-set randomization for commodity systems. In *ACSAC'10: Proceedings of the 26th Annual Computer Security Applications Conference* (New York, NY, USA, 2010), ACM Press, pp. 41–48.

[41] ROLLES, R. Unpacking virtualization obfuscators. In *WOOT'09: Proceedings of the 3rd USENIX Conference on Offensive Technologies* (Berkeley, CA, USA, 2009), USENIX Association, pp. 1–10.

[42] SCOTT, K., AND DAVIDSON, J. Safe virtual execution using software dynamic translation. In *ACSAC '02: Proceedings of the 18th Annual Computer Security Applications Conference* (Los Alamitos, CA, USA, 2002), IEEE Computer Society, p. 209.

[43] SCOTT, K., KUMAR, N., VELUSAMY, S., CHILDERS, B., DAVIDSON, J. W., AND SOFFA, M. L. Retargetable and reconfigurable software dynamic translation. In *CGO '03: Proceedings of the International Symposium on Code Generation and Optimization* (Washington D.C., U.S.A, 2003), IEEE Computer Society, pp. 36–47.

[44] SHARIF, M., LANZI, A., GIFFIN, J., AND LEE, W. Automatic reverse engineering of malware emulators. In *SP'07: Proceedings of the 2009 30th IEEE Symposium on Security and Privacy* (Washington, DC, USA, 2009), IEEE Computer Society, pp. 94–109.

[45] SITES, R. L., CHERNOFF, A., KIRK, M. B., MARKS, M. P., AND ROBINSON, S. G. Binary translation. *Communcations of the ACM 36* (February 1993), 69–81.

[46] SMITH, J., AND NAIR, R. *Virtual Machines: Versatile Platforms for Systems and Processes (The Morgan Kaufmann Series in Computer Architecture and Design).* Morgan Kaufmann Publishers Inc., San Francisco, CA, USA, 2005.

[47] SRIDHAR, S., SHAPIRO, J. S., NORTHUP, E., AND BUNGALE, P. P. HDTrans: an open source, low-level dynamic instrumentation system. In *VEE'06: Proceedings of the 2nd International Conference on Virtual Execution Environments* (New York, NY, USA, 2006), ACM, pp. 175–185.

[48] STARFORCE. Starforce crypto. `http://www.star-force.com/`, 2008.

[49] SZOR, P. *The Art of Computer Virus Research and Defense.* Addison-Wesley Professional, 2005.

[50] UDUPA, S., DEBRAY, S., AND MADOU, M. Deobfuscation: reverse engineering obfuscated code. In *WCRE '05: Proceedings of the International Working Conference on Reverse Engineering* (Los Alamitos, CA, USA, Nov. 2005), vol. 0, IEEE Computer Society, pp. 45–54.

[51] VMPROTECT SOFTWARE. VMProtect. `http://vmpsoft.com/`, 2008.

[52] WANG, C., DAVIDSON, J., HILL, J., AND KNIGHT, J. Protection of software-based survivability mechanisms. In *DSN'01: Proceedings of the International Conference on Dependable Systems and Networks* (Goteborg, Sweden, 2001), IEEE Computer Society, pp. 193–202.

[53] WANG, C., HILL, J., KNIGHT, J., AND DAVIDSON, J. Software tamper resistance: Obstructing static analysis of programs. Tech. rep., Charlottesville, VA, USA, 2000.

[54] YOUNGDALE, E. Kernel korner: The ELF object file format: Introduction. *Linux Journal 1995* (April 1995).

[55] YOURST, M. PTLsim: A cycle accurate full system x86-64 microarchitectural simulator. In *ISPASS'07: Proceedings of the IEEE International Symposium on Performance Analysis of Systems and Software* (2007), IEEE, pp. 23–34.

[56] ZAMBRENO, J., CHOUDHARY, A., SIMHA, R., NARAHARI, B., AND MEMON, N. SAFE-OPS: An approach to embedded software security. *Transactions on Embedded Computing Systems 4*, 1 (2005), 189–210.

Protecting Applications Against TOCTTOU Races by User-Space Caching of File Metadata

Mathias Payer
Department of Computer Science
ETH Zurich, Switzerland

Thomas R. Gross
Department of Computer Science
ETH Zurich, Switzerland

Abstract

Time Of Check To Time Of Use (TOCTTOU) race conditions for file accesses in user-space applications are a common problem in Unix-like systems. The mapping between filename and inode and device is volatile and can provide the necessary preconditions for an exploit. Applications use filenames as the primary attribute to identify files but the mapping between filenames and inode and device can be changed by an attacker.

DynaRace is an approach that protects *unmodified* applications from file-based TOCTTOU race conditions. DynaRace uses a transparent mapping cache that keeps additional state and metadata for each accessed file in the application. The combination of file state and the current system call type are used to decide if (i) the metadata is updated or (ii) the correctness of the metadata is enforced between consecutive system calls.

DynaRace uses user-mode path resolution internally to resolve individual file atoms. Each file atom is verified or updated according to the associated state in the mapping cache. More specifically, DynaRace protects against race conditions for all file-based system calls, by replacing the unsafe system calls with a set of safe system calls that utilize the mapping cache. The system call is executed only if the state transition is allowed and the information in the mapping cache matches.

DynaRace deterministically solves the problem of file-based race conditions for unmodified applications and removes an attacker's ability to exploit the TOCTTOU race condition. DynaRace detects injected alternate inode and device pairs and terminates the application.

Categories and Subject Descriptors D.4.6 [*Operating Systems*]: Security and Protection; D.3.4 [*Programming Languages*]: Processors — Run-time environments

General Terms Security

Keywords Security, TOCTTOU races, Race protection, File-based TOCTTOU race protection, Dynamic protection, Virtualization

VEE'12, March 3–4, 2012, London, England, UK.

1. Introduction

Attacks to local security by privilege escalation are a challenging problem because a potential attacker already has access to some privileges on the same machine. An attacker can use these privileges to exploit local bugs in an application to escalate privileges and/or to impersonate a different user.

File-based race conditions are a typical form of Time Of Check To Time Of Use (TOCTTOU) attacks [4, 5]. The application process leaves a window of opportunity to the attacker where a specific bug is exploitable. A second process may interfere on a shared resource whereas the original process assumes that it is using the resource exclusively. These interferences can be used to replace accessed files between checks or, e.g., to deadlock privileged processes. As multicore systems become more and more popular, we expect an increase in attacks that employ multiple (concurrently) executing processes. Multicore systems enable an attack to run alongside the original program; the attacking process can then use cache effects, or other timing issues to exploit a process.

In a Unix-like system file accesses are particularly prone to race conditions. Potential race conditions arise because the mapping from a filename to a unique inode and device number can change. Filenames are volatile and the corresponding inode and device number can change upon every system call invocation. If a path and filename are passed to a system call then the kernel dynamically resolves the path and filename. The kernel then maps the resolved inode and device number (which corresponds to the file at that moment in time when the system call was executed) to a file descriptor that is then passed back to the application. The mapping from inode and device number to a file descriptor is unique and race-free but the mapping from filename to inode and device number is volatile.

File-based race conditions can occur either in the path to the file (i.e., a directory is a symbolic link that can be changed by the attacker), or in the final file atom (i.e., the last file atom is an attacker-controlled symbolic link). The POSIX community tried to address the problem of file-based races by introducing new system calls that work relative to a specific file descriptor [1, 2]. These new system calls can be used to, e.g., test permissions of files relative to a given base directory. A programmer can use these system calls to, e.g., authorize a directory (e.g., using user-mode path resolution) and then safely create a file atom in that directory provided that the directory is validated appropriately. If used properly the new system calls solve the problem of race conditions in the path to the final file atom, but they do not solve the problem of race conditions if the final file atom is a symbolic link.

Much work has been done by the system security community to resolve TOCTTOU races [3, 9–13, 15, 16, 18–20, 22, 23, 27–33, 35–37]. Recently a practical, portable solution has been found that can deterministically solve the problem without requiring modifications to the kernel or its API: user-mode path resolution [30]. This solution, however, suffers from a serious drawback: a programmer must manually identify and modify all pairs of system calls that are vulnerable to TOCTTOU races.

DynaRace builds on and extends user-mode path resolution by removing the burden of manual program modification. DynaRace deterministically performs safe user-mode file path resolution[1] for *unmodified* applications by applying some user-defined action to every atom along the file path in a race-free manner. The key idea is that DynaRace defines user-defined actions such that they guarantee that the metadata of file atoms do not change between invocations of vulnerable system call sequences. DynaRace then dynamically intercepts and replaces these vulnerable sequences with their deterministically-safe alternative. To this end, DynaRace maintains a cache holding the metadata of accessed files and a state machine that quickly identifies periods of vulnerability.

DynaRace is an approach that protects unmodified applications from file-based TOCTTOU race conditions. DynaRace adds a hidden layer between the unmodified application and the operating system that keeps state and metadata in a mapping cache for all accessed files. This mapping cache is used to verify the integrity and consistency of consecutive file accesses according to a state machine. Each accessed file has an associated state. The mapping cache is either updated with the current metadata or the existing metadata is enforced for the accessed file according to the state of the file. Each file can be in four different states: *new* for new files, *update* for files where the metadata is updated between system calls, *enforce* for files where the cached metadata is enforced between system calls, and *retire* for files that are no longer used in the application.

Individual unsafe system calls like `access` followed by `open` are redirected dynamically to race-free implementations. These race-free implementations are part of the DynaRace framework. They check the state of the file according to the internal mapping cache and the state machine. If the system call executes without a race condition then the mapping cache is updated and the result of the system call is returned to the application.

Our implementation prototype uses user-space binary translation and system call interposition to weave a deterministic race protection framework into the application. An important aspect of our implementation prototype is that neither the application nor any library must be aware of the safe system calls. The system call replacement system works in the background of the process without any coordination. The user-space application can use unsafe system calls and our approach ensures that no file system race conditions are possible.

The contributions of this paper are as follows:

1. DynaRace, a lightweight approach to protect unmodified applications from file-based race conditions.
2. An evaluation and discussion of a DynaRace prototype implementation.

DynaRace keeps state and metadata for each accessed file in an intermediate layer between the application and the operating system. DynaRace redirects all file-based system calls to a stateful inspection framework. This inspection framework uses a state machine and the cached metadata to validate that the metadata of a file has not changed between system calls that test file properties and system calls that use or change files or file metadata.

[1] See [30] for a detailed description of user-mode path resolution.

2. Attack model and background information

This section describes the attack model used for the DynaRace approach and presents background information on file-based TOCTTOU race conditions. File-based race conditions enable an attacker to escalate privileges, e.g., to access, read, or write privileged files.

2.1 Attack model

An attacker has user-access to the system and tries to escalate privileges. The user has no root-privileges and the attacker has no direct hardware access. The DynaRace protection runs with the same privileges as the protected application. A successful attack breaches the security of the application and enables additional privileges to the attacker. DynaRace terminates the application if an attack is detected; denial of service attacks are not part of the attack model.

2.2 File-based TOCTTOU race conditions

Table 1 shows a classic TOCTTOU race condition presented by Mazières et al. in [19]. A privileged (SUID) garbage collector script cleans the `/tmp` directory. An attacker prepares a temporary directory containing an empty file with the same name like the target file. The script reads the directory and relies on the fact that the directory will not change between individual system calls. The attacker removes the temporary directory and replaces it with a link to an existing directory. The script then deletes the file with the same name in the privileged directory.

SUID program	Attacker
	`mkdir("/tmp/x")`
	`creat("/tmp/x/passwd")`
`readdir("/tmp")`	
`lstat("/tmp/x")`	
`readdir("/tmp/x")`	
	`rename("/tmp/x", "/tmp/y")`
	`symlink("/etc", "/tmp/x")`
`unlink("/tmp/x/passwd")`	

Table 1. A potential attacker can race against the privileged application and delete a critical system file.

Table 2 shows a typical TOCTTOU race condition presented in [5]. The `access` system call is used to check permissions of the user in a SUID program. A privileged application relies on the fact that the mapping from a file to an inode and device id remains the same over subsequent system calls. An attacker replaces the file with a link to a privileged file. The privileged application then uses the sensitive file instead of the original file that was authenticated.

SUID program	Attacker
`access("file")`	
	`unlink("file")`
	`link("sensitive", "file")`
`fd = open("file")`	
`read(fd, ...)`	

Table 2. A potential attacker can race against the privileged application and read a privileged file.

3. The DynaRace approach

DynaRace adds a hidden abstraction layer between the application and the operating system. This abstraction layer keeps track of all file-based system calls and keeps information about accessed files and directories in a metadata cache. The monitoring of all file-based system calls allows DynaRace to keep track of all directories and files that are accessed. Our implementation prototype extends a dynamic system call interposition framework to dynamically monitor all file-related system calls of an application as well as all loaded libraries.

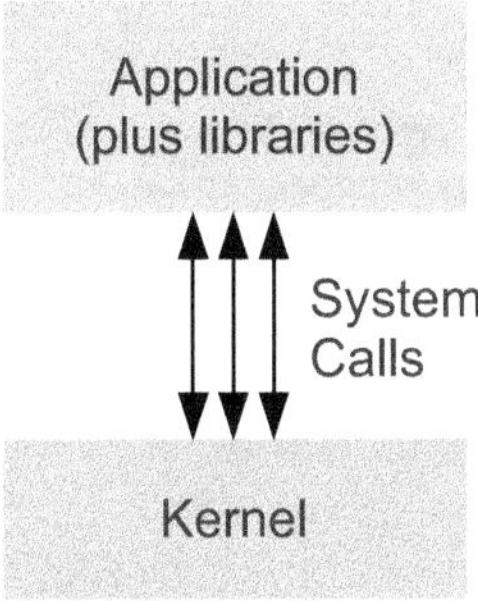

Figure 1. Execution *without* DynaRace checks for file-related system calls.

Figure 1 shows a system without DynaRace. Potentially unsafe system calls are executed directly by the kernel without additional checks for race conditions. Each system call is executed in isolation and without knowledge of the results of prior system calls. Applications without special checks (e.g., storing file state internally, or checking for safe accesses using hardness amplification, see Section 7.5) for these unsafe system calls are prone to race conditions.

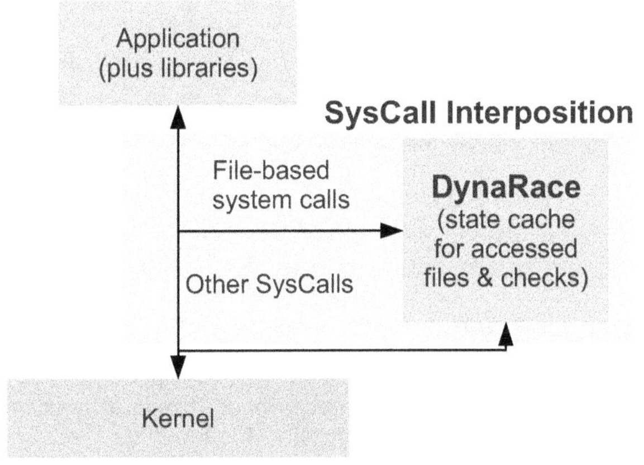

Figure 2. Overview of the DynaRace approach.

Figure 2 shows the DynaRace system. All file-related system calls are intercepted using system call interposition and are redirected to the DynaRace module. DynaRace keeps state for each accessed file and dynamically checks for file-based race conditions. Unsafe system calls like `access` followed by `open` are replaced dynamically with the new and safe race-free sequence of system calls. File-based system calls are no longer executed in isolation but use the state and metadata from prior system calls to validate the current system call. Neither the application nor any library must be aware of the safe system calls. The system call replacement system works in the background of the process without any coordination. The user-space application can use unsafe system calls and DynaRace ensures that no file system race conditions are possible. Due to the replacement strategy of system calls DynaRace can be applied to pre-existing libraries and applications. The DynaRace module works as an independent additional module and can be used in combination with other approaches.

Filenames and directory names can be changed by a concurrent process, e.g., by using symbolic links to redirect a file to a different location. The presented approach uses two security concepts: (i) A chain of trust of known directories from the root directory (/) to the directory of the file is constructed by iterating through all the different file atoms. This chain enables the use of the new system calls that are relative to a specific directory. (ii) A thread-local transparent mapping of file statistics that keeps track of all accessed, opened, stated, and modified files.

3.1 File states

The general rewriting policy for unsafe system calls replaces an unsafe system call with a set of dynamic atomic checks. These checks ensure that if a filename is equal to an already accessed filename then the following `open` system call can rely on the subsystem to ensure that the files are also equal.

Equality is defined as *same inode number, device id, and parent directory* for existing files. For files that do not exist equality is defined as *same parent directory and an error code*. The file metadata that is stored in the mapping cache must contain the complete metadata to show equality between different files or, if the file does not exist, information about the base directory and the fact that the file does not exist. The metadata of a file includes a pointer to the metadata of the directory of the file.

Every file that is accessed has an associated state. Depending on the system call that is executed on the file and the state of the file different checks are executed.

Figure 3 shows the different states and the checks that are executed during a transition. Nodes correspond to the states with associated checks and edges to different groups of system calls that force transitions between states. The three states are *update*, *enforce*, and *retire*. A file can be in any of these three states if the same filename has already been used in the program, or in the start state *new* if the file is used the first time.

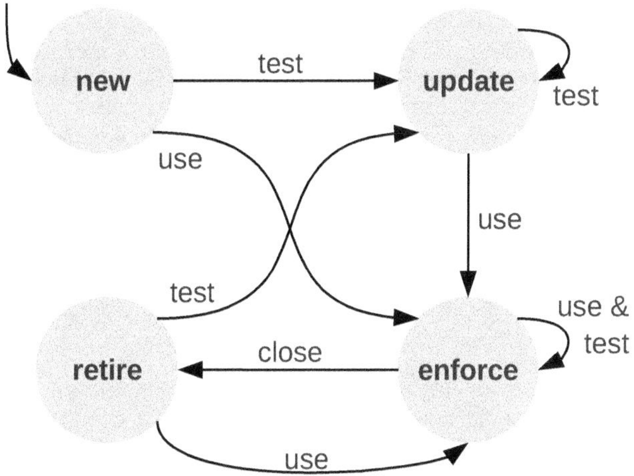

Figure 3. State machine with file states and dynamic checks.

The edges of the state machine correspond to different groups of system calls. The transition from one state to another depends on the system call and the current state. The system calls are separated into different sets depending on their function:

Test: the application uses system calls in this set to gather information and to check file metadata (e.g., permissions, or status).

The system calls in this group do not change the file or any associated metadata. Examples for *test* system calls are `access` or any of the `stat` system calls.

Use: this group of system calls works with files or changes file-related metadata. The system calls in this group modify the file or the associated metadata. Examples for *use* system calls are `open`, `creat`, or `chmod`.

Close: the group of system calls that closes or deletes files: `close`, `unlink`, and `unlinkat`. The application uses these system calls to close or delete files. These system calls signal the kernel that the application no longer works with the specified files.

Depending on the prior state of the file and the new state (as determined by the system call) a set of checks is executed. The metadata is updated if the file has not been changed by the application (e.g., in the states new, update, and retire). If the file transitions from the update state to the enforce state (or stays in the enforce state), then DynaRace enforces the correctness of the available metadata. If the file is a new file that has not been used by the application then DynaRace adds the metadata into the metadata cache. If the file has been closed then DynaRace updates the metadata and warns if there is a mismatch in the metadata cache. This "check and warn" case is used for files that have already been used in the application but were closed.

The state machine in Figure 3 is updated depending on the type of the system call.

Update: all state transitions that end in the update state (*new* → *update*, *retire* → *update*, and *update* → *update*) update the information of a file in the metadata cache or create a new entry for a new file in the metadata cache. This state gathers information about the different files used in the application.

Enforce: whenever a file is used (i.e., either the file itself or the metadata of the file changes) in the application then the state of the file changes to enforce. Enforce ensures that the application can always work with the same file. DynaRace enforces equality if valid information about the file is available in the metadata cache (this holds for the transitions *update* → *enforce* and *enforce* → *enforce*). If a system call of the use group is used for a new file (*new* → *enforce*) then DynaRace adds the information to the cache and changes the state of the file to enforce. If a file has been closed by the application and a system call of the use group is executed (*retire* → *enforce*) then DynaRace checks and updates the metadata and emits a warning if there is a mismatch between the cached and the current information.

Retire: a file ends in this state if it has been closed or discarded by the application (*enforce* → *retire*). This special state discards and retires files that are no longer used by the application after they have been in the enforce state.

The retire state offers the possibility to retire files that are no longer used by the application. A retired file can be changed by a concurrent process without a security violation. This feature is important to enable ownerships transfers like, e.g., log rotation. Process P_1 checks and opens a log file for writing. A second process P_2 rotates the logs (compresses the open log and creates a new, empty log file). Process P_2 then signals process P_1 to reopen its log files. Process P_1 closes the log file (thereby retiring the metadata information), checks, and reopens the new file.

3.2 File resolution

All file-based system calls are replaced by safe handler functions that dynamically use the mapping cache to verify that identical filenames conform to the same file identified by a unique inode number and device id. File resolution is performed in a manner similar to the `chk_use` algorithm presented by Tsafrir et al. [29, 30]. DynaRace uses the user-defined function in the `chk_use` algorithm to verify and update the mapping cache as the file is resolved atom by atom. The handler functions resolve files in the following way:

1. Split path names into (i) a directory path that contains the directory and (ii) the actual filename.
2. Rewrite relative directory path names to absolute paths according to the current working directory.
3. Identify and check the directory using the directory path.
   (a) If the directory path is already in the mapping cache then the handler function can open the directory and verify that the current directory and the data in the mapping cache are identical.
   (b) Otherwise the handler function builds a chain of trust from the root of the file system to the directory path by opening every single directory on the way and adding the information about the directory to the mapping cache, e.g., for `/var/tmp/file` the directories `/`, `var` relative to `/`, and `tmp` relative to `/var` are checked and added to the mapping cache.

   This function returns a file descriptor that can be used for system calls relative to the verified directory.
4. Next the filename is resolved using the resolved and checked directory. The file is opened and parameters are checked in the handler function (using the new relative system calls `openat` and `fstat64`). If the file is already in the mapping cache then the handler function ensures that the current file and the cached metadata is identical. Otherwise the new file information is added to the mapping cache.

If there is a mismatch between any metadata of either a directory or the file then the application is terminated with a race warning. After the file is resolved the system call handler is executed. This handler might then add new file information to the mapping cache or change existing information, according to the system call that is executed.

4. Implementation

The current prototype implementation of DynaRace relies on several software layers. A binary instrumentation toolkit detects and rewrites all unsafe system calls related to file handling. These system calls are then redirected transparently to the DynaRace module. The application (and all libraries used by the application) still issue the original (unsafe) system calls. Using binary rewriting, DynaRace keeps track of all accessed directories and files.

DynaRace extends the interposition layer from the libdetox framework [21] to check all system calls that modify files. All system calls that execute unsafe file operations are redirected to special handler functions. Each handler function handles one system call. These handler functions either (i) update the mapping cache between filenames and inode and device information for files that have not been used before, or (ii) use available information in the mapping cache to ensure that the filename still maps to the same physical file.

Related work [15, 28, 35] often matches specific predefined pairs of system calls to identify potential races. DynaRace introduces a new mapping cache that keeps track of all accessed files; all file-related system calls are rewritten to use this new mapping cache. This approach detects potential race conditions between any combination of file-related system calls.

The handler functions first resolve the file according to Section 3.2 and then check the actual system call or rewrite specific parameters. Handler functions exist for the following system calls:

Test: the following system calls are in the *test* group:

- **stat*:** all `stat` related system calls (e.g., `stat`, `stat64`) are rewritten to ensure that the specified file ends up in the cache. `fstat64` is used as the actual system call.
- **access:** this unsafe system call has no replacement that uses a file descriptor, so the handler function implements this system call using `fstat64`.

Use: the following system calls are in the *use* group:

- **open:** check flags, if `O_CREAT` is used then the handler ensures that `O_EXCL` is set as well, handling potential errors. `openat` is used as the actual system call, relative to the current directory.
- **creat:** reuses the check for the open system call.
- **chmod:** the handler ensures that the current metadata of the modified file is equal to the cached metadata and changes the system call to use `fchmod` with the tested file.

Close: the following system call is in the *close* group:

- **close:** the handler closes the file and reduces the number of open instances of the current file. If the counter reaches 0 then the file enters the *retire* state.

Section 3.1 explains the different states in more detail. The current implementation prototype emits a warning and terminates the application if an unimplemented system call is used, but the implementation can easily be extended to include other system calls as well.

DynaRace is released as open source. The prototype implementation is included as a module of the libdetox binary translation framework. The source code can be downloaded from the libdetox homepage at `http://nebelwelt.net/projects/libdetox`.

4.1 Tracking of file states and metadata

A transparent file mapping cache keeps the information of all used files and directories. This file mapping cache enables a secure way to identify files and is used in the handler functions of unsafe system calls. These handler functions rely on the file mapping cache to identify files that have already been used in earlier system calls, e.g., a rewritten `open` system call that is preceded by a (rewritten) `access` system call uses the file mapping cache to ensure that if the filenames passed to the system calls are equal then the files themselves are also equal.

The data structure for file entries contains the following fields:

- **state:** the current state of the file. Possible states for files are either *update*, *enforce*, *retire*, or *new* (see Figure 3). Directories are in one of two possible states. A directory is either accessible or in an error state.
- **nropen:** the number of open file descriptors for this file that are in use by the application. A file can only transition to the *retire* state if all open instances of a file are closed.
- **fd:** this field contains either 0 if the file is OK, the open file descriptor if the file is currently opened for DynaRace checks, or the error code if the file is invalid.
- **filename:** a string that contains the file atom for files or the full path for directories.
- **stat:** holds the result of the `fstat64` system call when the file was last accessed. This field is used to check equality of files.
- **dir:** a pointer to a file data structure that contains information about the directory of the file. A file is always verified alongside the directory that it is in.

The file mapping cache is constructed lazily. Whenever a new file is used by the application then the file's metadata and state are added to the mapping cache. If a file or directory is reused then the current state of the file system must conform to the data in the mapping cache. The handler functions update the mapping cache for system calls that change metadata after the system call is executed but before control is returned to the translated application.

4.2 File resolution

File resolution is split into two steps according to Section 3.2. The first step constructs an authenticated chain from the directory of the file to the root of the file system to authenticate the path. The second step uses the base directory to authenticate the remaining file atom (the last component in the path) against the already authenticated base directory using the new file-based race-free system calls. The following sections discuss the implementations to resolve directories and file atoms.

4.2.1 Directory authentication

Path authentication starts with a full path and recursively authenticates single directories moving towards the root directory. The recursive function first checks if the current directory is already in the cache, otherwise a new cache entry is constructed. Newly constructed entries are linked to the parent directory, and the correct parent directory is also verified. Each directory is stored in the cache with the full path to enable a fast lookup.

Directory authentication is implemented using an approach similar to `chk_use` [30]. `chk_use` consumes a path one atom at a time, starting with the root directory. The intention of `chk_use` is to specify a check function (e.g., `access`), and a use function (e.g., `open`) which are then executed after another in a race-free way. DynaRace uses the `chk_use` function to authenticate the directory by traversing the path one atom at a time and inserting the metadata information of each sub-path into the cache.

A notable difference to the original `chk_use` implementation is that DynaRace uses the new system calls like `openat` to traverse the directory path. This setup removes the need to change the current working directory of the process in the `chk_use` function and allows DynaRace to support multiple concurrent threads.

The path authentication function checks each directory once. If the check fails then an error is recorded in the list of paths. If there is an error during the authentication of the chain then this error is propagated upwards to the initial directory (and to the caller as well).

Path authentication takes a full absolute path as an argument and returns either a valid open directory or an error. The opened directory can be used for further authentication of files in that directory.

4.2.2 File authentication

File authentication takes an authenticated directory and authenticates a file atom in that directory. This function keeps track of the state of individual files and validates correctness according to Figure 3. New files are initialized and added to the list of accessed files, existing files are authenticated according to their current state and the target state.

File authentication first searches the list of already accessed files using the authenticated directory and the file name. If there is a cache hit then the file metadata is either updated or verified according to the state of the file. If the directory and the file are not in the cache (i.e., this combination is used for the first time) then a new entry is constructed with the available information.

This function throws two types of warnings. The first type warns if a file was changed by an external process during the runtime of this process. This type of warnings shows potential attacks against the program that were fixed. The second type warns if files are used without validation (e.g., opening files without checking the permissions first). This type shows protocol violations by the application. If a race attack is detected (i.e., the cached information changes in the *enforce* state) then the application is terminated.

4.3 Replacing system calls

The system call interposition framework checks all system calls and redirects all file-based system calls to handler functions. These handler functions implement the DynaRace core and keep state for each accessed file and all used directories.

The handler functions use directory authentication from Section 4.2.1 and file authentication from Section 4.2.2 to update the state cache of individual files and directories. These authentication functions abstract the bookkeeping problem and enable clean and simple handler functions.

The current implementation provides handler functions for the `stat`, `access`, `open`, `creat`, `chmod`, and `close` system calls. This section shows one system call from each state, `access` for the *update* state, `open` for the *enforce* state, and `close` for the *retire* state. Functions of the form `systemcall_int` (e.g., `fstatat_int`, `openat_int`, `close_int`) are helper functions in the virtualization layer that execute the real system calls.

The prototype implements a subset of all file-based system calls. Missing system calls can be added using the available authentication functions and the existing handler functions.

4.3.1 access system call

The `access` system call handler intercepts `access` system calls and rewrites them dynamically to use `fstat64`. The handler function takes the given filename and splits it into an absolute pathname (resolved using `getcwd` if the path is relative) and a file atom.

The absolute path is authenticated according to Section 4.2.1. All directories on the path are consequently added to the directory cache. Directory authentication returns an open file descriptor for the directory of the used file. This file descriptor is then used to execute a `fstat64` system call. The stat information is needed to construct the state information of the file atom. The file metadata entry is then constructed depending on the return values of directory authentication and the following `stat` system call using the file authentication function.

The `stat64` struct contains all information needed to reimplement the `access` system call. A macro uses the stat information, the user id, and the group id to return the same information like the access system call. The return value of the `access` handler function is either an error value for invalid files or 0. The state update can trigger warning messages that are logged.

4.3.2 open system call

The `open` system call handler intercepts all `open` system calls and rewrites them to use the safe alternatives. The given pathname is split into a file atom and an absolute path similar to the `access` system call handler. The absolute path to the file atom is then authenticated using directory authentication.

The file atom is then opened using the `openat` system call relative to the authenticated base directory. If the application uses the truncate attribute to remove the file's contents then the attribute is removed from the executed `open` system call. The truncating is delayed until after the authentication and the update of the metadata. The handler function then updates file metadata using the file authentication function.

The handler function either returns an error value or the open file handle. If there are authentication errors then the program terminates. If the application opens unchecked files that are in the "new" state then DynaRace emits a warning (in the file authentication function).

4.3.3 close system call

Similar to the `access` and the `open` system calls, the `close` system call is redirected to a handler function. The `close` system call has the advantage that the file is already open and there are no potential race conditions when accessing this open file descriptor.

The handler function searches the cache using the unique inode number and device id. If the file is opened multiple times then the number of open files is reduced. If the last file descriptor of a specific file is closed then the state of the file is updated to the special *retire* state.

4.3.4 New system calls

DynaRace can coexist with applications that already use new system calls that use relative directory file descriptors (`accessat`, `openat`, `fstatat64`, etc.). The new system calls are handled just like regular file-based system calls and redirected to a handler function by the interposition framework. The handler function then updates the file metadata and executes the new system call using the information provided by the application.

5. Implementation alternatives

Our prototype implementation of DynaRace uses and extends the libdetox binary rewriting framework for the execution of untrusted code. Three other implementation approaches are possible. The first approach extends the Linux kernel and implements the DynaRace approach, e.g., as a kernel module. The second approach extends the standard libc and implements the DynaRace approach on top of the library. The third approach uses the `ptrace` debugging framework to implement DynaRace in a concurrent process.

5.1 Kernel DynaRace implementation

An alternative implementation could extend the kernel with a module that implements the DynaRace approach and keeps a cache of accessed files on a per-application basis. This state cache could then be used whenever the application requests an unsafe system call.

An advantage of this implementation approach is that there is no overhead for binary translation and that the kernel can also keep track of all accessed files for all running applications.

A disadvantage is that a kernel-based implementation needs kernel level access. The kernel-based implementation can contain bugs and lead to exploits. Another point is that the Linux kernel already provides file-based system calls relative to open directories. These system calls can be used to implement safe applications. DynaRace is only needed for potentially unsafe applications. New functionality should only be added to the kernel if a user-space implementation is not feasible.

We argue that the risk of potentially exploitable code in the kernel is not worth the advantage of the lower overhead. In addition a user-space implementation is preferable if safe alternatives already exist in the kernel like the set of safe system calls that DynaRace uses.

5.2 libc-based DynaRace implementation

A second alternative implementation could extend the standard libc library. This library contains wrappers for most of the file-based system calls. These wrappers are then used by the application. The implementation would extend the wrappers for all file-based system calls to implement the DynaRace approach. A static cache of accessed files and states would be initialized during the standard libc initialization and used whenever a file is accessed.

An advantage is the lower overhead compared to our prototype implementation because no binary translation is needed to redirect and catch the system calls.

A disadvantage is that the application can still execute native system calls in using an unpatched ("third-party") library. This third-party library breaks the security of the race detection. A second potential problem is that the DynaRace race checks are executed at the same privilege level as the application. Our implementation uses binary translation for the application; the file-based system calls are then intercepted from the sandbox and redirected to the DynaRace implementation in the privileged part of the sandbox in user-space.

We argue that the risk of a third-party library that executes a direct system call is too high compared to the performance overhead for binary translation. A possible implementation should offer "complete" protection for all system calls, and not only the system calls that are executed through the libc.

5.3 ptrace-based DynaRace implementation

A third alternative implementation leverages the `ptrace`[2] system call to implement the DynaRace approach. A separate DynaRace process controls the target process and observes all system calls externally. The DynaRace process intercepts and inspects all file-related system calls.

DynaRace replaces the unsafe system call with a piece of code that executes a set of safe system calls and some checks. The DynaRace process would inject that code into the running process and redirect the execution flow to the injected code. This injected code would then replace the original system call and return the result from the kernel to the unmodified application code.

An advantage of this approach is that the application does not need to be translated and virtualized. Depending on the implementation of the DynaRace process this setup could lead to some performance speed-up compared to our prototype implementation.

A disadvantage is that the DynaRace process must either stop the traced process upon every system call, a setup that leads to high context-switching overhead, or DynaRace must inject new code into the application that could lead to unwanted side-effects. The implementation of the DynaRace process and the code-injection technique is critical to keep the overhead low. Original system calls must be permanently redirected to injected code to reduce the task switching overhead between the DynaRace process and the application process. Another disadvantage is that the application process does not profit from the additional protection that the sandbox offers.

We argue that a feasible `ptrace`-based implementation will be too complex due to the need to inject code in the application domain. A virtualization-based implementation adds new code naturally and instruments the executed system calls using simple redirection. Binary rewriting tools provide additional opportunities for error checking that are hard to replicate with external debugging techniques like `ptrace`.

[2] The `ptrace` system call is used to remotely control a process. The tracing process can read and write memory locations and registers of the target process, controls signals and signal delivery, and can inspect system calls and parameters.

6. Evaluation

The DynaRace prototype is implemented on top of the user-space security toolkit libdetox. This section evaluates (i) the raw performance of the DynaRace prototype implementation using several microbenchmarks, (ii) end-to-end performance of the DynaRace prototype implementation using a complex Apache setup, and (iii) evaluates DynaRace using several application scenarios. The discussion of the application scenarios shows how DynaRace protects from file-based race attacks in these scenarios.

6.1 Performance evaluation

The set of features and the security guarantees raise the question about the total overhead for libdetox. Optimizations in the dynamic translation process result in an average overhead of between 6% to 9.3% for the SPEC CPU2006 benchmarks, depending on the set of security guarantees that is used [21].

The prototype implementation of DynaRace is not yet optimized and there is potential to reduce the number of executed system calls and to use better data-structures for the mapping cache. Table 3 shows overheads for specific microbenchmarks depicted in Listing 1. Every microbenchmark executes the code sequence 1,000,000 times in a loop. The microbenchmarks are executed on an Intel Core i7 950 CPU at 3.07GHz using a 64bit version of Ubuntu 10.10 and the most recent libdetox version 0.3.0. The benchmarks are compiled using gcc version 4.5.2.

```
/* 1) long test */
if (access("input", R_OK|W_OK)==0) {
  int fw = creat("test", 660);
  if (fw == -1) perror("Creat");
    int fr = open("input", 0);
    if (fr == -1) perror("Open");
    close(fw);
    close(fr);
} else {
  printf("Unable to open dir");
}

/* 2) access test */
int j = access("input", R_OK|W_OK);

/* 3) open/close test */
int j = open("input");
close(j);
```

Listing 1. Microbenchmarks used for the evaluation (C code).

	Native	libdetox	DynaRace
1) long test	4.73ms	4.00ms	20.96ms (4.4x)
2) access test	1.59ms	1.62ms	6.11ms (3.8x)
3) open/close test	1.93ms	1.00ms	6.90ms (3.6x)

Table 3. Results of the microbenchmarks compared to native performance.

An interesting result of Table 3 is that libdetox is able to outperform the native execution for raw system call throughput in the open/close test. Two reasons for this behavior are (i) trace linearization inside the code cache (of the binary translator) for the translated standard libc function and (ii) the inlining of all system calls from the `ld-linux.so` library.

The DynaRace prototype implementation uses multiple system calls to verify that already accessed files have not changed between system calls. For new files additional system calls are used to gather information for the mapping cache. This setup leads to an overhead for file-based system calls of around 3-4x (for raw system call performance) to remove potential race conditions. Only the small set of file-based system calls that check or modify file metadata incur overhead. The overhead can be reduced through future optimizations that reuse more information or keep frequently accessed files open. All other (non file-related) system calls do not incur overhead.

The overhead is tolerable as system calls used to check the metadata of files and to open/close files are rare compared to read or write operations or computation. There is no overhead in the access to a file's data (e.g., reading from a file or writing to a file). Any overhead caused by DynaRace is associated with file metadata management. For most programs system calls that modify file metadata are not on the hot path. The time spent for I/O dominates the time spent for metadata management. The additional checks' overhead is small compared to the cost of a potential exploit.

6.2 Apache web server study

This section presents an end-to-end performance evaluation using the Apache web server. The web server study compares the performance of a system with active DynaRace protection for the Apache server and all scripts to a system without DynaRace. This study shows the completeness and end-to-end performance of our prototype implementation. The study uses Apache 2.2 on 32bit Ubuntu 10.04 LTS on a Core i7 950 CPU at 3.07 GHz in a VirtualBox virtual appliance using a single core. Apache uses the default Ubuntu configuration (multiple processes multiple threads, full support for the dynamic PHP interpreter and other modules). The study uses the `ab`[3] Apache benchmark in a different virtual machine on a different core on the same CPU to download four different files from a server. Each file is downloaded 100'000 times and Apache is restarted between iterations.

The four different files are `index.html`, a 5kB HTML file; `picture.png`, a 1mB image; `test.php`, a short PHP script that generates 90B output; and `test2.php`, a PHP script that executes `phpinfo()` and generates 48kB of output.

The evaluation uses three different system configurations: (i) native, Apache runs unmodified and unprotected; (ii) libdetox, Apache runs in a protected environment under the control of libdetox[4]; (iii) DynaRace, Apache runs in a protected libdetox environment with a DynaRace module that protects all file accesses as well. All three configurations run inside a virtual machine.

	Native	**libdetox**	(ovhd.)	**DynaRace**	(ovhd.)
index.html	1464	1675	-14.5%	1601	-9.4%
image.png	48	51	-6.3%	47	1.6%
test.php	1773	1562	12%	1498	15.5%
test2.php	463	343	26%	320	30.9%

Table 4. Results for the Apache benchmark showing the number of requests per second. The benchmark uses four different files to compare native performance, libdetox performance, and DynaRace performance.

Table 4 shows the performance numbers of the Apache benchmark. The three different system configurations are evaluated for each file. Each column shows the number of completed requests per second, the libdetox and DynaRace columns also show the overhead compared to native performance. The relative overhead shows that libdetox and DynaRace exhibit a small performance improvement compared to the native performance for static files. The improvement comes from the binary translation that results in greedy trace extraction for hot code.

For the dynamic files (`test.php` and `test2.php`) libdetox results in 12% and 26% overhead due to the translation of the dynamic PHP interpreter (which results in many indirect control flow transfers). Comparing the libdetox and DynaRace columns shows that DynaRace results in roughly 6% more overhead than libdetox alone. This overhead comes from the additional system calls for the directory and file atom authentication.

The overhead of both libdetox and DynaRace is tolerable, especially when considering that only a prototype implementation is evaluated. The prototype implementation still leaves room for additional performance optimization (e.g., additional caching of open file descriptors, better code optimization, and other optimizations). The current prototype implementation shows that the DynaRace approach is feasible and the overhead is tolerable. Additional optimization is left as a topic for future work.

6.3 Evaluation of the protection for file-based race conditions

DynaRace relies on the handler functions for the different system calls and the state of each file to protect and to remove potential race conditions. The file state is updated using transitions from one state to another.

This section shows three important usage scenarios that are common in applications. The usage scenarios are (i) checked file access where access permissions for a file are checked before it is used, (ii) temporary file creation where a file is created in an unsafe directory, and (iii) log rotation where files are replaced by an external process. Each usage scenario is dissected into the individual system calls and what (implicit) assumptions are used between the system calls. The described usage scenarios are prone to race conditions in their original form. DynaRace adds additional state to each file and enforces the assumptions between the system calls.

State transitions between system calls are shown in the following way:

$$oldstate \xrightarrow[targetstate]{systemcall} newstate$$

The state associated with a file transitions from *oldstate* to *newstate* if a *systemcall* system call is executed that induces the *targetstate* state. Both *newstate* and *targetstate* are needed for files that are in the *enforce* state. If a system call would induce the *update* state (e.g., the `access` system call) and the file is currently in the *enforce* state then the file remains in the *enforce* state.

6.3.1 Checked file access

The checked file access pattern consists of four steps to work with a file. The first step checks access permissions of the existing file using the `access` (or `stat`) system call. The second step opens the same file using the `open` system call, returning a file descriptor. The third step uses the file (e.g., reading from, or writing to the file descriptor using the `read` and `write` system calls; `read` and `write` system calls do not change the state of the file). The fourth step closes the file again using the `close` system call, completing the usage pattern.

A potential attack races to exchange the checked file after the first validation step and before the second opening step. Using mazes of connected directories [6] an attacker can win this race every time if he or she can inject a symbolic link into any part of the file name (see Section 7.4).

With DynaRace the following four state transition sequences are possible:

[3] The command used for the measurements is: `ab -c 2 -n 100000 http://${VM}/${FILE}`.

[4] Libdetox [21] protects applications from code-injection exploits, return oriented programming [26], and other control-flow oriented attacks

The file has not been accessed/used before by the application:

$$new \xrightarrow[update]{access} update \xrightarrow[enforce]{open} enforce \xrightarrow[retire]{close} retire \quad (1)$$

The file has been used before but was closed by the application:

$$retire \xrightarrow[update]{access} update \xrightarrow[enforce]{open} enforce \xrightarrow[retire]{close} retire \quad (2)$$

The file has been accessed by the application:

$$update \xrightarrow[update]{access} update \xrightarrow[enforce]{open} enforce \xrightarrow[retire]{close} retire \quad (3)$$

The file is still opened by the application:

$$enforce \xrightarrow[update]{access} enforce \xrightarrow[enforce]{open} enforce \xrightarrow[retire]{close} enforce \quad (4)$$

The above state transition sequences leave no opportunity for a potential attacker to change files between a check system call and a "use" system call. An attacker could swap files in the *update* or *retire* state but not if the current state or next state is *enforced.*

A potential attacker tries to change a file after the `access` system call and before the `open` system call. Using the DynaRace states an attacker can change the file only before the `access` system call in Equation 1; in Equation 2 and Equation 3 a warning is printed, and in Equation 4 the application is terminated with a race condition error message. DynaRace guarantees that in all cases no unchecked file can be injected between the `access` and the `open` system call. A potential attacker can change the files before the permissions are checked but never between the permission check and the system call that uses the checked file.

As soon as a file transitions into the *enforce* state the last checked or accessed information is fixed and verified. This setup results in a guarantee to the program that the last checked information of a file is enforced when that information is used later.

6.3.2 Temporary file creation

Safe temporary file creation is an important and hard problem. An access test using an `access` or `stat` system call first checks that the file does not exist. A following `creat` system call (or an `open` system call with the create exclusive flag) then creates the file. An attacker can try to race between the existence check and the file creation to add a link to an already existing file that will then be overwritten.

$$new \xrightarrow[update]{access} update \xrightarrow[enforce]{open} enforce \quad (5)$$

Equation 5 shows the state transitions when a new file is created. The state information contains a valid directory and the error code for the file after the `access` or `stat` system call. The directory where the file will be placed in must exist but the temporary file must not exist.

6.3.3 Log rotation

Log rotation is a technique that is used by many daemons to renew/rotate their log files. A daemon opens a log file and writes information to that file. A rotation daemon moves these log files to a different place and signals the original daemon to reopen the log file. The daemon then closes the old file and reopens the log file (which no longer points to the same inode and device id).

DynaRace's *retire* state enables log rotation. When a file is closed it can be reopened even if the metadata of the file has changed. The *retire* state is similar to the *new* state where we do not know anything about the file. The information in the cache is updated and enforced only if there exists a valid set in the cache.

```
...
lfd = open(tmp, O_CREAT|O_EXCL|O_WRONLY,
           0644);
...
if (lfd < 0) {
  unlink(tmp);
}
...
write(lfd, pid_str, 11);
/* unchecked relaxation */
chmod(tmp, 0444);
...
```

Listing 2. TOCTTOU vulnerability in X.org (os/utils.c, C code).

$$enforce \xrightarrow[retire]{close} retire \xrightarrow[update]{access} update \xrightarrow[enforce]{open} enforce \quad (6)$$

Equation 6 shows a sequence of system calls that is used during the rotation of a log file. The file is closed by the daemon, checked, and reopened. The `access` system call following the `close` system call prints a warning message that the file has changed. The daemon continues in the *update* state and enforces the information from the check when the file is opened.

This scheme leaves a window of opportunity for the attacker where he or she can change the log file after it was closed but before it is accessed. The access check in the daemon catches these attacks and the state information is later enforced.

6.4 X.org file permission change vulnerability

Version 1.4 to 1.11.2 of the X.Org X11 X server had a severe TOCTTOU race condition [34]. The X server creates a temporary lock file and relaxes the permissions of the lock file using unsafe system calls. Any local attacker with permission to run the X server can exploit this vulnerability to set the read permission for any file or directory on the system.

Listing 2 shows the code containing the race condition. The variable `tmp` contains a fixed string of `/tmp/.tXn-lock` where X is the n-th X display running on that computer. An attacker executes the SUID X binary as P_1. The attacker stops P_1 after the `write` system call and before the `chmod` system call. In a second execution P_2 of the X binary the `open` system call fails and the temporary file created by P_1 is removed using the `unlink` system call. The attacker kills P_2 and links `/tmp/.tXn-lock` to an arbitrary file (e.g., `/etc/shadow`) and continues P_1. P_1 will then set the arbitrary file to world-readable.

DynaRace would protect from this TOCTTOU race condition. As soon as the file identified by the `tmp` variable is in the *enforce* state it can no longer be modified by a concurrent process. Equation 7 shows the states for the temporary file for P_1. Before the `chmod` system call P_1 is stopped and P_2 depicted in Equation 8 is executed. P_1 then continues and DynaRace throws an error because the metadata of the enforced temporary file has changed.

$$P_1 : new \xrightarrow[enforce]{open} enforce \xrightarrow[enforce]{chmod} FAIL \quad (7)$$

$$P_2 : new \xrightarrow[enforce]{open} enforce \xrightarrow[unlink]{retire} retire \quad (8)$$

7. Related work

DynaRace is a dynamic TOCTTOU race detection mechanism that is implemented as a libdetox extension. File-based race detection can be built on different techniques. Static race detection analyzes the program source code or the binary of the application before execution; dynamic race detection uses code that is added during the compilation of the program to detect races at runtime; dynamic race prevention uses added code to prevent possible races; and novel race-free APIs change the available file system API to remove or reduce potential races.

7.1 Static race detection

Static source-code analysis [10, 11, 23, 33] can be used to detect potential file-based race conditions. A scanner reads the source-code of the application and observes calls to library functions or system calls. If a sequence of calls opens a race condition then the static analysis tool emits a warning.

Static analysis tools often have a high number of false positives because they rely on pattern matching and they cannot use runtime data to verify potential races. Due to the high error rate these approaches are not feasible for online services that must meet some response time constraints.

The DynaRace approach adds state to each accessed file. Due to the classification of system calls into groups and the additional state DynaRace decides for each system call if a potential race condition occurs.

7.2 Dynamic race detection

A dynamic approach can observe all system calls as they happen. These system calls can either be logged and analyzed post-mortem [18] or an online analysis can evaluate the pair of system calls according to a given policy [28]. Aggarwal and Jalote [3] use static binary translation to add dynamic guards that are executed at runtime.

IntroVirt [16] uses OS virtualization and a virtual machine monitor to run predicates outside of the OS scope. These predicates check the health of system software and also check for file race conditions if the programs have the right predicates. Wei and Pu [35] enumerate likely TOCTTOU pairs that are used for common tasks. Goyal [15] uses the `strace` framework to collect system call traces and detect TOCTTOU attacks.

The technique of enumerating pairs of system calls misses the opportunity to detect race conditions dynamically between any combination of system calls. This approach is similar to black-listing several pairs of system calls without looking at all possible combinations. Only an approach like DynaRace that takes care of all file-based system calls can protect from all race conditions. Due to the added state DynaRace looks at all possible combinations and sequences of system calls and therefore provides complete coverage.

7.3 Dynamic race prevention

RaceGuard [12] defends against several classes of TOCTTOU attacks using an in-kernel cache but is limited for file swap attacks where the file itself is changed from one execution to the other. Tsyrklevich and Yee [31] implement pseudo-transactions in a kernel module to detect specific combinations of check/use system calls targeting the same file. Multiple similar approaches followed [20, 27, 32, 36].

Several novel race-free APIs have been proposed to replace the POSIX-like system calls for file handling. Some of these novel APIs use transactions to run a set of related system calls atomically [22, 37]. The OS insures that no other application may interfere with these system calls.

Dean and Hu prove that no deterministic solution to prevent races exists (with the set of available system calls in 2004) and introduce a probabilistic way to prevent races [13]. They rely on the assumption that an attack is unable to win all races. Therefore they propose hardness amplification. Hardness amplification executes the check multiple times in a loop (a so called K-loop) and checks if all results are as expected.

Transactions of system calls need kernel modification. In addition to the new code in the kernel the applications must be rewritten to include transactional code. DynaRace supports a gradual approach that adds protection from file-based TOCTTOU races. Applications and libraries can use a mix of old file-based system calls and new file-based system calls. Using the file-state and the new system calls DynaRace deterministically protects every file-based system call.

7.4 Maze-based race attacks

Borisov et al. break the probabilistic approach by enabling an attacker to win all races [6]. If all races are won by the attacker then the check proposed by Dean and Hu [13] is unable to detect the race condition. An attacker constructs so called mazes. A *maze* is a chain of temporary directories that contains a link to the next chain as the leaf. The attacked program needs time to go through the maze (e.g, once for `access` and once for `open`) and in that time the attacker swaps the final link.

7.5 Hardness amplification-based race protection

Mazières and Kaashoek [19] propose an alternate approach that uses inodes (low level file objects) instead of filenames. If the binding between inode and filename is immutable then no file swap race conditions are possible when the target file changes. Tsafrir et al. [29, 30] implement a similar approach in user-space. Their approaches render the maze attack from Borisov et al. [6] impossible. User-space checks guard applications from TOCTTOU attacks. A file is resolved step by step. The algorithm checks for each part of the filename if the current part is a file or a symlink. Files are opened using an approach similar to Dean and Hu [13] using a K-loop probabilistic check. Symlinks are opened using a recursive check using the same algorithm.

Chari et al. take a different approach and extend Tsafrir's work to implement a `safe-open` mechanism [9] that ensures that all elements of a path are safe to open by the current user id. Safe file elements can be modified only by the same user or root.

DynaRace introduces a hidden mapping and state cache and rewrites unsafe system calls. This technique gives similar guarantees as Mazières and Kaashoek without the need to change the implementation of the application or the libraries. DynaRace resolves a file step by step similar to Tsafrir et al. but uses safe system calls. Using the new system calls DynaRace is deterministic and does not rely on a probabilistic approach.

7.6 System call interposition in binary translators

System call interposition adds an intermediate layer between the application and the operating system. This intermediate layer intercepts every single system call and enables checks based on the system call, the parameters, and the state of the application.

Binary translation is a natural solution to this problem as it translates the running program and can intercept any instruction or any memory location. Static binary translation is limited to statically known code, dynamic binary translation enables loadable modules as well. Dynamic binary translation can be used to weave additional security guards into the running application by modifying the executed machine code with low overhead. libdetox [21], Vx32 [14], Strata [24, 25], Program shepherding [17], and DynamoRIO [7, 8] enable low overhead dynamic binary translation.

We choose libdetox for our implementation because it contains many additional security guards that protect the running application from other attack vectors like buffer overflows, code injection, and (to some extent) data attacks.

8. Limitations and weaknesses

This section discusses limitations and weaknesses of the DynaRace approach and highlights insights obtained through the DynaRace prototype implementation. The idea of DynaRace is to associate state to each file. Files are identified using a mapping cache that maps filenames to unique inodes and device numbers.

Using the state machine in Figure 3 enables specific checks for file-based system calls, whereas the state transitions are decided based on the group that the current system call is in and the state of the file. All usage cases of a file inside an application are covered using the state diagram that never throws an exception if the file has not been changed between different system calls.

The *retire* state enables multiple concurrent processes to modify files in a safe way. Closing a file in one application retires the information in the mapping cache and the application no longer assumes that the state of the file remains the same. Ownership transfers in, e.g., log rotation, are only possible using the special *retire* state.

8.1 Retirement schemes

The current implementation keeps all files in the *enforce* state after they have been used with a system call of the *use* group. A possible extension of the state machine in Figure 3 would be a retirement scheme for system calls that change the file but do not return an open file descriptor (e.g., `chmod`, `chown`, or more general system calls in the *use* group without `creat` and `open`).

These system calls do not return an open file descriptor when they are executed. The application does not signal the kernel that it no longer expects to use the associated file (e.g., through the `close` system call for opened files). DynaRace therefore cannot check if a file is no longer used for these system calls. The retirement scheme for these system calls could be implemented through a timer that starts when the system call is executed. The timer would signal when these files can be retired and the state of the file would move from *enforce* back to *update*, thereby enabling concurrent modification without terminating the program.

A timer is of course a dangerous addition as it opens a new windows of opportunity for an attacker to delay the application until the timer runs out and the file state is no longer enforced. We leave this problem to future work.

8.2 Broken (legal) usage scenarios

DynaRace protects from changes to file-metadata from concurrent processes if the file state is enforced (i.e., if the application assumes that information from prior system calls is still valid). Possible broken usage scenarios are concurrent file/directory modification and polling.

If an application works with a file in the *enforce* state and a concurrent process changes the parent directory (e.g., by moving the directory, or by renaming the directory) then the directory verification will fail and an error is thrown. Two concurrent processes also cannot work together on a single file if it is in the enforce state in both processes.

Polling (i.e., checking metadata of the file) from concurrent processes works as long as the file is in the *update* state. If both processes want to work with the file (e.g., reading, writing, changing metadata), then DynaRace will terminate the second application due to a metadata mismatch.

DynaRace limits the number of modifiers of each file to a single process. If multiple processes try to modify a file at the same time then all processes except the first are terminated due to metadata mismatches.

9. Conclusion

This paper presents DynaRace, a novel approach to detect and prevent file system races in unmodified applications. DynaRace adds state to each file and keeps metadata for all accessed files in a mapping cache.

File system races are detected if the information in the mapping cache does not match the information of the current file. Our prototype application emits a warning and terminates the application if races are detected.

DynaRace ensures that there are no file-based races possible and dynamically rewrites unsafe system calls into safe versions that are race-free. A benefit of the DynaRace approach is that it protects all file-based system calls. DynaRace allows partial migration of individual libraries to the new set of file-related system calls. The new system calls are no panacea, even with new system calls a programmer still has to worry about the state of individual files. DynaRace removes this burden from the programmer and offers a state-based dynamic approach for all file-related system calls.

Currently programmers have to live with potential races when they use standard system calls, and it is hard to program race-free applications using the new system calls. The DynaRace approach enables programmers to use both the unsafe and the new system calls without the need to add explicit additional safety checks in the application while closing the door to attacks that attempt to exploit file system races.

10. Acknowledgments

We thank the anonymous reviewers for their detailed feedback and suggestions on how to improve the paper. Special thanks for pointing out [30].

References

[1] New system calls. https://lwn.net/Articles/164887/.

[2] openat syscall. http://linux.die.net/man/2/openat.

[3] AGGARWAL, A., AND JALOTE, P. Monitoring the security health of software systems. In *ISSRE'06: 17th Int'l Symp. Software Reliability Engineering* (nov. 2006), pp. 146–158.

[4] BISHOP, M. Checking for race conditions in file accesses. Tech. rep., University of California at Davis, 1995.

[5] BISHOP, M., AND DILGER, M. Checking for race conditions in file accesses. *Journal for Computing Systems* (1996), 131–152.

[6] BORISOV, N., JOHNSON, R., SASTRY, N., AND WAGNER, D. Fixing races for fun and profit: how to abuse atime. In *14th USENIX Security Symposium* (2005), pp. 303–314.

[7] BRUENING, D., DUESTERWALD, E., AND AMARASINGHE, S. Design and implementation of a dynamic optimization framework for Windows. In *ACM Workshop Feedback-directed Dyn. Opt. (FDDO-4)* (2001).

[8] BRUENING, D., GARNETT, T., AND AMARASINGHE, S. An infrastructure for adaptive dynamic optimization. In *CGO '03* (2003), pp. 265–275.

[9] CHARI, S., HALEVI, S., AND VENEMA, W. Where do you want to go today? escalating privileges by pathname manipulation. In *NDSS* (2010).

[10] CHEN, H., AND WAGNER, D. MOPS: an infrastructure for examining security properties of software. In *CCS'02: Proc. 9th ACM Conf. Computer and Communications Security* (2002), pp. 235–244.

The source code of the DynaRace framework and additional examples can be downloaded at `http://nebelwelt.net/projects/libdetox`.

[11] CHESS, B. V. Improving computer security using extended static checking. In *S&P'02: IEEE Symp. on Security and Privacy* (2002).

[12] COWAN, C., BEATTIE, S., WRIGHT, C., AND KROAH-HARTMAN, G. RaceGuard: Kernel protection from temporary file race vulnerabilities. In *Proc. 10th USENIX Security Symposium* (2001), p. 12.

[13] DEAN, D., AND HU, A. J. Fixing races for fun and profit: how to use access(2). In *Proc. 13th USENIX Security Symposium* (2004), SSYM'04, pp. 14–14.

[14] FORD, B., AND COX, R. Vx32: lightweight user-level sandboxing on the x86. In *ATC'08: USENIX 2008 Annual Technical Conference* (2008), pp. 293–306.

[15] GOYAL, B., SITARAMAN, S., AND VENKATESAN, S. A unified approach to detect binding based race condition attacks. In *CANS'03: Intl. Workshop on Cryptology & Network Security* (2003).

[16] JOSHI, A., KING, S. T., DUNLAP, G. W., AND CHEN, P. M. Detecting past and present intrusions through vulnerability-specific predicates. In *SOSP'05: Proc. 20th ACM Symposium on Operating Systems Principles* (2005), pp. 91–104.

[17] KIRIANSKY, V., BRUENING, D., AND AMARASINGHE, S. P. Secure execution via program shepherding. In *Proc. 11th USENIX Security Symposium* (2002), pp. 191–206.

[18] KO, C., AND REDMOND, T. Noninterference and intrusion detection. In *S&P'02: Proc. 2002 IEEE Symposium on Security and Privacy* (2002), pp. 177–187.

[19] MAZIÈRES, D., AND KAASHOEK, M. F. Secure applications need flexible operating systems. In *HotOS'07: Workshop on Hot Topics in Operating Systems* (1997), pp. 56–61.

[20] PARK, J., LEE, G., LEE, S., AND KIM, D.-K. RPS: An extension of reference monitor to prevent race-attacks. In *PCM'04: 5th Pacific Rim Conf. on Multimedia* (2004), pp. 556–563.

[21] PAYER, M., AND GROSS, T. R. Fine-grained user-space security through virtualization. In *VEE'11: Proc. 7th ACM SIGPLAN/SIGOPS Int'l conf. Virtual execution environments* (2011), pp. 157–168.

[22] SCHMUCK, F., AND WYLIE, J. Experience with transactions in quicksilver. In *SOSP'09: Proc. 13th ACM Symposium on Operating Systems Principles* (1991), pp. 239–253.

[23] SCHWARZ, B., CHEN, H., WAGNER, D., LIN, J., TU, W., MORRISON, G., AND WEST, J. Model checking an entire Linux distribution for security violations. In *Proc 21st Computer Security Applications Conference* (2005), pp. 13–22.

[24] SCOTT, K., AND DAVIDSON, J. Strata: A software dynamic translation infrastructure. Tech. rep., University of Virginia, 2001.

[25] SCOTT, K., AND DAVIDSON, J. Safe virtual execution using software dynamic translation. *ACSAC'02: Annual Computer Security Applications Conference* (2002), 209.

[26] SHACHAM, H. The geometry of innocent flesh on the bone: Return-into-libc without function calls (on the x86). In *CCS'07: Proc. 14th ACM conf. Computer and Communications Security* (Oct. 2007), S. De Capitani di Vimercati and P. Syverson, Eds., ACM Press, pp. 552–61.

[27] SPILLANE, R. P., GAIKWAD, S., CHINNI, M., ZADOK, E., AND WRIGHT, C. P. Enabling transactional file access via lightweight kernel extensions. In *FAST'09: Proc. 7th conf. on File and storage technologies* (2009), pp. 29–42.

[28] SUK LHEE, K., AND CHAPIN, S. J. Detection of file-based race conditions. *Int'l Journal Information Security 4*, 1-2 (2005), 105–119.

[29] TSAFRIR, D., HERTZ, T., WAGNER, D., AND DA SILVA, D. Portably solving file TOCTTOU races with hardness amplification. In *FAST'08: Proc. 6th USENIX Conf. on File and Storage Technologies* (2008), pp. 13:1–13:18.

[30] TSAFRIR, D., HERTZ, T., WAGNER, D., AND DA SILVA, D. Portably preventing file race attacks with user-mode path resolution. Tech. Rep. RC24572, IBM T. J. Watson Research Center, June 2008.

[31] TSYRKLEVICH, E., AND YEE, B. Dynamic detection and prevention of race conditions in file accesses. In *Proc. 12th USENIX Security Symposium* (2003), pp. 243–255.

[32] UPPULURI, P., JOSHI, U., AND RAY, A. Preventing race condition attacks on file-systems. In *SAC'05: Proc. ACM Symposium on Applied computing* (2005), SAC '05, pp. 346–353.

[33] VIEGA, J., BLOCH, J., KOHNO, T., AND MCGRAW, G. ITS4: a static vulnerability scanner for C and C++ code. In *ACSAC'00: Ann. Comput. Security Applications Conf.* (2000).

[34] VLADZ. Xorg file permission change vulnerability (CVE-2011-4029). http://vladz.devzero.fr/Xorg-CVE-2011-4029.txt.

[35] WEI, J., AND PU, C. TOCTTOU vulnerabilities in UNIX-style file systems: an anatomical study. In *FAST'05: Proc. 4th conf. USENIX Conf. File and Storage Technologies* (2005), pp. 12–12.

[36] WEI, J., AND PU, C. A methodical defense against TOCTTOU attacks: the EDGI approach. In *ISSSE'06: IEEE Int'l Symp. on Secure Software Engineering* (2006).

[37] WRIGHT, C. P., SPILLANE, R., SIVATHANU, G., AND ZADOK, E. Extending ACID semantics to the file system. *Trans. Storage 3* (June 2007).

V2E: Combining Hardware Virtualization and Software Emulation for Transparent and Extensible Malware Analysis

Lok-Kwong Yan[†‡] Manjukumar Jayachandra[†] Mu Zhang[†] Heng Yin[†]

[†] Department of Electrical Engineering & Computer Science
Syracuse University, Syracuse, New York, USA

[‡] Air Force Research Laboratory
Rome, New York, USA

{loyan, mjayacha, muzhang, heyin}@syr.edu

Abstract

A transparent and extensible malware analysis platform is essential for defeating malware. This platform should be transparent so malware cannot easily detect and bypass it. It should also be extensible to provide strong support for heavyweight instrumentation and analysis efficiency. However, no existing platform can meet both requirements. Leveraging hardware virtualization technology, analysis platforms like Ether can achieve good transparency, but its instrumentation support and analysis efficiency are weak. In contrast, software emulation provides strong support for code instrumentation and good analysis efficiency by using dynamic binary translation. However, analysis platforms based on software emulation can be easily detected by malware and thus is poor in transparency. To achieve both transparency and extensibility, we propose a new analysis platform that combines hardware virtualization and software emulation. The essence is *precise heterogeneous replay*: the malware execution is recorded via hardware virtualization and then replayed in software. Our design ensures the execution replay to be precise. Moreover, with page-level recording granularity, the platform can easily adjust to analyze various forms of malware (a process, a kernel module, or a shared library). We implemented a prototype called *V2E* and demonstrated its capability and efficiency by conducting an extensive evaluation with both synthetic samples and 14 realworld emulation-resistant malware samples.

Categories and Subject Descriptors D.4.6 [*Operating Systems*]: Security and Protection—Invasive software

General Terms Security, Performance

1. Introduction

Malware analysis is an important step to defend against malware. Given a piece of unknown malware, the objective of malware analysis is to reverse engineer it and quickly reveal its inner workings. As malware is often heavily obfuscated to thwart static binary analysis, dynamic binary analysis becomes increasingly prevalent. In this approach the analyst runs a malware sample of interest in an emulated execution environment (e.g., QEMU [30]) and then monitors and analyzes its malicious behavior in a fine-grained manner (at the instruction level). A great deal of research efforts take this approach [4, 8, 9, 15, 21, 24, 27, 32, 34, 40, 41].

The main advantages of this analysis approach are flexibility and efficiency for code instrumentation. Since the emulator is a regular user-level program, it is relatively simple for security analysts to add instrumentation code (such as taint analysis and symbolic execution). Due to dynamic binary translation, the performance overhead for such heavy instrumentation is often acceptable. However, its prominent drawback is lack of transparency. Because it is extremely difficult (if not completely infeasible) to emulate every aspect of real hardware, malware can take advantage of these discrepancies to detect the emulated environment and stay dormant to avoid analysis. Researchers have investigated this problem extensively and identified a large number of different detection methods [16, 26, 31]. Our measurement study in Section 5.2 shows that emulation-resistant malware has become a prevalent threat in the wild.

To address this transparency issue, Dinaburg et al. proposed to leverage hardware virtualization and developed a system called Ether [13]. Since the malicious code is executed on bare metal hardware and the in-guest changes caused by analysis can be intercepted and hidden by the hypervisor, this approach can achieve ideal transparency. However, Ether is not the ultimate solution. It incurs a prohibitive performance penalty to conduct instruction-level analysis by simply enabling single-step mode. Our experiment shows an approximately 3000 times slowdown by enabling single-step, not to mention the extra heavy instrumentation needed by in-depth malware analysis. Moreover, it is far more challenging to implement the code instrumentation tools within a hypervisor (i.e. Ring -1) than an emulator (i.e. Ring 3).

In this paper, we aim to bring the best of these two worlds. We aim to develop a malware analysis platform that is both transparent and extensible to facilitate custom fine-grained malware analysis. The essence of this platform is *precise heterogeneous replay*. That is, we record malware execution using hardware virtualization for transparency, and then replay and analyze the malware's execution using dynamic binary translation for flexibility and efficiency of in-depth analysis. The idea of heterogeneous replay was first proposed and implemented in Aftersight [10], which records the virtual machine execution from VMware and replays it in QEMU, for heavyweight analyses (such as bug detection) on production workload. In contrast to Aftersight, our platform needs to work under the malicious context: the emulator should exactly replay the execution recorded from the hardware virtualization platform in spite of the fact that malware is trying to detect every possible heterogeneous property in these two systems.

One challenge of precise heterogeneous replay is how to strike a balance between the recorder and the replayer. On one hand, if the recorder does not record enough events and states, the replayer

VEE'12, March 3–4, 2012, London, England, UK.

cannot precisely reconstruct the execution. On the other hand, if the recorder gathers complete information for every single instruction or event and leave an easy task to the replayer, the recording performance would become unacceptable. We carefully classify various operations and instructions into several categories and handle them properly to ensure precise replay.

We implemented a prototype system, called *V2E*. The recorder has been implemented in KVM [23], and TEMU (a dynamic binary analysis platform [37]) has been modified to precisely replay the execution. With minimum changes, the existing analysis plugins (such as taint analysis, unpacker, and tracing) work properly, achieving the advantages of transparency and greater analysis efficiency.

We have evaluated V2E using both synthetic and realworld emulation-resistant malware samples. These same samples were successfully recorded and replayed on our modified TEMU revealing the behavior hidden from the original TEMU platform.

In summary, this paper makes the following contributions:

- We propose a new technique that combines hardware virtualization and dynamic binary translation to achieve both transparency and efficiency for fine-grained analysis.
- We designed and implemented a prototype called V2E. While the recording component was implemented in KVM to record malware execution in a transparent fashion, the replay component was built in TEMU, largely by modifying its dynamic binary translation logic. Consequently, existing TEMU plugins have gained transparency and higher analysis efficiency after minor changes.
- We conducted extensive experiments and analysis, using both synthetic and realworld emulation-resistant malware samples. These samples utilize a large variety of methods for detecting emulated environments, so we believe our evaluation is well rounded. All emulation-resistant malware samples were successfully analyzed completely.

The rest of the paper is organized as follows. The next section lists the design goals that are essential for in-depth malware analysis and gives an overview of our approach. Section 3 and Section 4 describe the design and implementation of the recording component and replay component, respectively. Section 5 presents our experimental results. Section 6 discusses the limitations of the current implementation. Section 7 surveys the related work. Finally, the paper concludes with Section 8.

2. Design Goals & Approach

We first list the design goals for in-depth malware analysis, and then explain how our approach is able to address these design goals.

2.1 Design Goals

The following design goals are essential for in-depth malware analysis:

- **G1: Transparency.** The presence of the analysis environment should remain invisible to malware, voiding its intent to escape investigation.
- **G2: Instrumentation Support.** It should be relatively simple to add custom instrumentation on malicious code execution. In many cases, this instrumentation can be heavyweight, such as dynamic taint analysis and instruction-level tracing.
- **G3: Efficiency.** The efficiency for malware analysis is two-fold: 1) it should be efficient enough to monitor computation intensive and highly interactive malware; and 2) performance overhead for heavy code instrumentation should be acceptable.

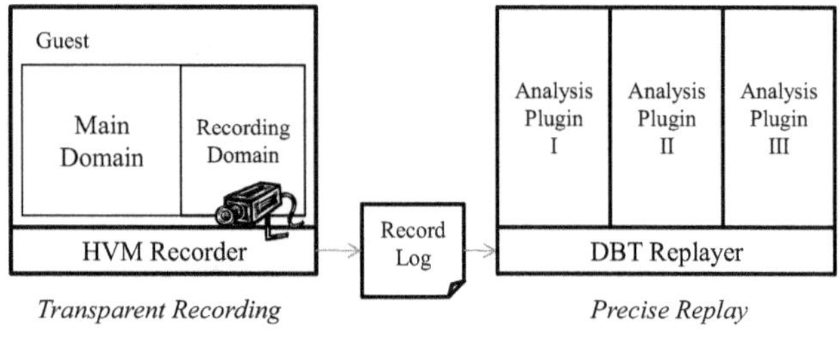

Figure 1. Architecture Overview

- **G4: Adjustable View.** Malware can present itself in various forms, such as user process, shared library, dynamically injected code, kernel module, etc. It should be easy to adjust our analysis focus to concentrate on malware's behavior instead of the execution of the rest of the system.

2.2 Architecture

The overall architecture is depicted in Figure 1. The malware sample under investigation is loaded into the guest system using hardware virtualization, to achieve transparency (**G1**). Although hardware virtualization may still be detected under certain circumstances [31] and a remote time source can be used to measure the real timing difference [12], as hardware virtualization has been widely deployed on production systems, detecting hardware virtualization environments becomes increasingly irrelevant. Ether demonstrated that hardware virtualization can achieve transparency in a practical sense [13].

The guest system is partitioned into two realms. The malware resides in the *recording realm*, and the rest of the guest system (such as the guest OS and the other applications) remains in the *main realm*. Depending on where the malware is present, we can put a user process, a shared library, a kernel module, or any combination of them into the recording realm to have a closer look at the malware's behavior. Such a separation fulfills the design goal of adjustable view (**G4**). It also partially addresses the efficiency issue (**G3**), because the irrelevant system execution is excluded from the recording realm. Some analysis techniques (such as Panorama [40] and HookFinder [41]) do need to observe the entire system execution. In this case, the recording realm includes the entire guest system, falling back to the whole-system recording.

The record log obtained from the recorder is then fed into the replayer. Using the dynamic binary translation technique, the replayer is able to offer acceptable performance for fine-grained code instrumentation, and thus achieves analysis efficiency (the second part of **G3**). The replayer facilitates any existing malware analysis platforms that are based on dynamic binary translation. Therefore, the existing analysis plugins on these analysis platforms can continue to work with minimum changes. It addresses the instrumentation support (**G2**).

2.3 Precise Heterogeneous Replay

Using hardware virtualization, we can record the malware execution in a transparent and efficient manner. To support various in-depth malware analysis techniques, we need to *precisely* replay the execution using dynamic binary translation. That is, at every single execution time, the program state in replay is exactly the same as in recording in spite of the fact that the malware execution is trying to detect various discrepancies between the real hardware and the emulated system.

Formal Definition. At each time i, S_i represents the program state (including CPU registers and memory) and I_i specifies the input. I_i may be null if no input occurs at time i. Then a transition function f characterizes the real hardware: $S_i = f(S_{i-1}, I_{i-1})$. Similarly, there is a transition function f' for the emulated hardware. Suppose that $f' = f$, given S_0 and I we can replay the whole execution. However, according to automata theory, determining if $f' = f$ is equivalent to the problem of determining whether two Turing machines are equal, which is known to be undecidable [35]. In practice, $f' \neq f$, because it is nearly impossible to correctly emulate some aspects of hardware. That is, for some i, $S'_i = f'(S_{i-1}, I_{i-1})$ and $S'_i \neq S_i$. Therefore, in addition to recording S_0 and I, for any moment j when $S'_j \neq S_j$, we need to record the state change $\Delta_j = S_j - S_{j-1}$. Then the new transition function f'_r is defined as below:

$$S'_i = f'_r(S'_{i-1}, I_{i-1}, \Delta_i) = \begin{cases} S'_{i-1} + \Delta_i & \text{if } \Delta_i \neq null \\ f'(S_{i-1}, I_{i-1}) & \text{Otherwise} \end{cases}$$

In other words, during replay, whenever a state change Δ_i has been recorded for time i, we will directly apply the recorded state change such that $S'_i = S'_{i-1} + \Delta_i$. Using simple induction, we can prove that with (S_0, I, Δ) and f'_r, $S'_i = S_i$ always holds true for all $i \in [0, n]$.

From Theory to Practice. From the formal discussion, we can see that the key to successful replay is to determine when to use f' and when to apply Δ. In other words, if we are confident that certain instructions and events can be correctly emulated in software, then we simply emulate them. Otherwise, we should record the state changes and then during replay apply these changes.

Fortunately, for general instructions like data transfer (e.g., `mov`, `push`, `pop`), control transfer (e.g., `call`, `ret`, `jz`, `jmp`), and integer arithmetic (e.g., `add`, `shl`), it is fairly easy to emulate them correctly in software because of their semantics are simple and remain the same across processor series.[1] Moreover, these instructions are the vast majority in program execution. As a result, the efficiency of both recorder and replayer can be ensured. We believe that this is a valid assumption, because these common instructions are tested over and over again in many different application contexts. Even if there is an emulation bug in one of these common instructions, because of its simple semantics, it should be easy to fix.

External interrupts, memory-mapped IO (MMIO), port IO, direct memory access (DMA), and timestamp counter are inputs I to the guest system. Like other deterministic replay systems [10, 14, 36], we choose to record these events if they happen in the recording realm.

Software exceptions, model-specific registers, and the `cpuid` instruction are not generally treated as inputs in previous replay systems. However, it is extremely difficult to emulate them right. Software exceptions are triggered when certain condition checks fail in the processor. It is fairly complicated to emulate all these condition checks in the exactly same way as in the real processor, not to mention that a specific processor may have CPU bugs that raise incorrect exceptions. The behaviors of model-specific registers and the `cpuid` instruction are processor specific. It is a daunting task to correctly emulate all the specifics to support at least the common CPU series. Therefore, we choose to record and replay exceptions, model-specific registers and `cpuid` as state changes Δ.

Floating point instructions and SIMD (Single Instruction Multiple Data) instructions (e.g., MMX and SSE) are generally difficult to be emulated correctly as well. We could also record the results of these instructions as Δ. However, for programs that heavily perform these operations, the performance for both record and replay may greatly degrade. Alternatively, we choose to pass these instructions directly to the hardware processor during replay. This solution assumes that the replayer is running on a machine supporting this set of floating point and SIMD instructions. This assumption can easily hold by running the recorder and the replayer on the same kind of machines (or even the same machine).

Operation Type	Solution
Data Transfer / Control Transfer / Integer Arithmetic	Emulate
Interrupts / MMIO / Port IO / DMA / TSC	Replay as I
Exceptions / System Registers / CPUID	Replay as Δ
Floating Point / SIMD Instructions	Pass through

Table 1. Operations and Corresponding Solutions.

As a summary, Table 1 lists these operations and their corresponding solutions: *emulate*, *replay*, or *pass-through*. We emphasize that the platform following this design principle does not immediately become transparent completely, because we do not preclude that the emulation of some of these common instructions may still be buggy. However, once identified, these bugs can be easily fixed and the transparency of the platform will be further improved.

3. Transparent Recorder

For successful replay, we need to capture S_0, I and Δ in a transparent and efficient manner. In this section, we describe how we are able to achieve this goal by leveraging hardware virtualization.

3.1 Mediating Recording Realm

In order to monitor malware in various forms, including kernel modules, shared libraries and processes, the recording realm needs to be defined at the page-level granularity and the interaction between the recording realm and the rest of the system needs to be mediated.

In hardware virtualization, Two Dimensional Paging (TDP) is a memory virtualization mechanism. While the conventional page table pointed by CR3 in the guest will be used to translate a Guest Virtual Address (GVA) into its Guest Physical Address (GPA), the second-layer page table maintained by the hypervisor will translate the Guest Physical Address into the Host Physical Address (HPA). The maintenance of the second-layer page table is invisible to the guest. AMD and Intel have different implementations: Nested Page Tables (NPT) for AMD and Extended Page Tables (EPT) for Intel.

We take advantage of TDP to mediate the recording realm. Specifically, we create two TDP tables, which partition the guest physical memory into two memory spaces, one for the recording realm and the other for the rest of the guest system. The code pages that belong to the monitored malware will be loaded into the recording realm, such that the interaction of the monitored malware with the rest of the system can be mediated by the TDP page faults and other VMExit (transitions from the guest to the hypervisor) events. Once again, these VMExit events are invisible to the guest system.

This TDP-based recording realm is flexible enough to monitor a small code module, a full user process, and even the entire guest system, depending on what pages are loaded into the recording realm.

3.2 Basic Scheme

In the basic design, the two guest physical memory spaces are mutually exclusive. That is, each individual guest physical page can only be present in either the recording realm or the main realm, but not both. This basic design ensures mediating all the inputs and events for the recording realm is simple.

We use a simplified *adore-ng* rootkit [1] as an example to illustrate this basic scheme. The C source code and the corresponding disassembly are shown in Figure 2. Briefly speaking, the orig-

[1] Note that these common instructions may still cause discrepancies in exceptions, which are handled separately.

```
1. int adore_root_filldir(void *buf, char *name,
     int nlen, loff_t off, ino_t ino, unsigned x)
2. {
3.   struct inode *inode = NULL;
4.   int r = 0;
5.   uid_t uid;
6.   gid_t gid;
7.
8.   if ((inode=iget(root_sb[current->pid% 1024],
                       ino)) == NULL)
9.      return 0;
     //lines 10 to 20 are omitted for brevity
21. }
```

(a) C source

```
d88888550 <adore_root_filldir>:
550:  push  %ebp
 551...56C: //set up stack,
               //%eax = current @L8
56C:  mov   0x6c(%eax),%edx  //%edx=pid @L8
56F:  xor   %edi,%edi
571:  test  %edx,%edx
573:  mov   %edx,%eax
575:  jns   57d <adore_root_filldir+0x2d>
577:  lea   0x3ff(%edx),%eax
57D:  push  $0x0
57F:  push  $0x0
581:  and   $0xfffffc00,%eax
586:  sub   %eax,%edx
588:  pushl 0x1c(%ebp) //push ino @L8
58B:  pushl x0(,%edx,4) //push root_sb[...] @L8
              // call iget @ line 8
592:  call  593 <adore_root_filldir+0x43>
   //The rest is omitted for brevity.
```

(b) disassembly

Figure 2. adore_root_filldir

inal pointer to `root_filldir` has been replaced by a pointer to `adore_root_filldir` to hide certain files. Suppose we want to record the execution of this kernel rootkit. So we move the code page of this kernel module from the main realm to the recording realm. We may treat this first code page as S_0. Figure 3 (A) illustrates this situation.

When the guest system is about to call `root_filldir`, the execution is redirected to `adore_root_filldir`, with virtual address $0xd88888550$ and physical address $0x16876550$. Since the physical page $0x16876000$ is not present in the main realm any more, this control flow transition will trigger a TDP page fault. The recorder located in the hypervisor will capture this TDP page fault and switch the memory space to the recording realm, which is shown in Figure 3 (B). In addition, we record the current CPU state (all the registers and flags), as input I_0.

On fetching the first instruction in `adore_root_filldir`, two more TDP page faults will be triggered for the page table directory page (PD) and the page table entry page (PTc) respectively. This is because the TLB has been flushed during the realm switch, and the CPU needs to look up the page table for the physical address of the first instruction. We will also move these two pages in the recording realm and record their contents as another input. This is a desired behavior, because the replayer will need the page table pages for address translation. Moreover, by including the page table pages, the problem of page swapping and re-mapping is automatically handled in both recorder and replayer. Figure 3 (C) shows this moment.

This first instruction (`push %ebp`) writes onto the stack. As the stack page is absent in the recording realm, this operation triggers the TDP page faults for the stack page (MS) and the corresponding page table pages (PD and PTs). as shown in Figure 3 (D). In this example, PD has already been moved into the recording realm, so no TDP page fault happens for PD.

Then the execution continues without causing any VMExits until $0xd888856c$. This instruction (`mov 0x6c(%eax), %edx`) reads a data page (D), which is not present in the recording realm. Similarly, this data page (D) and its corresponding page table page (PTd) are moved into the recording realm and recorded (see Figure 3 (E)).

The execution further proceeds to the instruction located at $0x169f7592$. It calls a kernel function `iget`. A TDP page fault is raised because the jump target is absent in the recording realm. By checking the faulting EIP, we determine that this EIP does not belong to the malware module. So we decide to switch back to the main realm (see Figure 3 (F)). In addition, we record a "JumpOut" event at this point, indicating that the execution has transferred out of the recording realm.

The kernel function `iget` now resumes its execution in the main realm. While it accesses the parameters, another TDP page fault will occur because the stack page (MS) has been moved to the recording realm. So we will move the stack page (MS) and the corresponding page table pages (PD and PTs) back to the main realm. This behavior is also desirable, because next time when the recording realm reads one of these pages, we are able to capture it and record the new page content as a new input. Figure 3 (G) illustrates this situation.

When `iget` finishes and returns, a TDP page fault will occur because the jump target is not present in the main realm. Thus, we switch the memory space to the recording realm, which is shown in Figure 3 (H). The CPU state is recorded and the execution resumes in the recording realm. The subsequent execution of `adore_root_filldir` will follow a similar cycle.

3.3 Other Inputs

The previous example only shows how to capture inputs from CPU states and memory. We need to handle other kinds of inputs as well. Control transitions such as interrupts and exceptions are naturally handled in the basic scheme. As the Interrupt Descriptor Table (IDT) is never present in the recording realm, any interrupt or exception will trigger a TDP page fault. We will treat this fault as a control transition and a new CPU state will be recorded when the execution returns to the recording realm. When executing in the recording realm, instructions like `cpuid`, `rdmsr`, `in` and `rdtsc` need to be recorded as inputs I and state changes Δ. With hardware virtualization support, we are able to trap these instructions into the hypervisor, and record their results when they are executed in the recording realm. DMA transfers may change memory pages in the recording realm without CPU intervention. When DMA writes into a page resident in the recording realm, we need to record that page as a new input. The DMA controller is emulated in software. So we can intercept this DMA write and record this input.

3.4 Optimizations

The basic scheme enforces two mutually exclusive realms. In many cases, this is unnecessarily expensive. If two realms read a shared page alternately, the basic scheme would repeatedly remove that page from the recording realm, and later move it back and record it, even though the page contents have not changed. We employ several optimizations to allow these two realms to share pages.

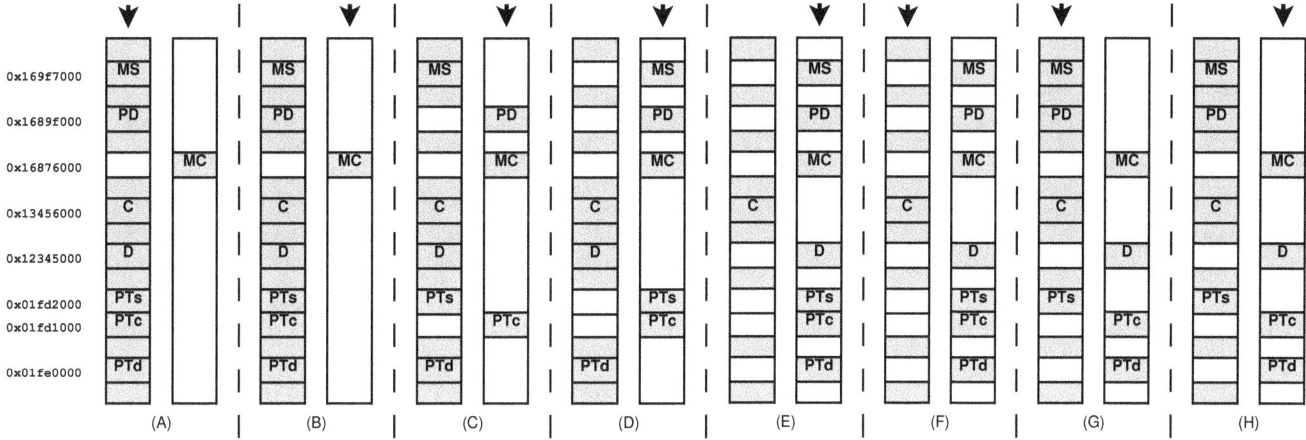

Figure 3. TDP snapshots for adore_root_fill. The two columns represent two guest physical memory spaces for the main realm and the recording realm respectively. A shaded block represents a present page, while a blank block indicates an absent page. The arrow on top signifies which realm is active.

Sharing Data Pages. To enable sharing data pages, we use a "Remove-On-Write" (ROW) principle, which is similar to Copy-On-Write. More specifically, we allow two realms to share pages, and these pages are set to be read-only. When one realm attempts to write to a page, a TDP write violation will be triggered, and that page will be removed from the other realm. This optimization works especially well for the page table pages, because both realms need these pages for address translation, and these pages do not change so often.

Sharing Code Pages. When recording a full process, we encounter a problem where both realms need to access shared library code pages. These code pages will be moved back and forth between the main realm and the recording realm, according to the basic scheme. Similar to sharing data pages, these code pages present in the both realms and are marked to be read-only. In addition, we manipulate the NX (Non-Execute) bit for these code pages, to capture the moment when the execution transitions into these code pages in the monitored process. More specifically, we monitor the context switch by intercepting CR3 writes. When the execution context switches to the recorded process, we switch from the main realm to the recording realm. However, there is a gap between this context switch and the user-level execution, because the context switch is performed in the kernel space and the execution will continue in the kernel space for a while before it transitions to the user space. In order to capture the entry point to the user space, we mark all the pages in the recording realm as Non-Executable. Although the kernel execution will trigger TDP page faults and in turn these pages will be loaded into the recording realm, we do not record these pages. We wait until we observe a TDP execute violation with the faulting EIP in the user space. Then we detect the entry point. The pages loaded during the kernel execution will be removed, so we can capture when the execution transfers back to the kernel later and pages marked NX will be restored. Fortunately, the kernel execution within this gap is normally very brief, so the overhead for capturing the entry point to the user space is very small.

3.5 Bridging the Semantic Gap

We usually specify which malware to monitor by its executable name, whereas the recording realm operates directly on guest physical pages. Therefore there exists a semantic gap. We leverage the VM introspection technique to bridge this semantic gap [17, 20]. More specifically, we intercept system calls and parse kernel data structures in the guest system to extract the OS-level semantics, such as the process list and the module memory map. By this way, we map the process name to the corresponding CR3, and module name to its virtual memory range. Then by looking up the guest page table, we further map the guest virtual address to the guest physical address.

The mapping from guest virtual to guest physical address may change over time due to page swapping. The newly mapped physical page will be captured and recorded when it is accessed later, but the physical page that is no longer mapped needs to be removed from the recording realm immediately. To do so, we need to capture the page table changes that affect the pages in the recording realm. According to our data page sharing mechanism, the page table pages associated to the recording realm are shared in both realms and set to be read-only. Therefore, any changes to these page table pages will be trapped to the hypervisor. Therefore, by checking which page table entry has been modified, we can determine which guest physical page needs to be removed from the recording realm.

3.6 Shadow Time Stamp Counter

As extra TDP page faults and other VMExits are needed for recording the malware execution, malware may detect the underlying recording behavior by examining the advance of the Time Stamp Counter (TSC). This can be done by `rdtsc` and reading the TSC model-specific register. We maintain a shadow TSC to hide this artifact.

The shadow TSC is an estimate of how much time the guest actually runs. We calculate it as follows: Let t_i be the value of the host TSC before VMRESUME[2] is executed. Let t_o be the value of the host TSC right after the CPU returns to the host. Let t_e and t_x be the time it takes to enter the guest and exit to the host and t_g be the actual execution time for the guest, then $t_o - t_i = t_e + t_x + t_g$. We approximate $t_e + t_x$ by turning on `rdtsc` and running `rdtsc` in a loop in the guest to obtain the average of $t_e + t_x$, which we used to calculate t_g. Then t_g is used to increment the shadow TSC, which is returned to the guest whenever the guest queries the TSC.

3.7 Implementation

We implemented the recording component in KVM in the Linux Kernel 2.6.32. The code base of KVM is well organized. While

[2] VMRESUME is the Intel instruction for entering the guest, non-root mode

`vmx.c` and `svm.c` contain the hardware specific code for Intel and AMD virtualization extensions respectively, `mmu.c` contains the memory management unit code that is common to both architectures. Within `mmu.c` is the `tdp_page_fault` function that is called by both VMX and SVM, and is where we implemented our realm control and enforcement logic. All memory based inputs are handled at this location. All non-memory based inputs to the *recording realm* are handled in the architecture specific implementation files.

Memory Management. For KVM, a virtual machine runs as a user process on the host. The guest physical memory is just virtual memory in that process. The guest physical pages can be swapped in and out, depending on the system workload. Therefore, the TDP table is rather dynamic. To tackle these dynamics, KVM registers *mmu_notifiers* with the Linux kernel. With these in place, any changes made to the page tables of that specific process, such as swapping a page or re-mapping a virtual page to another physical page, will notify KVM through *mmu_notifier*. As we manage two TDP tables, both tables need to be updated accordingly. Thus, we implemented our own versions of the *mmu_notifiers* so changes in the page table of the host process are reflected in the TDP page tables for both realms.

Logging. Being a kernel module, KVM cannot directly write to files. To enable logging, we implemented a user-level program that commits the changes to a log file. In the current implementation, when we load a page into the recording realm and record it, we record the full page content. Obviously, this is only necessary when the page is recorded for the first time. When the page is modified in the main realm and loaded back again, it is very likely that only a small portion of the page has changed. As a simple optimization, we may keep the old copy and only record the "diff". We did not implement this optimization. Instead, we simply zip the log. We found this simple solution sufficient in practice, because the compressed logs are usually small enough.

Event Landmark. We need a landmark to tell at what execution point a log event is recorded, such that we can replay the same log event at the same moment. Previous replay systems used the branch counter as a landmark. The branch counter increments when each branch instruction is committed and thus serves as an accurate landmark. In our current implementation, we simply used the CPU state (including the EIP, registers and flags) as the landmark. It is simple but might not be as accurate as the branch counter, because two execution points may happen to have the same CPU state. In practice, we found this simple solution good enough. As described later in Section 4, most of the events (such as memory accesses, regular control transitions, and special instructions) are replayed on demand, the role of the landmark is not as important as in the other replay systems.

4. Precise Replayer

We replay the execution using dynamic binary translation technique to provide good instrumentation support and analysis efficiency.

4.1 Dynamic Binary Translation

Briefly speaking, software emulation based on dynamic binary translation works as follows. When the emulator is about to run a block of code for the first time, it will translate that code block into a piece of code that can execute on the host and will store the translated code into the code cache. When the same code block needs to be emulated, the emulator can skip the translation procedure and directly fetch the translated code from the code cache and execute it. Special care is needed to emulate memory accesses. The *softmmu* is a software implementation of the Memory Management Unit, which looks up the page table and performs virtual-to-physical address translation. To speed up the address translation, the *software TLB* (Translation Look-aside Buffer) is implemented as a cache for the address translation results.

This design is mainly for improving emulation efficiency. However it deviates from the real execution in at least the following ways. First, a block-by-block translation procedure is introduced, which does not exist in the real processors. This translation procedure is normally invisible to the emulated execution, except when the block translation crosses the page boundary. This extra page access can be observed if it causes a page fault.

Second, for efficiency, dynamic binary translation often performs a lazy calculation of flags: a flag is calculated only when it is needed. For example, in "`cmpl $1, %eax; jz 0x401020;`", EFLAGS are not calculated on the first instruction, and then on the second instruction, only `ZF` is calculated to determine which branch to go. This lazy approach is good for efficiency but can be exploited to detect emulation.

Third, again for efficiency, interrupts are checked and served only at the block boundary. In contrast, on real hardware, interrupts may happen on any instruction. We have seen that realworld malware samples repeatedly measure the cpu cycles consumed by a simple `mov` instruction (using a sequence like "`rdtsc; mov %eax, %ebx; rdtsc;`") in a loop and only exit the loop when the number of cpu cycles is greater than a relatively big threshold to detect the presence of an interrupt in between.

In addition to the above discrepancies that are unique to dynamic binary translation, several more are common in software emulation. First of all, due to the complexity of x86 instruction set, some special-purpose instructions (e.g., System Management Mode and Trusted Execution Technology instructions) are hard to emulate and thus have not been implemented in software. We have seen that a malware sample executes `rsm` instructions and leads to a crash in QEMU. Moreover, accurate CPU timestamp emulation is nearly impossible. For simplicity, current CPU emulators (like QEMU) choose to fetch the time stamps on the host. It means that an instruction would consume much more CPU cycles in emulation than on the real hardware. Finally, the logic of checking and raising exceptions in the hardware is fairly complex and thus the software emulation for this logic is often error-prone.

4.2 Changes for Precise Replay

Considering all these challenges in software emulation and dynamic binary translation, we come up with several design changes in the work flow of software emulation to ensure precise replay. Particularly, we have modified the implementation of dynamic binary translation in QEMU to comply with these design changes.

New Translation Logic. According to Section 2.3, during dynamic translation, we classify the instructions into three categories: general-purpose, FPU, and others. General-purpose instructions include data transfer, control transfer, and integer arithmetic. They are translated according to their simple semantics. To avoid discrepancies in flag calculation, we disable the lazy flag calculation. That is, EFLAGS are immediately calculated after each instruction that changes EFLAGS. Assuming the control transition caused by exceptions be correctly replayed, the logic for checking and raising exceptions is completely removed, except for page fault. This is because we rely on the page fault logic to load memory pages at right moment.

Floating point and SIMD instructions execute on FPU. To ensure correctness, these instructions will be translated to wrapper functions that pass the operations directly to the real FPU. For example, in the software emulation approach, a floating point instruction `fadd %st1, %st0` would be translated to call a helper function helper_fadd_ST0_STN, in which this instruction is emulated in software. In our pass through approach, we will directly insert a piece of assembly code as: __asm__("fadd %st(1), %st(0)"). As this instruction takes two FPU registers. We can pass the same instruction to the FPU. If an instruction takes any operands from memory or the general-purpose registers, we need to copy the operands from the guest environment to the host or vice versa. For example, the instruction fadds %0xc(%ebp) adds a memory operand with st(0) and saves the result in st(0). Since this memory operand is loaded in the guest system, we have to copy its value into a temporary value on the host and then performs the floating point operation natively on the host, as shown in the following code snippet:

```
unsigned long temp = ldl(A0);
__asm__("fadds %0;" : : "m" (float)temp));
```

These natively executed FPU instructions may raise exceptions. We register exception handlers to catch and ignore them. We expect to replay the exceptions from the execution log.

Other instructions will be translated into "nop", expecting that the results of these instructions be correctly replayed from the log. That is, no translated code will be generated except advancing the program counter to the next instruction.

While translating each instruction, we check and ensure the program counter should not across the page boundary. Otherwise, we will stop translating the current code block and leave the current instruction to the next block.

Replay Logic. As our page-level recording is based on TDP, we will need the same page table mechanism in software emulation to correctly replay log events on demand. We introduce a *physical page container* for this purpose. This physical page container indicates if a physical page has been loaded from the log and thus is present. Generally speaking, during replay the physical page container replicates the TDP page table of the recording realm. When the replayed execution accesses a page that is absent in the physical page container, we will load the missing memory page and update CPU states from the log at the right moment.

In addition, in the end of each instruction we will compare the current CPU state with the landmark of the next log event. If the landmark matches, we will replay this log event. This log event may be a control transition caused by interrupts or exceptions, or a state change made by special-purpose instructions.

4.3 Example Walkthrough

We use the same *adore-ng* example to walk through the replay logic. As the first log event, the code page MC is loaded in the physical page container. This initial state is the same as that of the right column in Figure 3(A).

Then the second event is the CPU state for the entry point of adore_root_filldir. The replayer updates the CPU state accordingly. The code block starting with the EIP *0xd8888550* needs to be translated and put into the translated code cache before executed. This translation triggers looking up the page table for the physical address of that EIP. Consequently, the page table pages (PD and PTm) are loaded from the log on demand, because they are not present in the physical page container.

Now we start to execute the translated code. The first instruction pushes onto the stack. At this moment, we will load the page table page PTs during page table lookup and then the stack page MS for the memory write. Similarly, we will load the page table page PTd and the data page D at the right moments.

At the end of the call instruction at $0xd8888592$, which is about to jump to the kernel function iget, we know that a control transition happens at this moment. This log event is followed by several events for removing pages (MS, PD, PTs). Subsequently, we see an event to update the CPU state. After executing all these log events, we skip the execution of iget and directly arrive at the instruction $0xd888885a7$, where iget returns to. Now we arrive at the same state as the right column of Figure 3 (H). As this point, we also need to flush the TLB, because changes may have been made to the page table during the skipped execution.

It is worth noting that the replayer literally replays the log. As this example describes the basic scheme, we can see that quite a few pages (such as page table pages) are removed and then loaded back later. Given a log recorded using the optimizations discussed in Section 3.4, the replay will proceed more efficiently.

4.4 Implementation

We implemented the replayer on TEMU, a dynamic analysis platform in the Bitblaze binary analysis infrastructure [37]. A handful of plugins have been developed on TEMU to perform malware analysis. TEMU is based on QEMU version 0.9.1. So we modified the existing dynamic binary translation code in QEMU to support precise replay.

With the modifications in TEMU, the existing analysis plugins should work automatically, except for a small change. Each regular TEMU plugin needs to check if the current execution is within the context of interest (e.g., if the current process is the malware's process). However, for a plugin that works with replay, all execution is of interest. This is ensured by the recorder. So we can remove this context checking in the plugin. In particular, we modified two plugins. The first plugin is an unpacker, which is the implementation of Renovo [21]. The second is an instruction tracing tool called tracecap, which performs taint analysis and dumps detailed information for each instruction. Having a detailed instruction trace with taint information has been demonstrated to be crucial in many malware analysis projects [7–9, 22].

5. Evaluation

We conducted a systematic experimental study for V2E from the following aspects: 1) we studied the existing emulation detection methods and examined the effectiveness of V2E against these methods; 2) we conducted a measurement study on the severity and prevalence of emulation-resistant malware; 3) we evaluated V2E's capabilities in tackling real-world emulation-resistant malware samples; and 4) we measured its performance impact in various settings.

Experimental setup. The host machine has a Core i7 860 Quad Core processor with 4 GB of memory running Ubuntu 10.04, with our modified 2.6.32.29 kernel. The guest systems are Windows XP SP2, Ubuntu 9.04 and Redhat 7.

5.1 Study of Existing Anti-emulation Attacks

We collected a list of existing anti-emulation methods that are available in the literature [16, 22, 31]. To evaluate if V2E can defeat these techniques, we tested both synthetic and realworld samples whenever available. For those techniques without samples, we speculated their internal mechanisms and then made careful decisions. Descriptions of these methods are listed in the Table 2.

Among these detection methods, six of them, including "cmpxch8b", "double fault", "reserved MSR", "instruction length", "alignment checking" and "invalid opcode", cause aberrant exception behavior. As V2E accurately replays the exceptions from the real hardware, these detection methods will be automatically taken care of. We verified *instruction length* and *invalid opcode* using synthetic samples.

Then, "cpuid", "MSR fingerprinting" and "rdtsc" have deviated values returned from certain instructions. These values are hardware specific and thus hard to emulate correctly. V2E defeats these

Description	Defeated?
`cpuid` returns processor specific information. QEMU returns generic information. [16]	✓
`rdtsc` returns the contents of the TSC. [16, 22, 31]	✓
`cmpxch8b` conditionally writes to the memory operand, but a #GP exception is always generated if the memory operand is not writable. QEMU only raises #GP when the memory is written indeed. [16]	✓
A *double fault* exception is generated if the #GP handler can't be retrieved from the IDT when a #GP occurs. QEMU generates #GPs repeatedly. [16]	✓
Writing to *reserved MSRs* should generate #GP, but QEMU does not. [31]	✓
A #GP is generated if the *instruction length* is more than 15 bytes, but certain prefixes like `rep` can break this rule in QEMU. [22, 31]	✓
If the *alignment check* flag is set, then an alignment exception is thrown when an unaligned memory address is accessed. This exception is not thrown in QEMU. [31]	✓
CPU bugs or *errata* results in behavior that are either unexpected or does not follow the published logic, thus the emulator does not handle these like specific hardware would. [31]	✓*
MSR fingerprinting uses the `rdmsr_safe` macro to find the MSRs supported by the CPU. The list of MSRs can be used to help determine the CPU model. [31]	✓
The *fnstcw* instruction pushes the FPU Control Word register onto the stack. As it turns out, bit 3 of this register is reserved in Intel's implementation but is always 1. QEMU always returns 0. [22].	✓
`icebp` is an *undocumented instruction* that simply raises an exception. In QEMU this instruction hangs the emulator. [22]	✓
`rep stosb` can be used to overwrite a range of memory with `nop`. When paired with a `jmp` to nowhere, QEMU and singlestepping will throw a segmentation fault. Hardware executes successfully. [16]	N/A

Table 2. Survey of Emulation Detection Techniques.

methods by recording the values from the real hardware. We further verified "cpuid" and "rdtsc" using both synthetic and realworld malware samples.

"fnstcw" causes a deviated state in the FPU. V2E passes FPU/MMX/SIMD instructions directly on hardware, so no deviations in FPU would be possible for V2E. We have verified using several realworld samples, thus we are confident that it is defeated.

The "CPU errata" method needs special considerations. If a CPU bug causes a totally unpredictable result, it would be extremely hard to handle. The CPU bugs used for emulation detection in the literature [31] all cause incorrect exceptions. These CPU bugs can be handled correctly by V2E, because exceptions are recorded and replayed. In any sense, the effectiveness of this detection method is very limited, because a CPU bug is specific to a CPU family.

The "rep stosb" detection method exploits a cache coherency bug for self-modifying code in earlier Intel processors. This bug has been fixed in all current Intel processors. Therefore, this method is no longer relevant.

5.2 Malware on Existing Malware Analysis Platforms

We would like to see how well the existing malware analysis platforms handle realworld malware. So we collected 150 realworld malware samples from a live malware repository (`http://malc0de.com/database`) and security researchers, and tested them on three malware analysis platforms: Anubis [2], CWSandbox [11], and TEMU [37]. While Anubis and TEMU are based on software emulation, CWSandbox uses API hooking technique. We found that out of 150 samples, 51, 88, and 14 crashed or exhibited no behaviors in Anubis, CWSandbox, and TEMU respectively. Note that all these samples run properly in KVM, which means that they intended to escape from either of these analysis platforms. Interestingly enough, 14 samples that are resistant to TEMU also escaped Anubis and CWSandbox. Evidently, emulation-resistant malware has already become a prevalent threat.

5.3 Analyzing Realworld Malware with V2E

To evaluate how well V2E handles realworld malware, we ran the these 14 emulation-resistant samples with V2E. We ran each sample for up to 2 minutes and then stopped recording. For each sample, we configured V2E to record the entire user-level process and spawned child processes if any. We chose the time-out threshold of 2 minutes to be consistent with the settings of Anubis and CWSandbox. We did not observe any sample installing kernel rootkits, but if indeed a kernel module is installed, the recorder can be configured to record the execution of that kernel module as well.

V2E was able to record and replay the malicious behaviors for all these samples. During replay, we tested three settings: 1) replay with no plugin provides a baseline for the replay performance; 2) replay with tracing produces a complete and detailed instruction trace for the recorded execution; and 3) replay with unpacking extracts hidden code and data from the packed malware. A summary of the results is presented in Table 3. For each sample, we list its MD5 hash, the executable size, and the size of the recorded execution log. Then the runtime for replay with no plugin is listed. With regards to tracing, we list the instruction count and the runtime for tracing. As for unpacking, we show the number of memory dump files, and the runtime for unpacking.

From Table 3, we can make the following observations. First, the execution logs (after compression) are fairly small (up to 55MB). It is worth noting that unlike the logs in the other execution replay systems, these logs are self contained with all necessary code and data included. We can directly feed these logs into the replayer for in-depth malware investigation, and no other environment setup (e.g., virtual machine images and configurations) is needed. Second, due to the efficiency of dynamic binary translation, the baseline performance of the replayer (with no plugin) is satisfactory, from less than 1 second to 79 seconds. The very short replay runtime (less than 1 second) on some samples indicates that these samples are mostly idle. This is reasonable because many of the samples are bots and the networking is disabled during recording. Note that some samples are very computation-intensive, with over 1.3 billion instructions executed within 2 minutes. Third, with good instrumentation support (especially the support for shadow

MD5SUM	exe sz	log sz	Null runtime	Tracing runtime	Tracing # ins	Unpacking runtime	Unpacking dumps
27eb815f101a9295fbb601986f393d01	105KB	29.07MB	76.76s	2h19m	1347M	96.5s	78
43de1618764daf7e5887bd8ac9cadb52	105KB	28.46MB	76.69s	2h18m	1346M	96.09s	79
03f322365b844d8faf9236aab34b4214	106KB	30.75MB	77.09s	2h19m	1349M	97.02s	79
4f12dfb4b613abc4ddf56d087223a868	115KB	35.93MB	78.87s	2h20m	1366M	98.8s	57
f01cdf6e5052aeb5c6510bd8f8d88636	103KB	29.95MB	77.21s	2h19m	1348M	98.94s	81
f068b4362c646dae42cc3b1b8fe20c12	110KB	30.13MB	77.2s	2h19m	1350M	97.17s	77
1686739bc81a407dd9944e2d9bbcf2e1	23KB	2.44MB	0.65s	46.8s	7.73M	0.71s	8
0b8b2c0926630c69a6c75bba67b24a3e	39KB	3.25MB	0.97s	99.7s	16.8M	1.2s	55
c5ff7232868333107fa3efe895f12361	245KB	55.36MB	29s	27m15s	248M	39.33s	39
36e5fdcdbe0bcdc59ea001b162bfb97d	243KB	37.48MB	20.91s	1150s	175M	30.56s	22
c1a66699820fdeb7242e884e6d2f8bcb	119KB	676KB	0.57s	55.7s	9.55M	0.66s	10
dabec78d489f1e783fb23d6e726bd1a4	108KB	2.00MB	0.19s	23.2s	4.09M	0.22s	1
ef0458e196fbd1b4cc1613ba2ca3c43b	280KB	3.30MB	0.36s	54.8s	9.51M	0.46s	1
7ce6cd9837e1a7837c2b491c21ff5b69	101KB	7.10MB	34.35s	294.4s	43M	35.4s	30

Table 3. Analyzing Realworld Emulation-Resistant Malware with V2E

memory), the unpacker built on top of the replayer demonstrated good efficiency. It was able to finish replaying 2-minute execution logs in up to 99 seconds, and at the same time successfully extract hidden code and data from the packed malware samples. Interestingly enough, all these samples are packed. Without V2E's support, it would not be possible to unpack them successfully. Finally, tracing is substantially more heavyweight than unpacking, because it has to disassemble each instruction, fetch instruction raw bytes and operands, and write these details into the instruction trace. We have obtained complete instruction traces for all the samples within a reasonably short period (from tens of seconds to a couple of hours).

5.4 Performance

Without ground knowledge about the realworld malware, it is difficult to accurately measure the performance of V2E. Instead, we choose to measure its performance in controlled experiments.

Recording adore-ng. This experiment shows how well V2E analyzes kernel rootkits. We installed the adore-ng rootkit in Redhat 7 and exercised it by decompressing the linux source with about 17,000 files. This workload took 3s without recording and 52s when recording was enabled, generating a 14MB execution log. A roughly 17x slowdown seems high, but is reasonable for this workload with frequent context switch between the rootkit and the rest of the kernel.

Recording Internet Explorer. We use this test to show how well V2E performs on analyzing a highly complex, computation-intensive, and interactive application. In this experiment, we measured the load time of IE with and without recording. Without recording, IE started up and loaded the MSN homepage in 2.5s. With recording, it took 13.8s. That is about a 5x slowdown. A 52MB execution log was generated. We expect that the recording performance impact decrease as the IE continues to run, because more pages would remain stable in the recording realm. While recording, the IE was very responsive, so it should not be a problem to record any user interactions. In general, as we design V2E in favor of the flexibility of page-level recording and the self-containment of execution logs, its recording performance is likely less efficient than other recording systems. We believe this trade-off is reasonable for malware investigation.

Comparing with Single Stepping. We then enabled single stepping on KVM and measured the performance overhead of single stepping by executing a loop with 8 million instructions. On KVM, it took approximately .008s vs. 25s when single stepping was disabled and enabled respectively. That is more than 3000x slowdown. We can anticipate the performance of obtaining a complete instruction trace based on single-stepping to be much worse. By contrast, using V2E, the same 8 million instructions were recorded with negligible performance penalty. The baseline replay runtime was 0.3s, and it took only 0.8s to perform unpacking analysis and 48s to obtain the complete instruction trace.

6. Discussion

We discuss the limitations and potential evasion techniques in this section.

Bugs in Common Instructions. To achieve transparency, we assume that common instructions be emulated correctly. This assumption does not necessarily hold in the current implementation of V2E. If malware exploits one of the emulation bugs in the common instructions, V2E cannot successfully replay the malware execution. Once the replay failure is found, we can identify the bug and fix its emulation code in V2E. Over time, V2E will be improved to be increasingly more transparent.

Attacking the Landmarks. As mentioned in Section 3.7, the landmark mechanism is not perfect because the CPU state is not a unique identifer of execution point. A malware author may take advantage of this limitation to force an imprecise replay. We leave it as future work to resolve this issue by implementing a branch counter landmark.

Multi-core Support. The current implementation of V2E only supports a single-core guest environment. Since we use two-dimensional paging for separating the main and recording realms and each virtualized core has its own TDP table, recording malware's execution on multi-core environment is feasible by design. We leave the multi-core support as future work as well.

Denial-of-Service Attack. It is feasible for the malware to induce a large number of exits (e.g., TDP page faults and exceptions) to the hypervisor, so as to launch a denial-of-service attack to the recorder. In addition, the malware could detect the analysis environment by measuring this slowdown using an external clock. In general, this kind of limitation is not unique to V2E. It is also shared by other platforms (like Ether). The analysts will have to analysts make case-by-case solutions once they actually arise.

7. Related Work

Malware Analysis Platform. Here we compare different analysis platforms with respect to the degree of transparency, the breadth of analysis view, the support for fine-grained instrumentation, and fine-grained analysis efficiency.

DynamoRIO [6], Pin [25], and Valgrind [28] provide convenient and efficient support for fine-grained instrumentation on a user-level program, by performing dynamic binary translation. However, as they can only instrument a single user-level process, they cannot analyze kernel malware. TEMU [37] is an analysis platform based on QEMU [5], which is an efficient CPU emulator by performing dynamic binary translation. With a whole-system view, TEMU can analyze both user-level and kernel-mode malware. Cobra [38] is a malware analysis platform in form of a Windows kernel module. It uses a technique called localized execution to instrument and inspect malware's behavior. The localized execution technique is in spirit similar to dynamic translation techniques. Since Cobra resides in the kernel, it also has a whole-system view. However, it is unclear if Cobra has support for instruction-level instrumentation. The downside for all the above systems that are based on dynamic binary translation is lack of transparency. Incapable of correctly emulating all the complexities of a real CISC computer system, these analysis systems can be easily detected [16, 26, 31]. By design, Cobra is able to defeat some known anti-analysis techniques. However, Cobra does not address the transparency problem in a general context.

Ether [13] makes use of hardware virtualization techniques to observe malware's execution in a stealthy manner. However, Ether is not an ideal platform for in-depth malware analysis, which requires instruction-level instrumentation. Although fine-grained instrumentation can be achieved through single-step mode, its significant performance overhead (thousands of times slowdown) is unacceptable for the context of in-depth malware analysis.

V2E outperforms all these analysis platforms by combining the advantages of both hardware virtualization and dynamic binary translation techniques, and thus can achieve the highest standard in all the four metrics.

Emulator Detection and Countermeasures. Researchers have studied the problem of detecting emulators extensively [16, 31] and identified numerous detection methods. We have carefully examined these methods, and confirmed that V2E is able to defeat them effectively.

To address the anti-emulation problem, several techniques have been proposed. Balzarotti et al. proposed an automatic method to detect the emulation-resistant behavior by comparing if a piece of malware behaves differently on the real hardware than in the emulated environment [3]. This technique is effective as a detection tool, but it does not help defeat this anti-emulation problem. In order to successfully emulate these emulation-resistant malware, Kang et al. proposed a differential analysis method by comparing two execution traces, one from Ether and the other one from QEMU [22]. By performing trace alignment, this technique is able to automatically detect the root cause for the divergence and generate a runtime patch. However, this approach is not scalable if malware has many anti-emulation checks in many different paths (which is often true in practice), because one runtime patch can only apply to one point in one execution path. In comparison, V2E takes a more radical approach to defeat this problem. With the assumption that the emulation for common instructions should be correct, it should be able to analyze all emulation-resistant malware correctly. This assumption may not be entirely true, but once a bug is found for one of these common instructions, we should be able to fix it easily.

In fact, EmuFuzzer can help discover emulation bugs by fuzz testing[26]. According to the results, a large number of deviations are found for exceptions and floating point operations for QEMU. As V2E directly replays exceptions and executes floating point instructions natively, these deviations are irrelevant. Most of deviations in CPU flags would also disappear, as V2E disables the optimization for flags calculation. The rest deviations (37 in total) are for CPU general registers and memory states, some of which may indeed be bugs in the common instructions. If so, we should fix them and the transparency of V2E would be further improved.

Execution Replay. Building a reliable and efficient execution replay system is a challenging task, especially in the malicious context. Some replay systems record and replay the program execution of a single user-level process [18, 19, 29, 33, 36]. So they cannot monitor the malicious activities happening in the kernel (e.g., kernel rootkits). Moreover, completely intercepting and recording all the inputs taken by a user-level process is also difficult. Other than system calls, a user-level program may also take inputs from CPU timestamps, and the memory regions shared with other processes and the kernel, etc. Most of the above systems cannot completely capture all these inputs, and thus they are only partial solutions. To solve this problem, Jockey [33] makes use of binary rewriting technique. The program to be recorded needs to be disassembled, and the problematic instructions are replaced with functionally equivalent functions that can be intercepted. This approach becomes ineffective when dealing with malicious code, because it is commonly known that correctly disassembling malicious code is an open problem.

Revirt [14], VMware [39], and Aftersight [10] record and replay the execution of an entire virtual machine. Thus, they can observe malicious activities in both user and kernel space. V2E shares some similarity with Aftersight in terms of heterogeneous replay. Aftersight records a whole virtual machine execution from VMware and replays it in QEMU, enabling heavyweight analyses (e.g., kernel bug detection) on production workload [10]. Unlike Aftersight, V2E is specially tailored for malware investigation. Instead of monitoring the entire virtual machine, V2E takes a targeted approach: it directly monitors malware's execution, and can potentially achieve higher efficiency. More importantly, V2E is able to record malware's execution in a transparent fashion and then during replay faithfully emulate the execution for heavyweight analyses.

8. Conclusion

In this paper we presented V2E, a new malware analysis platform that is both transparent and extensible. It first records an execution log for a given malware sample under hardware virtualization to achieve transparency goal, then it replays the execution using dynamic binary translation to facilitate custom code instrumentation and in-depth investigation. The key challenge is to ensure that this replay process is precise. We conducted well-rounded experiments by analyzing a large number of realworld emulation-resistant malware samples and comparing with other malware analysis platforms. While these emulation-resistant malware samples are able to evade the other analysis platforms, the successful analysis of these samples in V2E demonstrated the efficacy and efficiency of our approach.

Acknowledgements

We thank the anonymous reviewers for their insightful comments for improving this paper. This work is supported in part by the US National Science Foundation NSF under Grants #1018217 and #1054605. Any opinions, findings, and conclusions made in this material are those of the authors and do not necessarily reflect the views of the NSF or the Air Force Research Laboratory.

References

[1] adore-ng. adore-ng rootkit. http://stealth.openwall.net/rootkits/.

[2] anubis. Anubis: Analyzing Unknown Binaries. http://anubis.iseclab.org/.

[3] D. Balzarotti, M. Cova, C. Karlberger, C. Kruegel, E. Kirda, and G. Vigna. Efficient Detection of Split Personalities in Malware. In *Proceedings of the Network and Distributed System Security Symposium (NDSS)*, San Diego, CA, February 2010.

[4] U. Bayer, P. Comparetti, C. Hlauschek, C. Kruegel, and E. Kirda. Scalable, behavior-based malware clustering. In *Proceedings of the 16th Annual Network and Distributed System Security Symposium (NDSS 2009)*, 2009.

[5] F. Bellard. Qemu, a fast and portable dynamic translator. In *USENIX Annual Technical Conference, FREENIX Track*, April 2005.

[6] D. Bruening, T. Garnett, and S. Amarasinghe. An infrastructure for adaptive dynamic optimization. In *International Symposium on Code Generation and Optimization (CGO'03)*, March 2003.

[7] J. Caballero, H. Yin, Z. Liang, and D. Song. Polyglot: Automatic extraction of protocol message format using dynamic binary analysis. In *Proceedings of the 14th ACM Conference on Computer and Communication Security (CCS'07)*, October 2007.

[8] J. Caballero, P. Poosankam, C. Kreibich, and D. Song. Dispatcher: Enabling active botnet infiltration using automatic protocol reverse-engineering. In *Proceedings of the 16th ACM Conference on Computer and Communication Security (CCS'09)*, Chicago, IL, Nov. 2009.

[9] J. Caballero, N. M. Johnson, S. McCamant, and D. Song. Binary code extraction and interface identification for security applications. In *Proceedings of the 17th Annual Network and Distributed System Security Symposium (NDSS'10)*, San Diego, CA, Feb. 2010.

[10] J. Chow, T. Garfinkel, and P. Chen. Decoupling dynamic program analysis from execution in virtual environments. In *Proceedings of 2008 Usenix Annual Technical Conference (ATC'08)*, June 2008.

[11] cwsandbox. CWSandbox::Behavior-based Malware Analysis. http://mwanalysis.org/.

[12] C. da Wang and S. Ju. The dilemma of covert channels searching. In *Information Security and Cryptology (ICISC'05)*, pages 169–174, 2005.

[13] A. Dinaburg, P. Royal, M. Sharif, and W. Lee. Ether: malware analysis via hardware virtualization extensions. In *Proceedings of the 15th ACM Conference on Computer and Communications Security*, pages 51–62, 2008.

[14] G. W. Dunlap, S. T. King, S. Cinar, M. A. Basrai, and P. M. Chen. Revirt: Enabling intrusion analysis through virtual-machine logging and replay. In *Proceedings of the 5th symposium on Operating Systems Design and Implementation (OSDI'02)*, December 2002.

[15] M. Egele, C. Kruegel, E. Kirda, H. Yin, and D. Song. Dynamic Spyware Analysis. In *Proceedings of the 2007 Usenix Annual Technical Conference (ATC'07)*, June 2007.

[16] P. Ferrie. Attacks on virtual machine emulators. Symantec Security Response, December 2006.

[17] T. Garfinkel and M. Rosenblum. A virtual machine introspection based architecture for intrusion detection. In *Proceedings of Network and Distributed Systems Security Symposium (NDSS'03)*, February 2003.

[18] D. Geels, G. Altekar, S. Shenker, and I. Stoica. Replay debugging for distributed applications. In *Proceedings of the 2006 USENIX Annual Technical Conference (ATC'06)*, pages 27–27, 2006.

[19] Z. Guo, X. Wang, J. Tang, X. Liu, Z. Xu, M. Wu, M. F. Kaashoek, and Z. Zhang. R2: An application-level kernel for record and replay. In *Proceedings of the 9th Symposium on Operating Systems Design and Implementation (OSDI'08)*, pages 193–208, 2008.

[20] X. Jiang, X. Wang, and D. Xu. Stealthy malware detection through vmm-based "out-of-the-box" semantic view reconstruction. In *Proceedings of the 14th ACM conference on Computer and Communications Security (CCS'07)*, October 2007.

[21] M. G. Kang, P. Poosankam, and H. Yin. Renovo: A hidden code extractor for packed executables. In *Proceedings of the 5th ACM Workshop on Recurring Malcode (WORM'07)*, Oct. 2007.

[22] M. G. Kang, H. Yin, S. Hanna, S. McCamant, and D. Song. Emulating emulation-resistant malware. In *Proceedings of the 2nd Workshop on Virtual Machine Security (VMSec'09)*, November 2009.

[23] kvm. Kernel Based Virtual Machine. http://www.linux-kvm.org/.

[24] A. Lanzi, M. Sharif, and W. Lee. K-Tracer: A system for extracting kernel malware behavior. In *Proceedings of the 16th Annual Network and Distributed System Security Symposium (NDSS'09)*, February 2009.

[25] C.-K. Luk, R. Cohn, R. Muth, H. Patil, A. Klauser, G. Lowney, S. Wallace, V. J. Reddi, and K. Hazelwood. Pin: Building customized program analysis tools with dynamic instrumentation. In *Proceedings of the 2005 ACM SIGPLAN conference on Programming Language Design and Implementation (PLDI'05)*, june 2005.

[26] L. Martignoni, R. Paleari, G. F. Roglia, and D. Bruschi. Testing cpu emulators. In *Proceedings of the 18th International Symposium on Software Testing and Analysis (ISSTA'09)*, pages 261–272, 2009.

[27] A. Moser, C. Kruegel, and E. Kirda. Exploring multiple execution paths for malware analysis. In *Proceedings of the 2007 IEEE Symposium on Security and Privacy(Oakland'07)*, May 2007.

[28] N. Nethercote and J. Seward. Valgrind: a framework for heavyweight dynamic binary instrumentation. In *Proceedings of the 2007 ACM SIGPLAN conference on Programming Language Design and Implementation (PLDI'07)*, pages 89–100, 2007.

[29] M. Olszewski, J. Ansel, and S. Amarasinghe. Kendo: efficient deterministic multithreading in software. *Proceedings of the 12th International Conference on Architectural Support for Programming Languages and Operating Systems (ASPLOS'09)*, Mar. 2009.

[30] qemulink. Qemu. http://fabrice.bellard.free.fr/qemu/.

[31] T. Raffetseder, C. Krügel, and E. Kirda. Detecting system emulators. In *the 10th Information Security Conference (ISC'07)*, pages 1–18, October 2007.

[32] R. Riley, X. Jiang, and D. Xu. Multi-aspect profiling of kernel rootkit behavior. In *Proceedings of the fourth ACM european conference on Computer systems (EuroSys'09)*, 2009.

[33] Y. Saito. Jockey: a user-space library for record-replay debugging. In *Proceedings of the sixth International Symposium on Automated Analysis-driven Debugging (AADEBUG'05)*, pages 69–76, 2005.

[34] M. Sharif, A. Lanzi, J. Giffin, and W. Lee. Automatic reverse engineering of malware emulators. In *Proceedings of the 30th IEEE Symposium on Security and Privacy (Oakland'09)*, pages 94–109, 2009.

[35] M. Siper. *Introduction to the Theory of Computation*. International Thomson Publishing, 1996.

[36] S. M. Srinivasan, S. Kandula, C. R. Andrews, and Y. Zhou. Flashback: a lightweight extension for rollback and deterministic replay for software debugging. In *Proceedings of the 2004 USENIX Annual Technical Conference (ATC'04)*, June 2004.

[37] temu. TEMU: The BitBlaze dynamic analysis component. http://bitblaze.cs.berkeley.edu/temu.html.

[38] A. Vasudevan and R. Yerraballi. Cobra: Fine-grained malware analysis using stealth localized-executions. In *Proceedings of the 2006 IEEE Symposium on Security and Privacy (Oakland'06)*, pages 264–279, 2006.

[39] vmware. Vmware. http://www.vmware.com/.

[40] H. Yin, D. Song, E. Manuel, C. Kruegel, and E. Kirda. Panorama: Capturing system-wide information flow for malware detection and analysis. In *Proceedings of the 14th ACM Conference on Computer and Communication Security (CCS'07)*, October 2007.

[41] H. Yin, Z. Liang, and D. Song. HookFinder: Identifying and understanding malware hooking behaviors. In *Proceedings of the 15th Annual Network and Distributed System Security Symposium (NDSS'08)*, February 2008.

Author Index

www.ingramcontent.com/pod-product-compliance
Lightning Source LLC
LaVergne TN
LVHW061241100826
845148LV00008B/999
* 9 7 8 1 4 5 0 3 1 3 7 3 5 *